A general history of the world, from the creation to the present time. ... By William Guthrie, Esq; John Gray, Esq; and others eminent in this branch of literature. ... Volume 8 of 12

William Guthrie

ECCO
PRINT EDITIONS

Eighteenth Century
Collections Online
Print Editions

Gale ECCO Print Editions

Relive history with *Eighteenth Century Collections Online,* now available in print for the independent historian and collector. This series includes the most significant English-language and foreign-language works printed in Great Britain during the eighteenth century, and is organized in seven different subject areas including literature and language; medicine, science, and technology; and religion and philosophy. The collection also includes thousands of important works from the Americas.

The eighteenth century has been called "The Age of Enlightenment." It was a period of rapid advance in print culture and publishing, in world exploration, and in the rapid growth of science and technology – all of which had a profound impact on the political and cultural landscape. At the end of the century the American Revolution, French Revolution and Industrial Revolution, perhaps three of the most significant events in modern history, set in motion developments that eventually dominated world political, economic, and social life.

In a groundbreaking effort, Gale initiated a revolution of its own: digitization of epic proportions to preserve these invaluable works in the largest online archive of its kind. Contributions from major world libraries constitute over 175,000 original printed works. Scanned images of the actual pages, rather than transcriptions, recreate the works *as they first appeared.*

Now for the first time, these high-quality digital scans of original works are available via print-on-demand, making them readily accessible to libraries, students, independent scholars, and readers of all ages.

For our initial release we have created seven robust collections to form one the world's most comprehensive catalogs of 18th century works.

Initial Gale ECCO Print Editions collections include:

History and Geography
Rich in titles on English life and social history, this collection spans the world as it was known to eighteenth-century historians and explorers. Titles include a wealth of travel accounts and diaries, histories of nations from throughout the world, and maps and charts of a world that was still being discovered. Students of the War of American Independence will find fascinating accounts from the British side of conflict.

Social Science

Delve into what it was like to live during the eighteenth century by reading the first-hand accounts of everyday people, including city dwellers and farmers, businessmen and bankers, artisans and merchants, artists and their patrons, politicians and their constituents. Original texts make the American, French, and Industrial revolutions vividly contemporary.

Medicine, Science and Technology

Medical theory and practice of the 1700s developed rapidly, as is evidenced by the extensive collection, which includes descriptions of diseases, their conditions, and treatments. Books on science and technology, agriculture, military technology, natural philosophy, even cookbooks, are all contained here.

Literature and Language

Western literary study flows out of eighteenth-century works by Alexander Pope, Daniel Defoe, Henry Fielding, Frances Burney, Denis Diderot, Johann Gottfried Herder, Johann Wolfgang von Goethe, and others. Experience the birth of the modern novel, or compare the development of language using dictionaries and grammar discourses.

Religion and Philosophy

The Age of Enlightenment profoundly enriched religious and philosophical understanding and continues to influence present-day thinking. Works collected here include masterpieces by David Hume, Immanuel Kant, and Jean-Jacques Rousseau, as well as religious sermons and moral debates on the issues of the day, such as the slave trade. The Age of Reason saw conflict between Protestantism and Catholicism transformed into one between faith and logic -- a debate that continues in the twenty-first century.

Law and Reference

This collection reveals the history of English common law and Empire law in a vastly changing world of British expansion. Dominating the legal field is the *Commentaries of the Law of England* by Sir William Blackstone, which first appeared in 1765. Reference works such as almanacs and catalogues continue to educate us by revealing the day-to-day workings of society.

Fine Arts

The eighteenth-century fascination with Greek and Roman antiquity followed the systematic excavation of the ruins at Pompeii and Herculaneum in southern Italy; and after 1750 a neoclassical style dominated all artistic fields. The titles here trace developments in mostly English-language works on painting, sculpture, architecture, music, theater, and other disciplines. Instructional works on musical instruments, catalogs of art objects, comic operas, and more are also included.

The BiblioLife Network

This project was made possible in part by the BiblioLife Network (BLN), a project aimed at addressing some of the huge challenges facing book preservationists around the world. The BLN includes libraries, library networks, archives, subject matter experts, online communities and library service providers. We believe every book ever published should be available as a high-quality print reproduction; printed on-demand anywhere in the world. This insures the ongoing accessibility of the content and helps generate sustainable revenue for the libraries and organizations that work to preserve these important materials.

The following book is in the "public domain" and represents an authentic reproduction of the text as printed by the original publisher. While we have attempted to accurately maintain the integrity of the original work, there are sometimes problems with the original work or the micro-film from which the books were digitized. This can result in minor errors in reproduction. Possible imperfections include missing and blurred pages, poor pictures, markings and other reproduction issues beyond our control. Because this work is culturally important, we have made it available as part of our commitment to protecting, preserving, and promoting the world's literature.

GUIDE TO FOLD-OUTS MAPS and OVERSIZED IMAGES

The book you are reading was digitized from microfilm captured over the past thirty to forty years. Years after the creation of the original microfilm, the book was converted to digital files and made available in an online database.

In an online database, page images do not need to conform to the size restrictions found in a printed book. When converting these images back into a printed bound book, the page sizes are standardized in ways that maintain the detail of the original. For large images, such as fold-out maps, the original page image is split into two or more pages

Guidelines used to determine how to split the page image follows:

• Some images are split vertically; large images require vertical and horizontal splits.
• For horizontal splits, the content is split left to right.
• For vertical splits, the content is split from top to bottom.
• For both vertical and horizontal splits, the image is processed from top left to bottom right.

A GENERAL

HISTORY of the WORLD,

FROM THE

CREATION to the present Time.

INCLUDING

All the EMPIRES, KINGDOMS, and STATES; their REVO-
LUTIONS, FORMS of GOVERNMENT, LAWS, RELIGION'S,
CUSTOMS and MANNERS; the PROGRESS of their LEARN-
ING, ARTS, SCIENCES, COMMERCE and TRADE;

Together with

Their CHRONOLOGY, ANTIQUITIES, PUBLIC BUILDINGS, and
CURIOSITIES of NATURE and ART.

By WILLIAM GUTHRIE, Efq;
JOHN GRAY, Efq;
And others eminent in this Branch of Literature.

——————— *cui lecta potenter erit res*
Nec facundia deferet hunc, nec lucidus ordo.　　HOR.

VOLUME VIII.

LONDON:

Printed for J. NEWBERY, R. BALDWIN, S. CROWDER, J. COOTE,
R. WITHY, J. WILKIE, J. WILSON and J. FELL, W. NICOLL,
B. COLLINS, and R. RAIKES.

M DCC LXIV.

A
GENERAL HISTORY
OF THE
WORLD.

The History of Persia.

Introduction.

S O much has been said concerning the history of this country, in the preceding part of our work, that we shall be very concise upon it here. The family of the modern emperors of *Perfia* is called *Sofian*, from one *Sefi*, or *Sofi*, who, for his sanctity, was held in great veneration by *Tamerlan*, whom he prevented from murdering, in cold blood, great numbers of his unhappy countrymen and others. Upon *Tamerlan*'s departure, the *Persians*, in a manner, adored *Sefi*; and, upon his death, continued to respect his descendants as their head.

History of Juneyd.

The most powerful amongst them was one *Juneyd*, who, after a variety of adventures, acquired a very considerable principality; but, in endeavouring to render himself quite independent of the *Koyounlu* princes, who then reigned in *Persia*, a conspiracy was formed against him at *Shirwan*, and he was cut off. He left a son, one *Hayder*, who was king of *Frellizand*, both in his father's life-time and after his death, and he had two sons, *Potshah* and *Ismael*; but was himself killed in endeavouring to revenge his father's death. *Ismael* survived him, and assumed the family name of *Sofi*; and, though he was but fourteen years of age, he put himself at the head of seven thousand followers, devoted to his family; and, after conquering and killing *Ferozad*, prince of *Shirwan*, who had defeated and slain his father and grandfather, he took possession of that principality, and, by degrees, of the greatest part of *Persia*, by defeating the *Turks*, of which nation the *Koyounlu* family was. He was, however, about the

He is succeeded by Hayder, and he by Ismael.

His wars with the Turks. year 1514, defeated by the *Ottoman* emperor *Selim*, who conquered great part of his dominions, but was obliged to march into *Egypt*; by which *Ismael* passed the rest of his reign in tranquility. He died in the year 1523, and may be called *His death and character.* the founder of the *Sosian* dinasty. He is said to have been a great but a cruel prince. He took advantage of the natural enthusiasm of his subjects, to make them look upon him as something more than man; and he sustained that character by his vast abilities. This is all we can say with certainty, or indeed with propriety, of *Ismael*; so miserably contradictory are all authors concerning him, notwithstanding the lateness of the period in which he lived.

Succeeded by Thamas, *Ismael* was succeeded by his son *Thamas*, or *Thomas*, who retook the city of *Tauris* from *Solyman*, the *Othman* emperor, with whom he had great wars with various success. In the year 1575, he was poisoned by the mother of *Hayder*, one of *who is murdered.* his sons, whom she wanted to advance to the empire; but that young prince, in going to visit his father's treasury, was murdered by his sister. Other writers say that *Hayder* had the presumption to appear before his father, when he was upon his death-bed, with a crown upon his head, though he had an elder brother, who refused, on account of his religious turn, to accept of the empire.

Death of Hayder. *Hayder* reigned but four days, being killed when he was but seventeen years old; and was succeeded by his brother *Ismael shah.* *Ismael*, who, from jealousies of state, had been twenty-five years in prison. Though he owed his advancement entirely to his sister, yet one of the first actions of his government was to order her to be put to death; and, in all his other conduct, he proved himself a bloody and inhuman tyrant. *His death.* He reigned, however, only twenty-two months; some said he was poisoned, and others that he was assassinated, by some of his grandees, who had disguised themselves like women, and were headed by his sister, whose name was *Periakokonna*, in resentment of his ingratitude.

Character of his sister. This lady is said to have been equally devoted to ambition and gallantry; and intended to have advanced one of her lovers, *Amir Kan*, to the throne after her brother's death: but the eldest of her brothers, *Mohammed*, was still alive. He had been spared by his brother, the late tyrant, only because he was thought too insignificant to be put to death; and he was called *the Blind* from a weakness he had in *He is succeeded by Mohammed, who puts his sister to death.* his eyes. Upon *Ismael's* death, the grandees of *Persia* made it a point of conscience for him to ascend the throne; which with great difficulty he was at last prevailed upon to do, but not before the head of his sister was brought him. Authors are greatly divided with regard to his character. Some represent him as weak, indolent, and pusilanimous; but others, with greater appearance of truth, say he was a brave and active prince. It is certain, at least, that he was engaged in wars with the *Turks*; and, that his generals often defeated

feated them, and sometimes were defeated by them. One *Moham-*
of his generals, *Arez Beg*, in particular, was defeated and *med's wars*
hanged by the *Tartars*. But *Mohammed*'s eldest son, *Hamza*, *with the*
amply revenged his death, by defeating them in their turn, *Turks and*
taking their general, and cutting in pieces prodigious num- *Tartars,*
bers of them. The *Georgians*, ever since the reign of *Tho-*
mas, had refused to be subject to the *Persians*, who had subdued them. *Georgia* was then governed by a *Christian* prince,
called *David*; and *Mohammed* sent an army to reduce him,
which forced *David* to fly: upon which, his brother *Simon*,
who had turned *Mahometan*, mounted the throne of *Georgia*,
with the title of khan, and under the protection of *Mo-*
hammed. He could not, however, afford him sufficient pro- *and Geor-*
tection against the growing power of the *Turks*, who, not- *gians.*
withstanding the prodigious valour of *Hamza*, made themselves masters of *Tauris*.

So amazingly ignorant are authors of the modern affairs of *Uncer-*
Persia, at this period, to which we are greater strangers than *tainty of*
to transactions in that country two thousand years ago, that *th-Persian*
it is uncertain who was the successor of *Mohammed*. *Hamza* *history.*
probably was, tho' some say that he was put to death in his
father's life-time, and by his order; but that is improbable,
and contradictory to the accounts of the most creditable travellers who were then in *Persia*. It is certain that *Hamza*
was a very brave prince, and, in his father's life-time, had
given many surprising proofs of valour. The *Persian* court *Degene-*
was, at that period, the theatre of unpunished incest, lust, *racy of*
and murder. The sovereign was despotic; and the people, *the court.*
the greatest, equally as the meanest, subjects, the most abject
of slaves: so that nothing was more common than for the
wives of the most considerable noblemen there, to prostitute
themselves, with the knowledge and consent of their hus-
bands, to the reigning prince. Fratricide, however shock- *Hatred of*
ing it is in all senses, was, though not the least, the most ex- *the blood-*
cusable, of the crimes of their monarchs: for their sons, be- *royal to*
ing begotten upon different mothers, who mortally hated *one ano-*
each other, and instilled the same sentiments into their chil- *ther.*
dren, did not think themselves relations in blood so much as
rivals in interest, and, with their first milk, they sucked in
a detestation for one another. Such are the dreadful effects
of polygamy in an arbitrary country; and, from that source,
most of the evils have proceeded which shock humanity to
read.

Hamza had a brother, named *Ismael*, who is said to have *Shah Iss-*
murdered him; though others pretend that he was killed in *mael III.*
battle in the year 1585. He was succeeded by *Ismael*, the *is mur-*
third of that name, whose throat was cut by his barber; an *dered.*
assassin employed for that purpose by the partizans of his
brother *Abbas*, whose death he had resolved upon. Neither
Hamza, nor *Ismael* III. reigned above eight months; for

which

which reason, they, by some writers, are left out of the list of *Persian* monarchs.

Succeeded by *Abbas* the *Great*. *Abbas*, who next mounted that throne, had a governor, called *Murshed*, assigned to him by his father; and to this *Murshed* he was principally indebted for the death of his brother and his own accession to the crown. We must not forget that the barber, who cut *Ismael*'s throat, was instantly torn in pieces, and his body burned by the conspiring lords who **who kills his governor *Murshed*.** were present. *Murshed* could not preserve his moderation after so many important services, and, presuming to treat *Abbas* still as his pupil, that monarch, attended by four of his principal lords, broke into *Murshed*'s apartments, and made one of the grooms kill him with a hatchet; for which he was rewarded with the dignity of khan, and the government *Herat*.

He recovers the provinces of *Persia*. *Abbas* was a man formed for the re-establishment of a tottering empire. The fairest provinces of his dominions had been dismembered by *Turks*, *Tartars*, and other barbarians; particularly the *Usbeks*, who were then possessed of the once glorious and flourishing empire of *Bukharia*; but were driven out of *Korasan* by *Abbas*. He next turned his arms against the *Turks*, and, by an incredible march, he surprized and made himself master of the city of *Tauris*, where they had built a strong fortress, and of many other places in *Georgia* **His treachery to the *Kurds*.** and its neighbourhood. Finding resistance at a place called *Remy*, and that he could not master it without the assistance of the *Kurds*, or mountaineers, who assisted the *Turks*, he dealt with them so effectually, that he took the place; but afterwards he most treacherously put all their chiefs to death; and he recovered all the provinces that had been dismembered from his empire, with a most horrible slaughter of the *Turks*, and the inhabitants, who opposed his arms.

The conquest of the great province of *Shirwan*, and its capital *Shamakiya*, cost him but seven weeks; and he made himself master of the rich principality of *Arran* about the same time. Upon this, the inhabitants of *Derbent* submitted to his yoke; tho', as we have already seen, it was deemed **Invades *Kilan*, and is in danger.** to be impregnable. His next expedition, which happened about the year 1593, was against the province of *Kilan*. Here, we are told, he was in danger of being drowned in passing a river, in which he lost four thousand of his troops; he, however, soon completed the conquest of the province with the slaughter of sixty thousand of its inhabitants; and made the country more accessible than it had been to strangers as well as to his armies.

The vast successes of *Abbas*, who, in history, is justly surnamed *the Great*, gave such jealousy to the *Turks*, that they invaded his dominions with an army of five hundred thousand men, by the way of *Tauris*. The intention of *Shah Abbas*,

Abbas, when this invasion happened, was to have given some repose to himself and his dominions; and he resolved to avail himself of the strength of the country, which was excessively mountainous, and to act on the defensive. For this purpose, he sent out flying parties, and promised every man, who should enter as a volunteer, which five thousand did, fifty crowns for each *Turk*'s head he should bring in. This had a great effect; and the *Turkish* general, *Chakal Ogil*, finding he could not force him to a general engagement, provoked him so, by bravading messages, that *Shah Abbas* gave him battle, and forced him to retire to the frontiers. But *Shah Abbas*, fearing a surprize, kept his army, for three days, under arms; nor did he himself, during that time, enter his tent. Though the *Turks* retired, yet a cruel war was continued between them and *Abbas*, who, about this time, narrowly escaped poison; and *Tauris*, after it had been taken by the *Turks*, was retaken by *Abbas*, who every day became more and more formidable, though he received, in the course of the war, several checks from his enemies. They, however, left him at peace for many years; and then the war between them broke out with more fury than ever. They were opposed by the *Persians* under *Kuchiki*, the ablest general *Abbas* had; who not only checked their progress, by defeating them in several engagements, but took many of their generals prisoners; all whom *Abbas* generously released without ransom, and with marks of favour. The next expedition of *Abbas* was into *Georgia*, where he defeated *Tamuras*, whom we shall mention more particularly afterwards, and he continued in that country for nine months.

But the military virtues of *Abbas*, to which were added many civil ones, were stained by the most inhuman, unheard of cruelties ever perpetrated. When he was upon his *Georgian* expedition, he ordered the noses and lips of all his soldiers to be cut off who made use of tobacco; and a poor merchant, who knew nothing of this order, having imported some tobacco into the camp, he was, by his command, placed upon a pile of faggots and burned to death. with the bags in which the commodity was, hung round him. The other instances of his cruelty are shocking to the last degree, for he knew no distinction between justice and barbarity. Under pretence of providing for the poor, he used to go disguised round the streets of his capital, and, upon the slightest offence, he would order a baker to be baked alive in his own oven, and a cook to be roasted upon his own spit; and, at one time, he was upon the point of putting to death the governor and all the magistrates of *Ispahan*, for some frauds practised in the markets. His great master of the ordnance, having, through jealousy, killed some people, he not only put him to death, but all his wives, children, and domestics. He sometimes caused, upon the slightest grounds of suspicion, the ladies of his harran, or seraglio, to be buried alive,

Marginal notes: His wars with the *Turks*, with various successes. His excessive cruelty to all ranks of people.

with

with the lovers they were accused to favour; and he often caused the bellies of those who offended him, to be ript up before his face.

Excuse for the same.

Those inhuman barbarities admit of no extenuation, but that the nature and genius of the *Persians* themselves, required such horrible examples to be made to keep them in awe. This excuse however, cannot be urged with regard to his unnatural treatment of his own sons and family. Two of them had their eyes burnt out, and by his command were shut up in prison. His eldest son, who gave extraordinary proofs of a military genius, was poisoned, by his father's command, and *Sefi*, his second son, met if possible, with a still more cruel fate. He was the darling of the people, and he had a son called *Sain*, the same who afterwards mounted that throne, by a beautiful *Circassian*, whom he had married. *Sefi* was the favourite of his father, and he strove to merit all his tenderness. For the cruelty of *Abbas* becoming intollerable to the grandees, written intimations were thrown into *Sefi's*

Conspiracy against him.

apartment, that he might if he pleased, immediately mount the throne of *Persia. Sefi* discovered the whole to his father; but the discovery, though attended with the warmest protestations of duty and obedience, instead of endearing him to the tyrant, proved his ruin. *Abbas* was struck with horror, in thinking he had a son about him, who had it in his power to dethrone him. His apprehensions deprived him of his rest, in so much, that he shifted his bed several times. every night. They were increased, by a trifling accident at hunting, the prince happening to shoot at a wild boar before his father; and the declared love the people had for *Sefi*, at last

He puts his eldest son to death.

determined his father to put him to death. He proposed that *Kuchuki* should undertake the execution, but he declined it with horror. One *Babut*, however, undertook it, and attended by some of his slaves, he stabbed the innocent prince dead, as he was returning from a bath, followed by a single page.

It was soon known by whose command this inhuman murder had been perpetrated; and it was with difficulty the people were prevented from pulling *Abbas* out of his palace.

His excessive grief for the murder.

Nothing could have appeased them but the excessive grief he discovered. It was so great that he suffered the prince's mother in her rage to pull him by the hair, and to beat him with her fists. In short, his mourning and grief for what he had done, was almost equal to his cruelty, in the commission; and ever after he wore the dress of one of his lowest subjects; for when *Herbert*, the traveller, afterwards saw him, though he was giving an audience to the *English* ambassador, he was drest in a coat of plain red callico, quilted with cotton. But he gave far more dreadful proofs of his grief, than fasting and mourning. For he invited all the khans, who had either given, or caused, a suspicion, or had encouraged his jealousy of his son, to a banquet, where he ordered poison to be administered ftered to them, and he faw them all expire, before he left the room. The tyrant however, probably fearing, that it might be difficult for him to get a future executioner of his cruelty, was fo far from putting *Babut* to death, that he rewarded him with the government of the principality of *Kafwin*. He forced *Babut* at laft, with his own hand, to cut off his fon's head, whom he tenderly loved, and to throw it at his feet. Obferving *Babut*, on this occafion, oppreffed with grief, " Think, *Babut*, faid he, what I muft have felt, when you " brought me the news of my fon's death. Be gone, and " comfort thyfelf with one reflection, that thy fon and " mine are no more; and that in this refpect, thou art " on a footing with thy fovereign " It is faid that *Babut* foon after was murdered by a confpiracy of his own flaves.

Story and death of the mur-derer.

Though the above relation of *Sefi's* death feems to be moft confonant to truth, and to the manner of proceed-ing in that country, yet *Herbert* has embellished it with many particulars, that have been feveral times worked up into a drama. He tells us, that *Abbas*, upon fome provoca-tion, purpofely given his fon, that obliged him to draw his fword in his prefence, ordered his eyes, as is ufual in that country, to be put out with a red hot iron; and that the prince, in a fit of phrenfy, ftrangled his own daughter, and was groping about to do the fame by his fon, when the mo-ther removed him; and that he perifhed a few days after by poifon. If this ftory is true, it muft be laid to another fon of *Abbas*, befides the prince who was put to death by *Babut*, which is by no means improbable, when we confider the in-humanity of this tyrant to his own family. For though he doated upon *Sam*, his grandfon by *Sefi*, yet had it not been for his mother's attention, who took care to give him proper antidotes, he foon would have poifoned him likewife.

Various relations of the murder.

Abbas found no relief from the ftings of remorfe, but in war; and about the year 1594, he reduced to his fubjection a vaft part of *Proper Perfia*, which had been feized by the *Kurds*, and then by the *Arabs*, but it was feveral years after be-fore he compleated the conqueft of the whole. But *Tamuras*, the *Georgian* prince, whom we have already mentioned, was at this time the moft formidable enemy *Abbas* had; and as we have fo good an authority, as that of Sir *John Chardin*, who was both judicious, and well informed, it may not be improper, to give here fome idea of the hiftory of that prince.

Abbas fubdues Pars.

Georgia is divided into two provinces, or as they are called, kingdoms, *Kaket*, and *Kardnel*. *Tamuras*, whofe true name was *David*, was the eldeft fon of *Alexander* king of *Kaket*, who, befides him, had two fons and two daughters. In his youth he had been a hoftage at the court of *Perfia*, where his education was the fame with that of *Abbas*. But upon his father's death, he was exchanged for his brother, after taking an oath of vaffalage to the *Perfian* crown. *Luarzab*,

Hiftory and ad-ventures of Ta-muras, prince of Georgia.

the

the king of *Kardnel*, was then a minor; but happening to be too familiar with the daughter of his first minister, *Meru*, who was but of a mean extraction, and refusing to fulfil a promise of marriage he had made her, for fear of family resentments; *Meru*, who had some reason to be afraid of his life, fled to *Ispahan*, where he put himself under the protection of *Abbas*, as being the sovereign lord of *Georgia*. It does not appear, that *Abbas*, at that juncture, was either able or willing to make war upon *Georgia*, merely upon *Meru's* account; but being of a very amorous complexion, he sent to

and of Luarzab, another prince of the same country.

demand in marriage the sister of *Luarzab*, the most celebrated beauty in all *Asia*. Nothing was more common, than for the *Christian* princes of *Georgia* to send their daughters to the haram of the *Persian* monarchs; and the mothers of all the children of *Shah Abbas*, had been *Georgian Christians*. *Luarzab*, however, flatly refused to comply, under pretence that his sister had been promised to *Tamuras*; and upon the demand being repeated, he even insulted the ambassadors of *Abbas*; who was then in no condition to force him into compliance. He proceeded therefore with art and caution, and though then very old, he pretended the princess was in love with him, and on this pretext, about the year 1610, he invaded *Georgia*; where by the help of gold, and *Meru's* intrigues, he found a great party among the *Georgian* nobility, many of whom turned *Mahometans*, to qualify them for holding places at the *Persian* court. But his chief dependence was upon his arts, to divide *Luarzab*, and *Tamuras*; by privately promising each of them the other's crown. It happened fortunately, that the two *Georgian* princes, were befriended not only by the *Russians*, the *Pope*, and other *Christian* powers, but by the *Ottoman* emperors, in hatred to *Abbas*, whose artifices they discovered; and they cemented the friendship between them still stronger, by *Tamuras* actually marrying the beautiful sister of *Luarzab*.

Barbarity of Shah Abbas.

Abbas, at that time, had not only a powerful army on the frontiers of *Georgia*, but had in his possession two sons of *Tamuras*, and a brother and sister of *Luarzab*, whom he kept as hostages; and whom he threatened to put to death. At the same time, he ordered his general to advance in person, at the head of thirty thousand horse, against *Tamuras*; who seeing his ruin inevitable, sent his mother *Mariana*, who, notwithstanding her age, was still lovely, to *Ispahan*, to intercede for the lives of her two grand-children. The tyrant fell in love with her, and offered to marry her. But she refused to turn *Mahometan*, and was therefore shut up in prison, where at last she expired, under the torments he inflicted upon her; while her two grand-sons were made eunuchs. *Abbas* then resolved to march in person against *Georgia*; and with infinite danger and difficulty he penetrated into the kingdom of *Kaket*; where he committed great ravages. Most of the *Georgian* lords being in his interest tereft, *Luarzab*, like *Tamuras*, was intimidated; and *Abbas* diffembled fo well, that he perfuaded him to repair to the *Perfian* camp; where, at firft, he was greatly careffed, and fent to *Shiras*. During his confinement the czar of *Mufcovy* ordered an ambaffador to fet out for the *Perfian* court, to interceed for him: which coming to the knowledge of *Shah Abbas*, *Luarzab* was privately put to death; and *Abbas* dif- avowed all knowledge of it to the czar.

Luarzab murdered,

Tamuras, by this time, began to be fenfible of his own danger, and obtained a powerful fupply of troops from the *Turks*, by which he gave feveral defeats to the *Perfians*, who were commanded by *Bagrat*, *Luarzab*'s brother, who had turned *Mahometan*, and had obtained from *Abbas* the government of *Georgia*. But the *Ottoman* forces being withdrawn, and *Ta-* *Tamuras* was obliged to fubmit to give *Abbas* his daughter in marriage; to receive the yoke of his authority, and to reign as a tributary prince. Upon this, *Abbas* not only bridled the *Georgians* with ftrong garrifons, but tranfplanted eighty thoufand of their families into other parts of his dominions.

Tamuras fub- dued,

At laft, well knowing their paffion for independency, he gave them a kind of charter of rights, exempting them from taxes; and confirming them in the poffeffion of their churches, without any mofques being built among them; he likewife granted them the priviledge of being governed by a prince of the royal blood of *Georgia*, provided he was a *Mahometan*; together with other privileges; with which all the other *Georgians*, during his reign were fatisfied.

but makes terms for the Georgians.

All this happened about the year 1613, when *Shah Abbas*, undertook an expedition againft *Baghdad*. He had been invited thither by *Bikir*, the *Turkifh* commandant there, upon fome difguft at the *Ottoman* court; but changing his mind, when *Abbas* came to demand the keys of the city, *Bikir* told him, he could give him nothing but powder and ball. Upon this *Abbas* ordered a general affault to be given, and carrying the place fword in hand, he put *Bikir* to death.

Abbas takes Baghdad.

The lofs of fo great a city enraged the court of *Conftan- tinople* fo much, that they made many efforts to retake it; and they feveral times befieged it but were always repulfed. *Kufchiki* continued ftill to be the favourite general of *Abbas*, and when the province of *Baghdad* was invaded by *Kalil*, a *Turkifh* bafhaw, at the head of five hundred thoufand men, *Kufchiki* gave them an entire defeat, near *Baghdad*, where *Abbas* was in perfon. Leaving that city to meet his general, he declared, as he approached him, that he could not have afked from God a greater victory: and would not be fatisfi- ed till *Kufchiki*, almoft by force, mounted the horfe on which *Abbas* rode, while he led him by the bridle. This great victory however, did not put an end to the wars between the

and de- feats a great army of the Turks. Joy of Abbas.

Perfians

Perfians and the *Turks*, which lasted all the remainder of the reign of *Abbas*, with various successes.

History of the conquest of *Ormus*, *Abbas*, equally politic as brave, had the art to turn every circumstance to his own account. In 1607, the *Portugueze* had taken the isle of *Ormus*, with some adjacent islands, from the petty king who reigned there; and, by this important conquest, they were in hopes to engross to themselves all the trade of the *Perfian Gulph*; and to dispossess the *English* of all commerce there. An officer, *Ruy Frera*, the *Portugueze* general and governor, accordingly, in the year 1621, attacked a squadron of *English* ships trading there, killed one *Andrew Shilling* their commodore; and obliged their ships to return to *India*. During their absence, *Shah Abbas*, who had reunited to his crown so many other dominions, ordered his governor of *Shiras* to besiege the city of *Ormus* with a great army. While he was lying before the place, upon which *Ruy Freras* had raised new fortifications, the *English* by the *English*. squadron being now augmented to nine ships, returned to drive the *Portugueze* out of *Ormus*, which they already found besieged by the *Perfian* army. The chief *English* commanders in this expedition were *Waddel*, *Blythe*, and *Woodcock*; and when they appeared before the place, it was intimated to them by the *Perfian* general *Kouli Kan*, that if they expected the benefit of trading in the *Perfian Gulph*, they must join his army against the common enemy the *Portugueze*. Upon this, a treaty was set on foot, and it was agreed, that the *English* should be put in possession of the castle of *Ormus*, with all its cannon and ammunition; but the *Perfians* were at liberty, if they pleased, to build another fort on the same island. The spoil was to be equally divided, and the *Perfians* were to pay half the expence of the warlike operations; but the *English* were ever after to be free from imposts in those parts. Those conditions being settled, the *English* commanders took a view of the dispositions of the siege, which had lasted seven months, without the *Perfians* making the smallest progress in it, according to the most authentic accounts received from the *English* and other *Europeans*, who The *Perfians* unserviceable soldiers. were present at the siege. The soldiers of *Shah Abbas the Great*, who had conquered so many great kingdoms, were most wretched practitioners in the art of war. The three captains above mentioned, besieged the castle of *Kishome*, which was defended by *Ruy Frera* in person; but he was obliged to surrender the place, and he himself was sent prisoner to *Surat*. In the mean while, the other six *English* ships landed a large body of *Perfians* upon the island of *Ormus*; and while the *Perfians* were making themselves masters of the town, which they did, the *English* cannonaded the *Portugueze* gallies, in which the chief strength of the besieged lay, and sunk five of them. This service took up about five weeks, but still the castle held out, being garrisoned by twenty-six thousand men, and defended by one

hundred

hundred and fourteen pieces of cannon. It is hard to fay
whether the *Perfians* or *Portugueze* were the more wretched
foldiers. The firſt were incapable of attacking, and the others
of defending. The *Portugueze* however, after a breach had
been made, repulfed the *Perfians* ; and the place would have
remained impregnable by them, had not the *Englifh* undertook the fiege, and forced the garrifon to furrender.

The reader, from the above relation, may eafily conclude,
that all the courage and fkill of the *Perfians*, who made fo
great a figure under *Abbas*, was only comparative, and that
in both refpects, they were as much inferior to the *Portugueze*, the moſt cowardly of the *European* nations, as they
were fuperior to their own barbarous neighbours. Great
hiſtorical inſtruction is to be gained from the fate of *Ormus*.
By its fituation in the mouth of the *Perfian Gulph*, it was Situation
once the greateſt mart of trade in the known world. It is and im-
celebrated by all antiquity on that account ; and even be- portance
fore the difcoveries of the *Portugueze*, it was talked of by of *Ormus*.
Europeans, as the paradife of the earth, and the mine of
riches. The *Portugueze*, about the beginning of the fixteenth
century, were the moſt enterprizing and the moſt infolent
people in *Europe*; and the kings of *Ormus* had formerly been
poffeffed of immenfe treafures, and territories upon the continent. After various revolutions in their government, *Albulquerque*, the famous *Portugueze* general and admiral, by
incredible efforts of courage and good management, rendered the king of the ifland tributary ; and in procefs of time
his flave. For though *Albulquerque* continued the government in the perfons of the royal family, yet they had no
power, but in fome very immaterial points of religion and
trifling difputes, over fubjects ; and they fubfiſted upon a
pitiful ſtipend allotted to them by the *Portugueze* governors;
nor were they even permitted, without leave, to depart from
the ifland. It was in vain for the kings of *Perfia*, who fome
time before the reduction of the ifland by the *Portugueze*,
had rendered it tributary, to complain of lofing their tribute, and of being infulted by a handful of beggarly *Europeans*, for fo the *Afiatics* confidered the *Portugueze* to be.
Albulquerque not only held them at defiance, but brought
them to treat with him upon the footing of a fovereign
prince. It would tire defcription to give an account of the
vaſt riches and luxury of the *Portugueze* fettlements in The *Por-
Ormus :* which was faid to contain forty thoufand people, *tugueze*,
though no more than feven miles in circumference. They
arrived to fuch a pitch of wealth and arrogance, as to boaſt,
that inſtead of gilding, as they did, the bolts and bars of
their doors and windows, they would make them of folid
gold and filver. In the fair time, the ifland itfelf was the
rendezvous of commerce. The foil of it being hid under the
moſt magnificient carpets below their feet, and rich pavilions
above their heads, made the whole ifland appear as a camp,

in which none but princes and general officers refided; while the air was impregnated by all the fineft odors and perfumes that nature can produce.

Its natural hiftory. After faying fo much with regard to this terreftrial paradife, the reader muft be furprized to underftand, that this delightful fpot was no other than a rock of falt; deftitute of water, herbage, trees, vegetables, and all thofe products of the earth which contribute either to the happinefs, or the fubfiftance of mankind. But trade, induftry, and a happy fituation, (it being no more than five miles diftant from the continent of *Perfia*,) fupplied them all; till all were deftroyed by luxury. The immenfe riches the *Portugueze* acquired, the adulations paid them by the flaves of the eaft, and the precautions taken by *Albulquerque*, and their wife predeceffors, to render the ifland impregnable, made them lofe all their virtue: animofities among themfelves fucceeded, and the pride inherent to their nation, with the defire of being revenged upon one another, finifhed their ruin, by a **Reflection** handful of *Englifh* failors, upon that once happy fpot. May the fame never be the fate of other *Europeans*, or their defcendants, who are now in circumftances of profperity and affluence, from valour and induftry.

The city goes to ruin. *Abbas* knew too well the importance of *Ormus* to think of preferving it. He knew his own ignorant and indolent fubjects never could fupport the ftate it was in, when it came into his hands; and that therefore, it muft in courfe fall a prey to any enterprizing *European* power who fhould attempt to reduce it. He therefore refolved to reduce it to the ftate in which it came out of the hands of nature, the moft uncomfortable and defpicable that can be conceived. The *Portugueze*, it is true, might have retaken it, had they been fupported properly by their governors at *Goa*; but all attempts of that kind proved unfuccefsful; and *Shah Abbas* **Ingratitude of Abbas to the Englifh.** was deaf to the moft flattering propofals of the *Englifh*, for making a fettlement there. Though the conqueft of *Ormus*, and the expulfion of the *Portugueze*, was entirely owing to them; and though a fair treaty had been concluded between them and the *Perfians*, yet after the fervice was performed, he moft ingratefully refufed to fulfil the articles; and, upon the whole, the *Englifh* were confiderable lofers by the fuccefs of their own arms. It is faid, that they did not carry off above the value of twenty thoufand pounds, though the money and effects, which fell into the hands of the conquerors, amounted to two millions fterling. But at the fame time, it is acknowledged, that they loft confiderable effects by ftorms and fhipwrecks. The trade of *Ormus* was, by *Shah Abbas* transferred to *Gambron*. The *Dutch*, partly by ftealth, and partly by connivance, carried off the materials of the fortifications; and by the lateft accounts we have, the whole ifland now appears like a wreck of nature.

The

The conqueft of *Ormus*, though ftained by ingratitude to Death and the *Englifh*, is reckoned among the moft fhining acquifitions made by *Shah Abbas*; who did not long furvive it. He had a particular affection for a place called *Farrbad*, in the province of *Mazenderan*; and in going to vifit it, he fell fick; but immediately, before the chief lords of his council, he named *Sain*, his grandfon by *Sefi*, whom he had murdered, his fucceffor. Some of them objected to his nomination, on account of a ridiculous prophecy made by a fortune-teller, who had foretold that that prince could not reign above eight months: but *Abbas* replied, That, as his father muft have inherited the crown had he been alive, he was refolved it fhould defcend to the fon, though he fhould reign but three days.

After this nomination, all kind of applications, that were in the power of medicine, were made for his recovery; but to no purpofe. His paffion that his grandfon *Sain* fhould fucceed him, was fo great, that he not only ordered his death to be concealed till the fucceffion was fecured to him, but that his body fhould be expofed, for fome time, in the fame ftate as he ufed in public audiences. We are accordingly told that this was done, and that his hand and lips were made to move by means of a filken chord which was fecretly pulled by a great officer of ftate; and, that this farce continued for fix weeks. At the time of his death, he was feventy years of age, forty-three of which he had been monarch of *Perfia*. He died in the year 1629.

All we can fay of this prince's character, is, that he had both courage and ability fufficient to deal with the barbarians, whom he either ruled over or fought with; and, perhaps, his horrid cruelties gave them impreffions which kept them in awe. He had notions of trade, but they were very impracticable. He wanted to be the chief merchant of filk in his kingdom, and actually fent an ambaffador with a merchant and a large cargo of filk into *Spain*. The ambaffador was fo ignorant of what he was about, that he offered the whole cargo in a prefent to the king, who treated him with great difdain; and, upon his return to *Ifpahan*, *Abbas* ordered his belly to be ripped up in the fight of his people. *Abbas* fent the like cargo of filk to *Venice*, where his project was equally unfortunate. For the perfon whom he had trufted, inftead of referving the profit to his mafter, fquandered it in fo high a manner of living, that the *Venetians* informed *Abbas* of his conduct: for which he returned them his thanks, and fent another merchant to receive what was left of the cargo. It is faid, that, finding the *Perfians* had little or no ideas of trade, he encouraged the *Armenians*, and that he broke his fubjects of the cuftom of vifiting *Mahomet*'s tomb at *Mecca*, by repairing himfelf in pilgrimage to the tomb of *Ridza*, at *Tus*, which is decorated with a leg of *Mahomet*'s camel hanging over it.

Shah Abbas.

His notions of commerce.

If

If he had any virtues, they confifted in his endeavours to keep the riches of his dominions within themfelves; for which purpofe, he difcouraged the fettlement of all *Jewifh* and *Indian* merchants in *Perfia*, becaufe of their ufury and

His great public works. exactions. We muft not, however, forget, that he erected fome very magnificent public works in his dominions; and that he feems to have been no perfecutor of the *Chriftians.* His perfon is faid to have been low and mean, and his countenance to have been very expreffive of his character.

Succeeded by *Sain Sefi.* When *Abbas* died, the mother of *Sain*, his fucceffor, was in her haram, bewailing her own misfortunes, and every day expecting that her fon, like her hufband, would fall a facrifice to the tyrant's jealoufy. *Zeynel* and *Kofrew*, two great minifters of ftate in the late reign, with the utmoft difficulty perfuaded her to give them admittance into her apartments, and not even without threats of breaking open the door.

His cruelty. When they entered, fhe delivered to them her fon, telling him, That fhe was putting him into the hands of his executioners. But fhe was foon convinced that they were leading him to his coronation, which was performed with all imaginable pomp and regularity, and he took the name of *Sefi.*

Abbas, notwithftanding all the enormous cruelties he was guilty of, was an innocent compared to *Sefi.* His cruelty was infatiable. As if *Perfia* could not furnifh executioners enough, he put to death, with his own hands, moft of his relations; and, foon after his acceffion to the throne, fcarce one of the blood of *Abbas*, but himfelf, was alive. The reader, from the following inftance, which we fhall give in place of thoufands that may be brought, will, perhaps, conceive fome idea of his character and that of his court.

Puts his uncle to death. and his fons. *Sefi* had an uncle, called *Ifa*, a man of great confequence, and a favourite with *Abbas.* He was married to a handfome witty lady, who bore him three fons, and was extremely agreeable to *Sefi* on account of her converfation. This familiarity produced a fatal effect; for prefuming upon it, fhe touched upon the poffibility of one of her fons fucceeding to the empire after the death of *Sefi*, who was childlefs. The monfter diffembled his indignation for that time, but next day he cut off the heads of the three youths, and was prefent when they were offered, in the moft opprobrious manner, to the mother, who fell at his feet, kiffed him, and wifhed him a long and happy reign. The father, *Ifa*, was then fent for; and, when *Sefi* infultingly fhewed him the heads of his fons, inftead of fhowing any refentment, he told the tyrant, That, had he known his majefty's pleafure, he would have cut them off with his own hands. This incredible meannefs, however, did not fave his life; for *Sefi*, thinking he had gone too far in provoking him, ordered his head likewife to be taken off.

The

The *Persians*, barbarous and abject as this story shews them to have been, could not bear their monster of a shah. The *Turks* had besieged *Baghdad*, and *Sefi* advanced as far as *Hamadan* to relieve it. There his nobility consulted amongst themselves about removing such a monster out of the world. Their consultation was discovered by *Zeynel*, an old and faithful servant of *Sefi*'s family, who was present, and who advised him to put the conspirators to death. *Sefi* replied, That he highly approved of the advice; and, to shew that he was determined to follow it, he put *Zeynel* to death with his own hand next day.

Conspiracy against him, discovered and the conspirators put to death.

Soon after, his high-steward, chancellor, and others of his great officers of state, met with the like fate; some from him, and others from the hands of executioners: and the tyrant, seeing one of his slaves turn his head aside from the horrible murders that were committing, ordered his eyes to be put out; saying, That, as they were so tender, they were useless to him. It is remarkable, that *Sefi*, when he committed all those barbarities, was only a boy; but so ingenious was he in cruelty, that he commonly ordered the nearest friend of the condemned to be his executioner. Not satisfied with that, he obliged sons to testify their approbation of their father's murder: for, at one time, after he had put some noblemen to death, he ordered their sons to behold their dead bodies; and one of them saying, That the death of a father was nothing to him, for he had no father but the shah, he gave the unnatural wretch his paternal estate. He even obliged a son to cut off the ears, nose, and head of his parent. His tyranny also enabled him to make *Mardid* deliver up *Kandahar*, as has been already mentioned, to *Auringzib*; and *David*, another of his great governors, fled into *Georgia*; for which reason, he most brutally revenged himself upon their wives and children. *Kouli Kan*, one of his great lords, who was governor of the *Sheres*, and had done the most important services to *Abbas the Great*, was wantonly beheaded by his order, and after him fifteen of his sons, upon a wicked suggestion that they were begotten by his father *Abbas*.

Farther instances of excessive cruelty.

About the year 1632, *Morad* IV. the *Ottoman* emperor, took *Tauris* and *Erivan*, and was within fifteen days march of *Ispahan*. But *Sefi*, ordering the streams to be cut off that supply the inland parts of *Persia*, they could not advance; and it is said that their whole army, consisting of one hundred thousand men, perished for want of water. It is uncertain in what year this event happened, because it is not mentioned by the *Turkish* historians.

Wars between the *Turks* and *Persians*.

Sefi being determined to retake *Erivan* from the *Turks*, led an army thither, and besieged it for four months; but finding the success did not answer his expectations, he came to the resolution of storming the place in person. His mother, from whom he is said to have inherited his thirst for blood, endeavoured to dissuade him from this rashness; but her advice was rewarded by blows. He dressed himself as a foot-boy, with

Obstinate resolution of *Sefi*, from who re takes *Erivan*.

a poll-ax

a poll-ax in his hand; and, though no breach was made, he put himself at the head of his troops to storm the place. It is almost incredible with what devotion the *Persians* consider the persons of their tyrants. Just as the attack was beginning, all the chief officers and great lords of his army fell at *Sefi*'s feet, and besought him, with tears, not to expose himself and his army to inevitable destruction; but to grant them twenty-four hours to make another attack. *Sefi* consented with difficulty, and they carried the place, though with the loss of fifty thousand men.

This was the most remarkable military action that happened during the reign of *Sefi*, who appears to have been endued with abundance of natural courage: for we are told that he defeated some of his rebel subjects, and obliged the *Turks* to raise the siege of *Baghdad*.

Sefi poisoned, but recovers.

Sefi's cruelties, at last, prevailed upon some of the ladies of his haram to conspire his death; and they gave him poison, but he recovered after a sickness of two months. They had been provoked to this by his having killed several of their companions with his own hand. Upon his recovery, he discovered the conspirators, at the head of whom was his uncle *Isa*'s wife. He ordered a pit to be dug in the garden of his palace; and next night forty ladies, amongst whom was his own mother, were thrown into it and buried alive.

He murders his mother and other ladies,

We have already hinted, that *Sefi* inherited great part of his cruelty from this lady; and some think, that she, and the esteemed *Adawlet*, or prime-minister, were the chief instruments of his cruelty. This minister and *Taketh* supplied the queen-mother with four hundred golden ducats a day, being about one one hundred and fifty pounds sterling, for her own use. Being an eunuch, in the compleat sense of the word, he had free admission, at all times, into her bed-room; and it was no secret that *Shah Abbas* had left with them instructions to put to death many of the great lords, amongst whom was *Kouli Kan* above-mentioned, the most magnificent and powerful subject in *Persia*. The surviving lords, knowing their danger, put the minister to death, and presented themselves in a body, with his blood upon their hands, before the shah, who seemed to approve of what they had done; but, in a day or two after, he put them all to death, as they were sitting in council. The truth is, *Sefi* was generally drunk; to which we must ascribe great part of his cruelty and inconstancy. He had a great kindness for a *Swiss* watch-maker; but the watch-maker happening to kill a *Persian*, who lay with his mistress, and refusing to return *Mahometan*, *Sefi* put him into the hands of the relations of the deceased, who killed him in 1637.

and his chief nobility.

He puts to death his queen.

But the effects of *Sefi*'s intemperance appeared most remarkably in the murder of his *Georgian* queen, the daughter of *Tamuras*, whom he killed in a fit of drunkenness, and next day he called for her. Being told he had stabbed her, he immediately

mediately publifhed an order againft drinking wine; and commanded that all the wine in his dominions fhould be thrown into canals or otherwife deftroyed. We are told of another queen he had, the daughter of a *Circaffian* lady, to whom his own mother had been a flave; and who had fpirit enough to tell him fo, when fhe fent him her daughter, not, as fhe faid, to be his concubine, but his wife. Mention is made of another wife, the daughter of an officer, who was originally a water-carrier; and who was the firft wife he married.

In other refpeds, he was very delicate in his choice of women; and he had three hundred of the handfomeft that *Perfia*, or the neighbouring countries, could afford. His fubjeds of all ranks endeavoured to buy his favour, by prefenting him with beautiful women; and fome of his greateft lords facrificed even their daughters and nieces to his luft. But it is now time to clofe the life of fuch a monfter.

Before his death, the *Turks* retook *Baghdad*. Either intemperance or poifon deftroyed him in the year 1642, after reigning above twelve years. When he was upon his death-bed, he had fenfe and fobriety enough to bethink himfelf of a fon he had of thirteen years of age, whom he had given orders to be blinded. The eunuch who was to have been the executioner, touched with compaffion, had faved the young prince's fight; and, upon hearing *Sefi* bitterly bewail the incapacity (for blindnefs is fuch in *Perfia*) of his fon to fucceed him, he produced him before the fhah; who, finding he had his eyefight, was fo well pleafed, that, it is faid, he lived twenty-four hours longer than otherwife he could have done. We are, however, to obferve, that the order for blinding his fon muft have been in the early part of his reign; becaufe he afterwards ordered the eyes of all whom he commanded to be blinded, to be dug out of their heads and brought to him in a golden difh.

Sefi was very handfome in his perfon and face, which gave no indications of his bloody difpofition. He was, at the time of his death, about twenty-eight years of age; nor is there a good adion recorded of him, but his replacing about three hundred *Georgians*, who had been removed out of their country by his grand-father. He ufed to excufe his cruelties to the *Europeans*, by telling them they were neceffary for keeping fuch a nation of brutes, as he reigned over, in fubjedion. Before he died, he made all his great men recognize the right of his fon to fucceed him.

He accordingly mounted the throne by the name of *Shah Abbas* II. His entry into *Ifpahan*, from *Kafbon*, where his father died, was the moft fplendid of any that can well be imagined. He rode, for fix miles, upon carpets and cloths of gold and filver, which afterwards became the prey of the populace, they being trod upon only by his own horfe; and

the

the rejoicings made by the *Dutch* company, upon that occasion, coft them above three thoufand pounds flerling. His entrance, however, into *Ispahan*, was deferred for three days, becaufe an aftrologer told him that the lucky minute was not come.

About a year after his acceffion, the king of the *Ufbek Tartars* took refuge in *Perfia* againft his own fons, who had dethroned him. *Abbas* received him with the greateft politenefs and magnificence, and gave him fifteen thoufand horfe and eight thoufand foot, with a vaft fum of money, to re-inftate him. The fame year he recovered *Kandahar* from the great

Rebellion of the prince of Jafkes. mogul. The prince of *Jafkes*, an almoft inacceffible province in the fouth of *Perfia*, had rebelled in the late reign, and refufed to pay the tribute impofed upon him by *Abbas* I. after he had conquered *Ormus*. *Abbas* II. ordered the governor of *Ormus* to attack him with twenty thoufand horfe, but that governor died in a bog. He was fucceeded in his command by his brother, whom the prince of *Jafkes* defeated; but the fuperftition of the latter directing him to *Mecca*, to

Courage and good fortune of the princefs of Jafkes. return thanks to his prophet, he was furprized, and carried prifoner to *Ormus* by the new general. But the princefs of *Jafkes*, a woman of more than mafculine fpirit, hearing of her hufband's misfortune, put herfelf at the head of fix thoufand horfe; and, by prodigious marches, fhe furprized the quarters of the *Perfian* general by night; killed him with her own hand; and, having cut in pieces the greateft part of his army, fhe carried off her hufband, with about a dozen ladies of the general's haram. This difgraceful event fo exafperated *Abbas*, that he fent a third brother of the two deceafed generals, at the head of thirty thoufand horfe, to revenge the affront; but he was defeated by the prince of *Jafkes*.

Character of Abbas II. The character of *Abbas* has been differently reprefented. It is certain that he was a friend to the *Chriftians*, that he poffeffed fine natural parts, and that he had an inclination to do juftice; but that often, like his predeceffors, he degenerated into cruelty. He had a genius for drawing and the mechanical arts, which made *European* artifts come into high favour at his court. But the virtues he had were ftained or perverted by his exceffive intemperance in drinking and in women. He ordered feveral of the latter to be burned alive for mere trifles; and one in particular, who declined his embraces, becaufe fhe knew, that, if fhe had a child by him, fhe muft remain in the haram, inftead of being given, as generally happened to the ladies who had no children, to fome great lord in marriage.

His death. As other inftances of his brutal cruelty could convey no inftruction to the reader, we fhall now bring him to his death, which happened by the violence of venereal difeafes he had contracted; and which were heightened by his intemperance. He performed fome acts of juftice upon his oppreffive minifters; but not fufficient to attone for the cruelties he committed during his drunkennefs. His death happened in the thirty-feventh year of his age.

Abbas II. was fucceeded by his fon *Sefi* II. or *Solyman*, whofe mother thought that the officers were come to put him to death, when they knocked at the door of her apartment, that they might conduct him to the throne. Soon after his acceffion he fell fick; and feveral other calamities, particularly famine, afflicting *Perfia* at the fame time, the fuperftitious aftrologers contrived that he fhould be inaugurated again; becaufe, it feems, they had not chofen a lucky minute for his inauguration. This fecond inauguration was performed with many ridiculous ceremonies, though the effential part of it was, the putting a rich cap, adorned with feathers, upon the emperor's, or fhah's, head, and the girding him with a fword.

In this prince's reign lived a great man, who, in common with others of the fame quality, was called *Ali Kouli Kan*. He had often commanded the *Perfian* armies with fuccefs, but being of a temper too plain and boifterous for a court, when his expeditions were over, he was chained up; for which he was called the fhah's lion. Having been under one of thofe confinements for about five years, he prevailed with his keeper to fuffer him to go a hunting, promifing to return by fuch a time. He kept his word, but, upon his return, he baftinadoed the keeper feverely, for prefuming to fuffer a prifoner, whom the fhah had committed to his charge, to be at liberty.

This piece of humour procured him his liberty from *Sefi*; and, to the amazement of the whole court, he came into the fhah's prefence, and told him, That his lion was come to kifs his hands. Being gracioufly received by the fhah, the courtiers poured in prefents upon him; but being deftitute of ready-money, he applied to the *Armenian* merchants, who are *Chriftians* and the greateft traders in *Perfia*; but they refufed to lend him any money. As they were immenfely rich, he refolved to be revenged upon them; and he, one high-feftival day, conducted the fhah to their capital, where he was received by their patriarch, or high-prieft, at the head of their clergy, all of them dreffed in their canonical robes; habits which were fo ftrange to *Sefi*, that he afked his conductor, who their perfons were that wore them. " They are devils," replied *Kouli Kan*; and perfifting in his affertion, he raifed fuch a ftorm againft the *Armenians*, tho' he himfelf was originally a *Chriftian*, that they were obliged to buy their peace with large prefents to the fhah, and about fifteen thoufand pounds to *Kouli Kan*; foon after which the emperor died.

We have little more to add to the hiftory of this prince, but that *Perfia*, under him, was over-run with impoftors, who called themfelves aftrologers, who brought his government

Marginal notes:
He is fucceeded by *Sefi* II.

Remarkable hiftory of *Kouli Kan*,

who inftigates the fhah againft the *Chriftians.*

Death and character of *Sefi* II.

ment

ment into the utmost contempt, and that he suffered the *Us-beck Tartars* to insult him with impunity; and granted the demands of the *Dutch East-India* company, though they had taken from him the island of *Kismiss*, situated near *Ormus*. In short, superstition prevailed so much in his reign, that even armies were headed by astrologers; and, through their folly, ten thousand *Persians* were drowned in an expedition against the *Kusals*, who were not above one thousand in number.

We have a vast number of particulars, related by travellers, concerning the personal behaviour of this shah; but all of them tend only to let us know, that he inherited his family vices, those of drunkenness and cruelty; and the particulars are too shocking and indecent to be transmitted by history; being no other than the frolics and barbarities of a man mad by drinking. He was, in his person, a prodigy of strength, but very handsome; and was distinguished from the common ranks of his subjects only by his imperial cap of feathers. Towards the end of his reign, he grew excessively avaritious; and his vast debauches almost emaciated him. In short, he was, like his immediate predecessors, a reproach to human nature; and he died in the year 1694, aged forty-eight, of which he reigned twenty-nine.

He is suc-ceeded by *Hufeyu.*

Sefi, or *Solyman*, is said to have left behind him no fewer than threescore sons, and was succeeded by one of them. *So-lyman* appointed his eunuchs, and infamous favourites, to be the executors of his will; which was, that they should raise to the throne either *Hufeyu*, or his elder brother *Mirza Ab-bas*, a prince endowed with every royal accomplishment. *Hufeyu*'s indolence gained him the preference; and *Abbas*, upon *Hufeyu*'s being raised to the throne, was confined in prison: but *Hufeyu*, from a principle of religion, or, as some say, from a private contract between him and *Abbas*, could not be prevailed upon to deprive him of his sight.

Hufeyu's grandmother, by the mother's side, had been a great instrument of his advancement to the throne; and had brought over the eunuchs, who had then the management of the empire, to his party. *Hufeyu*, amongst many other weaknesses, had that of being superstitious to the last degree. This, joined to a puny natural constitution, formed a most despicable character; and he was extremely bigotted in the formalities of his religion, particularly in an aversion he had to wine. It was by no means for the interest of the eunuchs to have a sober sovereign upon the throne. They complained of it to the queen-mother as a breach of their covenant with her. There was a necessity for her inducing her son to get drunk; for the eunuchs, at that time, composed a tribunal, to which all other tribunals in the kingdom were subordinate; and the shah himself could be considered in no other light than that of being their creature, whom they could set

Str tagem to make him drink wine.

up, or depose, at will. The queen-mother was persuaded to appear sick, and the physicians were ordered to prescribe

wine

wine for her recovery. Her son, the shah, who tenderly loved her, presented it to her lips; but she refused to taste it till he had drank some. He objected the sin he must commit in tasting it; but she quieted his conscience by telling him, That a king of *Persia* could not be guilty of sin. He seemed to be persuaded, and drank up the bowl; which he found to be so pleasing, that he made it, ever after, his constant companion.

The eunuchs having thus succeeded, in keeping the shah almost perpetually drunk, took care to supply him with money for gratifying his other favourite passions; which lay in women, and magnificence in his buildings and equipages, which were so excessive, that the ordinary revenues of the crown could scarcely defray the expence. But the eunuchs took care to supply him, by oppressing the people to such a degree, that all *Persia*, for some time, may be said to have been exposed to the rapine and injustice of those wretches, who were put in by the eunuchs to govern the people; and who, having bought their places, were obliged to sell their justice, and reduce the subjects to the most deplorable situation. It would be both tiresome and uninstructive to the reader, to give particular instances of this. It is sufficient to say, that, at the time we now treat of, all regular government, all principles of morality, and almost all social intercourse, were lost amongst the *Persians*, who were abandoned to the scourges of those monsters, and the robbers whom they substituted for their governors. *His magnificence in buildings and equipages.*

His abandoned government.

As to the shah himself, he gave himself up to the most unmanly and ridiculous diversions, within the walls of his haram, without giving the least attention to government, and without once reflecting that he was a sovereign

It is almost incredible that any people could bear such tyranny from such wretches as the eunuchs, however they might bear it from their own king; but the *Persians* were made to be slaves, and the greater the burthens that were heaped upon them, the more they thought themselves obliged to crouch under them.

This happened not to be the case with the *Afgans*, a people partly subject to the *Moguls*, their residence lying in the province of *Kandahar*, in the eastern part of *Herat*, and in the mountains dividing the *Persian*, *Bukharian*, and *Indian* dominions. Though we call them *Afgans*, because that by that name they made the most considerable figure in the great scenes we are to open, yet, as is usual in those countries, they were divided into a great number of tribes; such as the *Balluchi*, the *Abdollis*, the *Khizi*, and many others. They had been subject to many different princes, according as the *Arabs* and *Tartars*, the *Moguls* of *India*, or the *Persians* had prevailed; and, not being perpetually galled by one yoke, they conceived ideas of liberty. The *Persian* monarchs, however cruel and oppressive to the subjects of the interior *Character and history of the Afgans.*

parts

parts of their dominions, found their account in treating the *Afgans* with lenity; an indulgence which they compensated by a faithful obedience to government. The oppressions of the infamous eunuchs made them feel and reflect that they **They** were men. They complained to the king; but his mini- **complain.** sters, or eunuchs, stiled their complaints treason; and their deputies were dismissed with contempt and neglect; which brought them into a disposition to become independent.

A gover- The eunuchs, who governed every thing at court, to re- **nor is sent** duce them, made one *Gurghim Kan*, who was governor of **them.** *Georgia* and *Kirman*, governor of *Kandahar* likewise. He was by birth a *Georgian*, and had once fought against the *Persians* for the liberty of his country; but perceiving that the prin- cipal men in it were corrupted by the *Persian* gold, he turned *Mahometan*, ingratiated himself with *Husseyu*; and, being of a bold and daring disposition, he undertook to keep the *Af- gans* in quiet. With this view, he marched, at the head of a body of *Persians* and *Georgians*, into the country of the *Af- gans*, and gave them up to the mercy of his soldiers, who inflicted upon them the most cruel indignities and oppres- sions.

History Amongst the other deputies sent to court by the *Afgans*, **and ma-** was one *Mir Wis*, the head of a tribe, and otherwise a man **nagement** of great quality, rank, and capacity. He had been privately **of the fa-** furnished with a large sum of money by his constituents; **mous** *Mir* and, by observing the course of parties that were formed at **Wis.** court, he put it to an excellent use; for he employed it in strengthening the party that had been formed against *Gur- ghim*; and he had interest enough, while *Gurghim* was in *Kan- dahar*, to get himself introduced to *Husseyu*. As his appear- ance was noble, and his eloquence graceful, natural, and pa- thetic, he prepossessed the shah in his favour, and inspired him with a jealousy of *Gurghim*, who, by this time, thought himself so secure, that he had dismissed the *Persians* who were in his army, and only retained the *Georgians*, as being by far the best soldiers, and the most faithful to his person.

Notwithstanding this advantage, *Mir Wis* had still a great point to gain. The *Afgans* were zealous *Mahometans* of the *Sunnis* sect; and it was a matter of conscience with them, how far their law authorized them to take up arms against their *Mahometan* prince, tho' a tyrant. *Mir Wis*, well know- ing that the doctors of *Mecca*, who were all *Sunnis*, mortally hated *Husseyu*, who was a *Shiite*, undertook a journey to *Mecca* and *Medina*, to consult the mollas, for so those doc- **Gets the** tors were called, upon this point; and, by painting the go- **Mahomet-** vernment of *Husseyu* in the most detestable colours, he ob- **an doctors** tained a full resolution in favour of taking arms against his **on his side** sovereign, who was not only a tyrant but a heretic; for so they esteemed the *Shiites*; and who, as *Mir Wis* falsly al- ledged, had disturbed the *Sunnis* in the practice of their devo- tion.

Mir

Mir Wis kept this festa, or opinion, secret. Upon his return to the *Persian* court, which he found alarmed by an ambassy from the czar, *Peter the Great*, of *Muscovy*, containing some intimations of a claim which the ambassador had, by birth, upon the crown of *Armenia*. Though this claim proceeded, perhaps, only from the vanity of the ambassador, who was originally an *Armenian*, yet *Mir Wis* magnified it into a plot between the ambassador and *Gurghim*, to possess themselves of the sovereignty of *Armenia* and *Georgia*, which were both of them *Christian*. This insinuation was so artfully propagated, that the prime-minister, who had been gained by *Mir Wis*, procured *Husseyn*'s consent that *Mir Wis* should be honoured with robes of state, and other distinctions of favour; restored to his rank amongst his countrymen, of which he had been deprived; and sent back to *Kandahar*, to be a check upon *Gurghin*'s ambition.

Upon the return of *Mir Wis* to *Kandahar*, *Gurghim*, who more than suspected his commission, by way of trying him, demanded in marriage his daughter, who was a celebrated beauty; a proposal which, he knew, a bigotted *Sunnite* never would agree to, when coming from a *Shiite*. When this demand was made, *Mir Wis* had occasion for all his dissimulation to concert the measures he was resolved upon; and he easily imposed upon *Gurghim*, who had never seen his daughter, by sending a young lady in her place magnificently dressed. In short, he dissembled so well, and railed so loud against his refractory countrymen, that *Gurghim*, at last, looked upon him as one of his best friends. *Gurghim* had about him, at that time (the year 1709) only a guard of about one thousand *Georgians*, but all of them picked men; and *Mir Wis* found means to persuade *Gurghim* to send off the greatest part of them to reduce the heads of a tribe whom he had secretly persuaded to refuse to pay their taxes, and to whom he professed himself an inveterate enemy. *Gurghim*, at this time, resided in *Kandahar*; but *Mir Wis* and his *Afgans* were encamped, as usual, in tents, and happened to be then near that city.

In the mean while, *Mir Wis* had engaged a large party of his countrymen to take arms for the recovery of their liberty as he called it, and to approach privately towards *Kandahar*, whence he invited *Gurghim* to a feast in his camp. The invitation was accepted of, and *Gurghim*, buried in sleep and wine, was murdered, with all his *Georgian* and *Persian* attendants; who, dressing themselves in the arms and habits of the deceased, got, that very night, possession of *Kandahar*.

The behaviour of *Mir Wis*, on this occasion, was wise and moderate. The town, as he had concerted, was full of his *Afgans*; yet he offered a licence for all the inhabitants of *Kandahar* to depart, with their effects, if they were not disposed to accept of the liberty he had it now in his power to

His success, and promoted dissimulation

He murders Gurghim.

C 4   give

give them. The inhabitants heard him with shouts of applause, and swore they would stand by him with their lives.

He takes the pass of Zibel. Soon after, the detachments of the *Georgians*, who, by the contrivance of *Mir Wis*, had been sent to reduce the rebels, returned towards *Kandahar*; but, though *Mir Wis* was greatly superior to them in number, he could make no impression upon them, and they fought their way into *Persia*, leaving *Mir Wis* to take possession of the important pass at *Zibel*.

His pretended enthusiasm. After this, *Mir Wis* pretended to commence enthusiast; and rejected, with texts taken from the *Koran*, in his mouth, all terms of accommodation offered by the *Persian* court; and even went so far as to imprison the messengers who brought them. After this, he defeated the khan of *Herat*, who advanced against him at the head of fifteen thousand horse, though he had no more than five thousand *Afgans*; and, multiplying victory upon victory, the *Persians*, at last, were obliged to employ *Kosroph*, who was governor of *Georgia*, and nephew to *Gurghim*, to suppress the rebellion. He **The Persians take Zibel, and besiege Kandahar** had an army with him of thirty thousand *Persians*, and one thousand two hundred *Georgians*, and soon made himself master of *Zibel*; and then marching on, he besieged *Kandahar*; while *Mir Wis* remained in the field, with a handful of forces, who continued faithful to him, but were soon increased by tribes of *Afgans* resorting to him from the mountains.

They are defeated. The inhabitants of *Kandahar* offered to surrender the place upon terms. *Kosroph* would hear of none; and drove the inhabitants to despair, till *Mir Wis* finding means to cut off his provisions, the latter gave him so total a defeat, that only seven hundred of his army escaped, he himself remaining **Death of Mir Wis.** amongst the number of the slain. This happened about the year 1710; and, though the *Persians* made several efforts to recover *Kandahar*, yet *Mir Wis* still remained victorious, reduced the whole province of *Kandahar*, and died, in peace, king of it, in the year 1715.

He is succeeded by his brother Abdollah, who is murdered *Mir Wis*, at the time of his death, had no sons of sufficient age for government; and therefore left his crown to his brother *Abdollah*. This prince was of a very different disposition from *Mir Wis*; and, entering into a negotiation with the *Persians*, he was upon the point of restoring the whole province of *Kandahar* to them, though upon very good conditions, when he was murdered by *Mahmud*, the eldest son of *Mir Wis*, then about eighteen years of age, and who was soon after proclaimed king of *Kandahar*.

Herat becomes an independent state. At the same time that *Kandahar* thus dismembered itself from the *Persian* monarchy, *Herat* did the same, by the means of *Ezadallah*. He was the son of one of the chiefs of the *Abdollis*, an *Afgan* tribe, which had submitted to the *Persian* government; and his father wanting to prostitute him to the infamous lust of the governor, *Ezadallah*, to avoid infamy
committed

committed parricide. He then put himself at the head of a small army; and every where routing the *Persians*, he became, at last, master of the whole province of *Herat*, and the capital itself, by favour of the inhabitants; who, like *Ezadallah*, were all of them staunch *Sunnis*, and therefore detested the *Persians*.

About the same time, the *Usbeks*, and other barbarians, broke into *Korasan* and *Sherwin*, and defeated great armies of the *Persians*. But the chief attention of *Husseyu* and his court was turned against *Ezadallah*, who defeated a great army of them, and killed their general, a youth of eighteen years of age, with his father, an old judge, who served as his lieutenant over eight thousand *Persians*, with the loss of three thousand of the *Abdollis*.

The government of *Husseyu* becoming now contemptible, the *Arabs* of *Maskat* made themselves masters of *Barayan*, and then went to take *Gomron*, to which city *Abbas the Great* had transferred the commerce of *Ormus*. *Fatey*, *Husseyu*'s first minister, offered his service to suppress them; but *Husseyu*, fearing to put him at the head of an army, gave the command of it to *Luft*, *Fatey*'s brother-in-law. This general endeavoured to engage the *Portuguese* in his master's service; but either the poverty or avarice of his court, or both, disabled him from paying them, and he was forced to remain upon the defensive.

Mahmud, on the other hand, raised an army to invade *Kerman*; and, after undergoing vast difficulties, he made himself master of the capital which bears the same name; and laid heavy contributions upon the inhabitants. *Luft*, or, as he is called, *Luft Ali*, who remained still at the head of an army, flew to their relief and recovered the capital; but put the inhabitants under more severe contributions than the *Afgans* had done.

This success emboldened the *Persian* court so much, that a very great army was raised to reduce *Kandahar*. Nothing could have prevented this but the envy of the *Kerman* lords, and others, who had suffered by him in their estates, and who brought the shah's almoner and his physician into their party. They had great influence with the shah; and he was prevailed upon to give orders for putting *Luft Ali* and *Fatey* under an arrest, and the latter to the torture; which was accordingly done. But, such was his stupidity, and such the dissentions that prevailed amongst their enemies, that even *Husseyu*, at last, was convinced of their innocence; and, though he had barbarously ordered *Fatey*'s eyes to be put out, he spared his life; and, had it been in his power, he would have restored both him and *Luft Ali* to his favour.

After this, the *Lesji* invaded *Sherwan*; and *Vustanger*, the *Georgian* general, would have defended it, had not *Husseyu* been prevailed upon to make a peace; upon which *Vustanger* retired in great disgust, swearing that he never would

again

Marginal notes:

Other rebellions.

Mahmud takes *Kerman*, but loses it again.

Husseyu is betrayed by his favourites.

His ar-
mies are
defeated.

The Af-
gans again
take the
field,

and Mah-
mud ad-
vances
against Is-
pahan.

His pro-
grefs.

Oppofed
by the
Perfian
army,

who,
through
treachery,
are de-
feated.

again draw his fword in the fervice of the fhah. The *Leffi*,
who had concluded peace only through fear of that general,
hearing of his refentment, recommenced their hoftilities;
and, after giving the *Perfians* repeated defeats, they made
themfelves mafters of all the province of *oberwan*, and defeated a body of forty thoufand *Perfians*.

In the mean while, the *Afgans*, who had been intimidated
into a fubmiffion by *Luft Ali*, hearing of his difgrace, and
that of his brother-in-law the firft minifter, with the other
diftractions of *Perfia*, recovered their fpirits; as *Mahmud*,
whofe glory had been eclipfed, did his credit. He raifed an
army of fifteen thoufand men, and he was joined by all the
tribes related to the *Afgans*. The miferable ftate the *Perfian*
empire was then in, gave him hopes of fuccefs in his enterprize, which was no lefs than to attempt the conqueft of all
Perfia and the dethronement of *Huffeyn* It is uncertain what
the number of the *Afgans* were with which he fet out; but it
is certain they could not be lefs than five thoufand difciplined men. He marched to *Kerman*, after paffing through
prodigious deferts, and reached it in *Faruary* 1722; but he
found himfelf unable either to take the fortrefs of that city or
that of *Yutzd*; and, after the lofs of four thoufand men, he
pointed his march to the capital, *Ifpahan*, which was but
ill provided to refift him.

Huffeyu and his court had flattered themfelves that it would
be impoffible for *Mahmud* to furmount fuch a march as he
did before he could reach *Ifpahan*; but, when they faw him
at the gates of their capital, they fent *Mohammed*, who was
then firft minifter, to offer him money, if he would defift
from his enterprize. This unadvifed ftep convinced *Mahmud* of the extreme weaknefs of the *Perfian* court; he rejected the offer, and advanced to *Gulnabad*, in *Englifh*, *The
Conferve of Rofes*, a town fituated within nine miles of *Ifpahan*. While he lay there, after many debates in the court of
Perfia, it was refolved to give him battle.

Never was there feen fuch a difparity in the looks of two
armies. The *Afgans*, through the incredible length of their
march, appeared emaciated, and were deftitute of cloaths;
even their officers had fcarce a rag to cover them; and without all kind of artillery but a few fmall arms; while the *Perfian* army appeared in all the pomp and luxury of their anceftors, under a *Xerxes* or a *Darius*. The battle joined;
and, at firft, went fo hard againft the *Afgans*, that *Mahmud*
had prepared fome of his dromedaries to carry him out of
the field; when, by the courage and good conduct of *Nafer*,
one of his generals, the fortune of the day changed in favour
of the *Afgans*. They were affifted by the treachery of an
Arabian general, who, after plundering *Mahmud's* camp,
marched off with the booty, and left the *Perfians* to be cut in
pieces. The *Afgans* made themfelves amends by taking the
Perfian camp, and all its rich furniture. The lofs is faid to
have been no more than two thoufand on each fide; but the

defertion amongft the *Perfian* troops amounted to thirteen thoufand.

It appears from the beft authorities, which notwithftanding the latenefs of the transaction, are precarious and contradictory to one another; that *Makmet*, the *Arabian* prince or wali, who had plundered the *Afgan* camp, was in fact *Huffeyn*'s general on this occafion; and, affifted by the natural cunning of his country, had found means notwithftanding all that had paffed, to preferve his confidence. *Ifpahan* was unguarded, being little more than an open city, deftitute of fortifications that were tenable, ammunition or provifions. Never did prince take more pains to ruin himfelf, than *Huffeyu* did upon this occafion. *Mahmud*, who had little experience in war, made no ufe of his victory; and had not fo much as carried off the artillery, which the *Perfians* had abandoned in the late engagement. His inactivity gave time for the *Perfian* generals to repair the old fortifications of *Ifpahan*, to add new ones, and to fill that city with large bodies of troops, and the inhabitants of the neighbouring country. *Heffeyu*'s prime minifter, was for having him retire to *Kafbin*, which was fortified, and there to make a ftand. But the *Arab* general, who on this occafion was made governor of *Ifpahan*, reprefenting the difgrace that muft attend fuch a ftep, and the contemptible number, and the pitiful condition of the rebels, it was refolved to defend *Ifpahan*.

Hesseyú betrayed by his general, who advifes him to defend Ifpahan.

Mahmud feems by nature to have been no great genius, neither in war nor politics, but experience gave him great abilities in both; and he had in his fervice great generals and wife minifters. He had heard, that *Huffeyu* had invited the prince of *Georgia*, whom he moft dreaded, to come to his affiftance. He underftood that troops were marching againft him from all parts of *Perfia*; and that the very garrifon of *Ifpahan* was more than fufficient to deftroy his army. But he was reaffured, by the intelligence he had of the divifions that prevailed in the *Perfian* court; and more than probably by fecret correfpondences he held there. Recovering his fpirits and refolution to the aftonifhment of the *Perfians*, he marched towards *Sherifan*, not far to the eaft of *Ifpahan*, and took poffeffion of the magnificent palace of *Ferebad*, which the cowardly *Perfians* deferted; and left in the hands of the *Afgans* all the cannon and artillery that was to have defended it. He then laid fiege to *Julfa*, a city inhabited by *Armenian* merchants, who for the benefit of commerce, had been fettled there by *Abbas the Great*. The merchants, fome of whom were very rich, made for fome time a vigorous defence, in hopes of being relieved from *Ifpahan*; but deceived in their expectation, and a breach being made in their walls, they were obliged to compound matters with *Mahmud*, and to ranfom the plunder of their city, by paying him about one hundred and feventy five thoufand pounds,

Diftreffes of Mahmud.

He takes Ferebad, and Julfa.

and

and fifty virgins, who were to be sacrificed to the lust of the conquerors. But money had more charms for the *Afgans*, than beauty, and all of them but a few, who were contented with their new lovers, were suffered to be ransomed; nay some of them without ransom, were sent back to their parents. The contribution imposed upon their city was severely and rigorously exacted, not without circumstances of injustice and cruelty by the conqueror.

He besieges Ispahan. As *Julfa* was one of the suburbs of *Ispahan*, *Mahmud* prepared to besiege that city, which is said then to have been of vast extent, and containing in the whole about seven hundred thousand inhabitants. The avenues to it, and the neighbourhood of it, are represented as most enchanting spots, and it was accessible only by bridges. The treachery of the *Arab* general began at this time to be suspected by *Husseyn* himself; and *Ahmed Aga*, a white eunuch, had been made governor of *Ispahan*. Before *Mahmud* begun the siege,

Treaty between him and Husseyu a treaty was set on foot between him and *Husseyu*, who to spare the effusion of blood, offered to confirm to him the sovereignty of *Kandahar*, together with the province of *Haffaray*; and to make him a present of a great sum in ready money besides. *Mahmud* could have no objection to this proposal, but being resolved to be treated with on the footing of a king, and a sovereign prince, he demanded *Husseyu*'s daughter in marriage, to prevent all future objections to his blood, or that of his descendants. This demand be-

broken off. ing imprudently refused by the proud shah, hostilities went on; and *Mahmud* attacked the bridge of *Sheraz*, one of the principal leading to *Ispahan* *Ahmed* was a brave man and a good soldier, and being served by an *European* engineer, he

Mahmud is defeated gave the *Afgan* so severe a repulse, that, had it not been for the private intelligence he had with the *Arab* general, he would have abandoned the siege. But being encouraged by the infidelity of the *Arab*, he turned the siege into a blockade, and endeavoured to cut off all provisions from the city, by ravaging the neighbouring plains, which are wonderfully extensive, populous, and fertile. He could not have succeeded even in this, had it not been for the dissentions of the *Persian* lords, who were marching to the relief of *Ispahan*, and who

but cuts off a grand convoy of provisions. refused to serve under *Ali Merdan*, the prince *Wali*, or *Loreftan*. Those dissentions gave an opportunity for *Aman*, the bravest of *Mahmud*'s generals, to attack and defeat them separately, and to cut off a grand convoy of provisions, which were marching to *Ispahan*.

Ispahan invested. But the want of discipline in the garrison, contributed still more effectually to the ruin of *Husseyu*. The *Georgians* were the flower of his troops, and were entrusted with the important pass of the bridge of *Abbas Abad* But receiving a supply of brandy, they intoxicated themselves so, that they were cut in pieces without resistance, and the pass was seized by the *Afgans*, who thereupon compleatly invested the

city.

city. This inveftiture proves either the rafhnefs, and ignorance of *Mahmud* in military affairs, or the vaft dependance
he had upon the traytors about *Huffeyu*'s perfon. The braveft
and moft fenfible of the *Perfian* generals reprefented to the
fhah how eafy it would be, with one brifk fally, to cut in
pieces the handful of miferable mountaineers, who kept fo
great an army cooped up, or at leaft to befiege the befiegers.
But this propofal, by the influence of the *Arab*, who pretend- *Huffeyu*
ed that every day would bring frefh fuccours, was rejected *again be-*
by *Huffeyu*; and, at the worft, that prince ftill flattered him- *trayed.*
felf with the poffibility of accommodating matters with his
enemy.

Mean while, *Aman* the *Afgan*, general, who continued Cruelty
with a flying army to fcour the plains of *Ifpahan*, had been of the
guilty of the moft fhocking cruelties and breaches of faith, *Afgans,*
towards the miferable peafants of *Perfia*. Having furprized
a large body of them who delivered up their arms, on promife of their receiving quarter, he put all of them to death
in cold blood, excepting thofe who could pay a ranfom for
their lives. The inhabitants of *Little Ifpahan*, and the neighbouring country, looked upon this as a common caufe; and
perceiving that the fatigues of the march had greatly dif-
ordered the *Afgans*, affembled in a body, and entirely routed is reveng-
them. On this occafion the baggage and plunder of the *Afgans* ed.
fell into the hands of thofe peafants; which exafperated *Mah-*
mud himfelf, who thought the honour of his arms fo much
concerned, that he purfued them with a body of horfe, but
the peafants facing about entirely defeated him; and, amongft
a great number of other prifoners, they took *Mahmud*'s
uncle, and younger brother, with his two coufins. *Mahmud*
was extremely mortified, at feeing his arms fuffer fuch
checks, and as he loved his relations, he even ftooped to
apply to *Huffeyu*, for his interceffion in their favour. This
was readily granted, but before the meffenger was able to
reach *Little Ifpahan*, the vindictive peafants had impaled their
prifoners, and he faw their bodies upon the ftakes; and at
the fame time was informed, that they had been put to death
by way of reprifals. This being related to *Mahmud*, he
ordered all his *Perfian* prifoners to be put to the fword without diftinction.

This feafonable act of valour by an undifciplined body, *Huffeyu is*
filled *Mahmud* with fuch apprehenfions, that he was about betrayed.
to have raifed the fiege, and had actually made difpofitions
for that purpofe It was in vain for the *Armenians*, and the
braveft of the *Perfian* officers, to remonftrate to *Huffeyu*, how
very eafy it would be to cut off his retreat. *Huffeyu* continued to be lulled by the treacherous arts of the *Arab*, who
had entirely regained his afcendancy over him, and filled
him with fufpicions of the fidelity of the *Armenians*. The
Arab therefore procraftinated matters fo much, on pretence
that the neceffary fuccours were not arrived, and that the
Armenians

His gere-
rals de-
feated.

Armemians were not to be trufted, that the fhah's troops returned ingloriouſly into *Iſpahan*, without attempting any
thing againſt the enemy. To compleat the misfortunes of
Huſſeyu, the khan of *Kokilan*, who was advancing to his
aſſiſtance with ten thouſand men, was defeated ; and the
other princes, either themſelves prompted by motives of ambition, or corrupted by *Mahmud*, or both, refuſed to act
under the generals he had appointed. *Mahmud*'s intelligence
was ſo good, that he reſumed his ſpirits, and recommenced
the ſiege of *Iſpahan*.

He puts
his ſon in
his own
place,

Notwithſtanding all the arts of the *Arab*, the voice of the
people at laſt convinced *Huſſeyu*, that he had been betrayed ;
but the *Arab* ſtill aitfully perſuaded him, that all the miſcarriages of his government weie owing to his not having a general of authority enough to make the *Perſians* obey him.
Huſſeyu, upon this, ſent for his eldeſt ſon, *Abbas*, and, as ſome
ſay, reſigned the government into his hands ; but, perhaps,
it is more proper to ſay, that he put him at the head of the

but im-
priſons
him.

adminiſtration. The young prince inſtantly ordered the
Arab, the chief phyſician, and their known accomplices, for
execution : but they perſuaded the father to ſhut him again
up in the priſon from which he had been taken. It thereby
appears that the father did not, at leaſt, reſign the crown to
him.

A ſhort trial was made of *Sefi*, the next ſon in order of
birth ; but, being found deſtitute of capacity, he too was remanded to his priſon : and the third ſon was ſet aſide on account of his religious turn : ſo that, in the end of *May*, 1722,
Thamas, the fourth ſon, was declared the preſumptive heir of
the crown ; and, breaking through a poſt which was commanded by *Aſhauf*, ſon to *Abdollah*, *Mahmud*'s murdered
brother, he reached *Koſbin*. There he met with cruel diſap-

He is be-
ſieged by
his ſub-
jects.

pointments. All the governors, princes, and great lords,
upon the frontiers, though ſubjects to *Huſſeyu*, and at the
head of armies, ſhewed a great coldneſs in his ſervice, and
Thamas was utterly incapacitated to advance to his father's
relief. This backwardneſs was occaſioned by the ſecret hopes
moſt of thoſe great men had of each erecting an independent
ſovereignty out of the ruins of his country.

Famine
rages in
Iſpahan.

The abſence of *Thamas* ſerved the treacherous views of the
Arab, becauſe it was a pretext for his not attacking the poſts
of the *Afgans* until the prince came up with his army, ſo as
to put them between two fires, and utterly to deſtroy them.
The people, however, having ſenſe enough to perceive that
the troops in the city were more than ſufficient for deſtroying
their enemies, inſiſted loudly upon their being attacked.
They were the more clamorous on account of the famine
that began to prevail amongſt them ; and the *Arab* was
obliged to give way ſo far to them, as to march out ſeveral
times ; but he always returned without fighting ; and generally

nerally pleaded in his excuse, that the astrologers told him, the lucky hour was not yet come.

Those pretexts, equally stale and ridiculous, at last exaf- Mutiny of perated the people into a kind of mutiny; and they beset the peo-*Husseyu*'s palace, demanding that he, in person, should lead ple. them on to action. He endeavoured to put them off till next day; but they persisting in an immediate compliance to their demand, they were fired upon by an army of eunuchs, who were always maintained within the palace walls. Upon this, the brave *Ahmed*, then the governor of the city, stepped in to his sovereign's relief, attacked the *Afgans*, forced their chief post, and would have entirely defeated them, had it not been for the infamous conduct of the *Arab*, who drew off his men just as victory was about to declare itself for the *Persians*. *Ahmed*, seeing the *Arab*'s treachery, or- *Ahmed* dered his *Persians* to fire upon his troops; and, both *Huf-* defeated, *seyu*'s bodies being thereby thrown into confusion, the *Afgans* rallied, recovered their post, and forced their enemies to retreat to *Ispahan*.

Upon their return, the *Arab* had the art to prevail upon *Husseyu* to disgrace and dispost *Ahmed*; but the loyal eunuch died a few days after, as is supposed, of grief, or by poison.

Nothing now remained before *Husseyu*'s eyes but the pro- as is the spect of inevitable ruin. It was compleated by *Mahmud*'s governor being able to buy off the governor of *Sejestan*, who was ad- of Sejestan vancing to the relief of *Ispahan* with ten thousand troops. The price was certain very rich presents, and the government of *Korasan*. This success, together with the indolence of the prince, or sultan, *Thamas*, from whom very great things were expected; and, above all, the famine which now raged in *Ispahan*, rendered *Mahmud* secure of his prey. The unhappy *Husseyu*, unable to resist longer the cries of his people and the sight of their miseries, offered the command of his armies to *Luft*, who had before acted at their head with so much success; but he had too great knowledge both of the weakness of the troops, and the treachery of the court, to accept it As his last resource, he renewed his negotiation with *Mahmud*; offered him his daughter in marriage; the provinces of *Korasan*, *Kirwan,* and *Kandahar*, in sovereignty; and one hundred and fifty thousand pounds besides, if he would draw off his army: but the *Afgan* haughtily an- Haughti- swered, that he had already in his own power all that *Huf-* ness of *seyu* offered; and thus the negotiation broke off. Mahmud.

The reduction of the whole province of *Korasan*, under Misery of *Meluk*, late governor of *Sejestan*, left *Husseyu* nothing to hope Husseyu. for, but his being received by the conqueror upon his absolute submission. Famine drove numbers of *Persians* out of the city, where their throats were cut by the *Afgans*, who gave them no quarter. All the treasures of *Husseyu*, both in plate and ready-money, with all the sums he had been able to borrow from the *English* and *Dutch* merchants, were now entirely

tirely exhaufted ; and, at laſt, about the end of *September*, he offered entirely to ſubmit to *Mahmud*'s power.

who con-
cludes a
capitula-
tion with
Mahmud.

It was the twenty-firſt of *October* following before the inhuman *Afgan* terminated the negotiation. His reaſon for this delay was, that famine might thin the city of its inha-bitants, ſo as that he might have nothing to fear from them ; for, when they had conſumed all other, even the moſt loath-ſome, animals, they were reduced to live upon one another, till the living were not ſufficient to bury the dead ; and a peſtilence muſt have enſued from the number of dead bodies, had it not been from the remarkable ſalubrity of the air and ſoil of *Iſpahan*.

At laſt, the capitulation, by which *Huſſeyu* was to dethrone himſelf, and become a voluntary captive to the conqueror, was ſigned. All that *Mahmud* deigned to grant, was, that no violence ſhould be offered to the perſons of the king's no-bility, or the ſurviving inhabitants of *Iſpahan*. *Huſſeyu* took a moſt mournful and melancholy leave of his ſubjects, im-puting his and their misfortunes to bad councils. On the twenty-third of *October*, he marched, with his principal at-tendants, conſiſting of about three hundred, towards the *Af-gan* camp ; and was obliged to wait for ſome time, becauſe

Pride of
the latter.
Interview
between
them.

his conqueror, as was pretended, was aſleep. Being intro-duced, he found *Mahmud* in the great hall of his own beloved palace of *Farabad*, ſeated on a cuſhion of gold. *Huſſeyu* gave him the firſt ſalute, which was returned by *Mahmud*. *Huſ-ſeyu*, at laſt, was conducted to a ſeat, from whence he made a ſhort ſpeech, in which he ſaid he chearfully reſigned the empire to *Mahmud*, and wiſhed him proſperity. He then took out of his own turban the royal plume of feathers, which, in *Perſia*, is the badge of ſovereignty, and offered it to *Mahmud*'s firſt miniſter. But this did not anſwer either the pride or the purpoſe of the *Afgan*. He continued in his ſeat, but refuſed to accept the plume from his miniſter ; ſo that *Huſſeyu* himſelf was obliged to ariſe and to fix it in his turban with his own hand, pronouncing theſe words, ' Reign ' in peace."

This ceremony, ſo mortifying to *Huſſeyu*, performed in ſight of all the officers and great men in both armies, was, by them, underſtood to convey to *Mahmud* an undoubted right to the ſovereignty of *Perſia*. When it was over, a re-paſt of coffee and tea was ſerved in ; and *Mahmud*, relaxing of his uſual ſeverity, promiſed to conſider *Huſſeyu* as his fa-ther, and to follow his advice in all he undertook. The re-paſt being over, a detachment of four thouſand *Afgans* took poſſeſſion of the city and palace ; and, on the twenty-ſeventh of *October*, he made a moſt triumphant entry into *Iſpahan*, at the head of his army, attended by all the great officers of ſtate, civil and military, *Perſian* as well as *Afgan*. The un-happy *Huſſeyu* rode upon his left-hand till he entered the ſuburbs, and was then conducted, by a private way, to the

palace.

palace. *Mahmud* not thinking it proper to lead him in triumph through a city where he had been so lately sovereign. This confideration, however, did not prevent *Mahmud*, when he was feated on his throne, in view of all the grandees and people, from obliging *Huffeyu* to come into the affembly, and to be the firft who faluted him king of *Perfia*. After this, the whole affembly took oaths of allegiance to his government.

It is here we muft clofe the reign of *Huffeyu*, which had lafted twenty-eight years; and he may, in fact, be confidered as the laft fovereign of the race of *Sefi*, who reigned independently in *Perfia*; for, though his fon *Thamas* afterwards mounted that throne, yet he held his power from a fubject. That dinafty had lafted about two hundred and twenty-three years in *Perfia*; and fuch an uninterrupted fucceffion of human monfters is not, perhaps, to be parallelled in the hiftory of any nation under the fun. *Huffeyu* is faid, indeed, to have been naturally a good-natured prince, even to a weaknefs; but his indolence and propenfity to pleafure, were as fatal to his people as the cruelty of his predeceffors had been; and his ruin was owing entirely to his own credulity, and obftinate confidence, in a traitor. It is faid, he never put on the red drefs, which the fhahs of his dinafty always wore when they pronounced fentences of death. *His character.*

Though *Mahmud* may be confidered as a rebel, and an ufurper, yet the *Perfians*, after he was eftablifhed upon that throne, found much more eafe under his government, than they had done under the execrable creatures of his good-natured predeceffor. Juftice was impartially adminiftered; the privileges of the *Europeans* were confirmed; and, what is more remarkable, the three great traitors, the *Arab* general, the chief phyfician, and the chief eunuch, in the late reign, had their eftates confifcated, and their perfons fentenced to perpetual imprifonment, in this, for infidelity to their mafter. It is faid they would have been put to death, as all other traitors, and inftruments of their iniquity, were, had it not been that *Mahmud*, who valued himfelf upon keeping an oath, had fworn that he would not take their lives. From the fame principle of juftice, or rather policy, *Mahmud* treated with the higheft honours and diftinctions the firft minifter, *Luft Ali*, and all thofe who had been faithful to *Huffeyu*. He likewife fhewed great marks of regard for that unfortunate prince, and took his daughter in marriage; upon which, *Huffeyu* publifhed a manifefto, directed to all his fubjects, recommending to them *Mahmud's* right to the crown. *His moderation.*

Thamas was then at *Kafbin*, where he had affumed the title of fhah; and *Mahmud*, having levied confiderable taxes upon his new fubjects, fent the monies, which amounted to three hundred and fifty thoufand pounds, to raife new troops in *Kandahar*. But the money was feized by the governor of *Bendor* in *Sejeftan*. In the mean while, *Ahman*, who was the *Thamas affumes the title of fhah.*

D right

right hand of *Mahmud*, attacked *Kafbin*, and took it in *December*; but his cruelty forced the inhabitants into an infurrection, and they drove him out of their city, *Ahman* himfelf receiving a wound in the fhoulder.

Thofe difgraces and loffes made *Mahmud* throw off the mafk, and return to his natural cruelty ; but, according to the beft accounts, it might have been the effects of frenzy, which fometimes feized him. He ordered all the *Perfian* noblemen in his fervice to be murdered at a banquet he had prepared for them ; two hundred fons of the *Perfian* and *Georgian* nobility to be butchered, as he did three thoufand of *Huffeyu*'s troops he had taken into pay, and all who had received penfions or falaries out of the royal exchequer, and numbers of the chief inhabitants of *Ifpahan*; fo that the butchery continued for fifteen days.

His indolence.
After thofe execrable cruelties, which he faid he committed to prevent any infurrections in that capital during his abfence, he fet out for *Tauris*, where fultan *Thamas* was leading a life of indolence and pleafure ; and entered that province at the head of ten thoufand men. who defeated the army of *Thamas*; and *Mahmud*, after taking feveral cities, gave the command of his army to *Zebir Deft*, and returned to *Ifpahan*.

His negotiation with the *Turks* and *Mufcovites*
Thamas, notwithftanding his father's misfortunes, was ftill in poffeffion of all the exterior parts of the *Perfian* empire ; but they were fituated fo that they were extremely convenient for two great princes, the emperor of the *Turks* and *Peter the Great* of *Mufcovy* ; both of whom, being no ftrangers to the diftractions of *Perfia*, invaded it about this time ; the one on the north, the other on the fouth. The czar foon made himfelf mafter of *Daghaftan, Derbend*, and the province of *Khilan*; as the *Turks* did of *Georgia*.

Thamas had nothing to oppofe to thofe mighty powers but the confideration of what was due to royal blood and of the diftreffes he fuffered ; and he fent ambaffadors with thofe reprefentations to the courts of *Conftantinople* and *Ruffia*. There was, at that time, no good underftanding between thofe two powers. The *Turks* pretended it was a fin for them to affift a *Shuite*, and that it was an affront to the *Mahometan* religion for *Thamas* to apply for relief to a *Chriftian* prince ; fo that *Thamas* met with no help at *Conftantinople*. The czar, more politic, gave his ambaffadors a favourable reception, and promifed to reftore him to the crown of his anceftors, upon his yielding up to *Mufcovy* all his right in the provinces of *Ghilan, Mazanderan*, and *Aftrabad*, together with the towns of *Derbend* and *Raku*.

When this treaty was publifhed, it gave *Mahmud* vaft uneafinefs ; which was increafed by the behaviour of *Aman Ollah*, who now began to claim the reward of his fervices, which was no other than an equal partition of all the conquefts he had made. *Mahmud* durft not abfolutely refufe him,

him, but found means, by reprefenting to him the unfettled
ftate of affairs, to quiet him with promifes, leaft he fhould
have joined *Thamas*. *Mahmud*, after this, had leifure to
extend his conquefts; but we are told of a very extraordinary adventure which befel him in *March*, 1724, as he returned to *Iſpahan*.

A *Georgian* lady, who had loft her hufband fighting againft Remark-
Mahmud, became fo defperate that fhe vowed to revenge his able ex-
death upon the *Afgans*; and, for that purpofe, fhe left two ploit of a
children fhe had to the care of her brother, and difguifed lady.
herfelf in man's apparel. Upon *Mahmud*'s entering a city,
when he was upon his journey to *Iſpahan*, fhe attacked his
guard of *Afgans*, and killed twenty of them before fhe could
be taken or difarmed; which, at laft, fhe was, and brought
prifoner before *Mahmud*, who appeared greatly furprized at
her refolution, ordered her wounds to be dreffed, and that
fhe herfelf fhould be taken care of; but we know not the fequel of her hiftory.

In the mean while, *Zeberdeft*, one of *Mahmud*'s favourite *Shiraz*
generals, took the city of *Shiras* by ftorm, and attempted to taken by
take *Gombroon*, but was repulfed by the refolution of a few ftorm.
Engliſh and *Dutch* who had factories there: fo pitiful are all
the boafted exploits of eaftern conquerors. After this, *Mahmud*, at the head of his *Afgans*, marched to *Kokhilan*, which
lies on the road to *Baſſora*, about ten days journey from *Iſpahan*. This expedition proved quite unfuccefsful; the
Arabs harraffed his army fo much that he was obliged to compound with them for its fafety: and, returning with difgrace
to *Iſpahan*, he was forced to beftow about one hundred and
twenty-five thoufand pounds as an indemnification to his foldiers for the loffes they had fuftained by the *Arabs*.

Being thus baffled by fo mean an enemy, it reduced *Mahmud* fo low in the eyes of the public, that, had *Thamas* be- *Thamas*
haved with common fenfe, he might have mounted his fa- opprefſes
ther's throne. Inftead of that, he oppreffed the *Armenians*, the *Arme-*
deprived them of their liberties, and fuffered the *Turks* to *nians.*
become mafters of *Georgia*. After that, they befieged *Erivan*,
the capital of *Armenia*, and took it after a great refiftance.
The bafhaw of *Von*, however, was repulfed at *Tauris* by the
inhabitants, and obliged to retire to *Khoy*. To be revenged He is op-
of this difgrace, the bafhaws of *Baghdad* and *Bafra*, which pofed by
two cities were then in the hands of the *Turks*, laid fiege to the *Turks.*
Hamadan, and took it. This conqueft was attended by a
kind of manifefto, publifhed by the *Turkiſh* refidents, or commiffaries, at the court of *Ruſſia*, declaring the treaty that had
been concluded between *Thamas* and the czar to be void, on
account of the precarious circumftances that *Thamas* was in,
which did not admit of his making any fuch ceffions, and becaufe the *Sublime Port* could not fuffer a foreign power to obtain footing in *Perfia*. In fhort, they required the czar to give

up

up all that had been yielded to him by *Thamas*, and all his conquefts upon the *Caspian Sea*.

His dominions partitioned. Upon this declaration being made, it was thought that a war was unavoidable between the *Turks* and the *Mufcovites* ; efpecially as the former were fo averfe to all treaties with a *Chriftian* prince in prejudice of the *Mahometans*. The grandvizir, however, and the czar's minifters, managed fo artfully, that they concluded a treaty ; by which a kind of a partition of territory was to be made between the emperor of the *Turks* and the czar of *Mufcovy* ; a certain portion being to be left for *Thamas*, if he fhould think proper to accept of it ; and they were to concur in fetting him on the throne of *Perfia*.

This treaty was figned on the eighth of *July*, 1725, and was equally refented by *Thamas* as by *Mahmud*. The latter recruited his armies, and befieged *Yezd* ; but he was obliged to raife the fiege with difgrace and lofs. In fhort, though *Mahmud* had mounted the throne, which *Huffeyu*'s pufillanimity and mifmanagement had loft, yet *Thamas*, both by *Perfians* and foreign powers, was regarded as the fhah of *Perfia*. *Mahmud*'s power lay entirely amongft his countrymen the *Afgans*, and he kept a ftanding army of them in pay. He could not, however, depend upon them ; and, at laft, he grew contemptible in their fight. His perfon was defpicable, and the plain manners of the *Afgans* had been effaced in him by effeminacy. His arms were no longer victorious, and his troops reproached him in the fame terms as the *Macedonians* did *Alexander*, That he was conquered by the people whom he had vanquifhed. This difcontent, at laft, grew outrageous, through the refpect which they paid to *Afhraf*, the fon of *Abdollah*, *Mahmud*'s uncle, whom the reader may remember had been murdered by *Mahmud*.

Rife of Afhraf. This young man, ever fince his father's death, had ferved in a military capacity under *Mahmud*; and was fo much the darling of the foldiers, that the tyrant durft never put him to death, though he knew that *Afhraf* was meditating his deftruction. In this undefirable fituation; he acted a prudent part ; for, having no children of his own, he declared *Afhraf* his fucceffor ; but he kept fo watchful an eye over him, that he was unable to difturb him. All *Mahmud*'s precautions,

Mahmud turns delirious. however, could not guard him againft himfelf. His brain appeared to be touched. He performed a fantaftical penance called the riadhiat ; by which he fhut himfelf up for fourteen or fifteen days, and, by continual agitations of the body and workings of the mind, all the time furrounded with darknefs, he loft the ufe of the fmall reafon that had been left

He butchers the royal family of Perfia. him. But his frenzy took a moft terrible turn, for he murdered one hundred princes of *Huffeyu*'s blood with his own hands, after ordering them to be carried into a court-yard, with their hands tied behind them, where he cut off their heads. The cries of one of *Huffeyu*'s fons reaching the unhappy

happy father, he run forth in an agony to save him, and received upon his own arm the wound that was aimed at the child, who was no more than five years of age. The sight of *Husseyn's* blood seemed to make some impression upon *Mahmud*; and, from that time, he stopped the butchery. He, however, never could recover his senses. His frenzy increased every day, and was discernable in the most extravagant actions of generosity as well as cruelty; no kind of superstition was omitted for his recovery; and no foolish ceremonies, either *Christian* or *Mahometan*, were left unpractised.

Ashraf, in the mean while, was meditating the destruction of the tyrant; and, for that purpose, had entered into a correspondence with *Thamas*, whom he invited to mount the throne of *Persia*. *Thamas* promised *Ashraf* his own terms; and, though *Ashraf* was under a kind of confinement, yet he managed so well, that *Thamas*, by his invitation, drew near to *Ispahan* with an army. The *Afgans* considered themselves as masters of *Persia*, and would not forego their right of raising a prince of their own race to that crown; for which reason they chose *Ashraf* for their king and freed him from his confinement, being headed in their attempt by the great general *Aman Ollah*. *Ashraf*, however, refused to accept of his new dignity, until, by way of atonement for his father's death, the head of the tyrant was brought to him; which it accordingly was, though his frenzy had proceeded to such a height, that, by the course of nature, he could have lived but a few hours, had not his head been cut off. *He is slain by Ashraf.*

The character of *Mahmud*, and his government, must give every considerate person the most despicable ideas of the people whom he conquered and over whom he ruled. His face and personal appearance were shocking; and, though he undoubtedly had courage, yet his failings, ignorance, and inconstancy, threw him even below the common level of mankind. His successes were owing to the valour of his countrymen the *Afgans*; but that valour degenerated when they became the conquerors of *Persia*, and were inured to the delicacies of that inchanting climate. If any thing can be said in favour of this frantic monster, it is the regard he seemed to pay to his word. This is exemplified in his not putting *Ashraf* and *Aman Ollah* to death, though he had reason to believe they were meditating his destruction. But the merit of his clemency receives great abatement when we consider, that both of them were more high in the esteem of the army than he himself was; and to have attempted to take away their lives must have precipitated his own destruction. In short, what was said of the *English Cromwell*, was, with more justice, applicable to *Mahmud*, That he was a fortunate madman. His successes were owing to temerity, and he was but twenty-seven years of age at the time of his death. *His character. Compared with Cromwell.*

Ashraf

Afhraf *Afhraf* began his reign with cruelties, which if poffible,
fucceeds exceeded thofe of his predeceffor, whofe minifters, favour-
him, ites, and guards, he immediately put to the fword. *Aman Ollah*
himfelf was killed; and it was with fome difficulty, and not
till after fhewing him great indignities, that he was prevailed
upon to fpare the mother of *Mahmud*, who had been the
means of inducing her fon to fpare his life. His diffimulation
was equal to his cruelty. For after putting out his brother's
eyes, and confining him, as he did to one of *Mahmud*'s fon's,
his policy. whofe mother he poifoned, he offered his throne to *Huffeyu*,
but that pitiful prince was better pleafed with being fuper-
intendant of the buildings then erecting within the inclo-
fure of the palace. Upon this he married one of *Huffeyu*'s
daughters, and took upon himfelf the title of fultan. But
his engagements with *Thamas*, who had ftill great authority
in *Perfia*, gave him vaft difquiet. At firft, he offered him
the crown of *Perfia*, but *Thamas* difdaining to take that
which he could command, and which was his by right, advanced towards *Ifpahan*, though he was obliged to fly by
Afhraf's fuperior power. In the mean while, the *Turks* had
again made themfelves mafters of *Tauris*, and fhewed fome
difpofitions for marching againft *Ifpahan*, from which they
were with fome difficulty diffuaded; but in *March* 1726, on
Wars with pretext of fome ridiculous controverfy in religion, they de-
the *Turks*, clared war againft *Afhraf*, took *Kafhin*, and *Maragha*, though
the former city was foon after reduced by *Afhraf*.

The indolence and mifmanagement of *Thamas*, at this
time, had made him fo contemptible, that the *Turks* refufed
to treat with him; and feemed to meditate nothing lefs than
the conqueft of all *Perfia*. This they certainly would have
effected, had not *Afhraf* found means to have diffeminated
amongft them, the doctrine of the impiety of *Moflems* cutting one another's throats, by which the *Turkifh* army was
divided. Their general however, being ftill at the head of
feventy or eighty thoufand men, attempted to cut *Afhraf*'s
army in pieces; but religious fcruples had got fuch a foot-
whom he ing among his troops, that he was defeated, and *Afhraf* re-
defeats. mained victorious. He maintained this fuperiority to the
year 1727, when the *Ottoman* court finding the backwardnefs
of their troops to fight againft a *Mahometan* power, every day
increafe, ordered a bafhaw or general, who commanded in
Treaty *Perfia*, to conclude a peace with *Afhraf*. The terms were,
with that the *Turks* fhould have the poffeffion of *Zengan*, *Soltainia*,
them. *Abher*, and *Tahiran*; but that *Khuyeftan* fhould be reftored
to *Afhraf*; who was to be acknowledged king of *Perfia*, and
named in the public prayers, immediately after the *Turkifh*
emperor, who was to be acknowledged the true fucceffor to
the khaliffs of *Baghdad*.

Hiftory Peace being made between *Afhraf* and the *Turks*, upon
and rife thofe, and fome other ridiculous terms; a new agent, who
afterwards

afterwards made the greateſt appearance of any man in the of *Nadir* eaſt, ſtarted up ; and was afterwards known by the famous *Shah*, or name of *Kouli Kan*, and *Nadir Shah*. He was a native of *Kouli Kan*. *Koraſan*, but by deſcent a *Tartar* ; or that ſpecies of *Tartars*, called *Turkmans*; and loſing his father, who was a kind of a taylor, when he was but thirteen years old, he was bred a ſhepherd, and ſupported himſelf and his mother, by carrying ſticks to market upon an aſs, and a camel; the whole of his patrimony. After this, about the year 1704, he was carried into captivity by the *Uſbeks*, with whom he remained about four years; but, after that, eſcaping, he commenced a robber and a murderer, and after various adventures, he killed his maſter, and fled to the mountains with his daughter, whom he made his wife. About the year 1714, he continued his trade of robbing ; and the courage and reſolution he ſhewed, recommended him to the governor of *Koroſſan*, who gave him a poſt under him, ſomewhat reſembling a gentleman uſher. In this ſtation, he found means to be preferred in the army, and behaved ſo bravely againſt the *Tartars* and *Buka- rians*, that he was not only made a colonel, but had a pro- ſpect of riſing to a much higher command. He was diſap- pointed in his expectation by court intrigues, and in the height of his reſentment, his tongue made ſo free with his patron the governor of *Koraſſan*, that by his order he was ſoundly baſtinadoed ; upon this he retired to *Kallat*, where his uncle, who happened to be at the head of a tribe, called *Aſhar*, commanded. His pride and preſumption did not ſuffer him long to remain in a ſubordinate quality, and it was eaſy for him to collect a party of ruffians and robbers, to the number of eight or nine hundred, who choſe him for their head; and in the year 1722, he lived by robbing travel- lers and caravans. A great man, one *Seyfoddin Begh*, hap- pening about that time to be in diſgrace at the court of *Perſia*, fell into the ſame courſe of life, and joining with *Nadir*, their party amounted to about three thouſand. *Nadir* now began to make ſo great a figure, that his uncle procured the ſhah of *Perſia* to pardon him ; and he requited his un- cle's kindneſs by ſeizing his caſtle of *Kallat*, and murdering him. After this he declared for *Thamas*, who was then at *Farabad*, in *Mazamdaran*, in very deſperate circumſtances, and depending upon *Fati Ali*, the governor of that province. The firſt ſervice that *Nadir*, who was now at the head of five thouſand men, performed for *Thamas*, was his taking the important city of *Niſhabur*, from the *Afgans*, and this ſucceſs procured him admitance to *Fati Ali*, who introduced him to *Thamas*, from whom he received a full and a free pardon.

Thamas, who appears to have been a very weak prince, Who be- had been ſecretly diſobliged with *Fati*'s aſſuming behaviour, comes ge- and *Nadir* eaſily ſaw it ; but finding that *Thamas*, on account neral to of an oath he had made, could not be prevailed upon to give *Thamas*. orders for *Fati*'s death, he murdered him himſelf : telling his master, that if he, *Thamas*, was fettered by an oath, he *Nadir*, was not. Upon *Fati*'s death, *Nadir*, who had obtained an entire ascendancy over *Thamas*, became his generalissimo and first minister, and was at the head of eighteen thousand men, with whom he drove the *Balluchis* out of *Mashad*, the capital of *Korasan*; for which service, *Thamas* ordered him to be called *Thamas Kouli Kan*, the addition of his own name, being the highest distinction he could bestow upon a subject. After this *Nadir* reduced the whole province of *Korasan* to his master's allegiance, and with twelve thousand men he subdued *Herat* itself, where he cut off the governor's head.

Ashraf defeated and he murders Husseya, with many of the royal family. *Ashraf* had not, at this time, above thirty thousand troops, whom he could depend upon, but most of them were *Afgans* and provincials, who were reckoned greatly superior to the *Persians*. *Thamas* however, had a general who supplied all defects; and though his numbers were inferior by five thousand, to those of *Ashraf*, yet he gave them battle, and, to the astonishment of all the east, he defeated them, and in two engagements cut fourteen thousand of them in pieces; obliging the remainder to take refuge in *Ispahan*. Here the bloody *Ashraf* murdered the old shah *Husseyu*, and all the males of the imperial family. He then loaded three hundred mules with spoils and treasure, and left *Ispahan*, at the head of twelve thousand of his *Afgans*. He had scarcely marched out of that city, when the *Persian* general *Kouli Kan*, arrived in it with his army, and having quieted the tumults, which were very outrageous, he went to meet *Thamas*, who was coming to *Tahiran*. He met him about six miles from the capital, was received with excess of honours, and he behaved in the most submissive manner. When *Thamas* entered his palace he was shocked by the sight of his father's murdered body, and those of his descendants. But as he was entering the womens appartment, an old woman slave threw her arms around his neck, with an excessive transport of joy; and he soon knew her to be his own mother, who had lived in that disguise, and conformed herself to her appearance, ever since the *Afgans* had obtained the mastery at *Ispahan*.

Insolence of Kouli Kan. *Ashraf* and his *Afgans* had marched no farther than *Shiras*, where they continued to rob and murder the people. *Thamas* expressed great concern for their hardships, but he soon understood, that he was to take law from his insolent general; whom he had made governor of *Korasan*, and promised to give him his aunt in marriage. *Kouli Kan* in return, said he was ready to march with the army against the *Afgans*, but that he did not chose to be exposed to his court enemies in his absence, of which he had known but too many instances; and he therefore demanded to have a power of raising money by his own authority, for paying the troops. *Thamas* saw the tendency of this demand, but was obliged to submit, though in fact he thereby gave himself a master. *Kouli Kan* then, though it was in the depth of winter, marched to

Astaker,

Aftuker, or the antient *Perfepolis*, and on the fifteenth of *January* 1730, he routed *Afhraf* and his *Perfians*; and pur- *Afhraf de-*
fued them with fuch vigour that they were all cut in pieces, *feated and*
and *Afhraf* at their head; though fome have reported that *flain.*
he was taken prifoner, and carried to *Ifpahan*, where he was
curried to death upon a public fcaffold.

Kouli Kan having performed thofe glorious fervices for his *Further*
lawful fovereign, was rewarded, by marrying his mafter's *conquefts*
aunt; and after ftaying for fome time at *Shiras*, he marched *of Kouli*
with the army to wreft from the *Turks* the city of *Hama-* *Kan a-*
dan, which they were in poffeffion of. He performed that fer- *gainft the*
vice, after giving them an entire defeat; and then out march- *Turks.*
ing the bafhaw *Cuproli*, he took *Tauris* and *Ardibel*; and next,
marching to *Herat*, which was in the hands of the *Abdoles*, he
recovered that city, and put the governor and the chief of the
rebels to death. This laft fervice he had fo much at heart,
that to be at leifure to purfue it, he granted a peace to the
Turks; and then he feems to have retired to his government
of *Korafan*; and to have applied himfelf to the forming an
army of *Tartars*, and other barbarians, whom he difciplined,
and attached to himfelf for his own wicked purpofes. In the
mean while, *Thamas* getting the better of his native indolence, and equally afraid of the *Turks*, and his own general,
marched to befiege *Irivan* with five thoufand men. At firft,
he met with fome fuccefs, but his provifions failing, he was *Thamas is*
obliged to raife the fiege, and in his retreat to *Tauris*, he was *defeated*
defeated by *Cuproli* and *Ali*, the two *Turkifh* generals, and *before*
forced to retire to *Hamadan*; by which means, *Tauris* *Laghdad,*
again fell into the hands of the *Turks*. Being joined by the
garrifon of *Hamadan*, he ventured to fight the bafhaw of
Baghdad, but he was defeated in a bloody battle, and the
Turks took poffeffion of *Hamadan* likewife. The diftractions that followed in *Conftantinople*, obliged the *Turkifh*
generals to propofe a peace, which *Thamas*, who was in
danger of lofing *Ifpahan* likewife, gladly agreed to in *Janu-* *makes*
ary 1732 but with the fhameful condition of refigning all *peace with*
his rights to *Armenia* and *Georgia*; the *Turks* engaging to *the Turks.*
affift him in driving the *Ruffians* from their conquefts upon
the *Cafpian Sea*.

It is more than probable, that *Thamas* found himfelf under
a neceffity, equally from the infolence of his general, as from
the power of the *Turks*, to make this peace. *Kouli Kan*, who
faw all his conquefts given up by it, had a plaufible pretext
for oppofing it, which he did in the moft earneft manner;
promifing to affift the fhah with an army. *Thamas* however
difbanded his army, and fent orders for his general to do
the fame. But *Kouli Kan*, far from obeying him, affembled
his army to the number of feventy thoufand men; and, by
expatiating upon the terms of the late inglorious peace, he
perfuaded the chief officers under him, to ftand by him and
by one another, againft the minifters and courtiers, who were
meditating

meditating their ruin; he then advanced with his army to *Iſpahan*, where it was ſecretly reſolved to depoſe *Thamas*, and to place upon his throne *Abbas* his ſon, who was but ſix months old. *Kouli Kan* being arrived near *Iſpahan*, made a general review of his army, at which the ſhah was preſent. As many of the common men were no ſtrangers to the deſigns on foot, *Thamas* might have ſaved himſelf, by ordering his general to be cut to pieces in the field, and by putting himſelf at the head of his army; for he was at that time extremely beloved for his humanity, and the mildneſs of his government; but he neglected the opportunity, and *Kouli Kan* ordering him to be ſeized, while he was intoxicated with wine, put him under arreſt in the garden of his own palace,

but he is deposed by *Kouli Kan*, and finally depoſed; all the great officers, civil and military, by choice or force, ſwearing allegiance to the infant in the cradle.

After this great event, *Kouli Kan* ſteadily purſued what he had profeſſed, the recovery of the ceded provinces from the *Turks*, and laid ſiege to *Baghdad* with eighty thouſand men. Upon this, war was proclaimed at *Conſtantinople*, and *Topal Oſman*, one of the greateſt and moſt remarkable generals the *Turks* ever had, marched to relieve it at the head of eighty thouſand men. *Kouli Kan* was in hopes to have taken the place by aſſault or famine; and though it was garriſoned by twenty thouſand men, it could have held out but a very few days, when *Topal Oſman* came up. A bloody battle was fought between him and the *Perſian* general, *Kouli Kan*, who was at the head of ſeventy thouſand men; and the *Turks* muſt have been routed, had they not been ſo ſeaſonably reinforced by the baſhaw *Mawſel*; while the baſhaw of

who is defeated before *Baghdad*. *Baghdad*, made a ſally which entirely raiſed the ſiege, after it had continued for three months. This battle coſt the *Turks* thirty thouſand men, and *Kouli Kan* loſt as many. He behaved with remarkable courage in it; and after having two horſes killed under him, he loſt all his baggage. This happened in the ſummer of 1733, and *Kouli Kan*, the better to diſguiſe his intention, ſent word to the baſhaw of *Baghdad*, that he was reſolved to pay him a viſit in the ſpring. But the genius of *Kouli Kan* was too active to brook ſuch a delay, for in *October* the ſame year, he penetrated into the *Turkiſh* dominions, as far as *Leyham*, a place within fifteen miles of *Kerkowd*.

But he defeats the *Turks*, and recovers his loſſes. Here he was oppoſed by *Topal Oſman*, at the head of one hundred thouſand men, which he had aſſembled with great difficulty. A battle was fought on the twenty-fifth of the ſame month, but to the diſadvantage of the *Perſians*. Next day brought on a general engagement, in which the *Turks* were totally routed, with the loſs of forty thouſand men, their military cheſt, and all their baggage; and what was ſtill more irretrievable, their excellent general was left dead on the field of battle. *Kouli Kan* was prevented from purſuing

ing

ing the advantages he might have gained by this great victory, by being obliged to march to *Shiras*, where he defeated one of his own generals, who had proclaimed the depofed *Thamas*; and the general, whofe name was *Mohammed*, being taken, hanged himfelf. Being now at leifure to refume his grand operations againft the *Turks*, who were difpirited, and divided amongft themfelves; he recovered all *Georgia*, and *Armenia*, and obtained many other advantages. His fame was then fo great, that in the year 1735, the emprefs of *Ruffia* concluded a treaty with him, by which he ceded all, or a great part of, the *Ruffian* conquefts, upon the *Perfian* territories. After this, *Kouli Kan* increafed his army to one hundred and twenty thoufand men, and, after defeating and flaying *Cuproli* the *Turkifh* general, and twenty thoufand *Turks*, in a bloody battle, he retook *Erivan*, and thus compleated the conqueft of many of the provinces that had been difmembered from *Perfia*. makes a peace with the emprefs of *Ruffia*,

Kouli Kan was now confidered both as the greateft politician, and the greateft general in the eaft. Though he fecretly coveted a peace with the *Turks*, yet he refufed to conclude it, but upon condition of their reftoring *Baghdad*, and paying the expences of the war. In the mean while, about the beginning of the year 1736, the young *Shah Abbas* died, but whether naturally or violently, we know not. Upon this the *Perfian* grandees were convoked in the plains of *Mogan*, to deliberate upon filling up the throne. *Kouli Kan* propofed *Thamas*, but the deputies infifted upon himfelf accepting of the crown. The reader may remember that the *Afgans* are *Sonnites* and hate the *Perfians* for being *Shiits*. *Kouli Kan's* chief dependance at this time was upon the *Afgans*, and he himfelf had been bred a *Sonnite*. Upon the chief men ftill preffing him to mount the throne, he confented on three conditions. Firft, that the crown fhould be made hereditary in his family; Secondly, that none of the defcendants, or relations of their late fhah's fhould receive fhelter, fupport, or entertainment in *Perfia*; and thirdly, that the cuftom of curfing *Abubeker*, *Omar*, and *Othman*, with that of commemorating *Huffeyn's* death, fhould be abolifhed in *Perfia*. Death of the young *Shah Abbas*. Conditions on which *Kouli Kan* accepts the crown.

Nothing can give us a higher idea of *Kouli Kan's* power over the *Perfians*, who in general are great biggots, than their agreeing to thefe propofals; which facilitated a peace with the *Turks*, who yielded up their rights to the conquered provinces; and confented that the *Perfians* might have liberty to vifit the temple of *Mecca*, without paying duty. After this, *Kouli Kan* endeavoured to abolifh all differences between the *Sonnites* and the *Shiites*; and he ftript the *Turkifh* clergy, and doctors, in the neighbourhood of *Ifpahan*, of all their revenues, which he beftowed upon his troops; faying that they were better priefts than the others, whofe Alterations in religion.

prayers

prayers had been ineffectual for procuring to *Perfia* that peace, which the others had obtained by their swords.

Nadir en-
deavours
to culti-
vate the
arts of
peace.

The peace with the *Turks* however, was far from giving tranquility to *Perfia*, which was moſt miſerably harraſſed and depopulated, and exhauſted by its civil wars. *Kouli Kan* indeed ſought to remedy thoſe evils, by fixing his reſidence in *Iſpahan*, and by encouraging commerce and agriculture. But he ſeems to have been void of all true ideas of the civil arts of life; though he ſometimes affected them, and even talked with the *Engliſh* and other foreigners upon thoſe ſubjects. The truth is, had he been better informed, and better diſpoſed, he could not have ſucceeded; for no ſooner did he begin to have ſome reſpite, after making peace with the *Turks*, than he was obliged to ſet out for *Kandahar*, to ſubdue *Huſſeyu Kan*, brother to the late *Sultan Mahmud*, who had ſeized upon that province and city. This was not amongſt the moſt glorious of *Kouli Kan*'s expeditions. For though he defeated *Huſſeyu*'s troops, yet having no heavy cannon, he could not take the city, and he was forced at laſt to accept of it, upon terms, from *Huſſeyu*, and to confirm him in his government. His ſon *Rizi Kuli*, whom he had made governor of *Maſhad*, was more fortunate in ſubduing the provinces of *Balk*, and *Bukharia*, and reducing the *Uſbek Tartars*, who were now become very formidable.

he is de-
feated.

Conqueſts
of his ſon
Rizi.

It was now about the middle of the year 1738, and *Kouli Kan* was then meditating his famous expedition into *India*, of which we have already given a full account, and which will render his name famous to future ages. But notwithſtanding the immenſe treaſures which he brought to *Perfia* upon his return, we do not find, that either that country, or his own court, were much improved by ſuch vaſt acceſſions of treaſure. He was by no means either ſo magnificient, or ſo poliſhed as *Jenghiz Khan*, or *Tamerlan*, and other conquerors, whom he reſembled in his riſe and fortune. At the ſame time it muſt be acknowledged, that notwithſtanding all his treaſons, bloodſhed and cruelty, he was far from being ſo great a deſtroyer of the human ſpecies, as the beſt of thoſe tyrants were. While he was in *India*, a report prevailed that his army had been defeated. Upon this his ſon *Rizi Kuli* endeavoured to ſeize upon the government, and actually murdered ſhah *Thamas*, in the fortreſs where he was confined. *Rizi* ſoon after found he had been miſinformed, and deſpairing of pardon from his father, he meditated his deſtruction. In the mean while, *Nadir Shah* returned from *India* to *Kandahar*, and finding that the *Uſbeks*, who were then in poſſeſſion of the once glorious *Bukharia*, and *Korafan*, had invaded *Perfia*, he marched at the head of fifty thouſand men to chaſtiſe them. The khan of *Bukharia* ſoon made his peace by ſubmitting, and was continued in his government; but the khan of *Korafan*, or, as it was now called, *Keyvea*, held out, and after loſing twenty thouſand men,

who mur-
der's Tha-
mas.

Nadir's
ſucceſſes

men, he was taken prifoner, and put to death with thirty of his principal followers, by way of retaliation, for his having murdered one of *Nadir Shah's* ambaſſadors.

As *Nadir*, for ſo we now call *Kouli Kan*, was returning to *Maſhad*, an *Afgan*, who had been hired by his ſon *Rizi* for that purpoſe, ſhot at him and wounded him in the hand; and, being ſeized upon, he accuſed *Rizi*, who was immedi- ately apprehended. *Nadir* was fond of this ſon, more than tyrants commonly are of their children; and, it is ſaid, he would have pardoned him for the attempt, but that the young man refuſed to make any ſubmiſſion, and even gave his father opprobrious language; upon which, *Nadir*, in a rage, deprived him of his eyes. *Rizi at-tempts to murder his father.*

After this, revolts and rebellions multiplied upon *Nadir*; ſo that, during the laſt five years of his reign, he cannot be ſaid to have been otherwiſe than unfortunate, though he ge- nerally was victorious. It was with difficulty he eſcaped be- ing, with his army, deſtroyed in an expedition he made in- to *Dagheſtan* againſt the *Leſghi*, after having been ſucceſsful in two others againſt the *Arabs* and *Uſbeks*. After that, he was embroiled with the *Turks*, who made war againſt him, and *Aſtarabad* and *Shiras*, with a great part of the domini- ons he had recovered ſince his acceſſion, revolted from him; while the *Turks* aſſembled a body of one hundred and thirty thouſand men near *Erivan*, and declared war againſt him. It is true, *Nadir*, in *Auguſt*, 1735, at the head of eighty thouſand troops, defeated them; killed their general *Abdol- lah Cuproli*, and twenty-eight thouſand of their men, with the loſs of eight thouſand of his own, he himſelf having two horſes ſhot under him. But this victory did not prevent daily revolts from happening in *Georgia* and *Koraſan*, which obliged *Nadir* to conclude another peace with the *Turks*; by which ſome ceſſions in point of religion were made; but he ſeems to have loſt a great deal in point of intereſt. *Nadir's defeat. War again breaks out with the Turks. Nadir's diſtreſſes,*

Perhaps the affair of religion contributed more than any other cauſe to the ruin of *Nadir*. The frequent revolts and rebellions againſt him appear to have ſowered his temper, ſo that he looked upon the native *Perſians* as his worſt enemies, and took into his pay a great number of *Afgans*, *Uſbeks*, *Turks*, and *Tartars*. To ſupport thoſe barbarians, he not only ſquandered upon them the vaſt treaſures he had brought from *India*, but laid very heavy impoſitions upon the cities of *Perſia*; ſo that the whole of that delightful country pre- ſented ſcenes of the deepeſt miſery, and the moſt ſhocking barbarity. *and op-preſſions.*

Marching from *Maſhad* to the plains of *Sollin Mcydan*, a conſpiracy was formed againſt him. It has been ſaid, that *Nadir*, finding he could not depend upon the *Perſians*, con- voked the chiefs of the *Uſbeks*, *Tartars*, and other barbarians, and that it was agreed amongſt them, that very night to put

all

all the *Perfians* that were in the camp to the fword. This refolution, we are told, was difcovered by a *Georgian* flave overhearing the defign and communicating the fame to the *Perfian* generals. But this difcovery is far from being probable, it not being likely that *Nadir*, upon the point of fuch a fcheme being executed, would have gone fo quietly and unguardedly to fleep in his tent as we find he actually did. But it is more probable, that the *Perfian* chiefs, having refolved upon the affaffination, wanted to juftify themfelves by this pretext. We are not even certain as to the name of the perfon who was *Nadir's* executioner. It is faid to have been *Shaleh Beg*, the captain of his *Afgan* guard. He took with him no more than four refolute men, and, rufhing into the haram, or womens apartment, they there killed an eunuch; and proceeding to enter the inner haram, they killed an old woman, who, it feems, made a noife at their appearance. They difcovered a particular tent of the haram, where *Nadir* lay with his wife, the *Indian* emperor's daughter, by the luftre of fome jewels which lay on a table near a burning lamp; and when they came to it they found him juft rifen, having probably been awaked by the old woman's outcries. He had a fword in his hand, which, on the fight of the confpirators, he drew, and demanded what was their defign. *Saleh Beg* then cut him acrofe the collar-bone; but *Nadir* defended himfelf fo bravely, that he killed two of his moft forward affailants, and would have efcaped, had he not been entangled in the ropes that interlaced the tents of his haram, fo that falling, *Saleh Beg* gave him a terrible wound. Upon this, *Nadir* cried out for mercy; but the confpirators told him, That, as he had always been a ftranger to mercy, he was to expect none, and they immediately cut off his head. This happened in the year 1747, in the fixty-firft year of *Nadir's* age, and the twelfth of his reign.

Nadir was one of thofe extraordinary perfons, in nature and conftitution, fomewhat between a man and a monfter, whom we have had fo often occafion to mention in the courfe of this hiftory. His natural parts and courage undoubtedly were very ftrong, and in his perfon he was fitted for the moft difficult and fatiguing warlike operations. He was fix feet high, of a majeftic awful afpect, and his voice was fo loud, that it could have been heard diftinctly by an army of one hundred thoufand men. He had great readinefs of thought in concerting, and equal quicknefs and refolution in executing, his defigns. Though he made religion his pretext for a great number of his unjuftifiable undertakings, yet he appears to have been very little affected by it; for, when the prieft, who acted as high-mufti of *Perfia*, prefumed to throw in fome remonftrances upon the head of religion, *Nadir* ordered him to be ftrangled. He feems to have been extremely rapacious, and, it is faid, he was perfectly well acquainted

with

Nadir Shah murdered.

His character.

with the state of his finances through every province of his empire, his memory being as extraordinary as the other talents he possessed from nature. He expressed a delight in precious stones, and wore them in his turband, which was the only finery he affected in his dress. His diet was plain; but, by what can be understood, his manners and address, upon the whole, were barbarous; and, that he was afraid of conspiracies, appears by his wearing a private coat of mail, and by his generally having in his hand a battle-axe, which he managed very dexterously, and even played with while he was giving public audiences.

The state of that country, since the death of *Nadir Shah*, has been so unsettled, and the accounts we have of it are so fabulous and unascertained, that we must here close our history of it.

The History of the Ottoman Turks to the Death of Bajazet.

IT is in vain for us to attempt to settle the particular country from whence the people we are now to treat of issued. The most probable opinion seems to be, That the word *Turk* originally carried with it no favourable signification, being little better than a vagrant and a barbarian; and that it was given by the people in the east indifferently to all strangers. As we have already observed, *Scythia, Tartary*, and even *China* itself, sent forth swarms of barbarians at different periods, who, from the several names of their leaders, were called *Ogusians, Seljukians*, or *Othmans*, but all of them were *Turks*; and they were known by that name even after they had obtained settlements; the very countries which they first conquered and inhabited, after leaving their own, being called *Turkestan* and *Turkamania*. *Conjecture. Name of the Turks.*

We shall not trouble our readers with the fabulous accounts given by the *Turkish* historians of the original of the *Othman Turks*; the most consistent is, that a great body of the *Ogusians*, headed by a leader called *Ertogrul*, or *Ortogrul*, were taken into pay, as soldiers of fortune, by some of the last princes of the *Seljukian* line, with whom they agreed in manners, language, and religion. *Ortogrul's* services were so great that he was highly rewarded by the *Seljukian* monarch, who probably was *Aladin*; and he seems to have obtained a settlement at a place called *Soguta*, or *the Willow Village*, upon the frontiers of *Mysia*. On the death of *Ortogrul*, he was succeeded by his son *Othman*, who, in like manner, assisted the *Seljukian* monarchs against the *Greeks, Tartars*, and other nations with whom they were at war. The *Seljukian* race *Their rise.*

a

at this time, declining, their generals, who, in fact, feem to have been, even under their fultans, independent princes, affociated themfelves, and, extending their conquefts all round over the divided and effeminate *Greeks*, they made a divifion of their territories, and *Bythinia* fell to the fhare of *Othman*. The *Turkifh* hiftorians, however, have endeavoured to conceal the truth; which is, that the dread of *Jenghiz Kan*'s arms, and thofe of his fucceffors, particularly *Hulacu*, obliged thofe mercenary barbarians to feek a refuge towards the weft; which they laid wafte as they proceeded.

Hiftory of Othman. *Othman* feems to have been a general of great addrefs, and both the *Chriftian* and *Turkifh* writers tell us, that a kind of a confpiracy was formed amongft the *Greek* governors, in which was the governor of *Hirman Katu*, called *Mikael Hofa*, or *Goat's Beard*, whofe daughter was to be married, and *Othman* was invited to the wedding at a caftle called *Bilejiki*, where the confpirators intended to difpatch him. *Kaufi*, it feems, difcovered the confpiracy, and was generous enough to put *Othman* on his guard. Upon this intelligence he difguifed forty of his moft refolute foldiers like women, with concealed weapons, and placed himfelf, with a ftrong body of troops, in ambufh. The difguifed foldiers being admitted into the caftle fecured the gates; and *Othman* coming up with his troops, deftroyed his enemies, and made himfelf mafter of that and fome other important places. The *Greek* emperor *Andronicus*, however, taking into his pay a body of fix thoufand *Alans*, the command of whom he gave, about the year 1289, to his colleague and fon, the young *Mikael*, greatly alarmed the *Turks*; but he behaved fo fhamefully, that they, recovering their confternation, fhut him up in *Magnefia*; from whence, with great difficulty, he efcaped; and the *Alans*, refufing to ferve longer under him, returned home.

His ftratagem.

The Alans defert the emperor.

The *Byzantine* hiftorians inform us, that, after this, the *Greek* emperors took another body of mercenaries into their pay; but their leader being put to death, they invited *Othman* into *Europe*, and joined with his *Turks*; and, the *Greeks* not daring to oppofe them, they laid wafte all the *Greek* empire wherever they marched; the inhabitants flying to walled and fortified places, which thofe barbarians were in no condition to befiege. In fhort, they pufhed their incurfions even to the *Bofphorus*.

Incurfions of the Turks.

According to other hiftorians, about the year 1304, the emperor invited one *Roger*, an *European* foldier of fortune, with eight thoufand of his troops, to his defence; but thofe mercenary auxiliaries were, if poffible, more cruel and oppreffive to the inhabitants than the *Turks* themfelves were; and *Othman*, taking advantage of their diffentions, at laft blockaded *Nice*, the capital of *Bythinia*; and defeated a large body of troops fent from *Conftantinople* to its relief. It appears, however, that *Othman*, as yet, was far from being the moft

Hiftory of Roger.

Othman blockades Nice.

moſt conſiderable leader amongſt the *Turks,* who had then
the ſake of money, one of thoſe leaders would make a ſhort
ceſſation of arms with the *Greek* governors; but then his followers immediately put themſelves under ſome other chief
who was in arms; ſo that perpetual ravages and blood-ſhed
went on.

In the mean while, the young emperor, *Mikael,* was
hunted from place to place; and, finding he could not remain ſafe in *Pergamus,* he went to *Cyzicus,* and from thence
to *Piga.* At laſt, he was obliged to call in *Kazam Kan,* a
Tartar chief, to his aſſiſtance. His alliance was of ſome ſervice to the *Greeks,* and at *Cyzicus* they formed an army of
ſixteen thouſand men; but *Mikael* was obliged to give the
command of it to *Roger,* who, for ſome time, had great *Roger de-*
ſucceſs againſt the barbarians, gave them ſeveral defeats and *feats the*
checked their inſolence. He could not, however, pre- *Turks:*
vent *Aliſuras,* one of the *Turkiſh* chiefs, from becoming
maſter of *Tripoli.* But *Roger,* preſuming on his ſucceſſes,
and finding all the open country of *Greece* to be a mere deſert,
by the ravages of the *Turks,* he entered the imperial cities,
put the richeſt of the inhabitants and governors to the torture, and ſometimes to death, to oblige them to diſcover
their riches; till, at laſt, the inhabitants of *Mogulſia* had
ſpirit enough to cut part of his troops in pieces, and to ſhut
their gates upon him and to ſecure the treaſures he had left in
the place.

Upon this, without minding the requeſts or threats of the *His op-*
emperor, he beſieged the place. He was, however, obliged *preſſive*
to raiſe the ſiege and to retire, being equally hated by the *cruelty,*
Greeks and *Romans* as by the *Turks.* Upon his retreat, he
went to *Calipoli,* and had the inſolence to go to *Adrianople,*
attended by no more than one hundred and fifty of his guards,
to pay a viſit to the emperor *Mikael.* Here he met with the re- *and death.*
ward of his injuſtice and cruelty, being killed by *George,* the
head of ſome *Allans* who had remained in the emperor's ſervice.

Upon this, the *Catalans, Roger*'s ſoldiers, maſſacred the
people of *Calipoli,* paſſed over to *Aſia,* and gave no quarter
to any of the *Greeks.* The emperor ſent troops who beſieged
the fort of *Calipoli,* which was in the hands of the infidels,
while they, in their turn, beſieged the city. *Mikael* endeavoured to raiſe the ſiege, but his generals were defeated; upon which he entered *Adrianople* at the head of an army, all
of it compoſed of mercenary *Allans* intermingled with ſome
Turks (for they contained ſo many clans, that ſome of them
had but little connection with others, whilſt all of them were
ready to take pay) and a few cowardly *Greeks* and *Italians.*
At laſt, the *Turks* and he came to a pitched battle; where

The Greek emperor defeated. The *Greek Mikael* shewed great personal courage, but, being basely abandoned by his mercenaries, he was defeated; and he and all his army must have been destroyed, had not the *Turks*, apprehending an ambush, desisted from the pursuit.

The Catalans and Turks quarrel. The *Catalans*, who gained this victory, were ruined by it. The *Turks* and they quarrelled, and they quarrelled amongst themselves. The reader, in the preceding part of this history, will see a great deal of the management by which the emperor of *Constantinople* prevented the progress of the *Turks*; but we are now to attach ourselves to the history of *Othman*. It is sufficient to say, that the differences between the *Turks* and the *Catalans* run to such a height, that they cut one another's throats wherever they met. *Othman* seems to have taken but little concern in those events, and to have entirely minded his own interest. It is said, that the emperor's sister,

Greek princess affronts Othman, who, as we have already seen, had been promised in marriage to the great *Hulacu*, affronted him, by threatning him with the power of that prince, who actually sent thirty thousand men to the emperor's assistance.

Notwithstanding this, the divisions in the imperial family grew to such extremes, that, about the year 1308, *Othman* had reduced to his power all *Bythinia*, and had made a considerable progress in the reduction of *Paphlagonia*. After this, being in no farther dread of *Hulacu*, he formed the siege of *Nicomedia*; but, being obliged to raise it, he built a strong castle to bridle it, and gave the command of it to *Targam*, one of his best generals. He then retired into winter-quarters, but was attacked in them by *Honorius*, the imperial governor

who defeats the Imperialists. of *Prusa*. *Honorius* was defeated, and *Othman* took *Kutahi*, but lost his grandson, who was drowned by the breaking down of a wooden bridge.

Those vast successes enabled *Othman* to form the siege of *Prusa* itself, once the capital of *Bithynia*. But, unable to

His policy take so strong a place, he built two forts, or castles, near it, to hinder it from receiving provisions; and ordered the governors of those forts to preserve them as sanctuaries for the people of the country; by which means, they were always plentifully supplied with provisions; and they, the inhabitants, became dutiful subjects to *Othman*.

He forms a small fleet. This barbarian seems to have been of a far more politic cast than his cotemporary countrymen. He even formed a small fleet, by seizing the ships of some pirates; and with that he made himself master of several islands in the *Archipelago*; which enabled him to plunder the sea-faring subjects of both the *European* and *Asiatic* powers, to the vast emolument

His civil conduct of his followers. To this policy his successes were, perhaps, greatly owing, as well as to the means he took to make his conquests durable. For, after a summer's campaign, he always dedicated the winter to the regulation of civil affairs, and the introduction of good government and œconomy amongst his

soldiers

foldiers and new fubjects. Sometimes the fummer was far
advanced before he took the field, as if he had been averfe
to harraffing his army ; but this he did with defign ; for he
knew that their impatience for plunder and action would
make them apply to him to head them againft their enemies.
When this, as it generally was, was the cafe, he then led
them to the field.

He happened, however, towards the latter end of his *and hypo-*
reign, for we muft then fuppofe him to have been an inde- *crify.*
pendent prince, to confume two or three years in thofe pacific matters, till his foldiers began to murmur for want of
action. He then called them together, and gravely told
them, That he himfelf being a good *Mahometan*, could not,
in confcience, march againft the enemies of his faith, without formally fummoning them, either to embrace it or be-
come.tributary ; and that, if they refufed both conditions,
they were to be proceeded againft with fire and fword. We
are accordingly told, that he fent his meffengers of ftate
round to the *Chriftian* princes and governors, with fuch fum-
monfes ; and, that fome of them, particularly his friend *Mikael Kofa*, actually turned *Mahometan*, while others of them
confented to pay tribute.

By thofe means, he gained fuch acceffions of power, that *Encreafe*
he reduced a vaft number of important cities. Becoming at *of his*
laft too formidable to the *Turks* and *Tartars*, who had feized *power.*
upon the eaft part of *Syria*, and were now mafters of *Iconium*
itfelf, they invaded his dominions, and filled them with blood
and rapine. But *Othman*, who feems to have had as much
fpirit as he had ambition and policy, drew together his army,
gave them battle, and entirely routed them, and incorporated all the prifoners he took, who were very numerous,
amongft his own fubjects.

His favourite fon, *Orchan*, or, as he is commonly called, *His fon*
Orchon, contributed greatly to his father's fucceffes, and fub- *Orchan's*
dued a vaft number of cities, of which we now know no *valour.*
more than their barbarous names ; but they were, at that
time, all of them populous and flourifhing. The *Greek* emperor made an effort to oppofe him ; but his troops, though
they are faid to have been well armed and difciplined, were
defeated by *Abdorrahmon*, another of *Othman*'s generals, very
few of them efcaping either death or captivity.

One of the laft and moft fignal actions of *Othman*'s life, *Othman*
was his reducing *Prufa*, one of the greateft cities in that part *takes Pru-*
of *Afia* ; the blockade of which was ftill continued. Au- *fa.*
thors are divided as to his manner of reducing it. Some fay
that it was ftored with eight years provifion, and that the
place was fo ftrong, that *Othman* employed his friend *Mikael
Kofa* to perfuade *Honorius*, the governor, to furrender it to
Orchon, upon promife that the lives of the inhabitants fhould
be fpared, and thirty thoufand crowns of gold payed by the
befiegers. Others, particularly *Knolles*, the *Englifh* hiftorian

of the *Turkish* affairs, say, that the place did not surrender before it was reduced to the greatest extremity by famine and the want of all necessaries. Other writers, who were then alive, and pretend to have been upon the spot, with no great probability, say that *Othman*, after he had reduced the town, found such resistance from the castle, that he ordered a report of his death to be spread abroad, and that he died with a desire to be buried in a *Greek* convent within the castle. They add, that the coffin, where his body was supposed to be, was filled with arms, and attended by himself and thirty-nine of his most resolute officers in mourning; and, that the credulous monks, prevailing so far as that they were granted admittance, by way of mourners for the deceased, they became masters of a gate, and the place thereby fell into *Othman*'s hands without blood-shed. Be this as it will, it is certain, that *Othman* was possessed of this important city and fortress; and, that he died soon after, having appointed his son *Orchan* to succeed him. He lived about sixty-nine years, of which he reigned about twenty-six. His death happened in the year 1327.

It must be confessed, that, though *Othman*, in conquests and military atchievements, came far behind *Jenghiz Kan*, *Tamerlan*, and many other conquerors of the east, yet he excelled them all in the wise disposition he made of his succession, by leaving his territories to his successor undivided; a principle upon which the present greatness of his descendants, who have ever since assumed his name, is founded. In other respects, it is, on all hands, allowed, that he was brave in the highest degree; and so generous to his friends, officers, servants, and the poor, that he left an empty treasury. It is said, that a little hat, which he used to wear, very different from the present *Turkish* turbans, and his green camblet cloak, are still to be seen hanging over his tomb at *Prusa*.

Orchan equalled, if not exceeded, his father, in all civil and military accomplishments. The young *Andronicus*, who was now emperor of *Constantinople*, thinking to take advantage of *Othman*'s death, invaded *Orchan*'s dominions; but was baffled, though, at first, he obtained several advantages. After this, in the year 1331, *Orchan* besieged *Nichomedia*, and reduced it, partly by policy and partly by force. He then became master of all the fortified places of *Bithynia*, excepting *Nice*, having improved the art of engineering far beyond what his father did.

The reader must observe, that this was not done before those places had undergone great variety of fortune; sometimes submitting to the *Greek* emperors, and sometimes to the *Othmans*.

We are likewise told, that many of the other *Mahometan* powers, who had erected sovereignties on the ruins of the *Greek* empire, joined with *Andronicus* against *Orchan*, who

appears

Stratagem reported of *Othman*.

His death,

and character.

Succeeded by his son *Orchan*,

who takes *Nicomedia* and reduces *Bythinia*.

Confederacy against him.

appears to have been the moſt poliſhed of the *Turks* his co- prefers his
temporaries. He aboliſhed the *Seljukian* money, and had a brother.
mint of his own; he treated his brother *Alladin*, who ſeems
to have been a brave and a worthy ſubject, with the utmoſt
diſtinction, by making him general of his armies, or prime-
miniſter. Before this time the *Ozugians*, or, as we now call
them, the *Othman Turks*, were no better than robbers; and,
notwithſtanding all the pains that *Othman* had taken, they
knew little of ſubordination, and were continually in mutinies. *Orchan* therefore inſtituted a ſeminary of ſoldiers for He forms
his army, conſiſting chiefly of young *Chriſtians*, taken from a militia.
their parents; to whom, after they had been inſtructed in
the *Mahometan* faith, he gave regular pay; but without hin-
dering ſuch of the *Turks* as were men of property from ſerv-
ing amongſt them. To theſe we may readily believe he gave
ſuperior advantages, by aſſigning them lands for their ſubſiſtence in time of peace,

By thoſe wiſe regulations, he had always at hand a diſci-
plined army, powerful enough to check the mutinous ſpirit
of his *Turkiſh* militia; ſo that, at laſt, he was able to lay
ſiege to *Nice* itſelf. The ſiege continued for two years, He takes
and, famine and peſtilence prevailing within the place, the *Nice*.
garriſon was obliged to capitulate. His behaviour, on His gene-
this occaſion, was magnanimous; he gave the inhabitants rous be-
leave, not only to retire to *Conſtantinople*, but to carry with haviour.
them all their effects. The inhabitants thought it much
more eligible to remain under ſo generous a conqueror, than
to be under the tyranny of ſo abandoned a court as that of
Conſtantinople; they therefore deſired leave to withdraw their
capitulation, and to remain under the protection of their
conqueror; which was granted them. *Orchan*, at the ſame
time, extended his clemency to a degree that, however
ſtrange and extravagant it may appear to modern times,
perhaps did not appear ſo to the parties themſelves; for, a
great number of women bewailing the death of their huſ-
bands during the ſiege, and their own deſtitute condition, he
ordered the chief of his attendants to make wives of them.
In ſhort, by his clemency and magnanimity, he ſoon peopled Effects of
Nice with *Greek* inhabitants, who fled to his protection from the ſame,
the tyranny and oppreſſions of their own governments; ſo
that it ſeemed to vie with the largeſt cities of the *Greek* empire in populouſneſs.

About the year 1334, *Orchan* made himſelf maſter of *Kam-* His far-
luk, after beſieging it a year; a place ſo ſtrong, that *Othman*, ther ſuc-
after various attempts, deemed it to be impregnable. But ceſſes, po-
this politic prince did not confine his practice to the arts of licy, and
war alone. He ſtudied to make it the intereſt of the *Greeks* love of
to ſubmit to his ſway. We know little of his private life learning.
or education; but it is highly probable that he had far other
inſtruction than what he could receive in a camp, or, rather,
a moveable city, of ſuch barbarians as his father commanded;

for such they were, and so they lived. *Orchan*, by his libe-rality and endowments to learned men, emptied even *Arabia* and *Persia*, those seats of eastern literature, of their men of knowledge. He erected a magnificent mosque, an hospital, and an academy, in the city of *Prusa*; to which all the stu-dents in the east, who wanted to be instructed in *Mahometan* learning, resorted.

His conduct, perhaps, in his political capacity, is not quite so defencible; though he appears to have done no more than make reprisals upon robbers. The heads of the *Oguzian* clans, who had been confederated with *Othman*, being far inferior to him and his son, in genius and capacity, had left the dominions of which they had robbed the *Greeks* and the *Seljuks* in a most miserable state, without providing for their defence; so that it was easy for *Orchan*, and his disciplined troops, to reduce them by force, had they refused to submit to persuasion. His sway was so mild, and his subjects so happy, that several princes put themselves and their subjects under his protection; and became, as it were feudatories to him; an institution well known in *Europe* at that time, and not unknown to the *Scythians, Tartars*, and the ancestors of the *Oguzian Turks* Some of those princes, however, had spirit enough to dispute *Orchan*'s command. *Turson Beg*, the prince of *Pergamus*, and of several other fine cities and coun-tries, had offered to hold them in vassalage, or fee, of *Orchan*. In this he was opposed by *Hajil*, who, under pretence of com-promising matters, stabbed his brother *Turson*, and shut him-self up in *Pergamus*, now called *Bergama*, which was be-sieged by *Orchan* He had little occasion to employ force, the inhabitants equally respected him as they detested the mur-derer, whom they delivered up to *Orchan*, and put themselves and their city under his protection. *Hajil Beg* died two years after in prison; and the governor of *Ulabad*, on suspicion of a revolt, was put to death. Such great successes struck ter-ror into the *Greeks*, and, about the year 1338, *Anakhor* and *Emrud*, two sea-port towns, submitted to *Orchan*, upon his threatning to besiege them.

Among the other leaders of the *Augzukian Turks*, was *Aydin*, who, and his son *Amir*, were become sultans of *Ka-ria*, and masters of *Lydia, Smyrna, Ephesus*, and several other cities of *Iconia*; which being a woody country, and at the same time lying upon the sea, furnished him with timber for building ships, so that this sultan *Amir* became soon a great maritime power. His fleet consisted of no fewer than seventy-five ships, and, crossing the *Egean Sea*, he subdued a great number of places on the sea-coasts of *Samo Thracia*; nor dared *Andronicus*, though he came in person, venture to fight him. Instead of that, he called to his aid *Sarkhan*, the *Turkish* governor of *Phocea*; who, upon his promise to deliver his son *Solyman*, then in the hands of the *Genoese*, who had made themselves masters of *Phocea*, furnished him with some

troops

His con-quests.

He takes Pergamus.

Amir a maritime power.

troops and shipping; and this seems to have brought about a peace between the emperor *Andronicus* and *Amir*; tho' we are told that the latter was prevailed upon, by the emperor's general *John Kantakazemus*, his old friend, to lend him thirty ships.

We know nothing from the *Turkish* historians, how *Orchan* was employed all this time; he seems, probably, to have been almost at perpetual war with the *Greeks*; and, like his neighbours, to have endeavoured to render himself a maritime power: for, in the year 1334, he fitted out a fleet of thirty vessels, to make a descent upon *Constantinople*, or its neighbourhood. We are told, however, that all those ships and their crews, excepting as many as filled one ship, were destroyed by the general *Kantakazemus*. A peace soon after followed between *Orchan* and *Andronicus*, by the management of *Kantakazemus*. The latter then had leisure to chastise *Sarkhan*, his master's new ally, who had recommenced his ravages in *Thrace*; and the imperial arms every where prevailed against the *Turks*, who were at war with the emperor; while the dominions of *Orchan* were in a flourishing tranquil state.

Kantakazemus was both the hero and historian of the *Greek* empire at this time; and, undoubtedly, was possessed of great virtues. *Andronicus* III. dying, left his son *John*, who was but nine years of age, under the tuition of *Kantakazemus*; but, being hated by the clergy, and *Anne*, the empress-mother, he was by her proscribed; but the army proclaimed him emperor. The faction, however, prevailed so strongly against him, that all his relations were imprisoned, his wife and children were besieged in *Didymothicum*, and he himself was obliged to retire into *Servia*. *Didymothicum* is a strong city of *Thrace*, or *Romania*, lying upon the river *Hebrus*. *Amir*, who was now called the sultan of *Iconia*, and whom we have already mentioned, no sooner heard of the distress of *Kantakazemus*, and his family, than he entered the *Hebrus* with three hundred and eighty vessels, which carried twenty-nine thousand men; and, raising the siege, he behaved towards the emperor, and his family, with a fidelity, and personal affection, of which there are but few instances amongst princes: for, after he had relieved *Didymodicum*, he wept for joy on hearing that *Kantakazemus* was safe; and gave God thanks for enabling him to come to his assistance. After this, he rejected all presents and offers made him by the court of *Constantinople*; and, when he joined his troops to those of *Kantakazemus*, he prostrated himself before that emperor as his sovereign; and it was with difficulty he was persuaded to remount his horse.

Kantakazemus being thus reinforced, proceeded victoriously against his enemies. but the intrigues of the court of *Constantinople* prevailed with *Amir*'s great officers to oblige him to return to his own dominions. It was with sensible regret he

Orchan fits out a fleet, which is destroyed by the Greeks.

History of Kantakazemus.

Fidelity of Amir towards him.

did this, and not till after he had performed a thousand brave
actions, in his own person, to serve *Kantakazemus.* Before he
returned, he earnestly advised the empress *Anne* to peace; and
promised, in fifteen days, to return with his troops, and to
serve *Kantakazemus* till the end of the war. But, when *Amir*
landed at *Smyrna,* he found the *Latins* there before him; and
it was with great difficulty he prevented that city from falling into their hands.

Amir re-
turns.

His wars. This unforeseen invasion preventing *Amir* from coming so
soon as he intended, to assist *Kantakazemus,* that emperor was
obliged to apply for auxiliaries to *Orchan,* whose territories
were much better situated, for giving him speedy assistance,
than those of *Amir* were. *Orchan,* we may now reasonably
suppose, was, by far, the most powerful prince of the *Ogu-*
zian Turks; and his territories appear now to have had a long
peace. He had been often courted, by the empress *Anne,* to
join her son; but he had declined it from prudential motives,
and readily entered into a treaty with *Kantakazemus,* who appears, by his assistance, to have got possession of *Constantino-*
ple and the imperial dignity.

Distress of
Greece.
The prodigious swarms of *Turks,* however, that filled all
Greece, the great power they had obtained by sea, and the
improvements they had lately made in the arts of war, rendered the imperial dignity a post of both trouble and danger.
Luckily for *Kantakazemus,* those barbarians were so divided
amongst themselves, that they did not form any very strong
body under one head; and, next to *Orchan, Amir* seems to
have been the most powerful amongst them. He had returned

Adven-
tures of
Amir.
with twenty thousand men to the assistance of *Kantakazemus,*
and had done him the greatest services under the most dis-
couraging difficulties. But some differences he had with
Sarkhan, who was called the sultan of *Lydia,* obliged him to
return home to defend his own dominions, which were invaded by a popish patriarch of *Constantinople,* at the head of
an *Italian* army. He killed the patriarch before the altar at
Smyrna, and put to the sword some of his chief followers;
but the main body of the *Italians* retired to a fort they had
raised in the neighbourhood.

The great distance in which *Amir's* territories lay from
Constantinople, rendered *Orchan's* friendship of the greater importance to *Kantakazemus.* The politic *Orchan* was sensible
of this, and formally demanded the princess *Theodora,* daughter to the emperor, in marriage. It may, perhaps, be proper to put the reader in mind, that, notwithstanding the vast
dismembering and mutations which the *Greek,* or, as some
call it with more propriety, the *Roman,* empire had sustained,
Kantakazemus was still a great prince, not only on account of
the territories he possessed, but because the *Greek* emperor
was held in veneration by the remotest and most barbarous
people in the east. It was a new and unheard-of thing that
an infidel, and the son of one who had, but the other day,

been

been no more than the captain of a band of lawless robbers and wanderers, should demand in marriage the daughter of a *Greek* emperor.

Notwithstanding the seeming advantage attending the alliance, the pride of *Kantakazemus* appears to have been shocked at the demand. He consulted his general officers upon it, and they understanding that *Orchan*, if his request was granted, had promised him to serve against all his enemies as his son and subject, unanimously advised him to close with *Orchan*'s demand, He also applied to his friend *Amir* on the same occasion; who most generously represented the advantages attending *Orchan*'s offer, on account of the situation of their mutual territories; and pressed him by all means to agree to the proposal. The answer therefore was favourable to *Orchan*'s courtship. A noble escorte, and a strong squadron of *Turkish* ships, were sent to conduct her to her future husband, to whose commissioner she was dilivered, by her father and mother, at *Seliverea*, with most extraordinary pomp.

Orchan demands and marries the *Greek* emperor's daughter.

It is not to be imagined, that either pride, disinterestedness, or love, influenced *Orchan* on this occasion. The consequences shew, that he courted this match and alliance, that his officers and troops might have opportunities of becoming acquainted with *Europe*. He behaved afterwards to his father-in-law with great affection, and all matters being accommodated between him and *Paleologus*, *Orchan* paid *Kantakazemus* a formal visit, at *Scutari*, the famous castle lying on the *Bosphorus*, opposite to *Constantinople*. The interview was exceedingly grand, and *Kantakazemus* and *Orchan* sat together at the same table. It does not however appear, that *Orchan* went to *Constantinople*, though his wife did; for he is said to have remained on shipboard. Soon after, *Orchan* sent a body of ten thousand troops to assist *Kantakazemus* in a quarrel, that had arisen between him and the prince, or kral, of *Servia*. The *Greeks*, on this occasion, had a melancholy specimen of what they were to expect from their new auxiliaries; who indiscriminately plundered and murdered, under pretence, that the inhabitants were the emperor's enemies. In short, whenever they had loaded themselves with booty they returned home; and the kral of *Servia* made use of that opportunity to besiege *Thessalonica*. The emperor renewed his demand for assistance, and *Orchan* ordered his son *Solyman* to march at the head of twenty thousand men for that purpose. But *Orchan* appears not to have been in earnest, for after having ravaged the *Greek* territories in *Bulgaria*, he received orders from his father to return; though we know of no enemy he had at that time. Next year however, being 1354, *Orchan* sent an army to assist the *Genoese*, settled at *Gallata*, a suburb of *Constantinople*, then at war with the *Venetians*, who were countenanced by the emperor. His motive for this, besides the capital one we have

His views in the match.

He assists the *Greeks*.

disorderly behaviour of the *Turks*.

already

Orchan assists the Genoese.

already mentioned, seems to have been avarice; the *Genoese* being very rich, and having promised him vast sums of money; and he sent an army, which encamped opposite to *Constantinople*, to their assistance.

He relieves the emperor's son.

Every day now more and more convinced *Kantakazemus* of *Orchan*'s real view, which was no other, than to get footing in *Europe*. Differences again breaking out between *Kantakazemus* and *Paleologus*, *Orchan* sent his son *Solyman* to the relief of *Matthew*, the son and successor of *Kantakazemus*, who was besieged in *Adriancple*. On the other hand, *Paleologus* was assisted by the *Servians*, and the *Bulgarians*; but they were defeated by *Solyman*, who had raised the siege of *Constantinople*. After this, *Paleologus* courted *Solyman*'s

Solyman's policy,

friendship, but the subtile *Turk* declined entering into any offensive engagements with him, though he promised not to be his enemy. The motive for this caution was soon discerned. For after the great services he had performed for *Kantakazemus*, he seized a great number of places in *Thrace*,

He takes Zimpe and other places;

and particularly the important fortress of *Zimpe*. As *Orchan* maintained a great shew of justice and moderation, *Kantakazemus* complained to him of his son's proceeding Solyman appeared upon this occasion, to be a little refractory, and, in collusion with his father, he refused to give up the fort, without having money to pay his troops. *Kantakazemus* accordingly gave him ten thousand crowns of gold; but *Solyman*, instead of fulfilling his agreement, seized upon *Kalipolis*, in *Thrace*, and a great many places upon the sea coast, which had been laid in a manner desolate by an earthquake; and after rebuilding and peopling them, he filled them with

and at last Kalipolis.

garrisons. The taking of *Kalipolis*, the most important city of the empire next to *Constantinople*, opened the eyes of *Kantakazemus*, as to the true design of the *Ottoman* princes. He complained to *Orchan* of his son's breach of faith, but received no satisfaction but delays and fair promises, though he had an interview with *Orchan* at *Nichomedia*. *Orchan* was then engaged in a war with the *Tartars*, and *Solyman* had taken *Ancyra*, and *Katea*, their two chief cities. Re-

A sham compromise.

turning from this expedition, a sham agreement was made, between *Orchan* and *Solyman* on the one part, and *Kantakazemus* on the other, for the redelivery of *Kalipolis*, and the other places in *Thrace*: but it was never executed.

Kantakazemus retires to a monastry.

It is no wonder, if, after this, *Kantakazemus* was out of love with the world. He entered into a treaty with his collegue *Paleologus*, and resigning his part of the empire to his son *Matthew*, he went into a monastry. About this time, some piratical powers of *Old Phocca*, happened to carry off *Khalil*, one of *Orchan*'s sons; *Paleologus*, who was determined to break with *Matthew*, purchased the young prince's freedom, upon condition that he should not take part with *Matthew* in their quarrel between one another. *Orchan* did not think that this compromise bound him up from assisting

his

his brother-in-law in other matters; for he lent him five thoufand troops, in a quarrel he had with the kral of *Servia*'s widow, who was immenfely rich. But fhe was fupported by *Palcologus*; and *Matthew*'s auxiliaries, after ruining the country, fled like cowards from the *Servians*, and he being taken prifoner, was forced to renounce all title to the empire. The account we have given, is the moft probable we have, of the firft fatal footing the *Turks* obtained in *Europe*. Their own hiftorians have reprefented it with very romantic circumftances attending it; as if *Solyman*, attended by three general officers, and no more than eighty men, had paffed on a raft from *Afia* to *Europe*; where under pretence of hunting, they made themfelves mafters of the places in queftion. But this relation is inconfiftent with all other hiftories, by which it appears very plainly, that *Solyman*, long before that, had commanded armies, in thofe very territories; and could be no ftranger to the fituation of the principal towns and cities.

About the year 1359, the whole province of *Karipolis*, followed the fate of *Kalipolis*, and came into *Orchan*'s poffeffion. Some pretend that the taking of *Kalipolis* did not happen till after *Matthew*'s refignation of the imperial authority; but nothing is more plain, than that it was at that time in the hands of the *Othmans*; though it is poffible, that he did not affert his claim to it as his own property, during the reigns of his father, and brother-in-law. *Orchan*, after this, exerted himfelf to the utmoft, to fecure and enlarge his footing in *Europe*. He fent his fecond fon *Morad*, with a ftrong reinforcement to *Solyman*, who took *Malgara*, *Ibfalam*, and *Epibatos*, which lies in the neighbourhood of *Conftantinople*. He then befieged, and, after lofing a great number of men, took *Chirli*, by which he cut off the communication by land, between *Conftantinople* and *Adrianople*. In all thofe undertakings, *Orchan* was ferved by three famous generals, who were commonly called *Ache Beg*, *Gazi Facil*, and *Ormus Beg*, the latter of whom was his favourite; and is faid to have been defcended from the emperors of *Tribezond*.

Solyman had exercifed fuch cruelties upon the inhabitants when he took *Chirli*, that *Morad* made himfelf mafter of *Pergus*, without a ftroke; and then returned to *Afia*. His brother *Solyman* did not long out-live thofe conquefts, for he was foon after killed by a fall from his horfe. Though this had a fatal effect upon the health of his father, whofe darling he was; yet fo intent was *Orchan* upon his *European* conquefts, that he ordered *Ache Beg* to purfue them; and that general is faid to have made himfelf mafter of *Dydmiothykon*, which we are told, though with no great probability, he ordered to be reftored to the *Greek* emperor, at the requeft of his old friend and father-in-law, *Kantakazemus*. Soon after this he died of heart-break, for the lofs of his fon; and of when, according to fome authorities, he was feventy years of age,

Marginal notes:
Orchan thoufand
Matthew, who is forced to renounce the empire. Improbable account.

Succeffes of Orchan.

Orchan fecures his footing in Europe.

His generals.

Death of Solyman,

Orchan.

age, of which he had reigned thirty; though others pretend he was eighty years of age when he died.

Orchan's character, If we diveft ourfelves of that partiality, and thofe pre-poffeffions, which we are apt to entertain againft a prince by birth a barbarian, and by religion a *Mahometan*, we fhall have many fhining and even amiable qualities to admire in *Orchan*. It appears, from all authorities, that, far from ex-tending his dominions merely by cruelty and force, the people whom he fubdued, became his fubjects on account of the lenity, and liberty they enjoyed under his government. In him, thofe liberal arts, that were practifed in the eaft, found a patron and protector; and he feems to have been a proficient in fome of them himfelf. Though, from the numerous religious houfes, of all kinds, that he built, he ap-pears to have been a ftrict *Mahometan*; yet he was fo far from offering violence to the religion of his fultana queen, that we learn from her own father, fhe not only had the free exercife of it, but made a great many converts in her hufband's court. It cannot, indeed, be denied, that he long had projected the footing he gained in *Europe*, in prejudice **virtues** of the *Greek* empire. But ambition was the virtue of his **and mode-** age and country, and *Kantakazemus* himfelf can be confider-**ration.** ed as little better than an ufurper. *Orchan*, however, ma-naged matters towards him with great decency and mo-deration, and in all but his favourite point of obtaining a footing in *Europe*, he proved a ufeful and faithful ally to him, and in fuch a diftracted ftate, as the *Greek* empire then was, few princes would have acted with fo much temper as *Orchan* did. The vaft difference between the *Byzantine*, and *Ottoman* hiftories, in dates and facts, in which both of them are miferably defective, leave us fo much in the dark, as to many particulars, that we only mention facts, in which all are agreed, and perhaps, if the chronology of thofe facts could be afcertained, the reign of *Orchan* might appear in a much more favourable light, than we, confiftently with our information, have dared to reprefent it.

Succeeded by his fon Morad, or Amurat, Nothing can give us a higher idea of the wifdom and policy of the firft *Othman* fultans, than by reflecting that they left their empires fo fettled, that, like almoft all the others in the eaft, they were not broke to pieces in a few years, by quarrels and difagreements amongft their defcend-ants. *Morad* mounted the *Othman* throne, and, amongft the firft actions of his reign, was his reducing *Adrianople*, by **his policy** means of *Atebeki*, his generaliffimo and firft minifter. He then extended his conquefts in *Thrace*, and brought the whole of his acquifitions in *Europe*, which were called *Rum Eli*, under a regular government. *Ormus* was fo fuccefsful that the *Sultan Amurat*, for fo we fhall call him, was able to make an improvement upon his father's military fyftem. For the number of the captives brought into his dominions be-ing very great, *Amurat* appointed commiffaries, who chofe every fifth of the moft robuft men amongft them; and

many

many thousands being thus set aside, he sent them to *Haij* and insti- His insti-
Bektash, a religious *Turk*, famous for his sanctity and mira- tution of
cles, desiring him to give them a banner, a name, and his the *Jani-*
blessing. The saint, in the true eastern spirit, selecting one *saries.*
of them, put the sleeve of his gown upon his head, saying,
" Let their name be *Yenghicheri*, let their visages be always
" bright, their hands be victorious, and their swords keen.
" Let their lances always hang over the heads of their foes,
" and wherever they march let them always return with
" white countenances." Such was the original of the order
of the *Yenghicheres*, known to us by the names of *Janisaries*;
and who have ever since continued to be the flower of the
Turkish armies; and to this day the caps they wear upon
their heads retain the form of the saint's sleeve.

Amurat soon reaped the benefit of this new military insti- His vast
tution, by many important conquests he made in *Europe*, as conquests,
well as in *Asia*. He became the arbiter of all the princes,
and governors in those parts, who had started out of the
ruins of *Jenghiz Khan*'s empire; and about the year 1389,
his dominions were so much extended, that the *Wallakians*,
Hungarians, Servians, Bulgarians, and other *European* nations,
entered into a confederacy against him, under the command
of *Lazarus*, the prince of *Servia*, who appears to have been
a *Christian*. A bloody battle was fought between the two
parties on the plain of *Kossovia*, in *Servia*; victory declared for
the *Othmans*, but a desperate *Servian* soldier, while *Amurat*
was walking over the field of battle, had strength, though
wounded, to stagger up to him, and to plunge a concealed
dagger in his breast, by which he immediately died. Such and death
are all the interesting particulars we can with certainty re- by a
late of this great sultan; who, besides many other places *Christian*
and countries, added to the empire left him by his father, soldier.
Ancyra, Adrianople, Felibe, Eski, Zaghanna, Ipsala, Malgara,
Batha, Zagara, and *Gumurjina,* and by marrying his son
Bajazet to the daughter of the prince of *Phrygia Major*, the
Othmans acquired *Kutahia, Egugoz,* and *Fushanlike.* The city
of *Elvadz, Emishahr, Arsherith, Karagais,* and *Seydgshri,* with
many others, became their tributaries. *Amurat* likewise Particulars
took, but with great difficulty, the two strong castles of of *Amu-*
Bobria, and *Kavallah*; with the greatest part of *Albania*, *rat*'s con-
and other territories. We only now know their names, quests.
which being *Seljukian*, were commonly those of the different
governors who possessed them, and are therefore immaterial.
Their situation and boundaries are equally unknown to us,
because of the many different hands through which they
passed, and their continual wars, by which they were still
either losing, or enlarging their territories. We have
thought proper to throw the names of the principal places
Amurat conquered together in this manner; because, though
we know he did conquer them, we have no historian to conduct us in the chronology, or order of his actions. He was
killed

killed in the seventy-first year of his age, and the thirtieth of his reign. *Amurat* is celebrated for his fortitude, abstinence, and modesty, after he came to his sovereignty; and he is said to have been always clothed in soff, or woollen.

He is succeeded by his son Bajazet,

Abu Yazid, whom in compliance with the *European* pronunciation, we shall call *Bajazet*, succeeded his father, who, according to the *Greek* writers, had put out the eyes of his eldest son *Sawy*, for conspiring against him. *Bajazet* had a younger brother called *Yakub*, who attempting to make some

His cruelty, and conquests,

disturbances upon his succession to the throne, was by his orders strangled, and *Lazarus*, the prince of *Servia*, who had been taken prisoner, was put to death, though some say he fell in the battle. *Bajazet*'s first exploits were against the *Servians*, whom he subdued. After that he conquered all *Iconia*, and banished *Yesse*, the son of *Atin*, to *Nice*. The prince of *Phrygia Major*, as we have seen, was his father-in-law, but that did not protect him from *Bajazet*'s ambition; which stript him of his capital *Kotiakum*, and all his kingdom; and then sent him a prisoner to *Ipsala*. His name was *Karmian Ogli*. The prince of *Karimania*, who was brother-in-law to *Bajazet*, by marrying his sister, to avoid the like fate, made war upon *Bajazet*'s enemies the *Moldavians*; whose country he ravaged; and at first defeated *Stephen*, the prince of it, a man of extraordinary spirit and valour. For being obliged to fly to *Nemps* after his defeat, his mother, who commanded the garrison there, refused him admittance, saying, that she would see him dead, rather than he should owe his safety to a woman. *Stephen*, ashamed, retires, and getting together twelve thousand of his subjects, he attacked and routed the *Karimanian* army. *Bajazet* was then upon his march to take *Jessi*, the capital of *Moldavia*, but *Stephen*

but is defeated by Stephen,

pursuing his good fortune, gave him a total defeat, and obliged the mighty *Bajazet* to fly, almost unattended, to *Adrianople*.

He reduces Karamania.

The prince of *Karimania*, who had great subjects of complaint against *Bajazet*, upon this, attacked his *Asiatic* dominions. But *Bajazet*, whose epithet was *Ildarim*, or the like name, for his incredible activity, while every one thought his affairs ruined, got together an army, defeated the *Karimanian*, and put him to death; by which all *Karimania* was reduced. After this, *Bajazet* passing into *Europe*, took several forts and towns upon the *Danube*; and returning to *Asia*, *Kadi Burhan*, the prince of *Kesaria*, besides many other fine cities and territories, surrendered to him the important city of *Scives*, or *Sebastia*; and continued ever after *Bajazet*'s faithful friend and servant. After this, he became master of a vast number of important places and countries; but unfortunately the *Turks* and *Greeks*, having different names,

Confusion of historians.

sometimes three or four for the same places and provinces, modern authors have been led into vast confusion and uncertainty upon that account. We are told that he seized

Karia,

Karia, and *Lycya*, and that *Kedar*, the prince of *Lydia* and *Jolia*, submitting to him, *Bajazet* gave him his daughter in marriage, but soon after had him difpatched by poifon. He then reduced *Philadelfia*, and returning to *Europe*, he repaired and fortified, in a very ftrong manner, *Kalipolis*.

While *Bajazet* was in *Europe*, his provinces in *Afia Minor* were attacked and laid wafte by *Kutrum*, who is called the prince of *Kaftamoni*; *Bajazet*, with his ufual celerity, repaffed the *Straits* with his army, and *Kutrum* happening to die, *Iffindar Beg*, upon his making his fubmiffions to *Bajazet*, took poffeffion of all his towns and territories. Notwithftanding all the confufion that we find in *Bajazet*'s hiftory, it feems to be pretty certain, that, about the year 1391, he was mafter of all *Bythynia*, *Phrygia*, *Bulgaria*, and *Karia*; and carried his arms into *Pamphilia*. The affairs of the *Greek* empire were then in terrible diforder. The emperor *John Paleologus*, and other princes of his family, had by their ambaffadors, and in their own perfons, endeavoured to roufe the *Chriftian* princes on the continent of *Europe* to a fenfe of their danger, from the growing power of the *Othmans*, but more efpecially the infatiable ambition of *Bajazet*. The popes, the *Venetians*, and fome other trading powers, had fometimes affifted the emperors with money, but it was fo miferably mifemployed, that they fhut up all the *Greek* empire in a manner within the walls of *Conftantinople*, which *Bajazet* earneftly wifhed to become mafter of. With this view he built greater naval armaments than the *Othmans*, or any *Turkifh* nation had ever feen before; and to take raifed a city to cut off the communication between *Europe* and *Afia*. This city lies at *Bogaz Geiheihd*, or *the Paffage of the Straits*, and is fituated between the *Propontis*, and the mountains of *Nicea*, from whence the people of *Conftantinople* ufed to draw their materials for fhip-building. Thofe precautions being taken, *Bajazet* marched and encamped his army under the very walls of *Conftantinople*, and prepared to befiege it.

But the *Greek* emperor *John*, though thus reduced, was ftill very powerful within the walls of his capital. Many of his fubjects, efpecially thofe who had fettled there for the fake of commerce, were immenfely rich; and it was not the intereft of the powers of *Europe*, that they fhould be plundered by *Othman Turks*. Add to this, that the place was well fortified, and the garrifon, as well as the inhabitants, who were incredibly numerous, was very ftrong, and while the *European* powers were mafters of the fea, as they were, *Bajazet* could have no profpect of being able to reduce the place by famine. The *Othman*, however, feemed to be infenfible to all thofe confiderations, and to be determined to proceed in the fiege. It was with difficulty he was diverted from this refolution, by his firft minifter, who advifed to fet on foot a treaty with the governor, as they haughtily called

Bajazet subdues Kaftamoni.

Diftractions in the Greek empire.

Bajazet attempts Conftantinople.

Strength of that capital.

called the emperor of *Conſtantinople*. *John* had no power to diſpute the terms propoſed, or rather preſcribed, by *Bajazet*. They were, that *John* ſhould pay an annual tribute to *Baja-zet*; that *Mahometans* ſhould be allowed places of worſhip, a hall of judgement, and a kadi or magiſtrate of their own in *Conſtantinople*, and that *Manuel*, the emperor's ſon, ſhould, with one hundred followers, attend *Bajazet* in an expedition he was juſt about to enter upon, againſt the *Turks* of *Pam-philia*; all which terms *John* agreed to.

The emperor becomes tributary to Bajazet.

Bajazet accordingly marched into *Pamphilia*, which war being ſucceſsfully finiſhed, he returned to *Europe*; but was alarmed when he ſaw that the *Greek* emperor, during his abſence, had made a vaſt number of additional fortifications to his capital. *Bajazet*'s fleet, in the mean time, had burnt the city of *Kiho*, and had ravaged the iſles of the *Archipe-lago*, and had endeavoured to cut off the communication between *Europe* and *Aſia*; which indicated that he was re-ſolved, at all events, to attempt the conqueſt of *Conſtantinople*. He ſummoned *John* to demoliſh the additional fortifications he had made, threatening, that if he did not, he would order the eyes of his ſon *Manuel* to be plucked out. Such re-peated misfortunes and indignities broke the heart of *John*, and *Manuel* had the good fortune to avoid the fate intended him, by eſcaping from *Perſia* to *Conſtantinople*; where he took poſſeſſion of the imperial throne. His eſcape highly exaſperated *Bajazet*, and, after ſending *Manuel* many inſo-lent meſſages, he returned once more into *Thrace*, which he filled with his ravages, and took *Theſſalonica*. After that, he ſent *Tarkan*, one of his generals, to lay the country waſte about the *Euxine Sea*, while another of his barbarians, *Abra-neſus*, falling into the *Morea*, ravaged *Ahaya*, and *Lacedemon*. Thus the once populous and flouriſhing ſtates of *Athens*, *Sparta*, and the other cities of *Greece*, the ſeats of liberty, literature, of all that was noble, and of all that was polite; ſtates that checked the invaſions of *Xerxes*, at the head of about a million of men, were abandoned to the ravages of brutal *Turks*; and by what appears from hiſtory, were obliged to ſubmit without ſtriking a ſtroke. *Bajazet* then, with his own army, formed the blockade of *Conſtantinople* in ſuch a manner, both by ſea and land, that the inhabitants not receiving their uſual ſupplies from *Europe*, were in danger of ſoon being in want of all the neceſſaries of life.

His inſolence to the Greek emperor, who dies and is ſucceeded by his ſon Manuel.

Bajazet ravages Greece,

and block-ades Con-ſtantinople

Manuel found means to let the pope, and the other princes of *Europe*, know the dreadful ſituation he was in; and a kind of cruſade, at the head of which was *Sigiſmund*, king of *Hungary*, immediately took place. The *Chriſtian* army conſiſted of one hundred and thirty thouſand *European* troops, chiefly *Engliſh*, or ſubjects to the king of *England*, *French*, *Italians*, *Germans*, and *Hungarians*; and, having rendez-vouſed in *Hungary*, they laid ſiege to *Nicopolis*. The count of *Nevers*, afterwards duke of *Burgundy*, commanded under
                                                        Sigiſmund;

He de-feats the Chriſtians

Sigifmund ; and, at firft, the *Chriftians* retook feveral places, and obtained many advantages againft the *Turks*.

Bajazet having intelligence of thofe proceedings, refolved to put the fate of his empire upon checking *Sigifmund* ; and therefore calling in his parties and armies, raifed the blockade or, as others call it, the fiege of *Conftantinople* ; and, after burning all his fcaling-ladders, and other machines, marched with the whole towards *Nicopolis*. *Sigifmund* was but a young man and covetous of glory ; he turned the fiege of *Nicopolis* into a blocade, and marched, with the main body of his army, againft *Bajazet*.

This was what the *Othman* moft wanted, for he was afraid that the *Chriftians*, having fecured their retreat over the *Danube*, would have forced him to attack them in their intrenchments. Underftanding that *Sigifmund* approached, he divided his army into two bodies : the foremoft was commanded by his generals ; and the latter, which was placed fo as to be concealed from the fight of the *Chriftians*, and confifted of his janifaries, and the beft troops he had, was commanded by him himfelf. The *Chriftians* thought that the whole of *Bajazet*'s army confifted of his firft divifion, and the *French* begged for the honour of beginning the attack. As ufual, they did it with fuch an impetuofity, that they bore down all before them ; and they were feconded by *Germans*, *Flemings*, and other nations, till, continuing their purfuit too far, *Bajazet* and his janifaries feparated the rear from their van, and began a moft amazing flaughter, very little quarter being given. The *French*, who were the moft forward, were all cut in pieces, excepting the count of *Nevers*, and a few principal officers, who were made prifoners, and fpared by the tyrant, on account of the great ranfoms they were afterwards obliged to pay. As to the rear, they were either cut in pieces or pufhed into the *Danube*, where they perifhed ; while *Sigifmund*, who had not borne his command with much equanimity, was fortunate enough to repafs the *Danube* in a pitiful yawl.

He defeats the Chriftians in a bloody battle.

Bajazet, after this great victory, refumed his operations against *Conftantinople* ; but he found it in a more formidable ftate than it was in when he left it ; and perceived that he could not reduce it without a vaft expence of blood. He had in his army a prince of the *Paleologue* family, named *John*. He was the fon of *Andronicus*, *Manuel*'s elder brother ; fo that, in fact, he was the lawful heir of the *Greek* empire. *Bajazet* made this prince his tool, and fent a public meffage, offering to defift from hoftilities, if *Manuel* would yield his throne to the lawful heir. At the fame time, he promifed *John* great advantages, if, as foon as he was poffeffed of *Conftantinople*, he would refign it to him. *John* feemed to agree to this propofal very readily, and diffembled fo effectually, that *Bajazet* left him with the command of ten thoufand *Turks*, and drew off his main body to a great diftance from the city.

He renews the fiege of Conftantinople.

but is out-
witted in
his defign
to become
mafter of
it.

The *Conftantinopolitans*, ever wavering, fhewed fuch difpofitions to embrace *Bajazet's* propofal, that *Manuel* could not
refift them. He entered into treaty with *John*, and, refigning to him the empire, he had liberty to fet fail, with his family and effects, on board the gallies that were in the harbour, for *Europe*. *John*, upon this, took quiet poffeffion of
Conftantinople; but *Bajazet*, who had promifed to make him
king of *Morea*, was amazed when he refufed to give up *Conftantinople*. *Bajazet*, at that time, however, was in no condition to force him; but, in lieu of *Conftantinople*, was obliged
to accept of *Salivrea*, the only other town that remained to
the *Paleologue* family.

The caufe of this moderation in *Bajazet* was the irruption
of *Tamerlan* (of which and its motives we have given an ample account) into his dominions. Some authors, not without great probability, fay that *Tamerlan* was implored, by
letters from the *Greek* emperor, to come to his relief. Be
this as it will, it is certain that *Tamerlan's* ambition, and the
growing greatnefs of *Bajazet*, were more than fufficient for
impelling him to make war upon the *Othman*; for, though
Bajazet was a *Mahometan*, yet, when his avarice or intereft
were concerned, he made no difference in religions, but
treated all with equal rapacioufnefs and cruelty.

Bajazet
attacked,
defeated,
and taken
prifoner
by *Tamer-
lan*.

The reader, in the former part of this hiftory, hath feen
the event of the war between *Tamerlan* and *Bajazet*, and of
the battle of *Ancyra*, in which *Bajazet* was defeated and taken
prifoner. We fhall therefore only mention that a body of
European troops in *Bajazet's* army were compofed of *Servians*,
and are reported to have been commanded by an *European*, by
fome called *Pafir Laus*, and by others *Stephen*. He is faid to
have been the fon of *Lazarus*, prince of *Servia*, who was killed
in, or after, the battle of *Kaffova*. His fifter had been married, as *European* authors pretend, to *Bajazet*, who allowed
Stephen, in confideration of her being diftractedly fond of
him, to keep part of his dominions. She retained the exercife of the *Chriftian* religion in her own apartments; and had
fo much influence over *Bajazet*, that fhe prevailed upon him
to drink wine, and to indulge himfelf in luxuries, to which
the princes of the houfe of *Othman* had always been ftrangers.

After the battle, this princefs fell into the hands of *Tamerlan*, who is faid to have been touched with her charms; but
finding fhe was averfe to changing her religion, fent her to
Bajazet. When we confider, however, who this princefs
was, and to whom fhe was married, we can have no exalted
opinion either of her religion or delicacy. I have, in another
place, given my reafons for believing that the ftory of *Tamerlan's* fhutting up *Bajazet* in an iron cage, is not fuch a fiction
as fome modern writers feem to imagine. There is reafon,
it is true, for believing that he afterwards releafed him from

that shameful confinement, and treated him with uncommon generosity.

Bajazet is said to have died at *Egridur*, on the twenty-third of *March*, 1403. But authors neither agree as to the place or manner of his death; some say that it happened by poison, and others by a fit of an apoplexy; while a third kind say that he dashed his brains out against the grates of his iron cage. *His death,*

We know little of his character but by his actions; wherein an amazing quickness of thought, and rapidity in execution, appear to have subdued all his enemies till he was himself subdued by a conqueror, who, in power, as well as in experience and policy, far exceeded himself, and, at least, equalled him in courage. He is said to have been very fond of architecture and works of magnificence, many of which he erected; and to have been implacable in his fits of passion. He died in the fifty-eighth year of his age, and the fifteenth of his reign. *and character.*

The History of the Othman Turks, from the Reign of Bajazet, in the year 1403, to the taking of Constantinople, in 1462.

BAJAZET, according to the best authorities, lost his eldest son, *Mustapha*, in the battle of *Ancyra*; but left behind him three others, whose names were *Solyman, Musa,* and *Mohammed*; all of whom tasted of empire, though the youngest was the only one who lived to possess his father's undivided territories. Happily for the *Othman* line, *Tamerlan's* more important concerns in other parts of his vast dominions, did not admit of his taking time to secure the conquest of *Bajazet's* countries, either for himself or his posterity. *Bajazet's* eldest son, whose sir-name was *Chelebi,* or *the gentle,* a common epithet, in those days, to the sons of sultans, escaped from the battle of *Ancyra* time enough there to secure his father's treasures, and the allegiance of the *European* army, by whom he was saluted emperor. *His empire divided.*

We are told, however, that the emperor *Manuel,* who had, for some time, been in exile in *Europe,* upon *Bajazet's* death, recovered his empire of *Constantinople*; and was applied to for assistance by *Solyman,* who made him great cessions of dominion upon *Manuel* promising him his protection and assistance; and, that *Solyman* proposed to reserve to himself, of all the territories his father had conquered from the *Greek* emperor, only the sovereignty of *Thrace.* This seems to agree ill with what we are told by other authors, as if *Manuel* had acknowledged *Tamerlan* his superior; nay, that *Solyman* himself had made his submissions to the conqueror. *Solyman reigns in Europe. His treaty with the Greek emperor.*

F 2 But

Oppofed
by his
brother
Mufa.

But thofe inconfiftencies are frequent in the hiftories of princes of the *Greek* and *Turkifh* dinafties. It is probable that *Solyman*, finding *Tamerlan* was obliged to leave thofe parts, behaved to him with fome haughtinefs; and that *Tamerlan*, on that account, beftowed on his brother *Mufa* the inveftiture of all his father's, *Bajazet's*, dominions; telling him, that he loved power lefs than he did a noble mind. *Tamerlan*, at the fame time, reftored to their dominions all the petty princes whom *Bajazet* had difpoffeffed; which, upon his departure, made thofe countries fo many fcenes of blood and ruin; but this does not fall within our plan to recount. Some were favoured by *Solyman*, who is likewife called *Mufulman*, and fome by his brother *Mufa*.

Character
of *Solyman*

Solyman was brave, and a good foldier; but debauched and luxurious; and, finding out *Tamerlan's* partiality to his brother *Mufa*, who refided at *Prufa*, he advanced againft him at the head of his *European* army. *Mufa* fled before him; and *Solyman* took poffeffion of *Prufa*, where he plunged himfelf into all manner of pleafures. At this time, his brother *Mufa*, being refufed fhelter by all the neighbouring princes, who ftood in awe of *Solyman*, croffed the *Hellefpont*, and fled even as far as *Wallakia*. Here he was joined by a number of foldiers of fortune, or rather free-booters, who enlifted under him in hopes of fharing the fpoils of his brother's empire. As to *Solyman*, he ftill continued his revels and debauches at *Prufa*; while his brother made himfelf mafter of *Adrianople*, in the year 1406.

He defeats
Mufa,

But *Solyman*, who, when fober, was one of the braveft and moft accomplifhed princes of the age, fhaking off his vices, affembled his army, and, advancing towards *Adrianople*, he obliged his brother once more to fly to *Wallakia*. His retreat proved fatal to *Solyman*, who, plunging himfelf once more into pleafures, forgot that he was either a king or a man; and fuffered the affairs of his empire to go to ruin. His thoughtlefs diffipation, and neglect of every thing relating to government, notwithftanding all his amiable qualities, difgufted his chief officers and minifters fo much, that they entered into a correfpondence with *Mufa*, who, favoured by them, affembled an army and furprized *Adrianople*, where

but is furprized in
his debauches
and killed

Solyman was. He had but juft time to efcape from thence at the head of a few horfemen, and directed his flight to *Conftantinople*; but he was killed upon the road; fome fay during a debauch that he made; and others, by the hands of three brothers, to revenge other two of their brothers, whom he had unadvifedly killed: and by this *Mufa* became poffeffed of *Adrianople* and all the dominions of *Solyman*, who, though he reigned near three years, is not reckoned amongft the *Othman* fultans.

Mufa defeats the
Hungarians.

Bajazet's empire had now two competitors for it. *Mufa*, who reigned at *Adrianople*; and *Mohammed*, who was poffeffed of *Amafia*, and feveral other territories in *Afia*. The
latter

latter, having chastised some robbing *Tartars*, prepared to march against *Musa*; who, terrified at his approach, offered to resign to him his pretensions upon all their father's *Asiatic* territories; and, as a proof of his sincerity, he made war upon the *Christians*, and invaded the territories of *Sigismund*, the king of *Hungary*, whom he defeated in a terrible battle near the city of *Samandria*, almost upon the banks of the *Danube*. This victory, however, and many other advantages he obtained, was, by the *Turks*, ascribed to his generals *Korshah Muluk* and the famous *Ormus Beg*.

Musa himself was gentle, generous, and a lover of justice and moderation; qualities which those barbarians construed into effeminacy and cowardice. *Mohammed*, therefore, being, in their eyes, a more active prince, the two generals above mentioned, with other principal officers of *Musa's* army, invited him to take possession of the whole of the *Ottoman* empire; which, they said, must be ruined if it continued to be divided. *Mohammed* took their advice, and *Musa* was obliged to fly to *Servia*; where that prince furnished him with the means of repossessing himself of *Adrianople*, which he did, *Mohammed* being obliged, by the advanced season of the year, to return to *Prusa*.

Musa, ignorant, perhaps, of the treachery of his two generals, or from a principle of clemency, pardoned them both, though they fell into his hands upon his retaking *Adrianople*; and both of them repeated their treasons, by again inviting *Mohammed* into *Europe*. According to the Greek historians, *Musa*, upon this occasion, shewed himself a true *Turk*, and fell upon the cities and countries that had been ceded by *Solyman* to *Manuel*; and, after committing prodigious ravages, he, at last, besieged *Constantinople* itself. Upon this, *Manuel* invited *Mohammed*, who, by *Musa's* successes, seems, at this time, to have dropped his pretensions to his *European* dominions, to his assistance. *Mohammed* and his army, accordingly, by the favour of *Manuel*, who promised him all his assistance for making him sole sultan of the *Othmans*, threw themselves into *Constantinople*; where they made a vigorous defence, but were defeated in two sallies. Upon this he proposed to the emperor to make a diversion, and to pass the *Propontis*; which *Manuel* agreeing to, the proposal had the desired effect; for *Mohammed* landing in *Europe*, divided his army into two bodies; one of which marched towards the *Euxine Sea*, the other towards *Adrianople*. *Musa* pursued them; but, his troops being corrupted by the treachery of his generals, who had once more gone over to *Mohammed*, he was deserted by them, and slain by a private man, whom *Mohammed* afterwards made a great general.

Accounts of the Greek historians.

Mohammed joins Manuel, and kills his brother.

The *Turkish* historians, however, speak nothing of *Musa's* besieging *Constantinople*; but say that he was taken prisoner

F 3   by by one of his brother's soldiers, and, by his order, put to death. But the former account, which is given by *Dukas*, the *Greek* historian, who was upon the spot at the time, is, by far, the most probable.

Moham-
med sole
sultan.
Mohammed was now without a competitor, and proclaimed sole sultan of the *Othmans* at *Adrianople*. His first warlike atchievement was to humble the prince of *Karamania*, called *Karaman Ogli*; whom, after twice rebelling, he generously pardoned, but took from him some of his strong places. He next marched against *Iffindar*, the prince of *Kaftamoni*, whom he defeated and killed, and seized upon his treasures and dominions.

As *Karaman Ogli* had surprized, plundered, and demolished the city of *Prufa*, *Mahammed* rebuilt it. But that sultan's memory is valuable for nothing so much as the fidelity with which he fulfilled his engagements to the emperor *Manuel*; to whom, for the assistance he afforded him against *Mufa*, he had promised him the places that had been taken from the *Greeks*, on the *Euxine Sea*, the *Propontis*, and in *Theffalia*; all which he faithfully restored upon *Manuel's* requisition. He told the *Greek* ambassadors, at the same time, that he considered *Manuel* as his father, and that he should be ever obedient to his will and direction. About this time, he also received ambassadors from the princes of *Greece*, with all whom he made peace, and wished that the God of peace might punish the party by whom it was violated.

The *Greek* empire, through the good faith of *Mohammed*, began now to raise its head; and that prince saw it without jealousy; for, after *Manuel* had successfully finished an expedition he had undertaken into *Morea*, he and the sultan had an interview together at *Kallipoli*; and *Mohammed* even dined on board one of the emperor's gallies.

Rebellion
of *Chuneid*
quashed
by the ful-
tan.
One *Chuneid*, whom *Solyman* had made governor of *Bulgaria*, had surprized *Ephefus*, *Smyrna*, and *Thyra*; and, in all those places, had been guilty of great cruelties. *Mohammed* went at the head of an army to reduce him; and, in this expedition, he was assisted by the princes of *Phocea*, the *Higher Phrygia*, *Karia*, *Lefbos*, *Chio*, and even the great master of *Rhodes*. The latter prince had had some footing in *Smyrna* during the usurpation of *Chuneid*, and had almost compleated a fort there. *Smyrna* being besieged and taken by *Mohammed*, with the assistance of those princes, the sultan gave orders for demolishing the grand-master's fort. The latter resented this proceeding so far as even to make reprizals at sea; but *Mohammed*, with great moderation, represented to him the necessity of demolishing that fort, which was a perpetual bone of contention between the *Turks* and *Chriftians*; till, at last, he pacified him, by giving him leave to build another fort upon the confines of *Karia* and *Lycia*.

The design of building such forts is not extremely creditable, they being intended, and maintained, as places of refuge

fuge for runnagate flaves, who were called "The freed of St. *Peter*," from the name of the fort.

Mohammed behaved with equal moderation and juftice to all the other princes who ferved in his army, many of whom were *Chriftians*, and all of them were charmed with his mildnefs and affability. We may place thofe tranfactions about the year 1417. *His moderation.*

Chuneid, finding himfelf unable to refift, fubmitted to, and was pardoned by, *Mohammed*, who fent a fleet to chaftife a prince called the duke of *Naxos*. This duke was an ally to the *Venetians*, and lord of feveral other iflands in the *Archipelago*; but had neglected to recognize the fupremacy which the houfe of *Othman* claimed over thofe iflands. The fleet fitted out againft him by *Mohammed* confifted of thirty gallies, all of which were deftroyed, and their crews put to the fword, by the duke's allies the *Venetians*, who were then extremely powerful by fea. After this, the *Venetians* bombarded and ruined the tower of *Lampfacus*, and then failed to *Conftantinople*, where they were received by *Manuel*, who feems to have made but very indifferent returns for *Mohammed*'s kindnefs to him. *His fleet entirely defeated by the Venetians.*

Theffalonica was one of the cities which had been ceded to *Manuel* by the houfe of *Othman*, and had, ever fince he came into poffeffion of it, been an eye-fore to *Mohammed*'s fubjects. *Muftapha*, the eldeft fon of *Bajazet*, was flain in the battle of *Ancyra*, but his body never had been found. According to *Dukas*, the fame *Bajazet* had a fourth fon, whofe name likewife was *Muftapha*, and who, on account of his tender age, had been left at home when that battle was fought. In the year 1419, *Mohammed*, underftanding that *Karaman Ogli* had been guilty of new exceffes, and had even been barbarous enough to burn the body of his father *Bajazet*, marched with his army into *Afia*, where he took the city of *Kogni*, or *Iconium*, which belonged to *Karaman*, and laid his other dominions wafte with fire and fword. *Hiftory of Muftapha, pretended or real fon of Bajazet.*

Upon his return to *Adrianople* from this expedition, he was alarmed with an account that one, pretending to be *Muftapha*, one of *Bajazet*'s fons, was in arms in *Wallakia*. *Mohammed* had made *Chéuneid* governor of *Nicopolis*, and, knowing his treachery, fufpected him to be the author of the impofture, and ordered his head to be ftruck off. *Chuneid*, however, evaded the blow, joined *Muftapha*, raifed a great army of *Turks* and *Wallakians*, and, falling upon *Theffalia*, they deftroyed *Zagara*, and even laid fiege to *Nicera*, if we may believe the *Turkifh* hiftorians. *Mohammed* was alarmed at the progrefs of the impoftor, who, by the abovementioned hiftorians, is faid to have been the domeftic of a petty prince; and, marching with an army to oppofe him, the rebels were defeated. But *Chuneid* was purfued and admitted into *Theffalonica*, by *Demetrius Lafcaris*, *Manuel*'s go-

vernor

vernor of that city. *Mohammed* demanded that the traitor should be given up to him; but readily agreed to wait till *Lascaris* could know the emperor's own sentiments on that head.

He is made prisoner. By the manner in which those princes proceeded, it is more than probable that he who is called the pretended *Mustapha*, was a real son of *Bajazet*, and known to be such both by *Manuel* and *Mohammed*. *Manuel* refused to deliver him up, but offered to keep him and *Chuneid* prisoners all their lives, upon the emperor's paying him three hundred thousand aspers a year for their maintainance. What is still more remarkable, *Manuel* was to have the entire disposal of them after the sultan's death; and was at liberty to act as his successor should deserve. This insurrection, however, drew *Mohammed*'s arms into *Wallakia*; where he took so many places, and built so many forts, that the country consented to pay a tribute and to give him hostages

Mohammed invades Wallakia.

A remarkable religious impostor
An impostor of a different kind caused likewise considerable trouble to *Manuel*. His name was *Prekligia*, by birth a peasant, but a prophet by profession. This impostor preached up a religion somewhat like the *Christian*, for he affected to be of that profession, in some points, but extravagant in others. It consisted in a kind of levelling principle, for he recommended an equality and community in all things but in women. His dress was modest and simple; and he preached up poverty to his disciples. He appeared in a place opposite to the isle of *Chio*, near the *Stilarian* mountains, at the mouth of the *Ionian Gulph*. Being assisted in his impostures by an old *Greek* monk of *Kandia*, who pretended that *Prekligia* could walk upon the sea, he obtained so g eat credit, that his followers defeated, with great slaughter, in two different battles, *Mohammed*'s two governors of *Iconia* and *Lydia*.

defeats the Othman generals,

but is himself defeated and put to death.
Upon this, *Mohammed* put his son *Amurat* at the head of an army, which was commanded, under him, by *Bajazet*, his favourite minister, who, with great difficulty, forced the fastnesses of the one coated men, so called from their imitating the dress of their prophet, and put them all to the sword. It is remarkable, that none of those wretches, at their death, could be prevailed on to abjure their profession; their leader was nailed to a cross, and carried through the streets of *Ephesus*, after suffering the greatest torments; and, after his death, his infatuated followers believed he would come again to life.

According to the order of time, this rebellion must have been suppressed six years before the death of *Mohammed*; for *Amurat*, his son, who commanded, was no more than twelve years of age. In his return through *Asia* and *Lydia*, *Bajazet* was so apprehensive of the effects of *Prekligia*'s doctrine, that he put to the sword all the *Turkish* monks who professed it.

As

As to *Amurat*, though so young, his father was so well satisfied with his conduct and capacity, that he made him governor of *Amasia*, but put about him able counsellors.

The rest of *Mohammed*'s reign was employed in regulating the affairs of his government. But, amongst the last actions of his life, was his reducing *Old Kalipolis*, *Tarkii*, and *Herghe*. *Mohammed*, upon his return from that expedition, was seized with a disorder, by some said to have been the apoplexy, by others a flux, which afterwards proved mortal. His eldest son, *Amurat*, was, at that time, at the head of an army in *Thrace*, and at a vast distance. *Mohammed*, finding his end approaching, was sensible of the great importance of keeping his death a secret till the arrival of his eldest son; and he gave a strict charge to his two vizirs, *Bajazet* and *Ibrahim*, for that purpose. *Conclusion of Mohammed's reign.*

The *Greek* historian, *Dukas*, tells us, that he recommended the care of his two younger sons (one of them eight, the other only seven, years of age) to *Manuel*, the *Greek* emperor, from a political as well as a natural reason; for he thought, that, besides thereby securing his children's lives from the jealousy of their elder brother, *Amurat* must be kept within the bounds of moderation by their being alive. He died in the forty-seventh year of his age, after having reigned a sole sultan almost nine years. The time of his death is fixed to the year 1421. *His dispositions, death,*

Tho' the reign of an *Ottoman* sultan is become almost another word for tyranny, cruelty, and perfidy, yet the history of few nations in *Europe* can match a prince endued with such sentiments of justice, friendship, and moderation, as *Mohammed* appears to have been. He mounted the throne of *Ottoman* at a time when the smallest efforts of confederacy amongst the *Christians* must have driven the *Turks* out of *Europe*, and have even recovered the *Greek* empire in *Asia*. *Mohammed* was sensible of that, and took care betimes to make *Manuel* his friend. *Manuel*, on the other hand, perceived it to be far more his interest to lye under obligations to *Mohammed*. Thus both princes, in fact, acted upon motives of interest as well as justice. *Mohammed* knew that he never could be much affected by the *Christian* powers, while *Manuel* was his friend; but we have scarcely, perhaps, in history, a parallel of such inviolable faith, honour, and confidence, as *Mohammed* shewed towards *Manuel*, notwithstanding all the provocations given him by the latter. His justice and gratitude is equally conspicuous in other respects. *and character.*

Upon the death of his father, and the divisions between his two elder brothers, he was eagerly sought for by *Tamerlan*'s orders. He was attended by a slave named *Bajazet*, and he fled to the mountains of *Galatia*, where he underwent such inexpressible miseries, that his feet being swelled, he must either have perished or been taken, had not *Bajazet* for several days carried him upon his back, and exposed himself *Fidelity of a slave.*

self

self to the extremity of misery for the prince's support, even to begging bread for him, habited like a religious person. After *Mohammed* came to the *Othman* throne he was so grateful for the services of his faithful slave, that he raised him to the highest post of the empire, for he and *Ibrahim* divided the prime vizership between them.

Mohammed's death concealed. It was of great importance for those two ministers to conceal the death of *Mohammed* till his successor could arrive. In this they were assisted by the ceremonies of the *Turkish* court, which permits no subject but the vizers, or such as they appoint, to approach the person of the sultan. By those means, it is said they concealed *Mohammed's* death from all but his physicians for forty-one days.

The Reign of Amurat, *or* Morad *the Second*.

Bajazet's son alive. NOTwithstanding all that has been said by the *Turkish* historians in honour of the *Othman* succession, it seems to be pretty certain that *Mustapha*, the eldest son of *Bajazet* was alive at the time of *Amurat's* accession. He had been protected, as has been already observed, by the *Greek* emperor *Manuel*; and he seems even to have reigned over part of the *Othman* dominions. His claim of blood rendered him a useful ally to *Manuel*. *Amurat* having buried his father at *Prusa*, received a message from *Manuel*, demanding that his two younger brothers should be sent to *Constantinople* in pursuance of the late sultan's will. But the vizier *Bajazet*, by *Amurat's* orders, flatly refused to suffer the *Othman* **Manuel protects him.** princes to be educated amongst *Christians* or infidels. Upon this, *Manuel* entered into a treaty with *Mustapha*, who granted him his own terms, and gave his son as an hostage for the performance. *Mustapha* was declared governor of *Thrace*, and he and *Chuneid*, (who still attended him) took possession of *Kallipolis*, and made themselves masters of the adjacent country. After this, he marched towards *Kariopolis*, but *Amurat* sent *Bajazet* against him, with an army of thirty thousand men. *Mustapha*, whose claim of blood seems to have been undoubted, by shewing himself to the enemy, and **His progress.** harranguing them from an eminence, persuaded a great part of *Bajazet's* troops to join him, and *Bajazet*, and his brother **He gains a victory over the sultan's army.** *Kamzas*, followed their examples and made their submission, but *Bajazet* was put to death by the instigation of *Chuneid*, whose son-in-law *Bajazet* formerly ordered to be castrated. It appears from the *Turkish* historians, that *Bajazet* had become extremely unpopular at the *Othman* court, and that the other great ministers sent him on this expedition to ruin him, which it effectually did. After this, *Mustapha* marched to *Adrianople*, which he entered without resistance.

It

It had been agreed between *Muftapha* and *Manuel*, whose great view was to reftore the antient majefty of the *Greek* empire, on the ruins of the *Othman*, that *Kallipolis* fhould be reftored to the *Greeks*. *Demetrius Leontarius*, *Manuel's* admiral and general, was by the emperor appointed to take poffeffion of the place, when both *Muftapha* and *Chuneid* refufed to deliver it up, the former fmoothly, the other contumaciously. *Demetrius* upbraided *Muftapha* with ingratitude, and the crimes of his family. This however, was all the fatisfaction he could obtain, and he carried his fquadron back to *Conftantinople*. *Manuel's* views did not fuffer him to put up with this difappointment. He offered, if *Amurat* would give up *Kallipolis*, and refign his father's will, directly to affift him againft *Muftapha*, who was now in quiet poffeffion of *Adrianople*, where he found immenfe treafures, which he expended in pleafure and indolence. *Amurat*, though voluptuous, refufed to agree to *Manuel's* terms; but he fent *Ibrahim*, his firft minifter, to treat with the emperor, and to offer him any other terms he fhould demand. *Amurat*, at the fame time, entered into a treaty for fome *European* fhipping to tranfport his forces to *Europe*. *Cineis* or *Chuneid*, who had hitherto continued faithful to *Muftapha*, reproached that prince with the inglorious life he led, and, with difficulty, perfuaded him to take the field, and endeavour to pafs the *Straits*. But *Amurat* had already taken poffeffion of the moft important paffes; particularly of the bridge of *Lopadion*, by which the progrefs of *Muftapha* was ftopped. *Muftopha* at this time, feems to have been in actual poffeffion of all the *Othman* empire in *Europe*, as *Amurat* was of that in *Afia*, which was far more extenfive and populous. *Muftapha's* progrefs being ftopped, *Amurat's* army encreafed every day. The bridge of *Lopadion* had been broken down, and the two armies were incamped on the oppofite fides of a great morafs. *Hamza*, the brother of *Cineis*, was one of *Amurat's* general officers; he had entered on a fecret treaty with *Cineis*, by means of a flave, who fwam over the morafs, by order of *Amurat*, who promifed to make him governor of *Iconia*. *Cineis* embraced the propofition, left *Muftapha*, engaged, defeated and killed the governor or prince of *Iconia*, who was defcended from the famous *Atin*; and made himfelf mafter of *Ephefus*.

As to *Amurat*, though but twenty years of age, and though, while at *Prufa*, he had been immerfed in pleafures, yet he acted with all the coolnefs and activity of a great general. Knowing the genius of his fubjects, he procured one *Seyd Bekhar*, who was efteemed a prophet and a faint, to gird him with a fword, and to give him his folemn benediction. This had a wonderful effect in his favour, and no fooner was the defection of *Cineis* known, than *Muftopha's* army abandoned him; and he was obliged to fly, almoft unattended, to *Kallipolis*. *Amurat* repaired the bridge of *Lopadion*,

He falls out with Manuel.

Muf'apha abandoned by Cineis.

Political conduct of Amurat.

dion,

dion, and, sending for *Adorno*, the admiral of the *European* shipping he had contracted with, and two thousand *Italian* mercenaries, he forced *Muftapha* to abandon *Kallipolis*, and to fly first to *Adrianople*, and then to *Wallakia*, where he was **Muftapha** made prisoner, and by *Amurat*'s order ignominiously hanged, **hanged.** to efface out of the minds of the people, the opinion of his high birth; and, to this day, fome of the *Turkifh* historians treat him as an impostor, but against all the evidence of facts.

Amurat *Amurat*, having nobly rewarded *Adorno* and his *Italian*
befieges foldiers, refumed his purpofe of uniting all the *Othman* do-
Conftanti- minions. *Karaman Ogli*, affifted by fome of the *Seljuk* gene-
nople, rals, whom we have fo often mentioned, had attacked *An-dalia*, but was defeated by *Gamza-Beg*, who, after that, reduced fome of the *Seljuk* territories. It was eafy for *Amurat* to
fee, that *Manuel* was at the bottom of all the difquietudes he
had met with, and *Amurat*, without ceremony, in the year
1422, raifed an army of two hundred thoufand men, to befiege *Conftantinople. John Paleologus*, at that time, governed
the *Greek* empire under *Manuel*, who was now aged and infirm; and he endeavoured to appeafe *Amurat* by his ambaffadors, but the *Othman* refufing to admit them to his prefence, actually laid fiege to *Conftantinople*. The *Greek* court
perceiving all endeavours for an accomodation to be vain,
perfuaded *Amurat*'s brother, called *Muftapha Chelebi*, to
rebel. In the mean while, the emperor *Manuel* died, and
Amurat being obliged to raife the fiege of *Conftantinople*, returned to *Adrianople*, and marched against *Nicea*, which had
been befieged by his rebel brother, or rather his abettors; for
Muftapha himself is faid to have been very young. *Amurat*'s
fortune prevailed, he furprifed *Nicea*, and taking his brother
puts his prifoner, he had him ftrangled before his eyes, and his
brother to guards cut in pieces. After this, he married the daughter of
death. *Laz Ogli*, defcended from *Lazarus*, the famous prince or
He mar- defpot of *Servia*. His next wife was the daughter of
ries. *Ifandiar-Beg*, the prince of *Sinope*, which he fubdued, and
fhe was mother to *Mohammed the Great*. Every thing now
feemed to give way to the *Othman* fortune. *Amurat* returning from his expedition against *Sinope*, prepared to reduce
Cineis, who pretended to hold the principalities of *Smyrna*,
independant of the fultan. *Amurat*, at first, only demanded
hoftages of *Cineis* for his good behaviour, but his demand
was attended with menaces, which *Cineis* feemed to difpife.
Cineis de- The truth is, *Cineis* appears to have been a prince of
feated. great power, as well as abilities, for though, through the
overheat of his fon named *Kurt*, or the *Wolf*, he was defeated by *Halil*, *Amurat*'s general, yet he made good his retreat,
first towards the mountains of *Smyrna*, and then towards
Hypfela, a city on the *Iconian Sea*, where he had a fleet, and
military ftores. In the mean while, his fon *Kurt* was taken
prifoner; and *Kamza*, the brother of the vizier *Bajazet*, who
had

had been faved by *Cineis* when *Bajazet* was put to death, was fent to purfue him, *Halil* being made governor of *Smyrna*. As to *Cineis*, he went to *Iconium*, and, though that prince had no reafon to truft him, he gave him a fmall reinforcement of men, and a large fupply of money. This enabled *Cineis* to return to *Hypfela*, where he was befieged by *Kamza*; *Kamza* happening then to be abfent upon other affairs, the fiege was carried on by *Halil*. But *Cineis* would have bidden defiance to all the *Othman* power, had not *Morat* fent him a fquadron of *Genoefe* fhips of war, under their admiral *Palavicini*, *Adorno* being now dead. The arts of artillery, as now practifed, were then in their infancy; and *Hypfela*, perhaps, was the firft city that had ever been battered by fhips from the fea with cannon. The novelty difmayed the inhabitants, and *Cineis* apprehending a revolt, furrendered the place to *Halil*, but capitulated for his life. This capitulation, though fworn to, was difowned by *Kamza*, and *Cineis* and his whole race, wherever they could and put to be found, were inhumanly put to death by him and *Amurat*. death. Thus died the brave, but unfortunate *Cineis*, who, by the *European* hiftorians, is called *Tzunites*, and is faid to have been defcended from the ancient princes of *Smyrna*, though perhaps his pedigree did not reach higher than the irruption of the *Othmans*.

About the year 1426, we find *Amurat* embroiled with the *Amurat* *Venetians*, who, during the late difturbances, had received takes under their protection *Theffalonica*, called by the *Turks*, *Salo- Theffalo- niki*. The *Venetians* would willingly have compromifed mat- nica. ters with him, but *Amurat* would hear of no terms, unlefs they would deliver up *Theffalonica*. The *Venetians* refufing to comply, *Amurat* befieged that city with an immenfe army, and took it, and then came to an accomodation with the *Venetians*. The conqueft of *Theffalonica* was followed by the reduction of all the places and cities that had been ced- ed to the late *Greek* emperor *Manuel*; and a great number of petty *Afiatic* princes fubmitting to pay him homage, and to hold their territories of him; he was now mafter of almoft all the antient *Greek* empire, excepting the *Morea*, and *Con- ftantinople*; but that city was a perpetual eyefore to *Amurat*. The *Greek* emperor then, was *John Paleologus*, a brave and a worthy prince; but finding himfelf in no condition to ftand out, he fubmitted to give up all the cities and forts, he held makes the upon the *Euxine Sea*, and to pay a yearly tribute of three *Greek* em- hundred thoufand afpers, by which he with great difficulty peror his obtained a temporary but faithlefs fufpenfion of hoftilities. tributary

Though *Amurat* was wife, brave, politic, and lefs inclin- He con- ed to blood, or to break his faith, than many of the eaftern quers tyrants were, yet he was a thorough barbarian. The inha- *Theffalo- bitants of *Theffalonica*, while their *Venetian* protectors efcap- nica. ed to their fhips, were either butchered, or referved for the moft painful and infamous ftates of flavery; and that noble city.

city, formerly the pride of the *Greek* empire, now rendered
destitute of its own inhabitants, was but poorly peopled, and
and Ephe- that by barbarous, despicable *Othmans. Ephesus* underwent the
fus. same fate, and all the scenes which freedom, arts, and learning, had formerly dignified, became now, in a literal sense,
so many dens of thieves.   Their inhabitants, indeed, under
the *Greek* emperors had greatly degenerated from those illustrious republicans who antiently did credit to human nature; but still it is certain, that learning maintained the
possession of her native *Greece.* She was driven by the
Othmans from thence to *Europe,* where she recovered and
improved all her former lustre.

Amurat's   *Amurat,* however, kept his court at *Ephesus* with a barba-
magnifi- rous magnificence, and sent ambassadors into *Wallakia,* and
cence and *Servia,* countries governed by princes under the denomina-
ambition, tion of *Waywods;* over whom he pretended a superiority.
opposed This superiority was disputed by *Dragul,* the natural son of a
by Dragul. *Wallakian* waywod, and he soon grew formidable to *Amurat,*
whose tributary waywod he defeated, and put to death.
Dragul, after this, assumed the sovereignty of *Wallakia,* and
defeated and killed the brother of the deceased waywod,
though he was acknowledged and supported by *Amurat.*
This revolution did not prevent *Amurat* from attacking
Gharmian Ogli, the prince of *Karamania,* and sultan of *Iconium.* It is none of the smallest injuries the *Turks* have done
Uncer- to learning, and history, in perverting the names of men
tainty of and places, and disguising them so in their own barbarous
history. jargon, as to render their situation and persons obscure, and
unintelligible.   This prince of *Karamania* was married to
Amurat's sister, and, next to *Amurat* himself, he seems to have
been the greatest monarch of all the western part of *Asia.*
He had had many disputes with *Amurat,* who had again
and again ravaged his dominions, and they had as often ac-
Amurat's commodated their differences.   The quarrel we now treat
wars with of, is said to have arisen from a beautiful *Arabian* horse,
Karaman which *Amurat* desired the *Karamanian* to send him, but the
latter refused to comply, with some expressions of contempt,
as incapable to mount and manage a horse of such fire and
mettle. *Gharmian,* or *Karaman,* soon found reason to repent
of so disobliging a refusal. *Amurat* entered his dominions,
which he subdued to the very gates of his capital, *Iconium,*
and *Karaman* was obliged once more to purchase his peace
by large cessions of territory, and costly presents, amongst
which was the celebrated horse. Though *Amurat* was perpetually victorious, yet he enjoyed but little tranquility. He
Invades carried the war against the *Venetians* into the island of *Zante,*
Zante. where he took *Ghiogherjinlek;* but, soon after, his arms received a check from the despot *Demetrius,* brother to the
Greek emperor.

His wars   But the most formidable enemies of the *Othman* power, at
with the that time, were the *Hungarians.* They were then a brave,

                                              a warlike

a warlike and a free people, and extremely dreaded by *Amu-*
rat. But here again, though the facts are recent, the history
of them is extremely confused. The. *Turkish* historians
mention great advantages gained by their countymen over
the *Hungarians,* none of which are mentioned by the
Christians. The histories of the latter, however, are far
more authentic than those of the *Othmans,* whose writers were
at once prejudiced and ignorant.

Albertus, archduke of *Austria,* dying, left his wife, the
daughter of the emperor *Sigismund,* and heiress to the crown
of *Hungary,* big with child. The *Hungarians* were sensible
of their danger from the neighbourhood of *Amurat,* who
was now in a manner master of *Servia,* and *Wallakia.* It
is true, those countries were ruled by princes of their own.
Wallakia, by *Dragul,* and *Servia* by *George,* its own despot,
the father of *Amurat*'s beloved wife; but *Dragul* thought
himself happy, if he could retain his newly acquired sovereignty, without endangering it by opposing *Amurat;*
George, on the other hand, though he detested his son-in-
law, had suffered so much from him, that he had been
obliged to buy his peace upon the most mortifying terms.
The *Hungarians,* therefore, saw themselves in a manner exposed to the first brunt of *Amurat*'s arms. Their danger
was the greater, as he had subdued the *Karamanians,* and
the other petty *Asiatic* princes, who were equally jealous of
his power. *Knolles,* the *English* historian of the *Othmans,* tells
us, not without probability, that it had been agreed upon
by the *European* princes and the *Asiatic* ones, who lay
nearest to the *Othman* dominions, that, as often as he
should attack the one, he should himself be attacked by the
other: but this confederacy being in fact broken by *Amu-*
rat's arms, the *Hungarians* had now nothing but their
own courage and troops to oppose his ambition. But unfortunately they were destitute of a head. The chief nobility, therefore, made a tender of their crown to *Uladislaus,*
king of *Poland,* a young prince of great courage and activity,
together with the person of their queen, when she should be
delivered. *Uladislaus,* with some difficulty, consented; but
during the negociation, the queen being brought to bed of a
son, formed a party for herself and him, who disputed the
government with *Uladislaus;* and thus *Hungary* was involved
in a civil war, the most favourable circumstance that could
possibly have happened for *Amurat*'s ambition. He instantly
sent *Mikhal-Ali-Beg,* one of his best generals, with some of
his bravest troops, who made themselves masters of the
principal passes and forts in *Servia, Moldavia, Transilva-*
nia, and the neighbouring countries. He was followed by
Amurat in person, who destroyed all before him, in hopes of
taking *Belgrade.*

That city, the famous bulwark of *Christendom* against the
Turks, lies on the confluence of the *Danube* and the *Save,*

and is reckoned one of the strongest, as well as most important places in *Europe*. It had belonged to the despot of *Servia*, who, fearing that *Amurat* would force it from him, gave it up to the *Hungarians*, who were better able to defend it. *Amurat*, in his progress, was greatly assisted by *Dragul*, who attended him to *Hungary*, who was highly caressed by the *Othman*. By what *Dukas*, a cotemporary *Greek* historian, has told us of this expedition, it does not appear that the use of fire arms, and great guns was known, or at least common in *Amurat*'s army. But he trusted to the valour of his troops, and the terror of his name, both of which were exceedingly powerful. In the year 1436, *Amurat* passed the *Danube* at *Nicopolis*, but found all the country before him a desart, the inhabitants flying into their cities. *Amurat* was but ill provided to attack fortifications defended by artillery, and we are told, that some of the *Hungarian* cities even threw their gates open without his venturing to approach them. Had

but mis-carries in the expedition. the *Hungarians* been united, this expedition must have been fatal to *Amurat*. He found himself incircled with strong cities, in the middle of an enemy's country; and he began to suspect that he was betrayed both by *Dragul* and the despot of *Servia*.

Character of *Hunniades*. It was about this time, that the famous *John Hunniades* appeared. He was a brave and a fortunate general against the *Turks*, and had raised himself to high rank in *Hungary*. Equally politic as valiant, he seems to have avoided the party rage which then divided that unhappy country; but at the time we now treat of, all he could do was to harrass the *Turks*, at the head of a small army he commanded, cut off their provisions, and, at last, he forced *Amurat* to repass the *Danube*, and to return to *Adrianople*. The *Christians*, in those days, thought it meritorious to keep no faith with heretics, or infidels. *Amurat*, with all his faults, was sincere, open and of good faith. Reflecting on his late expedition, he plainly enough perceived that the despot of *Servia* was in confederacy with his enemies. The despot's son, some say two of his sons, was then a hostage in *Amurat*'s hands, and suspected of giving intelligence to his father, who held a correspondence with the *Hungarians*. By the advice of *Fadulak*,

Amurat breaks with the despot of *Servia*. his chief vizier, upon his return to *Adrianople*, he ordered the despot to deliver up to him the strong fort of *Sendrew*, in *Servia*, which had been built by the despot; the latter refusing to deliver it, because upon the marriage of his daughter, some call her his sister, with the sultan he had purchased, leave to build it. *Amurat*, it seems, frankly owned that he could not defend the equity of the demand upon any other principle, but that he might disable the despot from betraying him farther; and, laying siege to the place, in three months time he took it by capitulation. After this, the vizier persuaded *Amurat* to put out the eyes of the despot's two sons who were in his hands, and to put *Dragul*, who had come to his

court,

court, in irons, till he ſhould give up two of his ſons as hoſtages for his fidelity, which he did.

Amurat imagining that by his ſucceſſes and the meaſures He be-
he had taken, he had removed all former obſtacles, reſumed ſieges *Bel-*
his expedition againſt *Belgrade*; and early in the ſpring he *grade.*
at laſt formed the ſiege of that city The efforts he made
to take the place were incredible. High mounts and towers
were raiſed in vain againſt it, the walls were battered with
the utmoſt fury, and the *Danube*, and *Saave* were covered
with *Othman* pinaces, and veſſels, to prevent the beſieged,
who were commanded by *Johannes Uranus*, a *Florentine*,
from receiving any ſupplies by the way of *Hungary*. The
defence however, which the garriſon made by means of
their tubes, and a duſt compoſed of nitre, ſulphur, and char-
coal, for ſo the *Greek* hiſtorian calls cannon and powder,
was ſo vigorous that *Amurat* loſt a vaſt number of his
braveſt troops. *Uladiſlaus* would gladly have entered into a
treaty with *Amurat*, but the latter rejected all terms, thinking it impoſſible that the city could hold out long. At laſt,
a breach was made in the walls, and it was mounted by the
janiſaries, but they were repulſed with the loſs of twelve
thouſand of the braveſt troops amongſt them. After that,
Amurat endeavoured to make a party in the city, by throw- but is
ing into it letters upon the points of arrows; but all prov- forced to
ing ineffectual, and ſeeing his vaſt army reduced to leſs than raiſe the
half its original number; he broke up the ſiege in great ſiege.
bitterneſs of mind.

Though the memorable defence of *Belgrade* did great The deſ-
honour to the *Hungarians*, yet *Amurat*, we ſhall not ſay pot of
with what juſtice, complained that it legally belonged to him, *Servia*
as being deſcended from *Bajazet*, who was married to the joins with
princeſs of *Servia*, and therefore, next heir to that country, the *Hun-*
farther alledging, that as *Belgrade* was part of *Servia*, it was *garians.*
not in the power of *George* to cede it to the *Hungarians*.
George, who appears to have been a prince of abilities, knew
by this, that *Amurat* had reſolved on his final deſtruction;
and as he held great eſtates in *Hungary*, ſome of which he
had got in exchange for *Belgrade*, and was poſſeſſed of large
ſums of ready money, he linked himſelf with *Hunni-*
ades, who was now raiſed to the chief command of the
Hungarians, and conſidered as the guardian of the infant ſon
of the queen, as *Uladiſlaus* was of the kingdom, tho' he had the
name of king. *George* and *Hunniades* joining their troops,
they formed an army of twenty-five thouſand men. *Amurat*,
to prevent the diſgrace of too precepitate a retreat, had left and de-
Iſa, one of his nephews, with a body of troops to ſcour the feats the
country about *Belgrade*, which he reduced to great ſtraits. *Othmans.*
Upon this, *George* and *Hunniades* paſſed the *Danube*, and encamped near *Sendrew*, and being followed by *Iſa*, (according
to the *Chriſtian* writers,) a battle enſued, in which *Hunniades*
obtained a compleat victory. Several other battles enſued with

various fuccefs, and *Amurat* in fome of them, commanded in perfon. The particulars are told with great contradictions and confufion by hiftorians. It is certain, however, that *Amurat*, alarmed by the *Chriftians* paffing the *Danube*, at laft gave an ear to propofitions for peace.

A negotiation being fet on foot, *Sendrew*, and the other places that had been taken from *George*, in *Servia*, was reftored; and it was agreed, that neither the *Turks* or *Hungarians* fhould pafs the *Danube* to attack each other.

This peace is a clear proof, that, notwithftanding the darknefs and confufion of hiftorians, *Hunniades* had, before then, gained many glorious victories and advantages over the *Turks*, who loft, in that war, above two hundred thou-

A folemn peace concluded between the Othmans and Hungarians. fand of their beft troops. This treaty was moft folemnly fworn to by *Amurat* and *Uladiflaus*, the one upon the *Alkoran*, the other upon the *Gofpel*. Accidents, however, might have appeared powerful towards concluding the treaty. *Karaman*, encouraged by the difgrace the *Othman* arms had fuffered in *Hungary*, again invaded *Amurat*'s dominions with great fury, and foon recovered the places taken from him. This brought *Amurat* with an army into *Karamania*, where he retook *Iconium*, with a vaft quantity of treafure; and he proceeded with great feverity till he was appeafed by his fifter, *Karaman*'s wife, who became anfwerable for her hufband's fidelity to the *Othman* government

Amurat refigns the government to Mohammed .This placability, fo uncommon in a *Turkifh* prince, was owing to a philofophic turn of mind, indulged by *Amurat*; he grew weary of greatnefs, and fought to retire to a private life. This defire for folitude was increafed, when, on his return from the *Karamanian* war, he heard that his fon *Aladin*, a promifing young prince of eighteen years of age, was dead. He immediately convoked an affembly of his great men, and formally refigned the imperial turban to his fon *Mohammed*, then about twenty years of age. The reftlefs *Karaman*, hearing of this great revolution, and that the great *Amurat* was buried in a philofophic retirement, he immediately fent ambaffadors through all the *European* and *Afiatic* ftates that were contiguous to the *Othman* dominions, exhorting them once more to refume their arms, as he himfelf intended to do, and exterminate the tyrants of *Afia*, now that their head had refigned his authority.

A confederacy againft him. The juncture for this was favourable. The *Greek* emperor, *John*, was then in *Italy*, and in high favour with the pope, for his endeavours to unite the *Greek* and *Latin* churches. That emperor had three brothers, each of them poffeffed of the eftates that ftill remained to the empire without the walls of *Conftantinople*, though, in fact, not only they, but the emperor himfelf, were no better than vaffals to the *Othmans*. They, however, could bring confiderable bodies to the field. The *Venetians* and the *Genoefe*, on their account, were extremely well difpofed to humble the *Othman* power; and all the

the populous states upon the borders of *Hungary* waited only for the signal from *Uladislaus* to rise in arms.

Uladislaus had ambition, and was not insensible of the ad- The treaty vantages which the juncture presented; but with what face broken by could he break a treaty so lately, and so solemnly, ratified; the *Chris-* and so well observed on the part of *Amurat?* His conscience *tians.* soon found a salve for perjury. Cardinal *Julian Cesarini,* the pope's legate in *Germany,* an enthusiast and a bigot, had long employed himself in bringing heretics, as they were called, to the stake, and preaching up crusades against infidels. On hearing of *Amurat*'s resignation, he repaired to *Hungary,* and, in his master's name, declared the peace, concluded between *Uladislaus* and the *Hungarians* on the one part, and *Amurat* on the other, to be void, because made against the consent of the pope; who, in his letter, which the cardinal pre-sented at the same time, said that the *Christian* princes had no authority to make such a peace without being impowered to do it by the holy see. In short, *Uladislaus,* and his *Hun-garians,* being absolved from their oaths by the legate, a re-solution, in which the great *Hunniades* concurred, was taken to recommence hostilities against the *Othmans.*

Amurat, at this time, was living in retirement at *Magnesia;* and his son, *Mohammed,* was in the actual exercise of sove-reignty at his court; and the great officers, both civil and military, hearing that a kind of general confederacy had been formed, both in *Europe* and *Asia,* against the *Othman* power, which, if not opposed, must end in its destruction, applied to *Amurat* to reassume the reins of government. At *Amurat* first, being not fully informed of circumstances, or being in resumes love with his retirement, he refused to leave it; but, upon the go- farther application, he agreed to their request; and, as if soli- vernment. tude had given a fresh spring to his body and spirits, he pre-pared to set out for *Adrianople,* there to take upon himself the command of his army. It is remarkable, that we know of no opposition made by *Mohammed* to this resolution, tho' he was one of the fiercest as well as the most ambitious princes that ever breathed.

In the mean while, the confederates proceeded with vast spirit and unanimity. The pope's and the *Venetian* gallies, to the number of one hundred and twenty-five, lay before *Calipolis* and at the mouth of the *Bosphorus,* to cut off all com-munication between *Europe* and *Asia.* Notwithstanding all He takes their precautions, *Amurat* passed the *Bosphorus,* in *Genoese* the field vessels, which he hired at an immense expence, and, reach- against the ing *Adrianople,* led his army to the field. That of the *Chris- Christians.* tians,* under *Uladislaus* and *Hunniades,* composed of *Hungari-ans, Poles,* and other nations, and volunteers from several parts of christendom, had already taken the field, and, tho' *October* was almost spent, they passed the *Danube* and burned the suburbs of *Nicopolis,* the capital of *Bulgaria;* which country, by the late treaty, remained in the poffeffion of the *Othmans*.

Here *Uladiflaus* muftered his army, but the generals of the greateft experience found it unequal to the attempt he was to make. *Dragul*, the waywod of *Wallakia*, one of thofe *Chriftian* princes who have no religion but intereft, would gladly have perfuaded *Uladiflaus* to have returned; but finding the pope's legate bore all the fway in his councils, he was obliged, not only to defift from his remonftrances, but, according to *Chriftian* hiftorians, to fend his fon with a body of troops to the *Hungarian* army. At firft, *Uladiflaus* proceeded with great fuccefs, and took feveral places of importance from the *Turks*. But certain accounts arriving that *Amurat* had paffed the *Bofphorus*, he was ftruck with confternation. He, and all the heads of the confederacy, had hitherto proceeded on the fuppofition of the *Bofphorus* being fo well guarded by the *Italian* fhipping, that it was impoffible for the *Othman Afiatic* army to get over to *Europe*. Though we are ignorant as to particulars, yet it is certain that the gold of *Amurat* removed this impoffibility; for it not only procured him tranfports for his troops, but relaxed the vigilance of the pope's and *Venetian* admirals. His army, according to the beft accounts, confifted of above one hundred and fifty thoufand fighting men. *Uladiflaus*, underftanding this, fell back to *Varna*, a city, near the *Euxine Sea*, in *Bulgaria*, which he had taken a day or two before from the *Turks*; and there he held a council of war, to deliberate whether they fhould give battle to *Amurat*, who, with his army, lay within four miles of them, or retire. *Hunniades* thought there was danger in both, but that there was leaft in a battle; and his opinion, with the heat of the pope's legate, carried the queftion for fighting.

Succefs of the latter.

On the tenth of *November*, 1444, was fought the great battle of *Varna*, between *Amurat* and *Uladiflaus*. The *Chriftian* army was drawn up by *Hunniades*. It was flanked, on one fide, by a morafs; and, on the other, with the baggage belonging to the camp; and behind it lay a fteep hill; fo that the *Chriftians* could not be advantageoufly attacked but in their front. *Amurat*'s indignation at the perfidy of the *Chriftians* appears to have hurried him into an overfight at the beginning of the battle; for he advanced in perfon, at the head of his horfe, too far before his infantry to be fupported; and met with fo fevere a repulfe from *Hunniades*, at the head of the *Hungarian* and *Polifh* cavalry, that he was in danger of being totally defeated. In this diftrefs, *Amurat* pulled from his bofom the original of the treaty he had lately made with the *Chriftians*; and, in the hearing of both armies, he appealed to God for the punifhment of perjury; at the fame time unfolding the writing to their fight, and ordering it to held aloft upon the point of a fpear. Putting divine vengeance

The battle of Varna.

Appeal of Amurat.

ance out of the queſtion, we meet with nothing in hiſtory better judged than this action of *Amurat* was. It damped the ſpirit of his enemies, and rekindled that of his own troops. Great part of the *Chriſtian* army was compoſed of over-zealous prelates, and church-men, and their followers, who were placed upon one of the wings; but, on the repulſe of the *Turkiſh* cavalry, they quitted their poſts and joined in a diſorderly purſuit. By this time, the janiſaries and the *Turkiſh* infantry, having come up, fell upon the weak wing, and forced *Hunniades* and the king to return from the purſuit; which they had, for ſome time, continued with prodigious ſlaughter. This gave *Amurat* an opportunity to rally his cavalry, and the battle was now renewed with fury. *Uladiſlaus* fought with great courage, and ſingling out *Amurat*, who was equally forward, his horſe was killed by a javelin thrown at him by the ſultan. The king falling to the ground, his head was inſtantly ſtruck off by a janiſary; and being, by *Amurat*'s orders, expoſed on the point of a ſpear, the diſpirited *Chriſtians* were every where put to the route. It was not in the power, even of *Hunniades*, to rally them, all he could do was to retire, in tolerable good order, with a body of horſe, towards the *Danube*, which he paſſed.

[margin: Total defeat of the Chriſtians and death of Uladiſlaus.]

It is ſaid, in this fatal battle, two thirds of the *Chriſtian* army were put to the ſword; and, that all who ſurvived periſhed miſerably in fens and bogs, or by the inclemency of the ſeaſon, or were carried into ſlavery. Of the *Turks* thirty thouſand are ſaid to have been killed.

[margin: Loſs of both parties.]

As to the brave *Hunniades*, he, having paſſed the *Danube*, and finding that his cavalry could not ſubſiſt in a body, was obliged to diſmiſs them; and moſt of them met with the fate of their fellow-ſoldiers on the other ſide of the *Danube*: for no ſooner did the deſpot of *Servia*, and *Dragul*, hear of the defeat of the *Chriſtians*, than they again changed ſides, and cut off the ſtraglers of the *Chriſtian* army wherever they found them. *Hunniades* being thus left alone, fell into the hands of *Dragul*, who would have put him to death had he not been afraid of the *Hungarians*. *Hunniades*, however, had afterwards his revenge upon him, by putting to death both *Dragul* and his ſon.

[margin: Hunniades eſcapes.]

As to the cardinal, that fire-brand of war, he likewiſe was killed in the purſuit, as were a great number of other churchmen and prelates. The clergy, in general, to palliate their own madneſs and perfidy, threw the blame of the defeat upon *Hunniades*, who, they ſay, withdrew from the battle with ten thouſand of the beſt troops, becauſe of a ſecret enmity he had towards the king. But this calumny againſt one of the braveſt and moſt ſucceſsful enemies the *Turks* ever had, carries along with it its own refutation.

Amurat bore his victory with great moderation. The loſs of thirty thouſand of his beſt men ſunk ſo deep into his mind that he appeared to be melancholy, and he reſumed his in-

[margin: Amurat again reſigns the government,]

clination

clination for retirement. Accordingly, when he returned to *Adrianople*, he again embraced a monaftic life at *Magnefia*; though, others fay, at *Prufa*. His retirement, however, proved extremely detrimental to his fubjects. *Mohammed*, to whom he again relinquifhed his empire, had not authority enough to curb the janifaries, who everywhere murdered and robbed the other fubjects of the empire, and threatened univerfal diffolution to the ftate. Add to this, that *Amurat's* fecond retreat gave frefh fpirits to the *Chriftians*; and *Hunniades*, upon his return to *Hungary*, had raifed a frefh army, with which he had obtained feveral confiderable advantages againft the *Othmans*.

but re-fumes it. All thofe confiderations, backed with the importunities of the greateft men of the empire, prevailed with *Amurat* again to refume the government, which he feems to have done with fome refentment againft his fon *Mohammed*; for we are told he fent him, in difgrace, to the cell which he himfelf had quitted in *Magnefia*. His firft care was the internal peace of his empire, and then he made preparations for fubduing the famous *Skander Beg*.

History of Skander Beg. The hiftory of this prince, fo well known to the *Chriftians* by the name of *Skander Beg*, is extremely uncertain. It does not even clearly appear whether he was a prince or a rebel, a *Chriftian* or a *Mahometan*. According to the moft accurate accounts, he was the fon of a petty defpot in *Albania*. His true name was *George Caftriot*; and, that country falling under the power of *Amurat*, the *Othman* obliged *John Caftriot*, the father, to deliver up to his cuftody *George*, and three of his elder brothers, as pledges of his fidelity. It is faid the latter were put under confinement by *Amurat*; which is not quite unlikely, when we confider how very ready thofe petty princes were to fuit their conduct to times and accidents.

George being too young to give any umbrage to the *Othman*, he was circumcifed and educated in the *Mahometan* religion. As he grew up, he difcovered fuch pregnancy of parts, with fuch amazing ftrength and agility in all his exercifes, that he became the greateft favourite *Amurat* had; fo that, before he was twenty years of age, he acquired the name of *Iskander*, or *Lord Alexander*, alluding to the *Macedonian* conqueror, the higheft compliment which the *Turks* can pay to a fubject; and he was fent upon an expedition againft the defpot of *Servia*. He behaved fo well in this, and many other commands, that he was preferred to the government of a province; but, in the mean time, his three elder brothers died of a dreadful plague which broke out at *Prufa*.

Young *Skander Beg* could not be ignorant that he was now the only furviving fon of his father, whofe eftates remained ftill in the poffeffion of *Amurat*; and the perpetual wars which, on all hands, furrounded the *Othmans*, prompted his

daring

daring spirit to attempt a recovery of his paternal dominions, however questionable the means might be. Growing every day more and more in favour with *Amurat*, he was again sent to command against the *Christians* under the bashaw *Carambey*, the governor of *Romania*, and brother-in-law to *Amurat*. *Carambey* was defeated by *Hunniades*, and taken prisoner. *Skander Beg* fled in the rout, but kept his eye upon the bashaw's secretary. It appears, from the evidence of history, that *Skander Beg* had held a continual correspondence with his countrymen, and that a conspiracy had actually been formed to support him in recovering his country. But the great difficulty was to get possession of *Croia*, the chief town of *Albania*. With this view it was that he and his men flying, with the bashaw's secretary, drew him into a solitary place, where they cut his attendants in pieces, and afterwards obliged the secretary to write, and seal with the bashaw's signet, a letter addressed to the governor of *Croia*, which was in *Carambey*'s province, commanding him instantly to resign his government of the city to *Skander Beg*, its new governor.

Stratagem of Skander Beg,

After this, he put the secretary likewise to death, and marched, with great quickness, towards *Albania*, attended with a body of his country-men, who had been in *Amurat*'s pay, the *Albanians* being then accounted the best soldiers in *Asia*. Every thing succeeded so well with them, that *Skander Beg* not only got possession of *Croia*, but found means to introduce a body of *Albanians*, and cut the throats of all the garrison, excepting a few who abjured *Mahometanism* to save their lives. His success raised such a spirit amongst the *Epirots*, and other *Albanians*, that, in a few weeks, many of the *Turkish* garrisons in *Epirus* were put to the sword; and, in short, all the *Turks* who were found in the country were massacred.

by which he gets possession of Croia,

Amurat, whose sincerity and good faith stands unimpeached, even in *Christian* histories, was not more exasperated by the massacre of his soldiers and subjects, than he was at the ingratitude, as he thought, of *Skander Beg*, and, tho' he had many more threatning wars upon his hands, he resolved, at all events, to reduce the rebels. It happened, fortunately for *Skander Beg*, that the *Venetians* were in possession of several ports of the *Adriatic Sea*, which lay on the coast of *Albania*, but were divided from the in-land country by vast chains of mountains. *Skander Beg* knew the genius of *Amurat* too well not to make the *Venetians* his friends, and to avail himself of every other advantage before the *Othman* could approach him.

and conquers the Othmans.

The severity, if not cruelty, with which he had hitherto treated the *Turks*, daunted the garrisons they still held in that country so much, that *Skander Beg* reduced them, one by one, almost without blood-shed, granting them the most favourable terms, which he punctually performed. *Sfeti-*

grade,

grade, the ſtrongeſt fort in all *Albania*, ventured to hold out；

and the courage of the garriſon, particularly of a common ſoldier, drove *Skander Beg* into an unmanly action ; for he ordered all the *Turks*, ſome of whom were of quality, who would not embrace *Chriſtianity*, to be put to death in ſight of the garriſon. This act of cruelty rather exaſperated than intimidated the garriſon ; ſo that *Skander Beg* was obliged, for that time, to raiſe the ſiege ; but, at the head of fourteen or fifteen thouſand choſen troops, he laid the neighbouring countries under ſuch contributions, and acquired ſo much plunder, that it was ſaid his ravages were all his revenue.

Such, in the main, is the hiſtory and riſe of this great champion of *Chriſtianity*, in whom we can hitherto diſcover nothing but diſſimulation, cruelty, and barbarity. He undoubtedly is defenſible, nay commendable, for reſcuing his country from a foreign yoke ; but he did it in a manner which a virtuous man and a real *Chriſtian* would not have followed. The hiſtory of that country and time is too rude and imperfect to inform us whether he re-eſtabliſhed the civil government of *Epirus* or *Albania* ; but we are told that he had a nephew, who was a brave young prince, the ſon of one of his younger brothers, and extremely ſerviceable to him in his wars. His name was *Ameſa*. The baſhaw *Ali*, one of *Amurat*'s great generals, marched againſt *Skander Beg* with forty thouſand men ; which obliged the latter to return to the de-

fence of *Epirus*. A battle enſued ; in which the *Othman*, too much deſpiſing *Skander Beg*'s force, was defeated, with the loſs of twenty-two thouſand men.

This victory, joined to *Amurat*'s paſſion for retirement, and his being involved in a multiplicity of other wars, ſeems to have given *Skander Beg* time to breathe. He entered into a correſpondence with *Hunniades*, and, it is ſaid, though with no manner of probability, by the *Chriſtian* writers, that he attempted to join *Uladiſlaus* before the battle of *Varna*; but that he was prevented by the deſpot of *Servia*, who fortified the paſſes of his country againſt him. *Knolles* and other hiſtorians have not only drawn a compariſon between *Skander Beg* and *Hunniades*, but likewiſe given the letters that paſſed between *Amurat* and *Skander Beg*, and *Skander Beg* and *Uladiſlaus*. Theſe, however, are manifeſt forgeries ; as, indeed, great part of *Skander Beg*'s hiſtory ſeems to be romance. All we know, with any degree of certainty, is, that, after the defeat of *Ali*, he fortified the mountains and paſſes into *Epirus*, and made himſelf maſter of *Sfetigrade*, and removed his family and principal effects to the *Venetian* territories.

The ſcarcity of hiſtorians amongſt the *Turks*, joined to the inſincerity, arrogance, and inaccuracy of thoſe few ſcraps we have from them, leaves us in the dark as to the internal tranſactions of the *Othman* empire at this time, and the reaſons why ſo great and active a general as *Amurat* was, left ſo formidable an enemy as *Skander Beg* was, ſo long at leiſure to render himself still more so. *Ducas* and *Khalkondylas*, the *Greek* historians, assist us, in part, to fill up the gap: for *Constantine*, the prince and governor of *Morea*, called, by *Khalkondylas*, the duke of *Peloponnesus*, like *Amurat*'s other enemies, taking advantage of his wars, made an irruption into the *Othman* territories, took the city of *Pindus*, and over-ran *Beotia* and part of *Akhaia*, and advanced to the very gates of *Athens*. *Amurat*, informed of this irruption, advanced in person, with a great army, to *Pharres*, which obliged *Constantine* to fall back to guard the *Heximilion*, or the wall, six miles long, built across the isthmus of *Corinth*, for the defence of the *Morea*; and is said to have run between the *Ægean* and *Ionian Seas*. *Amurat* knew how feeble a defence this rampart was, and what wretched soldiers *Constantine* commanded; and, continuing his march, his troops invested the whole length of the wall. *Constantine* would then have gladly made peace, but *Amurat* threw his ambassador, who was father to *Khalkondylas*, into irons; and, notwithstanding the incle-mency of the season, he attacked them with very little oppo-sition, took and demolished the celebrated *Heximilion*, and soon reduced all the *Peloponnesus*, or *Morea*, to the form of a tributary province. This expedition happened in the year 1448, or the beginning of the year 1449, though others have made it more early.

He forces Heximili-on, and renders the Morea tributary.

Here we are to fix the first expedition of *Amurat* in per-son against *Skander Beg*. Before he set out, he dispatched two of his generals, *Ferises* and *Mustapha*, at the head of fly-ing armies, but with orders to ravage the frontiers of *Epirus*, and prevent the incursions of *Skander Beg*; but, by no means, to advance into the country before his arrival with the main army. Both those generals were surprized and de-feated by the active *Skander Beg*, who had spies both in the enemies court and camp. It appears, as it often does upon such occasions, *Skander Beg* gave very little quarter; for, in one encounter with a party of the enemy, consisting of six thousand men, five thousand *Turks* were killed on the spot, and three hundred made prisoners, while all *Skander Beg*'s loss amounted to no more than twenty horse and fifty foot.

Renews the war with Skan-der Beg,

By this time, *Amurat* had advanced to the borders of *Epi-rus*, at the head of one hundred and fifty thousand men. He ordered a profound silence to be observed as to the place of their destination, and, entering the country, he immediately besieged *Sfetigrade*, which was defended by *Perlat*, one of *Skander Beg*'s best officers, and a chosen garrison. The place made a noble defence, not only against *Amurat*'s power, but his money, repeated offers of which *Perlat* and the garrison rejected with disdain.

and enters Epirus, and be-sieges Sfe-tigrade.

As to *Skander Beg*, he did all that could be done by a great and a wise general. He sent as many of the aged and infirm, with women and children, as he could into the *Venetian* ter-ritories,

Conduct of Skander Beg.

ritories, or towards the mountains, and ordered all the able inhabitants to march into *Croia*, and other fortified places, while he himſelf kept the field with ten or twelve thouſand choice horſe, and was perpetually alarming, harraſſing, and deſtroying the *Othman* troops. The efforts made by *Amurat* to carry the place, as deſcribed by all hiſtorians, ſeem to have been the effects of deſpair rather than thoſe of generalſhip: and, according to the beſt accounts, he loſt before the place thirty thouſand of his beſt troops. The force of money, however, prevailed where arms could not. The *Albanians* who defended the place were called *Chriſtians*, but their prieſts and teachers were ſo extremely illiterate, that their whole nation was more ridiculous and ſuperſtitious than the worſt of *Jews*. A traitor of the garriſon was bribed by *Amurat* to throw a dead dog into the only well which ſupplied them with water; and they who had braved all the thunder of the *Othman* arms, were ſubdued by a pitiful piece of ſuperſtition. There was not a common ſoldier of the garriſon who did not chuſe rather to periſh with thirſt than drink from that polluted well; ſo that the governor was obliged to propoſe a capitulation, after having defended the place from *May* to *September*, 1449.

Sfetigrade betrayed,

Amurat was ſo agreeably ſurprized, when the capitulation was propoſed, that he could ſcarce believe his own good fortune, and granted all the terms the garriſon required; which were, that all the military men and officers, as well as other inhabitants, if they choſe it, might depart with their arms and baggage; and that, if any choſe to remain, they might be permitted to live in the ſame manner as they did under *Skander Beg*; but that their houſes ſhould be built without the walls of the city. *Amurat* punctually performed all thoſe conditions.

and taken.

The taking of *Sfetigrade*, was all the fruit which *Amurat* reaped from this bloody and expenſive expedition. He had ordered freſh reinforcements of troops to be ſent him, in vaſt numbers, both from his *Aſiatic* and *European* dominions; and, the ſeaſon of the campaign not being quite over, he penetrated farther into the country and laid ſiege to *Croia*. Having engaged a great number of *European* engineers and matroſſes in the ſervice, he had a moſt formidable train of artillery, with which he battered the place, and made a breach which the janiſaries, the braveſt of his troops, deſperately endeavoured to ſtorm. The name of the governor was *Uranacontes*, a perſon of great courage, virtue, and conduct; and *Skander Beg*, in all other reſpects, had provided ſo well for the defence of the city, that the *Turks* were conſtantly repulſed in all their aſſaults; and, the weather becoming now intolerable, *Amurat* ſaw himſelf reduced to the mortifying neceſſity of raiſing the ſiege. *Skander Beg*, at the head of his choſen body of horſe, did not fail to harraſs him in his retreat;

Croia beſieged.

The ſiege raiſed.

10

so that he was in danger of having it cut off, and of perishing in the mountains, if he had not left the governor of *Romania*, with thirty thousand men, to make head against *Skander Beg* ; while he himself, at the head of the main body, with infinite difficulty, regained his own dominions, and passed the remainder of the winter at *Adrianople*.

Amurat remained there for several months, till he raised an army more numerous than the former, with which he again entered *Albania*, and penetrated to *Epirus*. He was, perhaps, encouraged to this by some differences which had fallen out, in the mean time, between *Skander Beg* and the *Venetians* ; but, upon *Amurat*'s approach, which each of them had equal reason to dread, they soon became greater friends than ever. *Amurat* having therefore, in vain, endeavoured to bring the *Venetians* over to his side, again laid siege to *Croia*. *Skander Beg* pursued his former conduct, and chose a strong camp in the mountains lying between *Epirus* and the *Venetian* territories, at a proper distance from *Croia* ; so that he could act as he saw occasion. *Amurat*, on the other hand, altered his former dispositions. He divided his vast army into two parts· one of them he employed in carrying on the siege; while the other was to face *Skander Beg*, and prevent his harrassing the besiegers as he had done during the last siege. *Amurat* again invades *Epirus*, and besieges *Croia*.

It is, on all hands, allowed that *Skander Beg*, on this occasion, performed prodigies of valour ; and the almost total silence of the *Turkish* historians, with regard to him, more than proves it ; because they could not mention him without notoriously perverting the truth, or throwing a shade upon the glories of their sultan ; which, amongst the *Turks*, is a capital crime. Valour of *Skander Beg*.

While the *Turks* were battering *Croia* with the most destructive fury, *Skander Beg*, and his chief general, who, in the history, is called *Moses*, fought a most terrible battle in the mountains ; where he defeated the *Turks*, and opened to himself a passage to *Amurat*'s camp, just as he had ordered a general assault to be given to the city. *Skander Beg* fell with such fury on the guards that had been left in the camp, that *Amurat* was obliged to reinforce them with four thousand men under one of his best generals, who was followed with a much greater body under prince *Mohammed* himself. who attacks *Amurat*'s camp.

Skander Beg was now in imminent danger. The love either of glory, revenge, or money, had drawn him too far from his soldiers ; and, in an instant, he found himself surrounded by *Othmans* in the midst of their camp. *Mose*, who commanded under him, giving him up for lost, had made an orderly retreat ; while *Skander Beg*, with the officers and soldiers that had followed him, by a most prodigious effort of valour, cut his way through the barbarians, who could make no impression with their weapons upon his armour ; and, at last, joined *Moses*, to the inexpressible surprize and joy of all his camp. *Skander Beg* in danger.

The

The siege of Croia continued

The tumult occasioned by *Skander Beg*'s irruption daunt-ed the ardour of the besiegers, so that the general assault of the city was but feebly carried on, and they were repulsed with great loss. A great number of bloody actions and attacks, greatly to the honour of *Skander Beg*'s memory, followed during the course of the siege, in all which the *Turks* were defeated. We are even told by cotemporary writers, that *Amurat* carried with him a large foundary, and vast quantities of metal for casting new cannon, to replace those which should be rendered unserviceable during the siege, and that prince *Mohammed*, proclaimed a reward of one hundred thousand aspers, to the soldier who should first mount the walls. But every day produced some new attack from *Skander Beg*, who held the *Othman* camp in perpetual confusion and alarm. The infidels at last, became convinc-ed of the superiority of *Skander Beg*'s troops and general-ship, so that it was with the utmost difficulty that *Amurat* and his son could prevail upon them to make fresh assaults. At last, the losses and disgraces they suffered every day, made them lose all courage, and *Amurat* was obliged to desist from his assaults, and to work by mines, but those likewise

but is raised.

proving ineffectual, he first turned the siege into a blockade, and then intirely abandoned it to return home

Reflection

We have been the more particular in our account of *Skander Beg*'s wars with the *Othmans*, because in fact, they have been misrepresented by most historians, and in so many different lights, that many have looked upon the whole to be little more than a romance. They have not even pre-served the chronology of the facts, recent and important as they are. The western historians in particular, have blend-ed the first and the last sieges of *Croia* into one, and have made *Amurat* die of despite under the walls of that city, because he could not take it. The truth is, before he raised

War with the Hun-garians renewed.

the siege, he received advices, that *Hunniades* and the restless *Hungarians*, had raised a fresh army to revenge their late defeat. This news had prevailed with him to offer *Skander Beg* the quiet possession of *Epirus*, provided he would sub-mit to pay ten thousand ducats, as tribute; but the offer was rejected. *George*, the despot of *Servia*, seems at this time to have been in *Amurat*'s interest, for he gave him the first intelligence of the motions of *Hunniades*. That general, ever since the death of *Uladislaus*, had acted as guardian of the kingdom, during the minority of *Ladislaus*, the son of *Albert*, and his army was both numerous and powerful, having at that time the *Wallakians* on his side. Having passed the *Danube*, he fell into *Servia*, and summoned the despot to join him and the *Christians*. The despot had had many differences with *Hunniades*, about the lands he had received in exchange for *Belgrade*, and he was exasperated at *Hun-niades* being preferred to him in the guardianship of the kingdom. He therefore evaded the summons of *Hunniades*, which

which indeed the latter had no right to send him. *Hunniades* was then obliged to content himself with threatening to be revenged of the despot, and he advanced against the *Othmans*. *Amurat* receiving exact intelligence from the despot, of the motions and strength of the *Christians*, suffered them to advance into his dominions as far as the great plain of *Kossova*, in *Bulgaria*, through which runs the river *Schichiniza*; both armies passed that river, being the same plain on which the battle that cost *Amurat* the first his life, was fought. *Amurat* attacked the *Hungarians* with great vigour, but was repulsed; his vast superiority of numbers however, enabled him to renew the fight, and the *Hungarians*, who had not fifty thousand men in the field, not being above a third of the number of the infidels, were at last surrounded. *Hunniades*, is said to have fled out of the field with great dishonour. But the circumstance, which all historians agree in, may serve to clear up his conduct. For we are told, that *Danus*, a *Wallakian* general, who commanded the left wing of the *Christians*, went over with eight thousand of his countrymen, who were esteemed the flower of the *Hungarian* troops, and offered to serve under *Amurat*, but that the latter suspecting, or detecting them, ordered his cavalry to surround them, and to cut them in pieces. This cowardice and treachery might have made *Hunniades* suspect he was betrayed, and might have prevailed upon him to have left the field of battle, sooner than otherways he would have done. By the best accounts, the battle or skirmishing lasted for several days, but at last ended in the total defeat of the *Christians*. It appears, that the despot of *Servia* remained all the time unactive, though he made professions of his friendship to *Hunniades*. About twenty thousand *Christians*, and forty thousand *Othmans*, fell in the battle. *Hunniades*, after being almost famished in the mountains, was made prisoner by the despot, and redeemed his liberty by giving his daughter in marriage to the despot's son.

Defeat of the Christians at the battle of Capora.

Upon the whole, it is by no means improbable, that *Amurat* had a secret intelligence with the chief of the *Christian* officers, who had great resentments against *Hunniades*. We are likewise told, that *Amurat*, out of resentment of the despot's having set *Hunniades* at liberty; invaded his dominions, and destroyed them with vast fury, which obliged the the despot to call in *Hunniades* to his assistance. Upon *Amurat*'s return to *Adrianople*, the marriage of his son *Mahommed*, with the daughter of a *Turkish* prince, many of whom still remained both powerful, and independant, in the more remote parts of *Asia*, was celebrated with great magnificence. It does not appear that *Amurat* long survived this event, for he died in a fit of apoplexy, in the beginning of the year 1451-2, after a debauch, for he very freely indulged himself in the use of wine, he was but forty-nine years of age at the time of his death, and that with other circumstances,

By what means effected.

Death of Amurat.

circumſtances, is ſufficient to give us ſome idea, how igno-rant the *European* writers are of that great man's hiſtory and character; for they repreſent him as being eighty five years of age, at the time of his death, and as dying under the walls of *Croia*, which he had beſieged.

His cha-racter.

Moderation, and equanimity, ſeemed to have formed the true character of *Amurat*; though a zealous *Mahometan*, he ſtrictly kept his faith with the *Chriſtians*, but he appears to have been greatly diſguſted at the breaches of faith towards him; he was according to his religion charitable, but though his reign in the main was glorious, his life cannot be ſaid to be happy, and this undoubtedly was the reaſon why he ſo often laid down and reſumed the reins of govern-ment, that he might retire to a private life. But even his remounting the throne, though unwillingly, when the ſtate of public affairs rendered it neceſſary, is perhaps, a greater proof of his moderation, and philoſophy, than if he had capriciouſly buried himſelf in his retirement.

The Reign of Mohammed *the Second, commonly called the* Great, *and the firſt Emperor of the* Turks.

Acceſſion of *Mo-hammed the ſecond*

THE vizier *Halil*, had long held the reins of the *Othman* goverment under *Amurat*, and upon his maſter's death he diſpatched a meſſenger to inform his ſon and ſucceſſor *Mohammed* of that event; upon which that prince immedi-ately repaired to *Adrianople*. Either through his own filial affection, or perceiving the reſpect which all his ſubjects re-tained for the memory of his father, he ſhewed great marks of affliction at firſt, but in a few hours after he aſſum-

his cruelty ed the throne, he put to death his brother, a child of no more than eight months old; forced his mother to marry a ſlave againſt her will, and even murdered the executioners of his own orders. This lady is ſaid to have been daughter to the prince of *Sinope*, and if ſo, ſhe was mother to *Mohammed* himſelf. This opinion received ſome countenance from what we are told by *Khalkondylas*, that he made *Iſaac* gover-nor of *Aſia*, that he might be ſecure from all danger. As to her, the daughter of the deſpot of *Servia*, he ſent her back to her father, and gave her ſome lands in jointure, and at the ſame time he ſhewed a great diſpoſion to cultivate a friend-ſhip with all the *Chriſtian* poweis, particularly with *Conſtan-tine*, the emperor of *Conſtantinople*.

and policy But this conduct was all diſſembled, that he might be at more leiſure to take meaſures for carrying his vaſt ſchemes into execution. His firſt care was to reduce *Karaman*, from whom his father had received ſo much trouble, and which he did in a moſt effectual a manner. The empire of *Conſtantinople*,

ſtantinople, was at that time extremely weak. All the princes of the imperial houſe, who had any dominions without that capital, were ſubjects or tributary to the *Othmans*. Notwithſtanding this weakneſs, *Conſtantine*'s miniſters ſent a very imprudent meſſage, inſinuating to *Mohammed*, that it was in their power, by means of a prince called *Orcan*, deſcended from the ſultan *Bajazet*, by *Muſſulman*, or *Soleyman*, to raiſe a rebellion in the *Othman* dominions, and that it would be eaſy for them to bring the *Hungarians* again to invade them. *Mohammed*, and the *Othmans*, had long conſidered the emperor of *Conſtantinople* as their ſubject. *Mohammed* was at this time in *Anatolia*, and being informed by *Halil* of the demands of the *Greeks*, he received the information with the utmoſt indignation, but he diſſembled his reſentment, and gave orders for the *Greek* ambaſſadors to attend him at *Adrianople*. He no ſooner was arrived there, than he upbraided them with their folly, and infidelity, and produced the treaty he had lately made with them, by which at their own requeſt, he had allowed *Orcan* three hundred thouſand aſpers a year. But looking upon the treaty as now being void, he ordered that allowance to be ſtopped, and having given orders for a prodigious quantity of cannon of the largeſt ſize to be made, he ordered two forts to be built at the mouth of the *Boſphorus*, by which *Conſtantinople* was in a manner ſhut up on that ſide. They were forts of amazing ſtrength, and the *Greeks* eaſily ſaw with what intention they were built. It was in vain for the emperor and his miniſters to deſiſt from all their high demands, and even to offer to pay a yearly tribute if *Mohammed* would ſtop the building. But the *Othman* equally diſpiſed their ſubmiſſions, as he had done their menaces. He told them, that the ground on which the forts were built, were part of his own dominions, that if he was again troubled upon that ſubject, he would order the ambaſſadors, or meſſengers, to be flayed alive.

Quarrels with the Greek emperor

Conſtantine finding all his remonſtances and treaties ineffectual, proceeded to put his capital in the beſt ſtate of defence he could. For this purpoſe, he applied to ſeveral *Chriſtian* courts; but the ſtate of affairs in *Europe* at that time not admittting his receiving any ſuccour from them, he was obliged to have recourſe to *Italian*, and other mercenaries. *Juſtiniani*, a brave *Genoeſe* of quality, was made general. An embargo was laid on all ſhipping, and about five thouſand troops were taken into pay, though the whole of the garriſon, even including the *Greeks*, did not conſiſt of above nine thouſand men. Before the two forts were finiſhed, *Conſtantine* had found means to provide the city with proper means of defence, and whatever was neceſſary for the ſubſiſtence of the garriſon; and he had even the ſpirit (finding *Mohammed* inexorable) to ſend him a defiance.

who applies in vain to the Chriſtian powers.

If

If all circumftances are rightly confidered, the defence made by *Conftantine* on this occafion was amazingly intrepid. *Mohammed* having compleated his forts, by which the city was blockaded towards *Europe*, and *Afia*, returned in a kind of triumph to *Adrianople*, where he made the neceffary preparations for bringing into the field an army of above three hundred thoufand fighting men. The *Greeks* on the other hand, though fenfible of their danger, were divided about immaterial points of religion, or rather fuperftition. The emperor wanted by all means an union between the *Greek* and the *Latin* church, but in this he met with a ftrong oppofition; and his own brother declared that the people would rather choofe to fee *Mohammed*'s turban, than the pope's tyara, upon their altar. This unfeafonable difpute, perhaps more weakened the place, than all the formidable artillery that *Mohammed* brought before it. His engineer is faid to have been a *Hungarian*, the dimenfions of his cannon, as reprefented by cotemporary hiftorians, exceed all belief; fo that they appear to have been mortars. Two of the beft hiftorians fay, they carried balls of a hundred pounds weight, and that each piece required feventy yoke of oxen, and two thoufand men to draw it. Other writers fay, that the *Turkifh* cannon threw balls of fix hundred weight.

Conftantinople itfelf is of a triangular form, two fides of which are bounded by the *Propontis*, and the port, or harbour; and the third is defended by a wall reaching from fea, to fea, before which the *Turkifh* army fat down. The wall towards the land was double, the outer wall being but indifferent, and trufted to its foffe, which was two hundred feet wide, but the inner wall high, ftrong, and regular. The entrance of the haven was fecured by a chain, within which was a fleet of fhips. *Mohammed*, after feveral fruitlefs attempts to take or deftroy thofe fhips, by the vaft navy he had before the town, would have defpaired of fuccefs, had
he not formed and executed one of the boldeft projects that ever entered into the breaft of man: this was no other than to tranfport fourfcore gallies over land, by main force. This amazing attempt, is faid to have fucceeded by placing the keels of the fhips upon ftrong planks befmeared with tallow and fat, by which being drawn to the eminences above the harbour, they were launched into it, in much the fame manner as fhips of war are now launched in *England* from their ftocks. Prince *Cantemir*, an author of great credit, obferves however, that the *Turks* in this exploit employed a number of ftupendous engines for tranfporting the veffels over the inequalities of the ground; and others add, that the *Greek* fhips were awed by the great and fmall artillery of the *Turks*. The infinite confternation of the *Greeks*, in feeing a fleet of fourfcore great gallies thus carried over a tract of land of above three *Italian* miles, can fcarce be conceived, when they faw them, next morning, riding in their harbour,

harbour, for the whole transportation was effected in one night. The operations of the besiegers were thereby greatly facilitated. It does not however appear, that any more than two *Turkish* ships were destroyed upon this occasion, or that *Justiniani*, and his mercenaries were dispirited; the emperor having promised them vast rewards, in case they should succeed in raising the siege. This was the case with the *Greeks*; they were daunted by the perpetual thunder of the *Othman* artillery, which exceeded all belief; by the mines which the *Turks* worked, the towers and machines they brought against the place, and, above all, by the vast breaches which now began to be made in the outer wall. After this, *Mohammed* ordered a wooden bridge, of a most amazing construction, to be built, on which a battery of cannon was erected, and, every thing being ready for a general assault, a negociation ensued. *Mohammed* offered the emperor, and his nobility, their freedom and effects, and the people great privileges, but denounced the severest vengeance if his terms were refused. The conditions were not complied with, and, according to the *Latin* and *Greek* historians, on the twenty-seventh of *May*, 1453, the general storm began; it was carried on with the utmost obstinacy, though it appears to have been that of the outer walls alone, which, at last, the *Turks* carried. But as the inner wall was still pretty entire, the besieged might have made a brave defence, had not *Justiniani* been wounded, and obliged to retire. His retreat dispirited his men, who abandoning their posts, gave the *Turks* an opportunity of mounting the outer wall, and of rushing by thousands through the breach. Here they were opposed by the emperor in person, who manned a narrow gate, which served for their admission through the inner wall into the city. The *Turks*, who were encouraged by the most magnificent promises of their master, and equally terrified by his threats, bent their whole force against the gate, which was called the gate of *Kartias*. Could the emperor have shut it, he might still have made a good defence, but that was impracticable, nor could *Constantine* himself return into the city, so great was the press. The *Turkish* officers perceived the advantage they had gained, and *Mohammed* in person, with an iron-rod in his hand, drove on his battalions towards the breach. It was here *Greek* emperor killed and *Constantine* was slain; being wedged up with the crowd, and unable to defend himself, he called for one of his followers to put an end to his life; but he was reserved to die *Constantinople* taken. by the hands of the *Othmans*, as did many of his nobility, and bravest officers.

It was about one in the morning, before the *Turks* got possession of one part of *Constantinople*, and in the assault they are said to have lost no more than three men, which if true, is an evident proof that *Constantine* and his followers were so wedged in at the time of their death, that they could do nothing for their own defence. A great many were killed after the infidels entered the city, from an opinion that the garrison and inhabitants were much stronger than they were.

Many ridiculous, and some improbable, accounts are added to what we have aboved recited. It seems, however, to be certain, that the loss of *Conftantinople* was, in a great measure, owing to the credulity, and amazing fuperftition, of the *Greeks*; for they had among them a general perfwafion which had been propagated by some impoftors, that, if the *Othmans* were fuffered to advance to a certain pillar, within the city, an angel from Heaven was to appear and drive them back with great flaughter.

The Turkish account of that affair.

The *Turkish* accounts, as given by prince *Cantemir*, make it probable that a treaty was on foot, between *Mohammed* and *Conftantine*, at the time the city was taken. They tell us farther, that *Mohammed*, after having had a conference with the *Greek* deputies, and having difmiffed them, fent a party of horfe after them to call them back, to add fomething to what he had faid. The *Greeks*, miftaking this party for affailants, fired upon them ; and, both parties being fupplied with frefh troops, the affault and defence became at laft general, till it ended, as we have obferved, by the death of the emperor before a poftern gate of the inner wall. But here the *Turkish* accounts, as collected by prince *Cantemir*, are much more candid and confiftent than thofe of the *Chriftians*, because the *Turks* did not get immediate poffeffion of the inner wall upon *Conftantine*'s death ; for, though *Mohammed* continued the affault with the greateft obftinacy, yet he ordered a ceffation of arms ; and, upon the befieged claiming the benefit of the terms that had been agreed upon, he inftantly ratified them, as to that part of the city which was not in his poffeffion ; but refufed to do it as to that part which he had taken by affault This conduct renders all the accounts given by the *Chriftians* of the cruelties practifed by the *Othmans*, after taking the capital, extremely fufpicious ; efpecially as fome of the authors were themfelves fufferers, while others of them had nothing fo much in view, as to give their readers the moft horrid ideas of the perfidy and inhumanity of the *Mahometans*.

Zogan, who was *Mohammed*'s head vizir and general in this fiege, acted towards the harbour, where his poft lay, much in the fame manner as his mafter had done in the land-attack ; for, feeing the inhabitants flying on all fides with their effects, he perfuaded moft of them to return with him, upon promife of fafety to their perfons and property. As to the *Italians*, and the other mercenaries, they feem to have fuffered but little, and to have got off in their fhips, as did great numbers of the wealthy inhabitants.

Barbarity of Mohammed,

Allowing, however, all that the *Turkish* accounts fay to be true, it is certain that a great deal of barbarity and rapine followed

2

followed, upon the taking and surrender of the city: nor is
this surprising, when we reflect upon the length and obstinacy of the siege, which continued for fifty-one days; and,
above all, the natural disposition which the *Turks* had to
plunder. *Mohammed*, however, was so much of a barbarian,
that, when the emperor's dead body was found, it was ignominiously exposed, and the head carried through all the
chief cities of his empire, to raise, in the princes and inhabitants, the higher ideas of *Othman* grandeur.

Other instances, related by the *Christians*, of *Mohammed*'s
inhumanities, are questionable; particularly with regard to
the death of *Notares*, who is called the great duke, and whose
credit in *Constantinople* was almost equal to that of the emperor. This nobleman, or prince, was indeed put to death; as
were some of his family; but it is uncertain whether he did
not provoke *Mohammed* by his imprudent intrigues, in expectation of troops and ships being sent from *Europe* to recover the city. But he died like a man of courage and
virtue. In other instances, *Mohammed*, heated, perhaps,
with wine, as well as success, put off humanity. He purchased many of the chief *Greek* noblemen from his soldiers,
who had made them prisoners during the siege, on purpose
that he might have a kind of a right to put them to death,
and to appropriate such wives and children as were handsome to his own lust.

*who puts
the grand
duke to
death.*

As to the great number of slaves made, and the severities
practised to extort ransoms, and to make the richer sort discover their effects, they were enormities which *Mohammed*
himself could not prevent; and all were reckoned slaves who
fell into the hands of the besiegers before *Mohammed* had ratified the terms of the capitulation. The like observation
may be made with regard to the profanation of sacred places,
holy books, vestments, vessels, and the like, which the *Turks*
held it as meritorious to profane, as the *Christians* did the
Turkish mosques, and *Alkorans*, and other implements of *Mahometan* superstition. But that some of those outrages were
exaggerated, appears highly probable from *Khalkondylas*, who
tells us, that the *Turks* threw away gold and silver to go in
quest of brass and baser metals; an ignorance too gross to
suppose of the meanest barbarian, amongst the *Othmans* especially.

Mohammed being now in full possession of *Constantinople*,
entered, in the most magnificent manner, into the grand
church of *Sancta Sophia*, where he commanded the worship of
Mohammed to be performed in his presence. He remained in
the city four days, and then crossed over to *Galata*, the fortifications of which he ordered to be destroyed, lest it should
tempt some of the *European* maritime powers to retake it.
He next ordered *Halil*, the prime-vizier, who had so faithfully served his father and himself, to be put to death. His
crime was his notorious avarice, by which he had amassed

*and enters
Constanti-
nople.*

H 2   immense

immenſe riches, and which had prevailed upon him to be bribed by the *Greeks*. This charge was ſtrongly urged againſt him, before his face, by *Notares*, the great duke, before his death: but *Mohammed*, perhaps, would not have regarded the accuſation, had he not reflected, that, ever ſince the beginning of the ſiege, *Halil* had ſtrenuouſly endeavoured to perſuade him to raiſe it.

In this place we are not to forget the famous ſtory of his cutting off the head of a beautiful *Greek* lady, with whom his ſoldiers thought he ſpent too much time. Though this act of barbarity is doubted by ſome authors, yet, not to mention the great credit it has obtained, it is by no means improbable, when we conſider the cruel cataſtrophe of *Notares* and his family, after receiving from the tyrant the higheſt marks of eſteem and affection; and that, very poſſibly, he might diſcover, that this fair *Greek* was a party in their intrigues.

Returns to Adria-nople.   *Mohammed*, having given orders for repairing and reſortifying *Conſtantinople*, and for preſerving to the *Chriſtians* the places of worſhip that had been ceded to them, returned to *Adrianople* on the eighteenth of *June*, being the twentieth day after *Conſtantinople* was taken. Here he appeared in all the glory of a great emperor, and was courted, even by *Chriſtian* princes, of whoſe intereſt he became the umpire. He ſeems to have ſpent the remaining part of the year 1453, and part of the ſucceeding year, in *Adrianople*.

He acquires Servia.   His next warlike expedition was againſt *Servia*, the inheritance of which he claimed, as his father had done. All he got by this acquiſition ſeems to have been a ſum of money from the deſpot, who, with the principal inhabitants, and their effects, had retired to *Hungary*, together with an acknowledgment of his ſuperiority; for he found himſelf unable to take the fort of *Sendrew*, which would have opened his paſſage over the *Danube* into *Hungary*. Soon after, the old deſpot died, and his ſons fell at variance amongſt themſelves.

Mohammed had not better fortune in the next attempt he made, which was againſt *Rhodes*, and upon which he had likewiſe pretenſions; but the knights refuſed to pay him tribute. His ſhips had, however, ſome better ſucceſs at *Leſbos*, and other iſlands in the *Archipelago*; the reduction of which he ſeems to have attempted chiefly with a view of raiſing a naval power, and for the ſake of commerce. This rendered them more formidable to the *Italian* ſtates than even the conqueſt of *Conſtantinople* had done; for the pope, and others of them, fitted out a fleet of forty ſail, which proved too ſtrong for that which *Mohammed* ſent againſt the prince of *Leſbos*.

In *July*, 1456, *Mohammed* attacked *Belgrade* with an army of one hundred and fifty thouſand men, and a fleet compoſed of three hundred veſſels. He was encouraged to this expedition

by

by his becoming now fole mafter of *Servia*. By the help of his mortars, of which he is faid to have been the inventor, he had, at firft, great fuccefs; but *Hunniades*, throwing himfelf into the city, with a great body of excellent troops, he was repulfed with vaft lofs. This ferved only to redouble *Mohammed*'s attempts upon the place, but all of them proved unfuccefsful, and he loft a great part of his artillery; fo that *Hunniades*, in a manner, befieged him in his camp. This brought on a general engagement, in which *Mohammed* behaved with great perfonal courage, but loft the braveft of his officers and troops, and was himfelf fo dangeroufly wounded in feveral places, that he was carried back for dead to his camp; and, when he recovered, he raifed the fiege, which coft him, in the whole, about forty thoufand men. The very remembrance and mention of this fiege is faid to have affected him vifibly ever after. Amongft his other loffes was that of his whole fleet, which he brought up the *Danube*, and of which the *Hungarians* took twenty fhips, and run the reft on fhore. This was the fevereft mortification that *Mohammed* ever received, but his grief was alleviated by the death of the brave *Hunniades*, which happened foon after; fome fay of his wounds, and others by the plague. This ftroke was fo fatal to the *Chriftians*, that the *Turks* looked upon it as a victory; and, on that account, they have reprefented the fultan as having the advantage of the *Hungarians*, tho' they do not diffemble his raifing the fiege of *Belgrade* with vaft lofs.

He is defeated before Belgrade.

Thomas and *Demetrius*, the late *Greek* emperor's two brothers, ftill held a fhadow of command in the *Morea*, where they were revered on account of their brother's high quality, and were, in a manner, neceffary both to the *Othmans* and the *Venetians*; the latter poffeffing moft part of the fea-coafts. But *Mohammed*, after taking *Conftantinople*, and raifing to himfelf a great naval power, thought thofe precautions needlefs. Upon his building the caftle upon the *Bofphorus*, he fent *Thurakan*, one of his beft generals, to keep the *Greek* princes in awe; but both *Thurakan* and his fon *Ahmed*, who fucceeded him in his command, were defeated.

Soon after, the news of his taking *Conftantinople* ftruck fuch a terror into the *Greek* princes, and the *Italians* of the *Morea*, that they entered into a refolution to abandon *Greece*, and to retire, with all their effects, into *Italy*. This refolution, if executed, would have crufhed all *Mohammed*'s purpofes. He therefore entered into a treaty with the two *Greek* princes, and promifed to continue them in his protection. But the *Albanians*, a hardy and unpolifhed race of men, inhabiting the mountains and inlands of the *Morea*, hearing of the defperate ftate of the *Greek* affairs, arofe in arms; and, chufing one *Kantakuzemus* for their leader, committed vaft depredations upon the ftates of the two brothers.

He fubdues the Morea.

The

The *Christian* writers, who have been moſt inveterate againſt *Mohammed*'s memory, by their own relation of facts, beſtow the greateſt encomiums upon his good faith in his proceedings with regard to thoſe two brothers: for, though the *Albanians* took and plundered many conſiderable places in the *Moroa*, and ſent a great many of the *Greek* inhabitants into ſlavery, yet they were bravely oppoſed by the two brothers, *Demetrius* and *Thomas*, the latter of whom was a great general. This made the *Albanians* ſecretly have recourſe to *Mohammed*, to whom they promiſed to deliver up all the places they had taken upon the ſea-coaſt of the *Morea*, provided they were left in poſſeſſion of the open country. Two *Greeks*, *Centerion* and *Lukanus*, privately managed this negotiation; but *Thomas* ſeized them both, and threw them into priſon; eſcaping from whence, they put themſelves at the head of the *Albanians*, and attacked *Patras*, one of the ſtrongeſt cities of the *Morea*; from whence they were bravely repulſed by prince *Thomas*. But the number of the rebels daily increaſing, they muſt, at laſt, have been ſucceſsful, had not *Mohammed* ſent an army to the aſſiſtance of the princes which reduced the rebels to their duty.

Could the two brothers have been prevailed upon to ſtand to the terms they had ſo often ſworn to obſerve with *Mohammed* and his father, in all probability they might have remained in quiet poſſeſſion of their ſeveral dominions: but they not only, upon every favourable piece of news they received from *Italy*, diſputed the payment of the tribute, but, upon the ſmalleſt reſpite they had, quarrelled with one another, each endeavouring to ſeduce the other's ſubjects. This made *Lukanus* renew his intrigues to cauſe the *Albanians* again to take arms, but with no ſucceſs; and the accounts, of the defeat of *Mohammed*'s fleet, arriving in the *Morea*, the two brothers again refuſed to pay the immediate tribute of nineteen thouſand ducats a year for poſſeſſion of the fineſt and moſt populous country in *Greece*, with the arrears of two years owing.

Mohammed invades the Morea. *Mohammed* underſtood, perfectly well, the motives of their refuſal, and the vaſt preparations that were making againſt him in *Italy*, and other parts of *Europe*, and he reſolved to obſerve no farther meaſures with ſuch faithleſs tributaries. Notwithſtanding all the provocations he received, he proceeded with great openneſs and honour. He ſent to let the two princes know that they muſt either pay him the three years tribute, or quit the country. Receiving no ſatisfactory anſwer, in the beginning of the year 1459, or the end of the year preceding that, he fell into the *Morea* with a great army. He detached part of his troops to beſiege *Corinth*, which was governed by one *Aſan*, commonly called *Aſanes*, who was related to *Demetrius*, and a man of great intereſt in the *Morea*. *Mohammed*'s approach alarmed *Deme-*

trius

tius so much, that he submitted, and delivered into his hands *Lakonia*, or the antient *Sparta*. Other places held out, but the garrisons and inhabitants of those who made any considerable resistance met with no quarter. This cruelty daunted others of the *Moreans*, so that, at last, all submitted to *Mohammed* but prince *Thomas*, who, for a whole year, defended the castle of *Salmenica* against the *Othman* power. At last, the place was no longer tenable, and he made his escape to *Italy* by sea, where he was received with those distinctions that were due to his high birth and courage.

Mohammed, who was a great judge of mankind, bestowed upon *Thomas* a very extraordinary compliment; for he said, That, during all his wars in the *Morea*, he encountered none but slaves, excepting *Thomas*, who was a man. *Demetrius*, his brother, found means to draw his wife and family out of *Epidaurus*; which *Mohammed* afterwards besieged and took. One of *Demetrius*'s daughters being excessively handsome, *and mar-* *Mohammed* is said to have fallen in love with her, and after- *ries a* wards to have married her. *Greek* *princess.*

Though *Mohammed* was a *Turk* and an infidel, yet he re- *princess.* ceived an education superior, perhaps, to any prince of his age. He understood *Latin*, he spoke *Greek*, *Arabic*, and *His ac-* *Persian*, and was a considerable proficient in the mathema- *complish-* tics and geography. He was so well skilled in drawing, that *ments.* he sent for the famous *Gentili Bellino* from *Italy* to paint him, and nobly rewarded him for his trouble. A prince so accomplished, and master of the country which was once the mistress of all arts, could not be without some degree of curiosity to visit the stupendous remains of antiquity in that territory. *Athens*, at that time, still possessed many monuments of its antient greatness; and it was governed by the *Italians* under the protection of the *Othman* court. *Mohammed* had a laud- *He visits* able desire to see the amazing remains of antiquity there; *Athens.* and, having gratified it, he took the city under his peculiar protection.

The prince of *Athens*, at that time, was *Nerio Acciaoli*, of *History of* a *Venetian* family, who dying, left his wife, and his young *that prin-* son, under the care and tuition of the *Othman* court. The *cipality.* princess, having youth and beauty on her side, soon made a party at *Constantinople*, which put her in possession of the government of *Athens*. She fell in love with *Palmerio*, a young *Venetian* merchant, but he was married. She offered, however, to make him her husband, and prince of *Athens*, provided he could get rid of his wife. *Palmerio*, equally amorous and ambitious as the princess, found no difficulty in becoming a widower, for he poisoned his wife, having gone to *Italy* for that purpose. The princess then married him, and, by her interest at *Mohammed*'s court, she put him in possession of the principality of *Athens*. But *Franko*, a near relation of her husband, throwing himself at *Mohammed*'s feet, made him sensible of the wickedness of the princess and

her

her hufband, who proved a tyrant to the people. *Moham-med*, being convinced of the truth, gave the government to *Franko*; who was no fooner in poffeffion of it than he imprifoned and murdered the princefs: and, in his turn, he experienced the juftice of *Mohammed*, who ordered his general, *Omar*, to take *Athens* and hold it for him. *Omar* performed his commiffion, but found fome difficulty in reducing the citadel. *Franko*, however, delivered it up in lieu of another government, beftowed upon him by the moderation of *Mohammed*.

We have been the more minute upon this hiftory of *Athens*, becaufe it places the character of *Mohammed* in a new light, and difcovers that he was far from being the faithlefs barbarian fome have reprefented him. He was not wanting in *Mohammed's policy.* policy as well as juftice; and his great care, about this time, feems to have been the peopling *Conftantinople*. *Chriftians*, with one accord, allow that the *Greeks*, after the *Turks* had taken the city, abandoned it. *Mohammed* well knew the indolence of his own fubjects, and how unfit they were to people the capital of a new empire. He therefore tranfplanted thither the inhabitants of all the places he conquered, and granted them peculiar priviledges.

The *Genoefe* had declared war againft him for not reftoring *Gallipoli*, or *Pera*; upon which he took from them *Amaflris*, and fent the inhabitants to people *Conftantinople*. About the fame time, he fubdued the empire, as it was called, of *Trebizond*, though it was no other than a pitiful diftrict of *Kolkis*; and its emperor *John* fubmitted to pay him a yearly tribute. The iflands of the *Archipelago* had the fame fate; and *Subdues iflands in the Archi-pelago.* their inhabitants, in confequence of *Mohammed's* favourite fcheme, were fent to people *Conftantinople*.

His chief general in all thofe conquefts was *Zogan*, who appears to have been a man of intrigue as well as courage, and was made governor of the *Morea* by *Mohammed*. It appears pretty plain that the *Othmans* were ftrangers to the ftrength and beauty of that country. It was fo populous that *Mohammed* every month found new enemies in it to fubdue; *His juftice* but, at laft, he compleated the conqueft of it. Amidft all his victories, *Mohammed* ftill kept up a fhew of juftice. for, having underftood that his favourite, *Zogan*, had made a tyrannical ufe of his power, he ftripped him of his command. He treated him, at the fame time, like a flave; for he obliged him to reform his manners, and then he reftored him to his places, after having forced him to put to death *Acciaoli*, the late duke of *Athens*.

When one reflects upon the ftate of chriftendom about this time, 1459, it is hard to pronounce who were the greateft barbarians, the *Chriftians* or the *Othmans*, perhaps the latter *and great fuccefles.* were now the more virtuous people. We cannot otherwife account for the amazing fuccefs of *Mohammed's* arms, fince nothing is more certain than that, if the *Chriftians* had been

united

united in any one principle, the *Turks* might have been driven out of *Europe*. But, far from that, *Mohammed* extended his conquefts into chriftendom itfelf, even to the fubduing two hundred cities and twelve kingdoms; by which we are to underftand petty provinces.

The reader may be amazed why we are not able to give a detail of thofe prodigious conquefts, which would have made fo great a figure in the hiftory of *Rome*, *Greece*, or *Bockaria*. The reafon is plain. The *Othman* policy and pride were equally enemies to letters; and *Mohammed*, though the moft accomplifhed prince of his age, trufted more to the renown of his great actions, than to literature, for diffufing his glory to pofterity.

Uzan Haffan, a prince on the borders of *Perfia*, but whofe territories at prefent cannot be defcribed either as to their extent or value, was a perpetual thorn in the fide of *Mohammed*. Prince *Cantemir* improperly calls him the king of *Cappadocia*, though it is certain that the greateft part of *Perfia* was fubject to him. He was in league with the prince of *Sinopi*, one of the ftrongeft cities in all *Afia*. *Mohammed* found means to detach the prince of *Sinopi* from his alliance with *Uzan Haffan*, by giving him up *Philippoli* in lieu of *Sinopi*. After this, having provided a moft immenfe fleet, which, in fact, was rather for fhew than fervice, he invaded *Uzan Haffan*'s territories, and obliged him to make peace. He then marched to *Trebizond*, which he conquered, and put the emperor to death, together with all his family. This tranfaction reflects great difgrace on the memory of *Mohammed*, becaufe we know of no motive he could have for fuch fhocking barbarity.

Conquers *Uzan Haffan*, and the empire of *Trebizond*.

The active *Skander Beg* continued ftill to be the fcourge of the *Turks*. *Hamza*, upon *Mohammed*'s acceffion to the *Othman* throne, was fent, with twelve thoufand chofen horfe, into *Epirus*; but he was defeated and taken by *Skander Beg* and his nephew *Amefa*. *Debreas*, another *Turkifh* general, at the head of a ftill greater army, met with the fame fate. Thofe defeats of the *Turks* left *Skander Beg* at liberty to act offenfively againft *Mohammed*. He propofed, at firft, to befiege *Sfetigrade*; but his chief general, *Mofes*, diffuaded him from the refolution, being corrupted by *Mohammed*; and *Skander Beg*, receiving a fupply of men from *Alphonfo*, king of *Naples*, laid fiege to *Belgrade*, upon the borders of *Epirus*. As it was a place of great confequence, *Mohammed* fent *Seballias*, one of his bafhaws, with forty thoufand horfe, to raife the fiege; and he defeated *Skander Beg* in a great battle, in wnich the latter loft the greater part of his *Italian* auxiliaries.

Wars with *Skander Beg*.

It muft, however, be confeffed, that there is fomewhat extremely unaccountable in this period of *Skander Beg*'s hiftory. We are told, that, after his defeat, *Mofes* abandoned him, and entered into the fervice of *Mohammed*, who fent him

Doubts concerning them.

him with an army into *Epirus*. This army was defeated by *Skander Beg*; and *Moses*, returning to his duty, was not only received and pardoned by that prince, but restored to all his former posts and dignities : a clemency that can scarcely be reconciled to common sense or prudence.

Mohammed then changed his measures, and, finding means to inveigle *Amesa* into his service, he proclaimed him king of *Epirus*; to which he seems to have had a right, as being the son of *Skander Beg*'s elder brother.

Here the history of *Skander Beg* is all confused and uncertain. The *Latin* writers represent him as being perpetually victorious against the *Turks*, and as defeating his nephew *Amesa*, and *Mohammed*'s other generals, with prodigious slaughter, in every encounter. The *Greek* writers, on the other hand, say that *Mohammed* forced him to abandon *Epirus*, and to retire to *Italy*, from whence he returned into *Albania*, and harrassed the *Turks* at the head of flying parties. This last seems to be the most probable account; and we are told that *Mohammed*, after committing the most horrible cruelties in *Albania*, about the year 1461, found himself under a necessity of making peace with *Skander Beg*, to whom he sent considerable presents.

Mohammed's great naval power.   But, whatever Mohammed's land-wars might have been, it is certain that he never lost sight of raising a great naval power, which he employed against the islands of the Archipelago. He subdued Mytelene, and left his grand-vizier, Mahmud, at the head of a great army, to besiege Lesbos, which he likewise took and depopulated after a brave resistance. Nicholas Gattiluzio was then prince of Lesbos, and, though all the inhabitants of that island are said not to have amounted to above twenty-five thousand souls, he murdered his brother that he might enjoy the sovereignty. The island being subdued by Mohammed's general Mahmud, Nicholas, and his cousin-german Lucius, who had been a party in his guilt, turned Mahometans to save their lives; but even this did not prevent their being put to death by Mohammed.

He subdues Wallakia.   While the latter was thus intent upon conquering the islands of the Archipelago, he was diverted from his purpose by Bladus, the son of Dragul, prince of Wallakia, who threw off the Othman yoke. This Bladus is represented as a monster of inhumanity, and is called the pale-maker, from the vast number of persons, his own subjects as well as foreigners, whom he impaled alive. Mohammed had always looked upon himself as sovereign of Wallakia, and the prince, or waywod, of it, to be no other than his substitute and tributary. He accordingly imposed upon Bladus an annual tribute of ten thousand crowns and five hundred young men, who were to be employed in the Othman service; and not contented with that, he insisted upon Bladus repairing to his court at Constantinople with the young men, and doing him homage.

Bladus

Bladus, far from complying with the imperious demand, impaled the meſſenger alive, and invaded the *Othman* dominions, which he laid waſte with fire and ſword. He was oppoſed by *Hanſa*, one of *Mohammed*'s chief generals, whom he defeated, and, as if he had been determined to ſhew the *Othman* that there was in the world a man more haughty, and cruel than himſelf, he impaled *Hanſa* alive, and all the other *Turkiſh* priſoners he had taken.

Mohammed upon this, fell into *Wallakia* with two hundred thouſand men, and ſent his fleet up the *Danube*. He is ſaid to have been inſtigated to the invaſion by *Bogdan* the prince of *Karabogdania*, who was at war with *Bladus*, and had beſieged *Kilia*, upon the *Danube*. *Mohammed*'s fleet burnt *Bidina*, and *Praylabum*, then the moſt conſiderable places in *Wallakia*, but his army advancing into the country, he found it deſtitute of inhabitants, *Bladus* having withdrawn them into the cities, and fortified towns. *Mohammed* purſuing his march, came to the ſpot where *Hanſa*, and the other *Othmans* had been impaled; the ſight of their bodies upon the ſtakes, ſtruck him with horror; and *Bladus*, who kept the field with a flying camp of ten thouſand men, attacking him with vigour, he ſuffered conſiderably. Had it not been for the cruelty of *Bladus*, he might have given a ſevere check to the *Othman* power. But he was ſo much deteſted for his cruelties, that *Mohammed* found means to ſet up his brother *Drakula* againſt him, by which he gained ſo ſtrong a party among the *Wallakians* themſelves, that *Bladus* was expelled from the waywodſhip, and, being equally hated by the *Hungarians*, as by the *Othmans*, he was ſent priſoner to *Belgrade*, but was afterwards killed by the *Turks*.

From what has been ſaid, the cruelties of *Mohammed* ſeem in ſeveral reſpects to have been neceſſary. It is certain, that he lived in an age when *Chriſtians* thought it meritorious to break their faith with *Mahometans*; and the greateſt part of *Hungary*, *Wallakia*, *Moldavia*, *Tranſilvania*, and the adjacent countries, were ſtill little better than idolaters, and if they were of any religion, it was worſe than *Mahometaniſm* itſelf. The *Venetians*, far more politic, but equally faithleſs, about the year 1462, again invaded the *Morea*, and made great conqueſts; but they were ſoon ſtripped of all, ſo that they gained nothing, but their having freſh ſeverities inflicted upon the *Chriſtians*, through *Mohammed*'s reſentment. We are told, that after he had recovered the *Morea*, he demoliſhed the church of the *Holy Apoſtles*, which was built in the middle of *Conſtantinople*, by the emperor *Juſtinian the Great*, and that in the place of it, he erected a moſque, or janie, which, though he was a tyrant, ſhews him to be no barbarian; for it was thought, next to the temple of *Sancta Sophia*, to have been then the largeſt place of worſhip in the world. One *Khriſtodulus*, a *Greek*, and a *Chriſtian*, was the architect, and rewarded by *Mohammed* with a whole ſtreet, that was given

and the prince of Karabogdania.

His farther conqueſts over the Chriſtians.

His magnificent moſque.

to him in property, befides other noble prefents. It is ab
furdly faid by *Chriftian* biggots, that *Mohammed* impaled him
alive, to prevent his rearing fo noble a ftructure for any o
his fucceffors. This ridiculous calumny has been applied t
other tyrants, particularly *Bafilides*, the great duke of *Mof*
covy.

**He fub-
dues *Bof-
nia*.**

About the year 1464, *Mohammed* fubdued, and flev
Stephen the prince of *Bofna*, and reduced all the tract of lan
from the *Iconian Sea*, to *Sclavonia*; upon this occafion
mention is made of *Sandal*, the prince of the *Illyrians*, who
had a difpute with his brother about the government *M-*
hammed took *Sandal's* part, but *Stephen* the other prince, fub
mitted to *Mohammed*, who by degrees made himfelf mafter
of all *Illyria*, and at laft, put the prince of that country to
death. Notwithftanding thofe vaft fucceffes, the *Venetians*,
and other *Italians*, again invaded the *Morea*, but with no
better fuccefs than before, though they were fupported by
the *Hungarians*, under *Mathias Hunniades*, the fon of the

**Lemnos
fubdued.**

famous *John*. They found means however, to fubdue
Lemnos, but they were defeated at *Mytelene*, in *Lefbos*. After
this, the *Venetians* applied for a kind of crufade againft
Mohammed; and the pope interefted himfelf fo much in the
fame, that he prevailed with *Skander Beg* to break the peace
with *Mohammed*. This pope, *Pius*, gave *Skander Beg* affurances, that he would in perfon invade the *Othman* dominions, and he actually had made intereft with the *Chriftian*
princes for that purpofe, but died before he could fulfil his
refolution. *Skander Beg* gave the *Othmans* feveral fignal
overthrows, by which the *Venetians* once more landed in
the *Morea*, and made an attempt upon *Pattras*, in which they

**Victories
of *Skander*
Beg.**

were again unfuccefsful. *Skander Beg* in the mean time, whofe
hiftory approaches fo near to romance that we dare not
give the particulars of it a place, heaped victory upon
victory, till at laft *Mohammed* found himfelf under neceffity
to employ affaffins to murder him. Perhaps the whole of
the infamous attempt is a fable, and calculated only to
blacken *Mohammed*, whofe affaffins, it is faid, were difcovered and executed. It is however pretty certain, that, about
this time, *Mohammed* invaded *Epirus*, and befieged *Croia* with
two hundred thoufand men, and even the *Chriftian* writers
allow that *Skarder Beg* was fo much diftreffed, as to be
obliged to repair in perfon to *Rome*, to follicit aids of pope
Paul the fecond. The *Turkifh* general who commanded at
the fiege of *Croia*, was *Balibanus*, and *Skander Beg* receiving
fome fuccours from the *Venetians*, defeated him, and raifed the

**Doubts
concern-
ing his
hiftory.**

fiege, but the particulars are told with fo much confufion,
and fuch difagreement amongft authors, that very little dependance can be had upon them. For though *Skander*
Beg is reprefented as being perpetually victorious, yet, according to the fame authors, we find him generally in *Italy*
folliciting aid of the pope, the *Venetians*, and other *Chriftian*
powers,

powers. Upon the whole, therefore, it is moſt probable, that the famous *Skander Beg*'s ſucceſſes had not always foundation in truth. *Mohammed*, in his laſt invaſion of *Epirus*, had built a city called *Valmes*, which greatly annoyed the dominions of *Skander Beg*, and he repaired to *Lyſſa*, a *Venetian* city, to conſult meaſures for taking it. All we know more of him is, that he died at *Lyſſa*, in the ſixty-third, or ſixty-fourth year of his age, and was held in ſuch reſpect, even among his enemies, that they wore pieces of his bones (which they dug out of his grave) by way of amulets, or charms, to procure them good fortune. It appears through all the miſts and clouds of hiſtory, that he was a great and a fortunate commander, though his real actions have been debaſed by, and intermingled with, fables. It is not even certain, though he was a perpetual enemy to the *Othmans*, whether he was by birth a *Chriſtian*. It is plain, that the *Chriſtian* powers had the greateſt opinion of his ſucceſs and abilities in war, and perhaps it was his intereſt to keep up that opinion, by magnifying his own exploits. After his death, which happened about the year 1466, *His death.* Epirus, and all *Albania*, fell under the *Othman* yoke, as all *Karamania* did ſoon after.

The *Venetian* fleet, however, and the *Hungarian* armies, *Succeſs of* kept *Mohammed* for ſome time in play, and recovered great *the Vene-* part of *Boſnia*, and *Servia*, together with ſeveral iſlands and *tians.* cities in the *Archipelago*. But the *Venetians*, at this time, began to degenerate. They were ſtill in poſſeſſion of the city of *Negropont*, lying in the antient *Eubea*, and deemed to be almoſt impregnable. *Mohammed* therefore reſolved at any rate to make himſelf maſter of the city and the whole iſland, and ſent no fewer than three hundred gallies upon the expedition, which were followed by himſelf in perſon, with a moſt immenſe army. The ſiege of *Negropont* was accordingly formed, and both that and the whole iſland was ſubdued. *Mohammed* is accuſed of being guilty of putting the *Venetian* general and garriſon to the ſword, contrary to his capitulation upon this occaſion. He is likewiſe accuſed of having put to death the governor's daughter, a young lady of exquiſite beauty, for refuſing to ſubmit to his embraces.

About the year 1470, the terror of *Mohammed*'s arms was ſo alarming to the *Chriſtian* princes, that they entered into a confederacy againſt him, and even engaged *Uzan Haſſan*, who had pretentions upon the empire of *Trebizond*: and in the ſame quarrel, the other parties were, pope *Sixtus* the fourth, the kings of *Naples*, and *Cyprus*, and the grand maſter of *Rhodes*. The *Venetians* under *Mocenigo*, joining ſeventeen gallies belonging to the king of *Naples*, committed prodigious ravages upon the *Othman* coaſts, and their fleet being afterwards increaſed by the pope's gallies, they even took *Smyrna*, and ſpread terror to the very gates of *Conſtantinople*.

tinople. This fuccefs induced the king of *Perfia* to offer to enter into the confederacy againft *Mohammed,* and that prince applied to the *Chriftian* powers for fome great guns, to begin the war. About the year 1473, *Mocenigo,* the *Venetian* admiral, ravaged the country of *Lydia,* and reftored the king of *Cilefia* to his territories, which he had been difpoffeffed of by *Mohammed. Uzan Haffan,* about the fame time, invaded the *Othman* dominions, both by himfelf and his generals, but his fon *Zeynoddin* was killed by *Muftapha, Mohammed's* eldeft fon, and his army defeated, though with prodigious lofs to the *Othmans.* This brought on a peace between *Uzan Haffan* and *Mohammed,* who reduced to his fubjection all the antient *Pefida.* The defection of *Uzan Haffan* from the grand confederacy, was fatal to the *Chriftian* intereft. *Mohammed's* general *Ahmed,* took from the *Genoefe, Kaffa,* and made fuch conquefts in *Tartary,* that *Mohammed* even appointed a crim, or head lord, to that country, and was acknowledged to be lord paramount of it.

The *Turks* were not equally fortunate upon the fide of *Europe,* where they were defeated by *Stephen,* the waywod of *Moldavia,* and their general, *Soleyman,* was killed ; all the fatisfaction that *Mohammed* had for the lofs, was to lay the country wafte, but it was abandoned by the inhabitants, who, upon the approach of the *Othman* arms, generally fled into the walled cities. The great *Skander Beg* being now dead, the *Venetians* pretended to be the protectors of his country, and defended *Croia,* when it was befieged by the *Othmans.* But they were defeated, and *Mohammed,* in his turn befieged *Skutari* with one hundred and thirty thoufand men. The fiege proved long and difficult, and the *Othman* troops brought before the place, are faid to have amounted at laft to three hundred and fifty thoufand men. This irrefiftable force drove the *Venetians* to defpair, and they purchafed a peace with *Mohammed,* at the expence of giving up *Skutari,* and all their pretentions to the ifle of *Lemnos,* and furrendering *Tenarus,* in the *Morea.* In fhort, they became to be little lefs than tributaries to the *Othman* court, for they paid eight thoufand ducats a year, for liberty to traffic upon the *Euxine Sea,* and other *Turkifh* dominions. The haughtinefs of *Mohammed,* however, could bear of no appearance of rivalfhip in power ; for, notwithftanding the peace he made with the *Venetians,* they took from *Leonardo,* who was called the prince of *Neritus, Zakynthus,* and *Cefalonia ;* but his army under *Ali Beg* was defeated by the *Hungarians,* near *Alba-Julia.*

The knights of *Rhodes* were, at this time, in high reputation for their piety and courage, which was a fufficient motive for *Mohammed* to invade that ifland. The grand mafter of *Rhodes* was, then, the famous *Peter D'Amboife,* who moft glorioufly defended the city, though attacked by eighty thoufand of *Mohammed's* beft troops, and conducted

ducted by secret traitors, who had discovered to the *Othmans* all the particulars of the place. One *Gervase Rogers*, an *Englishman*, is said to have signalized himself in the defence of *Rhodes*, by breaking down a bridge, from which the *Turks* battered the tower of saint *Nicholas*, the principal defence of the place. After this, the *Turkish* general *Masih*, is said to have employed some treacherous *Rhodians* to poison the grand master, but the treason was discovered, and the traitors were executed. The siege, however, went on with the utmost fury, and the *Othmans* in one assault lost five thousand men. This loss, with the great courage and resolution of the grand master, obliged *Masih* to raise the siege.

Mohammed, the longer he lived, contracted the greater hatred for the *Christian* powers. This perhaps may be easily accounted for; because though many brave and worthy *Christians* lived in his time, the governing *Christian* powers were biggotted, faithless, and entirely devoted to the see of *Rome*, which directed them to all actions of treachery and breach of faith. *Mohammed* was sensible that all his opposition in his wars which he had had with the *Christians*, lay in *Italy*; he therefore some time before his death fitted out an armament, and embarked an army at *Vallona*, a sea-port in *Macedonia*. He gave the command of this expedition to one of his bashaws named *Ahmed*, who landed in *Apulia*, and took *Otranto*, which he strongly fortified and garrisoned, in hopes of its serving the *Othmans*, as a key into *Italy*, and after ravaging that fine country he returned to *Constantinople*, intending the year after to renew the invasion.

Otranto conquered.

It happened luckily for the *Christian* powers, that the princes of *Asia* were equally jealous, as they were, of *Mohammed*'s greatness. The sultan of *Persia*, *Usan Hassan* the *Karamanian*, the sultan of *Egypt*, and several other *Asiatic* powers, confederated amongst themselves, and with the *Christians*, against *Mohammed*, who found himself obliged to raise the whole force of his empire to avert the danger. It is said by the *Christian* writers, that his son *Bajazet*, who at first commanded this army, was defeated by *Usan Hassan*. It is certain that *Mohammed*, being joined by his victorious bashaw *Ahmed*, could not renew his attempt against *Italy*, and was advancing in person against the *Asiatic* princes, when being encamped at *Maltepe*, near *Nicea*, he died of the gout, and a complication of other disorders, in the year 1481, in the thirty-first year of his reign, and the fifty-first of his life.

League against the Mohammed,

His death and

It has been already observed, that the *Christian* writers have perhaps been too severe upon the memory of this great prince and conqueror, on account of the barbarities he exercised against those of their religion. This is the more probable, because he was indisputably possessed of virtues that adorn the best of men, and several barbarities of which he

character.

was

was guiltless, have been charged upon him. He was the most learned prince of his age, for he spoke *Greek, Chaldee, Arabic, Persian, Latin*. This education seems to have been owing to his father's philosophic turn of mind, but a prince may understand the languages, and yet be a barbarian. That *Mohammed* was not so, appears from the encouragement he gave to fine arts, he was the best poet in his empire, he had an insatiable thirst after knowledge, when his warlike pursuits gave him leave, and in painting he had so good a taste, that he sent, as we have seen, for the famous *Gentili Bellino*, the great reviver of that art in *Europe*, to draw his picture. He was so well pleased with the performance of this artist, that he took him not only into his patronage, but into his friendship. He honoured him with a crown, and collar of gold, and rewarded him with three thousand golden ducats. He equally extended his favours to those who excelled in other arts and professions. He studied history, he was an excellent astronomer, and, as a prince, he is on all hands allowed to have been a great and an excellent justiciary amongst his own subjects. Though we are far from endeavouring to clear him from the charge of blood and cruelty, yet it may be proper to observe, that the *Othman* education of princes is very unfit for teaching them the sentiments of tenderness and humanity. In the course of this history we have observed, that the morals, and practice of the *Christian* princes were equally improper for giving him any exalted idea of their virtues. As to his person, he was below the middle size, but strong set, and his limbs were large. *Philip de Comines*, a cotempary writer, says, that he used seldom to appear abroad but in a chariot His complexion was sallow, and his looks, at once, full of sterness, and melancholly. At the time of his death he was, perhaps, the most powerful prince in the world, owing to the disunion that prevailed amongst his adversaries.

The Reign of Bajazet *the Second.*

He is succeeded by *Bajazet,*

ACCORDING to most historians, *Mustapha*, the eldest son of *Mohammed*, and one of his most successful generals, died in his father's life time, and some say, by his command, for having ravished the wife of a favourite bashaw. His second son, *Bajazet*, was appointed by *Mohammed* his successor, but had made a vow at the time of his father's death, to perform the pilgrimage to *Mecca*, which all *Othmans*, once in their life time, undertake. The first minister sent him an express, informing him of his exaltation to the *Othman* throne, and the danger of his delaying to take possession of it. *Bajazet* was too religious to put off his

pilgrimage,

pilgrimage, but ordered his great men to acknowledge his son *Korkud*, in his room. This *Korkud* was a young prince of remarkable virtue and modefty, and he accordingly mounted the throne, and performed all acts of fovereignty, prayers being made, and money ftamped in his name. *Bajazet* performed his pilgrimage as the fimple governor of *Amafia*, the ftation he was in at his father's death, and returning in nine months, he ordered his great men to continue to obey his fon as their fovereign, while he himfelf retired to a private life. It is juftly queftionable, whether *Bajazet* ferioufly meant that he fhould be obeyed, or whether the great minifters knew the fentiments of *Korkud*, as to his retaining the fovereignty. It is certain, that the young prince, hearing of his father's return, waited upon him at the head of his court and army, near *Necia*, where he was the firft to do him homage; and conducted his father to the member, or imperial throne, which he carried along with him for that purpofe. This was in the year 1581. *Bajazet* accordingly entered *Conftantinople*, as fecond emperor of the *Turks*, and nobly rewarded *Korkud*, who was then about nineteen years of age, for his filial piety. *Jem*, (whom the *Chriftian* writer call *Zizem*, *Zemes*, or *Zizemus*), the eldeft fon of *Mohammed*, born after he came to the fovereignty, was at that time fanjak, or governor of *Iconium*, and pretending that *Bajazet* was the fon not of an emperor, but of a private man, he laid claim to the empire. He likewife pretended, that the will of his father not being written, but refting only on the credit of a treacherous minifter, was of no force. *Jem* having courage, ambition, and more amiable virtues than *Bajazet*, took the title of emperor at *Prufa*, and foon raifed a great army of *Afiatics*. But *Bajazet*'s troops being in excellent condition, and headed by *Ahmed*, the beft foldier in the empire, foon defeated *Jem*, in a bloody battle near *Prufa*, and obliged him to fly to *Kayte Bay*, the fultan of *Egypt*, or, as he is called, king of *Mefer*. This *Kayte Bay* is faid to have been a great, and a politic prince, and, inftead of gratifying *Jem*'s revenge againft his brother, he advifed him to make a tour of pilgrimages to holy places, which *Jem* feemed difpofed to do, 'till he could fee what turn the affairs of the empire would take; but, after *Kayte Bay* had given him an equipage fuitable to his quality, *Jem* joined himfelf to the princes of *Karamania*, *Varfak*, and *Turgad*, and again was at the head of an army, which encamped between *Iconium*, and *Larenda*; once more he was defeated by *Ahmed*, *Bajzet*'s general, and his children were put to death by *Bajazet*'s order.

It is agreed on all hands, that *Bajazet*, at this time, began to be extremely unpopular, fo that nothing but the regard which the *Turks* had for the right of primogeniture, or rather the will of the late emperor, would have kept him upon the *Othman* throne. He is faid to have diftributed vaft fums

Marginal notes: who orders his fon *Korkud* to mount the *Othman* throne, who refigns to his father. Rebellion of *Jem*, who is twice defeated,

of money amongst his troops, to engage their fidelity. As to *Jem*, after being defeated, he wandered about from place to place, till he came to the sea-coast of *Cilicia*, where he provided a stout ship to carry him off, in case he was pursued. In the mean while, however, he applied to *Damboise*, the grand master of *Rhodes*, for shelter. *Damboise*, imagining that it would be of the highest importance for christendom, to give a retreat to the rival of its capital enemy, readily promised him not only shelter but support, and

and flies to *Rhodes* ordered a small quadron to bring him from *Cilicia* to *Rhodes*. But the pursuit after *Jem* was so hot, that he was obliged to go on board his own ship, from whence, according to *Christian* authorities, he shot upon the top of an arrow a stinging letter to his brother, who hearing of *Jem*'s escape, was thrown into the utmost terror and agony of mind.

Claimed by *Bajazet*. *Jem* arrived safely at *Rhodes*, where he was kindly entertained by the grand master, to whom he told his tragical story. But *Bajazet* countermined him, and sent *Ahmed*, of whose credit with the army he was now grown jealous, offering the grand master an advantageous treaty, and a pension of forty thousand ducats a year, for *Jem*'s maintainance, if he would keep him in confinement. *Damboise*, thought it neither for his honour or interest to comply; he knew the *Christian* princes, on whose protection he depended, would resent his accepting the offers, and, as the most prudent part he could act, he resolved to disoblige neither

Jem's adventures. them nor *Bajazet*, if possible. According to *Richer*, a *French* cotemporary author, he began to affect a distrust of *Jem*, which gave him a pretext for putting him under confinement, and thereby he was intitled to the forty thousand ducats, which he received of *Bajazet*. But the politicks of *Europe* did not admit of *Jem*'s continuing long in this confinement. *Charles* the eighth of *France*, was then meditating the conquest of *Naples*, and found that it would be extremely convenient for him to have *Jem* in his possession. The king of *Hungary* earnestly desired to be his keeper, because he could be useful in stirring up revolts upon the borders of *Turkey* against *Bajazet*; but the pope, as the common father of christendom, put in the fairest claim for the custody of his person. *Damboise* chose to oblige *Charles*, but in a way that he should not forfeit *Bajazet*'s pension. He sent *Jem* a kind of prisoner to one of the commanderies of his order in *Poictou*, called *le Bourneuf*. *Charles*, by this, becoming in fact master of *Jem*'s person, was applied to at the same time, by an ambassador from *Bajazet*, and by another ambassador from the pope, each desiring to have his person. Pope *Innocent* the eighth had the preference, and *Jem* was carried to *Rome*, where he was received with great pomp, but, according to the best testimonies, he refused, with great indignation, to kiss the foot of his holiness. We are likewise assured, that he continued a strict observer of the

Mahometan

Mahometan rites of religion, and practised them punctually even at *Rome*. From thence he went to *Naples*, under the pontificate of *Alexander* the sixth.

All the writers of that age agree in giving *Jem* the high-Character est of characters for address, politeness, courage, eloquence, and a fine person. But the cotempary *Turkish*, and *Christian* authors differ widely, as to the manner of his death. It is certain, that he was at *Tarcina*, in the kingdom of *Naples*, when *Charles* invaded it. The *Turkish* histories are very explicit, as to the manner of his death. They tell us, that an artful *Italian* renegate, who had been made barber-bashi, the sixth post of honour in the *Othman* court, or chief barber, for the fine hand he had in shaving, pretended to return to *Christianity*, and being admitted to *Jem's* service, he cut his throat at *Naples*, from whence he escaped to *Constantinople*, where *Bajazet*, according to the oath he made before the barber set out, raised him to the high post of prime vizier. But *Christian* writers give a more propable account of that event.

They tells us that *Alphonso*, king of *Naples*, applied to and death. *Bajazet* for assistance, against *Charles*, by a bishop his ambassador. *Bajazet* received the bishop politely, and sent back an ambassador of his own, with a large sum of money to be employed against *Charles*, and a private letter to pope *Alexander* the sixth. The contents of this letter were, an offer of two or three hundred thousand crowns, provided he would give up *Jem*, or consent to his being but to death; this profer is said to have opperated so well with his holiness, that *Jem* was poisoned. His death probably was effected by the *Italian* renegade, with the pope's connivance, though not in the manner he gave out; and it is very likely, that *Alexander* might, to save appearances, make a cloke of the *Italian*, saying, that he had cut the unfortunate prince's throat. But what destroys, in a manner the credibility of the *Turkish* account, is the silence of *Charles* himself, and cotemporary authors, with regard to it. His death happened in the year 1495, and his body was sent to *Prusa*, where it was interred.

We have anticipated, in point of time, the account of *Bajazet's* *Jem's* death, that we may without interruption attend the farther *Othman* history. About the year 1482, *Bajazet* fortified the conquests. *Morea*, and made himself master of *Kili*, and *Akkierman*, upon the *Danube*, the keys of *Moldavia*. After this, according to the *Turkish* historians, he conquered *Karamania*, and killed its prince in battle, though he was supported by the sultan of *Egypt*. All those, and other great conquests, are destitute of chronology in the *Turkish* histories; which, notwithstanding their inaccuracy, we are obliged to follow. *Christian* writers, however, have given us the motives for his invading *Moldavia*, which were as follow.

Upon

His defign
againſt
Ahmed,

Upon the return of *Ahmed* from *Rhodes*, *Bajazet* being in-ſtigated by an old baſhaw called *Iſaak*, whoſe daughter *Ahmed* had divorced, as being criminal with *Muſtapha*, *Bajazet*'s elder brother, reſolved to deſtroy *Ahmed*. To give ſome colour, beſides jealouſy, to the murder, it was given out amongſt the courtiers, that *Ahmed* had ſuffered *Jem* to eſcape, and had entered into dangerous intrigues with *Bajazet*'s eldeſt ſon. The emperor, however, was too great a maſter of diſſimulation, to ſuffer any mark of his deſign to appear; far from that, he received *Ahmed* on his return from his embaſſy, with unuſual honours, and gave him a noble entertainment, at which both he and his gueſt drunk to ex-ceſs of the richeſt wines; but when the company, according to cuſtom, had robes given them by the emperor, as a mark of his favour, and their diſmiſſion, that of *Ahmed* was of black velvet, which the *Turks* look upon to be the fore-run-ner of immediate death. *Ahmed*, like a brave moſlem, called the emperor a ſon of a ſtrumpet, and reproached him for ſuffering him to drink wine, as he intended ſo ſoon to put him to death; but whilſt the executioners were preparing to do their office, *Bajazet*, reflecting upon the conſequences, ordered the execution to be ſuſpended. *Ahmed*'s ſon, however, ſuſpecting the truth, raiſed the janiſaries, who adored *Ahmed*, into a mutiny, they beſet the imperial palace, they reviled the emperor, who appeared to them at a window, with the moſt approbious names, and forced him to deliver their be-loved general into their hands; but *Bajazet*, though obliged to diſſemble, ſoon after gave orders to murder *Ahmed* as he

whom at
laſt he
puts to
death.

ſat at ſupper. This threw the janiſaries into new commo-tions, to appeaſe which, *Bajazet* undertook the expedition into *Moldavia*, in which he made the conqueſts above-mentioned. The country, however, was far from being

His expe-
dition
againſt
Moldavia,

conquered, and in the year 1485, his troops again invaded it with great deſtruction. But the winter approaching, the waywod of *Moldavia*, according to the *Chriſtian* accounts, intercepted them in their return, and cut off forty thouſand of their beſt troops.

and his
wars a-
gainſt the
Mamlucks
of Egypt.

The next war of great conſequence, in which we find *Bajazet* engaged, was againſt the *Mamlucks* of *Egypt*, who were commanded by their prince. *Kayte Bay*, was ſupport-ed by the *Cherkaſians*, then reckoned the moſt warlike people in *Aſia*, and the moſt noble and independent. *Bajazet* knew that *Kayte Bay* had befriended his brother *Jem*, and had given him money. But *Kayte Bay* was ſo great a gene-ral, and ſo powerful, that *Bajazet* not chuſing to attack him directly, incited *Alidulet*, a petty prince of *Aſia*, to invade the *Egyptian* dominions; which he did with ſome ſucceſs, being ſupported by *Bajazet*'s troops. *Kayte Bay* being equally afraid of the *Othman* power, obſerved the ſame policy, and employed *Kior Shah*, another petty prince, to

attack

attack the *Othmans*; those wars continued for some time, with various successes, but at last the two principals declared war against one another. That part of *Syria*, which belonged to *Kayte Bay*, was invaded by the *Othmans*, and a general battle ensuing, the latter were defeated, though with an equal loss to the former; but the *Turkish* fleet being destroyed by a tempest, *Bajazet* was obliged to make peace upon disadvantageous terms, by giving up all his conquests to *Kayte Bay*. After this, *Bajazet* invaded *Cherkassia*, and subdued it, so as that *Kayte Bay*, despairing of any farther support from that country, is said to have broke his heart with grief. Upon the whole, *Bajazet* was rather a gainer than a loser by this war.

Bajazet having a religious turn, thought himself about this time obliged to assist the *Mahometans*, who were oppressed, and upon the point of being exterminated in *Spain*. As he could aid them only by sea, he sent a fleet into the *Mediterranean*, which did some damage to the *Christian* princes, but without being able to deliver the *Mahometans* in *Spain*. After this, about the year 1489, he sent *Yakub*, one of his generals, into *Kroatia*, and *Bosnia*, where he gave several severe defeats to the *Christians*, and made great conquests. It was about this time, that *Bajazet* married his daughter to *Ahmed*, the grandson of *Uzan Hassan*. About the year 1490, war again broke out between the *Othmans*, and *Egyptians*, in which the former made several conquests, and defeated their enemies. In the year 1492, *Bajazet*'s general obtained several advantages over the *Rhodians*, and his son-in-law *Ahmed*, flying from *Constantinople*, seized the principality of *Tauris*, after defeating the fifth sultan of the dinasty of the *White Sheep*. The *Christian* and *Turkish* authors differ so widely in point of chronology, that it is impossible to fix the precise periods of *Bajazet*'s *Asiatic* wars. We know however, that in the year 1499, he laid siege to *Lepanto*, in *Greece*, and took it at the first assault. He afterwards took *Modon* by storm, and *Koroni* surrendered to him. It is said by *Christian* historians, that he undertook those conquests against the *Venetians*, by the instigation of *Sfortia*, duke of *Milan*, and in resentment of what he had suffered from the *Venetians*. The latter were very unfortunate in the choice of their admiral, who suffered the *Christian* fleet to be defeated; for which he was afterwards banished by a decree of the senate. In this war, *Friuli*, and other parts of *Italy*, were ravaged by the *Othmans*. But in the year 1500, *Pisaurio*, the *Venetian* admiral, took twenty of the *Othman* gallies at one time, and being joined by the *Spanish* admiral, he reduced the isle of *Egina*, and took the city of *Cefalonia*, with the whole island, from the infidels. He afterwards burnt one of their greatest gallies, and took eleven of their vessels that were laden with stores of all kinds, together with the castle of *Pilas*. To counterballance those disasters, in the year 1501, the *Venetians*

He assists the Mahometans of Spain.

His farther conquests.

His son in law made prince of Tauris.

tians

tians, finding the vaſt trade they carried on for ſo many ages, and their naval power declining, grew weary of the war with the *Othmans*. They had loſt *Lepanto*, and *Durazzo*, and through the over great forwardneſs of ſome *French*, who joined them, they failed in an attack they made againſt *Mitelene*; after this the *French* ſeparated their ſquadron from the *Venetians*, and ſailed home, which obliged the latter ſeriouſly to think of peace with the *Othmans*. Previous to that, in conjunction with ſome of the pope's gallies, they took the whole iſland of *Neritos*; this rendered the terms of peace the more practicable; and indeed when we compare the loſſes and weakneſſes of the *Venetians*, with the power and ſuccefs of *Bajazet*, we muſt acknowledge the latter to **Peace con-** have acted with wonderful moderation. The agent who **cluded** managed on both ſides, was *Andreas Grittas*, then a ſlave at **with the** the *Othman* court, and the terms were, that *Leukas*, and *Ne-* **Venetians.** *ritos*, ſhould be reſtored to the *Turks*, and *Cefalonia* to the *Venetians*, who were likewiſe allowed to have a free trade to *Conſtantinople*, and the ports on the *Euxine Sea*, with a conſul at that capital, and other privileges.

Attempt From thoſe moderate terms, it is evident that *Bajazet* was **to murder** far from delighting in war; his real intention was, could he **Bajazet.** effect it, to live in peace. But the deſcendants of *Skander Beg*, at the time of making peace with the *Venetians*, raiſed up freſh commotions in *Albania*, which obliged *Bajazet* to march thither. Upon his return, a *Turkiſh* dervis, or monk, under pretence of aſking for alms, attempted to aſſaſſinate him, but miſſing his blow the traitor was torn in pieces. *Bajazet* having now put a period to his wars, diſmiſſed his army, that he might enjoy the ſweats of peace. But his **Rebellion** tranquillity was interrupted, by one, who was called *Shah* **of Shah** *Kuli*, or *the ſlave of Satan*, who broaching ſome hetorodox **Kuli,** opinions, in *Anatolia*, which he pretended to confirm with miracles, got together a great number of followers, out of whom he formed an army. The opinion of ſanctity this impoſtor had acquired, by his confining himſelf ſeven years in a cave, was ſo great, that even *Bajazet*, every year, ſent him ſeven hundred aſpers in charity. His actions, however, were far from correſponding with his profeſſions; for having formed an army of ten thouſand men, he plundered the country, and committed ſeveral acts of inhumanity. He afterwards defeated and took priſoner *Karagoſa*, beglerbeg, or chief governor, of the province, and ſummoned *Kutahia*, its capital, to ſurrender; upon its refuſing, he impaled *Kara-* *goſa* alive, in ſight of the garriſon. *Korkud*, *Bajazet*'s ſon, **who de-** was then governor of *Magneſia*, where he led a private philo- **feats the** ſophical kind of a life, and thinking it his duty to beſtir **Othmans.** himſelf againſt this rebel, he raiſed ſome troops, but he was defeated.

Bajazet, all this while, was indulging himſelf in the enjoyments of peace; and, notwithſtanding the danger of this rebellion,

rebellion, he never heard of it till he received a letter from *Korkud* acquainting him of his defeat. *Bajazet* was extremely exafperated with his generals and minifters, who had kept him fo long in the dark ; but ordered the bafhaw *Ali* to take the field, and his fon *Ahmed* to join him from *Amafia*, where he was governor. But the fhah *Kuli*, by this time, had entered *Karamania*, and had defeated and killed feveral of *Bajazet's* generals. He then advanced to the plain of *Zibbukia*, where a battle enfued between him and the bafhaw *Ali*, who fell in the field , on which his army was routed.

We are in the dark as to the fequel of the fhah *Kuli's* adventures; fome fay that he was defeated by *Bajazet's* generals, and that, after committing feveral acts of robbery, he fled to *Perfia*, where he was put to death by *Shah Ifmael*. Others pretend that that prince gave him a very favourable reception. Upon the whole, he feems to have been a very extraordinary perfon, and he merited from the *Turks* the title by which he was diftinguifhed. Scarcely was *Bajazet* rid of this rebellion, before an earthquake deftroyed a great part of *Con-* **Earth-** *ftantinople*, and buried thirteen thoufand of the inhabitants **quake.** in the ruins.

Bajazet ftill continued to lead a recluse voluptuous life. **Rebellion** His two fons, *Ahmed* and *Selim*, had active military difpofi- **of** *Selim,* tions ; while *Korkud* preferred retirement and ftudy. *Ba-* **Bajazet's** *jazet*, tired with the cares of empire, openly declared his **fon.** intention to refign it to his fon *Ahmed*, who was ftill governor of *Iconium*. But *Selim*, who governed *Trapezond*, trufting to his intereft amongft the janifaries, croffed the *Euxine Sea*, and advanced towards *Adrianople*, on pretence of paying a dutiful vifit to his father, whom he had not feen fince his acceffion to the empire.

Notwithftanding this plaufible pretence, which, amongft the *Turks* is held next to facred, *Bajazet* faw through his fon's defign ; and, fhaking off his lethargy, he put himfelf at the head of his troops, and met and defeated *Selim* at **He is de-** *Ogris*. *Bajazet* fhewed an uncommon moderation after his **feated.** victory ; for, contented with that, he fuffered *Selim* to efcape to his father-in-law, the khan of the *Krim*, who had been the principal abettor of his rebellion, and had affifted him with fhipping.

The moderation of *Bajazet* created in *Ahmed* fome fufpici- **Ahmed re-** ons, and he refufed to come to *Conftantinople* to receive the **bels.** empire, though preffed to it by his father. In fhort, according to the *Turkifh* hiftories, he turned rebel as well as *Selim*, and encamped at *Skutari*, oppofite to *Conftantinople*. In this diftrefs, *Bajazet* threw his eyes upon his dutiful fon *Korkud*, who had been obliged to retire to that capital, and offered to refign his empire to him. But he was no longer mafter of his own refolution. The janifaries were tired of peace ; and *Ahmed*, retreating from *Skutari*, had feized the

pro-

provinces of the *Leſſer Aſia*, which rendered him extremely unpopular.

Selim, on the other hand, entered into private connections with the great men of the empire, and the chief janiſaries, who inſiſted, even with threatnings, that he ſhould mount **[side: Bajazet forced to reſign his throne to Selim.]** the *Othman* throne. *Selim*, at firſt, ſeemed very backward to comply; but, finding his party too ſtrong to be diſappointed, he ſet out from *Kaffa* with his former pretext of paying his duty to his father, but with a ſlender attendance. The vaſt reſort of janiſaries to *Selim*, ſoon convinced *Bajazet* of what he was to expect. He preſſed *Selim* to come to viſit him, but that prince reproached him with his indolence and the miſmanagements of his government, through which the upſtart princes of *Perſia* and *Egypt* had aggrandized themſelves, at the expence of the *Othman* power; and inſiſted upon ſome examples of juſtice being made.

Bajazet, perceiving that nothing leſs than an immediate reſignation would ſatisfy his ambitious ſon, inſtantly diveſted himſelf of the empire in *Selim*'s favour, whoſe permiſſion he begged to live privately at *Dymotika* *Selim*, having compaſſed his main ends, preſſed his father to remain in his palace at *Conſtantinople*; but he declined the invitation, ſaying, That one ſcabbard could not contain two ſwords. He therefore took what he thought proper for his future ſubſiſtence, out of the imperial treaſury, and ſet out for *Conſtantinople*, attended by *Selim* and a few friends. *Selim*, taking leave of his father, left him to purſue his journey, but meditated how to deprive him of his life, as he had of his throne.

[side: His death and character.] This unnatural reſolution, ſo agreeable to the *Othman* policy, was carried into execution by one *Haman*, a *Jewiſh* phyſician, whom *Selim* bribed, and who poiſoned his father on his journey to *Dymotika*, when he had advanced but forty miles. The *Othman* ſovereigns live with ſo much reſerve, and the tranſactions of their ſeraglios are ſo ſecret, that the *Turkiſh* and *Chriſtian* writers differ widely with regard to *Bajazet*'s age at the time of his death. The former, who are not to be truſted, ſay that he lived to ſixty-two, and that he reigned thirty-two, years; while the latter make him eighty years of age when he died.

By what we have ſeen of this prince, it appears that he was brave, wiſe, and moderate. Indolence and ſuperſtition, however, got the better of his virtues, and, being naturally jealous, he is ſaid to have given private orders for putting to death his ſon *Mohammed*, a prince of great expectation and accompliſhments. The death of *Bajazet* happened in the year 1510, and ſeveral monuments of his magnificence and architecture, in various kinds, are yet to be ſeen in the *Othman* empire.

Selim I.

IT is plain that *Selim* owed his advancement to the *Othman* throne to the partiality of the janifaries in his favour, but he had many difficulties to encounter before he was fettled in it. *Korkud*, who was at *Conſtantinople* at this time, after his father's refignation, retired again to a private life at *Magneſia*; but, by many of the *Turks*, he was confidered as defigned by *Bajazet* to be his fucceffor, and therefore had great influence in the empire. But *Selim*'s greateſt danger aroſe from *Ahmed*, who was in the field at the head of an army. *Selim*, however, being in great reputation for his activity and courage, and having the janifaries on his fide, defeated and put to death *Ahmed*, after experiencing a great variety of fortune in the field.

Succeeded by Selim. who puts his brothers to death.

The next facrifice which the unnatural *Selim* made to his jealouſy and ambition, was the virtuous *Korkud*, whom filial piety could not fave from the bow-ſtring; for, being difcovered as he was endeavouring to efcape to *Rhodes*, he was ſtrangled by his brother's order. Before his death, he is faid to have written, in *Turkiſh* verfe, a letter to *Selim*, reproaching him for his inhumanity, which gave the tyrant terrible uneafinefs and remorfe. This, however, did not prevent him from wading farther in blood, for he put to death all the great men of his empire whom he fufpected of favouring either his brothers or his father.

Selim, thinking by thofe bloody meafures that his empire was fecure, proceeded to put to death many other princes of his houſe; and, the plague raging at *Conſtantinople*, he fixed his refidence at *Adrianople*.

It was there that he projected to invade the dominions of Ife de-*Iſhmael*, fophy of *Perſia*; which he did with a numerous army. This happened in the year 1514. Having advanced to the plain *Khaldrian*, near *Tauris*, he was oppofed by the *Perſian* troops, and made his treafurer his chief miniſter, for coinciding with him in opinion that the *Perſians* ought inſtantly to be attacked. A battle accordingly was fought; but it muſt have been fatal to the *Othmans*, had it not been for a kind of a maſked battery of cannon, which was opened againſt the *Perſians*, during the heat of the engagement, by *Sinan Paſha*. This gave the victory to the *Othmans*, who killed the beſt of the *Perſian* generals, and took all the treafures and equipages of *Iſhmael*. But *Selim* did not put his prifoners to death, or even carry them into ſlavery.

He defeats the Perſians.

Such is the *Turkiſh* account of this war. The *Chriſtian* hiſtorians, on the other hand, fay, that *Morad*, one of *Ahmed*'s fons, had taken refuge at the *Perſian* court. *Iſhmael* gave him his daughter in marriage, and, being difguſted with a perfonal affront he thought he had received from *Selim*,

ſent

sent *Morad*, with ten thousand horse, to invade *Capadocia*
Morad was supported by *Vast Ogli*, at the head of twenty
thousand horse more; and the main body of the *Persian* army
remained, under *Ishmael* himself, in *Armenia*. *Selim* flew, at
the head of forty thousand men, to repel the invasion; but
found that *Morad* had obtained several advantages in *Capadocia*. This obliged him to perform a long and a dangerous
march, till he arrived at the *Kaldarian* plains, near *Koy*, in
Armenia, where *Ishmael* still resided. Upon his arrival, some
conferences passed between him and *Selim* by heralds; but
Ishmael refusing to deliver up *Morad*, a battle ensued, in
which, after a long contest, the *Persians* were defeated. The
number of troops headed by *Selim*, on this occasion, are said
to have amounted to three hundred thousand. But the *Perfians*, though far inferior in numbers, were much better difciplined. *Ishmael* himself was wounded in the battle, which
was fought on the seventh of *August*, 1514; and, in his retreat, he ordered the city of *Tauris* to be surrendered to *Selim*,
which was accordingly done.

Loss of
***Selim*.**
But, though both the *Turkish* and *Christian* historians give
the victory to *Selim*, it is certain it cost him thirty thousand
of his best troops; and the remainder was so harrassed, that
they could make no farther progress. It is recorded, to the
honour of *Selim*, that a great number of *Persian* ladies being
taken in *Ishmael*'s camp, he set them all at liberty but one,
whom he gave in marriage to a bashaw; and many women,
dressed in mens cloaths and armour, being found dead upon
the field of battle, he ordered them to be honourably interred.
Upon the whole, it appears, from the consequences, that
Selim lost more than he gained by his victory. Though
Tauris had been yielded to him, he did not chuse to take possession of it, being distrustful of the inhabitants, and afraid
that *Ishmael*, who was getting together a great army, might
besiege him, cut off his provisions, and prevent his return
to *Constantinople*. But, in fact, *Selim* had been disappointed
by great numbers of the *Persian* nobility, who lay upon the
borders of the two empires, and who, having been disgusted
with *Ishmael*, had invited *Selim* to invade the *Persian* dominions; but they either retracted their engagements or were
over-awed by *Ishmael*. That prince soon recruited his army,
and the *Turks* prepared to retreat, to the great mortification
of *Selim*, who wanted to pass the winter in the neighbourhood of *Tauris*. This the janisaries would by no means agree
to; and, upon the approach of *Ishmael*'s army, the *Othmans*
retreated with such precipitation, that two thousand of them
who is
forced to
retire.
were drowned in the *Euphrates*. *Ishmael* followed in the pursuit; and the inhabitants of the mountains, which the *Othmans* were obliged to cross, harrassed them so much, that *Selim*, with the utmost difficulty, brought back the wretched
remains of his army to *Trebezond*.

Those

Thofe misfortunes are faid chiefly to have been owing to
Aliaudaulet, a mountain prince, who pretended to be in
friendfhip with *Selim*, but, in reality, betrayed him. From
Trebezond, *Selim* marched to *Amafia*, where he paffed the
winter.

Next year, the war continued with various fuccefs ; but,
at laft, by the valour of *Sinan Pafha*, *Selim's* chief general, the
Perfians were defeated, and their general put to death. It
appears, however, that, on the whole, the *Othmans* were the
greateft fuffers : but *Selim* had the higheft refentment againft
Aliaudaulet ; and, in the year 1515, he invaded his dominions. *Aliaudaulet* made a vigorous defence amidft his mountains ; but, being betrayed by *Ali Beg*, the general of his
horfe, he was defeated, taken prifoner, and put to death by
the order of *Selim*.

While *Selim* was engaged in the *Perfian* war, the *Europe-* His domi-
ans, the *Venetians* efpecially, harraffed his dominions, believ- nions in-
ing that he could not return alive to *Europe*. *Selim*, in order vaded by
to undeceive them, fent to *Venice* the head of *Aliaudaulet*, in the *Chrif-*
token of his victory. At the fame time, the *Hungarians* tans.
were defeated by the bafhaw *Yonus*, one of *Selim's* generals,
who not only recovered all *Bofnia* from the *Hungarians*, but
took feveral places of importance in *Hungary* itfelf. Thofe
fuccefes left *Selim* at leifure to fettle his new conquefts. He He con-
gave to *Ali Beg* part of *Aliaudaulet's* dominions, and made his quers *Ali-*
general *Sinan Pafha* governor of the reft, with a ftrong mi- *audaulet.*
litary force to protect him againft the *Perfians*. By this time,
the *Hungarians* had befieged *Semandria*, but *Selim's* generals
obliged them to abandon the enterprize.

In the year 1516, the *Kare Emid*, who inhabited the
country between *Urva* and *Van*, threw off the *Perfian* yoke,
and invited *Selim* to become their protector. *Selim*, at firft,
was averfe to trufting them ; but, at laft, he was prevailed
upon to give them *Mohammed Beg*, one of their own countrymen, and very popular amongft them, for a governor under
his authority. *Kara Khan*, *Ifhmael's* general, ftill kept the
field, and *Selim* was obliged to reinforce *Mohammed* with a
ftrong body of troops, to prevent his recovering the province. *Mohammed* then attacked, defeated, and put to and other
death, *Kara Khan*, and after that, he took the two great princes
cities *Mardin* and *Mufol* in *Mefopotamia*, and reduced all and
the kurds of that province, to the *Othman* allegiance, fo places.
that he even feemed to threaten the conqueft of *Perfia* itfelf.

Thofe rapid fuccefes of *Mohammed* being fufficient, as He under-
Selim thought, to fecure the *Othman* empire, on the fide of takes the
Perfia, he thought it high time to attempt a conqueft he had conqueft
long meditated, that of *Egypt*. It is certain that all *Europe* of *Egypt.*
and *Afia*, had, with great indignation, beheld the rife and
progrefs of the power of the *Othmans*, who, in fact, were a
nation of upftart vagabonds, and had raifed themfelves, by
the

the diſſentions amongſt their enemies. *Selim*, however, from the firſt time he mounted the throne, found that while the *Perſians*, and *Egyptians*, were united together, it would be difficult for him to extend the *Othman* empire, and he deemed it the worſt of impiety, to fall ſhort in that reſpect of his predeceſſors, who, all of them, had added nations, and provinces to the conqueſts of their forefathers; the inlargement of dominion therefore was, amongſt thoſe princes, a point of conſcience, and an article of faith. *Selim* fell behind none of them, either in ſuperſtition, or ambition, and being ſecure of *Perſia*, in the year 1517, he invaded *Egypt*, which was then governed by *Kanſu Gauri*, whom, in compliance with the *European* orthography, we ſhall, with other authors, call *Kampſon Gaurus*.

His motives Authors are divided, with the regard to the riſe, or rather the pretext of this war. It is certain, that *Selim*, after he had raiſed his army, pretended that ſeveral affronts and inſults had been offered him, by the *Egyptians*, and their allies the *Cherkaſſians*. His true motive was, to break the alliance between *Gaurus*, and *Iſhmael*. The former had brought an army into the field, and had threatened *Selim*, but hearing of the ſucceſſes of *Mohammed Beg*, he had endeavoured to compromiſe matters. *Selim* was inexorable, and *Gaurus* advanced with his army to *Aleppo*. The *Othmans* are conſcientious as to forms. Though *Selim* had entered into ſecret correſpondence with ſome of the principal *Egyptian* noblemen, and princes, who promiſed to deſert to him, and was reſolved to ſtake his empire upon the ſucceſs of the expedition, yet, before he undertook it, he conſulted his doctors, and learned men, as to its legality; they encouraged him to proceed, and, having a great army on foot, he marched directly towards *Aleppo*, having privately ſecured the governor in his intereſt; and he found *Gaurus* encamped under the walls of that city.

The reader is to obſerve, that the ſtrength of the *Egyptians*, at that time, conſiſted in their cavalry, who moſt of them were *Cherkaſſians*, but received from the *Turks* the opprobious name of *Mamlucks*, or *Slaves*, becauſe of ſome active ſlaves, trained to arms from their infancy, who were intermingled with them. The accounts we have of the valour and dexterity of this body, in feats of arms, would be incredible, did they not reſt upon unqueſtionable autho-

Account of the Mamluks, rity. But they ſeem to have been deſtitute of fire arms, and we are told their numbers did not exceed twelve thouſand, while the *Othman* army amounted to two hundred thouſand fighting men. *Gaurus*, by the advice of ſome of his ableſt generals, underſtanding that *Selim* had croſſed the mountain *oman*, and was within two days march of him, was inclined to retire to *Damaſcus*, and to ſtand upon the defenſive, till he could be joined by his allies the *Perſians*, and receive ſome artillery from *Europe*. But the *Mamluks* thought themſelves

themselves invincible, and perfuaded *Gaurus* to give the enemy battle.

The two armies being properly drawn out, the *Mamluks* who gave the *Othmans* fo furious a charge, that the latter muft have been deftroyed, had not *Selim*, after loofing the flower of his cavalry, led his janifaries up to the front of the battle, and plied the *Mamluks* with fo dreadful a difcharge of great and fmall artillery, that they were thrown into confufion, which was improved by the great fuperiority of the *Turks*, into a total defeat. *Gaurus* himfelf, after performing ftupendous acts of valour, fell from his horfe through the fatigue of the flaughter he had made, and the greateft part of the *Mamluks* were cut in pieces. It appears, however, by the relation of a *Turkifh* officer, who was kadi of *Conftantinople*, and who wrote the hiftory of this war, in which he ferved, that notwithftanding the fire arms of the janifaries, the *Mamluks* muft have been victorious, had not *Kayer Bay*, the governor of *Aleppo*, betrayed *Gaurus*, by going over to *Selim*, who treated him with great diftinctions of honour. As to *Gaurus*, hiftorians are divided concerning his character. It is moft probable, that he was vain and infolent, or at leaft, the inhabitants of the *Syrian* dominions imagined him to be fo, becaufe, in reality, they had invited *Selim* to invade them. This appeared by the great cities of *Aleppo*, and *Damafcus*, fubmitting voluntarily to the conqueror, and their example was followed by all the reft of *Syria*.

Selim, notwithftanding his favage difpofition, which was fo well known to his fubjects, that they gave him the title of *Yavaz*, or *the Fierce*, behaved with wonderful policy, in this expedition. He granted, with the beft grace in the world, all that was defired of him by thofe who fubmitted to his power. He exceeded, in acts of alms and devotion, and erected fumptuous monuments, to the memory of fome *Moflem* heroes, who were buried near *Damafcus*. All this fhew of piety, clemency, and generofity, gained *Selim* the hearts of the *Syrians*, in fo much that, in a few weeks, he begun his march againft *Cairo*, the capital of *Egypt*. Having lately habituated himfelf to affability, one of his general officers, upon his march, was imprudent enough to afk him, how foon they could reach *Cairo*. When it pleafeth God, replied *Selim*, but it is my pleafure that thou remaineft here, and he ordered his head inftantly to be ftruck off. Proceeding on his march, that he might keep up to that appearance of fanctity, which does fuch wonders amongft the *Mahometans*, he went flenderly attended, and paid his devotions, within the holy city of *Jerufalem*. After that, he reinforced a party which he had at *Gaza*, the entrance of *Egypt*, with fifteen thoufand men, under *Sinan Pafha*.

This precaution faved *Selim*'s army. *Tuman Bey* had fucceed *Gaurus*, as fultan of *Egypt*, and *Algazeli*, one of the braveft generals of the *Mamluks*, obtained leave from him,

The two armies being drawn out, the Mamluks who are defeated.

Policy of Selim.

he vifits Jerufalem.

Tuman Bey fucceeds to Gaurus.

to furprife the *Turkifh* pofts at *Gaza*. *Selim* was alway well ferved with fpies, in the courts of his enemies, by which *Algazeli's* intention was betrayed to him. When *Algazeli* advanced, he was ftartled to underftand, that his enemies were fo numerous; but though he had with him no more than five thoufand *Mamluks*, yet, depending upon their fidelity and courage, he refolved to attack his enemy. *Sinan Pafha*, on the other hand, left all his fick and wounded at *Gaza*, and advanced againft the *Mamluks*. The inhabitants of *Gaza*, feeing him leave the place, thought that it was in order to retreat to *Selim*, and inftantly cut in pieces all the fick and wounded of the *Othmans*, not even fparing the phyficians who attended them. After this, they fent a meffenger to *Algazeli*, informing him, that his enemies were retreated, while they were within an hour's march of his army. The *Turkifh* kadi, who has wrote the hiftory of this war, and who was himfelf prefent in the expedition we are defcribing, gives a moft curious account of the preparatives to the battle which followed. The *Turks*, being near their enemy, alighted from their horfes, girt their faddles, embraced, forgave, and afked pardon of one another, and then joined in folemn prayer, that they might prove victorious through the interceffion of *Mohammed*, and the four firft khaliffs his

His army defeated at *Gaza*.
affiftants. After that, they were harangued by their general *Sinan Pafha*, who told them, that all who were predeftinated to be killed, muft be killed, and that if the bodies of their flaughtered countrymen, could fpeak, they would call out, " killed, killed, by dogs, who have put us to death." He concluded, with promifing great rewards, in his mafter's name, to thofe who fhould behave well; he was anfwered by loud acclamations of applaufe, from his foldiers, who defired to be led inftantly to battle. Upon the firft charge, the *Mamluks*, as ufual, were victorious, but *Sinan* availed himfelf of his numbers, and difpofed his troops fo, that they furrounded the *Mamlucks*, a thoufand of whom, with fome of their beft officers, were cut in pieces, and the reft with difficulty efcaped.

Selim marches to *Cairo*,
The *Arabs*, who either inhabited, or fkirted the countries, through which *Selim* marched, were no friends to the *Othmans*, but the fire arms of the janifaries doing great execution amongft them, *Selim* made his way to within a very fhort diftance of *Cairo*. Through various accidents, he had heard nothing of *Sinan Pafha's* fuccefs, but being joined by him and his victorious troops, on his march, he gave them public teftimonies of his gratitude, and nobly rewarded them. It happened, however, luckily for *Selim*, that a three days rain which had fallen, laid the prodigious whirlwinds of duft and fands, over which he was to pafs, and to which the *Egyptians*, and *Arabs* principally trufted for their defence. By this unufual interpofition of providence, *Selim's* army was in excellent order, when arrived near *Cario*. *Tuman*

B. 3.

Beg, or, as the *Christian* historians call him *Tomom Bey*, was then encamped at *Rodania*, within six miles of *Cairo*, at the head of forty thousand men. He had by this time procured some artillery, but it appears that his engineers were extremly inexpert in the use of great guns. *Selim*, likewise, by his spies, was punctually informed of all his dispositions, and took care to disconcert them, by making his approaches, so as not to be annoyed by *Tomom Bey's* cannon. It appears from the relation of the kadi, that *Tomom Bey*, at this time, stood upon the defensive, and had fortified his camp; but the superiority of *Selim's* numbers obliged him to come to a pitched battle.

This battle, which is one of the most renowned in all the *Turkish* annals, has been most minutely described by the *Othman* historians. It is agreed on all hands, that it was fought on the twenty-fourth of *January* 1517, and that the courage of the *Mamluks*, must have been victorious, had it not been for the numbers of the *Othmans*, and the discipline and fire arms of their janisaries. Both armies prevailed by turns, and *Tomom Bey* rendered himself more remarkable by his courage and address in arms, than he was by his dignity, strength, and stature, in which he surpassed all the *Asiatics*. But he could not withstand the fortune of *Selim*, who every minute poured in fresh troops upon him, and obliged him at last to retreat to *Cairo*, with the loss of his camp, and artillery. This victory cost the *Othmans* dear, some of their best troops being left dead upon the field, and amongst the rest the renowned *Sinan Pasha*, whose death was sincerely bewailed by *Selim*; for he is said, on that account, to have taken no pleasure in the conquest of *Egypt*. *where he defeats the Mamlucks in a most bloody battle.*

Tomom Bey, notwithstanding his defeat, had still great resources. The loss of his artillery was indeed irreparable, and *Selim* had inhumanly caused all his officers, and troops, who had been taken prisoners, to be put to death. *Tomom Bey* bore up against all those misfortunes, and raising a new army, he encamped between the *Nile*, and *Cairo*. The *Othmans* had suffered so terribly in the late battle, that it was five days before they marched to attack him, though the distance between their armies was not above two miles; *Tomom Bey*, on the other hand, had imparted to his general officers a project he had, of breaking, by night, into the *Othman* camp, but this secret was disclosed to *Selim*, by his never failing spies. To prevent a surprise, he ordered fires to be lighted, all over his camp, so that when *Tomom Bey* attacked him, he was repulsed, and obliged to shut himself up in *Cairo*, where he barricadoed and fortified the streets, there being no walls, or regular fortifications round the city. *He attacks Tomom Bey in Cairo.*

Before we proceed, it is necessary to inform the reader, that, besides a superiority of force, and the advantage of of spies, *Selim* was but little opposed by the *Egyptian* natives. They were indeed a dastardly and inconstant people, but,

in

in general, they had a mortal averfion to the *Mamlucks*, who were foreigners and flaves, and had for fome centuries governed them by military law. *Tomom Bey*, being himfelf a *Mamluk*, or *Cherkaffian*, was, like his countrymen, unpopular amongft them, and having an equal averfion to the *Turks*, they were very indifferent which were their mafters. *Tomom Bey* feems to have been aware of this, for, we find none of the native *Egyptians* amongft his troops. The better fort, and the men of quality amongft them, were for the government of the *Mamlucks*, who left them in poffeffion of their properties, and an immenfely profitable trade, but the lower fort were fond of the *Turkifh* government, and proved as fo many fpies, upon *Tomon Bey*. *Cairo*, at that time, as now, was compofed of a vaft number of ftreets, fo narrow, that no wheel carriage could be introduced into them, and they were eafily guarded. It had, however, one great open ftreet, where *Tomom Bey* drew up his troops, and a kind of a citadel, but of very little ftrength. It would have been eafy for *Selim* to have reduced fuch an open, and defencelefs place, by fetting fire to their houfes, but he was unwilling to do any thing that could alienate the affections of the native *Egyptians* towards him, and befides, he did not chufe to deftroy a capital, in which, within a few days, he hoped to reign.

who defperately defends himfelf.

Tomom Bey, by the difpofitions he made, feems to have been fenfible of all this. He had received a frefh reinforcement of *Mamluks*, *Ethiopians*, *Moors*, and *Arabs*, whofe troops were no way inferior to the *Mamluks*. He had lined both the ftreets and the houfes, even to the flat roofs, with foldiers, and had drawn out of the arfenals, vaft quantities of offenfive, and defenfive weapons of every kind. *Selim* was aware of all this, but he, and his *Othmans*, now were acquainted with the *Mamluck* way of fighting, and they depended upon their numbers, difcipline, and artillery. Early in the morning the attack began upon the great ftreet, where *Tomom Bey*'s chief force was, by the janifaries, with their artillery in front, while the *Othman* force attempted an entrance, through the narrow ftreets, which were interfected by ditches filled with ftakes, and flightly covered over. The encounters all over the city were extremely bloody, and every quarter prefented the moft horrid fcene that can be poffibly imagined. But the *Turks* were under inexpreffible difadvantages, by the annoyances they met with, from the tops and windows of the houfes, and the vaft number of barricades, and blind ditches, which they had to pafs. They perfevered, however, thus furrounded by thoufands of deaths, for two entire days. *Tomom Bey*, and the braveft of his *Mamluks*, ftill facing them in the ftreets, and fighting them, with a courage, amounting to defpair, fometimes on horfeback, and fometimes on foot.

It

It may eafily be conceived, that during fo long, and but the
doubtful a difpute, the face of victory was often changed; Othmans
and the daftardly *Egyptians*, accordingly, fought with that at laft
party which prevailed. But fome fugitive *Mamluks*, and prevailed.
Arabs, going over to *Selim*, informed him, that in an oppofite
quarter of the city, there was a fquare, to which the *Mamlucks*, if defeated, intended to retire, and that their horfes
ftood ready bridled and faddled, to gallop off. Upon this
intelligence, *Selim* detached *Muftapha*, one of his beft generals, with orders to attack the city on that fide, while he
himfelf continued the main attack, with fuch fury, that he
forced the *Mamluks* to retire, and was in hopes of a compleat victory; when, all of a fudden, the *Mamluks*, as if
afhamed of furviving a defeat, attacked them with fuch fury,
that deftroyed the braveft of his officers and troops, and
forced the reft to fly in their turns. *Selim* then, filled with
fury, fhame and defpair, had recourfe to his laft expedient,
and gave orders for the city to be fired, in feveral places at
once; this was upon the third day of the battle, and altered
the fcene of horror, for the noife of the artillery was inter-
mixed with the falling of houfes, and the fhrieks of men,
women, and children, befet with flames, or perifhing in
them, and imploring mercy. As to the *Othmans*, they had
fuffered fo much, that they trufted to the conflagration,
rather than to their arms, and were acting upon the defenfive, when, all of a fudden, *Selim* was informed, that *Muftapha* had made his attack good, and had forced the oppofite
quarter of the city, where he had taken all the *Mamluks*
horfes, and their accoutrements. Upon this, *Selim* ordered the
foldiers to do their utmoft to ftop the flames from fpread-
ing, which by furprifing good fortune they did, and then
his troops, taking frefh courage, again fell upon the *Mamluks*, who had been difpirited by feeing their city on the
point of being reduced to afhes. But no fooner did they fee
the flames abated, than they again pufhed the *Othmans*, and
the fight was renewed with fuch fury, that the ftreets
ran with blood; and, at laft, the *Mamluks*, perceiving they
were in danger of being hemmed in by *Muftapha*, fled towards the *Nile*, but fifteen hundred of the moft refolute retreated to a mofque, which they had fortified, and in which,
they are faid to have held out, for three days and nights.
It was however, at laft taken by the *Othmans*; and this may and take
be faid, to have compleated the reduction of *Cairo* by *Selim*. the city,
As to *Tomom Bey*, he efcaped over the *Nile*, in a boat, in
difguife.

Such is the hiftory of this mighty conqueft, as related by
hiftorians who lived at that time, or were prefent in the
war. It muft appear plain, to the thinking reader, that
both parties were, at once flaves, and enthufiafts, believing
the doctrine of predeftination, as all *Mahometans* do, and
that enthufiafm alone fupported them, under the incredible

Reflection upon standing armies.

fatigues they suffered. When *Selim* first undertook the reduction of *Egypt*, it was a great, and a flourishing monarchy, its sultans being masters of *Syria* and *Mesopotamia* at the same time ; but the fate of this empire is a sufficient evidence of the danger of making a standing army the sole defence of a state. The sultans of *Egypt* had employed *Cherkaffians* to defend the *Egyptians*, who are naturally indolent, and the *Cherkaffians*, under the name of *Mamluks*, or slaves, became the standing army of the empire, while all the rest of the subjects were ignorant of the use of arms. Thus the defeat of the standing army decided the fate of that great empire ; a consequence, which *Selim* seems to have wisely foreseen.

Selim's conduct after his conquest

Authors are not agreed, with regard to the use which *Selim* made of his good fortune. He knew that great numbers of the *Mamluks* had escaped, and he had nothing to fear but from them. According to some authors, after *Cairo* submitted, he made proclamation, that all the *Cherkaffians*, who surrendered themselves in three days, (though others say in twelve hours) should be pardoned, while, at the same time, he denounced the severest penalties upon those *Egyptians* who should harbour any of them, but after great numbers had surrendered themselves, they were most faithlesly put to death. Perhaps, *Selim* made a distinction between the *Cherkaffians*, and the other *Mamluks*, who were *Egyptian*, or *Ethiopian* slaves. It is certain, the janisaries, and the other *Othman* soldiers, made a most unmerciful use of their victory, for they plundered the city, butchered many of the inhabitants, and tortured others, to oblige them to discover their treasures. Those excesses, soon made the *Egyptians* weary of their new masters, and understanding that *Tomom Bey* had fled to the country of *Saetha*, which lies to the west of the *Lower Egypt*, and that he was raising fresh forces, they privately sent to invite him back, promising, that if he came by night, they would make an insurrection in his favour. *Omer*, one of the greatest noblemen in that country, out of hatred to the *Mamluks* and *Tomom Bey*, discovered this correspondence to *Selim*, who nobly rewarded him for his intelligence, and took such measures, as were most likely to disappoint *Tomom Bey's* attempt.

Algazeli submits to him.

In the mean while, *Algazeli*, or as he is called, *Gazeli*, who seems to have been an *Arab*, returned from his own country, and finding *Cairo* in the hands of *Selim*, he made his submission to the conqueror, who raised him to a greater dignity than that which he held under *Tomom Bey*, and placed equal confidence in him. For some of the *Arabs*, and *Moors*, as they were called, having attacked the outposts of the *Othmans*, and made incursions to the very gates of *Cairo*, *Gazeli* was intrusted with an army to chastise them, which he did so effectually, that he plundered and took *Kayta*, put the *Moors* within it to the sword, and, to use the

Othman

Othman phrase, he rendered the rest of the inhabitaints as tame as hens.

Though the *Cherkaffians* were mercenaries, and, as they called themselves, slaves, yet being masters of *Egypt*, it was with the utmost reluctance that they beheld it under the *Othman* dominion. Finding *Tombm Bey* in a disposition to command them, he soon was at the head of five thousand *Cherkaffians*, and ten thousand *Arab* cavalry, all of them select, choice troops. The news of this, and the discontents of the *Egptians*, being made known to *Selim*, he sent two of the principal noblemen of his court, and the kadi of *Cairo*, to treat with *Tomom Bey*. According to some authors, he even offered to continue him in the government of *Egypt*, provided he would hold it of the *Othman* court, and agree to some other moderate conditions, of which, one seems to have been the dismiffion of the *Mamluks* from his service. *Tomom Bey* was by no means averse to those proposals, and, according to some, even embraced them, and for some weeks he served as vice-roy of *Egypt*, under *Selim*; but the fact is improbable, nor is it mentioned in the kadi's history. It is certain, however, that the offer was made, and that the *Mamluks* about *Tomom Bey* put all *Selim*'s ambassadors to death.

The motives which *Selim* had for proposing such advantageous terms to *Tomon Bey*, were various and powerful. He was at a vast distance from his hereditary dominions, from whence he could recruit his army, which was prodigiously reduced. He was surrounded by a faithless people, and expecting to be attacked by an enemy, whose courage and resolution he had reason to dread, and whom he had defeated only by his superiority in artillery and numbers. But *Tomom Bey*, had a fleet at that time, cruising against the *Portugueze*, in the *Arabian Gulph*, with three thousand *Mamluks* on board it, which *Selim* knew, and he every day expected it. His greatest apprehensions however, arose from the state of affairs upon the frontiers of *Persia*, where he was afraid *Ifhmael* might retake *Tauris*, and cut his army there in pieces, which would render his return to *Constantinople*, from whence he had, as yet, received no supplies, very precarious, and might shut him out of *Syria*, and the *Leffer Asia*.

Such were the motives that influenced *Selim*'s conduct when he heard of the murder of his ambassadors, by the broken *Mamluks*. This stifled in him, all consideration, but how to be revenged, and he ordered his general *Muftapha* instantly to throw a bridge over the *Nile*, by which his whole army could march at once against *Tomom Bey*; this could not be done before *Tomom Bey* had intelligence of it, and he formed a noble, but wise project for revenge. He put himself at the head of fifteen thousand choice *Mamluks*, and *Arab* horse, and travelled with such incredible expedition, that he came up with his enemies, just as the *European*

Tomom Bey receives the news the war.

Treaty between him and Selim.

But it is broken off.

division of their army had croffed the bridge. The *Othmans* imagining that *Tomom Bey* was at fome hundred miles diftance, thought themfelves fecure, when on a fudden they found themfelves attacked with great flaughter. *Muftapha*, who was then paffing the bridge, flew to fupport his troops, but found them in a manner routed, and that *Tomom Bey's* great aim was, to break down the bridge of boats, that no more of his enemies might pafs over. *Muftapha*, however,

Tomom Bey defeated,

with great intrepidity oppofed them, and gave time for frefh troops to pafs. Notwithftanding this, *Selim's* army muft muft have been cut to pieces, had he not got together a vaft number of little boats, in which he fent over his janifaries to fupport *Muftapha*. This zeal and activity of the *Othman* troops turned the fortune of the day, and *Tomom Bey*, with bitter expreffions of paffion, faw himfelf once more obliged

purfued,

to fly, with a handful of his faithful *Cherbaffians*. He was purfued by *Muftapha*, for four days and nights with the flower of *Selim's European* cavalry, and at laft he traced the unhappy *Tomom Bey* to a farm-houfe, where fatigue and wearinefs obliged him, and his attendants, to repofe. *Tomom Bey* thought he might do this with more fecurity, as the place belonged to an *Arabian* fheykh, pretending to be defcended from *Mohammed*, and as the *Arabians* were famous for their hofpitality; but he was deceived. *Muftapha* and and his party, befides being very much fatigued, were unwilling to commit hoftilities upon the fheykh's eftate. *Muftapha* however, by letters, prevailed with the fheykh, to place a guard round the farm, to prevent *Tomom Bey's* efcape; and *Selim* making moft magnificient promifes to the fheykh by letters, perfuaded him to give him up. The *Mamluks*, however, made a brave refiftance, but to no purpofe, for they were killed, or taken prifoners, and the unhappy

taken

Tomom Bey was taken in a lake, ftanding to the middle in water.

Some of the *Turkifh* hiftorians pretend, that, after this, *Selim* admitted his illuftrious prifoner to his friendfhip, familiarity at table, that he defigned to have reftored him to the government of *Egypt*, and that he was not put to death, till *Selim* could no longer, with fafety to himfelf, keep him alive. But this is an artful mifreprefentation of the fact, for whatever favour of that kind was defigned, or promifed, happened before, in the manner we have explained; nor was *Selim* of a difpofition to commiferate fallen greatnefs, or unfortunate courage. The kadi of *Conftantinople's* account, which is chiefly to be depended upon, becaufe he was prefent, fays, that *Tomom Bey*, when fent by *Muftapha* to *Selim*, was not admitted into that conqueror's prefence, but lodged under a ftrong guard in a neighbouring tent, from whence in a few days he was ignomioufly conveyed

and executed.

on a mule to *Cairo*, where he was ftrangled, and hanged by the neck, under the arch of a gate. It is faid, upon good authority,

authority, that, before his death, he was put to the torture, to make him difcover the place where the, treafures of his predeceffors were hid, and that he endured it with wonderful conftancy. His death put an end to the government of the *Mamlu's* in *Egypt*, which has ever fince been under the *Othman* dominion.

The ignominious death of fo great a prince as *Tomom Bey*, ftruck fuch terior into the cowardly *Egyptians*, that *Alexandria*, and all the ftrong places in that country, yielded to *Selim*, without refiftance, and he made *Khair Beg*, governor of his new conqueft. To compleat *Selim's* good fortune, *Rais Soleyman*, one of the admirals of *Tomom Bey's* fleet, perceiving that his mafter was put to death, killed *Aziz* the other admiral, and went over with his fhips to *Selim*. By this time, the *Othman* fleet was arrived at the port of *Alexandria*, and *Selim* having fettled every thing in *Egypt*, removed five hundred of the chief *Egyptian* families to *Conftantinople*, for which city he prepared to fet out, upon his return to *Cairo*. But before he departed, the garrifon which he was to leave at *Cairo*, petitioned him for an augmentation of their pay, upon this, *Selim* ordered *Yonus Pafha*, who commanded the army under him, and was grown formidable to *Selim* by his great popularity, to gratify their requeft. But *Yonus*, who envied *Khair Beg's* advancement, left *Cairo*, in company with *Selim*, without taking meafures for that purpofe. *Selim* being overtaken with an exprefs from the garrifon, complaining of the neglect, he ordered *Yonus* to be put to death in his prefence, which was executed. When he came to *Gaza*, he rafed that city to the ground, and gave the government of *Damafcus*, *Paleftine*, and *Syria*, to *Gazeli Bey*, who had fo faithfully ferved *Tomom Bey*. His fucceffes were followed by the voluntary furrender of many of the chief cities of *Afia*, who thought themfelves happy, to be under his protection; and even the prince of *Mecca*, from being a fovereign, became his tributary. So that before his return to *Conftantinople*, all the *Arab* tribes were, by this prince's means, brought to his fubjection. The power of the *Cherkaffians* was reduced, and, upon the whole, he added to his empire, territories equal in extent, to all that were left him by his forefathers.

But thefe immenfe conquefts had drained his treafury fo much, that he found himfelf in no condition to carry on the vaft projects he ftill meditated. This is a kind of a proof, how tender *Selim* was of oppreffing his new fubjects with frefh impofitions, for it is certain, had he proceeded in the oppreffive, arbitary way, practifed by other barbarous conquerors, he could have been at no lofs for the finews of war, in a country fo immenfely rich, as *Egypt* then was. The *Perfians*, however, now trembled at his name, and fent ambaffadors, who met him on his return, and flattered him with the moft fulfome compliments, to which *Selim* paid fo

Confequence of Selim's conquefts.

His wife conduct.

K 3

little

little attention, that he solemnly swore, he never would take rest till he had utterly subdued the *Persian* monarchy. With this view, he applied himself to raise money necessary for the war, and, in the mean while, he paid a visit to the tombs of his ancestors at *Adrianople*, where he was seized with a slight fever, and then with an imposthume, which **Death,** put an end to his life, in the fifty-fourth year of his age, and the tenth of his reign. He was buried at *Constantinople*, in a new mosque.

and character of *Selim*, *Selim* was by far the greatest conqueror of his time, not only with regard to the extent of territory, but to the numbers, power, courage, and discipline of those he subdued. His conquests therefore, considering the shortness of his reign, are as wonderful, as the wise and political dispositions which he made, to preserve them to his successors. He considered intelligence, as the soul, both of government and war, and he had spies, both in the councils of his enemies, and the bed-chambers of his great subjects, so that it was a common saying, that the emperor to morrow would know, what passed to night, between man and wife. This art of intelligence contributed to the tranquility of his reign. But all his political and moral qualities, which were very great, were stained by his ambition and cruelty, for he committed general massacres, upon the slightest occasions. He is noted amongst the *Othmans* for his wit and repartees, though, perhaps, a polished *European*, would not be apt to admire either. He was the first *Othman* monarch who, after his accession, shaved his beard, which being somewhat inconsistent with the precepts of the koran, was taken notice of by his mufti, and his excuse was, that he did it, that his ministers might have nothing to lead him by. The pictures we have of him, represent him, with a club in his hand, an instrument of which he was so fond, that, in the eastern stile, he called himself the father of clubs.

The Reign of Soleyman the First.

Who is succeeded by Soleyman. THIS great prince was named *Konuni*, or the *Institutor of laws*, he being, in fact, the legislator of the *Othman* empire. *Selim*, who had been so terrible to all his adversaries, being dead, *Gazeli Beg*, whom he had made governor of *Damascus*, attempting to render himself independent, besieged *Aleppo*, but being obliged by *Ferhad Pasha*, *Soleyman's* chief general and minister, to raise the siege, he was followed, defeated, and killed by *Ferhad*, who immediately took possession of *Damascus*, and gave it to another governor. *Soleyman* was then at leisure to pursue the schemes of his father, who, before his death, had altered his system, and thought,

thought, that his interest led him to subdue the *Christians*, before he prosecuted his war against the *Persians*. This is the more probable, as we perceive from *European* histories, particularly that of *England*, that all the churches in *Europe* resounded with exhortations to the people, to contribute money for the suppressing the growing power of the *Othmans*. *Selim* had left his son a considerable navy, which *Soleyman* improved, and he sent one squadron into the *Archipelago*, and another to the *Black Sea*, to support his opperations by land. He then committed the government of *Asia* to *Ferhad*, and falling into *Hungary*, he made himself master of the strong city of *Belgrade*. Returning to *Constantinople*, he understood that *Ali Beg*, whom his father had raised to the goverment of *Aliaudaulet*'s principality, was preparing to shake off his yoke, he sent orders to *Ferhad Pasha* to take off his head, which he did.

The island of *Rhodes*, which was then possessed by the Knights *Templars*, was by sea the bulwark of christendom. *Soleyman*, therefore, determined to employ the whole power of his vast empire in reducing it. *Philip de Villiers Lisle-Adam*, a man of the greatest virtue and courage, was then grand master of the order; and perceiving *Soleyman*'s resolution, he endeavoured to alarm all *Europe* in its defence; but all the forces he could trust to were six thousand men, of whom six hundred were knights of the order. Before *Soleyman* begun hostilities, he summoned the order to surrender, and then he landed upon the island with two hundred thousand men, of whom sixty thousand were pioneers. Though the brave grand master found his sollicitations for succours from the *Christian* princes ineffectual, yet, with the small garrison he had, he made as a glorious defence, as any recorded in history. The formidable artillery of the *Othmans*, played night and day upon the city, and one of the *Turkish* mines taking effect, it blew up the *English* bastion, with the destruction of a great number of *Englishmen*. After this, a vast number of assaults were made by the *Othmans*, who were bravely repulsed by the garrison, the very women doing duty at the breaches. *Soleyman*, thus finding his greatest efforts were disappointed, notwithstanding the numbers, and desperate resolutions of his troops, in a rage ordered his two generals *Mustapha*, and *Piri*, whom the *Europeans* call *Pyrrhus*, to be put to death, and the sentence would have been executed, had it not been for the intercession of the other generals. *Soleyman*'s chief admiral however, was by his command publickly whipped, and reduced to the station of a galley slave, because the city was supplied, by sea, with men and provisions. It is probable, that *Soleyman*, seeing he had lost twenty thousand of his best troops, would have raised the siege, had it not been for a secret correspondence he held within the city, by which he was informed of the weakness of the garrison, and directed how to make his

He besieges *Rhodes*.

K 4   attacks.

attacks. By this means, he made a great breach, and giving a general assault, though he lost five thousand men, he made lodgments so near the walls, that he thought himself sure of carrying the city. But, previous to another general assault, he sent a message to the grand master, promising him all kind of favour, if he would yield up the place. *Lisle-Adam* would have defended it to the last extremity, but he was over-ruled by the other knights, who, knowing the city not tenable, persuaded him to capitulate, which he did upon very honourable terms. *Soleyman* gave a noble testimony of his merit, by treating him with vast respect, calling him father, and expressing his sorrow, that he was obliged to turn him, in his old age, out of his habitation.

Soleyman takes Rhodes.

Mustapha, *Soleyman's* general, resented the disgrace and danger he had lately incurred, and was meditating to revolt from his master during the siege of *Rhodes*, when *Soleyman* received in his camp, an account of the revolt of *Egypt*. *Mustapha* was immediately detached to reduce it, and to take the government of it upon himself. He was so successful in his expedition, that the rebels were defeated, and he made himself master of the immense riches that had been left by his predecessor *Khair Beg*. But, during his absence, *Soleyman* supplied his place of prime vizier, with *Ibrahim*, a common janisary. *Mustapha*, disgusted at this, sought to make himself master of *Egypt*, independent of *Soleyman*, and opened his mind to *Mehemmed Effendi*, the chief scribe or secretary of the divan. But *Mehemmed* continued so faithful to *Soleyman*, that he disappointed all the ambitious designs of *Mustapha*, whom he defeated and killed, and, as a reward for his loyalty, he obtained from *Soleyman* the government of *Egypt*. But the affairs of that country still remaining unsettled, *Ibrahim*, who had married the emperor's sister, repaired thither, and after extinguishing the remains of the rebellion, transferred the government to *Soleyman Pasha*, the same who had commanded *Tomom Bey's* fleet, and had submitted to *Selim*. The peace of *Asia* being thus secured, *Soleyman* turned his arms against *Hungary*, which was then governed by *Lewis* the second, a young, head-strong prince. *Soleyman* invaded his country with two hundred thousand men, and advanced against *Buda*, the capital. He was opposed by *Lewis*, at the head of no more than twenty-five thousand forces, which, under him, were commanded by *Tomoreus*, archbishop of *Colossa*. The infatuations of the *Hungarians* were such, that *Tomoreus* engaged the *Othmans*, before he was joined by the waywod of *Transilvania*. The battle was fought at *Mohatz*, and proved fatal to the *Hungarians*, who were, all but a few, cut in pieces. The young king *Lewis* was drowned, in a ditch, into which his horse plunged him, and his fate was even bewailed by *Soleyman*; this battle was fought the twenty-ninth of *October* 1526. *Buda* then opened her gates to the conqueror, as did many

He subdues the rebellion in Egypt,

and defeats the Hungarians.

of

of the moft important cities in *Hungary*, and *Soleyman* made an unmerciful ufe of his victory, by ravaging the country, and depopulating it, by killing, and carrying into flavery one hundred and fifty thoufand of its inhabitants.

During this expedition, a report was fpread in *Afia* of *Soley-* **and *Ka-*** *man*'s death, which raifed a rebellion under *Kalender*. This re- **lender.** bel made fo formidable a progrefs that he fubdued all the *Afiatic Turkey*, and fhook the throne of *Soleyman*, till he was defeated by *Ibrahim Pafha*, who killed thirty thoufand of his men.

Soleyman, though a great legiflator, was a cruel and unjuft judge. His cuftom was to put whole communities to death for the crimes of one or a few, according to a maxim, if not a law, of the *Othman* government. He ordered all the *Alba-nians* in *Conftantinople* to be cut in pieces, without diftinction, becaufe fome robbers of that nation had robbed and murdered a *Chriftian* merchant. Soon after, he ordered all the inha- **He de-** bitants of *Aleppo* to be put to the fword, for the fault of a few **ftroys the** who had killed fome troublefome ecclefiaftics; and it was **inabitants** with great difficulty that *Ibrahim* could prevail upon him to **of *Aleppo*.** mitigate the rigour of the fentence, by putting to death only the moft guilty, and fending the others into banifhment.

The commotions of *Afia* had a bad effect upon *Soleyman's* **His expe-** affairs in *Hungary*. *Ferdinand*, king of the *Romans*, having **dition into** defeated *John*, the waywod of *Tranfilvania*, who had been **Hungary.** elected king of *Hungary*, retook *Buda*, in right of his wife, who was fifter to the late king *Lewis*. After this, *John* threw himfelf upon the protection of *Soleyman*, who again at- tempted to invade *Hungary*; but, the weather rendering the roads impaffable, he was obliged to defer his expedition till next year, which was 1529. He then befieged *Buda* with an army of one hundred and fifty thoufand men. The city was defended by a *German* garrifon, commanded by *Nadafti*, an **Takes** *Hungarian* officer of great courage and reputation. The *Hun-* **Buda.** *gnians* and *Germans* hated one another, and the garrifon mu- tinying, they threw their governor into irons, and gave up the city, upon terms of having their lives and arms fecured to them.

It is faid, by fome writers, that *Soleyman*, when he took poffeffion of that city, ordered all the *Germans* to be put to the fword for the injuftice they had done the governor; but others fay, that this was done in direct breach of the capitu- lation.

The recovery of this important city was attended by the fubmiffion of *Bogdan*, the prince of *Moldavia*, who confented that his country fhould become a fief of the *Othman* empire, with a falvo of the religion of his fubjects. This fubmiffion was extremely agreeable to *Soleyman*, who prefented that prince with a military cap, or cockade, by the *Turks* called kukka, made of oftrich feathers, and jewels, with other badges of command.

Elated

**Befieges
Vienna.**

Elated with this great acceſſion of power, *Soleyman* fell into *Germany*, and, deſtroying the country wherever he came, he, at laſt, laid ſiege to *Vienna*. This city, tho' the capital of the *German* empire, was poorly fortified, but it was defended by a garriſon of twenty thouſand men, commanded by a prince-palatine of the *Rhine*. The numerous forces of *Soleyman*, however, blocked it up ſo cloſe that it could receive no ſupplies from *Frederick*, duke of *Bavaria*, who was general to the king of the *Romans*.

Soleyman, who knew the valour of the *Germans*, would have given the garriſon any terms, but they were rejected. Upon this the ſiege proceeded with great vigour but little ſucceſs. The heavy artillery of the *Turks* was ſunk by the *Germans* in bringing it up the *Danube*; and the different attacks made upon the city coſt *Soleyman* eighty thouſand troops. He again made magnificent promiſes to the citizens, perſuading them to ſurrender, but they were alſo refuſed; and, the rainy ſeaſon coming on, *Soleyman*, after cauſing all his pri-

**but is
forced to
raiſe the
ſiege.**

ſoners to be butchered before his face, raiſed the ſiege, and, with great difficulty, carried the broken remains of his army to *Buda*. His miſcarriage and loſſes in this expedition is ſaid to have affected him ſo much, that he pronounced a curſe upon ſuch of his ſucceſſors as ſhould attempt to beſiege *Vienna*.

**Defends
Buda.**

Soleyman, upon his return to *Buda*, confirmed *John*, the waywod of *Tranſilvania*, in the tributary government of *Hungary*, which he now conſidered as part of his own hereditary dominions. Returning to *Conſtantinople*, the circumciſion of his three ſons, *Muſtapha*, *Mohammed*, and *Selim*, was celebrated with a magnificence which took up ſo much time in preparing, that the king of the *Romans* took that opportunity of beſieging *Buda*. The garriſon, however, made a noble defence; and the beſiegers, being ſtruck with a panic, on account of the reſolution ſhewn by a *Jewiſh* woman who fired off a canon with the ſleeve of her ſhift, which ſhe tore off and lighted; and with a report that the great *Ibrahim*, prime vizir, was coming to relieve the city, that they precipitately abandoned the ſiege.

**Affairs of
Hungary.**

According to the *Turkiſh* hiſtorians, who are extremely partial to the glory of their own emperors, *Soleyman*, next year, at the earneſt requeſt of his tributary king of *Hungary*, invaded the dominions of *Ferdinand*, defeated him, and reduced a great deal of territory to his ſubjection. But the reverſe of this was the truth: though *Soleyman* invaded the *German* dominions with five hundred thouſand men, it was with difficulty he could take the little town of *Gunz*; and his detached parties, which were very ſtrong and numerous, were every where cut in pieces by the *Germans*. *Charles*, the emperor, and his brother *Ferdinand*, king of the *Romans*, remained, with the main body of their army, at *Vienna*. *So-*
leyman,

leyman, not thinking proper to attack them, returned to *Belgrade*, and *John*, the king of *Hungary*, was obliged to raise the siege of *Gran*, which he had undertaken.

Could the emperor *Charles* have been persuaded by his brother to have pursued the advantages they had gained this campaign, the *Turks* might have been expelled out of *Hungary*; but the affairs of *Italy* ingrossed the mind of *Charles* so much, that he hastily returned thither. His admiral, *Doria*, however, took the city of *Koron*, with the city and castle of *Patrass*, and several other castles in the *Gulph of Lepanto*. But the *Christians*, after *Doria* left that coast, could not maintain their footing at *Koron*, or in the other places they had taken in the *Morea*. In this *Soleyman* was greatly favoured by the friendship of the *Venetians*, with whom he had lately concluded a treaty, and whom he strove by all means to oblige *Gritti*, the son of the doge of *Venice*, was then at the court of *Soleyman*, and, notwithstanding the difference of religion, was his principal favourite. *Soleyman*, understanding that *John*, the king of *Hungary*, was tampering with the court of *Vienna*, sent *Gritti*, with a magnificent retinue of seven thousand persons, to controul him. This expedition proved fatal to *Gritti*: the *Transilvanians* and *Hungarians* paid but little regard to his authority; and some of his attendants having basely murdered the bishop of *Varadium*, who was likewise a waywod, and a man of great consequence in *Transilvania*, the bishop's friends confederated together, besieged *Gritti* in the castle of *Mege*, became masters of his person, and cut off his head.

It was about this time that the famous *Barbarossa*, *Soleyman*'s admiral, began to make a great figure. His original name was *Khairoddin*; his father was a *Greek* renegado of *Mitylene*; and he and his brother being bred, from their infancy, to the sea, came, at last, to command a squadron of pirates, who were taken in pay by *Selim*, king of *Algiers*, against his brother *Mohammed*. *Horrukkius*, the elder brother, afterwards killed *Selim*, and succeeded to his throne; but being himself slain by the *Spaniards*, his brother took the command of the fleet, and signalized himself so much, that he was taken into *Soleyman*'s service, as being the only match in those seas for *Doria*.

His first expedition was to *Italy*, where he plundered several towns and took the city of *Fundi*. He then alarmed and insulted all the coasts of *Naples*, filling every place he came to with blood and desolation. His name being thus terrible, he undertook to place *Rashid*, the son of *Mohammed*, king of *Tunis*, upon his father's throne, which was occupied by his younger brother *Muley Hassan*. He accordingly, pretending that *Rashid* was with him, though, in fact, he had left him at *Constantinople*, got possession of all the kingdom of *Tunis*, and afterwards proved a most useful sea-officer to *Soleyman*, who, having nothing to fear from *Europe*, was carrying on

the

Adventures and death of Gritti, Soleyman's favourite.

Rise and history of Barbarossa.

the war againſt *Perſia*. He had there been joined by *Mozaf-fer*, the king of *Ghilan*, the antient *Hyrchania*, and other princes of the country, who became his tributaries : but meeting with great difficulties in this expedition, he turned off towards *Baghdad*, which he entered and fortified.

It appears, in this expedition, that the *Perſians* had cor-rupted his difterdar, or high-treaſurer, who was put to death after he had accuſed *Ibrahim*, the prime-vizier, of being as guilty as himſelf. *Soleyman* carefully diſſembled this infor-mation, which he received in writing from the treaſurer while he was at the foot of the gallows. But, as the *Turks* think that the words of dying mèn are the ſtrongeſt of all evidence, he put *Ibrahim* to death.

After this, he marched againſt the ſhah of *Perſia*, who, terrified by his approach, ſued for peace. *Soleyman* then ſet out on his return for *Conſtantinople* ; but was ſo much har-raſſed by the *Perſian* horſe that he loſt fifteen thouſand men, as his army did the greateſt part of its baggage ; circum-ſtances carefully concealed by the *Turkiſh* hiſtorians, who make *Soleyman* return in great triumph to his capital.

During *Soleyman*'s abſence in this expedition, *Charles* V. ordered his generals to invade *Boſnia* and beſiege *Sulten* ; but they were defeated by *Haſrud*, the governor of the province. This event, and the ravages which *Barbaroſſa* continued to make on the coaſt of *Italy*, alarmed the emperor ſo much that he prepared a powerful armament, in the whole amounting to ſeven hundred ſail, with a proportionable body of land-troops on board, and ſet ſail in perſon for *Africa*. With this force he had the good fortune to take *Gulletta*, which was the key of *Tunis*, by a general aſſault ; and thereby made himſelf maſter of the greateſt part of *Barbaroſſa*'s fleet, which defended it. Upon this, *Barbaroſſa* put himſelf at the head of his land-troops, but being defeated, he retired to *Tunis*, where ſix thouſand *Chriſtian* ſlaves he had knocked off their own fetters, and made themſelves maſters of the garriſon. *Barbaroſſa* fled to *Hippo*, while *Charles* entered *Tunis*, which the *Spaniards* plundered, and the *Germans* in revenge cut in pieces all the *Moors* and inhabitants they met with. *Muley Haſſan*, whom *Charles* had promiſed to reſtore to his throne, prevailed with him to ſtop the ſlaughter ; and vaſt treaſures were found in the place. *Barbaroſſa* had ſunk ſome gallies at *Hippo*, ſuſpecting what might happen, which he now weighed up ; and ſailed with them to *Algiers*. This was a great diſappointment to *Charles*, who, upon certain condi-tions, reſtored *Muley Haſſan* to his throne and returned to *Italy*. Though nothing can be better aſcertained in hiſtory than the whole of this expedition, yet it has been entirely ſtifled by the *Turkiſh* hiſtorians, who have made *Barbaroſſa* victorious in all places and upon all occaſions.

From *Algiers Barbaroſſa* ſailed to *Conſtantinople*, where he ſoon was put at the head of a new fleet, which went againſt

Charles, the em-peror in-vades Tu-nis,

and takes it.

Korfu,

Korfu, then in subjection to the *Venetians*; but, though *So-leyman*, without any blood-shed, subdued all *Albania*, yet his success in that expedition was very indifferent. Being soli-cited by the *French* ambassador, he, at first, invaded *Italy* and took *Castro*; but lost twelve of his best ships filled with janisaries, who were all killed or taken by *Doria*. Having landed upon *Korfu*, he proclaimed war against the *Venetians*, with whom, till then, he had lived in friendship, for the in-sults and injuries they had done to his flag; and he made vast numbers of the miserable inhabitants his captives, of whom *Barbarossa* had fifteen thousand for his own share. The city of *Korfu*, however, was so bravely defended by two *Ve-netian* senators, that *Soleyman* was obliged to raise the siege in *September*, 1537. He was afterwards somewhat indemnified for this loss and disgrace, by the successes of his admiral *Lutzi*, who subdued the islands of *Ægina*, *Paros*, and *Naxos*, whose princes agreed to pay tribute to *Soleyman*. In these islands the *Othmans* made an immense booty, and carried from them a vast number of captives. In the mean while the troops of *Ferdinand* besieged *Essek*, in *Hungary*, but with so little success, that they were obliged to raise the siege, and most of their troops were put to the sword by the *Turks*.

In the margin: *Successes of Doria.*

In the year 1538, *Soleyman*, who had the trade of his sub-jects greatly at heart, fitted out eighty large ships, under the command of *Hassan Beg* and *Soleyman Pasha*, the governor of *Egypt*, to cruize upon the *Portuguese* and the *Venetians*, who had ingrossed the trade of *India*. The reader has already seen that *Tomom Bey* had sent a fleet to the *Red Sea* for the same purpose. The basha's first step was to seize the effects and persons of all the *Venetians* who resided at *Cairo* and *Alexan-dria*; and then sailing down the *Red Sea*, or the *Arabian Gulph*, he arrived at *Adin*, which lies at the bottom of the same, and most treacherously hanged the king of that city, with four of his officers, whom, under pretence of friend-ship, he inveigled on board his ship, and seized the city.

After this he attacked *Diu*, a *Portuguese* settlement upon the coast of *Kambia*, but was obliged to raise the siege; and, in his return through the *Red Sea*, he took off the head of the king of *Zibid*, for not shewing him a proper respect. He then landed at *Jaddah*, the sea-port of *Mecca*, for the purpose of paying his devotion in that city, and sent *Hassan Beg* to *Suez* with the fleet.

In the mean while the sultan, in person, had invaded *Mol-davia* with great cruelty, and obliged the *Moldavians* to pay him tribute; but they prevailed upon him to let them retain the shadow of electing a prince, whom he confirmed; but he took care to plunder them of all the ready-money and treasures that were found at *Soczava*, their capital. During this expedition, *Barbarossa* continued his depredations in the *Mediterranean*, but was repulsed at *Kanea*, in *Candia*, by *Gritti*,

In the margin: *Moldavia invaded.*

Sea war
with the
Venetians.

Gritti, the *Venetian* governor there. The *Venetians* entered
into a confederacy with the emperor, whose fleet was commanded by *Doria*, and the pope; so that the match between
Doria and *Barbarossa* was pretty equal.

The *Christian* fleet being rendezvoused, sailed forth to the
bay of *Ambracia*, where the *Turkish* fleet then rode; but *Doria*'s great ships being becalmed, the engagement which followed was to his disadvantage and disgrace. *Doria*, however, took *Castello Nuovo*, and garrisoned it with four thousand *Spaniards*, but the *Venetians* were then obliged to sue for
peace, which they accordingly obtained, though, soon after,
Barbarossa's fleet suffered so dreadfully by a storm, that he is
said to have lost twenty thousand men. Next spring, being that of the year 1539, *Barbarossa* besieged and retook
Castello Nuovo; but a peace being clapped up between the
emperor *Charles* V. and *Francis* I. of *France*, these two
princes invited the *Venetians* into a confederacy with them
against the *Turks*. That republic was, in fact, more afraid
of those two powers than of the *Turks* themselves; and, instead of joining with them, they made fresh concessions to
Soleyman for a renewal of the peace.

Buda be-
sieged and
seized on
by Soley-
man.

This left *Soleyman* more at leisure to attend the affairs of
Hungary, where *Ferdinand*, brother to *Charles* V. had attacked the infant king *Stephen*, who was under the protection
of *Soleyman*, and besieged *Buda*. *Soleyman* immediately sent
the basha *Hamed* with an army to raise the siege; and promised queen *Isabella*, mother to *Stephen*, that he would, in
person, support *Hamed*. He was as good as his word: the
Germans before the city were defeated with immense slaughter; but *Soleyman* treacherously made himself master of *Buda*,
with all *Stephen*'s territories, and sent both the mother and
son, who was yet in his cradle, into a kind of honourable
exile in *Transylvania*, under pretence of their being unfit for
government. He then ordered the churches to be converted
into jamis, or mosques, and *Hungary* to be reduced to the
form of an *Ottoman* province, and under a *Mahometan* governor.

Ferdinand, whose army was destroyed through the inactivity of his general, endeavoured most abjectly, by his ambassadors, to prevail upon *Soleyman* to suffer him to reign in
Hungary; and offered him the same tribute as had been paid
by the late kings, and even engaging himself to bring off his
brother, *Charles* V. from the *Christian* confederacy, that *Soleyman* might be more at leisure to attend the *Persian* war:
but the sultan was so far from complying, that he insisted upon *Ferdinand* delivering up all the places that was yet in his
possession belonging to *Hungary*; upon his indemnifying him
for the charges of the war, and even paying a tribute for *Austria*. Notwithstanding this roughness on the part of the sultan, who denied even to agree to a truce, he magnanimously

suffered

suffered the *German* ambassadors to take a view of his camp, that they might have an opportunity of admiring and reporting the excellent dispositions and discipline of it.

The basha *Mehemed*, a haughty severe general, was then made governor of *Hungary*; and *Soleyman*, partly by treachery, and partly by force, made himself master of all *Transylvania*, which he nominally gave to young *Stephen*, as being most agreeable to the inhabitants. It was about this time that the emperor, *Charles* V. made his ill-judged expedition against *Algiers*; in which his army and fleet, by famine and storms, were almost entirely destroyed. *Expedition against Algiers.*

About the year 1542, the ambition of *Charles* V and that of *Francis* I. of *France*, dividing all *Europe*, the latter's resentment got so far the better of him, that he sent an ambassador, one *Rinco*, to solicit the sultan *Soleyman* to declare war against *Charles*. *Rinco* was killed in *Italy* by some *Spaniards*, and was succeeded in his commission by *Polinus*, who, upon his arrival at *Constantinople*, found the divan greatly divided upon the subject of his ambassy, which was to solicit the fleet under *Barbarossa* against the emperor's dominions. The vizier *Soleyman* thought that *Barbarossa* was already too great, and, at first, refused to see *Polinus*; but the distribution of some money amongst other ministers, procured him an audience of the emperor, whose ambition was so agreeably flattered by one of the most powerful princes in christendom suing for his assistance, that he ordered *Barbarossa* instantly to fit out a fleet; which he did, to the amount of one hundred and ten gallies and forty galleons; with which he bore down towards the *Fare of Messina*, and took and plundered *Reggio*. He then sailed to *Ostia*, and filled all *Rome* with the terror of his arms; so that it was with difficulty the *French* ambassador, by his letters, prevailed with the inhabitants not to abandon the city. *Reggio plundered by the Turks.*

Though this unnatural alliance between the *French* and the *Othmans* was a matter of convenience for *Francis* at that time, yet it has since operated fatally both upon the interests of *Christianity* and the liberty of *Europe*, because it has, ever since, been the favourite alliance of the *French* in all their differences with other *Christian* powers. *Barbarossa*, after insulting the wastes of *Italy*, sailed to *Marseilles*. This was in the year 1543; and the active *Barbarossa* began to think that the *French* had imposed upon both himself and his master, as he saw no likelihood of their performing their mighty promise, by joining him with a very large force. At last, however, the *French* fleet was put in readiness, with eight thousand land-forces on board; and the combined fleets laid siege to *Nice*. After the preparations for that had been formed, the city capitulated to surrender to the *French*; but the castle under *Paul*, its governor, held out. The janisaries, understanding that, by the capitulation, they were to be deprived of the plunder of the place, and the powder and *Alliance between the French and Turks.*

shot

shot of the *French* auxiliaries being quite exhausted, were scarcely restrained from putting *Polinus* to death; and *Barbarossa* could scarcely be prevailed upon to stay longer from *Constantinople*, when a letter was intercepted from the *Spanish* general, promising *Paul* relief in two days. Upon this

Siege of *Nice* raised. the janisaries broke into, plundered, and fired the city, and *Barbarossa* raised the siege.

It was thought, after this, that he would have attacked *Doria*, who lay with his fleet at *Villa Franca*; but those two great admirals seem to have had their private reasons for not coming to a decisive action; and it is even said, upon good authority, that *Doria*, to preserve his countrymen, the *Genoese*, from being plundered by the *Turks*, supplied *Barbarossa* with necessaries for refitting his fleet, which, before winter, separated into two squadrons. One of these, under his kinsmen *Salek* and *Hassan*, ravaged the coasts of *Spain*, and wintered in *Algiers*; as the other, under himself, did at *Toulon*.

Character of *Barbarossa*. *Barbarossa* was not the barbarian he is represented to have been by *Christian* writers. During this expedition he fell in love with a *Spanish* lady, and made her his wife. He had notions of gratitude; for he obliged an *Italian* governor to set at liberty a young *Jew*, the son of one of his friends; and he was so welcome to his father, that the latter expired with joy in embracing him. His moderation in all his conquests, and his behaviour to the *French* after he thought they had deceived him, were virtues not common to a barbarian; while his valour, discipline, and the care he took of his men, would have done honour to the greatest character. It is true, he, without any remorse, ravaged the *Christian* territories; but the *Christians*, when ever they had an opportunity, did the same by those of the *Othmans*; but he is not accused of any acts of perfidy; on the contrary, he was capable of requiting kindnesses, and seldom, or never, broke his word. In his return from *France* to *Constantinople*, he burnt the city of *Porto Hercole*, ravaged the isles of the *Archipelago*, and spread desolation and distress wherever he came; but failed in a design he had upon *Puteoli*. The greatness of spoil, and the number of captives, he made in this expedition, was incredible; for he is said to have carried off, from the little island of *Lipaza* alone, which he laid waste, seven thousand prisoners. He returned, according to *Knolles*, to *Constantinople* in the beginning of autumn, 1544; where he was received with high honours, and caressed by his master, and had the good fortune to die in peace three years after viz. in 1547.

Crusade against *Soleyman*. *Ferdinand* finding *Soleyman* so intractable with regard to *Hungary*, formed a kind of a crusade amongst the *German* princes against him. The princes and free states chose the marquis of *Brandenburg* for their general, and raised thirty thousand foot and seven thousand horse, besides *Ferdinand's* troops, which joined them at *Vienna*, and a large body o

Hungarian

Hungarian and *Stirian* horse, with three thousand choice *Ita-lian* foot, sent by the pope under *Aleſſandro Vitellio*. They directed their march towards *Buda*; but the whole of the expedition was rendered shameful and unsuccessful by the dilatory conduct of the *German* generals, particularly the marquis of *Brandenburg*. Instead of marching directly to *Buda*, they laid siege to *Peſt*; but their operations were so ill conducted, that, had it not been for a handful of *Italians*, under *Vitellio* and *Medici*, another *Italian* who commanded the fleet, they muſt have been entirely deſtroyed; and, in the end, they were obliged to make an inglorious retreat to *Vienna*, where their mighty armament was diſbanded; while *Ferdinand*, to cover his disgrace, ordered *Perenus*, an *Hungarian* nobleman of great quality, to be thrown into prison, on suspicion of his aspiring to the throne of *Hungary*.

Soon after this, *Soleyman*, in person, fell into the imperial part of *Hungary*, with great cruelty; and, after reducing many important places, he laid siege to *Gran*, which was basely surrendered to him by two *Spaniſh* officers; and then he laid siege to *Alba Regalis*. Here the attack and defence were equally obſtinate. The women fought upon the walls, and a female *Hungarian* ſtruck off the heads of two *Turks* with one sweep of a ſcythe. The place, however, was, at laſt, taken by *Soleyman*; who is ſaid to have broken the capitulation, and to have put many of the principal citizens to death for their attachment to *Ferdinand* in prejudice of their lawful sovereign. The truth is, of the two the *German* yoke was the leaſt galling. *Hungary invaded.*

Amidſt all thoſe victories, *Soleyman* received a severe blow by the death of his son *Mohammed*, for whom he expreſſed an unuſual degree of ſorrow. The *Turks* thus continued victorious in *Hungary* till the year 1547, when a truce, for five years, was made between them and the *German* princes. *Death of Soleyman's ſon.*

Tahmaſp I. was then ſhah, or ſultan, of *Perſia*; and, having diſobliged *Alkaſib Mirza*, who is ſaid to have been king of *Shirwan*, and his own brother, the latter applied to *Soleyman*, whom he persuaded to bring a large army into the field, and promiſed to make him maſter of all *Perſia*. While *Soleyman* was on this march, his two sons, *Bajazet* and *Muſtapha*, came from their governments of *Iconium* and *Amaſia* to pay him their ſubmiſſions; but their father, ſuspicious of their entertaining ambitious thoughts, received them coldly and sent them back to their governments. Proceeding to *Perſia*, he made himself maſter of *Tibris*, *Van*, and *Amzeh*; and, by means of *Alkaſib Mirza*, his troops over-ran the whole country, and ſeized the ſhah's treaſures. *Alkaſib* relenting, would have returned to his duty; but, being diſcovered, he fled to *Georgia*, and from thence to *Arabia*, or *Irak*, where an *Arab* prince delivered him into the hands of *Thamaſp*, who put him to death. *Soleyman*, by this time, seems to have returned to *Conſtantinople*, and left the war to be *War with Perſia.*

be finished by the pasha *Mehemed*, who reduced above twenty cities, and placed garrisons in a great number of fortresses. The reader, however, in turning back to our *Persian* history, will find a different account of this expedition.

Adventures of Muley Hassan. *Muley Hassan*, whom *Charles* V. had made king of *Tunis*, being afraid that *Barbarossa*'s armament was designed against him, fled to *Naples*, to throw himself at the feet of *Charles* for protection. He was at *Naples* when *Barbarossa* was obliged to retire from *Nice*, and he there received an account that his son *Amid* had declared for himself, and usurped his government. Upon this, *Muley Hassan*, being well provided with money, hired some *Italian* soldiers of fortune, who served under one *Lofredi*, and passed over to *Tunis*; but, in attempting to remount his throne, was defeated; and, being taken prisoner, his unnatural son cut out his eyes. *Tonaries*, the *Spanish* governor of the *Guletta*, for the emperor, upon this, sent for *Abdol Mulek*, who was *Amid*'s elder brother, and who, by a stratagem, made himself master of *Tunis*, but he died after enjoying his royalty but twenty-six days. He was succeeded by his son, a child of twelve years of age; but, being under the tuition of three barbarians, their government grew so intolerable to the people, that *Amid* was re-admitted to *Tunis*; where he cruelly put all his enemies to death, his father alone escaping through the favour of *Tonaries* who gave him shelter in the *Guletta*.

Dragut's conquests. During this confusion, *Dragut*, a famous *Turkish* pirate in those seas, made himself master of several cities in the kingdom of *Tunis*, particularly *Mohammedia*; and, being countenanced by *Soleyman*, he committed prodigious depredations on the *Christian* powers. Upon this, the emperor *Charles* ordered his admiral, *Doria*, to suppress the pirate, and to raze *Mohammedia*, his chief haunt; which, by the help of some knights of *Malta*, he accordinlgy did. *Dragut* applied to *Soleyman*, who, exasperated by *Doria*'s successes and ravages, furnished *Dragut* with one hundred and forty sail, commanded by the pasha *Sinan*, who landed in *Sicily*. Here they took the castle of *Augusta*, and, making a fruitless attempt upon *Malta*, they sailed to *Goza*, from whence they carried off above six thousand captives. From thence they sailed to *Tripoli*, then, by the emperor's gift, in possession of the knights of *Malta*; and which, after a brave resistance made by the garrison, they took, through the treachery of a *French* renegado; but the *Othmans* broke the capitulation by depriving the garrison both of their freedom and their effects.

War in Hungary. In the year 1553, *Isabella*, the mother of *Stephen*, the young king of *Hungary*, was obliged to surrender *Transylvania* to *Ferdinand*, being unable to oppose the progress of the *Turks*, who besieged and took *Temeswar*; but, as usual, they most perfidiously broke the capitulation. They likewise took the castle of *Zolnuk*, but were repulsed in their attempt upon

upon *Erfam* and *Agria*, with the lofs of above fix thoufand men. To the infamy of the *French* government, this year the infidels, by the inftigation of *Henry* II. of *France*, defolated the coafts and iflands of the *Archipelago*.

It muft be admitted that the *Turks* are barbarians in almoft every refpect, and the beft of their own authors afford us nothing better than a glimmering of their hiftory; while thofe of the *Chriftians* are equally uninformed as to the *Turkifh* affairs. *Soleyman* had fo great a genius for conqueft, that his arms were employed in every quarter of the globe. In *Perfia* he met with but very indifferent fuccefs, though he had the inhuman pleafure of defolating the country. In his own family he was far more unfortunate. A confpiracy againft his domeftic peace was formed between *Roxolana*, his favourite miftrefs and wife, and her fon-in-law *Ruftan*, the grand-vizier. *Roxolana* had children whom fhe wanted to raife to the empire; and *Soleyman* had two fons, *Muftapha* and *Jehan Ghir*, who ftood in their way. *Chriftian* writers, very poffibly from the prepoffeffions they had againft *Soleyman*, have exalted *Muftapha*'s into the moft amiable of characters It is certain that his father was long jealous of his ambition, and that of his other fons, and had them narrowly watched.

Whatever paffes within the walls of the feraglio, or wherever the refidence of the *Turkifh* emperor is fixed, is kept fo fecret, or rendered fo uncertain by different reports, that an author is very unfafe in defcending to particulars, either of facts or characters. It is, however, agreed that *Muftapha* was the darling of the empire; and, that *Roxolana*, as is common with ambitious, wicked, women, confidered him as the chief bar between her off-fpring and the throne. *Soleyman* was now old, and fhe therefore had the more power over his affections. She prevailed with him to fend *Muftapha* and his mother to the diftant government of *Cayamania*, and *Ruftan*, who had married her daughter, attempted to cut off fome part of his revenue. The better to fucceed, fhe affumed an extraordinary fit of devotion, and could not be perfuaded to cohabit again with the fultan till he folemnly married her, which he therefore did. She then inftilled into *Soleyman* notions of his danger from *Muftapha*; and, if we may believe *Chriftian* writers, attempted to poifon him. But this wickednefs not fucceeding, *Soleyman* ordered *Ruftan* to raife a great army, under pretence of marching againft the *Perfians*; but, in fact, to feize upon *Muftapha*, and fend him in chains to *Conftantinople*.

It was eafy for *Muftapha* to perceive the danger which both his perfon and title to the crown were in; and he was fo well beloved, that he had intelligence of the defigns againft both. He raifed feven thoufand horfe, and began his march towards *Syria*; which was fufficient to fhew *Ruftan* that his

Sidenotes:
Conquefts of Soleyman.

Hiftory of Muftapha, his eldeft fon,

who is fummoned to Aleppo,

design was discovered; and he suddenly marched back to *Constantinople*, pretending that *Syria* was in quiet.

A tyrant thinks, that every act of just precaution in a son or subject, is an act of rebellion; and, next year, which was 1553, he put himself at the head of a great army, and ordered *Muftapha* to repair to him at *Aleppo*, where he lay encamped. The prince, perhaps knowing his resistance would be in vain, endeavoured, by a generous confidence, to win his father over, and presented himself at the door of the sultan's tent dressed in white; but perceiving he had his dagger by his side he left it without. Entering the tent he was met by seven mutes, who threw him upon the ground; but, either through the vigour of the prince, or their own disinclination, they were some time in strangling him; upon which, the unnatural father, from a traverse window, reproached and threatened them for their backwardness, and then they put an end to his life.

and put to death by *Soley-man*'s cruelty.

This was so secretly executed, that *Jehan Ghir*, so called from his deformity, knew nothing of the matter. He was a kind of favourite with the sultan, who imagined that he would be pleased with his elder brother's death, and intended to make him a present of *Muftapha*'s effects and treasures; but *Jehan Ghir* no sooner saw the dead body, than, either out of affection for his brother, or apprehension of what must be his own fate, flew himself upon the spot.

When the murder came to be made public, it had almost cost *Soleyman* his life and empire, through an insurrection of the janisaries and soldiers that *Muftapha* had brought along with him. It was, however, appeased; partly by the intrepidity, and partly by the well-timed compliances, of the sultan, who was obliged to strip *Ruftan* of his power. But the danger was no sooner removed, than he put to death *Achmet*, *Ruftan*'s successor, who had been the main instrument of quelling the mutiny, and *Ruftan* was re-instated in

peace was concluded, and the cities of *Van Marash* and *Mojul* were added to the frontiers of the *Othman* dominions on that side.

By this time two of *Soleyman*'s sons by *Roxolana* were grown to man's estate; the one *Bajazet*, and the other *Selim*. *Bajazet* was the favourite of the mother, and each hated the other. This encouraged an obscure person, at the head of no more than forty men, to appear upon the confines of *Moldavia* and *Wallakia*, and pretend to be the late prince *Mustapha*, or one of his sons; and, perhaps, he really was, the other son having been put to death soon after his father. Some, but we think with very little appearance of truth, say, that this pretended *Mustapha* was set up by *Bajazet*, in hatred to his brother. If there was any thing in this, it must be owing to the pretender's being the real son of *Mustapha*, and to *Bajazet*'s joining him, that he might put aside *Selim* from the succession, of whom he was to expect no favour. Be this as it will, it seems to be certain that *Selim* impressed his father, who was now old and infirm, with an opinion of his pretender being the creature of *Bajazet*, and the sultan ordered both of them to their respective governments. *Bajazet*, in fact, refused to obey, and retiring to *Ancyra* he raised a great army.

Differences between Soleymam's sons.

In the mean while, *Soleyman* committed the prosecution of the war against *Mustapha* to his sanjiacks, or other generals; and *Mustapha*'s soldiers deserting from him, he was taken prisoner and sent to *Constantinople*; where being put to the rack, he discovered his confederacy with *Bajazet*, and was then thrown into the sea. The *Christian* writers make this execution to have been performed while *Bajazet* was at court, and in his father's power; and that he was pardoned at the intercession of *Roxolana*. But the *Turks* are more to be depended upon, who tell us, that *Bajazet* was the chief means of suppressing *Mustapha*'s insurrection; and, that, far

be finished by the pasha *Mehemed*, who reduced above twenty cities, and placed garrisons in a great number of fortresses. The reader, however, in turning back to our *Persian* history, will find a different account of this expedition.

Adventures of Muley Hassan. *Muley Hassan*, whom *Charles* V. had made king of *Tunis*, being afraid that *Barbarossa's* armament was designed against him, fled to *Naples*, to throw himself at the feet of *Charles* for protection. He was at *Naples* when *Barbarossa* was obliged to retire from *Nice*, and he there received an account that his son *Amid* had declared for himself, and usurped his government. Upon this, *Muley Hassan*, being well provided with money, hired some *Italian* soldiers of fortune, who served under one *Lofredi*, and pass'd over to *Tunis*; but, in attempting to remount his throne, was defeated; and, being taken prisoner, his unnatural son cut out his eyes. *Tonarte*, the *Spanish* governor of the *Guletta*, for the emperor, upon this, sent for *Abdol Malek*, who was *Amid's* elder brother, and who, by a stratagem, made himself master of *Tunis*; but he died after enjoying his royalty but twenty-six days. He was succeeded by his son, a child of twelve years of age; but, being under the tuition of three barbarians, their government grew so intolerable to the people, that *Amid* was re-admitted to *Tunis*; where he cruelly put all his enemies to death, his father alone escaping through the favour of *Tonarte*, who gave him shelter in the *Guletta*.

Dragut's conquests. During this confusion, *Dragut*, a famous *Turkish* pirate in those seas, made himself master of several cities in the kingdom of *Tunis*, particularly *Mohanmedia*; and, being countenanced by *Soleyman*, he committed prodigious depredations on the *Christian* powers. Upon this, the emperor *Charles* ordered his admiral, *Doria*, to suppress the pirate, and to raze *Mohammedia*, his chief haunt; which, by the help of some knights of *Malta*, he accordinlgy did. *Dragut* applied to *Soleyman*, who, exasperated by *Doria's* successes and ravages, furnished *Dragut* with one hundred and forty sail, commanded by the pasha *Sinan*, who landed in *Sicily*. Here they took the castle of *Augusta*, and, making a fruitless attempt upon *Malta*, they sailed to *Goza*, from whence they carried off above six thousand captives. From thence they sailed to *Tripoli*, then, by the emperor's gift, in possession of the knights of *Malta*; and which, after a brave resistance made by the garrison, they took, through the treachery of a *French* renegado; but the *Othmans* broke the capitulation by depriving the garrison both of their freedom and their effects.

War in Hungary. In the year 1553, *Isabella*, the mother of *Stephen*, the young king of *Hungary*, was obliged to surrender *Transylvania* to *Ferdinand*, being unable to oppose the progress of the *Turks*, who besieged and took *Temeswar*; but, as usual, they most perfidiously broke the capitulation. They likewise took the castle of *Zolnuk*, but were repulsed in their attempt
upon

upon *Erfam* and *Agria*, with the lofs of above fix thoufand men. To the infamy of the *French* government, this year the unfidels, by the inftigation of *Henry* II. of *France*, defolated the coafts and iflands of the *Archipelago*.

It muft be admitted that the *Turks* are barbarians in al- Conquefts moft every refpect, and the beft of their own authors af- of *Soley*- ford us nothing better than a glimmering of their hiftory; *man*. while thofe of the *Chriftians* are equally uninformed as to the *Turkish* affairs. *Soleyman* had fo great a genius for conqueft, that his arms were employed in every quarter of the globe. In *Perfia* he met with but very indifferent fuccefs, though he had the inhuman pleafure of defolating the country. In his own family he was far more unfortunate. A confpiracy againft his domeftic peace was formed between *Roxolana*, his favourite miftrefs and wife, and her fon-in-law *Ruftan*, the grand-vizier. *Roxolana* had children whom fhe wanted to raife to the empire; and *Soleyman* had two fons, *Muftapha* and *Jehan Ghir*, who ftood in their way. *Chriftian* writers, very poffibly from the prepoffeffions they had againft *Soleyman*, have exalted *Muftapha*'s into the moft amiable of characters. It is certain that his father was long jealous of his ambition, and that of his other fons, and had them narrowly watched.

Whatever paffes within the walls of the feraglio, or where- Hiftory of ever the refidence of the *Turkish* emperor is fixed, is kept fo *Muftapha*, fecret, or rendered fo uncertain by different reports, that an his eldeft author is very unfafe in defcending to particulars, either of fon, facts or characters. It is, however, agreed that *Muftapha* was the darling of the empire; and, that *Roxolana*, as is common with ambitious, wicked, women, confidered him as the chief bar between her off-fpring and the throne. *Soleyman* was now old, and fhe therefore had the more power over his affections. She prevailed with him to fend *Muftapha* and his mother to the diftant government of *Cayamania*; and *Ruftan*, who had married her daughter, attempted to cut off fome part of his revenue. The better to fucceed, fhe affumed an extraordinary fit of devotion, and could not be perfuaded to cohabit again with the fultan till he folemnly married her, which he therefore did. She then inftilled into *Soleyman* notions of his danger from *Muftapha*; and, if we may believe *Chriftian* writers, attempted to poifon him. But this wickednefs not fucceeding, *Soleyman* ordered *Ruftan* to raife a great army, under pretence of marching againft the *Perfians*; but, in fact, to feize upon *Muftapha*, and fend him in chains to *Conftantinople*.

It was eafy for *Muftapha* to perceive the danger which both who is his perfon and title to the crown were in; and he was fo fummoned well beloved, that he had intelligence of the defigns againft to *Aleppo*, both. He raifed feven thoufand horfe, and began his march towards *Syria*; which was fufficient to fhew *Ruftan* that his design was difcovered; and he fuddenly marched back to *Conftantinople*, pretending that *Syria* was in quiet.

A tyrant thinks, that every act of juft precaution in a fon or fubject, is an act of rebellion; and, next year, which was 1553, he put himfelf at the head of a great army, and ordered *Muftapha* to repair to him at *Aleppo*, where he lay encamped. The prince, perhaps knowing his refiftance would be in vain, endeavoured, by a generous confidence, to win his father over, and prefented himfelf at the door of the fultan's tent dreffed in white; but perceiving he had his dagger

and put to death by *Soley-man*'s cruelty.

by his fide he left it without. Entering the tent he was met by feven mutes, who threw him upon the ground; but, either through the vigour of the prince, or their own difinclination, they were fome time in ftrangling him; upon which, the unnatural father, from a traverfe window, reproached and threatened them for their backwardnefs, and then they put an end to his life.

This was fo fecretly executed, that *Jehan Ghir*, fo called from his deformity, knew nothing of the matter. He was a kind of favourite with the fultan, who imagined that he would be pleafed with his elder brother's death, and intended to make him a prefent of *Muftapha's* effects and treafures; but *Jehan Ghir* no fooner faw the dead body, than, either out of affection for his brother, or apprehenfion of what muft be his own fate, flew himfelf upon the fpot.

When the murder came to be made public, it had almoft coft *Soleyman* his life and empire, through an infurrection of the janifaries and foldiers that *Muftapha* had brought along with him. It was, however, appeafed; partly by the intrepidity, and partly by the well-timed compliances, of the fultan, who was obliged to ftrip *Ruftan* of his power. But the danger was no fooner removed, than he put to death *Achmet*, *Ruftan's* fucceffor, who had been the main inftrument of quelling the mutiny, and *Ruftan* was re-inftated in his power.

Such is the manner, in general, in which the *Chriftian* hiftorians tell this event. The *Turkifh* hiftorians feem to admit that *Muftapha* was guilty; and fome, with probability on their fide, fay that *Jehan Ghir* was poifoned by his father's order.

New war with *Perfia*.

Perpetual action is the fureft means of keeping mutinous troops in order. The fpoils of chriftendom and *Perfia* were always agreeable to the *Turks*; and, in the year 1554, *Soleyman* denounced war againft the fhah of *Perfia*, and laid fiege to *Erivan*, which he took and deftroyed, though the fineft city in that empire. He laid wafte all the tract between *Tibris* and *Maragha*; and feveral of the *Perfian* governors, or rather princes, put themfelves under his protection, and favoured his operations. In the following fpring he marched to *Baghdad*, where, upon the fhah's humble application, peace

peace was concluded, and the cities of *Van Marash* and *Mo-ful* were added to the frontiers of the *Othman* dominions on that side.

By this time two of *Soleyman*'s sons by *Roxolana* were grown to man's estate; the one *Bajazet*, and the other *Selim*. *Bajazet* was the favourite of the mother, and each hated the other. This encouraged an obscure person, at the head of no more than forty men, to appear upon the confines of *Moldavia* and *Wallakia*, and pretend to be the late prince *Muftapha*, or one of his fons; and, perhaps, he really was, the other fon having been put to death soon after his father. Some, but we think with very little appearance of truth, fay, that this pretended *Muftapha* was fet up by *Bajazet*, in hatred to his brother. If there was any thing in this, it muft be owing to the pretender's being the real fon of *Muftapha*, and to *Bajazet*'s joining him, that he might put afide *Selim* from the fucceffion, of whom he was to expect no favour. 'e this as it will, it feems to be certain that *Selim* impreffed ', father, who was now old and infirm, with an opinion of .'s pretender being the creature of *Bajazet*, and the fultan ..dered both of them to their refpective governments. *Ba-izet*, in fact, refufed to obey, and retiring to *Ancyra* he ..fed a great army.

In the mean while, *Soleyman* committed the profecution of the war againft *Muftapha* to his fanjiacks, or other generals; and *Muftapha*'s foldiers deferting from him, he was taken prifoner and fent to *Conftantinople*; where being put to the rack, he difcovered his confederacy with *Bajazet*, and was then thrown into the fea. The *Chriftian* writers make this execution to have been performed while *Bajazet* was at court, and in his father's power; and that he was pardoned at the interceffion of *Roxolana*. But the *Turks* are more to be depended upon, who tell us, that *Bajazet* was the chief means of fuppreffing *Muftapha*'s infurrection; and, that, far from behaving undutifully, he continued in quiet during the remainder of his mother's life.

The war being now renewed between *France* and *Spain*, the coafts of the latter were again ravaged by *Soleyman*'s fleet, commanded by *Karli Ali Beg*; and we are told that they took and ranfacked *Durazzo*, which was retaken by the *Venetians*. The *Othmans* feem now to have been a formidable maritime power; for, befides the ravages they committed in *Europe* this year, they invaded and plundered *Ormus*, and the adjacent countries in the *Perfian Gulph*, and then returned by the Streights of the *Red Sea* to *Suez*; from whence the rich fpoils of the expedition were conveyed to *Conftantinople*.

We are likewife told, that, in the year 1555, *Soleyman* fent another fleet to the affiftance of the *French*; which, as ufual, made vaft depredations upon the iflands and coafts of the *Mediterranean*, and returned with great fpoils to *Conftantinople*. But, though the *Turks* mention every attempt they

Differ-ences be-tween So-leymam's fons.

His fleets ravage Spain.

made, and ravages they committed, as so many conquests, yet it is certain they kept none of the places they attacked; plunder being the only end they had in view. Their chief admiral in this expedition was *Kapudan Piala Pasha*.

His civil regulations. *Soleyman* snatched a small interval of peace, at this time, to make certain civil regulations; and, for that purpose, he drew up the *Kanun Namh*, or, *The Book of Rules*; which is, to this day, of great authority at the *Othman* court. It contains a kind of a system of the posts, precedencies, expences, and revenues of the empire. He likewise ordained, that, from thence forward, the sons of emperors should not have governments assigned them, but that they should be maintained in or near the court. Neither was he wanting to his own character in magnificence, for he now finished the jami, or mosque, which, after himself, he called *Soleymanyeh*. It stands on an eminence looking towards the harbour of *Constantinople*; but, though it undoubtedly is a most superb building, they who say, that no structure in the world is to be compared to it, exaggerate too much. *Soleyman* is said, by the *Turkish* writers, to have spent ten years in these important regulations; but we are not from that to conclude he was not, during these ten years, engaged, either by his admirals or his generals, in many warlike undertakings.

Hungarian war. *Ali*, pasha of *Buda*, after surprizing *Buboza*, in *Hungary*, made an attempt upon *Sigeth*, one of the most important places in that kingdom. Failing in this attempt, in *June*, 1556, he laid a regular siege to the same place, and pressed it, for some time, with the utmost fury; but, being continually repulsed by the courage of the garrison, under *Horwath*, he raised the siege, on the twenty-second of *July* following, after losing above two thousand men before it, and retired to *Quinque Ecclesiæ*. Notwithstanding this, he renewed the siege next year; but *Ferdinand's* generals, *Pelccher* and *Serini*, attacked and defeated his army, upon which they abandoned *Bubsza*, and many other places in the neighbourhood, and again retired, with great loss in their retreat, to *Quinque Ecclesiæ*.

Death of Roxolana. In the year 1557, died *Roxelana*, the mother and protectress of *Bajazet*; upon which, *Selim*, to prevent *Bajazet's* retreat into *Syria*, where he was sure of great support, made himself master of *Iconium*. Though this was a great disappointment to *Bajazet*, yet, being very popular, he got together an army at *Ancyra*; and, refusing all terms of accommodation proposed by *Soleyman*, he marched to attack *Selim*, or, at least, to open his way into *Syria*; but, before he could reach *Iconium*, *Soleyman* had taken care to re-inforce *Selim* with a large body of his best troops and a great train of artillery (of which *Bajazet* was destitute) and some of his best generals. Notwithstanding all this, *Bajazet*, presuming on his own popularity with his father's soldiers, ventured to give him battle. Forty thousand *Turks* fell in it; But *Bajazet*,

whole

whose chief strength lay in his *Arabian* cavalry, was, at last, obliged to retire; but did it in such good order, that *Selim* durst not pursue him; and he got more credit by that battle, on account of the vast odds of every kind which were against him, than he had done in all the preceding actions of his life.

This obliged *Soleyman*, old as he was, to pass over to *Asia*; which he did in *June*, 1559. He was followed by *Busbequius*, the *German* resident, whose entertaining letters are the most authentic accounts we have of the *Turks* at this period. He gives us a wonderful idea of the discipline, the abstinence, and the modesty of their soldiery; and he tells us, that, when certain presents arrived in the camp sent from the emperor of *Germany*, *Soleyman* received them formally in the sight of all his army, that he might shew them in what high esteem he was held amongst the *Christian* powers. His going over to *Asia* defeated all the designs of *Bajazet*, who now wanted to make his submissions; but being informed that his father was determined to destroy him, he, with great difficulty, fled with no more than twenty followers to *Persia*, where he was received by the shah *Tahmasp*.

Soleyman passes over to Asia.

Soleyman understanding this, sent two officers, *Hassan Aga* and the pasha of *Marash*, to prevail with *Tahmasp* to put him to death. The shah, at first, refused to do that, but he threw him into prison; and, the *Othman* envoys tempting him with a considerable sum, *Tahmasp* gave them leave to put him to death; which *Hassan* did with his own hands, by strangling him and three of his children, in prison. We are, however, given to understand, that, a great number of *Bajazet*'s followers repairing to him, he had the face of an army, which made *Tahmasp* uneasy. He therefore gave orders for billeting them around the country, and, being thus divided, they were all put to the sword. A fourth son of *Bajazet*'s was strangled at *Prusa*.

Puts his son to death.

Those dissentions in the imperial family at *Constantinople*, encouraged the *Christian* powers to think of recovering *Tripoli* in *Barbary*. A considerable armament, for this purpose, was fitted out by the knights of *Malta*, with the assistance of the pope and the king of *Spain*, and, in *February*, 1560, they sailed for the island of *Zerbi*, and took the strongest castle upon the island. In the mean while, *Piala Pasha*, the *Turkish* admiral, landed a body of men upon the island from eighty-five gallies, and, before the *Christians* could perfect the new fortifications they intended, attacked the remainder of the fleet, a part of it being before returned to *Malta*, and destroyed it.

Tripoli invaded.

The infidels then laid siege to the castle, which made a noble resistance. *Dragut* considering himself as the proprietor of the whole island, having taken it from a petty *Moorish* prince called *Karawan*, poured in reinforcements for carrying on the siege, and the garrison's water entirely failing them, the place was surrendered on promise of having their lives faved. In this expedition, befides their fhips, the *Chriftians* are faid to have loft eighteen thoufand men. Some *Spaniards* of great quality were made prifoners, who were obliged to ranfom their lives. *Piala* is faid to have conceal- ed the moft confiderable of them, who was fon to the duke of *Modena*, intending to put his ranfom into his own pocket. But, finding *Soleyman* very inquifitive after the young noble- man, he privately put him to death, fo that he never was more heard of. The *Turks* thus victorious, renewed or continued their depredations upon *Italy*, *Sicily*, and *Malta*, during all the year 1561. The king of *Spain*, *Philip* the fecond, indeed, fitted out a fleet againft them, under the command of his admiral *Mendoza*; but it was difperfed by ftorms, and twenty- five of his gallies, together with the admiral, were loft.

Succeffes of Soley- man. *Bufbequius*, who was then at *Conftantinople*, informs us, that *Soleyman* received the news of his great fuccefs at *Zerbi*, and, from a gallery, beheld the captive *Chriftian* fleet, and prifoners, which were brought in great pomp, with as much coldnefs and ferenity of countenance, as if the matter had not concerned him. His admiral *Piala*, and the *Othmans* in general, did not behave with the fame moderation. *Piala* intimated his conquefts, by a galley, which dragged at the poop of it one of the *Chriftians* great enfigns, with the pic- ture upon it of *Chrift* crucified, and the prifoners were treated with great indignities and inhumanity. Thefe vaft fuc- ceffes, and growing power of *Soleyman*, who now had made fuch warlike preparations, as threatened the deftruction of the *German* empire, prevailed with the emperor *Ferdinand*, to whom his brother *Charles* had refigned the empire two years before, to think in earneft of a peace with *Soleyman*, as they were then upon very precarious terms together. A diet of the empire affembling at *Franckfort*, *November* 24, 1562, for electing a king of the *Romans*, *Soleyman* fent *Ibrahim Pafha* thither, with prefents and a letter, in anfwer to the application *Bufbequius* had made, for an eight years truce. The fultan's titles, and the preamble to that letter, came up to the height of extravagance, but the conditional **Treaty with the Germans.** parts of it are very plain and equitable. The firft con- dition is, that *Ferdinand* fhould pay, as a pledge of the league, thirty thoufand ducats yearly, with two years arrears. This truce being concluded, *Ferdinand* furvived it only two years, and then it was broken, but by which party firft, is hard to be determined, for they who pretend that *Melchior Balas*, the imperial lieutenant of *Hungary*, firft began hofti- lities, allow, at the fame time, that the *Turkifh* governors were equally ready to make incurfions upon the emperor's territories, which is generally the cafe, in all governments diftant from the court, vefted with difcretionary powers, and confequently not eafily brought to trial. Be that as it will, in the year 1564, hoftilities recommenced with as much fury as ever, between the *Germans*, and the *Othmans*. The

Turks,

Turks took *Haden*, and besieged *Ungar*. As *Suendi*, the imperial general, did *Tokay* and *Erden*.

All this time, *Soleyman* was making the most prodigious preparations for war, which threw the *Christian* powers into the utmost consternation, as not knowing where the storm would break. The imperial minister at *Constantinople*, assured *Ferdinand*, that he intended to fall upon *Germany*, while *Soleyman* negociated at the court of *Vienna*, for the continuance of the peace. Mean while, hostilities continued, the *Turks* retook *Erden*, and invaded *Stiria*, where they were cut in pieces by *Charles* the archduke of *Austria*; and the fortune of the war was so various, that it was hard to say, which side suffered most. *Soleyman* carried his dissimulation so far, that his agents in *Hungary*, after suffering themselves to be taken as spies, declared, that he intended speedily to besiege *Sigeth*, *Raab*, and other important places in *Hungary*.

But the *Hungarian* war was not the chief object which *Soleyman* had at this time in his eye. *Kossum*, *Barbarossa*'s son, and *Dragut*, persuaded him, that he never could be master by land till he was so by sea, and for that purpose he must reduce *Malta*. Upon this, *Soleyman* ordered *Piala* to take thirty thousand of his best soldiers on board one hundred and forty-two gallies, seventeen galliots, twenty-three ships of burden, and other transports. The land forces were commanded by *Mustapha Pasha*, a man of seventy-five years of age. Those ships landed at *Porto Majore*, on the north-west of the island, which is no more than twenty miles long, and twelve broad. The chief strength of the island, or rather the city, of *Malta*, lay in three castles, Saint *Angelo*, Saint *Michael*, and Saint *Elmo*, which last the *Turks* determined to besiege.

The grand master of *Malta* then, was the famous *Valette*. He had had so good intelligence from *Constantinople*, that he knew of *Soleyman*'s intention, and had made preparations to receive him, but his garrison was weak, compared to the force which was to attack it. He had not above three thousand men, who properly could be called soldiers, for he could not depend upon five thousand of the country people, who had thrown themselves into the city, to avoid the enemy. The *Turks* attacked Saint *Elmo*, with amazing obstinacy, and were twice as bravely repulsed, but at the third assault they made a lodgment, which enabled them to renew their attack. Still they were repulsed by the incredible courage of the knights, and in one repulse they lost two thousand men, among whom was the brave *Dragut*. This resistance, and the vast train of artillery, and engines they had, served only to render them more resolute, and after battering down the walls of the castle to the very rock, on which it stood, they prepared for another general assault. The garrison of the castle was now reduced to a handful, and the grand

Stiria invaded.

Design upon Malta.

Preparation for its defence.

master

master offered to carry them off in pinnaces, but they refused; and the *Turks* prevailing, every man of them was put to the sword. The resistance *Mustapha* had met with amazed him, and he sent to *Soleyman* for fresh supplies, which he received under *Kossam*, who undertook the siege of the castle of Saint *Michael*.

Its siege, The brave grand master was not so fortunate in his applications. *Spain* was the power most interested in the preservation of *Malta*, and he sent to the vice-roy of *Sicily* for succours. All he could obtain, was a liberty for the knights residing there to depart, with a few gallies and some soldiers on board; but they found the ports of *Malta* so closely blocked up by a *Turkish* fleet, that they were obliged to return to *Messina*. The siege of Saint *Michael's* castle under *Kossum*, who is called king of *Algiers*, and of Saint *Angelo's* under *Mustapha* himself, was still carried on with all the destruction that artillery, engines of every kind, mining, sapping, and a more than human intrepidity, could effect. The defendants had the advantage of possessing more cool, and therefore more true, courage; and the more desperate the attacks of the *Turks* were, the more dreadful was their loss of men, for they continued to be beat off in all quarters, till at last *Mustapha* began to think of raising the siege. The grand master, by this time, had received a few inconsiderable reinforcements, and *Mustapha* had certain intelligence by deserters, that the vice-roy of *Sicily* was ordered to fail with a powerful armament for the relief of the island. At the same time he understood, that the castle of Saint *Michael* was now but slenderly garrisoned, and that one other resolute attack would carry it. This intelligence determined *Mustapha*, who had reimbarked some of his men, to recommence the siege. He attacked both castles and the town, with a fury next to madness, and they were defended with a courage that did honour to the name of *Christians*. Every person in the forts and the city, from the grand master down to the tenderest youth of both sexes, ran to the breaches and plied the infidels with such arms as they could manage, till, at last, after seven assaults with all their army and artillery, every succeeding one being more desperate than the other, they were beat off with prodigious slaughter. The attack upon what was called the new town, was renewed in like manner next day, and must have been carried, had not the grand master flown to its defence, and forced the infidels there to retire, with the loss of two thousand of their best men. *Mustapha* then attempted the breaches of Saint *Michael's* castle, but courage still prevailed over despair. The assailants found new works run up in the night behind the breaches they made in the day, and, though they repeated their storms with unusual fury, they not only were repulsed, but suffered greatly by sallies from the garrison

It

It muſt have been beyond the powers of humanity, for either the beſiegers or the beſieged to have exerted themſelves much longer than they had hitherto done. In the intervals of the attacks, *Muſtapha* attempted to treat, but the grand maſter rejected all his advances with diſdain; and in reſentment of the butchery at Saint *Elmo*, and other inhumanities exerciſed on the dead bodies of the knights, he ordered that no quarter ſhould be given to any *Turk*. *Muſtapha* was likewiſe very aſſiduous in procuring ſpies and intelligence; and the *Chriſtian* fleet being retarded by contrary winds, after the ſiege had laſted above four months, he prepared to give a general aſſault. But, on the ſeventh of *September*, *Garcias*, the vice-roy of *Sicily*, arrived at *Malta* with the long expected ſuccours, which conſiſted of ten thouſand men, on board ſeventy-two gallies. Upon this, the *Turks* broke up the ſiege with great confuſion and reimbarked before the ſuccours could throw themſelves into *Malta*. This vice-roy, upon landing his men, returned to *Sicily* with his ſhips, and *Muſtapha* having falſe intelligence that the ſuccours did not exceed three thouſand men, landed ſeven thouſand of his troops ſo as to intercept them in their march to the city; but the *Chriſtians* ſoon put them to the rout, with the loſs of two thouſand of their men; and had they known the ground none of the infidels could have eſcaped back to their ſhipping. Soon after, they ſailed out of ſight of the iſland, having loſt, during the ſiege, twenty-four thouſand of their beſt men, and twenty-four pieces of great ordnance. The loſs of the *Chriſtians* was two hundred and forty knights of the order, and about five thouſand ſoldiers. is raiſed.

Thus, to the immortal glory of the grand maſter, ended a ſiege, one of the moſt memorable we have in hiſtory. Many circumſtances occurred during the courſe of it, which we have not room to inſert; and, more than probable, many more did occur, that never came to the knowledge of the public; for it appears that the grand maſter was well ſerved with intelligence, even amongſt the *Turks*. Upon the return of the fleet to *Conſtantinople*, *Soleyman* behaved with unuſual moderation, in not inflicting the ſmalleſt puniſhment upon his unſucceſsful generals, thinking, perhaps, that the vaſt loſs he had ſuſtained was a proof of their having done their duty. He ordered *Piala*, however, to ſeize upon the iſland of *Scios*, becauſe its governor had kept a correſpondence during the ſiege with the grand maſter, and had been tardy in paying the arrears of his tribute. *Piala* executed his commiſſion with great punctuality; he ſent the governor and the principal perſons of the iſland in chains to *Conſtantinople*, and eſtabliſhed the *Mahometan* worſhip there inſtead of the *Chriſtian*. He then renewed his uſual ravages upon the coaſt of *Italy*. Modera-tion of *Soleyman*.

While the ſiege of *Malta* laſted, hoſtilities between the *Turks* and *Germans* continued in *Hungary*. *Maximilian* was *Hunga-rian* war then continues.

then emperor, and had on foot a very fine army, raised by himself and the princes of the empire, by which his troops were successful. The waywod of *Transilvania*, had assumed the title of king of *Hungary*, in hopes of obtaining the kingdom by gift from *Soleyman* his patron and protector; and this made him extremely active on the side of the infidels, who at first had some success, and *Soleyman*, old as he was, marched from *Constantinople* to support them. The pasha of *Buda* besieged *Palotta* by *Soleyman*'s order, but he was obliged by *Hoffenstein*, an imperial general, to raise the siege with loss. After that, he took *Wrisboun*, where he put to death all the *Turks* of the garrison, in revenge for the cruelties they exercised against the *Christians*. Count *Salm*, another imperial general, reduced *Dotis*, where he took the governor and the pasha of *Buda* prisoners, and put to death all the *Turks*, except fifty. After this, he reduced the forts of *Gesles*, *Witha*, *Ischolika*, and *Samboc*, without any loss. Count *Serini*, the governor of *Sigeth*, surprized a great convoy of of the *Turks*, near *Quinque Ecclesiæ*, and not only routed them with great slaughter, but took all they had in charge, which was very valuable. *Soleyman*, however, was still advancing with a vast army, and, by menacing the pashas who superintended the work with death, he threw a bridge, said to be a mile in length, over the *Drave*, in order to besiege *Sigeth*, which he actually did. The governor of the place was count *Serini*, who made so brave a defence that the anguish *Soleyman* thereby conceived, concurring with other maladies of age and sickness, he fell into a slow fever, which carried him out of the world. So profound is the secrecy of the *Turkish* government, that it is uncertain, whether he lived to see the place taken. *Christian* writers say, that he withdrew to *Quinque Ecclesiæ*, where he died on the fourteenth of *September* 1566, which was some days after the place was taken by his vizier, who was favoured by a dreadful conflagration that broke out in the town, and which, the *Turks* say, was the effect of *Soleyman*'s dying prayers for the prosperity of the *Othman* arms. When *Serini* found the place no longer tenable, he drest himself in a new suit of cloaths, and plunging with the remaining part of his garrison into the thickest of the infidels, they were all, but a few, put to the sword. The defence made by *Serini*, though not so successful, was, if possible, still more glorious than that made by the grand master. The *Turks* own that they lost before the place seven thousand janisaries, and twenty-eight thousand other soldiers, besides great officers, and volunteers, whom they did not muster. The brave *Serini*'s head was cut off after his death, and after being exposed to the rage of the infidels, it was sent by the vizier to count *Salm*, with the following short, but remarkable letter, " In token of love, I send thee the head of a most " resolute and valiant commander, thy friend. The re-
" mainder

" mainder of his body I have decently buried, as became
" fuch a man. *Sigeth* bids thee farewell for ever." The
taking of *Sigeth* and *Giula*, which was betrayed for a great
fum of money by the governor to the infidels, who, contrary
to agreement, put all the garrifon to death, as they did himfelf afterwards, was all the fruit of *Soleyman's* mighty
preparations for fubduing not only *Hangary*, but the *German*
empire.

Soleyman lived, according to *Chriftian* hiftorians, feventy- *Death and*
fix years, of which he reigned forty-fix : the *Turks* fay two *character*
years lefs. He was a prince of extraordinary endowments, *of Soley-*
he was a more elegant poet than any of his empire, the civil *man.*
policy of which he founded, and thereby he deferves the
character of being a great legiflator. He knew the *Perfian* and
the *Arabic* languages : he was magnificient, magnanimous,
faithful when rightly informed, generous when well ferved,
indefatigable to a miracle, brave in his perfon, and punctual
in his religion. With thefe great qualities, he is faid to
have been fcandaloufly uxorious, though temperate as to all
other pleafures ; and the almoft inceffant wars he carried on,
with the victories he atchieved, prove him to have been im-
moderately ambitious. His ftature was tall, and both his
perfon and features were flender, his nofe long and hooked.

The Reign of Selim the Second, furnamed Meft, or the Drunkard.

NOTwithftanding all the precautions which *Mohammed,* *Acceffion*
the prime vizier took to conceal the death of *Soleyman,* *of Selim.*
for fear of the infolence of the janifaries before the arrival
of *Selim* from *Magnefia*, whom he inftantly informed of his
father's death, that turbulent body fufpected the truth.
The vizer, to conceal it, is faid to have ordered all the phyficians and apothecaries who had attended *Soleyman* to be
ftrangled, and the dead body to be expofed to the public in
a litter, as if ftill alive, but wrapt up, as if in a fit of ficknefs, which fatisfied the janifaries.

Selim was then about forty-two years of age, and pofting
from *Magnefia* to *Conftantinople*, he there mounted the
Othman throne, and gave the ufual largeffes to the janifaries.
He next fet out for *Sigeth*, but he no fooner appeared in the
camp than the foldiers ran to their arms to defend the perfon
of their aged emperor, whom now, for the firft time, they
knew to be dead. The time between *Soleyman's* death and
his fon's arrival at the camp was forty-one days. *Selim*
having no competitor for the empire was unanimoufly acknowledged emperor by the army, and by all degrees of his
fubjects. On his acceffion to the throne, he gave twenty *his bounty*
dollars

dollars to every one of his janifaries, who were in all forty thoufand, and twenty-five to every fpahi, whofe number were fifteen thoufand. He gave a magnificent interment to his father, whofe memory is held in the utmoft reverence by the *Turks* to this day. Upon his mounting the throne a rebellion broke out in *Arabia*. The *Perfians* fhewed difpofitions to attack him, and his arms had been unfortunate in *Hungary*. All this made him defirous of a peace with the emperor *Maximilian*, which was concluded in *January*, 1568, for eight years, upon the fame terms as the former. The rebellion in *Arabia*, however, continued to rage under *Ulian Ogli*, but at laft was fuppreft by the *Othman* generals.

and fitua-
tion of his
affairs.
After this, *Selim*, for the better carrying on the war with *Perfia*, formed a project of joining together the *Don* and the *Wolga*, in that place where thofe rivers are but fix miles diftant, by a navigable canal, by which he was in hopes to fail through the *Euxine Sea*, to that of *Azof*, or the *Palus Mæotis*, and fo into the *Cafpian Sea*, and landing his army to penetrate into *Shirwan*. The care of this work was committed to the khan of *Crim*, who paffing through *Aftracan* begun the canal, but the labourers were obliged to abandon the undertaking, on account of the inclemency of the weather, and want of provifions. This project mifcarrying, rendered *Selim* more tractable as to a peace with the fhah of *Perfia*, whofe ambaffadors and prefents he received with great complacency, and the peace was concluded. He likewife made a peace with the *Venetians*, though he feems to have been ignorant of the terms of it; and his generals fuppreft a frefh infurrection in that part of *Arabia* that is called *Yaman*.

Attacks
Cyprus.
About the year 1570, *Selim* took it into his head to attempt the conqueft of *Cyprus*, then belonging to his new allies the *Venetians*, defigning with the revenues of the ifland to endow fome religious houfes he was building at *Adrianople*. While he was meditating this conqueft, the *Moors*, or *Mahometans* of *Spain*, chofe for their king *Manfur*, who was defcended from the ancient *Saracen* princes, and applied to *Selim* for fupport, but he excufed himfelf on account of his preparations againft *Cyprus*. The prime vizier *Mohammed*, a man of moderation, was againft the *Cyprian* war, but *Piala* and *Muftapha*, the fecond pafha, being for it, all that the *Venetian* ambaffador could obtain was, that one *Kobad* was fent ambaffador from *Conftantinople* to *Venice*, to make a demand of the ifland for his mafter, to indemnify him for the injuries he had fuffered from the fubjects of the republic. This demand being rejected with indignation, preparations went on on both fides, for attacking and defending the ifland. Early in the year, *Selim* begun hoftilities againft the *Venetian* territories on the continent, to prevent their affifting the *Cypriots*, and *Piala* failed with two hundred fhips of war, befides tranfports, for *Cyprus*, where he landed the

army,

army, and besieged *Nicosia*, the capital of the island, which was provided with a garrison of eight thousand horse and foot. The attack of the *Turks*, though furious, was so injudicious that they lost a vast number of men before they took the place, which they at last did, by pretending a retreat, then suddenly returning mounted the walls and carried the city by storm on the ninth of *September*; fourteen thousand of the besieged, amongst whom were the bishop, and *Dandalo* the governor, on this occasion were put to the sword by the barbarous infidels, who made a prodigious booty, the place being immensely rich, and took two hundred and fifty pieces of cannon. *Cyrina*, standing on the north-west of *Nicosia*, tho' very strong, fell next into their hands, through the cowardice of the governor; and *Mustapha* who commanded the land troops in this expedition, at last formed the siege of *Famagusta*, the strongest fortification on the island; but the season advancing, he thought proper to abandon it for that year.

During those misfortunes, the *Venetians* were not idle in soliciting succours from the *Christian* powers, and after many delays, their fleet with that of *Spain* under *Doria*, and the pope's under *Colonna*, the whole consisting of one hundred and ninety-two gallies, one hundred and twelve galeasses, or large ships, besides smaller vessels, sailed to the relief of *Cyprus*. This was about the middle of *September*, and before they landed they heard that *Nicosia* was lost Upon this *Doria* refused either to proceed, or to fight the *Turkish* fleet, and returned to *Messina*, notwithstanding all the remonstrances made by the other two admirals, who upon the departure of *Doria* thought themselves too weak for action, and failed to *Corfu*, from whence the *Venetian* admiral *Zani*, was, by order from the senate discharged from his office, and sent prisoner to *Vinice*. He was succeeded by *Venieri*, who after gaining several important advantages over the infidels in the *Mediteranean*, threw nineteen hundred men into the garrison of *Famagusta*, with a proportion of provisions, and ammunition, and bravely defeated the *Turkish* gallies. This procured the disgrace of several great officers amongst the *Othmans*, and amongst the rest of *Piala*, who was succeeded in his command by the pasha *Parten*, but the governor of *Scio* was put to death. In *April* 1571, *Mustapha* renewed the siege of *Famagusta*, the garrison of which consisted of five thousand men, and two hundred *Albanian* horse, all of them experienced troops, under *Baleoncus* and *Bragadino*, who was governor of the city. *Mustapha* proceeded by raising up mounts higher than the walls of the city, which lay low, by driving vast masses of combustible wood against the gates, and by mining the principal towers, in which they chiefly succeeded. Great part of the wall was blown up, and the *Turks* endeavouring to enter the breach were repulsed with the loss of four thousand men. Notwithstanding

Preparations of the Venetians.

The Turks defeated.

ing this, they plied the city so furiously with their artillery, that they discharged eight thousand balls against it in a day, and repeated their mines so often, that the garrison was reduced to three hundred men and seven barrels of powder. This prevailed with *Bragadino* to listen to the cries of the citizens for a capitulation ; and the *Turks* agreed that the inhabitants should enjoy life, liberty, and estate; and that the garrison should be carried to *Candia* with the honours of war. *Mustapha* perfidiously broke this capitulation, by putting *Bragadino*, and the other chief commanders, to the most torturing deaths that ingenious cruelty could devise. After this, all the fine island of *Cyprus* fell under the power of *Selim*.

but they reduce Cyprus.

During the siege of *Famagusta*, the two *Turkish* pashas, *Parteu* the admiral, and *Ali* the general, together with *Kilj Ali*, called by the *Christians Uluz Ales*, viceroy of *Algiers*, made an attempt upon *Candia*, the antient *Crete*; from whence they were driven with loss by the *Venetian* general *Justiniano*. They then plundered the now almost defenceless islands, and carried six thousand of the inhabitants into captivity. After this, *Kilij Ali* went, with a separate squadron of sixty gallies, to *Karzola*, a *Venetian* island, which was abandoned by the governor and all the inhabitants, except eight women and twenty men, who all of them took arms, and defended the town, till a storm arising, obliged the barbarians to return to their ships.

The Christian powers alarmed,

The dreadful progress of the *Turks*, as a maritime power, at last united the *Christian* princes. *Mohammed*, the prime-vizier, had foreseen this union, and strove to prevent it by opposing the *Venetian* war, and, even while *Famagusta* was besieged, the *Venetians* had a minister at the *Porte* treating of peace. The pope and the king of *Spain* understanding this, without farther deliberation, offered to enter into a league with the *Venetians*, who accepted of the same; and it was signed on the twenty-fourth of *May*, 1471. It was agreed that fifty thousand foot, and four thousand five hundred horse, should be ready, every year, in the spring, together with two hundred gallies, and one hundred other ships; and, that *Don John* of *Austria*, the king of *Spain*'s natural brother, should command the whole. The *Venetians*, at the same time; sent an ambassador to persuade the shah of *Persia* to attack the *Turks*, but he met only with evasive answers. The confederates, at the time of signing the league, had a great naval force ready, and they invited the other popish powers of *Europe* to join them.

and confederate together.

The first intelligence which *Selim* received of this formidable confederacy, was by some letters taken at sea; but, far from being daunted, he ordered his forces, both by sea and land, to proceed more vigorously than ever against the *Venetians*. They obeyed him, by committing the most horrible outrages upon the territories of that republic; and proceeded

ceeded so far, that *Venice* itself appeared to be in danger: the news of the league, however, obliged the *Turkish* admirals to re-unite all their fleet, which sailed to the bay of *Lepanto*. The rendezvous of the *Christian* ships was at *Messina*. The *Venetian* fleet consisted of one hundred and eight gallies, six galeasses, two tall, and some other smaller ships, commanded by *Venieri*. The pope sent twelve gallies, under the command of *Colonna*. *Doria*, the *Spanish* admiral, brought with him eighty-one gallies, three of which were *Maltese*; and the land forces on board, which were twenty thousand, were the flower of all *Europe*. Amongst them was *Alexander Farnese*, prince of *Parma*, afterwards the ablest general of his time. After some debates, it was resolved to attack the *Turks*, whose fleet consisted of three hundred and thirty-three sail, and their commanders were as determined as the *Christians* were upon a battle. Two so great navies never perhaps had encountered before, and had the *Turks* that day prevailed, they stood fair for universal empire. Both sides were animated with the deepest hatred to each other, and the fate of the engagement was for some time doubtful, but at last the *Christians* obtained a compleat victory. Thirty-two thousand of the infidels are said to have perished in this fight, which is the more credible, as the *Christians* were so exasperated against them, that they seldom gave quarter, and amongst them killed were all their great officers except *Parter*, and *Kiliy Ali*, who escaped with twenty-five ships. One hundred and sixty-one *Turkish* gallies were taken, forty were sunk or burnt, and about sixty smaller vessels were taken.

The Turks defeated at Lepanto.

This victory did great honour to *Don John*, who was but twenty-four years of age, and he had the generosity to ascribe it chiefly to the courage and conduct of *Venieri*, the *Venetian* admiral, before the battle, with whom he had been at variance. The loss of the *Christians* were seven thousand five hundred and sixty-six killed, many of them of the best blood of christendom, and about seven thousand wounded, amongst whom was *Don John*. Incredible were the rejoicings throughout all *Europe* for this victory, and it must fairly be owned, that the *Turks* have never, to this day, recovered the blow. When the certainty of it was reported to *Selim*, he received it with great seeming composure. Some say that he was almost choaked with grief, indignation, and despair, and that it was with difficulty that *Mohammed* dissuaded him from the barbarous resolution of ordering all the *Christians* in his dominions to be immediately massacred; but this barbarity does not agree with his general character. On the arrival of *Kiliy Ali*, who reported, that the *Christian* fleet was almost destroyed likewise, the sultan made *Kiliy Ali* his high admiral, and gave orders, throughout all his empire for fitting out a more formidable armament than that which he had lost. On the other hand, the *Venetians* retook *Suppoto*, in *Epirus*, and intercepted the *Turkish* gallies that

Progress of the Venetians.

were carrying home the spoils of *Cyprus*. They likewise obtained many other advantages. The other *Christian* confederates were not equally alert, and when *Foscarini*, who succeeded *Venieri*, put to sea, he was joined but with a very inconsiderable force, nor did *Don John* at all appear ; *Foscarini*, however, was at last joined by *Superantio*, another *Venetian* admiral, who had performed great exploits at *Corfu*, and by twenty-two *Spanish* gallies sent him by *Don John*, and with the pope's gallies, so that the whole *Christian* fleet consisted of one hundred and fifty-five gallies ; six galeasses, and twenty tall ships. *Selim*'s orders, on the other hand, had been so punctually obeyed, that, before the *Christians* had formed their junction, which they did in *August* 1572, his fleet consisted of two hundred and fifty gallies. The naval spirit of the *Turks*, however, was irretrievable, and almost all their best seamen had been destroyed in the battle of *Lepanto*. The *Spaniards*, on the other hand, being then embroiled with both *France* and *England*, acted with great caution ; and tho' *Don John*, at last, joined the confederates with fifty-three gallies, and eighteen ships of war, at *Corfu*, nothing decisive was done this season, *Don John* opposing all the vigorous measures proposed by *Foscarini*. The *Turkish* fleet under *Kilij Ali*, consisted of one hundred and sixty gallies, sixty galliots, and four great ships. But though *Kilij* was a brave experienced officer, he kept alof from a general engagement. *Superantio* and *Foscarini*, however, attacked part of the *Turkish* fleet and damaged it, but not being supported, the infidels got into the harbour of *Modon*, where *Foscarini* could not persuade *Don John* to attack them, and though they attempted to take both *Modon* and *Navarino*, the antient *Pylos*, they failed in both undertakings. *Don John*'s backwardness was very detrimental to the *Christian* cause, for it was thought, that, had *Foscarini*'s advice been followed, the fleet of the infidels must have been totally destroyed. *Don John* returning to *Messina*, *Foscarini* sailed to *Venice*, and the republic perceiving it was unsafe to trust to the confederacy, was obliged to accept of the terms *Selim* was pleased to prescribe ; and, after various negotiations, a peace was concluded in *February* 1574, by which the *Venetians* were obliged to pay to *Selim* three hundred thousand ducats, and to restore all their conquests, while the *Turks* were to keep all theirs. Such was the end of the naval operations of the year 1572.

Devotions of *Selim*. The year 1573 was mostly spent by *Selim* in the discharge of religious duties, and building or repairing houses of devotion, to conciliate the favour of heaven. The *Germans* besieged *Nova*, in *Bosnia*, but were obliged to retire with loss, while *Selim*, to wipe out the disgrace he had suffered at *Lepanto*, ordered his admirals and generals to attack *Messina* with a great armament, but all they could do was to ravage the adjacent country. In the mean while, upon the representations fentations of *Amed*, the king of *Tunis*, Don *John* failed with one hundred and five gallies, and forty ships to *Goletta*, where being joined by the pope's and the *Maltefe* fquadrons, he furprized *Tunis*, but, far from reftoring it to *Amed*, he ordered the monfter's eyes to be put out, for his unnaturality to his father, and brother, and threw him into chains. He then appointed *Mohammed* to be king of *Tunis*, and, having given orders for building a ftrong fort between that city and the *Goletta*, he returned to *Sicily*.

In the year 1574, *John*, the waywod of *Moldavia*, and natural fon to the waywod *Stephen*, having been raifed from a private ftation to that dignity by *Selim*, renounced *Moham-medifm*, upon which *Selim* appointed *Peter*, the brother to the waywod of the *Leffer Walachia*, to fucceed him. *John*, who appears to have renounced *Mohammedifm* only for political reafons, refufed to refign his government, and took into his pay a body of *Polifh* kofaks, commanded by *Sujercevius*. Upon this, *Selim* fent thirty thoufand *Turks*, and two thoufand *Hungarians*, to affift the palatinate of the *Leffer Walachia* in depofing *John*, and thefe being joined by the palatine's own forces, his whole army, confifting of one hundred thoufand men, paffed the *Moldaw*; but obferving no difcipline, they were furprifed by *John*, and *Sujercevius*, and almoft to a man cut in pieces, except the palatine, and his brother the expectant king, who paffing the river reached the caftle of *Brahilow*. *John* made a moft inhuman ufe of his victory, by defolating the country, and taking the caftle of *Brahilow*, he put to death every living creature within it, to the very dogs, and then razed the caftle. While he was befieging that place, *Sujercevius* killed fourteen thoufand out of fifteen thoufand *Turks*, who were advancing to relieve it, and the remaining thoufand threw themfelves into the caftle of *Tyma* or *Teina*, leaving the town to the mercy of *John*, who maffacred every perfon within it.

Selim, alarmed by *John*'s progrefs, ordered public prayers to be put up for the fuccefs of the *Othman* arms, and two hundred thoufand men to march againft him. At the fame time he employed agents to tamper with *Jeremiah Czarnieviche*, *John*'s favourite, who was trufted to defend the paffes of the *Danube*, and who, for a prefent of thirty thoufand *Hungarian* ducats, not only fuffered the *Turks* to pafs that river, but in a battle which enfued, went over to the infidels with thirteen thoufand of *John*'s beft troops, who being placed in the front of the army, were all of them cut to pieces, either by the *Chriftians* or by the *Turks* themfelves, who fufpected their fidelity. *John*, after performing wonders in the battle, was at laft obliged to give way to fuperior numbers, and retired to a ruined fortification, where he was, by the *Turkifh* agents, perfuaded to furrender himfelf, which he did upon terms for himfelf and his followers; but he no fooner came into the power of the pafha *Kejouji*, who

The Turks in Moldavia.

to which the Turks march with a great army

M 2   commanded

commanded the *Turkish* army, than he and his *Moldavians* were all men perfidiously put to death. The *Poles* fell with their swords in their hands, and only the brave *Swircovius*, with a few of the principal officers who were made prisoners, survived the massacre. After this, the infidels in a manner depopulated *Moldavia*, by either putting the inhabitants to the sword, or transplanting them to distant colonies.

and depopulates the country.

This year, *Selim* ordered his admiral, the pasha *Sinan*, to sail with three hundred gallies to retake *Tunis*, which service was performed with great success, in about three months time, during which the *Turks* lost thirty thousand men; so bravely was the *Goletta* and the new castle defended under the two commanders S. ... and *Salazar*, who were both taken prisoners. It is add'd, that *Sinan* most unmanfully struck old *Serbellio* when brought before him, and ordered his son to be put to death before his eyes. After the reduction of the *Goletta*, and the new fort, the *Turks* possessed themselves of *Tunis*, and king *Mohammed*'s person. Such are the chief transactions of this last year of *Selim*'s life, except the defeat of a body of fifteen hundred *Hungarians*, by the governor of *Giula*, as they were marching to surprise *Sigeth*.

They take *Tunis*.

Selim's death and character.

All we know of the sultan's death is, that, having built a magnificent bath, he entered it before the mortar was quite dry, having previously fortified himself with a large quantity of wine, against the exhalations of the mortar, and thereby contracting a head-ach, which, by degrees, threw him into an apoplexy, that carried him out of the world on the eleventh day of his illness, on the ninth of *December* 1574, after living fifty-two years, of which he reigned eight years, five months, and nineteen days. It seems to be agreed, both by *Christian* and *Turkish* writers, that he was excessively addicted to women and wine, but the latter pretend that he was never intoxicated, but inspired with divine enthusiasm. Notwithstanding this, he appears to have been of a more amiable personal character than any of his predecessors, and to have possest more private virtues. He never was guilty of cruelty, unless we charge to his account the horrible cruelties practised by his admirals and generals. Notwithstanding his favourite vices, he possest a sound judgment, and great intrepidity: he was secret, he was generous, steady, and constant, as appears by his attachment to *Mohammed* his prime vizier, though he often acted contrary to his advice. After he came to the empire he seldom took the field in person, but, notwithstanding his defeat at *Lepanto*, he may be said in general to have made a judicious choice of his great officers, both by sea and land. His being so soon able to establish his marine, is a proof of his excellent public oeconomy, and his successes against the *Christians* were wonderful, when we consider that the latter, during his

reign

reign, were arrived at a far higher pitch of power than ever they had known before. The *Venetians* were in poffeffion of a vaft marine, and the king of *Spain, Philip* the fecond, (who was the foul of the *Chriftian* confederacy) of the mines of *Peru* and *Mexico.* Add to this, that no age before, or, perhaps, fince, produced fuch a number of great *European* generals and admirals, as thofe were whom he had to fight againft. He is faid to have been conftant in his devotions, eafy even to jocofenefs and familiarity with his domeftics; a great favourer of the learned, and to have been fond of that kind of buffoonry which is in ufe among the *Mahometans.* As to his perfon, it is faid to have been clumfy, and of a middle ftature, and his face was bloated through the effects of wine.

The Reign of Morad the Third.

SELIM the fecond, was fucceeded by his fon *Morad* the third, by *Chriftian* authors called *Amurath* the third, who, after gratifying fome exorbitant demands of his infolent janifaries, ordered his brothers *Muftapha, Soleyman, Abdollah, Ozman,* and *Jehan Ghir* to be ftrangled before his face; an inhumanity of which even *Chriftian* writers talk with coolnefs, becaufe it is cuftomary and political. *Morad,* however, is faid to have dropt a tear, when he faw the mother of *Soleyman,* in defpair for the lofs of her fon, plunge a dagger into her own breaft.

After difcharging the neceffary and popular parts of government, he wrote a letter to the *Polifh* diet, recommending to them for their king, in the room of *Henry de Valois,* who had abandoned them for the crown of *France, Stephen Battori,* the waywod of *Tranfylvania.* The emperor *Maximilian,* and the great duke of *Mofcovy,* were then competitors for that crown, and *Morad* fearing leaft the election fhould fall upon *Maximilian,* conceived his letter in terms which fhewed he expected to be obeyed; which, in fact, he was, for they chofe the princefs *Anne,* of the *Jagellonian* family, for their queen, on the exprefs condition of her marrying *Stephen.* She performed the condition, and *Morad* ever after had, in the perfon of *Stephen,* a faithful and a ufeful ally.

In the firft year of his reign he gave orders for invading *Podolia,* but the kofaks broke into the dominions of *Peter,* the new waywod *Walachia,* fo that nothing paffed on that fide but mutual ravages. But the great object of *Morad,* at this time, was the war with *Perfia.* The reader in our hiftory of that country, will fee in what ftate it then was. *Morad* intending to take advantage of its diftractions, fpent three years in fecuring himfelf, both at home and abroad,

Succeeded by Morad, or Amurath.

Affairs of Poland.

Podolia invaded

by regulating his empire, and fortifying his frontiers towards *Europe*, or making peace with those *Christian* princes from whom he had most to apprehend. In the year 1576, his army consisting of two hundred and one thousand men, under *Mustapha*, encamped in the plains near the mountains of *Khieldar*, between *Khers* and *Teflis*; *Mustapha* then divided his forces, and part of them, under the pasha of *Ezerum*, attacked *Diarbeker*; *Tokmate Khan*, the *Persian* general, who had not with him above twenty thousand horse. But the *Turks* received, on this occasion, a terrible sample of the discipline and courage of their enemies; the pashas were defeated with great slaughter, till *Mustapha* moved with the main army to support them, and though the *Persians* were at last obliged to retire, *Mustapha* durst not venture to pursue them. This battle, and the mortality that immediately followed it from the stench of the dead bodies, is said to have cost the *Turks* thirty thousand men. Five thousand *Persians* were killed upon the spot, and three thousand who were taken prisoners were put to death. All their heads were ostentatiously piled up by *Mustapha* in a barbarous pyramid. That general then marched towards *Teflis*, the capital of *Georgia*, which he took possession of; but in his march his army was harrassed by the *Persians*, and distressed by famine. *Mustapha*, after dismantling *Teflis*, and receiving the submissions of several *Georgian* princes, marched towards *Shirwan*, where his army was in such want of provisions, that he detached ten thousand men to forage, but every one of them was cut off by *Tokmak*. *Mustapha*, however, afterwards surprized the *Persians* as they were dividing their spoil, and destroyed them all, excepting *Tokmak*, and a few who escaped by swimming the river. *Mustapha* then proceeded towards *Shirwan*, but the distress of his army was so great, that they mutinously refused to pass the river *Kanak*. *Mustapha*, on this occasion, discovered great intrepidity, he told the mutineers, that he was commanded by his master to pass it, and that he would pass it, though not a man should follow him. He accordingly plunged into the water, and being followed by the great officers, all the army prepared to do the same, but before half of it had entered the current, eight thousand of the most forward were drowned, nor would the passage have been effected, had not a ford been discovered at some distance, by which the rest got over. Coming into a plentiful country, the *Turks* forgot what they had suffered, and refreshed themselves for twenty days at *Eres*, where *Mustapha* left a garrison of five thousand men, and giving the province of *Shirwan*, which was now entirely reduced, to the pasha *Osman*, he prepared to return to *Constantinople*. In his march thither he lost a great many men by the *Georgians*, but he every where received submissions from the princes of the country. As to particulars, I must refer to our *Persian* history.

When

War with Persia.

Distress of the Turks.

When the winter came on, the *Persians* attacked the *Turks* Sequel of
in their quarters, and cut off vaſt numbers of them, which the *Persian*
obliged the paſha *Osman* to make a winter campaign, in
which both parties ſuffered greatly. *Osman*, however, having a communication with *Derbent*, called to his aſſiſtance
the *Tartars*, who prevented his entire ruin. *Hamzeh*, the
ſhah of *Persia*'s eldeſt ſon, defeated the paſha *Kaytas*, the
Turkiſh governor of *Eres*, and retook that city. Then
marching to *Shamakhiya*, he cut in pieces a great body of
Tartars, and forced the paſha *Osman* to abandon *Shamakhiya*,
and fly to *Derbent*, the only place in *Shirwan* that now belonged to the *Turks*. This *Persian* expedition, in twelve
months time, coſt the *Turks* ſeventy thouſand men. So great
a loſs and the difficulties which the remaining part of their
army was under to leave *Persia*, encouraged the khan of the
Crim Tartars to rebel, but he was ſurpriſed by *Muſtapha*,
who entered his country by the ſtraits of *Derbent*, and his
head was ſent to *Conſtantinople*. The *Persians* as well as the
Turks were now heartily tired of the war, and though hoſtilities ſtill continued between them, both parties, for ſome
time, did little more than endeavour to ſecure their territories by barriers of ſtrong forts.

In the ſpring of the year 1579, *Muſtapha* marched from and the
Erzerum to *Kars*, and detached the paſha *Haſſan* to relieve *Georgian*
Teflis, then beſieged by the *Georgians*. In his march *Haſſan* war.
defeated *Ali Kouli Khan*, and *Simon*, the *Persian* generals, who
way-laid him at the ſtraits of *Tomanis*, and took the former
priſoner. *Haſſan* having relieved *Teflis*, was again way-laid
on his return, and muſt have been deſtroyed by *Simon*, had
not *Ali Kouli Kan* inſtructed him how to deliver himſelf,
upon promiſe of his liberty, which the *Turk* ungenerouſly
refuſed to fulfil. *Simon*, however, cut off his rear, and took
all his treaſure, and when *Haſſan* joined *Muſtapha*, at *Kars*,
the place of the general rendezvous, the whole of the
Turkiſh army was ſo much reduced, that, being unable to
attempt any thing of importance, *Muſtapha* diſbanded them.

Morad had ſet his heart ſo much upon this expedition,
that he ordered *Kilij Ali*, his admiral, to build forts in *Min-*
grelia, to facilitate the paſſage into *Georgia* by the *Euxine Sea*,
but thoſe forts were ſoon demoliſhed by the inhabitants.
Thus far the *Persian* war may be ſaid to have been highly
diſgraceful, and detrimental to *Morad*. He threw the blame
of his miſcarriages upon *Muſtapha*, whom he diſgraced, and
gave his command to the paſha *Sinan*, whom he likewiſe
made grand vizier; *Mohammed*, who had ſo long enjoyed
that poſt having been publicly ſtabbed by a ſoldier, whoſe
pay he had withheld. This happened in the beginning of the
year 1580, when *Morad* ordered *Sinan*, the new grand vizier
to march with a freſh army againſt the *Persians*, who now
begged for peace, but it was refuſed them by *Morad*, and
their

their ambaſſador impriſoned. Upon this, hoſtilities proceeded, *Teſti* was again beſieged by the *Georgians*, and the *Turks*, under the paſha *Mohammed*, were defeated in attempting to relieve it. *Sinan* was not more fortunate than *Mohammed*. The *Perſians*, under *Tokmak* and *Simon*, cut off nine thouſand of his troops as they were foraging, and all he could do was to ſupply *Teſis* with proviſions, while the rains prevented his building a fort to ſecure the important paſs of *Temaris*. Unfortunately for *Moral*, his generals hated one another. *Mohammed* endeavoured to deſtroy a *Georgian* prince who turned *Mahometan*, and aſſumed the name of *Muſtapha*, but the *Georgians* bravely killed one of the *Turkiſh* paſhas, and cut off the ear of another, and wounded *Mohammed* himſelf. Thus he not only eſcaped from his danger, but having informed *Morad* of the plot laid againſt him, he was diſtinguiſhed by the ſultan with an imperial veſt, as a mark of his approbation, while *Sinan* was diſplaced from his vizirſhip, and was ſucceeded by the paſha *Shans*. The management of the *Perſian* war, in the year 1582, was then committed to *Ferhat*, a general of great reputation, which he loſt by his conduct, for he was defeated by the *Perſians*; and *Muſtapha*, the *Georgian*, renouncing *Mahometiſm*, he was obliged to return to *Erzerum*, while the paſha *Oſman* was appointed to ſucceed him in the command of the army, in which he met with ſuch difficulties, through the jealouſy of the other paſhas, that *Morad* was obliged to ſend *Kily Ali* with a fleet to aſſiſt him.

Venetian affairs.   *Morad* was, at this time, ill of the falling ſickneſs, and the war between him and the *Venetians* was upon the point of being renewed, through the horrid barbarities committed by *Limo* the *Venetian* admiral, in the *Adriatic Gulph*, upon ſome *Turkiſh* ladies, bound for *Tripoli*. But upon *Morad's* complaint *Emo* was put to death by the *Venetian* ſenate, and all that *Emo* had deprived the *Turks* of was reſtored, but the honour and lives of the ladies, who had been firſt raviſhed, and then thrown into the ſea. *Morad*, the ſame year, was farther embarraſſed, by the miſmanagement and corruption of his governors in *Egypt*, where the paſha *Ibrahim*, whom *Morad* had intended to be his ſon-in-law, was guilty of the greateſt cruelty and rapaciouſneſs, but made his peace with the ſultan by making him a preſent of a prodigious ſum, which he had plundered from the *Egyptians*.

Great loſſes of the Turks.   The poſt of prime vizier being at this time vacant, it was beſtowed upon the paſha *Oſman*, the *Othman* general againſt the *Perſians*, who recovered *Tibris* in the year 1585; but, like his predeceſſors, he was guilty of great cruelty and rapaciouſneſs, and was defeated by *Hamzeh*, the *Perſian* prince, in ſeveral bloody battles, but at laſt *Hamzeh*, in his turn, was routed by *Oſman*, who, at the ſame time died, of an ague and flux. His victory, which coſt him twenty thouſand men,

was,

was, in fact, a defeat, for his successor was harrassed in his march by Hamzeh The Turks, however, reached Wan, where they found they had lost eighty-five thousand men in the expedition ; and all they could do was to send some relief to Teflis; so their army was disbanded. This encouraged the Persians to besiege Tibris; but Ferhad in the year 1586, obliged them to raise the siege, and lay with his army in the neighbourhood four years. Christian authors give us more particulars of this campaign, for they tell us, that prince Hemzeh, who continued to do wonders against the Turks, was betrayed by the turkmans in his service, who abandoned the siege of Tauris, and set up Hamzeh's younger brother for king, but prince Hamzeh soon defeated them, and struck off the head of the khan Mohammed their general. He then that returned to the siege of Tauris, which he was obliged to abandon by fresh commotions, and his being a second time betrayed by the turkmans, and other great lords, whom the Turks had privately bribed. This conspiracy was more general than he at first imagined, and, being encouraged by his brother Ismael Hamzeh, who by some is said to have been king of Persia at that time, he was murdered, and thus the Othmans were delivered from their most formidable enemy

In December, this year, hostilities recommenced between the Hungarians and the Turks, and in 1587, they took several places from one another; but count George Serini, in an inroad they made into the imperial territories, attacked them while they were on their return loaden with plunder, and carrying with them a great number of Hungarian captives, with so much success, that he killed two thousand upon the spot, made thirteen hundred prisoners, with fifteen hundred horses, and recovered all the captives and booty; he himself losing only eleven men, though a great many of his army were wounded. Morad, understanding that the Turks had begun those hostilities, ordered the pasha of Buda to be strangled for violating the league, and gave his command to the pasha Sinan, who was equally turbulent as his predecessor, but was defeated by the imperial general, with the loss of three thousand men killed, besides two hundred drowned. The Turks, after this, lost several places in Upper Hungary, and Morad disapproving of Sinan's conduct removed him likewise

Hunga-rian war.

Abbas, commonly called the Great, was now shah, or king of Persia, and Ferhad still continued to command the Turkish troops in that country; but, in the middle of his career against the Georgians, he was checked by a mutiny of his army. Notwithstanding that, he still kept his footing in Persia, so that the shah was obliged to purchase peace by giving up to the Turks the provinces of Revan, Ghiurjeh, and Herabag, and all the conquests the Othmans had made in his dominions, together with his brother as a hostage.

This

Queen
Elizabeth
applies to
Morad.

This peace with *Persia* was for ten years, and is by *Christian* writers said to have been concluded in the year 1588, which was so famous for the defeat of the *Spanish* armada, by queen *Elizabeth*. That princess had not disdained to apply to *Morad* for assistance against the king of *Spain*; and she sollicited him to employ his fleet against her enemies, and for succour to *Don Antonio* king of *Portugal*, who had been dispossessed by the *Spaniard* of his crown. She had likewise informed *Morad* of *Philip*'s immoderate ambition, and the vast riches he drew from his *American* dominions, and of the overthrow she had given his fleet. *Morad* answered her letter in very courteous terms, but if this letter is genuine, and the date of it right, viz. the fifteenth of *September* 1589, the peace with *Persia* could not have been concluded, for *Morad* there speaks of his being on the point of subduing that people, whom he calls, " accursed heretics."

A Mutiny

Be that as it will, in 1589 the *Othman* court, as indeed it generally is, being split into factions, a strong party was formed against the defterdar, or high treasurer of the empire, and the janisaries, who are always the foremost in commotions at *Constantinople*, accused him of adulterating the coin in which he paid them, and laying them under unnecessary taxes. As it is easy to see the beginnings of a commotion at *Constantinople*, by the flocking together of the mutineers, the aga, or commander of the janisaries, was ordered to appease them, but he not succeeding was displaced, and another person who was to have been *Morad*'s son-in-law appointed aga in his room; but when he wanted to exert his authority, he was obliged to fly to save his life. A fire, either wilful or accidental, breaking out, the janisaries were so far from endeavouring to quench it, that they hindered others from doing it, so that it consumed above fifteen thousand houses, (if the number is not mistaken for fifteen hundred), with a great number of public buildings, and continued to demand the person of the defterdar, who had taken refuge in the imperial palace. According to the *Turkish* historians, *Morad* gave an uncommon specimen of magnanimity on this occasion. Far from gratifying the insolence of the mutineers, who had blocked up his palace, and threatened death to his ministers and himself, he armed his domestics, who in the *Othman* court are very numerous, and of a sudden throwing open the gates, the janisaries were attacked with such vigour that one hundred and seventeen were instantly killed, and, before the rest could recover their consternation, they were suppressed. But

suppress-
ed.

Morad thought it sufficient that he had by this well timed active resolution, preserved the imperial dignity from contempt, for he suffered the pasha *Sinan*, now his prime vizier, to interceed for the mutineers, whom he pardoned, all but the

ring

ring-leaders, who were thrown in the fea. He even ordered the janifaries to be paid in good money, abolifhed the taxes complained of, and gave the authors up to the fury of the people, who put them to death.

About this time, the long fubfifting peace between the *Poles* and the *Othmans*, received fome intermiffion, by the *Polifh* kofaks, invading *Koflan*; as the *Tartars*, who were tributary to the *Turks*, did *Podolia*. But when thofe mutual incurfions were on the point of producing a breach between *Morad* and *Sigifmund*, king of *Poland*, an accommodation was effected by the mediation of queen *Elizabeth*. *Peace with Poland.*

That great princefs had, at this time, vaft influence in the *Othman* councils. For when *Morad* faw it neceffary to keep his foldiery employed in fome foreign war, a party in the divan follicited him ftrongly to declare againft *Spain*, and it was thought that he would have followed that advice, had it not been that *Ofman*, now grand vizier, and the pafha *Haffan*, of *Bofnia*, determined him to break with the emperor of *Germany*, *Rodolph* the Second. Pretences were always ready for a war between thofe two ftates; and, though *Morad* made a fhew of his being unwilling to break the eight years truce, yet he ordered *Haffan* to invade *Croatia* with fifty thoufand men, in refentment of the injuries he pretended his fubjects had received from the *Auftrians*. This happened in the year 1591, and, next year, *Haffan* befieged and took *Wihitz*, the capital of *Croatia*, but the chief command in this war was given to *Sinan*, who hoped thereby to retrieve his character, and gratify his avarice. The emperor found himfelf unable, at firft, to withftand the torrent: fix thoufand of his foot, and five hundred of his horfe, were cut to pieces in one place, and feven thoufand in another; but the latter fold their lives fo dearly, that they killed twelve thoufand of the infidels. It was reckoned, at this time, that the *Turkifh* army in *Croatia*, and *Hungary*, amounted to one hundred and fixty thoufand men. The flownefs of the *Germanic* body, prevented the emperor from being able to oppofe this vaft force; and, about *September* this year, the infidels made a confiderable progrefs in *Hungary*. The emperor, at laft, found means to draw together about forty-five thoufand men, and threw a bridge over the *Drave*. The plague, at this time, began to rage in the *Turkifh* army, thro' its communications with *Conftantinople*, and, not caring to venture a general engagement, they drew off to winter quarters, in their own territories. All this time the hoftilities had been carried on with the utmoft fury. War had not been formally declared on either fide, and the emperor complained by writing, of the manifeft injuries and infults he had received, particularly in the perfon of his embaffador, whom the *Turks* had imprifoned; but was anfwered by *Sinan* only with recriminations, for his not fending the ftipulated tribute; and thus hoftilities went on. The *Turk-* *Affairs of Germany.*

ifh

ish garrison of *Petrina* spread great devastations through the imperial territories, where they took the town of *Martenize*, with the forts of *St. Hedwig* and *Isna*, and other places, putting the inhabitants, at the same time, to death, or which was worse, carrying them into captivity. They, however, were checked, in attempting to surprize *Nubusel*, in *Hungary*.

Courage of an abbot,

Hassan Pasha, of *Bosnia*, the most active general against the imperialists in this war, understanding that *Sifeg*, one of the strongest towns in *Croatia*, and built near the confluence of the rivers *Kulp*, and *Save*, and the bulwark of the imperial territories on that side, was governed by an abbot, he sent him an insolent letter, requiring him to give up the place; and, at the same time, to make sure of it, he corrupted the abbot's chief domestic to betray it. The abbot received *Hassan's* letter, at first, with great complacency, and having discovered the treachery of his domestic, he learned as much as he could from the messenger, and then ordered them to be bound together, and thrown into the *Save*. Another messenger was dispatched to know what had become of the first. He was assured, by the abbot, that he had been dismissed some days before, and, that he was very willing to give up the place, if *Hassan* would send some officers of rank, with a proper number of men, that it might justify his not holding it out. *Hassan* complied with this, and, in three days time, a large body of *Turkish* horse arrived before the castle, and, finding the gates open, five hundred of them entered it; when a port-cullis, being suddenly dropped, barred the rest from entrance, and every *Turk* **who puts a body of Turks to death.** who had got within the place was put to death. This resolute action greatly exasperated *Hassan*, who swore he would raze the castle, and pull the abbot's skin over his ears. He accordingly advanced with an army of thirty thousand men, and, having taken *Trenschin*, in *June*, 1593, he laid siege to *Sifeg*, which he battered so furiously, that it was in danger of being taken, had not a detachment of the imperialists, under general *Eggenberg*, about the twenty-first of *June*, seasonably advanced to its relief. The number of the *Christians* was not above four thousand men, but they were encouraged by count *Averfberg*, to attack the infidels, which they did with so much resolution, that the latter, after a long dispute, were broken, and *Averfberg*, cutting off **Eighteen thousand of them killed.** their retreat, by a bridge they were to pass, eighteen thousand of them were put to the sword, or drowned, no quarter being given on either side. Amongst the slain, was *Hassan* himself, with almost all the chief officers. The troops whom *Hassan* had left to continue the siege, hearing what had happened, attempted to destroy their powder and provisions, and fled with the utmost precipitation, while the *Christians* made themselves masters of their tents, baggage, and artillery.

This

War with
Germany.

This glorious defeat of the *Turks* exasperated *Morad* so
much, that he formally declared war against the emperor,
and the beglerbeg of *Greece*; about *September*, took *Sifeg*,
and put the brave garrison to the sword, whilst *Sinan Pasha*,
at the head of forty thousand men, took *Weisbrun*, and
Palotta, the garrisons of which, contrary to the capitulati-
ons, were put to the sword, and made himself master of all
the country adjacent, to the lake of *Balaton*. By this time,
the *Christian* army in *Hungary*, amounting to about eighteen
thousand men, besieged *Alba Regalis*, under count *Hardeck*,
governor of *Raab*, but was obliged to raise it about the beginning of *November*, by the approach of the pasha of *Buda*,
with twenty thousand men, to relieve the place. *Hardeck*
had just time to draw up his army, and, under vast disadvantages, he attacked and defeated the infidels, who lost eight
thousand men on the spot, with all their artillery and convoy, which was intended for the relief of the place. *Hardeck*, after this, set fire to the suburbs of *Alba Regalis*, and
returned to *Raab*. Though the season was far advanced,
count *Teffenbach*, another imperial general in *Upper Hungary*,
with about fourteen thousand men, on the nineteenth of
of *November*, took by storm the fortress of *Zubalak*, which,
till then, was deemed to be impregnable, and put all the
garrison to the sword; it being now the common practice of
the *Christians*, as well as the *Turks*, to give no quarter. He
then marched against *Filek*, and understanding that the
pasha of *Temeswar* was advancing to relieve it, with eighteen
thousand men, *Teffenbach* left half of his army to continue
the siege, and, with the other half, he totally defeated the
pasha, who was killed, as were six thousand of his soldiers.
The booty made by the *Christians* on this occasion, was very
great, both in artillery and provisions. Upon *Teffenbach's*
return to the siege, he was joined by count *Palfi*, with six
thousand men, and they pressed the place so furiously, that,
though it was strong and resolutely defended, they carried it
by storm, and put all the garrison to the sword, excepting
eight hundred, who, having retired with their wives and
children, to an inner castle, were admitted to a capitulation.

The *Turks*
defeated.

So many repeated blows and losses, as the *Turks* had suffered this campaign, threw them into such a consternation,
that they abandoned *Dirstein*, *Somosko*, *Setichine*, *Blavestein*,
Sallek, *Ainache*, *Sollock*, *Westhe*, and many other places *Peter
the Hussar*, a *German* officer, defeated the sanjak of *Palotte*;
as count *Grafwin* did a detachment of three thousand *Turks*,
most of whom were either killed or drowned. In short, it
was thought that a territory, equal in extent to the *Lower
Austria*, was this year recovered from the infidels, when the
severity of the season obliged the imperialists to go into winter quarters.

It

It was no wonder if a war, ſo ſucceſsfully and ſo furiouſly carried on by the *Chriſtians*, exaſperated the *Turks* at *Conſtantinople* to the laſt degree. *Morad* fell into a kind of a melancholy, and, being naturally ſuperſtitious, his clergy interpreted certain dreams he had been haunted with, as if his prophet had threatened him and his empire with deſtruction, if he did not direct the whole of his force againſt the *Chriſtians*; which he vowed to do. The campaign, therefore, of the year 1594, was carried on with equal fury as the preceding, and ſo reſtleſs were the *Turks*, that it may be ſaid to have laſted through all the winter; for, in the middle of *January*, *Teffenbach* put to the ſword one thouſand five

hundred *Turks*, who were making inroads. The archduke, *Matthias*, now commanded in chief for his brother the emperor, and opened the campaign ſo early, that, on the eighth of *March*, he beſieged and took *Novograd*, which ſurrendered by capitulation. This important acquiſition was followed by that of *Breſenza*, *Sigeſt*, and *Baboſtche*; all of them ſtrong places, and taken by count *Scrini*. *Hatwan*, in *Upper Hungary*, was beſieged by count *Teffenbach*, who defeated the paſha of *Buda* in his attempt to relieve it. In this action, the *Turks* loſt two thouſand five hundred men, and thirteen pieces of cannon; and, at the ſame time, *Jaſprim*, and *Zabola*, fell into the hands of the imperialiſts, and *Teffenbach* reſumed the ſiege of *Hatwan*.

By this time, the ſiege of *Gran*, the ancient *Strigonium*, and once the capital of *Hungary*, was undertaken by the archduke, with forty-four thouſand men; but though he made a great progreſs in it, the defence of the garriſon was ſo obſtinate, that he was obliged to raiſe it, on the twenty-eighth of *June*, as *Teffenbach*, whoſe army was greatly weakened by his numerous encounters, was obliged to do

that of *Hatwan*. It was during this campaign, that the *Raſcians*, a people who live on the banks of the *Danube*, rendered deſperate, through the oppreſſions of the *Turks*, threw off their yoke, ſeized their veſſels, beat the paſha of *Temeſwar*, at the head of fourteen thouſand men, in two battles; took *Baczkerek* and *Ottadt*, again beat the paſha of *Temeſwar*, killed ten thouſand of his men, and took eighteen pieces of cannon; and, at laſt, took *Werſetza* and *Lutz*. After that, they put themſelves under the emperor's protection.

Sinan Paſha was all this while aſſembling his army, which conſiſted of one hundred and fifty thouſand men, and providing for the ſecurity of his maſter's frontiers, and, after taking ſeveral leſs important places, in the end of *July* he laid ſiege to *Raab*, the garriſon of which conſiſted of about five thouſand men, under count *Hardeck*. As this was a city of the utmoſt importance, for the ſafety of *Vienna* itſelf, the utmoſt efforts were made by the archduke to relieve it,

but

but, though the *Turks* loft a prodigious number of men, they at laft defeated the *Chriftians*, in the ifle of *Schut*, and carried on the fiege with fuch refolution, after this victory, that twelve thoufand of them were killed in two attacks. Their obftinacy, however, at laft prevailed, and count *Haideck*, after obtaining a proper certificate from his officers, that the place was no longer tenable, furrendered it *and taken* to *Sinan*, for which he afterwards, according to the bloody *by the* politics of the court of *Vienna*, firft loft his right hand, and *Turks.* then his head, upon a fcaffold, as if he had been corrupted by the infidels. This was the greateft blow the imperialifts had received fince the beginning of the war, and was far from being counter-balanced, by their taking *Caftrowitz*, *Petrina*, *Sifeg*, and *Gara*.

After the conqueft of *Raab*, *Sinan* laid fiege to *Komorra*, *Progrefs* about four miles from *Raab*, fituated in the ifland of *Schut*, *of the war.* both by land and water. But, being abandoned by the *Tartars*, who returned home, and in their return, did incredible mifchief to the inhabitants of the places through which they paffed, and being hard preffed by the archduke, *Matthias*, he was obliged to raife the fiege, and put his army into winter quarters. Before the end of this campaign, a confpiracy was difcovered, by which the *Tartars*, in conjunction with fome *Tranfylvanian* lords, engaged to deprive *Segifmund Battori*, of that principality, and to give it to *Balthazar Battori*: but *Sigifmund* being put upon his guard, found means to trepan the confpirators, and put them all to death, in his capital of *Claufenburg*. *Sigifmund*, perceiving that the *Othman* court was at the bottom of this confpiracy, immediately entered into an alliance with the emperor *Rodolph*, and perfuaded the waywod of *Walachia*, and the palatine of *Moldavia*, to do the fame. This defection was of infinite prejudice to the *Othman* intereft. *Michael*, the waywod of *Walachia*, cut in pieces one thoufand janifaries, and all the *Turks* and *Jews*, who, againft his will, had been fettled in his dominions, and then he laid in afhes *Dziurdzowa*, a large *Turkifh* town on the *Danube*. After this, he furprized and put to death, a body of *Turks* who fought to kill, or to carry him off prifoner, and put to the fword all the *Turkifh* inhabitants of *Phlokh*, a great open town on the *Danube*, lying between *Vrofczok* and *Nicopolis*. He then marched over *unfuccefs-* the *Danube*, which was then frozen, and, having on the ice, *ful for the* defeated a large body of *Turks*, he furprifed and rifled, the *Turks.* rich city of *Brailowa*. Being unable to take the caftle, he repaffed the *Danube*, and routed a large body of *Turks* drawn from their adjacent garrifons. After this, he took and plundered *Silifhria*, a great city of *Bulgaria*, put the inhabitants to the fword, and burnt it to the ground.

According to the *Chriftian* writers, thofe difgraces and *Death and* loffes made fo great an impreffion on *Morad*, who was now *character* afflicted with the ftone, and a complication of diftempers, *of Morad.*

parti-

particularly the falling sickness, that he died on the eighteenth of *January*, 1595, in the fifty-second year of his life, and the nineteenth of his reign. By the best accounts we have of his person, his look, and manner, were more graceful and mild, than those of his predecessors. He was temperate, just, and religious, but he was thought to be too much under the power of his female relations, and to be too avaricious. His frequent changes of ministers and generals, shews that he was neither constant, nor cruel.

The reign of Mohammed the Third.

Cruelty of his successor. THIS emperor began his reign with a more than usual act of cruelty. He was the eldest son of *Morad*, and had nineteen brethren alive. *Morad*'s death being concealed from them, he invited them to a feast, where he ordered them all to be strangled; and, to compleat the horror of the entertainment, he is said to have caused ten of his father's wives and concubines, to be thrown into the sea, for fear they should have been pregnant. As the accession of this emperor, was owing to the nomination of the pashas, without consent of the army, the janisaries mutinied, and it was with difficulty they were appeased. But another insurrection broke out, when *Mohammed*, as it were, to shew the public he had no rival of his own family to fear, ordered a tent to be set up, and the dead bodies of his father and his nineteen brethren, to be exposed to the view of the people. The whole city flew to arms, while the emperor, after this inhuman exhibition, was feasting with his great pashas. But the grand vizier, partly by fair words, and partly by the terror of the artillery drawn out of the arsenal, quieted the disorder.

Confederacy against him. The confederacy formed between the emperor, and the *Moldavian*, *Walachian*, and other *Transylvanian* princes, at the end of the late reign, still subsisted, and in the beginning of this, they gained many advantages over the *Turks*, and took from them several places of importance. The *Walachians* in particular, intercepted *Sinan Pasha*, upon his return to *Constantinople*, and stripped him of all the plunder he had been so long amassing. *Mohammed*, looking upon those princes to be so many rebels, bestowed *Walachia* upon one *Bogdanus*, a descendant of its ancient princes, and ordered the *Tartars* to support him, but in their march they were defeated by the *Walachians*, with the loss of eight thousand men. *Aaron*, the waywod of *Moldavia*, was equally fortunate. He encountered the khan of *Tartary*, as he was advancing, by *Mohammed*'s orders, to dispossess him of his dominions;

dominions, and having, in three battles, put twelve thousand of them to the sword, he retook *Bender*, *Schinitz*, *Tigna*, and *Mekhnis*, with the country of *Bobraga*; and, afterwards, encountering *Janikula*, *Bogdan's* son, he killed eight thousand of his men, and thus cleared his country of the *Tartars*.

Had the princes of this confederacy been true to one another, it is probable they would have driven the *Turks* out of *Hungary*. The famine which, at that time, reigned amongst the *Tartars*, who had entered the country, was such, that their women eat their own children; so that scarcely eight thousand, out of eighty-five thousand, were alive. The waywod of *Walachia*, took *Schimele Orosiga*, where the *Turkish* magazines were preserved, *Kilek*, *Galempe*, *St. George*, and then laid siege to *Laganok*. To support this success, *Rodolph* sent above seventy thousand men into the field, under the command of the archduke, *Matthias*. The pasha of *Buda* was defeated near *Temeswar*, and the pasha *Ferhad*, in *Walachia*, with the loss of eight thousand men, by *Nadasti*, the imperial general. During all these successes, *Sigismund*, the prince of *Transylvania*, became jealous of the waywod of *Moldavia*, as deserting the common cause, by holding intelligence with the *Turks*; and his suspicions being confirmed, by certain intercepted letters, he seized him, his wife, and sons, sent them to *Prague*, and, gave the waywodship to *Stephen Rozwan*. *Mohammed*, perceiving that *Sigismund* was the soul of the confederacy that had done him so much hurt, endeavoured to detach him from it, by offering him the waywodships of *Moldavia*, and *Walachia*, but *Sigismund* stood firm to his engagements with the emperor. Every day added to the losses of the *Turks* in those countries, and the discontent at *Constantinople*, for continuing the war, grew so great, that the emperor was reproached to his face, by one of the old janisaries, for his perfidy, and the mismanagement of his ministers. After this, *Gran* was besieged by count *Mansfeld*, an imperial general. The pasha of *Buda* endeavoured to relieve it, but was defeated, with the loss of fourteen thousand men, by the counts *Palfi*, and *Swertzenburg*. And that important city, after a vigorous resistance, and seeing a fresh army of the *Turks* defeated under its walls, was obliged to surrender to the imperial arms. The *Turks* next lost *Vicegrad*. The prince of *Transylvania* defeated a body of thirty thousand of them, and besieged *Fagiat*, which ten thousand *Turks* endeavouring to relieve, they were all of them, excepting five hundred, cut in pieces. *Mohammed*, exasperated beyond all temper, by those and many other losses, ordered the pasha *Ferhad* to be put to death, and restored *Sinan* to the command of the army. He accordingly passed the *Danube*, but his numerous troops were encountered and defeated by the *Transilvanians*, with vast slaughter, as was the pasha of *Bosnia*, who invaded *Croatia*

Progress of it.

Losses of the Turks;

afia, with twenty thousand men. The infidels were not more fortunate in their other attempts in this country. They were obliged to raise the siege of *Petrina*, and the *Zakulians*, a people to the north-east of *Transilvania*, throwing off the *Turkish* yoke, joined *Sigismund* with forty thousand men. Upon which, the pasha *Sinan*, who had passed the *Danube* with seventy thousand of the best *Turkish* troops, retired to *Bukhorest*, and *Sigismund* stormed *Fergovisla*, where he put all the garrison, but the *Turkish* governor, to the sword, as he did four thousand more *Turks*, who came to reinforce it. *Sigismund* continuing his progress, advanced against *Buckhorest*, which *Sinan* abandoned, and then he took *Zorga*, with such loss to the infidels, that, in the twelve last days of *October*, twenty-six thousand of them were put to the sword, with the loss of no more than two hundred and fifty *Christians*; and then *Sigismund* returned to *Alba Julia*.

who employ the *Crim Tartars* against the *Christians*.

The policy of the *Turkish* court seems to have been, to employ the *Crim Tartars* against the *Christians*. Accordingly, in the year 1594, the khan invaded *Moldavia* with seventy thousand men, to make one *Sudriak* waywod of *Zamoski*. The great chancellor of *Poland*, out of hatred to *Sigismund*, invaded it at the same time, and, prevailing on the khan to return home, he displaced the waywod *Stephen*, and put one *Jeremy* in his room; who, though the vassal of *Poland*, agreed to pay tribute to *Mohammed*. The hatred of the *Poles* to the *Turks*, thus giving way to their enmity with *Sigismund*, the latter sent the degraded waywod, *Stephen*, with an army, to drive them out of *Moldavia*; but he was defeated and put to death, and the new waywod called the *Tartars* in to his assistance. The war now raged with more fury than ever all over *Hungary*, *Transylvania*, and *Moldavia*, but in general, greatly to the disadvantage of the *Turks*; who, if the *Poles* had joined the *Christian* confederate princes, might have been driven to the walls of *Constantinople*.

War proclaimed.

Such was the state of affairs in the beginning of the year 1596, when *Mohammed* ordered war to be proclaimed at *Constantinople*, against the emperor, and *Sigismund*. Being dissatisfied at the conduct of *Sinan*, who was now above eighty years of age, he recalled him, with intention, as was believed, to put him to death. But *Sinan*, making his peace with his money, died, as it was thought, of grief, for his bad success against the *Christians*. About the same time, the *Georgians* again took arms against the *Othmans*; and *Abbas*, the shah of *Persia*, as may be seen in the history of that reign, obtained vast advantages over them. But *Mohammed*, intent to subdue the *Christians*, declared that he would march to *Hungary* in person, at the head of the greatest army that the porte had ever sent to that country. *Lippa* was besieged by the *Turks*, but with no effect. They, however, recovered

Klissa,

Kliſſa, in *Dalmatia*, and count *Palfi* took *Sambok*, lying between *Buda* and *Alba Regalis. Sigiſmund* laid ſiege to *Temeſwar*, which forty thouſand *Turks* and *Tartars* attempted to relieve, but tho' he defeated them, and killed five thouſand of them, they repeated their attacks ſo vigorouſly, that he was obliged to abandon the ſiege. Towards the end of *July, Maximilian*, of *Auſtria*, the head imperial general, took poſſeſſion of *Vatchia*, and, in the middle of *Auguſt*, laid ſiege to *Hatwan*, a ſtrong fort in *Upper Hungary*, lying between *Buda* and the *Egra*, and, having taken it, put four thouſand of the *Turks* to the ſword, with the loſs of only three hundred of the imperialiſts.

Mohammed, at laſt, took the field, and left *Buda* at the head of two hundred thouſand men, purpoſing, as he gave out, to carry the war to the gates of *Vienna*, which the imperialiſts actually began to fortify. Upon his approach with this mighty army, the garriſon of *Hatwan* abandoned it; and, after detaching forty thouſand men to *Temeſwar*, he laid ſiege to *Egra*, which had often baffled the arms of his predeceſſors. A reader who runs over the particulars of one ſiege, by the *Turks*, may form an idea of them all, obſtinate and inceſſant attacks, a dreadful carnage, and perpetual minings and batterings, made up the whole. *Mohammed*, afraid that the imperial army was advancing to relieve the place, attacked it with ſo much fury, that, after a brave reſiſtance, he took it by an honourable capitulation; which was violated by the *Turks*, in revenge of ſome cruelties that had been committed upon the garriſon of *Hatwan. Mohammed*, however, is ſaid to have puniſhed the authors of this violation, and to have ſet at liberty the remaining priſoners. Winter now approaching, *Mohammed* began to think of putting his army into winter quarters, In the mean while, *Petrina* being beſiged by the *Turks*, they were obliged to abandon it with great loſs; and *Maximilian*, having united all his troops, was now at the head of thirty-two thouſand horſe, and twenty-eight thouſand foot, with a train of one hundred and twenty field pieces, and every thing elſe in proportion; while the grand army of the *Turks* was encamped near *Egra*. The *Chriſtians* were eager to come to a general engagement, but the *Danube* parting the two armies, no action of any importance, for ſome days, happened. At laſt, *Mohammed* ordered ten thouſand of his beſt troops to paſs the river. The *Chriſtians* not only defeated them, but purſued them over the river, and filled the camp of the infidels with ſuch terror, that they took one hundred and ninety pieces of artillery, while *Mohammed*, with his vizier, fled with the utmoſt precipitation; the former, through grief and vexation, even ſhedding tears, which he wiped away with a piece of *Mahomet*'s, the prophet's, garment, which he carried about him as a relick.

Mohammed takes the field.

he is defeated.

Night

Night now drew on; the *Turks* were endeavouring to recover from their conſternation, and *Maximilian* was about to order a retreat, when *Sigiſmund, Palſi,* and the other imperial generals, perſuaded him to puſh his good fortune, without giving the infidels time to breathe. The imperialiſts, accordingly, attacked the firſt line of the *Turks,* and, having routed it, with vaſt ſlaughter, they attacked the main body, which was drawn up immediately before their camp, but not till after ſtrict orders had been given, againſt all plundering and diſorders. The charge of the imperialiſts was ſo furious, that, having routed the enemy, they broke into the *Turkiſh* camp; by which, they not only loſt the fruit of the great victory they had gained, but were, in their turn defeated. The *Hungarians,* and *Germans,* were not proof againſt the amazing riches of the *Turkiſh* tents; and, breaking into *Mohammed*'s own pavilion, inſtead of purſuing their enemies, they fell to plunder. The paſha *Sigala,* an *Italian* renegade, obſerving this, rallied the infidels, and, while *Maximilian,* and the other *Chriſtian* generals, in vain, endeavoured to call their troops from the plunder, they found themſelves abandoned to the fury of the infidels, who killed twenty thouſand of the imperialiſts. This battle, called that of *Kareſta,* coſt *Mohammed* ſixty thouſand men. Luckily for the *Chriſtians,* the conſternation of the *Turks* continued to be ſuch, that they did not purſue their victory; and *Sigiſmund,* whoſe troops were under excellent diſcipline, retreated in good order, with the loſs of no more than two hundred of his men. Some of the *German* hiſtorians, however, are far from agreeing with thoſe particulars. They ſay, that the battle was fought on the twenty-fifth of *October,* that the loſs of the *Turks* was about twelve thouſand men, and that of the imperialiſts, about five thouſand, but they agree that the imperialiſts were not purſued, though the infidels are ſaid to have loſt great numbers in their retreat to *Egra,* and from thence to *Belgrade.*

Mohammed was ſo proud of his late conqueſt, that he was ſirnamed *Egra.* The paſha of *Boſnia* beſieged *Petrina,* but was defeated by *Herberſtein,* the imperial general, with great loſs. The conſequences, however, of the battle of *Kareſta,* in the year 1597, were detrimental to the *Chriſtian* intereſt. The confederacy began now to languiſh, and *Michael,* the waywod of *Walachia,* being no longer protected by his allies, again ſubmitted to be tributary to *Mohammed,* but without acting againſt the emperor. This defection from the common cauſe, obliged the brave *Sigiſmund* to reſign *Tranſylvania* to the emperor *Rodolph,* for ſome other eſtates and penſions; ſo that nothing, of any great conſequence, paſſed in the field that year.

In the year 1598, the *Tartars* made a peace with the emperor, upon the payment of a ſum of money; and the counts

Swit-

but recovers the field,

without purſuing.

A paſha defeated.

Swertzenburg, and *Palfi*, being informed by two *Italians* who had escaped from *Raab*, of the state of that important fortress, they had the good fortune to surprize, and make themselves masters of it, after a most desperate resistance, two of the *Turkish* pashas being killed. The booty the imperialists made in this place, is said to have been incredibly rich. Encouraged by this success, *Palfi* attempted to take *Buda*, but was obliged to raise the siege, as the *Turks* did that of *Waradin*, in *Upper Hungary*, which had been undertaken by the pasha *Ibrahim*. *Michael*, the cautious waywod of *Moldavia*, this year, again threw off the *Turkish* yoke, defeated the pashas of *Silistria* and *Badoua*, took *Nissa*, in *Bulgaria*, and harrassed the *Turkish* territories with his inroads.

Raab re-covered by the imperialists.

In the year 1599, the *Heyduks* of *Walachia* defeated the pasha of *Anatolia*, intercepted a reinforcement of three thousand *Turks*, marching to *Buda*, and took prisoner the pasha of that city. After this, they surprised and defeated the pasha of *Bosnia*, at the head of ten thousand men; and *Swertzenburg*'s regiment put to the sword, or drove into the *Danube*, a great number of ravaging *Tartars*. *Mohammed*, all this time, remained in *Constantinople*, where he gave himself entirely up to luxury. He took care, however, to support his troops in *Hungary*; but count *Palfi*, this year, intercepted a great convoy designed for the relief of *Buda*, and other cities belonging to the *Turks*, with a vast sum of money. Towards the end of the summer, however, the pasha *Ibrahim*, came to *Buda*, at the head of one hundred thousand *Turks*, and made some overtures for peace, which came to nothing. This year, *Sigismund*, repenting of his bargain with the emperor, resumed the government of *Transylvania*, where he was joyfully received by the states, who equally dreaded the *Austrian*, as the *Turkish*, tyranny. It is even said, that *Sigismund*, after all the great actions he had done against the infidels, chose to depend on them, rather than the emperor, and that he resigned his dominions to cardinal *Bathori*, who was to hold them of *Mohammed*, but who was defeated and killed by the waywod of *Walachia*. And thus all *Transylvania* came again under the emperor's dominion. This was a dreadful blow to *Mohammed*, who gave the pasha *Ibrahim* orders to resume the negociations for peace; but these, like the preceding, came to nothing; while the plague and famine continued to make prodigious havock among the *Turks* in *Hungary*.

War in Walachia.

So many calamities falling upon the *Othman* empire, on that side, encouraged *Kusachin*, the pasha of *Caramania*, who is said to have been of the blood of *Othman*, to rebel. Being an excellent officer, he defeated ten thousand of *Mohammed*'s troops, took *Iconium*, and charging *Mohammed* himself with cowardice and mismanagement, and his ministers with corruption, he prepared to advance to *Constantinople*. *Mohammed*, *Sinan*'s son, was sent to command against him, but

Rebellion in Turkey.

N 3

he

he, avoiding a battle, laid out some money so judiciously amongst *Kusachin*'s infantry, that they abandoned him, and the rebel retired with his cavalry to *Arabia*. Next year he prepared to attack the pasha *Mohammed*, who had wintered at *Aleppo*, but, the latter proclaiming a pardon to all who would come over to him, *Kusachin* was abandoned, and, being taken prisoner, was put to a tormenting death at *Constantinople*.

War in Hungary

We are now arrived at the year 1600, which opened with a mutiny of one thousand two hundred *French* and *Walloons*, in the garrison of *Pappa*, for want of pay, and they bargained to give up the place to the *Turks*, but it was recovered by *Swertzenburg*, who lost his life in the attempt, while the *Heydu's* surprised the town of *Giula*. In the end of *August*, the pasha *Ibrahim* took the field with two hundred thousand men, and begin his operations by taking *Babotska*, which lies within four miles of the *Danube*, and twenty-eight south-east of *Kanissa*, which important city, he likewise besieged. The imperial army consisting of forty thousand men, was commanded by the *French* duke, *de Mercoeur*, who attempted to raise the siege, and fought a drawn battle with the *Turks*; but provisions failing, and dissentions amongst the *Christians* arising, the place was delivered up by capitulation, which was observed; and *Ibrahim* endeavoured to serve his master, chiefly, by proceeding against the *Hungarians* gently and moderately. He died, however, soon after, having been nobly rewarded by the sultan.

Rebellion in Asia.

Matters did not go on so well on the side of *Asia*, where *Kusachin*'s rebellion was revived, by one *Skrivano*, who defeated the pasha *Mohammed*, after a bloody engagement. In *Persia*, shah *Abbas* ordered the *Turkish* embassador to be bastinadoed, for presuming to demand one of the shah's sons as a hostage to the *Othman* court; so low was the credit of the *Turkish* government fallen in *Asia*. The pasha, *Mohammed*, however, was sent against *Skrivano* with a fresh army of one hundred and twenty thousand men, but he was defeated by the rebel, who now proclaimed himself the defender of the *Mohammetan* faith. He was, however, again attacked by the pasha *Mohammed*, and thought proper to retire to the mountains. Here he recruited his army, and, falling into the lower countries, he ravaged the possessions of all who would not join him, and prepared to advance against *Constantinople* itself; but, being prevented by death, he was succeeded by his younger brother. The pasha *Hassan* was sent to suppress the new rebel chief, but he was both defeated and killed, and the rebels laid a great part of the *Othman* dominions, in *Asia*, under contribution, by which they raised vast sums. Their general, who is said to have been a *Tartar*, was now at the head of forty thousand men, laid siege to *Ancyra*, the inhabitants of which gave him two hundred thousand ducats to raise it. The *Turkish* governor resenting

resenting this composition, the *Ancyreans* cut his garrison in pieces, and drove him out of the city. The rebels then laid siege to *Prusa*, in *Anatolia*, which they took, and in it a vast booty, besides military stores in great abundance. After this, they were joined by the governor of *Baghdad*, and their progress became so formidable, that *Mohammed* was forced to comply with their demands, and to give the pashaship of *Bosnia* to their leader, who is called *Zel Ali*. The insolence of the rebels, who now appeared triumphantly at court, adorned with marks of imperial favour, exasperated the army at *Constantinople* so much, that their officers entered into a conspiracy with one of the sultana's, to place her son upon the throne; *Mohammed*, according to them, being now unfit for government, equally through incapacity and cruelty. This conspiracy being discovered by an intercepted letter, the sultana, her son, fifty of the conspirators, and the astrologers, who had promised them success, were put to death. But we are now to attend the affairs of *Hungary*.

In the year 1601, the duke *de Mercoeur*, began the campaign with the siege of *Alba Regalis*, and by fording a part of the lake, which the *Turks* did not think fordable, he sieged and took the city by storm; though the defence the infidels made was so obstinate, that most of it was ruined. *Hassan*, who had succeeded *Ibrahim* in the command of the *Turkish* army in *Hungary*, sought to surprise this important conquest, before the place could be repaired, but he was defeated by the duke *de Mercoeur*, with far inferior numbers, and the pasha of *Buda*, six sanjacks, many general officers, and six thousand common soldiers were killed. The duke then besieged *Kanissa*, and would have taken it, had not the inclemency of the season obliged him to raise the siege. This year, the plague raged through almost all the parts of the *Othman* empire, and the janizaries had the insolence to demand the heads of certain courtiers, who had offenced them. Having deputed their aga for that purpose, *Mohammed* put him to death, but the janisaries, in revenge, would have pulled him out of his palace, had they not, as usual, been appeased by money.

To counterballance those and a great many other misfortunes and disgraces, which the infidels suffered, during the course of this war, in the year 1602, the pasha *Hassan*, having an army of one hundred and fifty thousand men, besieged and took *Alba Regalis*, upon a capitulation of safety to the persons and goods of the garrison. But the imperial soldiers beginning to plunder the citizens, whose riches were otherwise to fall into the hands of the *Turks*, the *Tartars*, who served in the infidel army, broke in, and slaughtered both. *Yslan* the governor, who had made a most admirable defence, was with the chief officers, carried prisoner to *Constantinople*; and soon after, followed by the *Turkish* general and his army.

Alba Regalis taken.

The Turks defeated.

Alba Regalis retaken.

N 4

The

The imperialifts, this year, took the *Lower Buda*, and the city of *Peft*, partly by ftorm, and partly by ftratagem. The pafha *Haffan*, endeavoured, but in vain, to retake *Peft*, while count *Nadafti* reduced the towns of *Adom* and *Veldwar*. The *Upper* city of *Buda*, being ftill unreduced, the imperialifts befieged it with great vigour, but were obliged to raife the fiege with lofs, and likewife to abandon the town of *Adom*.

Campaign upon the Danube. The campaign of the year 1603 began upon the *Danube*, which was that year fiozen over. Six thoufand *Tuiks*, who ferved as a convoy of two hundred waggons of provifions, to *Alba Regalis*, were put to the fwoid by the imperialifts, who had no fooner poffeft themfelves of the waggons, than they were retaken by part of the garrifon of *Buda*, who, in their return, loft them to an ambufcade, formed by the garrifon of *Peft*. In *Walachia*, the war was carried on againft the *Turks*, by the new waywod, *Radul*. *Colonitz*, the imperial general, cut in pieces fix hundred *Tuiks*, in one party, but failed in his attempts upon a great convoy, as well as upon *Babotz*, and he retreated to *Komorra*. After this, though the *Tartars* entered *Hungary* through *Walachia*, in fuch numbers, that the vaft flaughter of them did not fenfibly diminifh them, *Colonitz* took *Loqua* and *Boulouvenier*, while *Bafta*, the imperial general in *Tranfylvania*, took *Soiomofe*, and the *Walachians* defeating *Yakil Mofes*, a *Turkifh* or *Tartar*, general, the tranquility of that country was reftored. In the mean while, the *Turks*, to the number of one hundred thoufand, affembled, with a fhew to befiege *Peft*, but the garrifons of *Raab* and *Gran*, under the direction of a *Turkifh* officer, who had deferted, plundeied, and fet fire to the fuburbs of *Alba Regalis*.

Mutiny at Conftantinople. The fervices which the pafha *Haffan* had done this campaign, were thought to have been fo confiderable, as to merit the fultan's fifter in marriage, and he repaired to *Conftantinople*, for that purpofe ; but was confounded, when he arrived there, to hear the janifaries, and other foldiers, in a body, demand of the fultan, that he fhould be delivered up to them. As the mutineers were very numerous, *Haffan* appeared before them, and underftood, that the charge againft him was, for employing the chief ftrength of the army in *Hungary*, while the *Afian* rebels were within three days march of *Conftantinople*. *Haffan* threw the blame upon the fultan's mother, and the kapigi aga, and continued fo fteady in his charge againft them, that the mutineers with the moft bitter reproaches to the emperor, demanded their heads with fuch obftinacy, that thofe of the kapigi aga and fome other officers, were ftruck off, and the fultan agreed **and a rebellion in Afia.** that his mother fhould be confined After this, the rebels of *Afia*, renewing their infults, *Mohammed* entered into a fecret negociation for peace with the imperialifts, but the treaty foon came to nothing. *Buda*, at that time, was in

great

great diftrefs for provifions; and the pafha *Morad*, on the twenty-fecond of *Auguft*, endeavouring to relieve it, he was defeated by *Rufhworm*, the imperial general, in many repeated encounters, with the lofs of above eight thoufand men, befides a vaft number of prifoners, waggons and horfes. A great many fkirmifhes, with various fortune to each party, happened after this in the ifle of *Vicegrad*, near *Buda*; but count *Trantmeftorf* beat the infidels in *Stiria*; and *Bafta*, the imperial general, took the important town of *Lugaze*, in *Tranfylvania*. The imperialifts however, in the end, could not prevent a great fupply being thrown into *Buda*; and then the *Turks* drew their army from *Hungary*. Upon this, the imperialifts befieged, and with great difficulty took *Hatwan*, on the twenty-ninth of *November*. Five thoufand *Turks*, under the pafha *Beged*, were either cut in pieces, or taken prifoners by *Bafta*. But the infidels found a ufeful ally in *Bethlem Gabor*, the head of the revolted *Tranfylvanians*.

This year, *Zel Ali* the *Afian* rebel, whom we have mentioned to have been reconciled to *Mohammed*'s government, did, in *Hungary*. at the head of twelve thoufand of his men, fuch great fervice in *Hungary* against the imperialifts, that the fultan promifed him the government of *Bofnia* But the pafha *Jaffer*, who commanded in that province, either unwilling to refign his government, or encouraged by the fultan, not only refufed him entrance into *Baghnaluck*, the chief town of the province, but prepared to cut him off. *Zel Ali*, feigning a retreat, abandoned his camp, but while *Jaffer*'s foldiers were plundering it, he attacked them fo unexpectedly that he killed fix thoufand of them, and having in his turn, plundered their camp, the whole province fubmitted to him, and he made a triumphant entry into *Baghnaluck*. After this he gave out that he would join the imperialifts if he difcovered any more practices against him, and avoided all the traps laid for him by *Mohammed*.

Such was the untoward fituation of the *Turkifh* government, when the negociations for a peace were renewed, under the refpite of a truce for twelve days, in the beginning of the year 1604. But, before the truce was out, the emperor *Mohammed* died, in the forty-fourth year of his age, and after a reign of nine years, and two months. He appears, upon the whole, to have been a cruel, worthlefs, fenfual man, and to have held his empire only by the compliances he made with thofe who difturbed his government. He put to death, as we have related, his eldeft fon upon an idle furmife, but afterwards finding him innocent, his body was buried in the imperial fepulchre, and the pafha who accufed him was ftrangled. His fecond fon died young, the fourth was confined in the palace, and the third fucceeded him. **Campaign in Hungary. Death and character of Mohammed.**

The

The Reign of Ahmed the First.

Succeeded by Ahmed. AHMED was no more than fifteen years of age when he mounted the *Othman* throne, a circumstance that had never happened before to that government. His first care was, to give orders that the negociation begun by his father with the imperialists should be continued; and then he turned his thoughts to suppress the *Asiatic* rebels, who continued in arms under *Kallenden Ogli*, and *Tavil*. His prime vizier *Koja Morad*, undertook this war, and after defeating the rebels, drove them into *Persia*. *Ahmed* demanded that the two generals should be delivered up, which shah *Abbas* refusing to do, the vizier invaded *Persia*, but too late to do any thing effectual for that campaign. *Ahmed*, young as he was, next applied himself to domestic regulations, and removed his grandmother, who had been so much complained of in the late reign, from all her power in the government. The negociations for the peace in *Hungary* still went on, but were interrupted by the imperialists discovering a plot of the *Turks* to surprise *Pest*, during the time of a grand entertainment there, given to their chief officers by the imperialists. After this, hostilities were renewed with great rigour on both sides. The pasha *Jaffer* entered his government of *Bosnia*, from whence he drove his competitor *Zel Ali*, who however, was made governor of *Temeswar*, but he failed in an attempt he made to surprise *Lippa*. Another design, formed by the *Turkish* prisoners, to surprise or destroy *Kassova*, miscarried about the same time, but the important fortress of *Kanissa* was accidentally blown up by gunpowder.

Continuance of the war with the Christians It appears, as if neither the *Turks* nor the imperialists in *Hungary*, were in earnest for a peace. The pasha of *Buda*, disowned the design upon *Pest*, and profest himself willing to resume the negociations, but at the same time he took and burnt down the castle of *Semnin* Matters thus beginning to wear a more favourable aspect for the *Turks* in *Hungary*, the pasha *Hassan*, who was reckoned the best officer in their dominions, was sent thither, with one hundred thousand men, while the *Tartars* continued their usual ravages in *Walachia*. This obliged the waywod *Rodolf*, to put his country under the protection of the emperor, who, this year, received one hundred and fifty thousand crowns from the pope, for the defence of *Hungary*. The terror of *Hassan*, who was now made great vizier, was such, that the governor of *Pest* blew up that fortress, and retired to *Gran*, which was soon after besieged by *Hassan*. *Tambier*, the governor of *Lipta*, marching to its relief, was intercepted by *Bethlem Gabor*, at the head of the *Transylvanian* rebels, and four thousand *Turks*, who were all of them routed, and the defence

fence made by count *Schultz* the governor of *Gran*, was so good, that *Haffan*, on the tenth of *October*, raised the siege, and was harrassed in his retreat by *Basta*, the imperial general. *Potskay*, a *Calvinist* nobleman of *Poland*, now ruled in *Transylvania*, under the *Turk*, and calling himself the defender of the reformed religion, he established *Protestantism* at *Kaffova*, which he took, after defeating *Beligiosa* the imperial general under *Basta*. The truth is, the persecutions of popery were now become as ruinous to *Hungary* and *Transylvania*, as the arms of the infidels had been. The imperialists under *Basta* at last defeated *Potskay*, but turned their arms against the *Protestants* of those countries, who uniting under *Potskay*, he again recovered his power. This reduced *Basta*, whose army was very mutinous, to apply to *Potskay* for peace, but the latter, among other things, insisting upon each subject having the free exercise of his own religion, the war went on. The *Heyduks* and *Tartars*, surprised *Gokaza*, near *Gran*, but it was recovered by the imperialists, who likewise took *Palantwar*. The *Turks* however, by the means of the *Heyduks*, most of whom were in *Potskay's* interest, took *Vachia*, but were repulsed in an attempt they made upon *Gran*; though the *Heyduks* betrayed to them the town of *Vicegrad*, the citadel of which soon after capitulated.

Such were the chief military transactions of the year 1605. Though the *Christian* cause then appeared to be on the point of ruin, yet, such was the bigotry of the house of *Austria*, that the emperor considered the *Protestants* to be equally his enemies as the infidels. The *Protestants*, on the other hand, the *Heyduks* especially, felt the *Turkish* more light than the *Austrian* yoke, and though *Basta* offered an indemnity to all deserters who would return to the imperial standard; his offer was so far from producing any effect, that he saw himself in danger of being abandoned by his own army. The *Heyduks*, in the beginning of *February* 1606, took the castle of *Sakmar*, and were prevented only by the accident of the ice failing under them, from taking *Takay* likewise. They next attacked *New Hanfel*, and made themselves masters of the town, but were dispossessed of it by the garrison of the castle. They had better fortune before the important town of *Filek*, which was surrendered to them for want of water, and their success was such, that they at last forced the states of *Transylvania* to recognize the authority of *Potskay*, on whose side were likewise most part of the native *Hungarians*.

Notwithstanding the defeat and flight of the two *Turkish* rebels into *Persia*, the rebellion soon broke out again in *Asia*, where the pasha *Sigala* was defeated by the rebels in a bloody battle. Putting himself at the head of a fresh army, he again obliged them to apply for assistance to the court of *Persia*, and that shah sending his son to their aid, defeated *Sigala*,

Bigotry of the emperor.

The rebellion breaks out again in Asia.

and

and killed thirty thousand of his soldiers, and afterwards reduced all the country of *Shirwan*, excepting a few inconsiderable places *Ahmed* upon this, was inclined to have abandoned the *Hungarian* war, and to have sent the pasha *Hassan* against the *Persians*, and the rebels; but changing his mind, he continued *Sigala* in his command. That general, notwithstanding his great abilities, was again defeated by the *Persians*, who afterwards took *Baghdad*. In *Anatolia*, the rebellion still continued to rage, and the pashas of *Damascus*, and *Aleppo*, were at war with one another. And to compleat the misfortunes of the *Turkish* government, on that side, the janisaries mutinied, and a dreadful fire broke out at *Constantinople*. *Sigala* informed *Ahmed* of all his misfortunes, and, obtaining the command of another army, he was again defeated, and with difficulty he escaped with only three hundred soldiers to *Ardena*, a city near *Tarsus*. The pasha of *Trebizond* advancing to his relief, *Sigala*, with no more than ten soldiers, got secretly over the walls and joined him. The two pashas were again defeated, and *Sigala* was obliged to save himself in a little boat. So many repeated overthrows, with the loss of *Adena*, tired out *Ahmed's* patience. He ordered all *Sigala's* house and riches at *Constantinople* to be seized, and that a fresh army should be raised against the *Persians*. The janisaries however, absolutely refused to march, and *Ahmed* was obliged to appease the mutiny by putting to death his high treasurer.

War in Syria. In *Syria*, the war continued between the pashas of *Damascus*, and *Aleppo*. The former at first had the advantage, and obliged his rival to submit to his terms: but the agreement was not of long standing, and the pasha of *Damascus*, with the pashas of *Tripoli*, and *Gazera*, advancing against *Aleppo* with sixty thousand men, they were defeated by that pasha with half the number, and he, at the same time, took *Tripoli*; and affecting to act independently of the sultan, he imposed a tribute on the *Turks*, and reduced all *Syria*, making several regulations in trade, to *Persia* and the *Indies*, to enrich his new subjects. The beglerbeg of *Anatolia's* lieutenant, was totally defeated, in endeavouring to reduce him, and he had the good fortune to possess himself of a whole year's tribute of *Egypt*, by the ship which carried it being thrown on his coasts.

Affairs of Germany Such complicated misfortunes on the side of *Asia*, seemed to determine *Ahmed* to have peace on any terms, but the *German* emperor was equally embarrassed. *Potskay* refused to treat with him, without establishing such preliminaries as amounted to his renouncing *Hungary*. *Basta's* army again mutinied, and the *Heydukes* not only took *New Hansel*, but ravaged *Moravia*. *Basta*, however, having somewhat appeased his mutinous troops, obtained some advantages over the *Turks*, and *Tartars*, near the *Danube*, and the imperial garrison of *Komora* surprised and killed the pasha *Begedes*, and intercepted

cepted a rich convoy of money that was going to *Potſkay*. That nobleman, however, proceeded with ſuch amazing ſucceſs, that not only all *Tranſylvania*, and the greateſt part of the *Auſtrian Hungary*, ſubmitted to him, but he carried his arms into *Auſtria*, and *Stiria* itſelf. In ſhort, even the counts *Serini*, *Nadaſti*, and *Budiani*, who had done wonders againſt the *Turks*, ſeeing the emperor in a manner abandon all care of them, ſubmitted to *Potſkay* likewiſe. But the *Heyduks* were forced to raiſe the ſiege of *Odenburg*, with great loſs. *Potſkay* likewiſe loſt four waggon loads of money, which was intercepted by the *Germans*; it having been ſent him by the *Turks*, as the price of his having given up *Kaſſova*. To compenſate him for this loſs, *Dotis* ſurrendered to his party; and on the ſeventeenth of *October New Hauſel* was, after a long and obſtinate ſiege, delivered to the *Hungarians* in his intereſt.

Potſkay, all this while, proceeded upon the moſt plauſible pretexts. He inſiſted, that *Hungary* ſhould be governed by *Hungarians* only, that *Tranſylvania* ſhould be independent, and both countries free, with the full liberty to exerciſe the *Proteſtant* religion. The *German* emperor at laſt agreed, that he ſhould enjoy, during his life, the principality of *Tranſylvania*, and that his ſubjects ſhould profeſs *Proteſtantiſm*; but by the perſuaſion of *Ahmed*, who promiſed to give all *Hungary* to *Potſkey*, he rejected thoſe terms, and the *Turks* beſieged and took *Gran*, the governor, *Dampier*, being obliged to ſurrender the ſame by a mutiny of the garriſon, who were put to death for their cowardice, and treachery, at *Komorra*, to which place they were conducted in terms of their capitulation. So many repeated misfortunes determined the emperor *Rodolph* to liſten to freſh propoſals for peace made to him by *Ahmed*; but they ſtuck at the toleration of the *Proteſtant* religion, which was ſtill inſiſted upon by *Potſkay*. And on the other hand, *Shah Abbas* ſent an embaſſador to *Vienna*, to diſſuade that court from coming to any accommodations with the porte. While matters were in this ſtate of ſuſpence, between peace and war, the *Turks* miſcarried in an attempt they made upon *Raab*, while the *Hungarians* of *Potſkay*'s party reduced *Tokay*, and blocked up *Eſpieries*. The *Turks*, about the ſame time, attempted to take *Lippa*, but, after entering the town they were defeated with great loſs by the garriſon of the caſtle. Negociations for peace, however, were reſumed, and the treaty was concluded between the emperor, the ſtates of *Hungary*, and prince *Potſkay*, on theſe terms: That the *Catholics*, *Lutherans*, and *Calviniſts*, ſhould all have free liberty to exerciſe their reſpective religions in *Hungary*; that *Potſkay* ſhould remain, during life, prince of *Tranſylvania*; and that they ſhould endeavour to conclude a peace with the *Turks*; that the ſtates of *Hungary*, in the emperor's abſence, might take the archduke *Matthius* for their palatine or governor, that all

other

other offices fhould be exercifed by the natives of the country ; and that the jefuits fhould not be allowed to enjoy any property in that kingdom, unlefs *Rodolph* fhould pleafe

A peace to make them any prefents. A treaty then fucceeded between *Ahmed* and *Rodolph*, which, on the ninth of *November* 1660, was concluded on the following conditions :

Its terms. That the fultan fhould ftile the emperor, father ; and the emperor the fultan, fon, in all their letters and negotiations, that the king of *Spain*, if he pleafed, fhould be comprehended in the peace ; that the *Tartars* fhould alfo be included, on the *Turks* giving affurance, that they fhould make no incurfions upon the *Chriftians* ; that this truce, or fufpenfion of arms, fhould laft twenty years, to begin from the firft day of *January* 1608 ; that the two parties fhould reciprocally fend prefents every three years to each other ; that the emperor fhould begin immediately, by fending two hundred thoufand florins, which fhould be inftantly returned by the fultan, in a prefent of the fame value ; that each party fhould retain what they were poffeffed of ; that they fhould not lay any additional taxes on the cities and villages taken in the late wars, befides what they then paid, that they fhould not attack any place belonging to each other, on any pretence whatever ; that on both fides they might repair their refpective fortreffes ; and that the agreement made with *Potfkay*, prince of *Tranfylvania*, fhould remain in full force. *Vachia* was to he reftored to the emperor, and the fultan was

Peace to keep poffeffion of *Gran*. During thofe negotiations,
with Ger- *Potfkay* was fo much indifpofed that he could attend at none
many. of the conferences, and at the end of this year he died, with the character of being one of the greateft patriots of his time ; only he was under the misfortune of his being obliged to affert the liberties of his country, and of mankind, by the affiftance of infidels, who were enemies to all liberty both civil and religious.

War with *Ahmed* having thus concluded peace with the *Germanic*
the Per- body, employed all his thoughts towards recovering thofe
fians. beautiful provinces that had been rent from his empire by the *Perfians*. Previous to that, he was obliged to endeavour to reduce, either by arms or by treaty, the pafha of *Aleppo*. Negotiations failing, the grand vizier was fent againft him with an army of one hundred and thirty thoufand men, and had the good fortune, after various conflicts, to force the rebel to retire to *Perfia* ; but recruiting himfelf there, he, at laft obtained his pardon from the fultan, who now fpent two or three years in pleafure and inactivity. The negotiations, however, with the *Perfians* ftill went on, through the agency of the khan of *Tartary*, but *Ahmed*'s demands being too high, hoftilities were renewed. The *Perfians* invaded the *Arabian Irak*, and *Ahmed* fent againft them the pafha *Nafuh*, who was defeated with the lofs of twenty thoufand men. He was fucceeded in his command by the

pafha

pasha of *Aleppo*, who probably having his reasons for not acting vigorously against the *Persians*, was put to death by the sultan's order.

By this time, viz. in 1610, the archduke *Matthias* had been elected king of *Hungary*, upon the terms of toleration for religion, and ratified the late treaty with *Ahmed*. He was opposed by *Gabriel Bathori*, who had assumed the principality of *Transylvania*, and had put himself under the protection of *Ahmed*, who supported him against *Corstantine*, the waywod of *Moldavia*. This summer, *Ahmed* had a fleet at sea, but it was unfortunate in all its operations against the gallies of *Malta*, and the other *Italian* powers. The *Tuscans*, in particular, made a vast booty by sea, to the value it is said of one million five hundred thousand crowns, while the gallies of *Malta*, and *Naples*, ravaged the *Turkish* islands in the *Archipelago* The *Persians*, in the mean while, were still gaining ground upon the *Othmans*, but *Shah Abbas*, about the beginning of the year 1611, would willingly have made peace upon terms that were disagreeable to the sultan, who successively employed *Mrrad*, *Serder*, and the pasha *Nassuf*, against the *Persians*. A peace, however, was at last concluded, on condition of the shah's paying to *Ahmed* two hundred camel loads of silk, and making some other immaterial concessions. This year, a detachment from the *Maltese* gallies surprised and plundered *Corinth* in the *Morea*, without any loss of men.

The pasha *Nassuf* was now, both for his great abilities in peace and war, the reigning favourite of the *Othman* court. In the year 1612, he carried with him to *Constantinople* a *Persian* ambassador, for ratifying the late treaty; but the janisaries being now idle, begun again to mutiny. They refused longer to accept of bread and rice for their subsistance, and when a great conflagration happened at *Constantinople*, instead of assisting to quench it, they broke open and plundered the houses of the inhabitants. *Nassuf*, who was now first vizier, and was the only subject of the empire who had the liberty of breaking in upon the sultan's pleasures, was so far from giving way to the mutineers, that he ordered sixteen hundred of them to be sent to *Asia*, and he threatened the extinction of their order. Those vigorous measures were the more easily executed, as the sultan had no wars upon his hands. *Matthias* king of *Hungary*, had succeeded to the empire of *Germany*, and demanded the principality of *Transylvania*, which was denied him. This year, *Ahmed* concluded an advantageous peace with the *Dutch*, who were then a considerable maritime power, and he gave them freedom to trade in his ports, and to send an ambassador, or resident to *Constantinople*. About *Midsummer*, *Ahmed*'s sister was married to *Mehemed Pasha*, son to *Segala Pasha*, the unfortunate commander against the *Persians*, and his

daughter,

Opera-
tions of
theTurkish
fleet.

The jani-
saries
a mutiny.

Cruelty of daughter, to *Mahammed* the high admiral. The mother of
Ahmed. this lady, however, a few days after the weddings were over,
felt the fultan's fury. He, it feems, was in love with a
female flave belonging to his fifter, whom the fultana poifoned, and *Ahmed* in revenge ftabbed her in the face with a
dagger, and trampled her underfoot on the ground, befides
beating her moft feverely. Soon after this, the fultan retiring from the plague at *Conftantinople*, to one of his country feats, a dervife, or religious perfon, threw a ftone at him,
with an intention to murder him, but the affaffin, miffing
his aim, was next day put to death.

The troubles, which ftill continued in *Moldavia*, and
Tranfilvania, were now come to fo great a height, that
Bathori was killed by his own foldiers.

Loffes of   In the year 1613, the *Florentines* took fort *Agliman*, which
the *Turks* lies to the north-weft of cape *Bogas*, in *Cilicia*, as the *Portugueze*, and *Spaniards* did *Aden*, lying on the *Red Sea*, towards the fouth of *Arabia*. Thofe, and a great many other
loffes fuftained by *Ahmed*, from the *Italian* and other powers,
obliged him to have recourfe to his *Chriftian* fubjects for repairing his marine. He obliged the *Armenians* of his empire
to build nine gallies, and the *Greeks* twenty; all at their own
expences. His arms profpered little better by land, though
after the death of *Bathori*, his rival *Bethlem Gabor*, was, by
the pafha *Serder*, declared prince of *Tranfylvania*, yet,
that was of very little fervice to the fultan, who raifed a
vaft armament, and fet out, as was thought, to conquer
Tranfylvania for himfelf, but was deterred by *Bethlem*'s great
power. Returning towards *Conftantinople*, he received intelligence that the plague raged in that capital, and when it
was fomewhat abated, to prevent its breaking out again, he
ordered all the dogs in *Conftantinople* to be carried to a defert
ifland, where, contrary to the doctrines of *Mahometifm*, he
fuffered them all to perifh for want of fuftenance.

Intrigues   During thofe public calamities *Ahmed*'s court was filled with
at *Con-* intrigues. *Sigala*, now pafha of *Buda*, notwithftanding the
ftantinople unfortunate campaigns he had made againft the *Perfians*,
was ftill fuffered to enjoy his life and government; and his
wife being fifter to the fultan the pafha *Nafuf*, the prime
vizier, being extremely jealous of his credit at court, denied
him accefs to the fultan, and did him all the ill offices in his
power. *Sigala*, being a man of intrigue, gave a letter to his
wife, addreffed to the fultan, but not being able, through the
vizier's jealoufy to put it into his own hands, fhe difpofed of
it in his room fo as that he found it. The contents of this
letter, which was faid to have accufed the vizier of a confpiracy againft the fultan's life, determined *Ahmed* to fend for his
head; the pafha *Boftanji* was appointed to be the meffenger.
It was fufpected that the vizier intended to fly over to *Afia*,
for which reafon, the pafha was obliged to ufe a ftratagem,
by

by dreffing himſelf in the ſultan's robes, and having thus ſecured him, the vizier, after delivering up the ſeal, quietly ſubmitted to be ſtrangled. Perhaps, his greateſt crime was his treaſure, for about four hundred thouſand pounds ſterling, in ready money, was found in his houſe after his death. This ſum enabled *Ahmed* to finiſh ſome magnificent works he had laid out at *Conſtantinople*; and *Bethlem*, his tributary prince of *Tranſylvania*, by the aſſiſtance of the paſha *Sauder*, retook ſeveral towns in *Germany*, and received the ſubmiſſions of others, but upon the expreſs condition of their not falling under the power of the *Turks*.

About the year 1615, a real or pretended brother to the ſultan, who called himſelf prince *Jakaya*, is ſaid to have attempted to murder him. The ſtory of this perſon is extremely romantic, and ſeems to have been the invention of the jeſuits, who were at this time very buſy in making proſelytes of *Ahmed*'s ſubjects. He pretended to be the elder brother of *Ahmed*, and that his mother, who was a *Chriſtian*, by giving out he died of the ſmall-pox, had ſaved his life, and ſecretly educated him in her own religion. His pretenſions gained credit ſo far, that the *Aſiatic* rebels received him for their head, but being defeated and wounded, he had recourſe to the methods of aſſaſſination. Being recovered of his wounds, he came in diſguiſe to *Conſtantinople*, where he is ſaid to have entered into a conſpiracy with a derviſe, called by *Chriſtian* writers the vizier derviſe, to murder the ſultan. The derviſe dying unexpectedly, *Jakaya* was obliged to fly, and wandering on foot through *Walachia*, and *Moldavia*, he there eſcaped many dangers, but at laſt came to *Prague*. There he met with nothing but great honours, and fair promiſes. *Coſmo*, grand duke of *Tuſcany*, next invited him into his dominions, and treated him with all the honours due to his real or pretended birth, as did the courts of *Madrid*, and *Rome*. His behaviour was ſo plauſible, and his ſtory had been ſo well cooked up, that the *Roman Catholic* powers, for ſome time, had thoughts, by *Coſmo*'s advice, of putting him at the head of a force to diſpute the *Othman* throne, as it was more than probable, he would be ſupported by a vaſt party in that empire. But the diſſentions amongſt the *Chriſtian* powers themſelves, prevented any thing of that kind from taking effect. We are told by thoſe who were perſonally acquainted with him, that he was a plauſible, well accompliſhed perſon, and that at laſt he went to *France*, where he was ſupported by the duke *de Nervers*, where it is likely he ended his days.

Stephen, the tributary waywod of *Moldavia*, under the *Turks*, behaved with ſo much cruelty, that his nobility ſet up againſt him *Alexander*, the ſon of *Jeremy*, their former waywod, and obliged *Stephen* to fly to *Brahilow*. *Alexander* had no objection to his continuing to pay the uſual tribute. But the paſha of *Buda* ſeized on his ambaſſadors in

The impoſtor.

Affairs of Hungary.

their way to *Conftantinople*, and fent them to *Stephen*, who put them to death. The war was then renewed with greater fury than ever, but all the events of it were favourable to *Alexander*, who, in the year 1616, defeated the joint forces of *Stephen*, and the pafha *Skinder*, in a general engagement, in which the latter loft twelve thoufand men on the fpot, befides wounded and prifoners. After this, the boyars, or great lords of *Walachia*, offered him their principality, which he declined to accept of; and upon the difgrace of the vizier who was *Stephen*'s patron, the latter was fent prifoner to *Conftantinople*, where he faved his life by turning *Mahometan*. *Mikhna*, the *Turkifh* waywod of *Walachia*, was, upon this, by the *Turks*, proclaimed prince of *Moldavia*, and invaded that principality at the head of twenty thoufand *Walachians*, and *Turks*. *Alexander* could have made head againft all this force, had he not been deferted by the *Poles*, and kofaks, who ferved in his army, and by his own general *Bicho*. Thofe defertions fo weakened him, that he and his fon *Bogdan*, after being totally defeated, were taken prifoners and fent to *Conftantinople*, where they were fentenced to perpetual imprifonment, but evaded that punifhment by embracing *Mohametifm*.

Conduct of the jefuits.

The houfe of *Auftria*, and the *Germanic* empire, were too much interefted in thofe difputes to remain ftrictly neutral in terms of the treaty of 1606. But though many hoftilities were committed between them and the *Turks*, no formal declaration of war having been made, that treaty was now renewed and explained, and feveral commercial articles, to advantage of both parties, were added to it. The intercourfe which this negociation occafioned, gave vaft umbrage to the people of *Conftantinople*. *Ahmed* had given the *French* jefuits leave to fettle at *Pera*, which is confidered as part of the fuburbs of *Conftantinople*, though on the oppofite fhore. It was not long before they began to practice their intrigues in making converts; and the *Turks*, who of all people in the world are the moft attached to their religion, underftanding, that they taught, and practifed, the doctrine of king killing, reprefented them to *Ahmed* and his miniftry, as fo many fpies fent by the *Chriftian* powers, to raife an infurrection in his dominions. Many concurring circumftances brought *Ahmed* over to this belief, and in his laft tranfports, he ordered all the *Chriftians* in, and about *Conftantinople*, to be put to the fword. This barbarous command would have been executed, had it not been for the reprefentations of the grand vizier and mufti againft it. But upon its being countermanded, it was with difficulty, that the people of *Conftantinople* were reftrained from putting it into execution themfelves, and from even putting *Chriftian* ambaffadors to death. The *French* ambaffador however, had fo much credit with the fultan and his miniftry, that they interpofed in favour of the *Chriftians*, and, after much difficulty,

difficulty, the jesuits, who had been imprisoned, and were every day expecting death, were pardoned and resettled at *Pera*.

It is thought, with some reason, that the baron de *Sancy*, the *French* minister, could not have had so much influence at the *Othman* court, had it not been for the mighty designs that were on foot against christendom, at the porte, which rendered it extremely inconvenient for that ministry to make the *French* king, *Henry* the fourth, their enemy. For we are told, that the *Poles* having declared in favour of the son of *Simon*, the late waywod of *Walachia*, *Ahmed* raised a great army to subdue all *Poland*. He likewise had now at sea two fleets, one to act against the *Russians*, and kosaks, in the *Euxine*, commonly called the *Black Sea*, and the other in the *Propontis*, or the *White Sea*, against the gallies of *Malta*, and the other *Italian* states. But, before any effect followed those preparations *Ahmed* died, on the sixteenth of *November* 1617, in the twenty-ninth year of his age, and the fourteenth of his reign, leaving behind him three sons, *Othman*, commonly called, *Osman*, *Murad*, or *Morad*, and *Ibrahim*.

Great projects against christendom.

Death

We know little or nothing of the intellectual character of this prince, farther than he was liberal and magnificent, and for a proof of the latter, we are referred to the jami, or mosque, which he built, and ornamented at an incredible expence, in the *Hippodrome*, at *Constantinople*. In his person, he is said to have been handsome, but what we are told of his pleasures, and diversions exceeds belief; for his historians say, that he had in his seraglio thirty thousand women, all of them the daughters of *Christians*; and that he had such a passion for hawking, and hunting, that he maintained forty thousand faulconers, and almost as many huntsmen, and that he had greater bodily strength, than any man about his court. The *Turks* have an excellent custom, in requiring that even their sultans should profess some manual art, to encourage industry amongst the common people. That of *Ahmed*, was to make horn rings for drawing the bow, as that of his father was to make arrows. And the one perhaps, finished a ring, and the other an arrow, in the space of twelve months.

Character of Ahmed.

The Reign of Muſtapha.

THIS prince was brother to the preceeding emperor, upon whose accession he was preserved from the bow-string, on account of *Ahmed*'s youth, and his having no children; that in case of his demise issueless, he might have an indisputable successor in the empire. *Ahmed*, after

He is succeeded by his brother.

having children, several times was resolved to dispatch *Mustapha*; but was always prevented by remorse, apprension, or accident. During this short reign, prince *Koreški*, the brave friend of *Alexander*, late waywod of *Moldavia*, having been in the preceeding reign taken prisoner by the *Turks*, and refusing to turn *Mahometan*, was imprisoned in the tower of the *Black Sea*, but found means to escape by the assistance of *Martin*, secretary to the *French* ambassador. As the prince was a most formidable, and determined enemy to the *Othmans*, all the *French* ambassador's servants were tortured to discover where he was, and the ambassador himself put under confinement, and got his liberty only by a large sum of money, which at the porte is next to omnipotence itself.

who is taken from a cell, to which he is remanded. *Mustapha* having been sequestered in a cell during the preceeding part of his life, held his sovereignty only that he might gratify his lusts. Thus the design of advancing him to the throne on account of the nonage of his brother's children, not answering, he was by the grand vizier, and the other great officers of his court, remanded back to his confinement, after he had sat upon the throne about four months, and given sufficient indications that he was fit to be the scourge, but not the sovereign, of a people.

The Reign of Othman, or Osman the Second.

Succeeded by Osman. THE great men of the court being thus disappointed in *Mustapha*, placed upon the *Othman* throne *Osman*, the eldest son of sultan *Ahmed* the first. The hatred which the *French* ambassador and nation bore to his predecessor, has made them exaggerate the virtues of this prince, who, according to some, was but eight, but, according to others, twelve or thirteen years of age, (the last is the most probable account), when he mounted the throne. A romance of his life, has been published in two sizeable volumes, and intermingled with many plausible, if not true, anecdotes. But, though the *French* thus exaggerate on the one hand, other writers, the *Turks* particularly, seem not to have done justice to his virtues, and resolution, which far exceeded what could be expected from his age and education, and above all, the situation of his person and government.

General state of affairs The favourite measures with the porte at the accession of the young sultan, was a war with *Poland*, on account of the support which that republic, and the kosaks, had afforded to the *Moldavian*, *Transylvanian*, and *Walachian* princes, who had been set up in opposition to the tributaries of the porte. *Jehan Beg Ghieray*, khan of *Khrim Tartary*, was the ally, or rather tributary of the *Othmans*, and he perpetually incited
the

the *Polish* territories, who, in conjunction with the kofaks, made reprifals. This ftate of warfare, while no war was declared, produced mutual recriminations. The porte refufed to check the *Tartars*, who, they faid, were an independent people, but had tributary claims upon *Poland*. The *Poles*, on the other hand, for much the fame reafons, declined curbing the kofacks in their incurfions upon the *Turkish* territories. Such was the ftate of affairs with *Poland*.

In *Germany*, the inhuman bigotry of the houfe of *Auftria*, in *Europe*. raifed fuch cruel perfecutions againft the *Proteftants*, efpecially thofe of *Bohemia*, that the latter applied to *Bethlem Gabor*, now the undoubted prince of *Tranfylvania*, under the porte, for affiftance. *Gabor*, for good reafons, applied to *Ofman* for leave, aid, and fupport. All which the fultan readily granted in the moft ample terms, and under a moft folemn oath. In the mean while, *Gabor* made a moft rapid progrefs againft the *Auftrians* in *Hungary*, which ended in his being chofen and proclaimed fovereign of that kingdom, by the confent and approbation of the court of *Conftantinople*.

On the fide of *Afia*, the pafha *Ali*, the grand vizier, penetrated at the head of the *Othman* army to *Tauris*, which he made himfelf mafter of, and his progrefs was fo rapid, that the fhah was obliged to fue for peace upon the vizier's terms. Upon this *Ali* returned to *Ergerum*, from whence he wrote an account of his expedition, of which I have given the fubftance, to Sir *Paul Pindar*, the *Britifh* minifter at *Conftantinople*.

Nothing now remained in the way of negociation, but to fecure the chief neutral powers of *Europe*, from taking part againft the porte. Thefe were *James* the firft, king of *Great Britain*, and the *French* king. The latter thought himfelf highly injured by the treatment his ambaffador had received at the porte; and *Uri Chaufh*, was fent to *France* with a letter from the young fultan, apologizing for what had paft, and promifing that, for the future, the ambaffador of *France*, fhould be treated at the *Othman Porte* with diftinguifhed honour. Thofe fubmiffions being received, the chaufh repaired with the fame character to the court of *Great Britain*, where he made a fpeech, and prefented a letter to *James* the firft, in terms that, though lofty, are by no means extravagant, and fome part of his letter which contains the higheft encomiums on hereditary right of fucceffion to empire, is fo well adapted to that prince's known character, that one is tempted to think his ambaffador had a hand in compofing it, and it had a correfponding effect.

I have premifed the above incidents, which took up above Expedi- two years, that the reader may have the more perfect idea tion a- of the motives that determined the *Othman* court upon the gainft the famous expedition made by *Ofman* againft the *Poles*. I have *Poles*. only to add, that, by the peace made with *Perfia*, the *Afiatic*

rebellion

rebellion was extinguished, and the *Othman* ministry trusted to the power of *Bethlem Gabor*, which now alarmed *Vienna* itself, for giving a diversion to the imperialists.

In the beginning of the year 1621, *Osman*, though not yet, according to the best accounts, above fifteen years of age, gave a proof of his superior genius, by despising the superstitious apprehensions of his subjects, on account of a very hard frost at *Constantinople*, by marching with his army, which consisted of three hundred thousand fighting men, against the *Poles*; while his fleet, and that of *Algiers* took *Manfredonia*, and *Torca*, in the *Mediteranean*, to give a diversion to the king of *Spain*, and the *Italian* powers. The sultan's intripedity against the prepossessions of a people so excessively superstitious as the *Turks* are, proved fatal to his affairs and person. *Ali*, his first vizier, who appears have been a brave general, and an honest statesman, was the only minister at the porte who approved of the sultan's expedition. The other ministers, had been in hopes of having the empire, as happens in minorities, and weak reigns, relinquished to them as their prey, and the common soldiers were little better than dragged into a war, which their religion seemed to disapprove of; and where they had nothing to hope for, but fatigue, blows, and death. So devoted, however, are the *Turks* to the will of their sovereign, that, severe as the season was, they took the field about the end of *April* 1621, and laid siege to *Kochin*, in *Moldovia*. The situation of the place being strong, they abandoned that attempt, and passed the *Boristhenes*, in hopes of defeating the chancellor of *Poland*, who was intrenched near *Kamnitz*, with forty-eight eight thousand men, of whom eight thousand were imperialists. The incredible efforts of *Osman*, for thirty four days successively, to break into the *Polish* camp, are proofs at once of his resolution, and of his enemies valour, for the *Turks* were repulied in every attack; so difficult it is for a commander to conquer, when spirit and inclination is wanting in his soldiers. The *Tartars*, however, in the *Othman* army, having no such scruples, committed most miserable ravages in the very heart of *Poland*. At last, the *Turks*, by the best accounts, having lost eighty thousand men, and about one hundred thousand horses, (baggage horses we suppose to be included); gave ear to the mediation of *Radzu*, then waywod of *Walachia*, and a peace was concluded. The terms on both sides were, that the *Tartars* should desist from invading *Poland*, and the *Poles* and kosaks from invading *Tartary*. That the *Poles* should trade freely in the sultan's dominions, upon their merchants paying one hundred thousand chekins; and that they should have a resident at the porte. They were likewise to pay forty thousand florins, as a gratuity to the khan of the *Tartars*.

A treaty.

When

When all circumstances are considered, this treaty was rather detrimental than disgraceful to *Osman*; the remains of whose army were saved by it, from unavoidable destruction, though the *Poles*, at the same time, lost twenty thousand men. As to *Osman* himself, however he might resent his disappointment, we know of no violent measures he pursued upon it, only he seemed inclinable to declare war against the emperor, for the assistance he had given to the *Poles*; but the latter declaring, that they would look upon such a step as an infringement of the late treaty, he desisted. *Osman* next, to palliate those mortifications, punished his intention to march in person against the amir of *Sidon*, who had rebelled. This expedition was opposed by all his ministry, as being unsafe, idle, expensive, dangerous, and derogatory to his sublime dignity. *Osman* was then forced to give out, that he intended to fit out a vast naval armament, to be employed against the kosacks in the *Black Sea*, and against prince *Philibert* of *Savoy*, the vice-roy of *Sicily*, who was suspected of intending to favour the revolt of the amir of *Sidon*. But by this time, a deep scheme was laid for his destruction, not really on account of his mismanagement, but his virtues.

The aversion of the great men to his government, had occasioned prodigious abuses in *Constantinople*, and *Osman*, not thinking himself safe to trust to the reports of others, had somtimes privately gone through the streets, that he might be the better assured of the facts. This laudable curiosity, was represented as meanness; and at a time of universal licentiousness, was construed as such by the soldiery, the principal authors of the prevailing disorders. *Osman*, thinking he could not be safe, without finding employment for his mutinous armies, at a distance from *Constantinople*, had formed a scheme of frugality, and was laying up money for the support of his wars; which conduct, his discontented subjects termed sordid avarice, the worst vice an *Othman* emperor can be guilty of in the eyes of his janisaries. Certain engagements of love and honour, had induced him privately to marry a *Turkish* lady, his subject. And when the marriage was declared, it was objected to, as being inconsistent with the late practice of the *Othman* emperors. Matters, with regard to *Osman*, were in this untoward situation, when Sir *Thomas Roe*, so famous for his negotiations in almost every part of the globe, and for the accounts he has left of them; arrived at the porte, as ambassador from king *James* the first. He was instructed, First, to demand redress of some injuries done by the officers of the *Turkish* revenue, to the *English* merchants at *Aleppo*, *Smyrna*, and other places. Secondly, to offer his mediation for terminating the differences between the sultan and the republic of *Poland*, which were now reviving. Thirdly, to intercede for the release of some *Polish* noblemen, and *Scotch* gentlemen, who were

Disorders of Osman's government.

O 4

prifoners. Fourthly, to demand fecurity againſt the depredations of the pirates of *Tunis*, and *Algiers*, upon the *Britiſh*
trade; and fifthly, reſtitution of a large fum of money, that
had been taken by *Oſman*'s ſubjects, from *Arthur Garraway*,
an *Engliſh* merchant, and which had been often in vain
ſolicited before, and promiſed by the *Othman* miniſters.

The anſwers returned by *Oſman* to all theſe requeſts were
manly, friendly, and rational. With regard to the firſt, he
ſaid the ambaſſador might make his own terms. As to the
ſecond, he ſaid that the *Poles* had deceived him, and as matters ſtood between him and them, they could not, conſiſtent-
ly with his honour, admit of any mediation. That, as ſoon
as the peace was renewed, all the *Poliſh* priſoners, in compliment to his *Britannic* majeſty, prince *Koreſki* excepted,
ſhould be releaſed. By this it appears that prince had been
retaken. As to the fourth article, the ambaſſador was offered any ſatisfaction he could deſire; but, with regard to the
fifth, the affair in queſtion, was of ſo old a date, and had
been canvaſſed by ſo many viziers, who had not thought
proper to give any ſatisfaction, that his ſublime highneſs
deſired to be excuſed, for letting it reſt where it did. But
in the letter written by *Oſman*, to *James*, the former poſi-
tively promiſes, that ſtrict juſtice ſhall be done to *Garraway*.

Death and   *Oſman* had been diſcontented ever ſince his diſgrace in *Po-*
character *land*, and daily received new mortifications from his ſoldiers.
of *Oſman*. He obſtinately reſolved to go upon a pilgrimage to *Mecca*.
He was ſtopped in ſetting out upon his journey, by the janiſaries, and ſpahis, who demanded the head of his vizier,
with ſo much obſtinacy, that *Oſman* endeavouring to fortify
himſelf in his ſeraglio, found himſelf abandoned, even by
his domeſtics, and the janiſaries cut the vizier in pieces.
Oſman's ſpirit was now brought down, he would gladly have
eſcaped over into *Aſia*, but he could not. He then endeavoured to ſooth the janiſaries, and might have ſucceeded,
had it not been for the roughneſs of the ₐga, whom they
put to death, as they did ſeveral other courtiers, and
dragging *Muſtapha* out of his cell, they again proclaimed him
emperor, while they impriſoned *Oſman* in the ſeven towers,
where he was ſtrangled, after a very brave reſiſtance, by the
paſha *David*, the new prime vizier. The manner of his
death however, is omitted by prince *Cantemir*, who only
mentions, that he was a prince of great hopes, and murdered
by the ſoldiery.

Muſtapha

Muftapha *reftored.*

THE new vizier *David,* was fo ignorant of every cir- Short
cumftance of the late vizier, that he knew nothing of reign of
the treaty between the *Poles* and *Ofman,* when their am- *Muftapha.*
baffador came to ratify it; which was done under the mediation, and at the earneft requeft, of Sir *Thomas Roe,* the
Britifh ambaffador. *David* hating the new aga of the janifaries, he ordered him to be ftrangled, under pretence that
he had been acceffary to the death of the brave prince *Ko-
refki,* who had been ftrangled in prifon by order of the vizier
himfelf. The aga's death again threw the janifaries into a
ferment, and finding that their re-invefted emperor was
little better than a vicious ideot, things came to extremity,
and the whole empire was full of commotions; at *Baghdad*
particularly, the captain of the janifaries flew the pafha,
burnt the mufti, and all his family, and fet up for an independent fovereign. The houfes of the *Chriftians* were plundered, and at laft, the janifaries, fpahi, and populace, reflecting on the fufferings, the death, and the good qualities of
their late emperor, ftrangled the vizier *David,* in the very
room, and upon the very fpot, where but a few days before he
had ftrangled *Ofman.* For fome time, the janifaries fupported
Muftapha, againft the fpahis, and the populace; but a rebellion breaking out in *Afia,* on account of *Ofman's* death,
they agreed that he fhould be depofed. This fentence was
intimated to him by the new vizier the pafha *Huffeyu,* and
he received it with all the ftupid indifference imaginable.

Reign of Morad *the Fourth, furnamed* Ghazi.

THIS emperor was no more than fourteen years of age Who is
when he was inaugurated, and by his mother's in- fucceeded
ftructions, he behaved fo artfully, that the foldiers did not by *Morad,*
infift upon their ufual largeffes on the creation of a new the fourth.
emperor, becaufe of the lownefs of the treafury. His firft
meafure of government was to put the pafha *Huffeyu* to
death, and to fubftitute in his room the pafha *Halil.* To
recruit the imperial finances, a tax was laid upon all
military officers, and the court moft fcandaloufly demanded
from the *Chriftian* ambaffadors a loan of thirty thoufand
chekins. The infolence of the janifaries, began now fo
much to difguft the military officers, and in general all the
great men in the empire, that they had thoughts of joining
Abaza, the pafha of *Erzerum,* and the pafha of *Baghdad,*
who were ftill in arms, to revenge the death of *Ofman,* while
a large

a large body of *Othmans* were cut off by the *Crim Tartars*, an the kosacks, who rebelled likewise, and entering the *Bosphrus*, in gallies and large boats, they burnt a great number houses and villages, in the neighbourhood of *Constantinop.* itself; nor was their fortune better in *Hungary*, where man of them were cut off by *Esterhasi*, the imperial general.

Peace with *Poland* and *Germany*. The vizier *Halil*, to gain some respite, amidst so many calamities, offered to conclude a new peace with the *Poles* and the *Germans*. This did not prevent *Abaza*, though h was the enemy of the janisaries, from ravaging *Anatolia* and becoming master of the city, and province of *Baghdad* and then forming his army into four divisions, he took the title of shah, and marched at the head of the first into *Meso potamia*. He sent the second into *Syria*, the third toward the *Black Sea*, and the fourth to *Mecca*; and all the four divisions were victorious against the *Turks*. *Murad*, though young, gave many specimens both of prudence and activity The prime vizier was sent with a great army to besiege *Baghdad*, and he defeated *Abaza*, in a bloody battle, near *Kaysariya*. The siege of *Baghdad* was then reassumed, but *Murad*'s general was obliged to raise it with great loss. About the year 1626, the famous *Bethlem Gabor*, the friend of the *Turks*, and the enemy of the *Austrians*, made peace with the latter, to whom he promised restitution of all the places, and liberty to all the prisoners taken by the *Turks* in the late war This treaty was approved of by *Murad*, who next year concluded a treaty with the *German* emperor, at *Komorra*. The *Turks* gaining thereby some respite on the side of *Europe*, the *Persians*, to whom *Abaza* had resigned *Baghdad*, offered to enter into a treaty with *Murad*; but the vizier *Halil* insisting that the rendition of *Baghdad* should be a preliminary, the proposal came to nothing, and the vizier once more marched to *Baghdad*, but without success, as it was defended by *Abaza*, who after almost destroying the *Turkish* army, forced the vizier to a shameful retreat *Murad* about the same time lost *Asac* which was taken by the *Crim Tartars*; but they soon restored it, on promise of pardon for all that had passed, and of retaining their khan whom they had chosen.

The vizier displaced; The pasha *Halil*, upon his late defeat was displaced from the viziership by *Murad*, who appointed the pasha *Khosrou* to succeed him, both in his civil and military capacity. The new general set out with an immense army, and a most formidable train of artillery, against *Abaza*, whom he besieged in *Erzerum*, and obliged him to capitulate; but it is doubtful upon what terms. All we know is, that *Abaza* came to *Constantinople*, where, notwithstanding all his former rebellions, he was taken into great favour by *Murad*, and made beglerbeg of *Bosnia*. The suppression of *Abaza*'s rebellion left the vizier at liberty to pursue his operations against the *Persians*, and he again formed the siege of *Baghdad*, but was

cbsg

obliged again to raife it with great lofs, after battering the city for forty-one days. Next year he defeated the *Perfians* in the plains of *Hamadan*, and once more formed the fiege of *Baghdad*, but he was obliged once more to raife it, with greater lofs than before. Notwithftanding thofe repeated loffes, the vizier had the addrefs to retain his power and credit with the emperor; whofe diffolute manner of living, was the main fpring of all the misfortunes that befel his empire. The kofaks renewed their depredations. The new governor of *Erzerum* rebelled, but was fubdued and beheaded, and *Prufa* and *Magnefia*, were feized upon by two other rebels, one of whom, *Elias*, made terms with the beg'erbeg of *Anatolia*, but, when he came to *Conftantinople* he was ftrangled. In the mean while, the vizier, who had again taken the field againft the *Perfians*, was fo ill fupported that the *Turks* met with vaft loffes, fo that *Morad* was obliged to fend a *Perfian* nobleman, who was his prifoner, to follicit peace from the fhah of *Perfia*.

One of *Morad*'s brothers-in-law, was now prime vizier; but having difobliged the janifaries, he was forced to fend them his head, and thofe of the aga of the fpahis, and the defterdar, to appeafe them, and to accept, from them, of a new vizier. The fultan was fenfible, that nothing could fo effectually curb the licentioufnefs of the foldiers as his finding them employment, and appearing in perfon among them. He accordingly ordered them to be daily difciplined, and he himfelf afifted in their exercifes. By this behaviour he became fo popular, that he ventured, without incurring any danger, to ftrangle the prime vizier, and to cut off the heads of the late mutiny. His army being thus well difciplined, the beglerbeg of *Rumeli* forced the *Perfians* to raife the fiege of *Wan*, and defeated them in a general engagement. This brought on propofals from *Perfia*, which were accepted of. About the year 1633, peace was renewed with the *Hungarians* and *Germans*. *Morad* then turned his arms againft *Amir Fakroddin*, one of the princes of the *Drafeis*, who had now become formidable, having got poffeffion of *Sidon*. A large fleet was equipped and fent againft the rebel, under *Kapudan*, the pafha of *Tripoli*. The pafha on his voyage encountered two *Englifh* fhips, laden with corn, which was a prohibited commodity; and the *Englifhmen*, rather than furrender, fought the whole *Turkifh* fleet for feveral hours, killed their admiral, with great numbers of his men, and then blew up their own fhips. A great army of *Turks* being now affembled againft *Fakroddin*, who was at the head of twenty-five thoufand men, he divided his army into two parts, and put one divifion under the command of his eldeft fon *Ali*, who at firft defeated the *Turks*, but being overpowered by numbers, he was taken prifoner and ftrangled, upon which *Fakroddin*, and all his dominions fell into the hands of *Morad*. It is faid, that the

prifoner

[marginal notes:] his fucceffor beheaded.

Hiftory of Fakroddin.

prisoner behaved with so much address, that *Morad* was not only inclined to save him, but took him into such a degree of favour, as excited the jealousy of his great men, who representing him as an apostate from their faith, (for *Fakrod- din* had turned *Christian*), *Morad* thought proper to pronounce sentence of death upon him, and the unhappy *Fakroddin* was strangled before his face, in the seventieth year of his age.

War with Poland. *Morad* then turned his arms against *Poland*, but after his generals had passed the *Danube*, the *Poles* cut in pieces a body of the *Tartar Turks*, and received a considerable check from the *Polish* kosaks. Notwithstanding this, *Abaza*, the *Turkish* general, boasted to his master of the great exploits he had performed, and he was the more readily credited, as the *Poles* had sent an ambassador to the porte to negociate a peace. *Morad* at first treated this ambassador with infinite contempt, but being soon convinced of the mistake he was under, he put *Abaza* to death, and sued in his turn to *Uladislaus* king of *Poland*, who was with great difficulty prevailed upon to grant it. By this peace, the *Turks* renounced all demands of tribute from *Poland*, and the sultan was to confirm such waywods of *Moldavia*, and *Walachia*, as should be presented and recommended to them by the *Poles*.

Expedition of Morad *Morad* had received a shock by lightning falling in his room, which is said to have made some impression upon his understanding; but at the same time to have altered his way of living. He gave large sums to such of his subjects as had suffered by a great fire, which had burnt down twenty-five thousand houses at *Constantinople*; and he allowed the *Mahometans* to drink wine, upon their paying him a duty. Perceiving that his empire was exposed to continual danger, by the great city of *Baghdad* being in the possession of the *Persians*, he resolved to go in person against that city, and accordingly, in 1634, he marched over into *Asia*. In his march he reduced *Revan*, but returned to *Constantinople* without attacking *Baghdad*, leaving his vizier to continue the war against the *Persians*. *Morad*, upon his return, perceiving the bad effects which wine drinking had upon his subjects, by their caballing and murmuring at the losses of the public, he not only discontinued his licence for selling it, but shut up all the coffee houses, and prohibited all places of public resort from entertaining any company. The affairs of *Transylvania* were at this time in great disorder, and *Ragotzli* prevailed so as to establish himself in the government of that country, against his rival *Stephen Bethlem*, whose interest had been espoused by *Morad* He was then upon a new expedition against the *Persians*, and during his march he lived as laboriously and plainly, as the meanest soldier of his army, making use of no other pillow but his saddle. His army amounted to near three hundred thousand men, and sitting down before *Revan*, it was betrayed to *Morad* by the governor,

governor, for which great rejoiceings were were made at *Conftantinople*, where, by *Morad*'s orders, two of his brothers, *Bajazet* and *Orchan*, had been ftrangled, during his expedition.

Morad then penetrated into *Perfia*, where he committed into *Perfia* great ravages; but the *Perfian* cavalry cut off vaft numbers of his men, and he loft ftill more by the country people, who defended the ftrong paffes of the mountains through which he was to march. At laft he was obliged to put his army into winter quarters, and to return himfelf to *Conftantinople* Upon his departure, the *Perfians* rufhing from their fortreffes befieged and took *Wan*, and put all the *Othman* garrifon to the fword. Two thoufand janifaries revolted to the enemy, and a general fpirit of mutiny fpread itfelf all over *Morad*'s army. The *Tartars* catched the infection, and part of them difowned the fultan's authority, while the *Ruffians* made themfelves mafters of *Afoph*, the moft important city on the *Black Sea*. To retrieve fo many difgraces, *Morad* was not wanting in punifhing the viziers, pafhas, and great officers, to whofe mifconduct the people imputed them; and in the year 1637, he in perfon again laid fiege to *Baghdad*, and carried it on fo obftinately, that he drove on his troops with his drawn fcimiter in his hand, and even killed his vizier, whom he imagined to be fomewhat backward in his approaches. • In fhort, during thirty days, an inceffant ftorm of bullets was poured upon the city from the *Turkifh* artillery, which was at laft obliged to yield to *Morad*'s unremitting fury. Above thirty thoufand *Perfians* who had fubmitted to *Morad*, were by his orders cut in pieces before his face; a mufician, who captivated the fultan's ears with his art, and who was in the number of thofe who were doomed to die, at laft prevailed with him to put a ftop to the flaughter, and all who were not maffacred were faved. A *Turkifh* officer who ferved in this expedition, wrote an account of it, which was publifhed, and which differs in fome particulars from that of the *Chriftians*, and particularly as to the death of the vizier, who he fays was killed by a mufket ball, from the walls of the city. The vizier's fucceffor was *Muftapha*, who was the firft *Othman* that planted the *Turkifh* ftandard on the walls of *Baghdad*; and *Morad* left him to complete his conquefts, while he himfelf fet out for *Conftantinople*, where he arrived on the tenth of *June* 1639. He was followed by a *Perfian* ambaffador with propofals of peace, which were rejected at firft, but foon after a treaty was concluded with the vizier, by which *Baghdad* was to remain in poffeffion of the *Othmans*.

Morad then turned his thoughts to a war with the *Vene-* War with tians, for taking fixteen *Algerine* pirate fhips, in the port of the *Vene-* *Valona*. *Morad* at firft gave orders for the *Venetian* ambaffa- tians, dor at his court, and all his attendants to be cut in pieces,

in revenge of this infult; but he was perfuaded by his minifters to change his fentence into that of imprifoning the
ambaffador in his own houfe; and the *Venetians* fubmitting
to pay him a fum of money by way of indemnification, the
difference was made up. Soon after *Morad* died, in confequence of a debauch he made with his favourites, which he
furvived about eleven days. It is faid, he intended to have
made his favourite *Muftapha* his fucceffor in the empire, and
that he gave orders on his death bed, for putting to death
his brother *Ibrahim*, and the princes of his blood, together
with all the great officers of the empire, whom he fufpected
of being enemies to *Muftapha*, in whofe arms he expired,
on the eighth of *February* 1640. The authority which his
mother retained during his defperate illnefs, faved *Ibrahim*
from the bow-ftring, and the intrigues of *Morad*'s fifter,
who was in love with *Muftapha*, a handfome youth of about
twenty-five years, faved his life likewife; and upon his refigning the poft of kapudan pafha, or lord high admiral, he
was made pafha of *Temefwar*, and it is faid, that he was fo
much affected by his mafter's death, that he attempted to
deftroy himfelf.

Death

**and cha-
racter of
Morad.**

When we confider *Morad*, not only as a free liver but a
free thinker, with regard to fuperftition, which is pretty
much the fame in all religions, we need not be furprifed
that his memory has been branded with the charge of impiety, and difregard to all religion; and that he has been
reprefented as being an habitual drunkard, which led him
to be guilty of the moft horrid cruelties, and the moft ridiculous extravagancies; in which the *Mohametan* and *Popifh*
writers agree. That thofe charges have been greatly exaggerated, appears to be more than probable, from the other
parts of his character, in which writers are equally agreed.
In all the exercifes of arms, he was the ableft performer in
his dominions; in the conduct of great affairs, he difcovered wonderful fteadinefs and prudence, and he was a
great and fuccefsful general, often, by his own prefence
and perfonal conduct, retrieving the mifcarriages of his
generals. He amaffed a moft amafing treafure, which he
left behind him, and he raifed his prerogative to a pitch
higher than ever it had been known, under the greateft of
his predeceffors, and all this before he attained to the thirty-
fecond year of his age. All thofe circumftances being laid
together, prove that this emperor could not have been the
furious, frantic fot, that fome hiftorians have reprefented
him to have been; either perpetually drunk with liquor, or
raging after blood. The weaknefs of the imperial authority
when he was called to the throne, and the ruined ftate of
the public finaces, require the greateft abilities to retrieve,
both which he certainly effected.

The Reign of Sultan Ibrahim

SOME circumstances attending the history of the late reign, instruct us, that an *Othman* emperor is not so succeeded arbitrary as he is represented, and, that certain forms must be gone through before his will can be executed in great matters. As a proof of this, we are to observe, that though *Morad* had ordered his brother *Ibrahim* to be put to death, the mufti was obliged to sign the sentence, or fofta, before it could be carried into execution; and it was prevented by the mother getting it into her possession. It is equally certain, that though *Morad*, perhaps, in the delirum of his illness, wanted to transfer the succession from the blood of *Othman*, to another family, (it is doubtful whether to *Mustapha*, or the khan of the *Tartars*;) no regard after his death was paid to his will. *Ibrahim*, the only surviving prince of the *Othman* lime, was at the time of his brother *Morad*'s death, immured in a little dark prison, which he barricaded in the inside, when they came to take him out of it, in order for his inauguration. His mother's authority and address, had prevailed with the great officers of the empire and army, to acknowledge him for the heir of the government; and being convinced that they came to recognise, and not to murder him, he gave them admittance. He had been a prisoner for four years; at this time, he was not twenty-three years of age; and when he came abroad, through the habit of a continual sedentary life, he appeared infirm and aukward.

The ceremonies of his inauguration being over, he entered the seraglio, where he soon discovered that he intended, by giving a loose to his natural disposition, to make himself amends for his long imprisonment. He had, notwithstanding his confinement, been allowed to indulge himself in the use of women to an excess, which had impaired his constitution, but desire still subsisting, his mother, and his minister the first vizier, took care to supply him with every allurement of beauty that could divert him from business. His inclination was turned towards the favourite sultana of his brother *Morad*, but that lady being equally formed for ambition as for love, it did not suit the views of the sultana mother, that she should gain any ascendency over *Ibrahim*, and she chose to sequester herself in the apartments in the seraglio, destined for the wives of the deceased sultans, which e en the reigning emperor could not, without the highest breach of decency, invade.

The first attention of *Ibrahim*, or rather his ministry, after matters were settled at home, was turned towards the *Black Sea*, where *Azoph* was in the hands of the kofaks, who had got together so great a number of small vessels, which

they

Side notes: Who is succeeded by *Ibrahim*. His disposition. Expedition against *Azoph*.

they employed in acts of piracy, that they interrupted the navigation to *Constantinople*, and other parts of the *Othman* dominions. The kosaks defended the place so bravely, that they baffled and ruined a numerous army sent against it by *Ibrahim*; but a second, headed by the vizier himself, advancing against it, they applied for protection to the czar of *Russia*, who had just made peace with the *Turks*, and whose domestic affairs would not permit him to embroil himself in the quarrel; so that the kosaks were forced to abandon the city, after ruining its fortifications and houses, and bringing off their valuable effects. The *Othman* ministry next renewed the peace with *Persia*, but they failed in a treacherous attempt to surprise the strong fortress of *Raab*, in *Hungary*. *Mustapha*, the same, possibly, who had been the favourite of the late reign, was the first vizier, and acted with such a spirit, that he cut off the heads of sedition, particularly the pashas of *Halep*, and *Kaffa*; so that the emperor securely enjoyed his pleasures. It soon appeared, that *Mustapha* himself was only the agent of the sultana mother; for when he and the pasha of *Kapudan* began to assume some airs of independency, they were immediately cut off. The khan of the *Tartars* himself, who had been so powerful in the late reign, did not escape feeling her resentment, for he was deposed, after making an unsuccessful campaign against the *Poles*.

Alterations in the ministry.

The name of the new vizier was *Mohammed*, who had been governor of *Damascus* and *Beker*. The pasha of *Rhodes*, succeeded to the high post of pasha of *Kapudan*. However indolent the emperor might have been at this time in person, his ministers seem to have been enterprising and vigilant. Having cleared the *Black Sea* from pyrates, a resolution was formed for chastising the *Maltese*, the *Venetians*, and the other *Mediterranean* maritime states, who had of late made prizes of great numbers of rich ships belonging to *Othman* subjects, and killed some of the great officers who defended them; particularly the kislar aga, in his voyage to *Egypt*, whither he was bound, in order to avoid becoming the sacrifice of court intrigues. As there was peace at this time between the porte and the *Venetians*, the *Othman* ministry highly resented the shelter and assistance which the *Maltese* ships, who had made all the prizes met with in their ports; particularly in those of *Candia*, or *Crete*, and a resolution was taken in the divan, to employ the whole force of the empire in taking that island from the *Venetians*. This resolution was forwarded with great firmness, and the most impenetrable secrecy, while the emperor's seraglio appeared with such a face of gaity, that had it not been for the well-timed resolution of *Bendish*, the *English* resident, the merchants of his nation trading to *Constantinople* must have been considerable sufferers. That minister, understanding that many of their goods had been forced from them without

out

out payment, ordered lamps of fire to be affixed to the mafts of thirteen *Englifh* fhips, and that they fhould anchor under the walls of the feraglio. This was done in confequence of an eftablifhed cuftom at the *Othman* court, by which every man, who, with fire upon his head demands an audience of the emperor, muft be admitted to it; and the vizier underftanding the meaning of the application, chofe to fatisfy the *Englifh*, by paying them their demands, without carrying their complaints farther.

The *Venetians* were no ftrangers to the vaft warlike pre-   War with parations carried on by the porte, and though they were   the *Vene*-pretended to be defigned againft *Malta*, yet their baillo, for *tians.* fo their refident at the *Othman* court was called, foon faw by the manner in which he was denied an audience of the vizier, that the ftorm was to fall upon his republic. On the laft of *April* 1645, the *Othman* fleet fet fail. It confifted of feventy-three gallies, with eight more from *Barbary*, one great galleon, two galliaffes, and twenty two preffed fhips; befides a vaft number of lefler fhips, which ferved as tranfports, and the whole took on board fifty thoufand timmariots, common foldiers of different nations, fourteen thoufand fpahis, feven thoufand janifaries, and three thoufand pioneers. Upon their failing, war was declared againft the republic of *Venice*, and their ambaffador was feized and imprifoned. Though the *Venetians* had then a good fleet at fea, yet it was unable to withftand fo powerful an armament. They applied for affiftance to the pope, and other *Chriftian* princes, who at laft fent them reinforcements, but too late to be of effectual fervice againft fo formidable an enemy, and to compleat their misfortunes, a very bad underftanding fubfifted among their commanding officers. The *Turks* landed about the middle of *June* in *Candia*, defeated feveral bodies of the *Venetians* who ppofed them, and ftormed with a great flaughter of the befieged, the town of *Kanea*, which was reckoned to be the fecond place of ftrength and importance in the ifland. Next year, the *Venetian* general was killed in defending *Retino*, which was likewife taken by the *Turks*; while the diffentions amongft the *Chriftian* officers arofe to fuch heights, that inftead of fighting the *Turks*, they appeared prepared to fight one another; fo that the infidels met with very little refiftance in becoming mafters of all the ifland, the capital, which was likewife called *Candia*, excepted. *Morofini* was then admiral of the *Venetians*, and a brave, experienced officer. Arriving off *Candia* with a fleet of twenty-two capital fhips, and finding that the infidels could not be drawn out of their harbours to fight him, he directed his courfe to the *Dardanels*, thinking that the danger of *Conftantinople* might bring on a general engagement. Finding this expedient unfuccefsful, he returned to *Candia*; and while he was debating with the *Venetian* providitor *Grimani*, about intercepting the *Turkifh* fleet, it landed forty thoufand men upon the iſland. All that the *Venetians* could then do, was to endeavour to intercept the infidel fleet in its return, but in this attempt likewiſe, they were unſucceſsful, and the brave *Moroſini* loſt his life. To counterballance thoſe misfortunes, the *Venetians* were ſucceſsful in *Dalmatia*, where they defeated the *Turks*, and took ſeveral towns, but loſt great part of their fleet by ſtorms.

Revolution at Conſtantinople. In the mean while, a great and unexpected revolution happened at *Conſtantinople*. The miniſter there, with the ſultana mother, called generally the ſultana *Valide*, at their head, found their account in keeping the emperor, totally immerſed in the pleaſures of the ſeraglio, which he carried to the moſt extravagant lengths; and at laſt, a procureſs, whom he employed in his amouis, gave him hopes of enjoying the daughter of the mufti, of whom he was paſſionately fond, and who was eſteemed to be the greateſt beauty of the empire. *Ibrahim* propoſed to her father to make her his wife; but the old man knew that as the empire was already heired by his other wives, that honour ſignified nothing, eſpecially as he was no ſtranger to the levity and inconſtancy of the emperor. The mufti returned him an evaſive but reſpectful anſwer; and, by his private order, the young lady rejected the propoſition of marriage, and proved herſelf to be ſuperior to all the infamous arts made uſe of by the ſultan's agents to ſeduce her virtue. *Ibrahim*, determined to enjoy her, employed force, and, having gratified his brutal inclinations, he ſent her home to her father with diſgrace. The mufti, who was a man of ſenſe and reſolution, was at no loſs how to proceed in being revenged. He opened himſelf to the paſha *Mohammed*, and to the aga of the janiſaries, whom he convinced, that *Ibrahim*, being as vicious as he was weak, they could have no ſafety but by depoſing him. The ſultana *Valide*, was no ſtranger to the ſubject of their conſultations, and frankly owned that her ſon was incapable of governing, and that ſhe would readily agree to his being depoſed, provided he might be permitted to enjoy his life in a private ſtation. As the vizier *Ahmud* had been the chief inſtrument employed in the unworthy actions of the emperor, particularly in the rape of the mufti's daughter, he was ſtrangled, and the janiſaries obliged *Ibrahim* to give the ſtandiſh (for ſo the office of vizier is called) to the paſha *Mahommed*.

where Ibrahim is depoſed. The circumſtances of the depoſition of *Ibrahim*, were very formal, and proved what we have hinted at, that there is a law in the *Othman* empire, ſuperior to the will of the ſultan. This ſeems to ariſe from the conſtitution of the old califat, in which the temporal was ſubordinate to the religious authority in the ſame ſovereign, not without a mixture of popular interpoſition upon great occaſions. The janiſaries having carried their point in a vizier, demanded in general terms, whether a fool and a tyrant might not be depoſed from

from the government. The mufti, after real or affected deliberation, anfwered in the affirmative; upon which the affembly required him as the judge and interpreter of the law of their prophet, to fummon the emperor to appear next day in perfon, at the divan, that it might be known whether he was capable of adminiftring juftice to his people. A fefta, by way of fummons, was accordingly made out, and carried to the emperor, who tore it to pieces, as it implied, that he was by his religion, under an obligation of obeying it. He was proceeding to extremities, when the mufti hearing what had happened, fent him another and a higher fefta, declaring that every perfon, even the fultan himfelf, who did not obey the law of God, ceafed to be a true believer, and, by becoming a kafre or infidel, he had forfeited his dignity, ipfo facto, and was no longer fit to govern.

Ibrahim knew fo little of the meafures that had been taken **His death.** for his depofition, that, turning to his vizier, he ordered him to bring him the mufti's head, and, by not being inftantly obeyed, he was given to underftand, that he was no longer in a condition to command; upon which, all his fpirits forfook him, and he fled to his mother for protection and advice. Her intrepidity did not abandon her upon this trying occafion. She boldly faced the janifaries, and the other infurgents, who had by this time broken tumultuoufly into the palace, and prevailed with them to offer no violence to the perfon of their fovereign, but to fuffer him to return, under a guard, to his former place of confinement; where, growing impatient and furious, he was, a few days after, ftrangled, by order of the new government, as is moft probable, on the feventeenth of *Auguft*, 1648. His character was that of a ftupid, capricious, voluptuous prince, without having, fo far as we know, a fingle good quality to counterbalance his bad ones.

The Reign of Mohammed IV.

THE late emperor, *Ibrahim*, left nine fons; of whom *Mohammed*, whofe mother was the daughter of a *Greek* prieft, *Soleyman* and *Achmet*, were fucceffively emperors *Mohammed* at the time of his fucceffion, was no more than feven years of age; and, by the arrangements of the government, it fufficiently appears that the confpirators had perfectly well ftudied the nature of the cataftrophe they had acted, as well as the future diftribution of imperial power. This feems to have been owing to the great talents of *Mehemed*, furnamed *Kioprili*, the founder of a celebrated family of the fame name; all of them men of extraordinary genius for government, and afterwards, long filling the higheft places in that of the *Othmans*. He had on account of his poverty, which his countrymen attributed to his integrity, been overlooked in the storms that fell upon the pashas in the late reign; and though he had been preferred by the faction which dethroned *Ibrahim*, yet he was so far from approving of their conduct or principles, that he resolved to lose no opportunity of cutting them off. A regency of twelve persons, at the head of which was the sultana *Valide*, had been, appointed to manage the government before the death of *Ibrahim*, till the young emperor should come of age. *Kioprili's* first care was to replenish the treasury, and the sultana *Valide*, well knowing that a foreign, especially a *Christian*, war, was the only means that could work off the bad humours, and insolence of the soldiery, who made the streets of *Constantinople* run with blood, it was resolved to continue that with the *Venetians*. Its threatre was very extended, for it lay not only in *Candia*, but in *Dalmatia*, *Bosnia*, *Albania*, and the *Morea*, and in short all over the *Asiatic* possessions of that republic. Hitherto it had been carried on in general to the disadvantage of the *Turks*, but the distractions of the empire far from obliging the new regency, as the *Venetians* hoped for, to restore peace, determined them to continue the war with more vigour than ever. The same spirit pushed them on to send secret orders to their pashas to begin hostilities in *Hungary*, where they were beat by the imperialists with dishonour, and the pasha of *Buda* made prisoner.

Progress of the Candian war. The new regency made the *Candian* war their chief object. The command of it had been committed to the pasha *Hussyu*, who gained several important advantages, but lost them all, upon the arrival of six hundred men, and sixty knights from *Malta*, and *Hussyu's* army begun to be reduced to distress for provisions. This was occasioned by the *Venetian* fleet having blocked up that of the *Othmans* in the *Dardanelles*; but winter obliging the former to withdraw, the army in *Candia* soon received supplies of provisions. In the beginning of the year 1651, no fewer than eleven hundred sail, of all kinds, loaded with men, ammunition, and provisions sailed for the use of the *Othmans* in *Candia*, where they landed with a trifling loss, though pursued by the *Venetian* fleet. This armament, joined to that already in *Candia*, encouraged the *Turks* to provoke the *Venetians* to two sea engagements, in which the infidels were beaten, and lost the greatest part of their fleet. Those disasters occasioned a mutiny among the *Othman* land troops, and it scarcely was suppressed, when an account came of two rebellions breaking out, one in *Damascus*, and the other at *Grand Cairo*. This embarrassed the *Turks* so much that the *Venetians* had leisure to send such reinforcements to their troops in *Candia*, as changed the opperations there, from a

siege

siege to a campaign. The *Othmans* were equally industrious on their part to repair their losses, and in the year 1624, in a sea engagement with the *Venetians* off the *Dardanelles*, the *Turks* lost six thousand men, and seven ships of war, notwithstanding which their kapudan pasha forced his way to *Candia*, where he landed twelve thousand fresh troops. Next year, the *Venetians* gave a new defeat to the *Othman* fleet, which increased the public discontent so much, that viziers, pashas, admirals, governors and generals, were every day strangled or displaced, throughout all parts of the empire.

The regency, notwithstanding all those disgraces, continued firm, and perhaps were secretly not displeased, at seeing so many turbulent spirits removed. Far from being humbled, when the *Venetians* offered to treat of peace, they rejected all terms in which the entire surrender of *Candia* was not made a preliminary. All hopes of peace thus vanishing, the merchants and tradesmen of *Constantinople* rose tumultuously, forced the regency to renew the negociation, and put the grand vizier to death for opposing them. It appears, as if the mutineer factions had persuaded the sultan, though he could not then be above twelve years of age, to take the reins of government into his own hands. The negotiation for peace being renewed, the *Othmans* demanded an immoderate sum to defray the expences of the war, which broke off the treaty anew. To add to the public misfortunes of the state, the janisaries, and spahis, though in every other respect opposite to one another, united in their remonstrances against a maritime war, in which so many of their countrymen had already miserably perished; so that when the new grand vizier, who had been pasha of *Aleppo*, and had been indefatigable in recruiting the *Turkish* marine, ordered them to embark, they refused to obey him, and haughty as he was, he was obliged to purchase their compliance by advancing them four months pay. Their fellows at *Constantinople* were not so tractable. Perceiving the maritime war still to be continued, they in a manner took the government into their own hands, deposed the vizier, drove the mufti out of *Jerusalem*, and new modelled the state, and threatened even to dethrone the sultan if they were opposed. *Mohammed*, young as he was, found means to quell this sedition; and being sensible of the necessity of having a man of abilities and authority to be his first minister, he named to that post *Kioprili*, who was then pasha of *Damascus*; the pasha of *Silistria*, was made high admiral, and *Husseyn* was continued in his command in *Candia*. All this while, the most incredible efforts were making for fitting out from all the ports of the empire, a greater naval armament than ever. It consisted of sixty gallies, twenty-eight ships, and nine galleasses; by which we are to understand ships of war built after different constructions.

P 3   Though

Though the *Venetian* fleet was far inferior in force to this, yet their men were incomparably better sailors, and they lay at the mouth of the *Dardanelles*, waiting for the *Turks*, whom they attacked, and deftroyed all their large armament, excepting eighteen galleons. After this, the *Venetians* eafily became mafters of *Tenedos*, and *Lemnos*, and gave many other fevere blows to the *Turkifh* marine.

Mutiny at Conftan-tinople. It appeared on this occafion, that the fpirit of the *Othman* government was as unfubmitting as its refources were in-exhauftible; for when the *Venetians* again fignified their willingnefs to come to an accommodation, notwithftanding the great advantages they had obtained, *Mohammed* de-manded, that all *Candia* fhould be delivered up to him, with three millions of crowns for the expences of the war. This obftinacy was far from being agreeable to the common people, who now felt the price of bread raifed by the in-terruption which the *Venetians* fhipping gave to their tranf-portations by fea. *Mohammed* and his new grand vizier, finding that there was no end of conceffions, acted now with a becoming intrepidity: the emperor himfelf mounted his horfe, and being attended by his vizier, and fuch of his guards as continued firm in their allegiance, no fooner did he appear in public than he won the hearts of the populace. He proceeded to the moft mutinous parts of the city, where in his own prefence, the boldeft of the infurgents were dragged to juftice, and executed. In the mean while, orders were iffued for retaking *Tenedos*, and *Lemnos*, which was effected with great lofs, by the *Turks*, and entirely quelled, for a fhort time, the fpirit of mutiny at *Conftan-tinople*. *Mohammed*, encouraged by thofe fucceffes and dif-pofitions, ordered frefh levies to be made, and that his army fhould rendezvous at *Adrianople*, from whence he propofed to march at their head into *Dalmatia*, to drive the *Venetians* out of that province.

Rebellion of the pafha of *Aleppo*. It appears as if, at this time, the pafha of *Aleppo*, who was remarakably ambitious and turbulent, had formed a defign to be at the head of the government, and perhaps to dethrone the emperor. *Krioprili* fufpecting thofe defigns, no fooner arrived at *Adrianople*, than he put the pafha's brother to death, on pretence of his not being punctual at the time of the rendezvous. The pafha was then at the head of forty thoufand men, with whom he immediately marched towards *Scutari*, burning and deftroying the country where-ever he came; and his army being now increafed to feventy thoufand men, he alarmed *Conftantinople* itfelf; demanding at the fame time, that the heads of *Krioprili*, and four other counfellors fhould be fent him. To give fome colour of juftice to his proceedings, he proclaimed a young man, whom he carried along with him, emperor of the *Othmans*, pretending him to be the lawful fon of the late fultan *Morad*. This increafed his army to a more formidable number than

ever,

ever, and the grand vizier marching in person against him, was defeated, with the loss of all his artillery and baggage; but not being pursued, he rallied the broken remains of his army, and in a few days was joined by the sultan himself. Various expedients were then proposed for an accommodation, the imperial army being now as strong as the rebels. The pasha agreed to treat, *Mortaza* the pasha was nominated by the emperor to be his plenipotentiary on the occasion. *Mortaza* had the address, under pretence of respect for the imperial authority, not only to withdraw his army during the negotiation, but to treat in a retired place, where he had some men ambushed, who suddenly fell upon the pasha, and strangled him, and seventeen of his friends, whom he had brought along with him to be witnesses of the accommodation. The pasha's army hearing of the fate of their general, in whom all their hopes were centered, immediately lost all courage, and quietly dispersed themselves.

Kioprili discovered, or pretended to discover, that other great men of the empire had abetted the pasha in his rebellion, which gave him a pretext to take off their heads, and among others, that of *Husseyu*, the pasha of *Candia*. His suspicions seem not to have been without grounds, for the nephew of the pasha of *Aleppo* appeared at the head of another great army to revenge his uncle's death; but *Kioprili* acted with so much address, and knew so well how to place his money, that this insurrection came to nothing likewise. This year, by the advice of *Kioprili*, the forts at the mouth of the *Dardanelles*, called the *Queen Mother*'s castle, were built, by which the important communication between the *Propontis* and the *Black Sea* were secured. *(margin: Great men executed.)*

Kioprili, by the above, and many other bloody severities, which he exercised upon the great men of the empire, struck terror into all his opponents, while his own active disposition, though he was now far advanced in years, and the abilities of his son, which were superior to his own, secured to him the affections of his master. By this time, the flames of war had spread to *Germany*, and the grand vizier marched in person to *Belgrade*, where falling sick, he was carried back to *Adrianople*, but gave such directions to the general of the *Turks* in *Hungary*, and *Transylvania*, that he took *Waradin*, and made several other important conquests in those countries, and would have taken *Clausemburg* likewise, had it not been relieved by general *Schmeidau*. All this while the war seemed to languish in *Candia*, on the side of the *Turks*. Four thousand *French* auxiliaries had been sent after the peace of the *Pyrenese*, into that island, where they reduced some places; but were repulsed before *Kanea*, and indeed, the situation of the empire did not at this time suffer the *Othman* government to make the reduction of *Candia* its chief object. This year, viz. 1661, old *Kioprili* sunk under age and fatigue, and not only obtained permission *(margin: War in Hungary.)*

from

from the grand fignior, that his fon fhould be affociated with him in the vizierfhip, but that he fhould fucceed him in the fame, which he did on the very day his father died. His firft care, was to remove from his mafter's court and councils, all whom he fufpected to be diffatisfied with his adminiftration, among whom was the mufti, whom he banifhed to *Gallipoli*. Thofe precautions could not be taken without relaxing the war againft the *Venetians*, who thereby obtained fome advantages over the *Othmans*.

Arrival of an English ambaffador at Conftantinople.

In the year 1662, the earl of *Winchelfea* arrived as his *Britannic* majefty's ambaffador at the porte, where he met with a moft magnificent, and indeed cordial, reception; and obtained feveral favours from the emperor and his minifters, in behalf of the *English* nation, whofe fhips had been complained of by the *Algerines*.

Rebellion of Mor taza.

All the cares of *Kioprili* at this time, were employed in fecuring to his mafter his pleafures, particularly that of hunting, in which he was fo extravagant, that he often employed above thirty thoufand men to find him game. So intent was he upon this diverfion, that he left the affairs of government entirely to his vizier, who proceeded with great feverity againft all, whom he either knew, or fufpected to be, his enemies. Having reafons for being diffatisfied with *Mortaza*, the pafha of *Baghdad*, he obliged him to take refuge with one of the heads of the *Kurds*, who was his father-in-law; but, before the vizier could reduce him, a revolution happened in *Georgia*. After *Azerum* had been fubdued by the emperor *Solyman*, the government of *Georgia* was parcelled out under feven princes, of whom three were to be tributary to the *Othmans*, and three to the *Perfians*; but the whole to be immediately fubject to *Achick Pafs*, who was to poffefs the feventh divifion, without being fubject to either power. This prince dying, his wife took a fecond hufband, whom in prejudice of her fon, fhe raifed to the throne; but his authority was difowned by the three *Perfian* provinces, who chofe another head, as did the three *Othman* likewife, but both parties at laft fixed upon the choice of another prince, and thofe troubles fubfided. *Kioprili* being thus at liberty to purfue his revenge upon *Mortaza*, he gave orders for befieging him in *Ziari*, a fortrefs belonging to the *Zidi Kurds*, who at firft defeated the *Turks*, but being afterwards overpowered, they ftruck off *Mortaza*'s head, to fave themfelves from being put to the fword.

War with the Chriftians.

The vizier then had leifure to turn his mafter's arms againft the *Chriftians*, but before he took the field he punifhed fome of them, for having, againft his orders, repaired, or rebuilt fome of their churches, that had been burnt down at *Conftantinople*, and reformed feveral abufes that had been introduced in the coin by the *Jews*, and *Armenians*. War was ftill going on with the *Venetian*, who this year did confiderable damage to the *Turkish* navigation, by taking, or
deftroying

destroying a very rich fleet, bound for *Alexandria.* As the emperor of *Germany* knew that great preparations were making by the porte against his dominions; he endeavoured to enter into a negotiation with the pasha of *Buda,* but in 1663, all the conferences, which had advanced very far, broke up, and the sultan in person, attended by his vizier, took the field, and ordered the *Tartars,* who were at this time at war with the cosaks, to furnish them with a hundred thousand men. The grand army arriving at the *Danube,* its van was attacked in passing that river, by *Forgatz,* the governor of *New Heusel,* but his party were surrounded and cut in pieces; and the *Turks* then invested *New Heusel.* This place then made a very gallant defence, and the *Turks* are said to have lost fifteen thousand of their best troops, in the several desperate, but unsuccessful, assaults they gave it for forty-three days. At last, in the month of *September,* one of the powder magazines blew up, which obliged the besieged to surrender the place, after making an honourable capitulation.

The brave count *Serini,* one of the *Hungarian* generals, endeavoured to stop the progress of the *Turks,* who were now ravaging *Stiria,* and *Croatia,* but his force being very inconsiderable, he could not prevent their becoming masters of the *Leventz,* and *Novogrede,* and then taking up their winter quarters at *Belgrade.* In the spring of the year 1664, *Serini,* who, inconsiderable as his force was, had given the *Turks* several checks, was at the head of twenty-five thousand men, took *Berzenthe,* and *Bakokza,* and defeated a large body of the infidels; besides obtaining over them many other important advantages He took a *Palanka,* and *Quinque Ecclesiæ,* or *Five Churches,* where he put the garrison to the sword, and laid siege to *Sigeth* itself, but was obliged to raise it upon the approach of a large body of the infidels. This encouraged the vizier to besiege *Serinswar,* but his party was intercepted by the count *de Serini,* who killed two hundred of them, and took a great number of prisoners. It appears, as if a very bad understanding at this time, subsisted between *Serini,* and the other imperial generals, particularly *Montecuculi,* for when the former had laid siege to *Canysia, Montecuculi* refused to support him, so that he was obliged to retreat with loss to *Serinswar,* a fortress belonging to himself, which was immediately invested, taken, and razed to the ground by the *Turks,* while *Serini,* in resentment of the injuries done him by the imperialists, separated himself from their army.

On the other side, *Nitra,* and *Leventz,* were recovered by count *Suse,* another imperial general, who defeated two armies of *Turks,* each consisting of fourteen thousand men. The infidels endeavoured to retake *Leventz,* but they were defeated with great slaughter by count *Suse,* and besides six thousand men, lost all their artillery, baggage, and provisions,

Actions of count Serini against the Turks

in Hungary.

vifions, to a vaſt amount. In this battle, the imperialiſts gave no quarter to any but ſeven hundred *Moldavians*, and *Walachians*, who having inliſted in the *Turkiſh* army were puniſhed as traytors and deſciters, by being hanged with their muſkets ſlung round their ſhoulders. Count *Suſe* after this, reduced *Barkan*; but all thoſe were only detached actions, for the two grand armies under the vizier, and *Montecuculi*, had ſpent the ſummer in obſerving one another's motions. At laſt, on the firſt of *Auguſt*, the vizier ſent half his army over to *Raab*, with an intention to bring over the other half in perſon. *Montecuculi* before this could be effected, attacked the diviſion that had paſſed with great fury, and the waters abating during the battle, the reſt of the infidel army were paſſing over, when *Montecuculi*, ſummoning all his ſtrength, attacked the janiſaries, and ſpahis, with ſo much fury, that they were entirely routed, with the loſs of ſixteen thouſand men killed, or drowned in their flight. Sixteen pieces of cannon, the grand vizier's ſtandard, and one hundred and twenty-ſix colours, five thouſand ſcimitars, and a great number of horſes were taken. In ſhort, this was looked upon as being the moſt complete defeat that the *Turks* had ever received in *Hungary*. The loſs of the *Chriſtians* amounted to about three thouſand men.

The loſs of this battle diſpoſed the *Turks* as much as the imperialiſts had been before, towards a peace. The diſappointment, which their mighty expectations had received from their diſgrace, as well as defeat, produced a mutiny in their camp, which might have proved fatal to *Kioprili*, had he not convinced the troops that his paſſing the *Raab*, which the *Turks* looked upon as being ominous, was owing to the emperor's expreſs commands, and that he had always diſapproved of it. A treaty was then ſet on foot, and concluded in the following terms. " That *Tranſylvania* remain with its ancient limits and privileges, under the command of prince *Michael Apaſi*. That the emperor of *Germany* have liberty to fortify both *Gutta*, and *Nitra*. That the *Turk* ſhall not alter, or innovate any thing on the confines of *Hungary*, or any other part bordering on the emperor's dominions. That *Apaſi* pay ſix hundred thouſand dollars to the *Othman Porte*, for expences of the war That the two provinces of *Zatmar*, and *Zaboli*, granted to *Ragotzki*, by his imperial majeſty during life, return again to the emperor, to which neither the prince of *Tranſylvania*, much leſs the *Othman Porte*, ſhall ever pretend. That the ſtrong caſtle of *Zechilhyd*, which revolted from the emperor, be demoliſhed, in regard, neither party will relinquiſh his right thereunto. That *Varadin*, and *New Heuſel*, remain to the *Turks*, having conquered them by force of their own A peace   arms. That for confirmation of this peace, ambaſſadors be concluded interchangeably ſent with preſents of equal value."

                                                                 This

This peace gave equal satisfaction to both parties. The *German* emperor had many reasons arising from his own family and affairs in *Europe*, and the vizier *Kioprili*, or *Ahmed*, as he is called, besides the violent passion which his army expressed to be led back to their own country, knew that he had many powerful enemies about his master's person, who were endeavouring to ruin him. Vast rejoicings were made on both sides, and it was resolved that the interchanging of ambassadors should take place the following *May* It seems evident, that by concluding this peace, *Kioprili* shewed himself a greater politician, than either his enemies at his master's court, or the ministers of the *European* courts; because, had the imperialists pursued their blow, they might not only have recovered all *Hungary*, but have preserved *Candia* to the *Venetians*, which was of the utmost consequence at that time, to the common cause of christendom. But above all, he shewed wonderful abilities in managing his master *Mohammed*, who being disguisted at the frequent tumults that had happened at *Constantinople*, had retired to *Adrianople*. *Kioprili*, had the address to persuade him, that his late defeat and disgust was owing to the spirit of mutiny, which had possessed his troops, who were impatient to return to *Asia*, and had been justly chastised for their disobedience, and that the conquests he had made of *New Heusel*, and *Novigrad*, and which were entirely owing to his valour, more than overballanced all his losses. But his chief argument for the peace, was the expediency and necessity the porte was under, of turning the whole force of its arms against *Candia*; the reduction of which, was of infinite more consequence to the glory of the *Othman* empire, than that of all *Hungary* could be. These reasons appeared so plausible to *Mohammed*, that he received *Kioprili* into a greater degree of favour than ever.

By this time, *Mohammed* had a son by his favourite wife, which put him upon the execrable expedient of dispatching his brother. It appears however, as if this fratricide, if committed, must have been warranted by the *festa* of the *mufti*, who refused to grant it on account of the weakness of the *Othman* line. *Kioprili*, was then at *Belgrade*, to which place he sent for his mother, on pretence of testifying his filial piety, but in reality to obtain information concerning the state of affairs at court, which she perfectly understood, being one of the most artful women in the empire, and a most useful agent for her son about the person of the emperor; with whom she was a great favourite. *Kioprili* remained at *Belgrade* till the arrival of *Mohammed Bey*, pasha of *Romelia*, who had been nominated by the sultan for his ambassador to the court of *Vienna*, and upon the arrival of count *Lesley*, who was nominated ambassador on the part of the emperor, at *Belgrade*, he set out with that nobleman for *Adrianople*, where he was received in a manner more hohourable,

Conduct of Kioprili

nourable, and affectionate, than ever had been known to
be expressed by an *Othman* emperor to a subject. *Kioprili*,
by this time, had ordered great bodies of troops to defile
towards *Dalmatia*, and acted with such exquisite policy,
that, least his having laid the blame of his defeat at the
Raab, should come to his master's ears, he persuaded him to
pardon all the mutineers, and to forgive all that passed,
while they on the other hand were silent, as to the transaction, being sensible to what motive they owed their lives.
About the same time, the *Genoese* renewed their treaty of
commerce with the porte, notwithstanding all the opposition it met with from the *French* ambassador.

*Candian
war re-
newed.*

Kioprili employed the short respite he now obtained from
war, in making most amazing preparations for the reduction of *Candia*, where the *Othmans* still preserved their footing, but without being able to master the capital, which
was reckoned one of the strongest cities in the world.
Kioprili charged himself with the execution of this expedition ; but that they might proceed with some shew of moderation, he sent for *Balarino*, the *Venetian* minister at the
porte, and demanded from him, the surrender of *Candia*,
letting him know at the same time, that should his masters
refuse to comply, he was resolved to employ all the force of
the empire against it. All the answer *Balarino* could return
was, that he should communicate the demand to his masters.
Kioprili, in the mean while, omitted nothing that could secure the peace of the empire, during his absence on the
Candian expedition. He composed the disturbances that
had arisen in *Egypt*; he persuaded his master to return to
Constantinople, where he was received with great joy, and
every thing that had passed was forgiven It is remarkable, that the hearts of *Mohammed*, and his vizier were so
much set on the reduction of *Candia*, that, sensible of their
own inferiority by sea to the *Venetians*, they applied to the
earl of *Winchelsea*, to take into their pay fifteen *English* ships
of war; but his excellency soon convinced them, that his
master being then at war with the *Dutch*, could not then
comply with their request, and his apology was accepted of.

*History of
Sabata-
Sevi, the
impostor,*

Every thing being now ready, *Kioprili* leaving proper
persons about his master, embarked for *Candia*, where he
landed, and put his men into winter quarters. This gives
us an opportunity of mentioning one the boldest impostures,
that ever employed the pen of history. A young *Jew*, one
Sabatia Sevi, the son of a broker, at *Smyrna*, having been
banished that city for a tumult, had wandered through
many parts of *Asia*, and at *Jerusalem* he met one *Nathan*,
when it was agreed upon between them, that *Sevi* should act
the part of the messiah of the *Jews*, and *Nathan*, that of his
prophet. It would have been impossible for them to have
succeeded in this frantic design, without being themselves
possessed of a certain degree of enthusiasm. At *Gaza*, both

impostors

impoſtors began their operations, and *Nathan* announced
the miſſion of the ſham meſſiah. It happened on account
of ſome cabaliſtical jargon about numbers, that great expectations had been raiſed among the *Jews* in general, concerning the mighty events that were to happen in favour of
the *Jews*, during 1666; and thoſe ridiculous notions had
gathered ſtrength by time. *Sevi*, who, during the courſe
of his wanderings, had been guilty of ſome amorous extra-
vagances, was perfectly well qualified for the part he was to
act, being poſſeſſed of a graceful perſon, a fluent tongue, and
a winning deportment. *Nathan* performed his part ſo well,
that he ſoon brought the *Jews* of *Gaza* to believe in his
meſſiah; and moving from thence to *Jeruſalem*, he converted all his countrymen there, into the belief that their kingdom was to be reſtored by *Sevi*, and all the *Syrian Jews*
followed their example. The impoſtors were even ſo
daring, as to pretend that they would pluck the crown from
Mohammed's head, before the end of the year, and their
followers left off all kind of buſineſs, but that of repeating
portions of ſcripture, predicting the approaching reign of
their meſſiah.

Nathan choſe twelve of their followers at *Damaſcus*, to
preſide over the twelve tribes of *Iſrael*, while *Sevi* viſited
Smyrna, where he had intereſt enough to procure thoſe who
did not credit his miſſion to be turned out of the ſynagogue;
and the wealth of his nation, which was exceſſive, was laid
at his feet for his acceptance. This was perhaps, the true
reaſon why the reign of this impoſtor laſted ſo long, it
being in *Sevi*'s power to gratify the *Turkiſh* governors with
bribes, which they are ſeldom proof againſt. Being carried
before the cadi, or criminal judge of *Smyrna*, he was diſmiſſed without hurt, which was attributed to his divinity;
and many of his followers ſwore to miracles that he had
performed, and had recourſe to the moſt improbable fictions
in his favour. Even ſome of his moſt violent adverſaries
were converted, and *Sevi* iſſued his mandates with all the
majeſty of a prieſt and a prince. To perform his promiſe,
he ſet out for *Conſtantinople*, and arrived there with great
numbers of his followers, juſt at the time that *Kioprili*
was about to embark on his *Candian* expedition; and this
ſeems to have ſaved his life, for all that the vizier had time
to do, was to order him to be clapped up in priſon. His
ſufferings redoubled the zeal of his adherents, who were
ſuffered for money to throw themſelves at his feet, while he
was in chains. This gainful traffic was too enticing for his
jailors to diſcontinue it, and ſo infatuated were the *Jews* at
Conſtantinople, that they refuſed to pay their juſt debts without his order; which at the requeſt of the *Engliſh* merchants
he granted them. It was now dangerous for the government to continue him longer at *Conſtantinople*, but for the
reaſons we have hinted at, inſtead of being put to death he

was only removed to the caſtle of the *Dardanelles*, where he was reſorted to more than ever ; for all the *European Jews* came now to pay their reſpects to their meſſiah. All this could not be done without raiſing the curioſity of the emperor himſelf, who ſent for *Sevi*, and demanded if he was the meſſiah. The impoſtor anſwering in the affimative, the ſultan ordered him to be ſtripped naked, and to be ſhot at by his jacoylans, or archers, and if his body was proof againſt their arrows, he promiſed to own him for the true meſſiah. The trial was too ſevere for *Sevi* to undergo it, and falling on his knees he acknowledged his impoſture. Upon being offered the alternative to be impaled alive, or turn *Mahometan*, he readily choſe the latter. But ſuch was the infatuation of his followers, that they gave out, that the *Sevi* they ſaw in a *Turkiſh* dreſs, was only a phantom, and that the real *Sevi* had been received up into heaven, there to remain till the time ſhould arrive for the completion of his prophecies.

Juſt as *Kioprili*, who had returned to *Conſtantinople*, was about to ſet out a ſecond time for *Candia*, a war broke out between the *Tartars*, and the *Poles*, which was terminated by an appeal to the porte, to the ſatisfaction of both parties, and about the ſame time the rebellious paſha of *Balſora*, or *Baſran*, was quelled. Though *Kioprili* had the glory of recommencing the ſiege of *Candia*, yet it never had been intirely diſcontinued for almoſt ten years before; for the *Turks* during all that time, in a manner blocked it up by land; but the ſea being open to the *Venetians*, the operations of their enemies gave them little trouble. The chief ſtrength of the city of *Kanea* conſiſted of ſeven baſtions, *Sabionera*, *Vettari*, *Jeſus*, *Martinengo*, *Bethlem*, *Panigra*, and Saint *Andrea*, all of them regularly fortified with ravelins, and

and of the ſiege of *Candia*. broad deep ditches. *Kioprili*, when he landed on the iſland, found *Kanea* beſieged by the *Chriſtians*; but he ſoon obliged them to abandon their enterprize. He then muſtered the whole of his army, which amounted to ſeventy thouſand men, and by reconnoitering the city, he ſoon found that the preceeding *Turkiſh* generals had made wrong diſpoſitions for ttacking it, and he formed others with better ſucceſs in the h e end. Though *Kioprili* was one of the greateſt generals, as well as miniſters of the age he lived in ; yet, ſo great was his opinion of his mother's underſtanding, that he carried her, as well as his wife, along with him in this momentous expedition. The *Venetians* had not been wanting to themſelves in preparing to defend the city, and had employed the ableſt generals in *Europe* for that purpoſe. They had expended immenſe ſums in keeping up their marine, which was commanded by *Andrea Cornaro*, and every where beat the *Turkiſh* fleets, and in providing a ſtrong land force, which was committed to *Franceſco Moroſini*, the marquis of *Villa*, and a *French* officer, one *St. Andre Mombrun*.

On

On the fourteenth of *May* 1667, the *Turks* took up their encampment before the city, along the valley of *Gioffiro*, and carried on their works to the sea side. Three batteries were raised, which thundered upon the town, as is said, with artillery, which discharged bullets from sixty to one hundred and twenty pounds weight; but the dispositions of the besieged were equally masterly and resolute, for their mines did vast execution upon the *Turks*, who made their chief attacks upon the bastion of *Panigra*. *Kioprili*, by this time, began to be sensible of the difficulty of his undertaking, and above all, of the disadvantage he was under for want of engineers equal to those of the besieged; who were supplied with the best that *Europe* could afford. Difficulties seemed to encrease his resolution, but he could not perform impossibities; for though he made a large breach in the *Panigra* bastion, and had even made a lodgement there, yet the dreadful mines sprung, and the frequent sallies made by the *Christians*, rendered fruitless the most desperate efforts of the infidels. In the mean while, the enemies of *Kioprili* were not idle, and so incessantly plied the emperor with suspicions of his conduct, that he was at last staggered into distrust, and sent him messengers with a very severe letter, with some oblique charges against his courage and fidelity. *Kioprili* candidly acknowledged that appearances were against him, that the siege had already cost much more blood and treasure than he had thought of at first; but that they should see that he was neither destitute of courage, nor of zeal for his master's service. He soon convinced them of what he said, by leading his men next morning to a fresh breach, that had been made in the walls, and which he was the first man to mount; but all his followers being killed, he returned almost alone to the camp. The messengers, who had been sent in the nature of spies over *Kioprili*, did justice to his courage, and made so favourable a report to the emperor, that it wiped all suspicions from his mind; and he sent him a most magnificent present. It exceeds the bounds of this undertaking to describe all the particulars of this siege, which was one of the longest, and most extraordinary ever carried on. It is sufficient to say, that by the assistance of the pope, the *Maltese*, and other *Christian* powers, the *Venetians* were enabled to make a most amazing defence, and destroyed so many of their enemies, that nothing less than the spirit and perseverance of *Kioprili* could have continued it.

The winter of the year 1667, somewhat relaxed the fury of the *Turks*, whose camp was now depopulated by diseases, as it had been before by the *Venetians*; but all hopes of an accommodation, which had been faintly mentioned, soon vanished, and before the winter was over, hostilities recommenced with more fury than ever. But *Kioprili* employed a new kind of artillery against the besieged, for he ordered

great

great numbers of papers to be fhot into the city on points
of arrows, offering very flattering conditions to the garrifon
provided they would furrender; and containing the moft
dreadful threatenings if they did not. Thefe ftratagems
however, had little or no effect upon their fidelity; and the
vizier then applied himfelf to the fenate of *Venice*; but to
as little purpofe. *Kioprili* having thus loft all profpect of
peace, redoubled his affiduity in bringing fupplies of men,
and provifions from the continents both of *Afia*, and *Europe*;
fo that never was there any war better fupported than that
of *Candia*. The marquis of *Villa*, a nobleman of *Savoy*,
being at this time recalled by his mafter, *Mombrun* became
fecond in command, and difcharged his duty with the fame
addrefs, and intrepidity. Notwithftanding the gallant defence
made by the garrifon, foldiers of the greateft penetration
forefaw, that the place muft be taken, if the infidels obftinately continued the fiege. Volunteers of the beft blood in
Europe, daily poured in from all parts to the affiftance of
the befieged; and feveral ftates, who in other refpects were
far from being in a good underftanding with the *Venetians*,
furnifhed their quotas. By thofe affiftances, the befieged
were enabled to hold out during all the year 1668, and
volumes have been written, upon the great actions performed by thofe illuftrious volunteers during every period of this
fiege.

Progrefs
of the
fiege of
Candia. In the beginning of the year 1669, it became apparent,
that the methods taken by the befieged to defend them-
felves, if continued, muft force them to furrender. The
frequent mines that had been fprung, had fhaken the walls
of the place, and the ground was become fo porous, that
the befieged had in many places no fhelter againft the
enemy's fire, all the ground lying open, excepting where it
was covered by the ruins. It is faid upon good authority,
that *Kioprili* loft thirty thoufand men in two affaults, which
he made upon the baftions of Saint *Andrea*, and *Sabionera*,
upon which he at laft made a lodgement, but to no purpofe
in the end, not being able to penetrate farther. While
matters were in this fituation, the dukes of *Beaufort*, and
Noailles landed at *Candia*, at the head of feven thoufand
of the *French* king's beft troops, who were fent to the defence
of the place, befides many *French* volunteers, who had greatly
diftinguifhed themfelves in the fiege. Upon reconnoitring
the condition of the place, it was agreed upon all hands, that
nothing but fome extraordinary effort could fave it. It was
therefore refolved in a council of war, that the enemy fhould
be attacked in their works by a brifk fally, to be favoured by
the *French* fleet. This refolution was executed with an intrepidity that bordered upon romance. The *Chriftians* at
firft bore all before them, but a large magazine of powder,
unluckily taking fire, deftroyed fome of them, and among
the reft the brave duke of *Beaufort*. It is faid however,
that

that the explosion of the magazine was not so ruinous as it was represented to be, and that the *French* being thrown into disorder, the duke was killed in endeavouring to rally them. The *French* ships shared in the disaster of their land troops, for the wind suddenly chopping about, drove them from the shore with considerable damage, and one of the largest of them was blown up.

Even this disaster, great as it was, was retrievable, as the loss the *French* sustained in number, did not amount to above three hundred men. The best authorities among the *French* themselves, are puzzled to account for the behaviour of their countrymen on this occasion; for the duke de *Nooilles*, a few days after, declared his intention to carry the *French* shipping and troops back to *France*. It is probable, that he had received from his master a discretionary power, authorising him to take this step, which he endeavoured to justify by the desperate condition of the place, and by the disagreement of the *French* and *Italian* officers, each throwing upon the other the blame of the late miscarriage, which had given the infidels an opportunity of making lodgments on the very bastions of the city. Be this as it will, it is certain that the duke could not be diverted from his resolution, and he reimbarked his troops at the very time when the besiged had the greatest occasion for their service. His retreat gave fresh spirits to the *Turks*, who attacked the new thrown up intrenchments within the city, but were again beaten back with vast loss by the springing of a fresh mine.

The senate of *Venice* was sensible of the impracticability The city of saving the place, and gave a commission to *Molino*, one capitu- of their nobles, to treat of peace. At this time the emperor lates *Mohammed* had left *Adrianople*, and repaired to *Larissa*, that he might be near at hand to superintend the embarkations for the siege and, to correspond with *Kioprili*. Upon the approach of *Molino*, a chaimachan was sent to inform him, that he could be admitted to no treaty unless he had brought with him the keys of *Candia*, and that he was not to presume to approach nearer the court than the place where he was. It was with great difficulty, that *Molino* at last was referred to treat with *Kioprili* in *Candia*, whom he found by no means so inexorable as his master, owing, perhaps, to fresh reinforcements which he understood had arrived, or were about to arrive. About the time of *Molino's* arrival in *Candia*, *Morisini*, and the other *Venetian* generals met in a council of war, to deliberate upon the conduct they were to hold. Some were for blowing up the place, but from the complexion of history, *Morosini* seems to have been secretly determined to give it up; though, according to the *Turkish* historians, who, in this case, are not much to be depended upon, some parts of the city were still tenable. After various debates, it was found most advisable to treat; and two gentlemen were appointed to repair to the vizier's tent, one of them an *Englishman*, called *Thomas Amand*, and the other *Stefano Cordeli*, a young man of parts; and they secretly set out by water for the vizier's camp, to which they were admitted by means of a flag of truce, which they carried along with them. Upon proposing a conference, (*Molino* having by this time left *Candia*) they were given in resolute terms to understand, that the vizier was resolved to treat upon no conditions, but those of a surrender, which the *Christian* plenipotentiaries agreed to, and the place of conference was named. The plenipotentiaries for the *Turks* were *Ibrahim*, the pasha of *Halep*, *Ahmed Aga*, the kahiyabeg of the janisaries, the spahiler agasi, and *Paniaotti*, the vizier's interpreter.

and surrenders by a stratagem.
The last named plenipotentiary, was a most extraordinary personage. He was a *Greek Christian*, and the vizier's first counsellor, a distinction which he merited by a most faithful attachment to his person, an incredible sagacity, which made the *Turks* look upon him as possessing supernatural powers. According to some well attested memoirs, he privately informed *Morosini*, that the *French* fleet, which was every day expected, was sent by that monarch to carry off the *Venetians* who remained in the city, and to deliver it up to the sultan, in consequence of the secret treaty between him and *France*. Next day, it is said, that twelve *Turkish* ships, which had in the night time been sent out for that purpose, appeared in sight under *French* colours, and being met by twelve more under *Turkish*, they saluted and joined, and amicably sailed into port together. *Morosini*, who had no great reason to think well of the *French*, was deceived by this appearance, and persuaded the garrison into a surrender. This story probably was invented by *Morosini's* friends, as a colour for surrendering the place; for it is certain, that *Morosini* had been long tired of the siege, and was willing to lay hold of the first honourable opportunity to capitulate. Such an opportunity presented itself at those conferences. For though the *Turks* would not hear of allowing the *Venetians* any equivalent for *Candia*, which they looked upon to be as good as reduced, yet *Kioprili* consented that the inhabitants should have leave to embark with all their arms, provision, and baggage, and likewise with their cannon; *Kioprili* even offered them *Othman* ships, if those of *Venice* were too few to carry off the garrison. No more than two thousand five hundred soldiers were left, and those sickly, and otherwise in a most miserable condition. None of the inhabitants remained in the place, but two *Greek* priests, and about thirty-three decrepid *Jews*, and *Greeks*.

Kioprili observed this capitulation with the most scrupulous exactness. He presented the inhabitant who brought him the keys of the place with a sable vest, and five hundred zequins, besides giving two hundred more to his retinue; and the *Turks* and *Christians* lived together in a most amicable

manner

manner till the time of embarkation. This siege had continued for twenty-five years, though sometimes it went
languidly on. The operations of the last two years and Vast loss
four months, were vigorous and incessant. According to of both
Ricaut, who was in *Turkey* at the time, in those twenty- parties.
eight months the *Venetians* lost, in killed or wounded, thirty
thousand, nine hundred and eighty-five men ; and the *Turks*
one hundred and eighteen thousand, seven hundred and
fifty-four men. The reader, by this account, may judge of
the obstinacy on both sides. The batteries, says *Ricaut*,
which the *Turks* raised against *Sabionera*, and Saint *Andrea*,
consisted of fifty-nine pieces of cannon, carrying from fifty
to one hundred and twenty pound weight of bullet. The
storms which the *Turks* made upon the town were fifty-six.
The combats under-ground forty-five. The sallies made
by the *Venetians* ninety-six. The mines and fornelli, sprung
by the *Venetians* eleven hundred and seventy-three, and by the
Turks four hundred and seventy-two. The *Venetians* spent
barrels of powder fifty thousand, three hundred and seventeen. Bombs of all sorts by the *Venetians*, of fifty to five
hundred weight, were forty-eight thousand, one hundred
and nineteen. Granadoes, of brass and iron, one hundred
thousand, nine hundred and sixty : Granadoes of glass,
eighty-four thousand, eight hundred and seventy-four. Cannon shot of all sorts, two hundred and seventy-six thousand,
seven hundred and forty-three pounds. Pounds of lead,
eighteen million, forty-four thousand, nine hundred and
fifty-seven. Of match, pounds, thirteen millions, twelve
thousand, and five hundred.

During the siege of *Candia*, so great was the oppressions Affairs of
of the house of *Austria* upon the *Hungarians*, that *Serini*, Hungary.
Nadasti, and *Frangapani*, three of their principal noblemen,
who, after the example of their ancestors, had signalized
themselves against the *Turks*, joined in a confederacy,
and chose to throw themselves upon the protection of the
Othman emperor, rather than longer suffer the tyranny
of the *Austrians*. This being intimated to *Kioprili*, he offered them his master's assistance, provided *Hungary* was
rendered tributary to the porte. Those generous noblemen
rejected the condition, and offered to return to their allegiance, provided they could be secured in their privileges;
but the emperor knowing the *Turks* to be then engaged not
only in a war with the *Venetians*, but likewise with the *Persians*, instead of giving them satisfaction, poured his troops
into *Hungary*, and having come to the knowledge of all that
had passed between those noblemen and the vizier, they,
together with count *Tattembach*, another head of the confederacy, were arrested, tried, and executed.

Kioprili, probably must have fallen a sacrifice to the intrigues of his enemies, had he not been successful before
Candia ; and perhaps, the danger he knew he was in, con-

tributed

tributed to determine him to grant the capitulation. After he had signed it, he had an opportunity of conversing with the *Christian* officers, and their company is said to have given a new turn to his manners. He heaped favours upon *Morosini,* and the other generals, and was even persuaded, for the sake of his health, which suffered by the opiates so much in use among the *Turks,* to drink wine pretty liberally.

Tumults at Constantinople quelled. On his entering *Candia* he forbade all rejoicings for the reduction of a place, which had cost the *Othmans* such seas of blood; and he immediately dispatched expresses to his master with the joyful news of the event, promising to attend him at *Constantinople* at the head of fifty thousand victorious veterans, to quell the rebellious spirit that had lately appeared in that capital. The grand signior was then at *Salonica,* giving audience to Sir *Daniel Harvey,* the *English* ambassador, and indulging himself in all manner of pleasures, especially those of hunting, to which he was generally accompanied by his favourite sultana. He was so much overjoyed upon receiving *Kioprili's* letters, that his mind instantly lost all impressions to that minister's disadvantage. He declared him to be the greatest and most successful general, that had ever commanded the *Othman* arms. He sent him the most costly presents, and even shewed an impatience for the arrival of *Molina,* the *Venetian* ambassador, that he might ratify all that had been concluded upon by his vizier. He at the same time sent commissaries into *Dalmatia,* to settle boundaries with the *Venetians,* and to remove all difficulties that could in the least obstruct the conclusion of a firm and lasting peace. *Kioprili* pursued the same plan, and even impaled some of his soldiers, for violating his proclamation against doing any injury to the *Christians.* He did not, however, set out from *Candia* without repairing the fortifications all over the island, that he might render his conquest as permanent as it was important.

The drinking of wine prohibited. The emperor's mother was at this time at *Constantinople,* where she had full power from her son to transact all affairs of government. But, though she was a woman of great spirit and address, yet she found infinite difficulty in managing the janisaries, and other soldiers. But the approach of the sultan, at the head of his victorious army, soon quelled them. As their irregularities were judged to be owing partly to their inactivity, but chiefly to their drinking of wine, both cases were provided for; eight thousand of them were sent into *Moldavia,* and other detachments to other frontiers of the empire, and a strict general prohibition was issued all over the empire against drinking of wine, and all games of chance. This prohibition was so strictly executed, there being no exception in favour of *Franks,* or *Europeans,* that the *English* ambassador had the utmost difficulty to procure a drop of wine for himself and his family; and what they made use of, was of their own making from the grape.

Though

Though not only death, but the feverest tortures were pronounced against all who should disobey this order; yet, in about twelve months, the use of wine became as frequent as ever in the *Othman* dominions.

Another difficulty at this time perplexed *Mohammed*'s internal government. That emperor, before his leaving *Constantinople*, had given orders that his brothers should be put to death, which coming to the ears of the janisaries, they rescued those princes, and put them under the care of the sultana mother, and made her answerable for their safety; but upon the return of *Kioprili*, and quelling the tumults at *Constantinople*, sultan *Orchan*, the eldest of those brothers, was poisoned, or as some say strangled, by the emperor's orders, without the latter being any ways apprehensive of the consequences. *Kioprili* was at this time in the height of reputation, not only among the *Othmans*, but the *Christian* powers. He had, with great difficulty, put an end to all terrestrial, commercial, and other differences with the *Venetians*. He disregarded the *Genoese*, and the other *Italian* states; he was upon a good footing with the court of *Vienna*, he had little or nothing to apprehend from the *Russians*, and his only object now was a war with *Poland*, where a very powerful nation of the kosaks, inhabiting between the *Boristhenes*, and the *Neister*, had put themselves under the protection of the porte. It was of the utmost consequence, on account of the situation of the country of those kosaks, to prevent this defection; and the king of *Poland* sent a large army to reduce them. *Kioprili*, the *Turks* being religious observers of forms, sent a chaush, with a dehortatory letter, containing some menaces if he proceeded; but that having no effect, the vizier in the beginning of the year 1672, passed the *Danube*, on a bridge which he threw over it at *Sacki*, at the head of one hundred and fifty thousand men; and after a long painful march through *Moldavia*, he encamped near *Kochin*. From thence he sent over the *Tyras* a party, that took *Zwanidez*, by which he effected his junction with the *Tartars*, who were headed by their famous khan *Selim Gyera*. While he was building a bridge over the *Tyras*, for transporting his artillery, it was discovered that *Duka*, the prince of *Moldavia*, secretly favoured the *Poles*, and was doing all he could to retard the work; upon which he was deposed, and one *Peter* set up in his room. *Kioprili* at last surmounting all difficulties, appeared before *Kaminieck*, the strongest town in *Podolia*, and opened his batteries against it. The *Poles* were so confident of the strength of this place, and trusted so entirely to it for stopping the progress of the infidels, that they at this time had no army in the field; but it was so furiously battered that it surrendered in ten days, to the amazement, not only of the *Poles*, but of all *Europe*.

War with Poland,

and Kaminieck taken.

Q 3

The

The conqueſt of *Kaminieck*, was one of the moſt im-portant the *Othmans* had ever made on the ſide of *Poland*; and according to prince *Cantenmir*, their power has been up-on the decline ever ſince. It opened all *Podolia*, and *Vol-hinia*, to their incurſions, and nothing lay now between them and *Upper Poland*, but *Lemberg*. *Mohammed* was ſo proud of this expedition, that he ſet out at the head of an army to ſupport it, and arriving at *Kaminieck*, he affected a conduct full of mildneſs, humanity and juſtice. He prohibied plund-ering, he protected the inhabitants who ſubmitted to his au-thority in their properties, without ſuffering any thing to be exacted from them; and gave a general invitation to the *Poles* to enter into his allegiance. All thoſe acts of clemency had ſo powerful an effect upon the natives, that they tried the experiment, and for ſome time found the *Turkiſh* yoke far more tolerable than that of their own lords. It is certain, that *Mohammed*, by this moderation, riſked a mutiny in his own army, which in all other expeditions had been enriched by the ſpoils of the conquered, but, in this, they met with nothing but impoveriſhment, and famine, though maſters of the fineſt countries in *Europe*. *Mohammed*'s moderation was the more remarkable, as the *Poles*, in the beginning of the war, had behaved with great intemperance, and offered ſome inſults to the porte. *Mohammed*'s head quarters at this time was at *Buſhach*, which lay on the frontiers of the palatinate of *Lemberg*; and the *Poles* named ambaſſadors to wait upon the *Tartar* khan with propoſals of peace, offer-ing to deliver up forty eight towns and villages, in the pro-vince of *Kaminieck*, to pay annually twenty thouſand rix-dollars, by way of tribute; and to ſuffer the koſaks to re-main under the command of their hetman *Doroſhenko*, who had put himſelf under the protection of the porte. The great khan did not choſe to return any anſwer of himſelf to thoſe propoſitions, but ſent tnem to *Mohammed*, who accept-

Peace concluded ed of them; diſbanded his army, and returned to *Conſtan-tinople*. *Ricaut*, however, differs in his account of this tranſaction; for according to him, the king of *Poland* was to give up all the *Ukrain*, *Podolia*, and *Ruſland*, and the city and diſtrict of *Lemberg* were to pay annually a tribute of ſeventy thouſand crowns.

The war renewed. By this peace, *Doroſhenko* was left governor of *Verania*, and *Podolia*, under the *Turks*, whoſe progreſs, by this time, had alarmed all *Europe*; ſo that the ſultan repented his having diſbanded his army. The *Moſcovites* were the firſt who began to arm. The imperialiſts were threatening to take the field, and the *Poles* themſelves refuſed to ratify the late treaty, which refuſal was ſignified in a letter from the grand chancellor to the porte. *Doroſhenko*, was the firſt who gave the porte notice of this untowardly ſituation of its affairs in *Poland*. The account was ſo unexpected, that the grand ſignior was preparing to ſet out for a favourite reſi-dence, where he was to ſpend his time during the heats of

the

the summer; and it was with difficulty that he was diffuaded by *Kioprili* from his defign, that he might attend the affairs of empire. New levies were already made, but no army being at hand to afford *Doroſhenko* immediate fupport, he revolted, and ravaged the borders of the empire; and accounts came that the *Poles* had already taken the field. *Kioprili*, fenfible how much depended upon maintaining the dignity of an empire, once more advifed his mafter to abandon all other concerns, even that of fuccouring the malcontents in *Hungary*, that he might be revenged on the *Poles*. It was, however, the end of *July*, before it was refolved that the emperor fhould march againſt them in perfon; but though the utmoſt exertions of his imperial authority had been made ufe of, for the fpeedy raifing an army, yet the backwardneſs of the foldiers from entering into another expedition againſt *Poland* was fuch, that he was obliged to fet out at the head of no more than fifteen thoufand men; taking along with him *Kioprili* himfelf, who led his van.

Previous to *Mohammed*'s march, he had difpatched a threatening letter to the *Poles*, containing the moſt dreadful menaces, if they did not fubmit. This letter had no other effect, than that of rendering the *Poles* more alert in their preparations. All their internal differences, of which the infidels had availed themfelves during the laſt campaign, were now compofed, and the famous *John Sobieſki* had taken the field, and was in the neighbourhood of *Lemberg*, at the head of fifty thoufand men, before the fultan could come up. *Mohammed*, at laſt, having joined his vizier, they found all the paffes upon the *Tyras* poffeffed by the *Poles*. The paſha *Huffeyu*, at that time, commanded for the *Turks* in *Podolia*. Upon the approach of *Sobieſki*'s army, he had fummoned *Petrezeicus*, then the tributary prince of *Moldavia*, to join him with his contingent troops; but the number falling ſhort, the paſha ſtruck the waywod with his pole axe, and loaded him with the moſt abufive language. His fubjects refented the affront, which he diffembled, and fo great was the contempt of the paſha for the *Moldavian*, that he appointed him to command his guard that night. The *Moldavians* took this opportunity of carrying off their prince to the *Poliſh* camp, from whence he efcaped with fome difficulty and danger, and returning to *Mohammed*'s camp, this feeming act of fidelity, (which indeed was the effect of the moſt profound diffimulation,) gained him the full confidence of the fultan and his vizier, which he made ufe of to give fecret intelligence to *Sobieſki*, of all the difpofitions of the *Turks*.

By this time, *Mohammed*'s army had been fo greatly reinforced, that he refumed his threatenings to fubdue all *Poland*, and confidered the *Poliſh* army, which was encamped between the *Tyras*, and the *Danube*, as his prey. *Sobieſki*, by

The *Turks* defeated with grea ſlaughter.

means of the intelligence he had gained, broke into the weakeſt part of the *Turkiſh* entrenchments with irreſiſtable fury, and not only *Petrezicus,* but *Gregory,* ſon of the tributary prince of *Walachia,* turned their arms againſt the *Turks,* who immediately perceived that they had been betrayed. Notwithſtanding this, the *Turkiſh* general, and the vizier, acted with ſo much intrepidity and reſolution, that they are ſaid to have maintained the battle for fourteen hours. But *Sobieſki*'s fortune prevailed; the left wing of the *Turks* fell into confuſion, and the right was forced to retreat, which turned at laſt into a downright flight; and the rout of the infidels ſoon became total. In this great battle, eight thouſand janiſaries, who were the flower of the *Turkiſh* infantry, were cut in pieces, as were twelve thouſand of their other ſoldiers; and not only the whole of their baggage was taken; but their military cheſt, conſiſting of two thouſand purſes, fell into the hands of the *Poles,* with all their waggons of ammunition and proviſions, to the incredible number of twenty-five thouſand. This victory, one of the greateſt ever obtained by the *Chriſtians* againſt the infidels, opened to the *Poles* a way for the recovery of all they had loſt. They accordingly retook *Khochin,* and ſeveral other important poſts upon the *Neiſter;* but the death of their king *Michael,* diverted their arms, and their generals were obliged to attend the election of a new king, which fell upon *John Sobieſki,* then grand marſhal of the kingdom. *Mohammed,* on the other hand, who had eſcaped out of the late battle, not without ſome danger to his perſon, appeared to be more exaſperated againſt the *Poles* than ever, and gave out, that he either would reduce them, or loſe his life. He was favoured by the ridiculous jealouſies and confidence of the *Poles.* *Sobieſki* had detached great part of his army to beſiege and recover the important city of *Kaminieck;* and he was extremely urgent with the *Poles,* to bring the war to a deciſive iſſue by taking the field with all their force. But, after the defeat the infidels had lately received, the *Poles* ignorantly imagined, that they could not be, for ſome years, in a condition to take the field; and in ſecret they were afraid, leſt *Sobieſki* ſhould gain ſo great a power as to be able to render their crown hereditary in his family. In vain did *Sobieſki* endeavour to aſſemble the whole force of *Poland* to recover this important fortreſs, for all he could do was to ſtraiten the garriſon, ſo that in a few weeks it muſt have ſurrendered for want of proviſions; but during that time, *Mohammed* had aſſembled ſuch a force, that the *Poles,* to their amazement were obliged to raiſe the ſiege; and the *Turks* not only revictualled and reinforced the garriſon, but took ſeveral places in the neighbourhood. At this time, *Doroſhenko,* who ſeems always to have followed the prevailing party, again offered his ſervice to *Mohammed* againſt the *Poles,* but meeting with a repulſe, he was highly exaſperated.

Kaminieck *ſelieved.* ꞁ

But

But the luxury and indolence of *Mohammed*, at this time, *Moham-* was extremely prejudicial to his affairs, and even shook his *med gives* throne. His love of pleasure made him resolve upon a wife *himself* measure. That he might not be interrupted in his favourite *up to* diversions, he sought to secure to himself the quiet possession *pleasure,* of all he held in *Podolia*, and for that purpose he ordered all *Christian* inhabitants to be removed out of *Kaminieck* to other parts of his dominions. After that, he returned to *Adrianople*, and there gave himself up to the uninterrupted pursuit of pleasure; and to render it the more secure, he amassed an incredible treasure, by the marriage of his daugh- *amasses* ter to a favourite, one *Kul Ogli*, pasha of *Magnesia*, at which *large* ceremony, all the grandees of his empire were obliged, by *treasures.* custom, to make him large presents. About the same time, he circumcised his two sons *Mustapha*, and *Ahmed*. Nothing of importance happened on the side of *Europe*, during this interval, thus dedicated to luxury, till the *Poles* being rend- ered sensible, that they owed to the emperor's indolence the cause of their tranquility, in 1676 attacked the *Othmans* in *Moldavia*. The pasha *Ibrahim*, surnamed *Shayton*, or *the* **Danger of** *Devil*, from his cunning, was sent against them; and he had *the* **Poles,** the address to amuse the *Poles*, whose numbers were not above fifteen thousand men, with *Sobieski* at their head, so that he surrounded them with one hundred thousand men, who must have been destroyed, had not a mutiny broken out in the *Turkish* camp. The janisaries complained of their being exposed to the fatigues of war, and the rigour of the seasons, while the emperor was shamefully sunk in his luxuries; and the khan of the *Tartars* complaining, that he had nothing to expect by the war, insisted upon returning home with his army.

Such was the situation of the *Poles*, when *Sobieski* sent **Their de-** some agents into the *Turkish* camp to treat of peace. *Ibrahim* **liverance.** saw the necessity he was under to conclude a negociation of some kind or other; and not only received the ambassadors, but relaxing, or being obliged to relax, in his discipline, *Sobieski* and his army had an opportunity of breaking through their toils, and attacked the *Tartar* camp. *Ibrahim* reproached the *Polish* ambassadors, who were in his tent when he received this account, with their sovereign's breach of good faith, and immediately detached his cavalry to sup- port the *Tartars*. A bloody battle ensued, in which neither side could claim the advantage; and about seventeen days past in hourly skirmishes. This was far from allaying the spirit of mutiny in *Ibrahim's* camp, and at last he was obliged, notwithstanding all the opposition made by the court of *Vienna*, to consent to a peace, which was approved of by the states of *Poland*, and an ambassador was nomi- nated to go to *Constantinople* to confirm it.

This ambassador was so full of his national pride, that when he arrived at *Constantinople*, he insisted upon the grand

vizier

vizier meeting him at the city gate. This demand amazed the *Turks*, and might have deftroyed all the profpect of a peace, had not the vizier been meditating a mighty expedition, which was to carry the *Turkifh* arms to the gates of *Vienna* itfelf. About the fame time died, of a complication of diftempers, which was heightened by the immoderate ufe of wine, and ftrong liquors, the vizier *Kioprili*, one of the greateft, and beft men, the *Othman* empire ever produced. Naturally gentle, and moderate, he preferved the tranquility of government, without having recourfe to thofe fanguinary meafures, that were practifed by his father, and his predeceffors. He was free from avarice, the common vice of his nation; and having been educated to the knowledge of the civil laws of his country, he was a moft punctual adminiftrator of juftice, with, perhaps, a too fcrupulous adherence to forms. No minifter, of his time, was more tenacious, than he was, of national honour, or more attentive to the fulfilling all the engagements he concluded in his mafter's name; and he died regretted by the *Chriftian* powers, particularly that of *England*, for which he always expreffed an uncommon deference. He was no more than forty-feven years of age when he died of the dropfy, and jaundice. Some time before his death he ratified the peace with the *Poles*, notwithftanding the offence given him by their ambaffador. By the articles of this peace, the *Poles* entirely renounced their claim to *Kaminieck*, and likewife to all authority over the kofaks of *Podolia*, and the *Lithuanian Tartars*, who were *Mahometans*, were permitted to depart to their own country.

Upon the conclufion of this peace, the infidels turned their eyes towards *Hungary*, where count *Strazoldo*, the imperial general, had taken from the malecontents *Debrezin*, a town which paid tribute to the porte, who could not avoid confidering fuch a proceeding as an infraction of treaties. *Kara Muftapha* had fucceeded *Kioprili* as firft minifter, and he gave the *Turkifh* pafhas in general, on the frontiers of *Poland*, leave to favour the malecontents, who were foon joined by *Apaffi*, a *Tranfylvanian* prince. Count *Wefelini* was then at the head of the malecontents, and defeated the imperial general. They next applied to the porte for fome more effectual affiftance, but the new vizier being by this time engaged in a war with *Ruffia*; all he could do was to give them partial affiftances. The ftates of *Hungary* endeavoured to interpofe, but the violence and bigotry of the court of *Vienna* fruftrated the effects of all negotiations. Thus the war between the imperialifts on the one hand, and the *Turks* and malecontent *Hungarians* on the other, every day increafed; but would have been more bloody, had it not been for that between the porte and *Ruffia*. In the mean while, died *Wefelini*, and the command of the malecontents fell upon young *Tekeli*, who afterwards made

Death of Kioprili.

Unfuccefsful war againft the kofaks.

made so great a figure. *Doroshenko*, the kosak hetman we have already mentioned, resenting the indignities that had been done him by the porte, as well as to his country, offered to submit to the czar of *Russia*, in which he was seconded by his officers, as the only means of delivering themselves from the *Polish*, as well as the *Turkish*, tyranny. The czar readily accepted of this vast acquisition to his dominions, which were thereby extended beyond the *Boristhenes*, and the *Ukrain* was secured, besides a number of brave soldiers being added to his army. *George Kiemielniski*, son of the famous *Bogdan*, who had been likewise hetman of the kosaks, was then a prisoner at the porte, but released by *Mohammed*, and sent at the head of an army to dispossess *Doroshenko* of the hetmanship, all other means proving ineffectual. The *Turkish* general the pasha *Shaytan Ibrahim*, had orders, at the same time, to make himself master of *Chehrin*, the capital of the country. This was an expedition to which the *Turks* in general had a mortal antipathy, and was undertaken only through necessity.

Ibrahim ordered the *Tartars* to attend him, and he himself and the passed the *Danube* on the sixth of *June* 1678, and marched *Russians.* through *Podolia*, and *Moldavia*, towards *Chehrin*, near which, he found sixty thousand kosaks, in possession of a strong post. While he halted to be joined by the *Tartars*, who were but three days march behind him, the *Russians* sent a strong detachment from their main army, which surprised and killed ten thousand of the *Tartars*, among whom were the khan's son, and eight mirzas. The *Turks* hearing of this defeat, threw down their arms, and made a most precipitate retreat towards the river *Bog*, which they repassed, but with great loss. The sultan, ashamed to ask for peace, employed a minister, who went in the name of the khan of *Tartary*, to persuade the czar to abandon the kosaks, and restore *Chehrin* to the *Turks*. The czar saw through the artifice, and knew the motives of the embassy. He sent an ambassador to *Constantinople* with letters demanding, in a very peremptory manner, that the *Kosak Ukrain*, to which he had an undoubted right by *Doroshenko*'s submission, should be left in quiet, otherwise he threatened to conquer the rest of that country, and carry his arms as far as *Asof*. The *Turkish* ministers were startled on reading this letter, and most of them were for accepting the czar's proposal; but the vizier *Kara Mustapha* opposed it, for the very reasons which they gave for accepting it. None durst contradict him, when he declared that the *Othman* arms must be employed in revenging the loss and indignity they had suffered from the *Russians*, and immediately he put himself at the head of eighty thousand *Turks*, thirty thousand *Tartars*, and forty thousand kosaks, who had joined *George Kiemielniski*, and passing the *Bog*, he came in sight of *Chehrin*. The *Russians* and kosaks were at that time building a new fort,

near

near *Chehrin*; and being surprised by the approach of the
Turkish arms, they retired to the body of the place. The
vizier took advantage of their consternation, and ordered
his kyehaya, or high deputy, to attack the town; but the
latter, after a dispute of four hours, was obliged to retreat
with the loss of two thousand men. Various were the desperate
methods made use of by *Kara Muftapha*, to repair
tl i lofs, but all of them proved unsuccessful; and at last, he
understood that the *Russian* general *Romadanowski*, had passed
the *Boristhenes*.

The Turks defeated. Upon this, he ordered the pasha *Kara Mehemed* to fight
him; but understanding that the *Russians* declined an engagement,
before they had relieved *Chehrin*, the pasha
Koplan, one of the best officers in the *Othman* service, was
ordered to intercept them in their march. *Koplan* having
taken up his ground for that purpose, was so furiously attacked
by the *Russians*, that all his army must have been defeated,
had he not broken down all the bridges in his rear,
to secure his retreat. The winter of 1679 was now approaching,
and the vizier, who had continued his operations
against the place, at last sprung so many mines, and made
so many breaches in the walls, that he became master of it;
but the garrison, after springing a mine, which destroyed
great numbers of the *Turks*, retired towards the *Boristhenes*.
When the vizier entered *Chehrin*, he found it so much ruined
by the late siege, that he razed it to the ground, but could
not bring *Romadanowski* to a battle; the latter well knowing,
that as the *Turks* could not subfist in the country, they
must be destroyed in their retreat, which accordingly happened.
For when the vizier entered *Adrianople*, his army was
so thin, and in so bad a condition, that he appeared as if his
troops had escaped from a total rout; no fewer than thirty
thousand having been cut off, or dying in their retreat; besides
losing all their heavy artillery. *Kara Muftapha* would
then gladly have embraced the peace, which he had before
so haughtily rejected; but the kofaks laid waste all the
countries on the *Euxine Sea*, and rejected all terms of accommodation.
Upon this the vizier resolved to build a
town at the mouth of the *Boristhenes*, or *Nieper*, not far
from *Oczakow*, to prevent the communication between the
kofak shipping, and the *Euxine Sea*. The pasha *Koplan*,
and six regiments of janifaries were ordered to cover the
workmen; but both they and their guards, when they had
proceeded but a very little way in their building, were cut
to pieces by the kofaks, who, among others, slew *George
Kiemielnifki*, the hetman, who had been appointed by the
A peace concluded. porte. The impracticability of making any conquests upon
the *Russians*, upon that side, appeared now so plain to the
Turkish ministry, that they gladly treated of peace, which
was at last concluded, to the great satisfaction of both
parties.

The

The *Turks*, from the uncultivated wilds of *Tartary*, now War in turned their arms towards the rich provinces of *Hungary*. Hungary, The cruelty and injustice of the *Austrians*, had encreased the number of malecontents there ; *Tekeli's* army, by the assistance he received from the porte, was in excellent condition; but after various adventures, which have no relation to this part of our history, he was obliged to apply to *Mohammed* for further succours. This was occasioned by a peace, which the *Austrians* had just concluded with the *French*, and which had left the former at liberty to pursue the *Hungarian* war. *Tekeli*, to induce the porte to grant the succour he required, offered *Mohammed* a tribute of forty, some say eighty thousand dollars a year, and, what was of far greater importance, to assist him, if required, with a body of thirty thousand *Hungarians*. The manner of complying with *Tekeli's* proposals, occasioned great debates in the *Turkish* divan ; only the sultan and his first minister, were for granting assistance openly ; as the emperor of *Germany*, however he might have behaved to the *Hungarians*, had done nothing to break the long peace he had concluded with the *Turks*. But the sultan and his minister stood firm in their opinion, and at last, the sultana *Valide*, allured by the hopes given her by the vizier, that her appointments would be encreased, declared herself for *Tekeli*, and brought others, amongst whom was the mufti himself, over to the same opinion. Notwithstanding those great authorities, the bulk of the people appeared to be so averse from a *German* war, and discovered so many and such dangerous indications of their sentiments, that the government found it necessary to publish the reason of their conduct, which they did, in a manner well suited to the pride and genius of the people.

Tekeli, and his adherents, were declared to be under the protection of the porte ; and letters were formally sent to the court of *Vienna*, charging that emperor, as was the truth, with his having violated the terms he had agreed to with the malecontents, and requiring him not only to recall his troops, but to restore all he had taken from them ; and that under pain of the porte's displeasure. Though this was a language, to which that court was not used, yet *Leopold* had so many reasons for wishing the porte to stand neuter between him and the *Hungarians*, that he sent count *Albert Caprara*, as his ambassador to *Constantinople*, to employ all methods, by money, intrigues, or otherwise, to divert the storm. The vizier, who was determined on the measures he was to pursue, and was apprehensive of the consequences of this embassy, before the arrival of the count, sent *Ibrahim*, the beglergeg of *Buda*, with six thousand men to *Tekeli's* assistance ; and ordered *Apaffi*, the tributary prince of *Transylvania* to join him likewise. *Tekeli*, thus assisted, bore down all opposition, and drove the *Austrians* out of *Zatmar, Kossovia, Esperies, Loutschet, Levent, Lipschet*, and

T.llak,

Tillek, with several other places of importance; part of which were garrisoned by the *Turks*, and part by the *Hungarians*.

where
Tekeli is
declared
king. Those successes encouraged the *Othmans* so much, that *Tekili* was, by order of the porte, invested with the sovereignty of *Hungary*, by the pasha of *Buda*. This being done, the vizier thought it needless to keep any farther terms with the imperialists, and signified it to count *Caprara*, that his master would agree to a peace only on condition of restoring *Hungary* to its independency upon the court of *Vienna*; pay an annual tribute of five hundred thousand florins; demolish *Leopoldopolis*, and *Gutta*; resign certain forts and territories to *Tekeli*; and grant an amnesty to all the *Hungarians*. Those propositions, as the vizier had foreseen, being rejected, war was immediately proclaimed against the *Austrians*, and the sultan himself, attended by all his great ministers of state, set out towards *Adrianople*, to take upon him the command of the army. While they were on their march, they were attacked by most dreadful storms, which threatened the ruin of the expedition, and made a great impression upon the superstitious *Turks*.

The *Turks*
invade the
empire. It was the winter of the year 1683, before the army was in a condition to set out for *Belgrade*, and *Mohammed* having reviewed it, invested his vizier with *Mohamet*'s standard, by which he made him his generalissimo; and then he returned to *Constantinople*. Though the vizier had now the full command of the army, yet, as this expedition was one of the most important that had ever been undertaken by the *Othmans*, he was resolved to proceed with caution, that in case of ill success, he might throw the blame upon others.

Delibe-
rations
about be-
sieging
Vienna, Having met *Tekeli* at *Essek*, at the head of three hundred *Hungarian* noblemen, he affected to treat him with the highest respect; and calling a council of war of his chief officers, he first demanded *Tekeli*'s opinion, whether the siege of *Vienna* should be undertaken that year, or delayed to the next. Nothing could be more distant than this question was from *Tekili*'s thoughts, which were entirely confined to *Hungary*. Though some ill informed *Christian* writers have reported, that *Tekeli* gave his opinion for besieging *Vienna* that year; yet, it is certain, from the testimony of the *Turkish* officers themselves, that in the council of war, he remonstrated strongly against the danger and folly of besieging *Vienna* that year, as such a step, besides the immense difficulties attending it, would unite all christendom against the *Othmans*. He added, that they might easily reduce *Hungary*, through the dissentions that prevailed there, and, the imperial army not being able to withstand the *Othmans* in the field, proper magazines might be soon established in that fruitful country, which could not fail to facilitate the entire conquest of the *German* empire. The vizier dissembled his disapprobation of *Tekeli*'s opinion, but proceeded to take those of the other generals, who were too

well

well acquainted with his secret sentiments, to give their real sense of the question; but submitted themselves to his better judgment. The vizier perceived, from their behaviour, that he was, in fact, single in his opinion; and sending off to *Buda* the imperial ambassador, whom he had hitherto amused with hopes of peace, he ordered his army to march towards *Raab*, or, as the *Turks* call it, *Yavarin*, and on the way he was joined by the khan of the *Tartars*, with all his troops, by which his army became so formidable, that the *Germans* abandoned the passage of the river, or, as some say, it was betrayed to the *Turks*, who immediately passed the same, and encamped under the walls of *Raab*.

While he was making vigorous preparations for besieging that important fortress, his spies brought him intelligence of *Vienna* itself being in so untenable a condition, that the emperor and his court had removed to *Lintz*. Nothing could be more agreeable, than this account was (which in general was true) to the vizier's views. After treating with the aga of the janisaries, from whom he had the most to apprehend, he again called a council of the chief pashas, to take their opinion, which was now unanimous against undertaking the siege of *Vienna*, before they had reduced the places that lay between them and the city; and *Tekeli* repeated his former sentiments. The vizier, upon this, produced the sultan's khati sharif, or sign manual, impowering *which is agreed upon.* him to act as he pleased; and this struck the pashas with such respect, that they instantly declared their readiness to execute his commands, whatever they might be. The vizier upon this ordered his camp to be razed, and leaving a detachment to block up *Raab*, he set out for *Vienna*, before which place he appeared, to the terror of all christendom; after surprising and cutting off several parties of the imperialists in his march, besides taking all the baggage of some of their chief officers. This happened on the thirteenth of July 1683. As we shall, in other parts of this work, have occasion more than once to mention this celebrated siege, we shall here confine ourselves chiefly to the part which the *Othmans* bore there.

It is to this day uncertain, whether the vizier had a real *Views of* correspondence with any of the *German* generals, by which *the vizier.* he had a fair prospect of success, or whether he was not actuated merely by ambition. The first seems to be probable, without detracting from the influence of the other, which undoubtedly was very powerful in his breast. Many writers, and those of note, are of opinion, that he had secretly formed the scheme of an independent empire, in the west, for himself; every thing concurred to flatter him in his project. He was at the head of one of the finest armies the *Othmans* had ever raised, consisting of above one hundred and forty thousand regular, well disciplined, troops, besides the *Crim Tartars*, and the attendants of his camp; the

whole

whole amounting to above three hundred thoufand men. He was poffeffed of immenfe treafures, and all the European pafhas, except *Ibrahim*, the beglerbeg of *Buda*, was in his intereft; fo that in fact, he had nothing to fear even from *Mohammed* himself. On the other hand, the Chriftian powers were divided, and it was well known, that *Poland*, from whence the emperor chiefly expected relief, was upon bad terms with the houfe of *Auftria*. He had cut off all communication between the duke of *Lorrain*, the imperial general, and *Vienna*; the fortifications of which were in a bad condition; and the garrifon confifted of no more than eight thoufand regular troops, while the flight of the emperor had ftruck the inhabitants with the utmoft confternation, and dejection. To bring over to his views the beglerbeg of *Buda*, from whom he had the moft to apprehend, he is faid, but upon no certain grounds, to have propofed to give him the kingdom of *Hungary*, while he referved to himfelf all the empire of *Germany*, *Tranfylvania*, *Walachia*, and *Moldavia*.

Siege of Vienna. The trenches being opened, the *Othman* artillery played with fuch fury, that breaches were made in the walls, the outer works were taken, and it was thought, that, had the vizier proceeded with the fame vigour as he begun, he muft foon have become mafter of the place. The true reafon why he did not, was moft probably owing to his avarice. He had formed high ideas of the treafures concealed in *Vienna*; and as he knew the rapacioufnefs of the *Turkifh* foldiery, if the place was taken by ftorm, he flackened the fury of the fiege, and threw letters into the place, containing the moft magnificent promifes, and at the fame time the moft dreadful threatenings, to induce the garrifon to furrender. It is thought by many, that, befides the motives of ambition and avarice, we have mentioned, the immenfe courfe of luxury, in which he was plunged, contributed not a little to his relaxing the operations; but this agrees ill with his general character. He found his greateft refiftance from count *Staremberg*, whom the emperor, upon his retiring to *Lintz*, had appointed to be governor of *Vienna*; and who made moft excellent difpofitions for the defence of the place. He armed the citizens, and the ftudents, who regularly mounted guard, under the command of a phyfician. The vizier ordered only fmall parties to the attacks of the baftions, who were eafily repulled, or cut off; and he unwarily divulged the great expectations he had from the *German* treafures. Thofe expectations were confirmed by a feries of mifmanagements. He ordered proclamation to be made in his camp, that if his troops fhould force the walls of the city, they fhould immediately intrench themfelves, without prefuming to advance without his orders; and, all of a fudden, he retrenched the allowance of his foldiers for provifions, which became exceffively dear in
the

the camp, notwithstanding the immense magazines he had brought along with him. *Kara Mustapha* pretended at first, that he had retrenched the provisions, only that he might have sufficient to spare to the *Othmans*, who were to be left to garrison *Vienna* after it was taken ; but it soon appeared, that the *Austrian* garrisons had cut off all their supplies, which was the consequence, as *Tekeli* had foreseen, of his precipitate march for *Vienna*

The janisaries coming to the knowledge of all this misconduct, would have mutinied, had not their aga and the pashas been in the vizier's interest. They could not however conceal their indignation, but called out to the *Germans*, " Come on infidels, the very sight of your hats will " put us to flight." The scarcity becoming more intollerable every day, the vizier, to prevent a sedition, sent off a detachment of eight thousand men, with orders to join *Tekeli* and his *Hungarians*, who were at *Ternau*, with orders to besiege *Presburg* ; where the inhabitants seemed disposed to receive a garrison of discontented *Hungarians*. The duke of *Lorrain* had intelligence of this design, and sent off a reinforcement to the garrison of *Presburg*, the preserving of which was of the utmost consequence to the *Germans* as it cut off the communication between the vizier's army and *Buda*, from whence he could have drawn vast plenty of provisions. But the duke received an account, that the reinforcement he sent to the garrison of the city had been beat, that the inhabitants had received a garrison of *Hungarian* malecontents ; and that *Tekeli* having joined the *Turks*, was preparing to besiege the castle of *Presburg*. Upon this, he detached prince *Lewis of Baden*, with a strong party, which coming up with *Tekeli*, defeated him with a considerable slaughter, and cut in pieces the *Turks* who were guarding a convoy of a thousand waggons laden with provisions for the use of the vizier's army ; all which fell into the hands of the imperialists.

The news of this defeat reaching the *Turkish* camp before *Vienna*, increased the spirit of mutiny there to such a degree, that the vizier found himself under the necessity of giving orders for a general assault, which, though very furious, proved ineffectual, through the superior knowledge of the *Germans* in springing mines. For some days, however, the assaults were renewed by the *Turks* with the greatest obstinacy, and though they were generally worsted, yet it was easily to be perceived, that, if the besieged were not relieved, the city must be taken. The besieged sent off an officer disguised like a *Turk*, to inform the duke of *Lorrain* of their situation. By a most mastery address he passed the *Turkish* camp, and reached that of the imperialists, where he gave his dispatches to the duke, who immediately returned the messenger, with assurances of speedy relief ; the receipt of which the besieged immediately signified by playing off sky rockets, a signal that was understood by the *Austrian* army. Though we have no intimations from *Christian* writers, of the manner in which the *Turkish* army was all this time supplied with provisions; yet it seems certain, that *Tekeli* had found means to convey them by the *Danube*; for the siege, at this period, was carried on with greater fury than ever. The vizier had abandoned his dilatory mistaken precautions, and had actually made so many lodgments upon the works of the city, that, had it not been for some signals of approaching relief, which were given from the mountains of *Calemberg*, where the *Austrian* army lay, the besieged must have lost their spirits; but so much were they re-animated by those signals, that they drove the *Turks* from all their posts with incredible slaughter.

Which is raised by the king of *Poland* and the *Germans*.   The infidels, by means of deserters, found out at last the meaning of those rockets to be, that relief was at hand; and therefore they prepared for a decisive battle. With this view, the vizier ordered *Tekeli* to join him with his *Hungarians*, which he declined to do; but upon muster, the *Turks* found that, during the siege, they had lost above forty thousand men. They then made another desperate, and their last, effort upon the city, but were repulsed as before, with prodigious loss; upon which they prepared for a general engagement. The fires upon the heights of *Calemberg* announcing the approach of the *Christian* army, just at a time when the besieged were so much exhausted, that they could hold out no longer; the vizier, who amidst the consternation of his officers and soldiers, retained his presence of mind, and intrepidity, summoned a council of war, to take the opinion of his chief officers, in what manner he should proceed. The pasha *Ibrahim*, the beglerbeg of *Buda*, declared himself for raising the siege, and marching against the *Christians*, but to keep upon the defensive, by the infantry making a rampart of trees cut from the neighbouring woods, and fortifying it with cannon, while the cavalry should attack the *Christians* on their flanks. This advice, though backed by most of the pashas, was rejected by the vizier. He alledged, that, by drawing off from siege, the garrison would level all their works, and repair the walls, and that the *Christian* force was so inconsiderable, that they durst not venture to attack him, if his army was fortified in the manner *Ibrahim* proposed; but that in their present situation, they must attack him or see the city taken before their eyes. He added, that the janisaries, if the siege was raised, could not be brought to re-enter the trenches, where so many of their fellow soldiers had perished; and that the autumnal rains, if set in, must oblige him to raise the siege, as they had formerly done *Solyman* the *Great*. In this reasoning, *Ibrahim*, who was the only general in the army who was not daunted by the vizier's authority, answered, that, by leaving a few regiments to defend the works of the camp, which were in fact stronger than those of the city, they might be secure; but to this expedient, the vizier gave no other answer

answer than again producing his absolute powers under the sultan's hand. Upon the breaking up of the council, the vizier massacred all his *Christian* prisoners, who are said to have amounted to thirty thousand men.

On the eighth of *September* the king of *Poland*, who had now surmounted all the prejudices he had entertained against the emperor, having joined the auxiliary troops of the circles, arrived with his army at the heights of *Calemberg*; after passing the *Danube* without any resistance from the *Turks*. In his march he was joined by the imperialists, and other *Germans*, and the whole of the *Christian* army amounted to about sixty-five thousand fighting men; the imperialists being commanded by prince *Charles* of *Lorrain*. It has been generally allowed, that the vizier behaved in an unsoldier-like manner, in not disputing the passage of the *Danube*, and in contenting himself with sending ten thousand men to observe the motions of the *Christians*; but this omission, probably, was occasioned by the assurance he had of a victory, which he was in hopes would for ever exterminate the imperial power in *Germany*. On the eleventh of *September*, the day before that destined for the relief of *Vienna*, the order of battle was settled in a council of war, held among the *Christians*. The *Polanders* formed the right wing, the imperialists under the duke of *Lorrain*, the left, and in the center were placed the troops of the empire, under their respective princes. There the king of *Poland* in person took post; and in this order the whole *Christian* army descended from the heights of *Calemberg*. Had not *Kara Mustapha* been intoxicated by self opinion, he might have rendered this descent difficult, if not impracticable, by taking possession of the forest of *Vienna*, where he might have raised a battery that would have flanked the *Christian* army, which had made dispositions upon that supposition. Instead of that, the vizier extended his army from the *Danube* to the bottom of the mountain, and sent a party to attack count *Lesley*, who had raised a battery to secure a pass leading to *Vienna*; but they were repulsed by the duke *de Croy*, and this drew on the general engagement.

The vizier leaving a sufficient force to continue the siege, drew up his army likewise in three divisions. The pasha of *Buda* had the command of the left wing, the pasha of *Diyarbeker* of the right, and he himself commanded the center, where the janisaries were posted. Upon the first charge, the vizier had reason to repent that he had not followed the advice of the pasha of *Buda*. The *Turks* were every where driven from their open posts, which they had seized too late, and had neglected to fortify. This first advantage was pursued by the king of *Poland*, with irresistible fury. The *Turks* were attacked on all sides, and the *Christians*, from their manner of fighting, soon perceived that the day would be their own, which gave them incredible spirits. The vizier in person, at the head of thirty thousand

Defeat and flight of the Turks.

choice

choice troops, attacked the division led by the king of *Poland*, who being seasonably supported by some battalions of the *Germans*, drove the infidels back to their camp, which was filled with confusion and dismay. The soldiers upon the wings of their army, seeing their center defeated, retired precipitately to their camp, without regarding the orders of their generals, and the janisaries who had been left to continue the siege, under pretence of defending their camp, left the lines, till at last the whole *Turkish* army joined, as it were by consent, in a total flight, which prevented the entire destruction of their troops, who suffered but inconsiderably in the battle. The truth is, though this victory was glorious for the *Christians*, and for the king of *Poland* in particular, yet, it was greatly owing to the dislike which the janisaries had to the vizier, and it is said, that of the *Christians* not above two hundred were killed, and of the *Turks* a thousand.

When the vizier saw the division which he commanded broken, and unsupported by his two wings, he retired to his tent, which he found deserted, and securing the standard of *Mohammed*, he fled after the rest of his army. The *Christian* generals, amazed at the little resistance that had been made by the *Turks*, thought that an ambuscade had been laid for them, and this rendered them cautious of entering the *Turkish* camp along with the fugitives. But about seven in the evening their apprehensions were removed, by receiving undoubted intelligence, that the *Turks* had entirely abandoned their camp, and were flying with incredible speed to join their countrymen, who were still blockading *Raab*.

Booty found in their camp

The king and prince *Waldeck*, a *German* general, then entered their camp, and were amazed at the immense booty which it contained, of which we have the following general estimate. There were six thousand five hundred tents, four thousand five hundred barrels of powder, six thousand weight of lead, twenty thousand granado shells, eight thousand hand granados, eleven thousand shovels and pickaxes, one thousand six hundred weight of match, two thousand five hundred fire balls, five thousand two hundred weight of pitch, eleven thousand weight of oil of petrolium, and tar, five hundred thousand of linseed oil, nine thousand five hundred of salt petre, five thousand one hundred pieces of coarse linnen, two hundred thousand hair sacks, for carrying earth and sand, eight hundred and ten weight of iron bars and horse-shoes, one hundred ladles for melting pitch, two hundred weight of packthread, with thongs made of camels hides and buffler leather, for binding, four thousand sheep-skins, fifty-two sacks of cotton, one thousand five hundred empty wool-sacks, two thousand halberts, four hundred scythes and sickles, five thousand six hundred barrels of guns for the janisaries, two thousand plates of iron for covering targets, one hundred and twenty three hundred weight of greafe and tallow, two hundred and thirty

thirty powder horns, two thousand six hundred bags for powder, four pair of smith's bellows, eight thousand carts, one thousand great bombs, eighteen thousand cannon balls, one hundred and eighty cannon and mortars.

It is said, that the *Turks* who fled from *Vienna*, travelled fifty four hours without meat or drink, till they reached their countrymen before *Yawarin*, where the vizier had full leisure to reflect on the madness of his own conduct. To palliate it as well as he could, he threw his miscarriage upon the cowardice or treachery of his general officers, particularly the pasha of *Buda*, whom he accused of having misbehaved at the head of twelve thousand men, sent to attack the *Christians* upon their descent from the heights of *Calemberg* The sultan was then at *Belgrade*, where he received this apology from his vizier; and the pasha of *Buda* understanding what the contents of the dispatches were, recriminated in other letters, which laid before the emperor a true account of the vizier's misconduct. But before any answer could be received to them, the vizier ordered the pasha of *Buda*, and fifty officers of his army, to be strangled. The reason he gave out was, their having, in a manner, forced him to undertake the siege of *Vienna*, and then not supporting him in carrying it on. He then made the pasha *Kara Mehemed*, governor of *Buda*, and encamped under the walls of that city. After that, the *Christian* army went in search of the *Othmans*, to besiege *Barkan*, a fort opposite to *Gran*; but the *Poles* taking the vanguard, paid little regard to discipline, and advancing without being supported by the *Germans* under the duke of *Lorrain*, were defeated, with the loss of two thousand men, and all of them must have been cut off had not the *Germans* come up to their relief. Next The *Turks* day, the *Poles* and *Germans* being now united, a bloody defeated. battle ensued, in which the weight of the *Othman* fury fell upon the *Poles*, at whom they were particularly exasperated, but the latter being again supported by the *Germans* under the duke of *Lorrain*, the *Turks* were completely defeated, with the loss of ten thousand of their best troops, and *Barkan* was taken. This great victory produced so large a booty to the *Christians*, that the *Poles* and *Germans* quarrelled about the division of the plunder, and were with some difficulty reconciled by count *Staremberg*, who had so bravely defended *Vienna*.

The defeat of the *Turks*, raised such a spirit of mutiny among their surviving troops, that the grand vizier was obliged to have recourse to various artifices to screen himself from the resentment of his soldiers. In the mean while, the siege of *Gran* was formed by the imperialists, and *Poles*, and taken chiefly by the courage of the *Bavarian* troops. The duke of *Lorrain*, however, granted the *Othmans*, who held out the place for five days, an honourable capitulation; and treated them with great politeness. It is probable, that

R 3 had

had it not been for the approach of winter, and the growing misunderstanding among the *Christian* troops, the infidels at this time must have been driven out of *Hungary*. *Leventz*, *Rabonitz*, *Probenz* on the *Drave*, *Esseghet*, and *Brevenitz*, near *Kanisia*, surrendered to the *Christians*, and above three thousand *Turks* were cut in pieces at *Setzin*, which was stormed without a capitulation. Besides the abovementioned places, many others fell into the hands of the imperialists before they went into winter quarters. So many reiterated losses on the side of the *Turks*, reduced them to variance among themselves. Their great officers threw their miscarriage upon each other, but the prime vizier, to exculpate himself, blamed *Tekeli*, for advising him to undertake the siege of *Vienna*. *Tekeli* would gladly have come to a good understanding with the imperialists, but the haughtiness of the court of *Vienna* would hear of no terms but an absolute submission. All this while, the most dreadful cruelties were committed by *Petreczeicus*, the *Moldavian* prince, who had revolted from the *Turks*, upon the *Crim* and *Bujak Tartars*; who, soon after the battle of *Vienna*, severely revenged themselves, and would have cut off *Petreczeicus*, and his confederates, had not the *Tartar* horse been so much fatigued that they could not continue the pursuit. *Dukay*, another *Moldavian* prince in the *Turkish* interest, was carried prisoner to *Warsaw*, where he died in confinement; and *Demetrius Cantacazenus*, a descendant of the ancient *Greek* emperors, was substituted in his room.

The sultan *Mohammed*, intent only on his pleasures, was agreeably amusing himself with the pleasures of hunting, while his armies were thus destroyed; but he was kept in the dark by the vizier, who, as long as he could dissemble, gave him hourly expectations of his troops being put in possession of *Vienna*; and so much was the sultan persuaded of the truth of this intelligence, that he had made preparations for a solemn rejoicing in his capital. A few days undeceived him, for he received letters from his vizier, with an account of the dreadful defeats of his troops, and the loss of his chief fortresses in *Hungary*; but throwing all the blame upon *Tekeli*, and the pasha *Ibrahim*. With those letters, the vizier sent immense presents to the sultana *Valide*, and the principal courtiers about the sultan's person, which had so great an effect, that his sublime highness confirmed him in the viziership, and approved of his putting the pasha *Ibrahim* to death. Those stratagems, however, did not long avail him, for while he was contriving how to get rid of the aga of the janisaries, and other great officers, some generals, who had escaped from the great slaughter of the *Othman* troops in *Germany*, and *Hungary*, informed the sultan of the truth. The pasha *Ibrahim*'s widow, who was sister to the sultan, was at the head of the vizier's enemies; but so steadily did that minister persevere in his own justification, that he he gained admittance to the sultan, who signed a writing, promising never to take off his head upon any suggestions that could be brought against him. *Ibrahim's* widow understanding this, travelled in disguise from *Buda*, the place of her husband's government, to *Adrianople*, where the sultan resided, to throw herself at his feet, for justice against the murderer of her husband. When she arrived at *Adrianople*, she heard of the death of the sultana *Valide*, upon whose friendship she had great dependence; but she had the pleasure to be informed, that that princess, upon her death bed, had cautioned her son against the vizier, and had exposed his malversations. To complete his ruin, *Tekeli*, alarmed at the accusations which he understood had been laid against him by the vizier, came to the sultan's court, where he justified himself from all the charges against him; and the janisaries tumultuously demanded the vizier's head.

Mohammed was, by this time, sufficiently awakened to a sense of his own danger, and his minister's wickedness, but was at a loss how to proceed. He was afraid of having recourse to violent measures, and endeavoured to pacify the janisaries with large sums of money; but in the mean time he called a council of state, to deliberate on the present situation of affairs. The mufti, and the great officers who composed this council, or divan, were unanimously of opinion that the vizier should be strangled; but the sultan making some difficulty, the janisaries again rose in tumult, and demanded his head; and this determined his fate. He was then at *Belgrade* recruiting his army, and not without hopes of striking some blow that might yet save him from destruction. The sultan having signed the sentence of his death, committed the execution of it to the kyehaya of the capiji. The manner of the vizier's submitting to the bowstring, is an amazing proof of the *Orkmans* obedience to the will of their superiors. This kyehaya, with two, or at most three attendants, privately set out for *Belgrade*, where he was to take off the head of the greatest subject of the empire; while commanding a powerful army. When he approached *Belgrade*, he privately dispatched a courier to the aga of the janisaries, recommending to him to dispose matters so that the execution should be performed decently and without noise. The aga, the kyehaya, and the two executioners who attended them, arrived at the vizier's palace, where, though he more than guessed their errand, he received them with the utmost respect, and at their demand delivered up the standard and seals of his office, and submitting his neck to the bowstring, he was strangled; not without making some protestations of his innocence. Many of his friends shared the same fate, the chief of whom was the testerdar, or great treasurer; and their estates, which were confiscated to the sultan, were thought to amount to

The grand vizier strangled.

four

four millions of money; the seasonable distribution of which prevented a revolution in the empire.

The aga *Selictar*, a person of great accomplishments, was offered the seals of the viziership; but that high post was now thought to be so dangerous, that he excused himself with a well turned compliment, of his not being able to survive the thoughts of a separation from the person of his adorable sovereign; upon which the seals were conferred upon the pasha kaymakan, *Kara Ibrahim*. This minister entered upon a charge equally dangerous as disagreeable. Universal corruption had overspread the empire, and little regard was paid to the chief officers of state. The new grand vizier had married one of the sultan's daughters, who was not above eight years of age, and found himself involved in inextricable difficulties. Being of himself a wise, moderate man, he was inclined to make up matters with the *Christian* princes, that the empire, which was exhausted by its losses, might have some respite. This advice was so disagreeable to the sultan, that he threatened to hang him up in his robes of state, if he did not proceed in his revenge against the *Christians*.

The *French* ambassador was the first who felt the sultan's fury, by being committed a prisoner to the custody of the chaush pasha, on pretence of some damages received by the *Turks*, from the *French* ships at *Scio*. The ambassador, at first, made a resolute stand, but was obliged to submit to determined force, and all he could obtain was, that the satisfaction he was to make should be performed by his secretary, which was done with great formality. The secretary laid presents before the sultan's feet, supposed to amount to two hundred thousand crowns, though not worth the tenth part of that sum, while the imperial usher proclaimed aloud, *Behold the agents sent from the king of* France, *to humble themselves before our magnificent emperor, and in the name of their king to offer their presents, in satisfaction for that affront and insult which the* French *ships offered at the port of* Scio. Sir *John Finch*, the *English* ambassador, was in like manner obliged to pay some unjust demands made upon the *English Turkey* company; and the *Dutch*, and *Venetian* ambassadors were forced to submit to the like imposition.

The *Venetians* resented the injuries offered to their ministers, and, joining in a league with the emperor of *Germany*, and the king of *Poland*, against the *Turks*, they declared war, and the *Venetian* ambassador had the boldness to give the declaration into the hands of the kaymakan; but he afterwards left *Constantinople* in disguise. The *Turkish* empire was very ill prepared to sustain this confederacy. Their marine was in a most despicable condition, and their troops were few, and dispirited. The vizier apologized for what had happened to the *Venetians*; but they refused to hear of any terms without the concurrence of their allies. The

vizier

vizier, however, took the best measures he could to face the storm. He restored the *French* and *English* nations to their usual privileges. He appointed the ablest generals to command the *Othman* armies, against the *Poles* and *Germans*, and the high admiral to act against the *Venetians*, while he himself continued at *Constantinople*, to prevent any intrigues that could be formed for his destruction; and gave all his dependents strict orders to communicate to the sultan, only the agreeable part of public occurrences. In the mean while, the duke of *Lorrain*, the imperial general, about the middle of *June* 1684, at the head of forty thousand men, marched to *Vicegrade*, and gave several defeats to the *Turkish* generals, who attempted to interrupt his progress. In the beginning of *July*, *Witzen* surrendered to the imperialists and *Poles*, who again defeated the *Turks*, and soon after formed the siege of *Buda*.

The fortress of *Pest*, opposite on the *Danube* to *Buda*, was taken by the imperialists in a few hours; but the *Turkish* general *Shaytan Ibrahim*, attempting to raise the siege, or to succour the city, at the head of eighty thousand men, was defeated with great loss. A great number of skirmishes followed, generally to the disadvantage of the *Othmans*. But the latter seem to have been well commanded; for when the duke of *Lorrain* summoned the governor of *Buda* to surrender, on pain of his garrison receiving no quarter, he was so far from complying, that he ordered forty imperialists to be hanged on the bastions of the city, though the pasha seraskier *Shaytan Ibrahim*, all this time continued at the head of a powerful army, and made repeated attempts to raise the siege. He was seconded by the rains which fell during the month of *September*; and on the first of *November*, the imperialists finding the *Turkish* garrison to be above ten thousand strong, and that they could not cut off their communication with the *Danube*, raised the siege, and retired into winter quarters, with the loss of twenty-five thousand men. During this siege, count *Lesley* took *Wirrowit*, and beat the *Turks* in two battles. At the same time, *Tekeli* was defeated by the imperialists in *Upper Hungary*. To counterbalance those losses, the pasha *Ayncji Soleyman* defeated the *Poles*, at *Babadaghi*, and penetrated into *Moldavia*, and *Walakhia*. A grand design was then on foot to invade *Constantinople* itself, by means of *Serban Cantakuzenus*, the *Turkish* governor of *Walakhia*. This prince had entered into engagements with the emperor of *Germany*, and the czar of *Muscovy*, to drive the *Othmans* out of *Europe*, on condition of his being declared emperor of *Constantinople*, the imperial seat of his forefathers. For this purpose, he had prepared a train of artillery, and raised twenty-four thousand men; but it was thought, that he was poisoned by the practices of the *Turks*. His brother *Demetrius Cantakuzenus*, governor of *Moldavia*, was deposed at the same time by the *Turkish* seraskier,

(marginal note: War in Hungary)

ſeraſkier, who appointed *Conſtantine Cantemir*, father to the hiſtorian, to ſucceed him. This year, *Sobieſki* king of *Poland*, ſurprized *Quancze*, upon the river *Tyras*, which was only at the diſtance of two hours march from *Kaminek*; but being hemmed in by the ſeraſkier, he made ſo inglorious a campaign, that the *Turks*, in deriſion, ſaid he had been bribed by the *French* king, the only friend they had among the *Chriſtian* potentates. The *Venetians* were more fortunate, for they obtained great advantages in *Dalmatia*. Their fleet was commanded by *Moroſini*, the ſame who had ſurrendered *Candia*; and who, by his brave actions on this occaſion, effaced all ſuſpicions of his former conduct. He took *Leukos*, or *Santa Maura*, an iſland and city in the *Ionian Sea*, on the ſixth of *Auguſt*; and afterwards, the *Venetians* ſubdued ſeveral ports of *Epirus*, and the *Morea*, where they defeated the army of the *Turks*.

and *Moldavia.* Thoſe ſucceſſes of the *Venetians*, gave the grand vizier but little diſquiet, as the *Poles* and *Germans* were now diſabled from acting, by the great loſſes they had ſuſtained. In the beginning of the year 1685, *Schultz*, an imperial general, was entirely defeated by *Tekeli*; but the duke of *Lorrain* beat the ſeraſkier of *Hungary*, and took *New Hauſel*, where all the garriſon, which conſiſted, at firſt, of three thouſand men, were put to the ſword, excepting two hundred. This ſtruck the *Turks* with ſuch conſternation, that they abandoned the defence of *Novigrade*, and *Vicegrade*, which fell into the hands of the imperialiſts. Thoſe loſſes daunted the ſeraſkier of *Hungary*, (who had hitherto bravely ſupported the honour of his maſter's arms) ſo greatly, that he made advances for a peace with the imperialiſts, but they were rejected. Count *Leſley*, and general *Schultz*, were equally ſucceſsful in *Sclavonia*, and the *Lower Hungary*; but, though *Tekeli* and his troops were every where routed, they choſe to retire to *Kaſchaw*, and to wait for the *Turkiſh* reinforcements, rather than ſubmit to the imperialiſts. On the ſixth of *October*, *Kaſchaw* was inveſted by *Caprara*, the imperial general; and *Tekeli* ſent repeated diſpatches for aſſiſtance to the paſha of *Waradin*, who deſired his advice about the beſt method for relieving the city. *Tekeli* accordingly ſet out with about ſeven thouſand men, and met the paſha near *Waradin*; where, after receiving the greateſt honours, he was arreſted by the paſha, and ſent in chains to *Conſtantinople*. The paſha then ſent for *Petrozzi*, who was lieutenant-general to *Tekeli*, and was deſired to take upon him the command of the *Hungarian* army. *Petrozzi*, and the other officers, who had been ſtunned by the faithleſs conduct of the *Turks*, diſcovered no immediate ſhew of reſentment; but upon their return to their camp, *Petrozzi* held forth the villainy that had been practiſed towards *Tekeli*, ſo effectually, that their army reſolved to take ſervice under *Caprara*, who was ſtill carrying on the ſiege of *Kaſchaw*.

Caprara received them with joy, and the garrison hearing of the defection of their countrymen from the *Turks* to the imperialists, threw open their gates to the besiegers, and put them in possession of the place.

It is thought, with good reason, that *Tekeli* was arrested, and imprisoned, by way of atonement for the serafkier's own ill success, to save his head at the *Othman* court. *Tekeli*, however, had his agents at the same court, who justified him so well, that orders were sent from *Constantinople* to reinstate him with honour in his command. In the mean while, the king of *Poland* tampered with prince *Constantine Cantemir*, to revolt from the *Turks*, which that prince appeared inclinable to do, if he could have brought the states of the country, whose wives and children were hostages for their fidelity at the porte, to join him. This being found impracticable, the king sent an army under the command of two generals, *Potocky*, and *Yablanowski*, to subdue *Moldavia*. *Cantemir*, not much to his honour, kept a private correspondence with them, and advised them to begin with the siege of *Kaminiek*. The *Poles* despised this advice, and expressed a contempt for all the *Othman* power, advising *Cantemir* at the same time to join them, under the pain of being treated as an enemy. A bridge was run over the *Tyras* by the *Poles*, who were soon encountered by twenty-five thousand *Turks*, fifty thousand *Tartars*, and five thousand *Moldavians*. Both armies halted, and by the management of *Cantemir*, the *Turks* might have been persuaded not to have hazarded a battle; but the *Poles* imputing their caution to timidity, attacked the *Moldavians* under *Cantemir*, who being supported by the *Turks*, obtained, according to his son's account, a compleat victory. This was the only advantage the *Othmans* gained during the whole campaign; which was, in other respects, so unfortunate for them, that the *Maynottæ*, a people of the *Morea*, revolted from them; and the *Venetian* general count *de St. Paul*, besieged and took *Koron*, and put all the garrison to the sword. While *Koron* was besieged, the *Maynottæ*, who are reported to be the bravest people of *Greece*, and descended from the antient *Spartans*, besieged and took *Zarnata*, and *Gommenizza*; but were repulsed before *Zing*. Many other actions happened in the *Morea*, with various success; but they are differently represented by the *Turks*, and *Venetians*, and are of themselves unimportant in their consequences.

Those unfavourable events, occasioned vast uneasiness to the grand vizier, who had no other way to shelter himself from the fate of his predecessor, but by putting to death the generals who commanded in the unfortunate expeditions. The only pasha who held out against the bloody politics of the grand vizier, was *Soleyman*, who had defeated the *Poles*, and was thereby become extremely popular in the empire. The vizier not being able to destroy him, persuaded the

Campaign in Molda-via

and Hungary.

sultan

fultan to appoint him ferafkier, or general, againft the *Germans*; and he was fucceeded in his command in *Poland* by *Buikkli Muftapha*. Upon this appointment, the kifler aga, who was *Soleyman*'s friend, gave him intimation, that his preferment was a trap to ruin him; and advifed him to repair to *Conftantinople*. Being admitted, after his arrival, to an audience of the fultan, he laid before him the dangerous ftate of his empire, and being feconded by the kiflar aga, or chief of the black eunuch's, *Soleyman* was appointed grand vizier, and *Kara Ibrahim* was banifhed to *Rhodes*. It is certain, that, when this removal took place, the *Othman* empire was in fo deplorable a condition, that even the horfe-furniture in the imperial ftables, made of plate, was coined into money. The new vizier knew the difficulties he had to ftruggle with, and that the imperialifts were daily gaining ground in *Hungary*, and *Germany*. He ordered all the gold and filver veffels in the palace to be coined, and raifed an army; but one of the firft meafures of his adminiftration, was to free *Tekeli* from his imprifonment, and to reinftate him in all his former honours. That nobleman being thus delivered, endeavoured to raife the fiege of *Mongotz*, which was defended againft *Caprara* by his lady, with fuch invin-cible refolution, that, without his affiftance, fhe obliged the *Germans* to abandon their enterprife, about the middle of *April* 1686.

Siege of Buda.

On the eleventh of *July*, the fame year, the imperialifts made difpofitions for befieging *Buda*. This enterprife was greatly favoured by the dejection of the *Turks*, through a long feries of mifcarriages, and mifmanagements. Several actions, all of them to the difadvantage of the *Othmans*, preceded the fiege, which was at laft formed by the imperial general *Staremberg*; and on the thirteenth of the fame month, the *Turks* burnt down the lower town, having retired to the upper, which was well provided for a defence, and garrifoned by eight thoufand men, under the pafha of the place. On the fourteenth, the duke of *Lorrain* took upon himfelf the command of the fiege, and the ferafkier, who at-tended his motions with an army, found it fo much difpirit-ed, that he retired to the diftance of three leagues, with an intention (as he could not raife the fiege) of throwing fuccours into the place. The pafha of *Maroz* was ap-pointed to that fervice; but he was defeated by the *Germans*. The fiege was then vigoroufly preffed by the latter. The garrifon made a brave defence, and the pafha of *Buda* being killed, he was fucceeded in his command by *Shaytan Ibrahim*, This general was then eighty years of age, and incompara-bly the beft officer the *Turks* had in the field; but was confiderably indebted for his advancement to Sir *Jonathan Dawes*, an *Englifh* merchant. Several fallies were made from the town, and fome with fuccefs, on the part of the *Turks*; the ferafkier all the while hanging, with a large

body

body of troops upon the skirts of the *Christian* army. This obliged the duke of *Lorrain* to divide his troops; he took the command of one part of them, with whom he faced the seraskier, and left the other division to continue the siege, under *Staremberg*. This encouraged the duke of *Lorrain* to give orders for battering the town in breach, which was executed with vast success by the baron *de Asti*, who made himself master of the lower town, and the castle. On the twenty-sixth of *July*, the besiegers were advanced within sixty paces of the counterscarp, and both they and the besieged underwent vast difficulties. Every day produced sallies, in which the *Turkish* troops behaved so bravely, that had it not been for a seasonable reinforcement of *Bavarian* infantry, the siege must have been raised. The duke of *Lorrain*, exasperated at the unexpected resistance he met with, sent a desperate kind of a message to the garrison, threatening, that, if they did not surrender, all within the city should be indiscriminately put to the sword. *Shaytan*, the commandant of *Buda*, treated this message with so much disdain, that he ordered forty *Christians* to be put to death on the ramparts of the city, in sight of the *Christian* army; and sent for answer to the summons, that he would treat all the *Christians* who fell into his hands in the same manner, without either giving or receiving quarter. The siege then went on with redoubled fury, till such numbers of the *Christian* officers were destroyed, that the undertaking was looked upon as impractacible, especially after the arrival of a new vizier, with a fresh army of sixty thousand *Turks*. But in the mean while, the chief magazine of the besieged blew up, and several bodies of the janisaries, sent to enter the place, being defeated; the *Othman* army, both without and within the city, was entirely dispirited, and at last hung out a white flag. The *Germans*, who had suffered incredible which is hardships during the siege, were then intent upon storming taken. the place, and disregarding the signal, entered it sword in hand; and the pasha *Apti*, who had succeeded *Shaytan* in the command, being killed in the breach, the place was taken by storm. About two thousand *Turks* fortified themselves within their works, and resolutely demanded quarter, which, after a council of war was held, was granted them; and they were the only *Othmans* who were saved from the sword.

Buda being thus taken, in sight of the grand vizier, who was unable to relieve it, and with tears lamented the loss of it; the duke of *Lorrain* sent one division of his army, under the prince of *Baden*, into the *Lower Hungary*, and another, under the generals *Caraffa*, and *Heusler*, into the upper. The prince of *Baden*, on the fifteenth of *September*, took *Simonthorn*, and, soon after, *Kaposwiwar* by storm. He next attacked and took *Quinque Ecclesiæ*, or *the Five Churches*; and burned and destroyed a vast number of other places belong-

ing

ing to the *Turks* in the *Lower Hungary*. *Caraffa*, and *Heufler*, were equally fortunate in *Upper Hungary*, where *Veterani*, another of the imperial generals, after defeating the vizier with great lofs, took *Seghedin*. In the mean while, the emperor of *Germany*, that he might improve the advantages which fo many victories gave him, entered into a negotiation the with two czars of *Ruffia*, *John* and *Peter*, the latter of whom was afterwards the famous emperor of that name. As they had fome differences with the *Poles*, the negotiation met with feveral rubs; but at laft the *German* emperor prevailed upon them to give up to the czars, *Kiow*, and *Smolenfko*. Upon this, *Sobiefki* again marched an army into *Moldavia*, where he made a new attempt upon prince *Cantemir*, to declare in his favour. This prince, as before, expreffed vaft affection for the *Chriftian* caufe, and promifed to do, underhand, all that was in his power to favour the *Poles*; but declined doing any thing openly till fuch time as *Sobiefki* had defeated both the *Turks* and the *Tartars*. It appears that, at the time *Cantemir* returned this anfwer, he was actually in the *Othman* fervice; but all the benefit which *Sobiefki* reaped from his friendfhip, amounted to a few days of jollity, which he fpent at *Jeffi*, upon the provifions that had been there laid in for his ufe by that prince.

Unfuccefsful campaign of the Poles.

Danger of Cantemir. The ferafkier *Muftapha*, at laft, difcovered *Cantemir*'s practices with the *Poles*, and threatened to lay *Moldavia* wafte, and to treat him as a rebel; but *Cantemir* found means to elude his rage, by again joining his camp. *Sobiefki*, by this time, began to feel the inconveniency of devouring the magazines that had been laid up for him at *Jeffi*. His army was in want of provifions, and he repaffed the *Pruth* in hopes of feizing fome magazines belonging to the *Tartars*. He was followed by the ferafkier, who furrounded his army; and it was with difficulty that he repaffed the fame river, and thereby faved his army; but was guilty of many inhumanities againft the *Moldavians*, owing perhaps, to *Cantemir*'s treachery; as there is little reafon to believe, that he would be more faithful to the *Poles*, than he was to the *Turks*, under whom he held his command. Even the moft facred places were not free from his violations, but the inhabitants were fufficiently revenged upon him, by the epidemical diftemper which broke out in his army, and the difgraceful loffes he met with in his retreat.

Campaign of the Venetians. All this while, the *Venetians* were carrying on a brifk war againft the *Turks*, and took *Ottokh*, were they put all the garrifon to the fword. After this, the kapudan pafha, or high admiral of the *Othmans*, made an attempt, but without fuccefs, upon *Kielaffa*, which was relieved by the *Venetian* fleet, while their general count *Coningsmark*, after twice defeating the ferafkier of the *Morea*, befieged and took *Modon*; where he found one hundred pieces of cannon, with vaft magazines of provifions. *Morofini*, another *Venetian* general,

laid

laid siege to *Napoli di Romania*, and *Coningsmark* beat the serasker who was advancing to its relief; and after several very obstinate battles, the place was surrendered to the *Venetians*. Upon the close of this campaign, which had been very unfortunate for the *Turks*, the sultan sent a minister to negotiate a treaty with the emperor of *Germany*; but the latter refused to listen to any terms without the participation of the *Poles*, and the *Venetians*. This disappointment obliged the sultan's ministers to have recourse to very oppressive measures; and both the *Germans*, and *Venetians*, in the beginning of the year 1687, obtained such advantages, that even the inhabitants of *Constantinople* became apprehensive for their own safety, and at last, proceeded to sedition, demanding the deposition of the sultan himself. This alarming news obliged him to repair immediately to *Constantinople*, where he laid the blame of all the public miscarriages upon his ministers; and to quell the sedition, he sold all the jewels in his treasury, and gave the produce of them to his troops, to an immense value. But this liberality reached no farther than to those who partook of it, nor could it revive a warlike spirit in the rest of the *Othman* empire; for, of forty thousand troops who were expected from *Asia*, not above six thousand arrived at *Constantinople*. A negotiation was thereupon set on foot by the vizier, who offered to give up even *Tekeli*'s person; but nothing would content the emperor less than six millions of gold, (meaning we suppose ducats) and an absolute cession of all the places the *Othmans* held in *Hungary*; upon which the war went on. *Soleyman*, in this campaign, shewed great abilities as a general, for though he was at the head of no more than fifty thousand dispirited troops; and though the duke of *Lorrain*, who was reckoned one of the best generals in *Europe*, commanded sixty-four thousand men, all of them well disciplined, and flushed with victories; yet, he chose his camp so judiciously under the fortifications of *Essek*, that the duke of *Lorrain*, when he passed the *Drave*, in order to attack him, found himself under a necessity of intrenching his own army, and the *Turkish* cannon was so well served by *French* engineers, that the *Germans* were actually beat, and forced to repass the *Drave* with considerable loss. The *Othmans* impetuosity did not suffer *Soleyman* to make all the advantage he might have derived from this action; though they pursued the *Germans* so furiously, that they were drawn from their advantageous situation, to fight upon equal terms. Both armies behaved with great intrepidity in this battle, which was fought on the seventh of *August* 1687, at *Mohatz*; but the *German* discipline prevailed over the fury of the *Othmans*, which as first was next to irresistible. The elector of *Bavaria*, and prince *Lewis* of *Baden*, distinguished themselves greatly against the janisaries, and the spahis, whose spirits beginning to flag, were first put into confusion,

and

and then driven back on their camp, which the *Germans* entered at the fame time, when the rout of the *Othmans* was completed. Eight thoufand of the janifaries, with the aga at their head, were killed; three thoufand of their other troops were drowned in the *Drave*, and two thoufand taken prifoners; while the imperialifts loft no more than one thoufand men in the laft day's action, and remained mafters of the *Turkifh* camp; which, befides fixty-feven pieces of cannon, contained amazing quantities of all kinds of ammunition and provifions.

Cam-
paign in
Hungary
unfortu-
nate for
the *Turks*.

The vizier, notwithftanding his defeat, acted as an able general. He reinforced the garrifon of *Effek*, left fix thoufand men to guard the bridge of *Peterwaradin*, and retreated to *Belgrade*, there to recruit his army. The duke of *Lorrain* finding himfelf unable, from thefe difpofitions made by the vizier, to advance farther on that fide, made a feint, as if he intended to befiege *Temefwar*; which drew the *Turkifh* army down to defend that city. The vizier being thus weakened on the fide of *Sclavonia* and *Servia*, *Dunewald*, an imperial general, paffed the *Drave* at the head of ten thoufand men, and befieged and took *Burzin*. He next attacked *Wappo*, and not only reduced that place but *Effek* itfelf, which was deferted by its garrifon, as were almoft all the other forts in *Sclavonia* belonging to the *Turks*; fo that it was entirely reduced by the imperialifts. The duke of *Lorrain*, with the main body of his army, was, all this while, obferving the motions of the *Turks* in *Hungary*; but his army fuffered prodigioufly through the wetnefs of the feafon, and he was obliged to make good his quarters in *Tranfylvania*. *Mikhael Apaffi* was then waywode, or governor, of that province under the *Turks*; and he had, in the beginning of the campaign, entered into a correfpondence with the *Germans*, to whom he promifed winter-quarters in his government. When the duke of *Lorrain* advanced to *Zolnok*, he fent to demand the performance of this promife; which *Apaffi*, either becaufe he faw the weak ftate of the duke's army, or being really afraid of the *Turks*, evaded; alledging, that his promife extended no farther than quarters for a few regiments: upon which, the duke entered *Tranfylvania*; where he took *Klaufenburg* and *Hermanftadt* with little or no lofs; and, the other chief places of the province opening their gates to him, *Apaffi* and the ftates concluded a treaty, by which they recognized the emperor of *Germany*'s authority.

While the war was thus carrying on fo much to the difadvantage of the *Othmans* in *Hungary*, *Sclavonia*, and *Tranfylvania*, the *Ruffians*, who were in the confederacy againft the *Turks*, invaded *Crim Tartary* under prince *Galliczin*; who loft forty thoufand of his beft troops, partly by the fword and partly by difeafes; and, fome difturbances happening at home, he was recalled, as is faid, by the princefs *Sophia*,

who

who managed the affairs of that empire under her brothers *Iwan* and *Peter*. The *Poles* were not more fortunate under *James Sobieski*, their king's son, who besieged *Kaminiek*, but, upon the advance of the *Turks*, made an inglorious retreat. The fourth *Christian* confederate against the *Ottomans* (the *Venetians*) had better fortune in the *Morea*; where their general, count *Coningsmark*, entirely defeated the seraskier, and reduced all that had formerly belonged to them in that province, the important city of *Patras* being the first to submit. The *Venetians* owed these advantages chiefly to their superiority at sea in the *Gulph of Patras*. *Mehemed Pasho* surrendered the castle of *Rumelia*, but first blew up its walls. The fort of *Morea* capitulated at the sight of the *Venetian* fleet; and, at last, the strong city of *Lepanto*, after a slight cannonade from the *Venetian* gallies, surrendered likewise. These four important fortresses were reduced in the space of twenty-four hours, and all their artillery fell into the hands of the conquerors.

Morosini, the *Venetian* admiral, next appeared before the castles *Tornese* and *Misitra*, which immediately surrendered; and he bombarded, but with little effect, *Napoli di Malvasia*, the strongest fort in all the *Morea*. He then sailed to *Corinth*, the reduction of which he knew would shut the *Turks* out of the *Morea*, and be followed by that of their other forts. The seraskier who commanded in *Corinth*, though he had a garrison of four thousand men, abandoned that city after damaging its works and endeavouring to set fire to the magazine, which was extinguished by *Morosini*. As to the seraskier, he barbarously put to death all the *Greeks* who fell into his hands, and retired towards *Thebes*. Soon after this, *Coningsmark* advanced by land against *Athens*, as *Morosini* did by sea; and, landing his men within six miles of the city, began to throw into it red hot bullets; one of which falling into a magazine, blew it up: upon which the garrison, consisting of six thousand men, capitulated; and were allowed to march out of the city with what they could carry, but without their arms. Some *Turks*, who had intermarried with the *Greeks*, remained in the place, and embraced the *Christian* religion. *Megara* was next surrendered to the conquerors, who burnt it. The war was, all this time, going on between the *Turks* and the *Venetians* in *Dalmatia*; where the pasha of *Bosnia* laid siege to *Zirg*, but raised it upon the approach of the *Venetian* army. *Cornaro*, their general, being joined by the pope's and the *Venetian* gallies, then formed the siege of *Castello Nuovo*; which the pasha of *Bosnia* attempted to relieve; but he was obliged to retire with the loss of three hundred of his best men. Notwithstanding this, the place made a brave defence against the *Christians*, who entering the city by storm, both that and the castle capitulated. The *Christian* writers have greatly magnified the courage and conduct of their generals and soldiers in all those

as are those in Morea and Dalmatia.

actions and sieges; and it must be owned that a total despondency appears, at this time, to have prevailed through
all the *Othman* empire.

The army
in *Hungary*
mutinies,

The effects of this despondency were soon seen. As the
Turks generally impute all their defeats and disgraces to their
commanding officers, the vizier *Soleyman,* after losing the
battle of *Mohatz,* perceiving them ripe for a mutiny, endeavoured to appease them, partly by giving them money,
and partly by finding them employment. The important
town of *Erla,* or *Agria,* had been, for some time, blocked
up by a small body of the imperialists; and, being cut off
from all provisions, was in danger of surrendering, when
the vizier ordered one thousand janisaries and five hundred
spahis to relieve the place, who actually refused to go upon
the service unless he marched at their head. *Soleyman* saw it
was in vain to contend with a spirit which had grown too
strong to be subdued. According to the *Turkish* historians,
he imputed all the miscarriages of the late campaign to the
bad conduct of certain pashas, who, hearing they had been
complained of at court, sought to prevent their destruction
by fomenting the discontents of the army. At the head of
this mutiny was one *Siavus,* or *Chiaush Pasha*; and, according
to the *Christian* writers, one *Osman Pasha,* who peremptorily
demanded of the vizier three months pay that was due to
the janisaries. He informed them that the money was on
the road, and that they should be paid in a few days; but
this did not satisfy the mutineers, who demanded, either to
be immediately paid, or, that he should resign the viziership. The vizier found some pretext for withdrawing; upon which the mutineers immediately declared *Siavus Pasha*
their general. According to the *Christian* accounts, the chief
mutineers intended to murder *Soleyman*; and, entering his
tent, killed several of his attendants; but he himself escaped
in a boat down the *Danube.*

The mutineers dispatched a messenger to inform the sultan
of what they had done; but, before his arrival, *Soleyman* had
been at court, where he was well received by *Mohammed,* to
whom he related the story of his deposition, and laid the
chief blame upon *Siavus.* The sultan being satisfied of *Soleyman*'s innocence, desired him, with tears in his eyes,
to conceal himself, in the house of a friend, from all but
him and the kisler aga, which he obeyed. Two days after his flight, *Siavus Pasha* had a consultation with the heads
of the mutiny; where the *Turkish* historians say that a plan
was formed for deposing the sultan himself. The *Christians,*
on the other hand, think that *Siavus* did not intend to go so
far, and, that he joined in the scheme only because he saw
himself in danger from the army, if he opposed it. At first,
he affected a backwardness to take upon himself the viziership, till it was given him by the sultan, and he advised
them

them to proceed by way of petition. One was accordingly *marches* drawn up, in the nature of a remonstrance, informing the *to Con-* sultan, that the army was resolved to march to *Constanti-* *stantinople* *nople* to demand justice upon the vizier, who had treache- rously deserted them, unless he instantly sent them the head of that traitor, with the pay that was withheld from them by his great officers of state. The sultan being more and more convinced of his vizier's innocence, returned no other answer to this remonstrance, than that the money was ready; but the plot had been too deeply laid to be frustrat- ed by this compliance, for the soldiery immediately exclaim- ed, that the sultan was as much to blame as his vizier, and that both of them deserved the same fate; and upon this, they tumultuously began their march towards *Constantinople*. The sultan, who had ruined himself by not having resolu- tion enough, at first, either wholly to deny, or to grant, the demands of the mutineers, held a consultation with his ministers how to proceed. *Regeb* the kaymakan, a brave intrepid officer, advised him to defend himself in his seraglio to the last extremity; but the kisler aga, being of a different opinion, *Soleyman* sent the seals, and even the great standard of the empire to *Siavus*, who received them with respect; but told the selictar aga, who brought them, that the troops were not to be appeased unless they had the heads of the vizier, the testerder, and gyumrukchi, or receiver of the customs. This was reported to the sultan by the selictar aga, who informed him, at the same time, that the soldiers were in arms, and had actually put to death such of their officers as they suspected to be well inclined to the govern- vernment. *Mohammed*, by the kislar aga's advice, resolved to gratify them to the full; but in the mean time to send for the pasha *Mustapha*, brother to the late vizier *Kioprili*, whose memory was dear to the soldiery, and to employ him in bringing about a reconciliation. *Soleyman* the vizier was accordingly seized and strangled, as were all the great officers about the palace, who were thought to be disagreeable to the army, which was then at *Adrianople*. The pasha *Mustapha* was received with much affection by the sultan, and created kaymakan of *Constantinople*, with full powers of granting the troops all they could demand.

Mustapha accordingly offered them every thing, but the *and de-* deposition of the sultan, which was now their chief object. *poses the* *Siavus*, the new grand vizier, expressed great reluctance to *sultan.* come to farther extremities, and exerted all his authority to detain the army at *Adrianople*; but perceiving his own life to be again in danger, through his backwardness to head them, he brought them to *Constantinople*, where he waited with great respect upon the sultan, who promised to make him the greatest subject in his empire, if he suc- ceeded in quelling the tumult. The vizier, upon his return to his palace, assembled the chief conspirators, and employ-

ed

ed all his art in diverting them from their purpose of depofing the fultan. They heaid him with great coolnefs, and
feemed to agree to his reafons; but they no fooner left his
palace, than they affembled in the orta jami, or council
chamber of the janifaries, wheie it was refolved to include
the vizier among the number of their enemies, for favouring the fultan. This refolution being imparted to the
whole body of the janifaries, the flame of fedition was in
an inftant communicated to all orders of men in Conftantinople. The clergy, partly through choice, and partly
through fear, joined the foldieiy; and all the other inha-
bitan.s conftruing this as a divine mandate for the emperor's
depofition, fnatched up what weapons were next them, and
iepaned with a kind of a religious fury to the church of
Saint Sophia, wheie the grand confultation was to be held.
It appeais, that there was then no mufti at Conftantinople,
none having been created fince the banifhment of the laft
one, fo that the nakib, or holy overfeer, and the fheykh, or
prieft of Saint Sophia, prefided in the affembly. Their firft
meafuie was to fend for the kaymakan (Muftapha), whofe
prefence they thought would give a fanction to their refolutions. When he came, the fheykh laid before him the difgraces and loffes that had lately befallen the empire, and the
neceffity of depofing fo worthlefs and indolent a prince as
Mohammed, who minded only his diverfions.

While he was in the midft of his harangue, an account
came, that the emperor had attempted to put to death his
brothers Soleyman, and Ahmed, but that they had been faved
by the boftangi, who were then furrounding them with a
guard. This information encreafed the fury of the affembly, to fuch a degree, that they would not only have depofed
but murdered, the fultan, had they not been reftrained by the
wifdom and authority of the kaymakan, who advifed then
to fend the nakib, and the fheykh to the fultan, to impart
to him the fentence of his depofition, in the name of the
clergy, foldiery, and Moflem nation, and to requiie him, at
the fame time, to leave his palace, and refign his dignity to
his brother Soleyman. The fultan received the meffage with
great compofuie, entered upon a defence of his government, reproached the clergy, or uema, for having corrupted the minds of his people; and their mufti (who he faid
was at the bottom of the confpiracy) for having advifed the
unfuccefsful war againft the Germans, which was the fpring
of all his misfortunes. The nakib paid little regard to what
he faid, and told him, that he came not to reafon with him,
but to receive his abdication; which Mohammed at laft
folemnly pronounced on the twenty-ninth of October 1687,
in favour of his brother Soleyman. Upon this, Mohammed
was conducted to his apartment, where he was clofely
confined during the remaining part of his life, which was
four years, he then dying a natural death, a fate very uncommon

common to a depofed *Turkifh* emperor. Some however, have written, that he was poifoned by order of his brother *Ahmed*, at the inftigation of a wicked aftrologer, who had a pique at him, and who pretended to foretel, that, if he was fuffered to live, he would reafcend the *Othman* throne. *Mohammed* died at fifty-two years of age, of which he reigned forty, five months, and fixteen days. He is generally allowed to have been brave in his perfon, and juft in his inclinations; but, during the laft four years of his reign, he feems to have given up all concern in the government, that he might indulge himfelf in his pleafures; and this indolent difpofition was attended with the fame confequences, that would have attended weaknefs, injuftice, and tyranny.

Soleyman *the Second.*

IT is probable, that when the news of *Soleyman's* advancement was brought him by the boftangi pafha, or head gardener; he looked upon it, as a trap for his life. He continued obftinate for fome time in refufing the dignity, on account of the great regard he had for his brother *Mohemmed*; and at laft, the boftangi pafha was obliged, in a manner, to force him out of his room, and to carry him to the throne, which he mounted with fear and trembling; and not without many expreffions of reluctance. Having been long in confinement, he had addicted himfelf to habits of ftudy and devotion; fo that his new dignity, for fome time, fat aukwardly upon him. At laft, all the neceffary forms of his inauguration being gone through, he confirmed *Siavus* in the vizierfhip; and ordered him to quell the remains of the tumult. *Siavus* had a moft difficult tafk to perform in this. The janifaries demanded their pay, and the ufual donative beftowed upon them at the acceffion of every new emperor; but the vizier found no money in the treafury; fo that he was obliged to have recourfe to feveral fevere methods of taxation, and to amufe the officers with fair words, and promifes of great employments. This method fucceeded tolerably well for fome time, and the vizier diffembled certain affronts and injuries offered to his perfon, with a view of feverely revenging them in time. The brave pafha *Fegeb*, who had in the late reign, by his fingular addrefs and prefence of mind, efcaped the bow ftring which was fent him, was now ftrangled, his great abilities and firmnefs rendering him too formidable, even to the vizier himfelf. The latter permitted the janifaries to difplace their aga, and to chofe in his room a young man of twenty-five years of age, who had been bred a furgeon. The janifaries having thus thrown off all regard for military difcipline, the

Soleyman ſucceeds.

vizier

vizier found himself safe only by following their dictates, which always terminated in raising money, to gratify their avarice. All the surviving officers, and servants of the late sultan, were taxed, some of them to the value of all they were worth, and large ransoms were raised for those who lay in prison for state matters.

The sedition quelled.

Those expedients procured a temporary tranquility, and on the seventeenth of *November*, the new sultan went in a boat to the seray of *Ayub*, where he was girt by the nakib with the sword of state, an indispensible ceremony of his instalment. This ceremony being performed, he returned in state, and soon after a universal change of the administration took place. The expences of the court, which had been exorbitant in the late vizier's reign, were retrenched, by which a vast deal of money was saved; and the gold and silver utensils in the imperial stables were coined, but all was insufficient to satisfy the growing avarice of the soldiery, who, if possible, became more outrageous. Perceiving that the authority of *Kieprili* the kaymakan, stood in their way, he was removed from his place, and the vizier, in hopes that their insolence would some time or other render them odious to the people, especially the inhabitants of *Constantinople*, raised to the highest posts all whom they named. At last, a new war appearing inevitable with the *Christians*, the vizier set up the horse-tail as a signal of his intention to take the field, and produced a khatti sharif, or order from the grand sultan, demanding their obedience; as all their demands had been gratified, and threatened to punish as rebels all who were refractory. The vizier would not have ventured to publish this paper, had he not been well assured that the mutineers were now divided among themselves. When it was communicated to the aga of the janisaries, he and all the chief officers promised obedience to it; but *Tesfuji*, the most dangerous of all the mutineers, declaring, that the man was a villain who obeyed it; he was immediately put to death by order of the aga, who was soon after assassinated by *Tesfuji's* friends. The mutineers then openly ran through the streets proclaiming the vizier to be a traitor, and a breaker of his oath; and robbing the houses of all whom they had not yet plundered. The vizier thought to appease them by resigning his office, and shutting himself up with some friends in his palace, which the mutineers immediately beset, but upon their endeavouring to break open the gates, they were repulsed by those within, who were about a hundred in number, with the vizier at their head. But though great numbers of the conspirators were thus killed, yet the vizier and his party were too inconsiderable to hold out long, and the few of them who remained alive leaped from the house into the street, and thus the vizier was left alone. In this situation, he

Death of the vizier.

killed

killed twelve of the janifaries with his own hand, at the door of his chamber; but at laft he was fhot through the head and fell dead. His death feemed to encreafe the fury of the *Turks*, by their breaking into his women's apartment, whom they treated with the moft unmanly indignities, and cruelty. Their madnefs, as the late vizier had forefeen, ruined them; for the ulema, and all the inhabitants of *Conftantinople*, feeing no end of their tyranny, affembled under the ftandard of *Mohammed*, and made proclamation, that all who were not willing to be deemed infidels fhould join them. Upon this, the rioters fearing to be overpowered, offered to fubmit, but thirteen of their ringleaders were put to death. The mufti, whom they had fet up upon their own authority was depofed, and his predeceffor reftored to his dignity. The titles of the emperor were proclaimed afrefh, and folemnly recognized by the multitude; while an aged man, the pafha *Nifangi*, was created vizier, and another aga of the janifaries appointed. After the riot was fully quelled, many *Armenians* and other wretches, who had difguifed themfelves like *Turks*, that they might rob and plunder with the greater fafety, were detected and hanged; but an act of indemnity being proclaimed on condition, that all who were concerned in the late commotions, fhould reftore what they had plundered to the rightful owners, all was quiet.

Till then, the fultan's reign had been a continual fcene of uproar and rebellion; but, we are informed by *Chriftian* authors, that above one thoufand of the rioters were, in the night time, thrown into the fea. This coming to the knowledge of the janifaries, they again took arms; but the fultan threw the blame of thofe executions upon the new vizier, whom he banifhed to *Rhodes*, and reinftated in his favour the pafha *Kioprili Muftapha*. The fultan then appointed one *Tekkiur* to the vizierfhip. Here it may be proper to inform the reader, that this high preferment could be held with fafety only by a man of confummate abilities; becaufe the vizier's head, or difgrace, was an atonement offered up by the fultan for all mifcarriages of government; and it is plain, that the late fultan owed his depofition to his affection for his vizier. The public tranquility being reftored, the fultan began to difcover fome talents for government. He publifhed edicts againft taverns, and tobacco, which he perfonally enforced in difguife, with great feverity. But the diforders which had been fuppreffed in the capital, now fpread into the provinces, where the head of a gang of banditti, inftigated the fpahis to demand the gratuity due to them upon the inauguration of a fultan. The vizier pleading the poverty of the imperial finances, they raifed the money by laying the country under contributions, and *Conftantinople* itfelf muft have been laid open to their infults, had not the janifaries united and fuppreffed them.

Thefe

These intestine commotions in the *Othman* empire were of great service to the imperialists in *Hungary* Agric was obliged by famine to surrender ; and *Mongatz* was besieged by the imperial general count *Teci*. This castle was deemed to be almost impregnable, and therefore *Tekeli* had made it the repository of all his records and treasures That nobleman was then in a most disagreeable situation. He was distressed and ill treated by the infidels, and the emperor of *Germany* fought his ruin, and rejected all terms of accommodation in which his being delivered up was not a preliminary. His wife, who had an heroic spirit, defended *Mongatz* with invincible courage, but could not hold out against famine, and the place was surrendered on the sixth of *January*, 1688. The government at *Constantinople* had been obliged to set the *Tekeli* to his liberty, and to give him the command of some troops, with whom he laid waste a part of the imperial dominions ; but, on the sixth of *February* following, he was attacked and routed by general *Heuslar*, with the loss of about one thousand men. These, and many other, disagreeable accounts arriving at *Constantinople*, the common people, the most superstitious in the world, complained that their intention in advancing sultan *Soleyman* to the *Othman* throne had been frustrated ; and a dangerous conspiracy was formed, the effects of which, however, were prevented, partly by the prudence, and partly by the lenity of the vizier. At this time, the imperial finances were so much exhausted, that, when the emperor found it conducive to the public tranquility to remove to *Adrianople*, he was obliged to set up his jewels and plate at public sale, to defray the expence of his journey ; nor had he even credit enough to pay for the horses, and other beasts of carriage which he was forced to hire for transporting his furniture.

His removal to *Adrianople* saved his government, as the seditious at *Constantinople* had now no farther object of their malice. They had already plundered every man who held a place at court of all his substance ; and, with them, to be rich was to be criminal. Though they had advanced the sultan to the throne on account of his piety, yet it was now termed indolence and inactivity ; and, on his arrival at *Adrianople*, he affected a warlike character, but dispatched two of his ablest ministers to negotiate a peace with the emperor of *Germany*. An aga, or officer, was, at the same time sent to *Apaffi*, the prince of *Transylvania*, threatening him with an incursion of *Tartars*, unless he raised money for the payment of the *Turkish* garrisons upon the *Boristhenes*. So low were the *Othman* affairs, at this time, reduced, that *Apaffi* despised this threatening ; and, on the ninth of *May*, 1685, he put himself under the emperor's protection, renounced all allegiance to the *Othman* porte, and received *German* troops into his garrisons, on condition of himself and his subjects being protected in their religion and liberties. A war with *Ge-*

nua

many being now unavoidable, the vizier committed the command of the army to Regeb, the serafkier of *Hungary*, but, on the eighth of *May*, *Alba Regalis*, one of the most important fortresses in *Hungary*, was surrendered to the imperialists; as too, about the same time, took the city and castle of *Lippa* by storm, with a great number of other very considerable places. These successes encouraged the *Germans* to form the design of besieging *Belgrade* itself; upon which, *Regeb*, or rather *Hughen Bey*, a bold partizan who had risen by robberies and rebellion, took upon himself the command of the *Ottoman* troops in *Hungary*, and even demanded the seal and the prophet's standard; but this demand seems to have been refused him.

Belgrade besieged and taken.

The elector of *Bavaria*, at that time, commanded the *German* army in *Hungary*, the duke of *Lorrain* being indisposed; and the principal general under him was prince *Lewis* of *Baden*, and, after obtaining a vast many advantages over the *Ottomans*, the siege of *Belgrade* was, at last, formed. The empire of *Germany* never, at one time, brought so many great generals as then to the field, and *Ricaut*, the *English* consul of *Turkey*, has very justly characterised them. The duke of *Lorrain*, the elector of *Bavaria*, and count *Staremberg*, who had so gloriously defended *Vienna*, were noted for having besides an excess of personal courage. Count *Caraffa* added the accomplishments of the courtier to those of the general. The prince of *Salm* was esteemed for experience and wisdom as well as valour, and count *Rabota*, who was commissary general of the imperial army, as well as field-marshal, was a most provident officer. Among the other great generals that distinguished themselves at the siege of *Belgrade*, *Ricaut*, who wrote at the time, and upon the spot, mentions the famous prince *Eugene* of *Savoy*, a young man, with so much judgment and true observation, that he gives him the very character which he afterwards so eminently deserved.

Before the siege of *Belgrade* opened, the *Germans* took *Titul*, or *Tibel*, which secured their advances to that city. The main body of the imperialists then proceeded towards the *Save*, where they beat the serafkier, who commanded the *Ottomans* at *Sabats*, and obliged him to retire to *Semendria*. Upon the approach of the duke of *Bavaria*, who was then but a young man, the inhabitants of the suburbs of *Belgrade* crowded, with all the effects they could carry along with them, for different places which bordered on the *Danube*; but numbers of them were intercepted, killed, and plundered by the *Germans*. Upon their flight, the garrison, which the *Turkish* historians themselves say consisted of nine thousand men, set fire to the suburbs; where the imperialists, however, found a large booty. On the twenty-brin of *July*, the besiegers, having completed their works, began to play upon the fortress of *Belgrade*, with twenty-six pieces of cannon,

cannon, and fifteen mortars, from three batteries. The garison was commanded by *Ibrahim Pasha*, who was encouraged by *Yeghen*, or according to others by *Ozman*, pasha of *Aleppo*, to make a vigorous defence. *Yeghen*, who was at the head of twenty five thousand men, endeavoured to cut off the provisions of the *German* army; and the besieged did vast execution by the briskness of their fire. The danger of falling short of provisions seems to have determined the besiegers to a vigorous, but a desperate, measure; which was that of storming the city at four quarters at once. While this was under deliberation, the duke of *Lorrain*, being recovered from his indisposition, arrived in the camp of the besiegers, on the sixth of *September*; but committed the conduct of the siege entirely to the elector of *Bavaria*, who commanded the front attack; those of the other three quarters being committed to the prince de *Commercy* and the generals *Heusler* and *Pini*. The quarter which the elector of *Bavaria* undertook to storm was the principal; but the besieged made so gallant a resistance, that, had not the elector himself stepped into the breach, and threatened immediate death to every man who would not advance, the *Germans* would have fled. The presence of his electoral highness re-animated them; and, notwithstanding the bold defence made by the *Othmans*, all the four attacks succeeded, and that important city was taken by storm, in which all the garrison was put to the sword; and it was with the utmost difficulty that the elector of *Bavaria* saved the lives of the pasha and the aga of the janisaries.

Belgrade being reduced, the two *Turkish* ambassadors, whom we have already mentioned to have been dispatched to the emperor of *Germany*, arrived in the *German* camp; but the duke of *Lorrain* having no commission to treat with them, all they did there was to assist at a festival made on account of reducing that important city, from whence they proceeded to *Vienna*. In the mean while, the prince of *Baden*, who commanded the *Germans* in *Bosnia*, took a vast number of places, and defeated the pasha of that province, who lost five thousand of his best troops in the engagement, leaving the pasha and his principal officers dead on the spot, with the loss of no more than one hundred and fifty men to the imperialists. The affairs of *Germany*, then invaded by the *French*, requiring the presence of the elector of *Bavaria*, his command fell upon count *Caprara*, who took possession of *Semendria*, the capital of *Servia*, and other places in that province; upon which the *Rascians* rose in arms, cut in pieces all the *Turks* who fell into their hands, and submitted to the house of *Austria*. After this, all *Bosnia* was compleatly subdued by the emperor of *Germany*; and prince *Eugene* being recalled to command against the *French*, he was succeeded by prince *Picolomini*. Count *Tekeli*, all this time, was endeavouring, at the head of a party of *Turks* and *Tartars*,

tars, to animate the *Walachians* and *Transylvanians* against the tyranny of the *Germans*, but all without success.

This year, the war in the *Morea* was carried on by the *Venetians* with various fortune. The *Turkish* seraskier, having taken the field more early than the *Christians*, retook *Athens*; and, soon after, the *Venetians* were obliged to abandon the siege of *Negropont*, the capital of the antient *Eubea*, and former. called *Calchis*. This was the most considerable island of the *Archipelago*, and the siege of the place afforded great opportunities for both parties to display their valour; but the brave defence made by the *Turks* disheartened the *Maltese* and the *Venetians* so much, that they, at last, abandoned the siege with vast loss, though *Morosini*, the doge, commanded here in person. During this siege, the brave count *Coningsmark*, the *Venetian* general, to whom that republic had been so much indebted for her successes, died, as was thought, of heart-break, through the mismanagements of the besiegers. On the side of *Dalmatia*, the *Venetians* took many places, and some of them of importance. On the seventeenth of *August*, *Klin* was invested by the procurator *Girolamo Cornaro*; and, after a most obstinate defence, the pasha who commanded in the place, surrendered at mercy, on the twelfth of *September*. *Cornaro*, after this, reduced *Narim*, and thus the campaign ended on that side.

The *Turkish* ambassadors dispatched to *Vienna*, by this time, had reached that capital. Their open instructions were only to notify the accession of *Soleyman* to the *Othman* throne, the *Turkish* government being in hopes that the *German* ministry would take that opportunity to propose a peace: but they were deceived, and the ambassadors were obliged to make the first advances. The terms they offered were, to agree either to a truce or a peace. If the emperor chose the former, he was to retain possession of *Hungary*. *Transylvania* was to remain in its present situation, *Kaminieck*, when dismantled, was to be restored to the *Poles*; and *Belgrade* to the *Turks* If, lastly, peace was more agreeable to his imperial majesty, the *Othmans* offered to settle it upon the footing of *Belgrade* being restored to them, and their returning part of *Hungary*. *Leopold*, then emperor of *Germany*, affected, through the whole of this negotiation, a great superiority over the *Othmans*. He ordered their ambassadors to be told, That he would hear of no peace till their master should make an ample cession to him of all *Hungary*, with its dependent provinces of *Sclavonia*, *Croatia*, *Bosnia*, *Servia*, *Bulgaria*, and *Transylvania*; that the exercise of the *Romish* religion should be permitted through all the *Turkish* empire; and, that *Wallachia* and *Moldavia* should remain free. He likewise insisted upon count *Tekeli* being delivered up to him; and, that the *Franciscan* friars should be put in possession of the holy sepulchre at *Jerusalem*. The other confederates

and negotiation.

were

were equally ridiculous and exorbitant in their demands.
The *Poles* required not only that all their antient boundaries
should be restored, but that *Crim Tartary*, *Walachia*, and
Moldavia, should be delivered up to them; that all *Christians*
in the *Othman* dominions should be exempted from tribute,
and, that they should be put in possession of the country on
both sides the *Boristhenes* as far as the *Danube*. The *Venetians*
demanded the demolition of the havens of *Dolcigno* and *An-
tifari*, with the possession of the sea-coast of *Negropont* from
Corcyra to *Corinth*, with part of *Dalmatia*, and the cession of
the *Morea*, with all the cities and territories already in their
possession.

The
Turks
treat in
Hungary.

The reader will easily perceive, that some of those demands were inconsistent with each other; but, upon the
whole, exorbitant as they were, the sultan must have complied with them, had not the *French* king interposed, by
giving the porte the strongest assurances that he would enter *Germany* with four hundred thousand men, and disable
the emperor from acting against the *Ottomans*. This was a
policy, at that time, embraced by *France*, upon a most unworthy principle, that of keeping the house of *Austria* low
by means of the *Ottomans*. The *French* king even bribed the
Poles not to act with them vigorously, and promised, if
they conquered *Germany*, to cede *Hungary* to the *Turks*.
The *German* emperor, on the one hand, had very different
ideas; and, though *Soleyman* offered to yield up all that had
been conquered by the *Turks* in *Hungary*, the proposal was
not only rejected, but the ambassadors themselves were imprisoned; an indignity which seems not to have been relented by the *Othman* court.

No sooner were the *Germans* retired to winter-quarters,
than *Soleyman* cut off two rebels, *Ferri Osman' Passa* and
Gyalik Passa. This reduced the empire to a state of tranquility, and *Soleyman* made preparations against the *Venetians*
in the *Morea*. For this purpose he set at liberty one *Libeni-
us Gheralkhari*, who had been long imprisoned, and made
him prince of *Mama*, in hopes that all the people of the
Morea would revolt from the *Venetians*, who would impose
upon them the *Roman Catholic*, instead of the *Greek*, religion. *Soleyman* then gave out, that he would command in
person against the *Germans*; but, being informed of their approaching to fight him, he resigned the command to a seraskier, who was imposed upon by an ignorant astrologer to
venture a battle, which he lost, as he did a second, upon a
like prediction of success: and almost all *Servia* submitted
to the *Germans*. Prince *Lewis* of *Baden*, about this time,
reinforced the garrison of *Belgrade*, fortified *Semendria*, and
defeated an army of forty thousand *Turks* and *Tartars*. He
then received intelligence, that the *khan of Tartary* intended
to attack his army on the side of *Peterwaradin*, while a

seraskier, at the head of fifty thousand men, was to shut them up in an opposite quarter. As this danger was threatening, the prince, on the twenty-ninth of *August*, 1688, advanced briskly against the seraskier, whom he routed, and then he repassed the *Morava* to attack the khan's son, who is called the sultan *Galga*. The generals *Veterani* and *Piccolomini*, commanded under prince *Lewis*, and routed a body of three thousand janisaries, who had taken post at a very advantageous pass covered with thick woods. General *Heusler*, when the *Turks* were routed, occupied the same ground, till the main body, under prince *Lewis* of *Baden*, advanced. After this, a running-fight succeeded, but to the disadvantage of the *Turks*, who lost one hundred and five brass cannons, and three mortars.

Prince *Lewis* then marched towards *Nissa*, which lay at the distance of twenty leagues; but the seraskier quitted it upon his approach, and took up a camp on the side of the *Nissava*, from whence he was driven by the imperialists with the loss of ten thousand men, besides all his tents and provisions. Those actions fully proved the debility of the *Turks* at this time, as their army was composed of above seventy thousand men; and that of the imperialists was but fifteen thousand. Prince *Lewis* then ordered *Nissa* to be strongly fortified, and marched against *Tekeli*; whom he defeated, and took *Widdin*; which greatly distressed the *Turks*, as it cut off all communication between *Temeswar* and their army.

So many repeated defeats alarmed *Soleyman*, who came to *Adrianople*; from whence he sent fresh offers to the *German* emperor for peace, provided he would restore *Belgrade*; in which case, he offered to abandon to the emperor all the rest of *Hungary*. *Leopold*, the *German* emperor, would, at this time, have disregarded all the threatening of the *Turks*, had he not been pressed by the *French*, who had obtained vast advantages over him; but, low as he was, he refused to agree to the *Turkish* proposals. This he afterwards found to be an irretrievable error, and was owing to a foolish punctilio of pride, the offers of peace made by *Soleyman* being as follows.

"First, That he should use his utmost endeavours to conclude a peace, so much desired by all the people; who, notwithstanding the many arguments, allurements, and fair promises of the *French* to the contrary, would not trust to that nation, which had been false to them in all ages, and now also endeavoured to entertain them with a thousand false hopes. Secondly, That he should labour, by all means possible, to persuade the emperor to quit *Belgrade*, and to make that place the limit of their dominions; and the *Save* to terminate the frontier on both sides. And, if any scruple, or difference, should arise thereupon, that then, in lieu thereof, he

Their
proposals
for peace.

he ſhould offer *Caniſia*; or, if that ſhould be taken, then to propoſe *Giula*, *Temeſwar*, or *Great Waradin*. Thirdly, As to the *Polanders*, to content them, a propoſal ſhould be made to demoliſh *Kaminiek*; and, if that would not ſatisfy them, that it ſhould be ſurrendered. Laſtly, As to the *Ve-netians*, they ſhould enjoy and keep all that they had taken; and, that no mention ſhould be made of *Negropont*."

The war continues.　The *Ruſſians*, about this time, began to make a figure in *Europe*, and ſent a body of above three hundred thouſand men againſt the *Tartars* under prince *Galliczin*. The *Tar-tars*, at that time, were the tributaries of the *Othmans*; and the treachery of ſome of the great *Ruſſian* generals rendered their expedition fruitleſs. In *Albania*, *Picolomini*, the impe-rial general, demanded a ſupply of troops from prince *Lewis* of *Baden*, who ſent him three regiments under the prince of *Hanover*, with whom he over-ran, or reduced, the moſt of that country; but he himſelf fell a ſacrifice to an epidemical diſtemper, and was ſucceeded by general *Veterani*. In the *Morea*, the ſiege of *Negropont* was reſumed by the doge *Mo-roſini*, who had wintered with his fleet at *Napoli di Romania*. Notwithſtanding this, the *Turkiſh* admiral landed five hun-dred men, who repaired the breaches; which obliged *Moro-ſini* to convert his arms againſt *Napoli di Malvaſia*, and he blocked up that place with his fleet. He then attempted to deſtroy *Liborakhi*, the *Turkiſh* governor of the *Morea*. This perſon was a *Chriſtian*, but had taken ſervice under the *Turks*, and had married the prince of *Moldavia*'s widow, with a large fortune. *Moroſini* ſent one *Dambi* to debauch him from his allegiance to the *Turks*; but he excuſed himſelf, by alledging, that his wife, children, and two of his friends, were pledges for his fidelity. Notwithſtanding this, he gave *Dambi* a great number of hints which encouraged the doge *Moroſini* to beſiege *Napoli di Malvaſia*. The place was gar-riſoned by no more than ſeven hundred men, beſides the in-habitants, who made about one thouſand three hundred more; but the fort was ſtrong, and the upper rooms of the houſes were filled with earth, which rendered them bomb-proof. While this ſiege was going forward, *Liberakhi* was defeated by the country people, while he was endeavouring to force them to pay their tribute to the *Turks*. After this the ſiege of *Malvaſia* was turned into a blockade, the doge not having a ſufficient force to carry it on; and he himſelf, with the main body of the fleet, returned to *Venice*; but, while he was performing quarantine at *Spalato*, advice came that the proveditor-general *Molino* had gained poſſeſſion of *Trebigno*.

In the mean while, the internal affairs of the *Othman* em-pire underwent a great revolution. Sultan *Soleyman* appears to have been a more able prince than he is repreſented by his hiſtorians. His depoſed brother being deprived of his uſual exerciſes, petitioned him for ſome indulgence and li-berty;

berty; but all the anfwer he received from the fultan, was, That he could do nothing but pray for him, and that he muft continue under his confinement. Soon after, he put to death the ferafkier of *Hungary* for mifbehaving againft the *Germans*; and he banifhed his vizier, as being a man incapable of managing affairs of ftate, and gave the feals to *Kiopri- li Moftafa*, the kaymakan of *Conftantinople*. The vaft popularity of the *Kioprili* family made this promotion highly agreeable to the *Turks*; and the new vizier immediately affembled a divan, confifting of all the great officers of ftate, ecclefiaftical as well as civil, to deliberate upon the affairs of government. The mufti, and the reft of the ulema, being queftioned, whether it was eligible or lawful to afk peace of the infidels, in cafe of neceffity, pronounced in the affirmative: but the lord-chief-juftice, or kadiolafker, of the empire, faid, That it was more eligible for true *Moflems* to perifh by the fword, than to difhonour the empire and the prophet by begging peace from infidels. The vizier ftruck in with this opinion. He made a fpeech that would have done honour to *Greek* or *Roman* eloquence. He obferved, That the late misfortunes of the empire were owing to a univerfal degeneracy that had crept into all ranks of men; that the *Othman* generals who commanded againft the *Germans*, minded nothing but to raife great armies without difcipline; and to amafs riches by oppreffion. That the ulema, or clergy, in general, being funk in floth and fenfuality, foothed the common people in their vices, and fought only to indulge themfelves in the habits of indolence and luxury; by which all the principles that had contributed to the *Othman* greatnefs, had been totally obliterated. He concluded by obferving, That, could he put himfelf at the head of twelve thoufand true *Moflems*, of true primitive virtue, he made no doubt of continuing and finifhing the war with fuccefs.

The mufti applauded the vizier's fpirit, but expreffed great doubts as to the practicability of reviving the antient difcipline of the *Othmans*, or of continuing the war, efpecially as their ambaffadors at *Vienna* had propofed a peace. The vizier affected great furprize at the mufti's fpeech, demanding to know who thofe ambaffadors were, and what minifter durft be fo wicked as to proftitute the honour of the empire, by advifing the fultan to beg a peace from infidels. In fhort, he boldly pronounced, That all who had the leaft concern in fuch a tranfaction, were the worft of traitors, and deferved to be treated as fuch.

This fpirited conduct of the vizier was not entirely owing to himfelf; for it was, in a great meafure, dictated by the *French* ambaffador, whofe mafter was, at this time, meditating the conqueft of the *German* empire, and encouraged the *Turks* to continue the war. A galibeh diwan, or a council of the moft folemn and decifive nature, being called, it

Promotion of Kioprili.

was

was there unanimously resolved to continue the war with the utmost vigour. *Kioprili*, however, being sensible that the ambassadors at *Vienna* were considerably advanced in the treaty, did not fail to write to the imperial ministers, to acquaint them, that they had no authority, or a very surreptitious one, for what they were doing; and, that their powers had been given them by the former vizier, without the consent, or knowledge, of the sultan.

His excellent and artful regulations. Having proceeded thus far, he applied himself, with amazing art and success, to substitute enthusiasm among the subjects of the empire for military discipline and courage. He plainly perceived them to be so dispirited that it was impossible to bring them to the field against the *Germans* with any prospect of success; and he therefore changed the whole warlike system of the empire. Instead of issuing manifestoes, like his predecessors, to force the subjects to come to the field, he published a firman, importing, That, as he was determined to command in person against the haughty *Germans*, so he was resolved to have no soldiers under him who were not actuated by a spirit of religion, and devoted to martyrdom for the good and glory of their country, and for the extirpation of infidels. He added, That every person who was afraid of being a martyr, might, by staying at home, do his country as effectual service as if he took the field, by purging himself from all vice, and fervently praying for the success of the *Othman* arms.

Great effects of them. Incredible were the effects of this artful manifesto, which seemed to impress all ranks of men with new principles. Instead of absconding, and hiding themselves, as before, or bribing the pashas to be exempted from military duties, they rushed into the field, and appeared to be emulous for the crown of martyrdom, by serving against the *Germans*. Even they who had been dismissed from the service, by having served out their time, resumed their arms, and a greater army of volunteers was raised than any the *Otomans* had brought to the field for a century before. *Kioprili* next applied himself to the reformation of the public treasury. He perceived, upon enquiry, that his predecessors had been guilty of the most notorious corruptions; and, that they had, for the sake of a little ready-money, exempted great numbers of people from paying any tribute. The vizier, to remedy this abuse, obliged the defaulters to make good all that they had purloined from the public; and issued a general mandate to subject all the inhabitants of the empire to the payment of the charach. This mandate included all the *Greeks*, who, ever since the taking of *Constantinople*, had exempted themselves from paying any tribute, by a writing which they pretended had been granted by the prophet *Mahammed* to the monks of *Sinai*; but which *Kioprili* alledged to have been counterfeited. The general assessment was made under three heads, and was in the nature of a capitation tax.

The

The richeſt ranks of ſubjects were obliged to pay ten leonines a year, the middling ſix, and the pooreſt about fifteen ſhillings ſterling. The reader, however, is to reflect, that this tax was in lieu of all other taxes excepting the ſultan's hereditary revenue.

Kioprili, upon reviewing the ſtate of the empire, found that large ſums had been bequeathed to the jami, or religious uſes. All this money he ordered to be brought into the public treaſury, under pretence that religious purpoſes were beſt ſerved by making war upon infidels and the enemies of the holy prophet. He next purged the courts of law from corruption, and filled the benches of juſtice with men of character and integrity, ſeverely puniſhing all judges who had been guilty of peculation, and reſtoring to the injured all that they had been robbed of. Without diſtinction of country and religion, he ordered that no proviſions in corn, or any other kind, ſhould be exacted from the ſubjects of the empire. an immunity which rendered him extremely popular among the *Chriſtians*, and ſo greatly raiſed his character among the *Othmans*, that he took the field with vaſt advantages. Among other regulations, he ordered that all neceſſaries ſhould be paid for in ready-money.

Kioprili's ſchemes were greatly advanced by the progreſs of the *French* arms in *Germany*. The prince of *Holſtein* commanded the imperial army in *Albania* during the abſence of general *Veterani*, and took poſt at *Priſſeren* to repel the inroads of the *Turks*. From thence he ſent one thouſand ſix hundred men, under the command of the prince of *Hanover* and colonel *Straſſer*, to relieve the paſs of *Haſſeneck*, which the *Othmans* had beſieged. The *Turks*, however, having ſent a detachment of *Tartars* into the open country, found means to draw *Straſſer* from a very advantageous poſt he occupied, and ſurrounded him with thirty thouſand men. The *Germans* made a brave, but ineffectual, defence. The prince of *Hanover*, count *Solari*, *Straſſer* himſelf, and all the *German* generals of note, were killed on the ſpot; and it was with difficulty that *Picolomini*'s regiment, next day, eſcaped the ſame fate, and reached *Procopia*. *Veterani*, ſoon after this, fortified *Niſſa*; but the imperialiſts were obliged to ſurrender the paſs of *Kaſſeneck*. *Kaniſſa* being beſieged by the *Germans*, was ſo ſtraitly blockaded, that the *Turkiſh* commandant treated about a ſurrender; but all terms of that kind being rejected by the imperialiſts, it was given up to count *Bathiani*. This place was of the utmoſt conſequence to the *Othman* empire, and the paſha, when he ſurrendered the keys of it, termed it the ſtrongeſt fortreſs of the ſultan's dominions. Some writers ſay that it was given up chiefly through the diviſions that prevailed in the garriſon; and, that it had proviſions, arms, and ammunition, ſufficient for holding out a much longer ſiege than it had ſuſtained. Be that as it will, it is certain that the imperialiſts found upon

its walls fifty-six brass and ten iron cannon, and in its magazines about four thousand muskets.

The *French* minister had, at this time, great connections
with *Kioprili*; and, in fact, directed the motions of the *Othman* court. Observing that *Tekeli* was possessed of great abilities, and extremely popular among the *Hungarians*, he prevailed upon the sultan to grant him a commission, consti-
tuting him prince of *Transylvania*, with the same powers that
had been granted to the famous *Bethlem Gabor*. *Tekeli*, upon
this nomination, affected all the state of a sovereign; issued
mandates to his new subjects to disown all connections with
the *Germans*, and to join with him in delivering their country from the tyranny of the imperialists. The *Germans* were
then weak in *Walachia*, and they were obliged to collect
from *Transylvania* all the troops in the neighbourhood, with
whom they fortified the most important passes to stop the
progress of the infidels. The *Tartars*, however, about the
middle of *July*, 1689, appeared with some gallies before
Widdin, to the number of five thousand men, and began to
cannonade the place; but it was soon delivered by *Traut-
mansdorf*, who obliged them to fall down the stream; and,
after throwing a reinforcement into the garrison, he returned
to *Jagodina*.

In *August*, the vizier, who had now taken the field, prepared to besiege *Nissa*; but was opposed by *Veterani*, who,
after reinforcing the garrison, encamped at *Alexin*. The vizier, in the mean while, marched with his army towards *Belgrade*, and, in his march, detached a body of men who intercepted and cut in pieces a part of *Veterani's* troops. This
advantage, of late so unusual to the *Othmans*, gave vast spirits to the *Turks*, who offered up public thanksgivings at
Adrianople, *Constantinople*, and the chief cities of the empire.
Selim Gyeray, the khan of the *Tartars*, was, upon this occasion, extremely useful to the *Othmans*; and the vizier, that
he might keep up, to the full, the reputation of sanctity
which he had acquired, ordered all his *Turkish* and *Tartar*
officers to dismiss the boys, and other persons, whom they
kept for infamous purposes, on pain of death.

Advan-   Those regulations had a wonderful effect, and the vizier,
tages   in a few days, laid siege to *Piroth*, which he took by capi-
gained by   tulation. Notwithstanding that, the janisaries would have
the *Turks*. plundered the heydukes who were in the garrison, had not
the vizier strongly remonstrated to them the lasting dishonour that must attend such a violation of faith. Maxims like
this were unknown to the *Turkish* government, and *Kioprili*
carried them to their utmost extent. Before he dismissed the
garrison of *Piroth*, he acquainted them, that it was to be
understood, that they were not again to carry arms, for a limited time, against the *Othmans*; and that, therefore, if they
were taken in *Nissa*, which he intended to besiege, they
could expect no quarter. This admonition had no effect
                                                        upon

upon the heydukes, who immediately retired to *Niffa*, which was befieged by the vizier. The place was defended by count *Staremberg*, with three thoufand foot and one thoufand four hundred horfe. The defence the count made was next to defperate, becaufe he had intelligence that his main defign was to befiege *Belgrade*. The fiege was preffed by the vizier with fo much vigour, that, on the twenty fifth day, the garrifon capitulated, on condition of their being allowed to march out of the place with their arms. This capitulation did not protect the heydukes who had furrendered it *Pineth*. Some of them, though difguifed, were difcovered by the janifaries, and, being put to the torture, were obliged to difcover their companions, who were all of them delivered up by *Staremberg* to the vizier, who hanged part of them and condemned the reft to the gallies. He, at the fame time, advertifed *Staremberg* of his danger, if he or his garrifon fhould take refuge in *Belgrade*, which he fairly acknowledged he was determined to befiege.

The fpirit and fucceffes of the *Turks* threw a damp upon the *Germans*, who were unequal to the double war carried on by them on the one fide, and the *French* on the other. Prince *Lewis* of *Baden* had an interview, at *Jagodina*, with general *Veterani*, where meafures were concerted for the relief of *Niffa*; but *Heufler* having been defeated by *Tekeli* and the ferafkier of *Tranfylvania*, forced them to alter their plan, and to march towards *Servia*, where the *Germans* were very weak. This determined the vizier to undertake the fiege of *Widdin*, which was garrifoned by no more than eight hundred men, while his army confifted of above one hundred thoufand. So poor a garrifon could not pretend to make any refiftance, and they furrendered, on the twenty-ninth of *Auguft*, before a breach was made in the walls. The fiege of *Semendria* was next undertaken by the *Othmans*; and its garrifon, commanded by lieutenant-colonel *Weingartler*, confifting of no more than one thoufand men, ftood a ftorm, which ended in their being all put to the fword.

The vizier then proceeded to his main object, which was the recovery of *Belgrade*. This city, fince it was taken from the *Turks*, had been very ftrongly fortified by the *Germans*; fo that it became a matter of deliberation with the vizier, who called a council of war for that purpofe, whether he fhould proceed againft it by fiege or blockade. The majority of the council declared themfelves for the latter method, on account of the vaft ftrength of the place, and the infinite difervice which the newly renewed fpirits of the *Othmans* muft fuftain fhould they be repulfed; which was extremely probable, as the garrifon confifted of eight thoufand regulars, befides numbers of other troops. The advocates for this opinion added, That, if the vizier would fortify the banks of the *Save*, the *Germans* muft be obliged, by famine, to furrender the place. They obferved, at the fame time,

Belgrade befieged.

that

that the *Germans* were so pressed by the *French*, they could make no head against the *Othman* troops.

The vizier, who had adopted a system of politics very different from those of his predecessors, followed the sentiments of the majority, though contrary to his own, and drew lines of circumvallation round the city. He had soon occasion to repent of his conduct, by receiving intelligence that the imperialists were advancing to its relief; upon which he ordered one part of his army to guard the passages of the *Save*, and the other to carry on the siege in form. According to *Christian* historians, *Belgrade* was taken partly by accident and partly by treachery. The duke of *Croy*, who took upon him the defence of the city, arrived on the eighth of *October*, the city being invested on the first. The day of his arrival, the chief magazine belonging to the besieged blew up; by which the citadel was dismantled, one thousand of the garrison were destroyed, and the city itself rendered incapable of any farther defence, the duke of *Croy* himself having been wounded and narrowly escaping with his life. According to some accounts, the blowing up of the magazine was effected by a *Turk* disguised like a *German*; but others ascribe it to the treachery of some pretended *French* deserters. There appears to be great reason for suspecting treachery, for not only the great but the lesser magazines blew up one after another, which gave so much courage to the *Turks*, that they cried out, in fits of enthusiasm, " That the hand of God was with them;" and they advanced to the storm with such irresistible fury, that one thousand of them

and taken. perished by the blowing up of the last magazine. In a few minutes, the smoke being dissipated, they entered the place, where they met with no farther resistance, the garrison having been, in a manner, destroyed, and their works demolished. The *Germans* who survived the storm escaped by boats upon the *Danube*. Amongst those were the duke of *Croy* and general *Aspremont*, who was second in command, and whose conduct, on this occasion, has been severely censured, but was cleared by prince *Lewis* of *Baden*.

Belgrade being thus, to the amazement of all *Europe*, reduced by the *Turks*, through that spirit of enthusiasm which *Kioprili* had re-animated, he sent a party of spahis to relieve *Temeswar*, which the *Germans* had blockaded for three years, but without being able to take it. The place was defended by *Koja Jaffer Pasha*, and the garrison was reduced to the utmost distress; but, so scrupulous were the *Turks*, that they could not be persuaded to relieve their hunger by those animals which their religion held to be impure. Upon the arrival of the supply of provisions, the spahis and the janisaries quarrelled who should be the first to seize them, and many were killed on both sides; but the janisaries remained masters.

Afte

After this; *Kioprili*, having repaired the damage done to *Belgrade* during the siege, passed the *Danube*, took *Lippa*, and drove the *Germans* from *Orsova*. He next attacked *Essek*, but, the garrison being strong, and the winter approaching, he was obliged to abandon his design upon that place, after losing a great number of men in a general storm which they attempted. The deliverance of this place was owing to the duke of *Croy* and count *Staremberg*.

A new war, at this time, broke out, on account of the succession of *Mikhael Apaffi*, the prince of *Transylvania*, who died towards the beginning of the year 1689, and bequeathed his dominions to the emperor of *Germany*; but they were assigned by the porte to count *Tekeli*, who was supported by the seraskier of *Hungary*, the khan of *Tartary*, and *Brankovan*, the prince of *Walachia*, who took upon himself the imperial name of *Cantacuzenus*. *Tekeli*, by this powerful support, passed the mountains of *Walachia*, and surprized *Heysler*, the imperial general, who, notwithstanding the intrepidity with which he defended himself, was defeated and taken prisoner. *Tekeli*, after this, advanced further into the province, where the inhabitants received him as their lawful prince. *{margin: Campaign in Transylvania,}*

By this time, prince *Lewis* of *Baden*, hearing of *Heusler's* defeat, passed the *Danube* near *Semendria*, and entered *Transylvania* by a pass called *the Iron Gate*. On the third of *October* he arrived at *Hermanstadt*, which *Tekeli* abandoned upon his approach; and, in a short time, he was deserted by the *Walachians* and *Transylvanians*, and forced to retire again into *Turkey* by the pass of *Bocz*. Prince *Lewis* pursuing his good fortune, arrived at *Zatmar* on the first of *December*, and found the vizier's son in possession of all the country beyond that. It is remarkable, that, when *Orsova* fell into the hands of the *Turks*, the *German* governor insisted upon being conducted, with all his garrison, their wives, and children, to *Belgrade*. The *Turks* acquainted him fairly, That that city was in their possession; but, not believing them, he continued so obstinate in his demand, that he was conducted thither. The men, on their arrival, were thrown into prison, where all of them perished; and the women and children sold as slaves, and their effects seized by the *Othmans*.

In 1690, the king of *Poland* entered *Moldavia*, where prince *Cantemir* commanded for the *Turks*, and ordered the inhabitants to desist from all intercourse with the *Poles*, or to furnish them with any provisions. Upon this, the king sent off a strong detachment to *Soroka*, a city on the *Tyras*, where they secured a large magazine of provisions, and brought them to the camp. In the mean while, the *Turks* and *Tartars* were advancing against him; and, his provisions being devoured, he attempted to return to *Poland* through a mountainous country, where many of his troops were cut *{margin: and Moldavia,}*

T 3   off

off while they were ftraggling in queft of fubfiftence. According to *Cantemir's* account, none of them could have efcaped, had it not been for his father's moderation; who perfuaded the ferafkier to difcontinue the purfuit. The fame hiftorian tells us, that his *Polifh* majefty, on this occafion, acted in a moft unfoldierlike manner, his army being ruined by the *Tartars* without coming to an engagement, and numbers of their cavalry fubmitting to be made prifoners rather than perifh with hunger; fo that it was no uncommon fight for a *Tartar* to have feven *Poles* for his prifoners loaded with fetters.

In the *Morea*, *Malvafia*, which had been blocked up for feventeen months by the *Venetians*, was battered by fea and land; and, at laft, was furrendered to them: and, about the fame time, their admiral, *Delfino*, beat the *Turkifh* admiral, and deftroyed feveral of his fhips, at *Mitylene*. The *Venetian* general *Cornaro*, about the fame time, took feveral other places in the *Morea*; and the war profpered equally well with the *Venetians* in *Dalmatia*. On the feventh of *September*, the *Venetians* landed at *Vallona*; and, after obtaining fome advantages againft a body of feven thoufand *Turks*, who oppofed them, they laid fiege to *Kanina*, which they took; and, foon after, the *Turkifh* garrifon of *Vallona* gave up that place likewife. It is faid that one hundred and thirty-four pieces of cannon were taken by the *Venetians* in thofe two fortrefses. At *Hercegovina*, in *Dalmatia*, the *Turkifh* governor, *Pafha Kin Ali*, endeavoured, with three thoufand men, to furprize fome places that had been lately conquered by the *Venetians* in that country; and, the better to fucceed, he chofe the *Eafter* hollidays for his attempt, while the *Chrifhians* were intent upon their devotions. The people of *Nifkho*, however, having intelligence of his defign, left their churches, killed feven hundred of his men, and carried himfelf prifoner to *Katuro*. After this, the *Venetian* general, *Molino*, took and deftroyed *Filioporikh*, in the neighbourhood of *Glamez*. To counter-ballance thofe advantages, *Mezzo Morto*, the dey of *Algiers*, who commanded the *Turkifh* fleet, deftroyed two *Venetian* men of war near *Kandia*.

The *Turks* unfortunate in the beginning of the campaign.

The vizier *Kioprili*, having been this year victorious wherever he commanded, returned in triumph to *Adrianople*, where he found the fultan ill of a dropfy; and, his phyficians having advifed his removal to *Conftantinople*, the vizier attended him to that capital; where he was received with unufual honours, as the reviver of the *Othman* glory and the *Mofem* difcipline. The rejoicings made by the *French* ambaffador, for his fuccefses againft the *Chriftians*, exceeded even thofe made by the *Turks*; and the winter was fpent by the vizier in raifing a more powerful army than what he had commanded in the preceding campaign. In the mean while, he appointed *Muftapha Pafha* to act againft the *Poles*, and

Kaplan

Kaplan Ali Pasha against the *Venetians*, who abandoned *Kanina* and *Vallona*, which they had taken in the beginning of the summer. *Kaplan* then took up a camp near *Celidnus*, where he checked the *Albanians*, who were ripe for a revolt. In *Hungary* the war went on with various success. The prince of *Hanover*, who commanded against *Tekeli*, was killed in an encounter with the *Turks* near the village of *Sernist*. In the mean while, colonel *Pohland*, an imperial officer, defeated one of *Tekeli's* commanders near *Karasebes*, took the fortress of *Tacket* and *Waradin*, and defeated a large body of *Turks* and *Tartars* who were making incursions into *Transylvania*. Many other encounters and skirmishes happened in these quarters about the same time. Count *Nigrelli*, an imperialist, defeated the garrison of *Great Waradin*; while the *Turks* took the castle of *Novi*, but were afterwards beat by the *Kroats*, who killed one thousand of them upon the spot. Colonel *Pohland* drew the garrison of *Lugos* into an ambuscade, and, after cutting in pieces eight hundred and fifty out of one thousand, of which it consisted, he took possession of the place. After this, the imperial garrison of *Segedin* surprized the city of *Khonad*; upon which the *Turks* abandoned the castle in the night-time.

All those motions, so much to the disadvantage of the *Turks*, happened before the vizier took the field. In *March* the imperial garrison of *Essek* destroyed *Inik*, with all its inhabitants; and a *German* officer, *Percilia*, killed one thousand two hundred *Turks* and *Tartars*, from whom he carried off a large booty. One *Antonio*, a famous *Rascian* partizan in the *German* army, took the strong castle of *Karakowar*, and afterwards surprized four of ten ships which were carrying provisions from *Widdin* to *Belgrade*, and forced the others to return. He likewise dispersed one thousand *Turks* who were upon their march to surprize *Lugos*.

When the campaign opened, count *Guido*, of *Staremberg*, drew together an army at *Sauseberg*; while the imperialists surprized *Titul*; and *Veterani* defeated a strong convoy that was carrying provisions for *Belgrade*, and killed one thousand of their party that guarded it. There is some reason to believe that many of those actions are considerably magnified, and some of them multiplied, the same encounter being sometimes split into various relations; a common practice with the *German* authors. It is certain, however, that the *Turks* under *Kathina Mostafa* were defeated near *Mitrovitz* with the loss of one thousand five hundred men and that of the place.

Those ill successes, on the part of the *Turks*, were, in a great measure, owing to the vizier not taking the field, on account of the weakness of the emperor. Many considerations detained him about the sultan's person, particularly the apprehension he was under lest one of the sons of the late emperor *Mohammed* should be made sultan; in which case,

T 4 he

he, probably, muſt have loſt, not only the command of the army, but his head.

Death and character of Soleyman. On the eleventh of *June*, 1692, the ſultan *Soleyman* died of the dropſy, being fifty-two years of age, of which he reigned three years and nine months. *Ricaut* repreſents him as being ſhort in ſtature, with a lean, long viſage, large, ox-like eyes, with a black beard mingled with grey hairs. Tho' he is repreſented, by hiſtorians, as being dull and heavy in his intellects, yet, from the choice he made of *Kioprili*, as well as from the principal actions of his life, he appears to have had a ſound underſtanding. His great application to reading, a quality uncommon with the *Turkiſh* ſultans, rendered him deſpicable in the eyes of his ignorant, barbarous miniſters. But his government was, in general, venerated by his ſubjects on account of his ſanctity and devotion, and the regularity with which he performed all his religious duties. *Ricaut* obſerves, that his favourite *Kioprili* was one of the moſt learned men in the empire, and had a moſt noble library, which recommended him to *Soleyman*. The *Othmans*, in general, had ſo great an opinion of this ſultan's virtues, that they have even invented ridiculous miracles which they have aſcribed to him.

The Reign of Ahmed II.

Acceſſion, THE appointment of a ſucceſſor to the late ſultan *Soleyman* was a matter of the utmoſt importance to *Kioprili*. A powerful faction at court were for replacing upon the throne the depoſed emperor *Mohammed*, who was now looked upon as being the victim of popular inconſtancy; and many were for raiſing one of his ſons, who, contrary to the barbarous uſages of the *Othmans*, had received a liberal education in the palace. Both thoſe propoſals were inconſiſtent with the views of the vizier, whoſe vaſt ſucceſſes, during the laſt campaign, gave him a deciſive weight in the appointment of the new emperor. *Ahmed*, the younger brother to the two late emperors, beſt ſuited his views; and he was accordingly ſaluted ſultan before his brother's body was interred. He was a thoughtleſs prince, unverſed in the affairs both of life and empire; but ſo far from having about him any of the *Othman* ferocity, that he ſpent moſt of his time in compoſing verſes and playing upon muſical inſtruments. Sometimes he viſited his depoſed brother *Mohammed*, whom he diverted with variety of gambols, ſinging, dancing, and playing tunes in his preſence, exhorting him to patience under his confinement, and bidding him be merry. He put him in mind, however, that he himſelf had been a priſoner for forty years, while *Mohammed* was emperor and did what he pleaſed;

and,

and, that it was but just that he should have his turn of power and pleasure; but assured him, at the same time, that he never would put him to death.

A prince of his disposition was highly agreeable to *Kiopri-* and cha- *li's* views; and, being afraid of the inconstancy of the peo- racter of ple of *Constantinople*, he persuaded the sultan to remove to *Ahmed II.* *Adrianople*, where he would be both more safe and free while preparations were making for the next campaign. The spirit of enthusiasm still prevailed among the *Othmans* to an incredible degree, and the name of *Kioprili* brought to his standard such numbers of soldiers, that many of them were dismissed; while all of them called out to be led against the infidels and that they would serve without pay, rather than miss the opportunity of gaining a crown of martyrdom. *Kioprili* soothed them with gentle expressions, but under-hand give orders to the pashas to bring only a certain number to the field, as there might be some difficulty in finding them subsistence before they reached *Buda*. The prodigious reputation which *Kioprili* had acquired, and the influence he had in all affairs of government, soon formed a party against him in the sultan's cabinet. There the koltuks (so called from having the privilege of supporting the sultan under the armpits) or chief courtiers, taking advantage of the sultan's weakness, instilled into him a distrust of his vizier's designs, as if he intended to raise to the throne a son of the late emperor *Mohammed*, and, that he had brought the janisaries to favour the resolution as soon as he should depart from *Adrianople*. The sultan, being shaken with those suggestions, asked the kisler *Agasi*, who was at the head of the party against the vizier, how he should proceed. He advised him to send the captain of the battle-axes to desire the vizier to come to court, where he might be easily dispatched.

This conversation was held in the sultan's apartment, and Conspi-was observed by one of the mutes, whose office it was to racy keep the door while the sultan was in discourse with any of against his ministers. As these mutes have great sensibility in signs, the vizier. he easily perceived, from the emotions into which both the sultan and kisler fell, that something very extraordinary was in agitation; and, suspecting what it was, he privately hastened to the vizier, and, by signs, found means to make him understand what he had discovered. In the mean while, the baltajilar kyehayasi, or captain of the battle-axes, arrived, and acquainted the vizier, that the sultan was in haste to speak with him; and this confirmed all the intimations he had received from the mute. He acquainted the messenger, that he would immediately wait upon the sultan, and ordered his horse to be got ready for that purpose; but, in the mean while, he privately sent for the aga of the janisaries, and other chief officers of the army, whom he knew to be in his interest, and to them he communicated what he had discovered. He then recapitulated all the services he had

done

done to the empire, and preffed them to take upon themfelves the adminiftration of affairs in oppofition to the evil counfellors about his mafter, to whom he intended next day to refign the feals of his office. The aga, and the other officers, were amazed at this relation, and broke out into the moft indignant expreffions againft the ftupidity and ingratitude of the fultan towards the pillar of the ftate and the reftorer of the *Othman* glory; declaring, at the fame time, that they would rather depofe him than fee *Kioprili*'s life, or power, in danger. They then entered into an affociation, in which they bound themfelves to ftand, to the laft drop of their blood, by the vizier; and, that they would implicitly follow whatever he fhould command them.

Kioprili, who had only affected to refign the feals, being now fenfible that he could depend upon their friendfhip, ordered the reis-effendi, or high-chancellor, to write out a talkifh, or letter of the moft folemn kind, to the emperor, to inform him that he was detained by a fedition of the foldiers, who thought themfelves injured by certain courtiers; but, that, as foon as he had reftored tranquillity, he would give his imperial majefty his beft advice how to proceed againft the mutineers. Next day, he fent another talkifh, informing the fultan, that he had tried all means poffible to quell the fedition, but without effect, becaufe the foldiers infifted upon the kifler-agafi, or aga, with his fecretary, being delivered up to public juftice; and advifed his imperial majefty to comply with their requeft, that he might prevent more difagreeable confequences. The kifler-aga, on the fultan's receiving this mandate, for fuch it was, from the vizier, faw that his practices had been difcovered; but, either through policy or real magnanimity, he requefted, that he might pay his life as a forfeir, if it could be conducive to the public tranquility. This, probably, faved his head; for the vizier, perceiving that the fultan was extremely unwilling to facrifice a favourite, who had manifefted fo much difintereftednefs and loyalty, was contented with his being banifhed to *Egypt*; but the fecretary was hanged in the robes of his order, with a filver ftandifh at his girdle.

Treaty of peace. The Revolution having, by this time, taken place in *England*, in favour of king *William*, that prince, whofe ruling paffion was to humble the *French*, interpofed as a mediator, between the *Germans* and the *Othmans*. Sir *William Trumball*, who had been fent ambaffador, by the *Stuart* family, to *Conftantinople*, being recalled, Sir *William Huffey* was chofen by the *Ruffia* company to be their agent at the porte; and, being recommended to king *William*, he was invefted with the character of ambaffador, and empowered to offer to the fultan king *William* and queen *Mary*'s mediation between him and the *Germans*. *Huffey* was directed to call at the court of *Vienna* in his way to *Conftantinople*; but the ridiculous

lous forms of the imperialifts prevented his arrival at *Adria-nople* before the vizier had quelled the late confpiracy, and was preparing to fet out for *Belgrade* at the head of one hundred thoufand men. Though he was refolved as to the part he was to act, yet he gave *Huffey* a civil reception, and received his propofals; which were no other than that both parties fhould agree to an article of *uti poffidetis*, by each retaining what he then poffeffed. The vizier feemed not to diflike what *Huffey* propofed; though his real defign was to amufe the *Germans* till he could take the field, which he effectually did. Putting *Huffey* off on pretence of the neceffity of his affairs, he referred him to the kaymachan of *Conftantinople*, who gave him audience, and affected to treat him with the fame diftinctions that were paid to the *French* ambaffador, but without complying with any of his propofals. The truth is, that the *French*, at that time, entirely poffeffed the ear of the fultan as well as of his vizier, who was at the head of an army fo numerous, and fo well provided, that he deemed it to be invincible. He privately informed the *French* ambaffador, that all that had paffed between *Huffey* and the kaymachan was little more than grimace.

His moft *Chriftian* majefty omitted nothing to improve this good correfpondence between himfelf and the emperor of the infidels. He fent one of the beft engineers in his dominions to conduct his artillery, and twenty-two of his officers, with a phyfician to attend upon the vizier during his campaign; a prefent extremely agreeable to that minifter, whofe court had a very high opinion of *European* phyficians. By this time, count *Marfigli* arrived from the court of *Vienna*, with the character of fecretary to the *Britifh* minifter; but, in reality, to manage the *German* intereft at the porte. The *Dutch* minifter, *Colier*, had orders to co-operate with him; and, finding they could do nothing effectual with the kaymakan, they fet out for *Belgrade*, once more to treat with the vizier, and to propofe to him much more advantageous terms of peace. On the fixteenth of *Auguft* they arrived at *Adrianople*, where they heard of the total defeat of the *Turkifh* army, which we are now to relate.

The vizier's army, when he arrived at *Belgrade*, confifted of above one hundred thoufand fighting men; the beft, according to general information, the *Othmans* had ever brought to the field. Befides thofe land troops, the *Danube* was covered with his veffels, which were extremely ufeful in conveying and cutting off provifions; the imperialifts having no veffels nearer their camp than *Peterwaradin*. On board one hundred of thofe fmall veffels, the vizier fent four thoufand men, under a pafha, to attack *Titul*, which ftill remained in the hands of the imperialifts; and which was battered fo furioufly, that *Thos*, the imperial commandant, was obliged to capitulate on the fourth day, on condition that the garrifon, which confifted of no more than one hundred and

twenty

Battle of Slanke-men.

twenty *Germans* and one hundred *Rascians*, should be allowed to march to the imperial camp. When they came out, the pasha and his officers, seeing how few they were, detained them. This produced an altercation between *Thos* and the pasha, who then gave orders to put all the garrison to the sword, and, drawing his scymitar upon *Thos*, the latter shot him, and another officer, dead; and ordered his men to fight their way through the army. This they bravely attempted to do, and killed five hundred of the *Turks*, but, the latter over-powering them, only a few of the garrison escaped being put to the sword.

It was the twenty-ninth of *July* before prince *Lewis* of *Baden*, the imperial general, arrived at *Peterwaradin*, where he reviewed his army, which consisted of sixty-six thousand men. He marched first to *Carlowitz*, and then to *Slankemen*, which was then only a ruined castle on the south of the *Danube*. In the mean while, the *Turkish* army passed the *Save*, and was encamped at *Semlin*, a town near the confluence of the *Save* and the *Danube*. By the twelfth of *August*, the imperial army were advanced within cannon-shot of the *Turks*; but, upon reconnoitring their camp, the *German* generals judged it to be impregnable; and, not being able to get provisions by the *Danube*, prince *Lewis* resolved to march back to *Slankemen*. The *Germans* beginning their retreat, after many skirmishes had passed between the advanced parties of both armies, the *Turks*, imagining that the *Christians* were flying, attacked their rear, but were repulsed with considerable loss. Notwithstanding this, the *French* ambassador had such sanguine hopes of conquest, that he persuaded the vizier to make a forced march in the night-time; by which he got between the imperialists and *Peterwaradin*, with design to cut them off from that post; and fortified themselves with such incredible diligence, that they raised walls above five feet high, and bastions mounted with cannon round their camp. It must be acknowledged that this was a very masterly manoeuvre; because the magazines at *Peterwaradin* could not now supply the imperialists with provisions, and none could be had by the *Danube*. All farther junctions of men were likewise cut off, and one thousand four hundred recruits, in their march to the imperial army, were put to the sword by the infidels: but, in another sense, it was, perhaps, impolitic, to drive such an army as prince *Lewis* commanded to despair; and, in this, the *Germans* found their safety.

The *Turks* defeated. Hearing that all their provisions from *Peterwaradin* had been intercepted by the enemy, on the nineteenth, by day break, they drew up in order of battle, the prince of *Baden* commanding their right wing, and count *Dunewald* their left, and, about noon, both armies faced one another that of the *Turks*, had its left flank covered by the *Danube*, with a deep ditch on their front. The proper disposition

tions being made, the artillery began to play on both sides. The imperial generals ordered their army to advance all at once; but this was found impracticable, for their left was encumbered by bushes and high grass; so that, when the right wing began the attack, they received so smart a fire from the janisaries, that, at first, they fell into disorder; but, being rallied by the dukes of *Holstein* and *Aremberg*, who renewed the charge, they led their men up to the muzzles of the *Turkish* guns, though with prodigious loss, especially of their officers. The left wing of the imperialists was in equal danger, some of its oldest and best regiments being entirely cut off; but despair still re-animating the *Germans*, and their bodies of reserve, and even baggage-men, coming up to their assistance about the close of the day, they, at last, broke into the *Turkish* camp where it was weakest. The *Turks*, in their turn, were now driven to despair, and pent up in a narrow space between their entrenchments and the *Danube*; from whence only some of their horse found means to escape through an opening made by a motion on the right of the imperialists. The *Turkish* infantry, and the main body of their cavalry, still maintained the fight with admirable resolution; and, though they had lost their camp, they had almost gained the field, when their tubulkhana, or great warlike music, which is always played near their general's person, ceased. This was owing to the vizier's being shot through the head while he was bravely animating his men in their foremost ranks. The visible despondency which his fall occasioned among the *Turks*, redoubled the efforts of the imperialists, who now found but little resistance, the aga of the janisaries being killed at the same time. Twenty-five thousand *Turks*, of whom ten thousand were janisaries, were killed, drowned, or mortally wounded. Of the imperialists, three thousand, one hundred, and sixty-one, were killed; of whom by far the greatest proportion consisted of general officers: and they had about it one thousand, four hundred, and thirty-six, wounded, by their own account; though some say that their loss was far more considerable.

The booty found in the *Turkish* camp was very valuable; Their loss, and, perhaps, more so than was given out. All their mili- and contary chests, consisting of copper, silver, and gold coin, fell sequences into the hands of the conquerors, with one hundred and of the victory. four pieces of cannon, the grand-vizier's standard, ten tory. thousand tents, and all the beasts of burthen, of which the *Turks* carry along with them incredible numbers. The consequences of this battle was not so fatal to the *Turks* as might have been expected from so complete a defeat; but this seems to have been chiefly owing to the inability the Germans were under to prosecute their victory; which was well known to *Chateauneuf*, the *French* ambassador. The princes

Oi

of *Baden*, general of the imperialists, was no enterprizing officer, though brave and experienced; and all he did after the battle was to turn the blockade of *Great Waradin* into a siege; in which, after all, he failed; for, winter coming on, he was obliged to resume the blockade. On the other hand, general *Veterani* took *Lippa*, and the *Turks* abandoned *Brodt* in *Sclavonia*.

A new vizier appointed.

Ahmed received, at *Adrianople*, the news of his army's defeat; and immediately he appointed *Ali*, who had been kyehaya, or deputy, to *Kioprili*, to succeed him in the viziership. This minister is represented as having been very unequal to his post. He was, by the common people, called, by way of derision, *the waggon-driver*; either because his talents were not superior to that profession, or because he had exercised it. When he was preparing to set out for *Belgrade*, *Hussey*, the *English* ambassador, who was to attend him thither, died; and was succeeded, as plenipotentiary, by lord *Paget*; who proved to be a very proper minister for that court. The new grand vizier, when he first entered upon his ministry, seemed to give a favourable ear to the mediation of the *English* and the *Dutch* for putting an end to the war in *Hungary*; but he soon altered his behaviour. The *Poles* had made an unsuccessful incursion into *Bessarabia*, from whence they were forced to retire with loss. The strong fortress of *Garbusa*, in *Candia*, fell into the hands of the *Turks*, through the treachery, as is said, of a *Spanish* officer, who pretended that the *Venetian* commandant had ravished his wife. But, above all, the new vizier was encouraged to lay aside all thoughts of an accommodation by the information he received from *Germany* of the exhausted state of the imperial finances and dominions, and of the vast successes and preparations of the *French* against the empire.

Peace proposed,

The truth is, the demands made by the *Christian* powers were unreasonable, and shewed their haughty, intractable disposition. The emperor, notwithstanding his reduced condition, demanded that all he had conquered should remain to him; that he should be put into the entire possession of *Transylvania*; that *Tekeli* should be delivered up; and, that *Ragusa* should be exempted, for the future, from paying tribute to the *Turks*. The *Poles* required the surrender of *Kaminiek*, *Podolia*, and the passes of the *Nieper*; and the *Venetians*, that *Livadia*, *Athens*, and *Thebes* should be ceded to them in lieu of some places in the *Morea*. Thus all hopes of peace being laid aside, and the vizier unable to continue the war, in preference to so many other generals of service and abilities, he had recourse to the most infamous methods of dispatching out of the world every officer, military as well as civil, of whose capacity he was jealous; and, at the same time, he replenished the finances with their effects; besides various other oppressive methods he took to fill the treasury.

His

His practices were too bare faced to be longer borne with. Some men of confequence, who had efcaped his cruelty, had the courage to reprefent to the fultan, that all perfons of experience and abilities in the empire were in danger of being exterminated. The fultan, at that time, had been fo affected with the bad news of the late battle, and the death of his vizier, that, notwithftanding the fprightly turn of his difpofition, he fell ill of a fever; and the mufti, who was a man of parts and abilities, protected the vizier, who paid him an implicit obedience; fo that his fate feems to have been, for fome time, fufpended.

Mean while, the commonalty of the *Turks*, efpecially but fruf-about *Adrianople*, began fenfibly to feel the want of bread, trated. particularly after the remains of their army arived in that city from *Hungary*. This difpofed them to mutinies; but the great officers of the army affembling, came to a refolution to fupport the government and to continue the war againft the emperor. This refolution was fo difagreeable to the common people, that the *French* ambaffador was in danger from their refentment; and, indeed, nothing but the great fums which he diftributed among the chief officers and minifters, could have prevented a revolution, at this time, from taking place; efpecially as the people were farther exafperated by the vaft fums of copper money circulated from the imperial treafury, while the foldiery was paid in filver. Upon the appearance of *Tekeli* at court, he was treated with unufual diftinction by the grand-vizier, having magnificent prefents made to him; and, by his, and the *French* ambaffador's, advice, it was refolved, that two great armies fhould be immediately affembled; the one to act in *Hungary*, and the other in *Tranfylvania*. The khan of the *Tartars* was, by the influence of *Chateauneuf*, treated with equal diftinction; and he and *Tekeli* fet out at the fame time; the former for the *Crim*, and the latter for *Hungary*. A war being thus refolved on, the divan formed a fcheme for fupporting it by a more equal taxation both of men and money, and which was approved of; and, indeed, frequent experience demonftrated how inexhauftible their dominions were in both.

While matters were thus concerting for carrying on the war, the *Afiatic* foldiery difcovered great difpofitions towards a revolt; and even the petty princes of the *Arabs* infulted the *Turkifh* caravans that were going to *Mecca*. About the fame time, viz. in *February*, 1692, a moft magnificent ambaffy from *Perfia* arrived at *Conftantinople*, the ambaffador's retinue confifting of three hundred and thirty-eight perfons, many of them the fons, or relations, of princes; all his utenfils, even to the meaneft, were of filver; and fixty camels, magnificently caparifoned, were loaded with prefents defigned for the fultan. The jealous difpofition of the *Turks* made them look upon this ambaffador as being no better than a fpy, who was to inform his mafter of the weaknefs of their

empire;

empire; and therefore they were extremely uneafy during his ftay at *Adrianople*; the only declared object of his ambaffy being to congratulate the fultan on his acceffion to the throne. Their apprehenfions were fomewhat diffipated by the *French* ambaflador declaring, that his mafter had already fent off a body of able officers and engineers to ferve in the *Turkifh* camp; and, that he every day expected the arrival of two large fhips, laden with all kinds of military ftores and mufkets for the janifaries. He even offered, in his mafter's name, to maintain three regiments of that body; but that offer was rejected by the divan with fome indignation, as injurious to the honour of their empire.

The new vizier difplaced and banifhed. Upon the recovery of the fultan from his illnefs, frefh applications were made to him againft his vizier; who, befides the mufti, was greatly fupported by his own fon, a man of fenfe and experience. But all their art could not ftifle the public difcontent at a minifter, fo bloody and fo incapable, continuing fo long in office. At laft, he quarrelled even with the mufti, whom he banifhed from court, and fought the ruin of the kaymakan of *Adrianople*, the only perfon who, he thought, had intereft enough to hurt him during his abfence in *Hungary*. His life, however, was of too much importance, and he was too well beloved by the fultan, to be difpatched without an imperial mandate; and the vizier was infatuated enough, without any ceremony, to demand his head of *Ahmed*, who feems to have been prepared for this infolent requeft. The moment it was made, he called for a band of black eunuchs, or executioners, in waiting, and ordered them to remove the wretch into another chamber and ftrangle him. The eunuchs happened to be in the vizier's intereft, and, throwing themfelves at the fultan's feet, befought him to take compaffion on his minifter's decrepid age. The fultan relented, and converted his fentence into banifhment; and, ordering the kaymakan, who expected nothing lefs than death, to appear before him, he gave him the late vizier's feals. That minifter was too wife to accept of them; and, with great importunity, got himfelf excufed: upon which the vizierfhip was conferred upon *Tapafhi Ali Pafha*, governor of *Damafcus*, who had ferved with reputation under *Kara Moftafa* at the fiege of *Vienna*.

The new vizier being fent for from his government, at the diftance of one thoufand miles, created fome ftand in public affairs, and occafioned an application from fome of the foldiery in favour of *Halil*, the ferafkier of *Belgrade*, but the fultan remaining firm in his choice, *Halil*, perhaps to his joy, was employed in the *Negropont*; and every thing remained quiet, while the depofed vizier was confined to the *Dardanelles*, and his immenfe eftate feized, with that of his fon, for the ufe of the fultan.

I

It is said, that the new vizier, upon his arrival at *Adrianople*, was difposed towards a peace with the *Germans*; but the four ambafladors who had been fent to negotiate at *Vienna*, where they met with baibarous treatment, by being thrown into prifon, returned to *Adrianople*; and, being influenced, partly by *French* gold, and partly by their own refentment, they made fuch a report of the diftrefled ftate of the *German* empire, that the continuance of the war was irrevocably iefolved on. The foimer fchemes for recruiting the army were now put put in practice, but met with great difficulties, and the vizier, in the mean time, difpatched the ferafkier of *Hungary*, with what forces he had raifed, towards *Belgrade*, to cover the *Turkifh* frontiers, and he then appeafed a mutiny of the janifaries, who refufed to march without fix months pay. His next meafure was to remove the kaymakan of *Adrianople*, and to fubftitute in his place the pafha of *Aleppo*, one of his own creatures; and this he effected, fo fai as we can learn, by his own power, without any interpofition from the fultan, who, perhaps, was difobliged at that kaymakan for having refufed the vizierfhip.

Great Waradin, all this while, continued blocked up by the imperialifts; and the *Tartars* were fo much out of humour with the *Othman* court, that tney refufed to march to its relief. General *Heufler*, who commanded the blockade, perceiving that the garrifon held longer out than he expected, and underftanding that the *Turks* were preparing to throw provifions into it, refolved upon more vigorous operations, by drawing his lines nearer to the city; but he was interrupted in his works by two brifk fallies of the befieged, who were both times repulfed. At laft, *Heufler's* heavy cannon coming up, he fent them a fummons, requiring them to furrender, under pain of all within the town being put to the fword, without refpect to age or fex. The garrifon confulted their officers, and, as no relief was at hand, and the time was elapfed in which they expected it, they fent five deputies; the chief of whom, in a formal fpeech, agreed to give up the place, on condition of them and their goods being fafely conveyed to *Panzova*; which, with other reafonable terms, were complied with.

This was looked upon as a conqueft of great importance, and there were found in the fortiefs five thoufand meafures of barley, one thoufand of wheat, three hundred facks of rice, fifty vats of flour, fifty biafs guns, twenty-two mortars, feventy thoufand pounds of good powder, feven hundred and twenty-three thoufand of decayed powder, three thoufand five hundred cannon-balls, thirty thoufand pounds of unwrought, and four thoufand three hundred of wrought iron. The whole garrifon confifted of one thoufand two hundred men; and they, with the inhabitants, amounted to twelve thoufand: but, after they marched out of the fortrefs, they found themfelves furrounded in an open place prepared without the walls; and there detained till the *Ger-*

Great Waradin taken.

man and *Rascian* garrison of *Pescobara* was released, they having been detained by the *Turks* contrary to the capitulation by which the place surrendered. To make some amends for the loss of *Great Waradin*, the *Turks* attempted to make an irruption into *Sclavonia*, by the way of *Essek*; but the *Rascians* fell upon them unawares, and dispersed them with considerable loss. About the same time, a party of the *Othmans*, going on board some armed vessels, made a desperate attempt upon *Titul*; but here, likewise, they were repulsed with loss by the *Rascian* garrison.

Campaign in *Hungary*.

They had no better success against *Titz*, another fortress upon the *Danube*, which they attacked with fifty vessels; but, after an assault which lasted several hours, they were obliged to retire with loss. On the other side of the river *Una*, the imperial *Kroats*, a people as barbarous as the *Turks* themselves, with the governor of *Novi* at their head, burnt the suburbs and town of *Behatz*; where they put all to the sword, excepting twenty persons of quality, whom they reserved to be ransomed. The same *Kroats* then proceeded to *Ostrasatz*, which they destroyed in like manner, notwithstanding the brave resistance made by the *Turkish* garrison. So many miscarriages created vast discontent both at the court and in the army; and it appears, at this time, that a conspiracy was formed against the vizier, chiefly on account of his having displaced the kaymakan of *Adrianople*. The vizier had the good fortune to discover this conspiracy, but did not think proper to punish the chief conspirators with death; all he did was to remove the aga of the janisaries from his place, and to substitute, in his stead, *Ishmael Pasha*, who had been kaymakan of *Constantinople*; and, having had some part of his education in *Germany*, where he had been prisoner, he was esteemed to be a man of address and capacity. The testerdar was likewise involved in this conspiracy, and he too was removed. But nothing gave so much disquiet to the vizier as his finding that the janisaries likewise were in the plot against him. The truth is, that rapacious body had no attachment to any set of men but for money; and the vizier and his opponents were alike to them. The vizier out-bid the others, and gratified the mutineers; but he saw, at the same time, that he must be at the necessity of doing the same as often as those tumultuous troops should please to be discontented. It was owing to this delay that the *Turks* met with so many losses in *Hungary*, where they twice attacked the fortress of *Portsen*, near *Peterwaradin*, but were repulsed with loss. The *Kroats* and *Rascians*, about the same time, to the number of five thousand five hundred, made an irruption towards *Meydan*; where they had the good fortune to save from butchery four hundred *Christians*, who were sentenced to be executed next day; and to return home laden with plunder, besides making several prisoners of distinction. A large convoy of provisions sent to *Temeswar* was taken at the same time; and the *Ra-*

sians

ſians, breaking into the _Morava_, carried off two hundred thouſand crowns in ſpecie, and beat the _Turkiſh_ convoy.

The ſeraſkier of _Babadaghi_, with ſome other _Turkiſh_ general officers, in the end of _July_, entered _Moldavia_, where they were joined by the _Turkiſh_ waywode of that country with twenty thouſand _Tartars_. Their object was _Soroka_, which they were in hopes of ſurpriſing, the _Poles_ having been negligent of guarding it. The _Turkiſh_ army conſiſted of thirty thouſand men, including the _Tartars_, and the garriſon of no more than ſix hundred; but, ſo unſkilful were the _Turks_ in the methods of beſieging, that, though they inveſted it, and carried on their approaches with all the regularity they were maſters of, they were obliged, at laſt, to raiſe the ſiege, with the loſs of three thouſand men. This miſcarriage of the _Turks_ gave great ſpirit to the _Poles_; and, when the khan of _Tartary_ offered to reſtore _Kaminiek_, with all _Podolia_ and _Ukrania_, to that republic, provided ſhe would renounce her alliance with the emperor, the propoſal was rejected, as the _Poles_ were in hopes of recovering all _Moldavia_.

The _Venetians_ having, during the preceding campaigns, ſubdued all the _Morea_, began now to entertain hopes of recovering _Candia_. With this view they endeavoured to ſurprize _Canea_; but the _French_ in their ſervice deſerted to the _Turks_, whom they put upon their guard; and the _Venetians_, after beſieging the place for fifty days, were obliged to raiſe the ſiege with conſiderable loſs. This was attended with ſome other advantages gained by the _Turks_ in thoſe parts. But the ſeraſkier of the _Morea_ was repulſed, with great ſlaughter, in an attempt he made upon _Lepanti_; and _Ali Beg_, a _Turkiſh_ general, was taken priſoner in endeavouring to recover _Gracow_. In the year 1693, the _Turks_ celebrated, with the moſt extravagant rejoicings, the birth of twins by one of their ſultan's wives; but their joy was ſomewhat damped by the burning down of four thouſand houſes, and two hundred ſhops, at _Conſtantinople_.

Mean while, the vizier was carrying on ſecret meaſures for peace; which being diſcovered loſt him his poſt, as being done contrary to the knowledge of the ſultan and the opinion of the divan. He was ſucceeded by _Bulukyi Moſtafa_, who, endeavouring to carry on ſome works of reformamation, to ſignalize his acceſſion to the vizierſhip, an inſurrection was threatened, and conſpiracies were formed againſt him; but, finding means to engage the janiſaries on his ſide, the principal conſpirators were apprehended and puniſhed, and tranquility was reſtored to the empire.

The paſſion for war ſtill continued at the _Turkiſh_ court; and the grand-vizier was preparing to put himſelf at the head of an army which was encaped without _Conſtantinople_, when a ſedition broke out under _Miſr: Effendi_, the ſheykh of _Pruſa_. This rebel was an enthuſiaſt; and it was thought,

Operations of the _Venetians_.

A ſheykh raiſes a ſedition,

U 2　　　　　　　　　　　　　　from

from some poetical rhapsodies which he published, that he was a friend to the *Christians*. He erected a standard in *Prusa* for enlisting volunteers in the cause of *God*, who were to serve without pay or reward, without arms, or expence to the sultan. The vast reputation he was in for sanctity, soon brought above three thousand votaries, who stiled themselves derwishes, to his standard ; and he set out at their head for *Adrianople*. Meeting with no resistance, he entered that capital, and, marching to the mosque of *Selim*, he there harangued the people. He told them, after performing his devotions, That *God* had revealed to him the cause of the late ill success of the *Othmans*, and, that the crimes of seventeen great men, among whom he named all the principal officers of the state, had brought the divine vegeance upon them ; that the empire itself must be destroyed unless they were put to death ; and, that the *Othmans* had no occasion for powerful armaments, because he was ready, with his unarmed derwishes, to encounter the infidels, or, as the *Turks* call them, gyawrs, and to drive them out of the empire.

which is
quelled.   The people, even of the better sort, were, by no means, indisposed towards this doctrine. The preacher wore a green turban, as a descendant from *Mohammed* ; by which his person became sacred, even from the power of the sultan himself ; and his congregation was resorted to by numbers of the regular troops. The vizier was alarmed by those seditious appearances, and sent the kaymakan of *Adrianople* to the court, then residing in that city, to bring the sheykh before him ; but he refused to betray his divine mission by obeying such a gyawr as the vizier. The kaymakan perceived that nothing was to be done by force against the enthusiast ; and made his report to the vizier, that, unless he was speedily suppressed, the whole empire must be thrown into confusion, his discourses tending to rebellion against the sultan himself. Upon this report, the vizier held a consultation with the aga of the janisaries, and the other great officers whom the sheykh had doomed to destruction ; and the result was, to send a talkish, or formal address, to inform the emperor of his danger. *Ahmed* immediately doomed the traitor, as he could not be put to death, to be banished to *Prusa*. The vizier, well knowing the danger of proceeding against the sheykh, by violence, trapanned him by flattering his vanity. He again sent the kaymakan to him, with the aga of the janisaries, and a number of officers and soldiers, who appeared before him in the most respectful manner, attended by one of the sultan's chariots ; and acquainted him that his imperial majesty had so great an opinion of his sanctity that he wanted to enjoy the pleasure of his conversation, and would therefore be glad if he immediately repaired to the palace. The sheykh suspected their intention, and boldly answered, That, though he believed they were sent by *Sheytan*, or *Satan*, he would attend them ; but, that they would
soon

soon receive marks of a divine manifestation in his favour. The effects of enthusiasm are incredible. The enthusiast mounted the sultan's chariot, and passed through crowds of his votaries, but he was no sooner at a proper distance from them, than he was put into a covered waggon and transported to *Prusa*.

The army, all this while, continued to be encamped without the walls of *Constantinople*, and, in a day or two after the sheykh's disappearing from *Adrianople*, a most dreadful hurricane happened, attended with thunder and lightning, which consumed a vast number of tents in the camp, and threw all the rest to the ground. The common people immediately interpreted those judgments as so many marks of divine vengeance for the indignity that had been done to the sheykh, and the sultan himself was so much of that opinion that he sent the holy man a most respectful letter, asking him pardon, and imputing the hardships he suffered to the villainy of his ministers; requesting him, at the same time, to return to *Adrianople*, and bless his army before it departed. The sheykh, to keep up the reputation he had got, in his answer, paid a compliment to the sultan, whom he acquitted of the treachery that had been offered him; but informed him, that the same divine spirit which had led him to *Adrianople*, did not permit his return thither. Thus ended this religious frolic, as it may be termed. But we are told by *Ricaut*, that, upon the disappearance of the sheykh, his principal followers were put to death; and, among them, a rapacious pasha, two agas, and an astrologer., Another fire, which happened at *Constantinople*, wherein twenty thousand houses were consumed, confirmed the people in their opinion of the sheykh's sanctity; which was heightened by news arriving of an emir of the *Arabs*, who said that he was descended from the prophet *Mohammed*, having laid siege to *Bassora*, in the *Persian Gulph*, as being his property by lineal descent. Upon this, the pasha of *Bosnia* had orders to march against the rebels; but the latter opened the sluices which let the water into the flat country, and not only overflowed the *Turkish* camp, but drowned about seven thousand of their men. But we are now to attend the progress of the *Hungarian* war.

On the twenty-seventh of *June*, 1693, the imperial general *Heusler* took the strong fortress of *Jeno*, which he had, for some time, blocked up; and, soon after, that of *Philagoras*. Those losses obliged the vizier to hasten his departure from *Adrianople* with the army, which was composed of very indifferent soldiers. While he was upon his march, being informed of the taking of *Jeno* and *Villagethwar*, he was distracted how to proceed, or whether he should reinforce the garrisons of *Temeswar* or *Belgrade*. At last he resolved upon the former, and ordered a pasha to march to that city with *The Turkish army marches to Hungary.*

strong

a ftrong detachment of men and a convoy of provifions. The pafha, and fome of the other officers, prefuming to remonftrate, that *Belgrade* was in danger, and muft be loft, if *Temefwar* was fuccoured, the vizier was fo incenfed, that he put to death, with his own hand, fix of his general office s who were of the pafha's opinion ; and began his march towards *Temefwar*, as if his intention had been to fubdue all *Tranfylvania*.

By this time, *Belgrade* was actually invefted by the Auftrians under the duke of *Croy* ; but, either through falfe information of the vizier's movements, or, as is more probable, through the dilatorinefs and imbecility of the court of *Vienna*, he neither was provided with men or artillery for fo great an undertaking. It was the firft of *Auguft* when the fiege might be faid to begin ; but it went fo flowly on, that it was the fifth before a battery was finifhed , nor did the *Brandenburgh* troops join the army before the ninth. In the mean while, the vizier, underftanding at *Diftra* that *Belgrade* was befieged, changed his route, and, by a moft unexampled march through mountains, he advanced towards *Belgrade*, after the fiege had continued, without any fuccefs, for twenty days. The conduct of the imperialifts, on this occafion, was unaccountable. No care was taken to cut off fupplies to the town by the *Danube* ; nor was the proper artillery brought up for feveral weeks after the fiege was formed. This was not a little owing to the falfe intelligence the duke of *Croy* had received of the vizier's having marched into *Tranfylvania* ; but he no fooner heard of his advancing to the relief of *Belgrade*, than he plied the fiege with redoubled fury. But it was now too late. The vizier's approach not only animated the befieged to a brave defence, but difcouraged the *Germans*, who fuffered very feverely from the fallies of their enemies, in one of which they loft above one thoufand men ; and they were repulfed in an attempt to ftorm the counterfcarp.

and raifes the fiege of *Bel grade.*
A council of war being held, it was judged impracticable to continue the fiege with their reduced numbers, and, at the fame time, to make head againft the vizier, whofe march to the relief of the city was as incredible as it was unexpected. The outer walls of the place had been ruined by the artillery of the befiegers ; and, even the citadel itfelf, though defended by a garrifon of fixteen thoufand *Turks*, was fo fhaken, that it muft have furrendered in a few days, had it not been for the approach of the vizier, who was preparing to ftorm the *Chriftian* camp. A refolution being taken to raife the fiege, the troops no fooner began to march towards the *Save*, than the vizier difpatched a courier to the fultan, to inform him of his having gained a complete victory over the *Germans*, which was proclaimed with great oftentation at *Adrianople*.

The

The duke of *Croy* took up a strong camp across the *Save*; which the vizier not daring to attack, sent the *Tartar* khan *Selim Gyeray*, with a large body, to cut off their provisions, and to ravage the *Hungarian* provinces. At *Khonad*, the *Tartars*, whose strength consisted chiefly in their horse, were so artfully surrounded by the imperialists, under *Hofkirkhen*, that they were reduced to the melancholy alternative of either starving or surrendering. The khan, rather than submit to either, ordered his followers to alight, and each man to kill his horse, and then to attack the enemy on foot; which they did with so much intrepidity, that the *Germans* were, at first, thrown into confusion; but recovering themselves, all the *Tartars*, excepting the khan and a few of his followers, were slaughtered.

On the nineteenth of *October*, *Hofkirkhen* fell upon the *Turks*, who lay before *Giula*, and drove them from a palanka, though they consisted of forty troops of horse, one thousand two hundred janisaries, and two thousand eight hundred *Tartars*. A thousand of the latter were killed, two thousand five hundred beasts of burthen were taken, and all their provisions destroyed; but it is uncertain whether this action did not precede that which we have given an account of against the *Tartars*; because, in the close of the letter which *Hofkirkhen* writes, upon this occasion, to the duke of *Croy*, he says, "Had I come but eight hours sooner, I had also met " with the *Tartars* marching to *Debrezen*; howsoever, I am " now preparing to follow them, and hope to come up with " them to morrow, or the day following."

This year, the imperialists, under count *Bathiani*, attacked *Brunzein Maydan* at sea, where the *Turks* had a great magazine of artillery, the neighbourhood of the place being famous for iron mines. The *Turks*, at first, made a brave defence; but such was the impetuosity of the *Germans*, that they stormed the walls of the place, and put to the sword above five hundred men and women, besides taking prisoners some persons of note; and, after securing all the contents of the magazines, they reduced the town itself to ashes. This place stands on the river *Sanna*, between *Kastanovitz* and *Bhaiz*; and the loss of it, together with a vast quantity of iron and brass artillery, gave very sensible disquiet to the court of *Constantinople*; the fourth part of which city was burnt down on the twenty-sixth of *August*, by an accidental fire. In other quarters, the *Othman* arms met with various success. The *Poles* were amused by the artifices of the *French* court; and the *Venetians*, in *Dalmatia*, by turns, defeated and were conquered. But we are now to turn from the operations of the field to those of the cabinet.

His *Britannic* majesty, *William* III. had nothing more at heart than to effect a peace between the porte and the *German* empire, which he knew could not act, with any probability of success, against the *French*, while it had an *Othman*

Negociations for peace

U 4 war

war to fuſtain. *Lewis* XIV. on the other hand, employed his ableſt miniſters, and their moſt ſpecious arts, to prevent any accommodation between the porte and the houſe of *Auſtria*. *Chateauneuf*, his reſident at *Conſtantinople*, finding that the *Turks*, before the ſiege of *Belgrade* was raiſed, were wavering between peace and war, called for a new ſupply of credit, which was ſent him by the marquis *de Lorand*, who aſſured the vizier, that the *French* king was upon the point of conquering *Great-Britain*, and conſequently *Holland*; which would give ſuch a blow to the *Germans* on the ſide of *Europe*, that the *Othmans* muſt become maſters of all *Hungary* and *Tranſylvania*. The *Turks* believed him; and he had even the addreſs, not only to obtain a promiſe from the vizier, that the porte never would make peace with the *Germans* without the participation of *France*, but leave for him to attend that miniſter's perſon in *Hungary*, that he might diſappoint all attempts towards peace. King *William* gave Mr. *Harbord* the character of his ambaſſador at *Conſtantinople*; but, when he arrived at *Vienna*, he heard, with the moſt ſenſible concern, of the ſmall probability of his ſucceſs with the *Othmans*. In quality, however, of mediator, he received the propoſals tendered for a pacification by the imperialiſts, the *Poles*, and the *Venetians*; which, with many other curious original papers, are inſerted in *Rycaut*'s hiſtory. Being thus ſupplied with credentials, *Harbord* proceeded from *Adrianople* (where he had arrived, for the moſt part, by water) to *Belgrade*, where he had an audience of the vizier. According to *Rycaut*, he found that miniſter ſo entirely prepoſſeſſed by the *French* ambaſſador, who, on that account, behaved with great inſolence, that indignation and concern threw him into a fever, of which he died on the thirty-firſt of *July*, 1692. His death happening ſoon after that of *Huſſey*, afforded great matter of ſpeculation, as if both of them had been poiſoned by the practices of the *French*; but, as *Rycaut* ſenſibly hints, their intereſt was ſo firmly rivetted with the vizier, that they had no occaſion to have recourſe to thoſe nefarious acts.

prove in-effectual. Many of the other great officers of the *Othman* empire were not of the vizier's opinion; and, upon the death of the depoſed ſultan *Mohammed* IV. a divan being held, the queſtion of peace or war was warmly debated; and it was thought that the former would have taken place, had not the imperial and *Dutch* miniſters been ſo zealous for it, that the *Turks* imagined the *European* confederacy on the brink of ruin.

Lord *Paget*, who now acted as the ſole *Britiſh* miniſter at the porte upon the death of *Harbord*, had an audience in *March* with little effect; and, ſoon after, the affair of the mediation grew deſperate. It was, at this time, reported, that the ſultan was about to remove towards *Belgrade*, to give greater ſpirit to the operations of his generals; but he was diſſuaded from this reſolution by his phyſicians perceiving him to be far gone in a dropſy, the hereditary diſeaſe of the *Othman* family. Preparations for war, however, went on with infinite vigour againſt the *Chriſtian* confederacy; but, whatever general maxims may prevail amongſt the *Othman* miniſters, it is certain that the ſecret ſprings of action are moved by a few private favourites within the walls of the ſeraglio. This obſervation was exemplified in the fate of this **Removals** vizier, who had ſo ſucceſsfully raiſed the ſiege of *Belgrade*, and returned to *Adrianople* in full hopes of being received with diſtinguiſhed honour by his maſter. Inſtead of that, being accuſed, on the ſlight pretext of his neglecting the affairs of the empire, becauſe he one day went a hunting, he was diveſted of the ſeals, which were given to *Ali Paſha*, the governor of *Tripolis*; but (a rare inſtance among the *Othmans*) he enjoyed his eſtate and liberty, and was made governor of *Damaſcus*.

The porte, at this time, by the inſtigation and influence of the *French* ambaſſador, ſought to divide and deſtroy the *Chriſtian* confederacy. The *French* deluded the *Poles* ſo as to apply for a ſeparate peace; which muſt have been effected, had they not peremptorily inſiſted upon the ſurrender of *Kaminieck*, with all its dependencies, and upon a clauſe of *uti poſſidetis*; two terms which were too unpopular even for the *French* intereſt to carry through. The teſterdar, or treaſurer, was, at this time, diſplaced, and, according to ſome, ſtrangled; and one *Ozman*, a worthleſs paſha, a native of *Caraia*, was made kaymakan of *Adrianople*. As to the vizier himſelf, he was, in his own mind, for peace; but, ſo great was the *French* influence at the porte, that he durſt ſcarcely own his ſentiments. It muſt be owned, that the common *Othman* hiſtories, at this time, are extremely imperfect; and that many changes took place at court unknown to the public, as will appear by the following curious letter from lord *Paget* to a friend at *Vienna*, dated *April* 24, N. S. 1694; which contains a more true deſcription of the *Othman* court, at this time, than we find in any hiſtory.

"SIR,

"THEY ſo often change their miniſters here, that an
"ambaſſador can ſcarce come to treat twice with the ſame
"perſon. Since my arrival here at the porte, they have had
"three grand-viziers, three chimacams of *Adrianople*, four
"chimacams of *Conſtantinople*, three agas of the janiſaries,
"three teſterdars, or lord-treaſurers, two new cadileſchers,
"or judges, of *Aſia* and *Romelia*; and, in ſhort, all the
"great officers of the empire were changed, the mufti only
"excepted; by which, there was ſuch a new ſet of idiots
"and fools got into places, as would overturn the beſt ſet-
"tled government in the world: for, theſe officers being
"only

" only fuch as chance offers, it is a doubtful wager, whe-
" ther he proves a fool or a wife man; and, in cafe he
" fhould prove a man of parts, yet he is fuffered fo fhort a
" time to remain in his office, that he is in no capacity to
" improve them."

" Ambaffadors, unlefs it be at their firft audience, and at
" that of *Congedie*, have no converfation or accefs to the
" grand-feigniors; and then they affect fuch a fort of gran-
" deur, as may beft cover all their thoughts by a filence;
" fo that they give no place for any debate; and a man can
" never lay any foundation upon their words: for, as their
" ally of *France* fcorns to be a flave to his word, fo they
" hold it to be no difhonour to be open, and efteem nothing
" for a fecret. It is true, that, very feldom, or never, a
" minifter fhall receive a flat denial from a *Turk*, for he fhall
" train you on to the very laft point; and, when you come
" to the laft argument, and upfhot of all, then a fum of mo-
" ney muft make the conclufion."

Such was the confufed ftate of the *Othman* affairs at this
time, when the khan of *Tartary*, upon fome diffatisfaction
expreffed by the porte at feeing the applications of the *Polifh*
envoy chiefly addreffed to him, left the court in difguft, and
was followed by the *Polifh* envoy himfelf, whofe negotiation
was difowned by all the reft of the confederates, who retired
and in-   in difgrace from *Adrianople*. At this juncture, the intrigues
trigues at   of the court grew to a greater height than ever; and the vi-
court.   zier, with the other great officers without doors, applied
formally to the grand-feignior to remove the kifler-aga, and
fome other officers within the palace, whom they accufed of
meddling in affairs of peace and war, in which they had no
concern. The fultan, on receiving this application, broke
out into an unufual paffion againft the vizier, and told him,
That, if the kifler-aga deferved any punifhment, it was for
his having been inftrumental in his, the vizier's, promotion
to the high place which he fo unworthily filled. The vizier
then found that he was deprived of his chief fupport, by the
departure of the *Tartar* khan; foon after which, his wife,
who was fifter to the fultan himfelf, endeavoured to accom-
modate matters between her hufband and the kifler-aga,
but without any effect, for fhe was forbidden the court, and
the fultan's mafter of the horfe was fent to demand from him
the feals of his office, which he was obliged to refign. His
houfe was then fealed up by the kaymakan of *Adrianople*;
but, being rich, he had intereft enough to procure an order
for his being reinftated in his government of *Tripolis*. His
enemies procured a revocation of this order; and a capigi,
with feveral boftanjis, being fent after him, overtook him on
the road, and, having brought him back, he was fhut up in
a prifon, which few had ever been known to leave, but with
their lives, and his eftate was confifcated to the fultan.

He

He was succeeded by another *Ali Pasha*, who, as his predecessor, had likewise been governor of *Tripolis*. This minister had, at the time of his succeeding to the viziership, some experience in business; but was not looked upon by the public as a man of abilities or capacity for that high station. He too, like his predecessors, was inclined to pacific measures; but was overborne by the ulema and the favourites of the seraglio, and the war went on. The *French* ambassador, acquainting the sultan that the *German* army was neither numerous nor well disciplined, formed a plan for attacking *Peterwaradin*; which coming to the knowledge of count *Caprara*, in *Hungary*, he entrenched himself round the city; and, in this situation, the vizier found him when he arrived before the place. He saw the *German* entrenchments too strong to be forced, and, fearing to be attacked himself, he fortified his own camp, and began regular approaches against *Caprara's* works, as if they had defended a fortified city; while his fleet, which consisted of one hundred and ten vessels of all kinds, cast anchor within cannon-shot of the imperial ships. This was a new way of making war; as if, in fact, two sieges were carried on at once; that of the *German* camp, and that of *Peterwaradin*. The *Turks* being well supplied with artillery and *French* engineers, soon broke into the imperial camp; from whence they were dislodged, with difficulty, by the *German* hussars; and, some *Brandenburgh* battalions arriving on the nineteenth, their courage was greatly abated. While those operations were carrying on by land, a brisk cannonade was kept up between the *Turkish* and imperial ships upon the *Danube*; and the governor of *Titul* took twenty-five of their provision ships, and sunk three of their frigates; beside which, one thousand five hundred of their troops were cut off by *Bassompiere*, an imperial general. Among the latter was the son of the *Tartar* khan, who threatened vengeance; but, the rainy season coming on, and the *Turkish* troops working in the ditches to their knees in water, the vizier was, at last, persuaded to raise the siege; which he did by night: and, soon after, the *Germans* reduced *Giula*. It is observed, by *Marsigli*, who was no mean judge of military operations, that the vizier, during the whole of this campaign, acted in a most unsoldierlike manner; nor could he have taken the place, in the way he proceeded, had his army been double its number.

In other parts of the *Othman* frontiers, especially towards *Poland* and *Russia*, nothing of importance happened. The inhabitants of the island of *Khios* were of two kinds; part of them *Latins*, chiefly *Venetians*; and the rest *Greeks*, who thought themselves happy under the *Othman* government, by the distinguished privileges they enjoyed. After the *Turks* had miscarried before *Vienna*, the *Italian* part of the inhabitants became spies for the *Venetians*, and, at last, secretly invited them to invade their island; but founded the

Successes of the Venetians.

Greek

Greek part of the inhabitants upon the fubject. The latter, unwilling to change the government they lived under, gave intelligence to the kapudan-pafha of what was in agitation; but, fuch was the ftate of the *Othman* affairs, at that time, that he was unable to fave the ifland; which the *Othman* governor, *Silahdar Haffan Pafha*, was obliged to deliver up by degrees.

The reduction of this ifland gave opportunities for its po-pifh inhabitants to manifeft their zeal for their church, for they immediately fhut up all the places of worfhip belong-ing to the *Greeks*, many of whom they obliged to comply with their religion; and they broke, in almoft every article, the terms of the capitulation for the ifland. The *Venetians*, as much elated by this acquifition as the *Turks* were difpi-rited, agreed upon befieging *Smyrna*. This alarmed the *French*, *Englifh*, and *Dutch* confuls refiding there; and they remonftrated to the *Venetian* commanders, That the ware-houfes of *Smyrna* were full of merchandizes and commodi-ties belonging to their refpective nations; and, that their republic would be obliged to make amends for all the da-mage which might be done to thofe ware-houfes during the fiege. The *Venetians*, upon thofe reprefentations, returned homewards with their fleet; but their general, *Delfino*, took *Kiklu* and *Klobuk*, in *Dalmatia*; the *Turkifh* ferafkier endea-vouring in vain to retake them.

Rebellion of the *Arabs*, About this time, the *Arabs*, who, for fome ages, had af-fected an independency upon the *Othman* government, com-plained, that the furreh, or tribute, paid them for not rob-bing the caravans going to *Mecca* from different parts of the *Turkifh* dominions, had been withdrawn; and furprized fome of the caravans, in which the khan of *Tartary* was go-ing on a pilgrimage to that city, whom they made prifoner, and compelled him to carry their complaints to the porte. In the mean while, their general, *Amir Mohammed*, conti-nued to plunder the *Othman* fubjects; and the *Arabs* found the trade fo beneficial, that his army amounted to fuch a number as enabled him to befiege *Mecca* itfelf. but, accord-ing to the *Turkifh* hiftorians, being ftruck with the fanctity of the place, he defifted from his enterprize. By this time the vizier had returned to *Adrianople* with a difpirited army, and in a manner that looks fo much like a flight, that a tu-**and fedi-tion at *Adriano-ple.*** mult enfued. The people of *Adrianople* being affembled in the chief mofque of the city, a bold *Turk*, who had accom-plices attending him, mounted the pulpit, and harangued the people as follows:

"*Moflems*, or believers, You are all, at this time, obliged
"to ftand up for the faith, for your country, and govern-
"ment. You cannot but be fenfible, that the *Chriftians* at-
"tack us both by fea and land; that we have a fultan who
"attends to nothing; and a great vizier, who is not ac-
"quainted, or practifed, in affairs either civil or military.
"Where-

" Wherefore, let us all run to the gate of our mufti, and
" there cry out, and exclaim, for a change of government.
" Do you not obferve what a capricious fool we have for a
" vizier; how obftinate and ignorant, and how he daily
" commits a thoufand follies?

Intelligence of this feditious fpeech being carried to the
kaymakan, he mounted on horfeback, and, taking with him
a ftrong guard of janifaries, he feized the preacher, but
without daring to punifh him at firft. Finding afterwards
that the mutineers were divided among themfelves, he proceeded againft them more feverely, by putting to death the
moft culpable, and throwing their bodies into the fea. The
Arabs were all this while in arms; and *Amir Mohammed*,
who, we perceive, was a fharif, or defcendant of the prophet, was preparing to ftrike an important blow both againft
Mecca and *Medina*; but was diffuaded from it by the mufti,
and the other good *Moflems*, both civil and military; who
perfuaded him into more pacific fentiments. We are, however, given to underftand, that thefe were greatly owing to
his being deferted by many of the *Arab* chiefs.

Towards the end of the year 1694, the vizier, who continued with the army encamped without the walls of *Adrianople*, gave out, that he would attempt the recovery of *Khios*;
the lofs of which had occafioned an interruption of all correfpondence with *Smyrna*, *Rhodes*, or *Egypt*; and this had
heightened the price of coffee, rice, and fugar. This defign
was laid afide upon intelligence being received, that the *Venetians* had made proper difpofitions for defending it. Before
the clofe of this year, the prudence of the kaymakan of *Adrianople* alone prevented a general revolution from taking place
in the *Othman* empire.

In the beginning of the year 1695, the attention of the Death and
miniftry was turned towards finding employment for the ar- charaĉter
my, to divert its turbulent fpirit; and a frefh fire broke out of fultan
in *Conftantinople:* but fultan *Ahmed* died on the twenty- *Ahmed.*
feventh of *January*, in the fiftieth year of his age, and the
fourth of his reign. We have already given his charaĉter;
and all we have to add, is, that, during his reign, he fell
into the common error of the *Othman* princes; that of too
great an attachment to private favourites, who abufed his
confidence. *Rycaut* reprefents him, as being agreeable in his
perfon; but his belly was too prominent, occafioned by the
dropfy. The immediate caufe of his death was a defluxion
upon his lungs; and it is faid, that, in his laft agonies, finding his nephew, *Moftafa*, could not be perfuaded to fpeak to
him, he fent him a meffage, begging, that, if he fhould fucceed to the empire, he would fuffer his fon *Ibrahim*, who
was no more than three years old, to live.

The

The Reign of Moſtafa II.

Acceſſion of Moſta-fa.

WE have already obſerved, that, whatever ideas the public may entertain concerning the deſpotiſm of *Turkiſh* ſultans, their power is undoubtedly circumſcribed in matters of ſucceſſion, and all the great conſtituent parts of government. This appeared in the ſucceſſion of *Moſtafa* II. the ſon of *Mohammed* IV. to the *Othman* throne, in prejudice of the infant ſon of the late emperor *Ahmed*. The vizier *Ali* would gladly have placed this infant ſon of *Ahmed* on the throne, that he might have enjoyed his power during a long minority. The courtiers had determined otherwiſe; and the hazandar-baſhi, or treaſurer of the ſeraglio, freeing *Moſtafa* from his confinement, he immediately mounted the throne, and was recognized as ſultan by the great officers of ſtate. He was, at this time, about thirty-three years of age, healthy and active in his conſtitution; and, from what we can gather from the *Turkiſh* as well as *European* hiſtorians, like many of his predeceſſors, he ſtepped from a priſon to a throne. His mother, who was the favourite wife of *Mohammed* IV. had a perfect aſcendancy over the ſon's ſpirit; and ſhe was given out to have been the daughter of a *Chriſtian* biſhop. She was then at ſome diſtance from court; and, till her ſentiments ſhould be known, the new ſultan was pleaſed to confirm the vizier in his office. The firſt act of his government was to inſpect his finances, which he found to be miſerably poor. To recruit them, he obliged all his great officers, not excepting the vizier, to bring in their ready-money; and his own mother is ſaid to have contributed ſeven millions (of aſpers we ſuppoſe) or about four hundred thouſand pounds.

Altera-tions at court.

The vizier ſeeing *Moſtafa* upon the throne, was among the firſt of the courtiers to pay him his allegiance. The ſultan declared, that he was reſolved to command his armies in perſon. He iſſued orders for a new train of artillery to be caſt, and he made all the arrangements neceſſary for a vigorous campaign, without conſulting any of his miniſters. He then recalled to court many of his father's faithful officers, and, among the reſt, *Elmas Mohammed Paſha*, a worthy, able man, and unſtained with avarice, the common vice of the *Othmans*; and him he made niſhanji paſha, a poſt ſomewhat a-kin to our privy-ſeal; after which he was made rekiub kaymakan, or deputy to the vizier, when the latter was at war.

Many circumſtances concurred to render the beginning of this reign uncommonly auſpicious. All the meaſures of the ſultan declared him to be of a warlike diſpoſition. He publicly charged his vizier to take care how he behaved towards

wards his foldiers, and to tell him nothing but the truth. The *Tartars* had beat the *Poles*. The kapudan-pafha, or admiral of the *Turks*, had defeated the *Venetians* in two feveral engagements ; and, to the aftonifhment of all chriftendom, the latter meanly refigned, without a ftruggle, their important acquifition of the ifle of *Khios* ; which the *Turks* again took poffeffion of, to the great joy of the *Greeks* and difcomfort of the *Latins*, fome of whofe chiefs were publicly executed by the *Othmans* ; and all who remained on the ifland were obliged to conform themfelves to the *Greek* liturgy.

The fultan being now firmly feated on the throne, and his mother being arrived at court, all the great places of the government were new modelled. Some of the late minifters were ftrangled, others beheaded, an aftrologer was hanged, and banifhment was inflicted upon the leaft culpable, all by the direction of the fultana valide, or mother. The fultan himfelf, like fome of his predeceffors, often went in difguife to places of mean refort, that he might hear the opinions of the common people ; and his fecret difpleafure againft his vizier was encreafed by his underftanding that the people, in general, looked upon the fultan only as a nominal character ; and, that, in fact, the vizier managed all the great affairs of the empire. This determined that minifter's fate, for the fultan was refolved, at all events, to deftroy him. The vizier was fenfible of this, and did all he could to avert his fate. He fqueezed money from all ranks of people, and his expertnefs in that practice was fo agreeable to the fultan, that his life was fpared longer than he at firft intended. *The vizier, and others, put to death.*

All the cares of the fultan were now directed towards a vigorous campaign on the fide of *Hungary*. *Moftafa* perfifted in his refolution to command the army in perfon. The vizier, and the great officers of ftate, did all they could to diffuade him from this ; but his mother encouraging him to perfevere, they thought proper to congratulate him upon the magnanimity of his refolution. An encampment, as ufual, being ordered for the army, which was to confift of eighty thoufand men, about two miles out of the gates of *Adrianofh*, the foldiers clamoured for their donative. The grand-vizier applied to the fultan, and offered to find the money for pacifying them ; but the fultan replied, with great firmnefs, That he was not indebted for his throne to the foldiery, but to his own hereditary right ; that the mifconduct of the two former reigns had impoverifhed the treafury ; that the donative in queftion was originally no other than a gratuity granted by his predeceffors on occafion of fignal fucceffes ; and, that, in fhort, he was refolved to difcontinue it.

Before the army was affembled, the *Tartar* khan was ordered to be in readinefs with all the men he could raife. He endeavoured to excufe himfelf, on account of a war he was engaged in with the *Mufcovites* ; but the fultan infifted peremptorily

remptorily upon his attendance. The fultan, by the firmnefs he difplayed on this, and all other, occafions, found himfelf adored by his fubjects, and now thought that he might venture to execute his vengeance againft the vizier. That minifter had long forefeen his own deftruction, which made fuch an impreffion upon him, that his very words and actions, even in the prefence of the fultan, betrayed his apprehenfion. *Moftafa*, in one of his midnight rambles, underftood that his artillery carriages were not fufficiently fortified with iron; and this trifling circumftance induced him to charge his vizier with neglect in the important duties of his office. The vizier threw the blame upon the topachi-bafhi, or mafter of the artillery, who recriminated, and, as the fultan had refolved that the vizier fhould be in the wrong, he was banifhed to *Chefme*, on the coaft of *Anatolia*; from whence he was foon brought to *Adrianople*, and, being there put to death, his head was expofed in the moft ignominious manner. The mufti, who was efteemed an honeft, worthy man, was, about the fame time, difplaced; and the fultan's tutor, a perfon of a very oppofite character, was appointed in his room. The aga of the janifaries, and almoft all the domeftics of the court, were, in like manner, difplaced by the female faction, which directed every thing at court, and fubftituted, in their rooms, none but the moft infamous of mankind.

Elmas Mohammed made vizier. *Elmas Mohammed Pafha*, whom we have already mentioned, and who was looked upon to be one of the handfomeft men in the empire (his appellation of *Elmas*, or *Diamond*, being given him on that account) was raifed to the vizierfhip, to the great difguft of the old pafhas in office; and, every thing being now in readinefs for the march of the army, the fultan fet out at the head of it, but not before he had publifhed the following general orders. "That no man going to the wars fhould be ferved by young boys. That good order and difcipline fhould be obferved in the march. That no man fhould ride out of the common high-road, or by bye-ways, into the corn-fields, or vine-yards, or other grounds belonging to the hufband-man" In confequence of thofe orders, the fultan, who continued to go about in difguife, commanded feveral perfons, whom, he thought, had contravened them, to be immediately executed. The army, when it left *Adrianople*, by reafon of the *Tartar* khan not joining it with above five thoufand men, did not exceed fifty thoufand. On the tenth of *June* they began their march, and took the route of *Tranfylvania*; by which the elector of *Saxony*, who this year commanded the imperialifts, was difabled, through moft unaccountable miftakes, from coming up with them. The fultan paffed the *Danube*, and, on the feventh of *September*, 1695, attacked *Lippa*, which was then no better than an open place, and took it by ftorm. All who were in it were put to the fword, excepting the governor and

and a few of the principal officers, who were reserved to be evidences of the *Turkish* victory. The sultan then reduced and dismantled *Titul*. *Veterani*, the imperial general, was then upon his march, with seven thousand *Germans*, to join the elector of *Saxony*; and the sultan sent *Mahmud Beg Ogli*, beglerbeg of *Rumelia*, with the light-armed troops, to keep the *Germans* in play till the rest of the *Othman* army could come up. *Veterani*'s troops were reckoned to be the best that *Germany* ever produced, and they repulsed *Ogli*, with vast slaughter, in sight of the sultan; who, with his own hand, killed numbers of the runaways, and advanced in person to the charge. The *Turks*, animated by his presence, broke, with irresistible fury, into the *German* camp; where they were cut in pieces by the imperialists: and a total route of the *Othmans* must have ensued, had not their generals, stung by the reproaches of the sultan, a third time rallied their army and renewed the attack. The battle was fierce and obstinate, notwithstanding the inequality of the numbers; the *Turkish* army then consisting of forty thousand spahis and eighteen thousand janisaries: but, the brave *Veterani* being mortally wounded, his men retreated.

This astonishing action gave the sultan an idea of the *German* valour and discipline, very different from what he had entertained before. He privately applied to the mufti, to find out some honourable method for discontinuing the pursuit of an enemy, whose despair might yet render them victorious. The mufti, as that set of men are always fruitful in expedients, immediately published a fetvah, implying, that, according to the principles of the *Koran*, no *Moslem* could obtain a crown of martyrdom, if he was killed in the too close pursuit of a flying enemy. In this action, the beglerbeg of *Rumelia*, several of the best *Turkish* generals, and above ten thousand of the common men, and other officers, were killed. The *Germans* lost one thousand horse, and one thousand five hundred foot; and, though it was observed that the sultan, in all actions, took care not to expose his person, yet he wrote most magnificent accounts of his victories to his mother and the regency which he left at *Adrianople*. He then led his forces back to the *Danube*, and took *Logush* and *Karansebes*, places of very little strength or importance. Through the whole of this campaign, so rigorous a discipline was observed, that some *Turks* were hanged for so small a crime as robbing a bee-hive. But, however inglorious this campaign might be to the *Turks*, it was more so to the *Germans*, whose general sent his troops into winter-quarters without their coming to farther action.

The affairs of *Poland* this year are variously represented. The khan of *Tartary* made an irruption into *Podolia* and *Pokutia*, as far as *Leopolis*; and is said to have carried off fourteen thousand prisoners: but this is denied by the *Poles*, who say, that they forced the *Tartars* to retreat, though their ar-

The Campaign in Transylvania.

my confifted of above feventy thoufand men. About the fame time, *Peter*, czar of *Mufcovy*, attempted to take *Afoph*, one of the principal towns of *Krim-Tartary*; but mifcarried, through the inexperience of his foldiers.

Mezzo Morto de- feats the Venetians, and reco- vers Khios.

Mezzo Morto, fo called from his being half dead, occa- fioned by a wound he received in an engagement with the *Spaniards*, was, at this time, at the head of the *Turkifh* ma- rine, and one of the moft fkillful, as well as braveft, officers of his time. He was born in *Africa*, of *Moorifh* parents, and had been early accuftomed to a piractical life; nor could he be ever reconciled to the *Turkifh* manners, even in his drefs. After the *Turks* had loft *Khios*, though he was then only cap- tain of a galley, to which poft he had raifed himfelf by his merit, he was fo far from defponding, that he advifed the divan to carry on an offenfive war by fea. Some of the greateft officers of that board treated him as a madman for this propofal; but the ferafkier *Mifri Ogli*, who was to carry on the *Venetian* war, approved of his fcheme, and put him at the head of a fquadron with which he attacked the *Vene- tian* fleet in the chief harbour of *Khios*; and, to the aftonifh- ment of all the *European* powers, defeated it in two engage- ments. The *Venetians*, who had depended entirely upon their naval power, at firft, were inclined to have butchered all the *Greek* inhabitants, whom, perhaps, with fome rea- fon, they imagined to have favoured the *Turks*; but the powerful protection of the ferafkier, over-awed the *Veneti- ans*, and their troops fhamefully deferted the ifland. Such as remained were obliged either to embrace the *Greek* reli- gion, or to ferve in the gallies; which even the power of the *French* ambaffador could not exempt them from: and many of the military men, whom their fhips could not re- ceive, when the others left the ifland, were put to death.

The ful- tan de- feats the Germans.

Mezzo Morto, who fhut up all the *Latin* churches in *Khios*, in the fame manner as the *Latins* had fhut up thofe of the *Greeks*, obtained great applaufe from his conduct. The ful- tan made a kind of a triumphal entry into *Adrianople*, upon the recovery of *Khios*, and likewife upon the defeat of the re- bellious *Arab* fheykh *Mohammed*, who had fo often robbed the caravans travelling to *Mecca*; and made *Mezzo Morto* his high-admiral. The *Turks*, in general, recovered their fpi- rits, and flocked to the imperial ftandards to make a glorious campaign in *Hungary*; where the elector of *Saxony*, the im- perial general, had befieged *Temefwar*. The fultan flew to raife the fiege, which he effectually did; and the *Othmans* took up a fortified camp, which the *Germans* bravely endea- voured to ftorm; but they were defeated with great lofs of men and almoft their whole train of artillery. This victory was owing greatly to the new vizier *Elmas Mohammed Pafha*, who threw himfelf, with the janifaries, between the *Ger- mans* and the tent of the fultan, who had been almoft made a prifoner by the fudden irruption of the enemy into his camp.

The

The *Othman* loss in this engagement was very considerable. The vizier's brother, the governor of *Temeswar*, and some thousands of the janisaries, were killed; and the safety of the *Othman* army was, at last, owing to the bastanjis, a militia but lately instituted among the *Turks*, somewhat of the nature of the antient soccage-tenures in *England*, as they held their lands by military services. The sultan affected great moderation upon this victory; which he was so far from pursuing, that he ordered the mufti to issue a servant prohibiting farther blood-shed; and, to the great disappointment of the *Germans*, he put an end to the campaign. Such, in general, is the *Turkish* account of this important campaign; and, in the main, however disguised by the variety of the *Germans*, it is true. The precise loss of the imperialists is not ascertained; but that of the *Othmans*, by their own confession, amounted to above eight thousand men.

While matters went prosperously on for the sultan in *Hungary*, *John Sobieski*, king of *Poland*, died, but the truth is, soon after the campaign, in which he raised the siege of *Vienna*, the *Poles* made but a poor figure against the *Othmans*. On the other hand, *Peter the Great*, czar of *Muscovy*, took *Asoph* from the porte; and the *Venetians* obtained some advantages on the side of the *Morea*, where they repaired the famous *Hexamilion*, a wall of six miles long, which is built across the isthmus of *Corinth*. They had not equal success by sea, where the great abilities of *Mezzo Morto*, now the kapudan-pasha, introduced a new discipline in the *Turkish* marine, and baffled all the attempts of the *Venetians*, who had so lately been accustomed to despise the *Othman* fleet.

The sultan having led his army back to *Adrianople*, there disbanded it; and, by *Rycaut's* account, the revival of the *Othman* glory was, in a great measure, owing to the sultan's valour; or, at least, to the opinion the public had of it. From *Adrianople* he marched with his guards to *Constantinople*, which he entered in as great triumph as if he had returned from the conquest of *Vienna* itself. Three days after his entry, he was solemnly girt with a sword by a sheykh at the monument of *Ayub*, one of the most important ceremonies of the *Turkish* government.

On the first of *November*, this year, a *Persian* ambassador had audience of the sultan. His business was to complain of *Babek Soleyman Bey*, governor of *Karamania*, for his turbulent disposition, to sollicit a separate place for the *Persians* to worship in in the temple of *Mecca*, and to obtain a preference for the *Armenian* patriarchs in the *Holy Land*; but we do not find that his ambassy met with great success. The vast improvements that *Mezzo Morto* had made in the *Othman* marine, induced the sultan to apply more than ever to fitting out a large fleet, part of which he destined to act against the *Venetians*, and part against the *Russians*, who,

since

fince the taking of *Afoph*, had become formidable to the porte. His proceedings were fo vigorous, that the *Venetians* were kept in awe, nor did the *Ruffians* continue their conquefts. As to *Mezzo Morto*, the fultan heaped upon him all the honours he could beftow, and furnifhed him with as many failors and marines as he demanded. About the twenty-third of *May*, a ferman, or proclamation, was publifhed for a general rendezvous of the army about *Adrianople*; and, to give fpirit to the warlike operations, a thorough reformation of the coin was effected, to the great joy of the military, as well as the civil, part of the empire; and, among other favings that were made at the fame time, the allowance of count *Tekeli*, for himfelf, his wife, and his family, was reduced to five dollars a day; but, to make him fome amends, he was permitted to fell wine. This nobleman is a ftanding evidence of *Othman* ingratitude. No man was more careffed at their court than he was, while they had any occafion for his fervices; but their ends were no fooner anfwered than he was thrown afide, lodged in one of the moft difgraceful ftreets of all *Conftantinople*, and he and his followers muft have ftarved, had it not been for his wine-licence, which, indeed, amounted to a monopoly, none of the *Othman* fubjects being indulged in that privilege. The *French* ambaffador, it is true, continued to fhew him fome tokens of refpect; but his influence was foon at an end with the porte, when the *Othman* minifters found that he was treating of a feparate peace with the imperialifts and their other enemies.

Rebellion in *Afia*. A rebellion, at this time, was raging in the bowels of *Afia*, which retarded the *Afiatic* troops from joining the army that was to act in *Hungary* till the fultan emitted a proclamation of pardon; upon which ten thoufand of the rebels came over to ferve him in his army; which, when he fet out for *Hungary*, did not confift of above forty thoufand men. The ftruggle about the fucceffion to *John Sobiefki*, king of *Poland*, was then very high in that country; but the fultan being informed that it had gone in favour of the prince of *Conti*, he immediately wrote a letter to *Tekeli*, giving him the title of king of *Hungary*; but commanded him to repair to him at *Belgrade*. The meffengers found the poor prince in bed, emaciated, tortured with the gout, and full of difeafes; but, without regard to his rank or condition, they forced him from his bed into a common cart, in which they fet out with him for *Belgrade*. His new title did him little fervice; for, as the profpect of peace encreafed, fo did the difregard of the *Turks* for him and his caufe; but, in the mean while, he was highly careffed.

Expedition i to Hungary. The fuppreffion of the *Afiatic* rebellion foon raifed the fultan's army to the number of one hundred and thirty-five thoufand men, befides a vaft number of attendants which the

Turkifh

Turkish camps always have in their train. The imperial and
English ministers acquainted the sultan of the peace of *Ryſ-*
wick between the emperor and the *French* king, and renewed
their offers of mediation; which he rejected, having received
information, that the imperial army under prince *Eugene* of
Savoy, did not exceed fifty-ſix thouſand men; and, that he
had orders to act upon the defenſive, and only to cover *Peter-*
waradin and the forts upon the *Danube.* The ſultan calling
a council of war, *Tekeli* gave it, as his opinion, that the army ſhould move from *Belgrade* and march into *Tranſylvania,*
where the imperialiſts were weak, and where the *Othmans*
were ſure to be joined by fifty thouſand *Hungarian* malecontents. The *German* army was then lying at *Segedin*; but no
ſooner had the *Othmans* paſſed the *Danube,* in their march to
Temeſwar, than prince *Eugene* made a motion, as if he intended to attack *Belgrade*; and the ſultan, in another council of war, came to a reſolution to attack the imperialiſts at
Titul; and, in the mean time, he ordered his fleet to proceed up the *Danube.* The *Germans,* perceiving the *Oth-*
mans advance, fortified the banks of the *Teiſſe* with maſked
batteries. The ſultan, thinking himſelf ſecure of victory,
proclaimed a reward of fifty crowns for every *German* taken
alive, and twenty-five for every head that ſhould be brought
in. The *Turks,* animated by this reward, threw themſelves
directly into their dumbas, or boats, and paſſed tumultu-
ouſly, in great numbers, to the oppoſite bank, without reſiſtance; but, no ſooner were they arrived there than the
batteries, being unmaſked, killed three thouſand of their janiſaries; and the whole muſt have been cut in pieces, had
not their fleet advanced and ſecured a retreat for the janiſaries in an iſland lying in the middle of the *Teiſſe.* From
thence they croſſed the river lower down, and a ſecond engagement enſued; but the imperialiſts, perceiving the whole
Turkiſh army preparing to paſs the river, retired to a camp
in the plain of *Kobila,* lying between the *Danube* and the
Teiſſe, and ſo as to be in the neighbourhood of *Titul, Sege-*
din, and *Peterwaradin.*

The whole *Othman* army, after this, having paſſed the
Teiſſe, in a new council it was reſolved to beſiege *Peterwara-*
din before the *Germans* could advance to its relief. But this
could not be done till a bridge ſhould be conſtructed for
paſſing the army; and this took up ſo much time, that prince
Eugene, by a wonderful march, notwithſtanding all the oppoſition made by the *Tartar* cavalry, led his army from *Se-*
gedin, and encamped on a plain between the *Othmans* and
Peterwaradin. This expeditious march ſtruck the *Othmans*
with conſternation, and the ſultan called together another
great council of war, to deliberate, whether the imperialiſts
ſhould be immediately attacked, or the *Othmans* remain upon
the defenſive till they ſhould be attacked by the *Chriſtians.*
The members of the council were greatly divided on thoſe

points.

Debates
in the
Turkish
camp.

points. The vizier was of opinion, that, considering the uncommon ardor of the soldiers for battle, the enemy ought to be attacked; and, that it would be disgraceful for the *Othman* arms to lose so fair an opportunity, and, that, in such a a , the army would be apt to mutiny. His advice was opposed by *Jaffer Pasha*, a general of great experience in the *Christian* wars, and of as undaunted a spirit in council as in battle. He, very sensibly, observed, that the *Othmans*, even when superior in numbers, never engaged the *Germans* in the open field, but they were defeated; and, that their army, which was one of the best they ever brought to the field, was commanded by a general, whose abilities and valour would suffer him to slip no advantages, and who would not risk a battle without being assured of a victory. He therefore advised the sultan to keep upon the defensive, even though the enemy should march by them to take possession of the head of the bridge. He said, That, by such a conduct, the *Othmans*, though they should not prove victorious, would avoid being defeated; and, that, by surrounding the *Germans* with their works, they might oblige them to fight under vast disadvantages, or to repass the *Danube* for subsistence. The vizier, perceiving that *Jaffer* was favourably heard by the assembly, called him dog and infidel, and accused him of having been bribed by the *Germans*. *Jaffer*, without being moved, called out to the sultan to open the curtain, which, as usual, divided him from the assembly, that he might hear what he had to propose; which was, to submit to be laid in irons, and to die the death of a dog, if he was not defeated, should he attack the *Christians*, provided the vizier should be obliged to account for his temerity.

The emperor was at a loss how to proceed, and adjourned the debate, but inclined so far to *Jaffer*'s advice, that he commanded his chaush, who served as a kind of military provost, to order, and even to force, all the soldiers, many of whom had already ranged themselves in order of battle, to keep within the lines. This threw them into such discontent, that the mufti was forced to publish a fetvah, importing, That every soldier who should fall in such a battle, would forfeit his crown of martyrdom.

Prince *Eugene*'s army, in the mean while, was in the utmost distress by the thirst and heat it suffered; so that he was obliged to secure the possession of the head of the bridge, that his men might refresh themselves with the water of the river. The prince having, by the orders given out in the *Turkish* camp, been enabled to do this without opposition, the *Othmans* imagined that their generals were afraid to fight; which gave the vizier an opportunity of triumphing over *Jaffer*'s timid counsels, which had given the *Germans* possession of the *Danube*, and time to reinforce their army. But all he could bring the sultan to consent to, was, to undertake the siege of *Segedin*, which he pretended could not hold out above

above ten days; and the reduction of it would put the *Oth-mans* in possession of all the country between the *Teisse* and the *Danube*. He added, There was the less danger in this measure, as the *German* army was too much fatigued to be able to follow them, and far less to undertake the siege of *Belgrade*; to the government of which he advised the sultan to appoint *Jaffer Pasha*. The sultan easily perceived with what view this last piece of advice was given, and rejected it. Next day, he began his march, but left *Jaffer* the command of the rear; while he, with a body of horse, marched towards *Zenta*, a small castle on the banks of the *Teisse*.

Prince *Eugene*, hearing that the tubulkhana, or imperial music, was playing in the neighbourhood, expected a battle; but finding the *Othmans* were directing their march towards *Zenta*, he dispatched his *Hungarian* horse to harass their rear; while he himself followed, at the head of sixteen thousand troops, with such incredible diligence, that, that very night, they got up with *Jaffer's* division; every man of whom they killed or took prisoner, and *Jaffer* himself among the rest, excepting a chamberlain, who escaped to *Zenta* and informed the vizier of what had happened. That minister dreading the consequence, ordered the messenger's head to be struck off, to keep the news from spreading; and informed the sultan, that *Jaffer* had, indeed, been surprized; but that the *Oth-mans* had rallied, and entirely defeated the *Christians*. He was, however, very soon contradicted by the appearance of the *Tartar* horse, who informed the sultan, that the whole *German* army was at hand. The sultan could not conceal his indignation at his vizier, but, ordering a bridge to be thrown over the *Teisse*, which was compleated in four hours, and without suffering the vizier to pay his usual compliments, he passed it on horseback. The vizier saw now his ruin inevitable, unless he was saved by a desperate effort; and, instead of following the emperor with all the troops and artillery, as he had been ordered, he fortified his camp as well as time would permit; and, sending for the pashas, who had passed the river, he insultingly told them in a speech, That now was their time to be conquerors or martyrs; and immediately the whole army fortified the camp by a second ditch, before which they placed their waggons and other carriages.

The sultan, who seems, at this time, to have been on the opposite side of the river, beheld, from thence, the *German* army advancing; and sent repeated messages to the vizier, commanding him immediately to send over all the janisaries with the artillery. The vizier concealed those orders, which, indeed, happened to be impracticable, by the bridge being accidentally broken down. About three hours before night, the *Christian* army advanced to the charge; but they were repulsed with loss: and they perceived, with amazement, that the *Turkish* camp, instead of being defended only by

Battle of *Zenta*.

X 4   waggons,

waggons, was furrounded by two deep ditches; that the division of the army with the vizier was more numerous than all their own army; and that, when the bridge was repaired, they might be reinforced by the fultan. Upon those confiderations, prince *Eugene* altered the plan of his attack, and ordered a trench to be dug in the dry part of the channel of the *Teiffe*, below the *Turkifh* camp, into which he introduced feveral regiments, who thereby flanked the *Turks* within their camp, while he himfelf attacked its outfide. To prevent the bridge being repaired, he ordered two cannons to play upon it; while the fultan employed one of the ableft officers about his perfon to defend it; but the *German* artillery being better ferved, he was driven from his poft with fome lofs; and the bridge was damaged fo as but one man could pafs it a-breaft. During this cannonade, the two attacks formed by prince *Eugene* went brifkly on, but to the great difadvantage of the *Germans*, whom the janifaries drove from the outer ditch, but, returning to the inner ditch, they declared they would not follow their advantage, and that they would ftand upon the defenfive there only. This obftinacy appears to have proceeded either from a defire of being at hand to repel the attack from the river, or, which is more probable, from a difguft at the behaviour and haughtinefs of their vizier and the pafhas, to whom they attributed all that they had fuffered; and who, upon their refufing to defend the outer ditch, killed feveral of the moft forward mutineers. According to *Cantemir*'s account, this feverity drove them into fuch rage, that they maffacred the vizier, the pafhas, and all their other officers, excepting an aga who, from his impetuofity, was called *the mad*. While this fcene was acting in the camp, the imperialifts feized the outer ditch, and made difpofitions for attacking the inner; and this drew the main ftrength of the enemy from the attack on the fide of the river; fo that the *Germans* were likely to become mafters of the head of the bridge, and, confequently, the *Othmans* were in danger of lofing the only communication they had with the fultan.

Total defeat of the *Turks*.

The confideration of this was fo alarming, that their force was again directed towards the river; which gave an opportunity to the *Germans* to pafs the inner ditch with little or no lofs, and to attack the *Turks* in their rear. This completed their deftruction. They who fled from the fwords of the imperialifts, either threw themfelves into the river, where they were drowned, or were killed in feeking a paffage over the ruined bridge, by which only a very few efcaped. By the lifts it appeared, that, within the fpace of three hours, no fewer than fourteen thousand and feventy janifaries, with their aga, were killed; three thousand, feven hundred topchi and jobeji; feventy-three general officers, befides the vizier, *Elmas Mohammed*; fifteen pafhas of three horfe-tails, twenty-feven pafhas of two or one horfe-tail; and feven
thoufand

thousand arnauds, who were, by far, the bravest, and best disciplined troops, not excepting the janisaries, of the *Othman* army. In short, at a modeiate computation, no fewer than thirty thousand *Turks*, including attendants upon the camp, were drowned or killed in this battle. According to the letter sent by the empeior of *Germany* to king *William*, ten thousand of those fell by the sword, the rest being drowned; and the imperialists took seventy-two pieces of cannon, several thousand waggons laden with provisions; while the *Germans* had no more than five hundred men killed and as many wounded. There is reason, however, to believe, from the accounts given us of this battle, by prince *Cantemir*, who was present, that the loss of the imperialists was more considerable. It is, notwithstanding, agreed, on all hands, that, since the defeat of *Bajazet* by *Tamerlane*, the *Othman* power had never received so great a blow. Their defeat appears, in fact, to have been entirely owing to their want of discipline, and the hatred which the soldiers, especially the janisaries, had for the vizier; choosing rather to fall by the swords of the imperialists than to contribute to his glory. The *Othmans* behaved bravely when it was too late, but their efforts were those of despair rather than courage, and seived only to precipitate their fates.

The sultan, during the battle, remained a spectator on the opposite side of the river; and was often heard to bewail the loss of so many brave soldiers, without being in a condition to relieve them. Though he was naturally brave, though he was still at the head of an army, equal, at least, to that of the *Germans*; and though it might have been easily supposed that the latter were most terribly fatigued, yet a panic seized him; and he put to death a renegade *Venetian*, who had been made a pasha, only for advising him not to fly dishonourably. In the middle of a very dark night, unable to see the way, he let out with a great retinue; many of whom, by mistaking the road, lost their horses and equipages: and the sultan, in the morning, changing both his horse and habit, fled to *Temeswai*, where he ordered the governor to conceal his arrival, lest he should be besieged by the *Germans*. The soldiers, about noon, perceiving that the sultan and his great officers were not at their head, immediately concluded that they had been taken prisoners on their march by some of the *German* parties; and they fled, without the least order, towards *Temeswar*, where they found the gates shut against their admittance. This confirmed them in their apprehensions, but they could fly no farther. Besides their being every moment afraid lest the *Germans* should fall upon them, they were destitute of all provisions; and neither they, nor their horses, had any thing to quench their thirst. Thus all property ceased among them; the stronger robbed the weaker of whatever could support his life. The sultan, all this time, had no regard but for his own safety; and, expecting every

moment

moment to be befieged by the *Germans*, he prepared for a vigorous defence. Perceiving he was in no danger of a fiege, on the third day he appeared without the walls; and his army, at feeing him, received him as if he had returned in triumph, and feemed to forget all the miferies they had fuffered.

Their camp plundered by Tekeli.   *Tekeli*, who was at the head of a body of *Hungarians*, was in no hafte to follow the fultan; but, upon his and his army's precipitate flight, he pillaged the *Othman* camp, and made himfelf ample amends, by the vaft booty he got, for all the penurious days he had fpent in their fervice. As to the *Germans*, they, for fome days, were difabled to proceed; and, even after they had been recruited, they were apprehenfive of fome ftratagem having been formed by the *Othmans*. At laft, after fpending fome days in repairing the bridge, they paffed the *Teiffe*, and took poffeffion of all that *Tekeli* had left in the *Othman* camp.

On the fourth day after the battle, *Moftafa* began his march towards *Belgrade* with his army. He had, upon his arrival at *Temefwar*, difpatched a black eunuch, to inform his mother of his being alive, and at the head of an army. This was a wife precaution, as it quelled all infurrections and intrigues about his fucceffion. To quiet the minds of the people, and to fave the glory of the *Othman* arms, it was publicly given out, that a detachment of the fultan's army, under the vizier, had been attacked by one hundred thoufand *Germans*; and, that he, and the janifaries with him, had been cut in pieces; but that the emperor, with the main body of the army, were not in the engagement. As it ufually happens, the more the vizier was hated, the more the fultan was beloved, by the foldiery; who called out again to be led to the *Chriftians*, that they might revenge the defeat of their fellow-fubjects. *Moftafa* accordingly marched at their head towards *Belgrade*, as far as *Alibunar*; where he invefted *Huffeyu Pafha* with the vizierfhip. He then proceeded to *Belgrade*; from whence, after a ftay of a few days, he returned with his army to *Adrianople*, about the end of the year 1698.

Succeffes of the Germans.   The truth is, the feafon was now too far advanced for either army to undertake any thing of importance. The *Germans*, on the thirtieth of *October*, detached fome troops, under general *Rabatin*, towards *Karanfebes* and *Vipalanka*. On the fourth of *November*, the fiege of the latter was formed; and, on the fixth, the place was taken by ftorm; and the garrifon, confifting of eight hundred men, was put to the fword. The *Germans* likewife took the caftles of *Doba* and *Mogla*, and fet fire to *Saray*, the capital of *Bofnia*. The late defeat of the *Othmans*, at the battle of *Zenta*, feems to have thrown their affairs into fuch confufion, that the *Turkifh* troops in that province applied to *Daltaban Moftafa Pafha*, who happened to be then in *Bofnia*; and who, by his great actions,

actions while he was governor of *Baghdad*, had acquired the highest military character in the empire; and forced him to take upon himself the command of the army: which he no sooner did, than he drove the *Germans* beyond the *Saave*, and retook from them twenty-four castles, or rather palankas, situated on that river.

The domestic revolutions that happened this year in *Muscovy* and *Poland*, prevented any remarkable actions in those parts; only the *Russians* employed the summer in fortifying *Asof* and *Luktikh*, without being interrupted by the *Othmans*. In the islands of the *Archipelago*, the infidels had a great number of officers called begs; each of whom commanded one or more vessels to cruize upon the *Venetians*, or the other *Christian* powers at war with the *Turks*. The most eminent of these begs was one *Mehemed*, who, at his own cost, maintained three gallies. This free-booter attempted *Tino*, one of those islands, but was repulsed by the *Venetian* governor; and, the *Turks* having several times declined to engage the *Venetian* fleet, the latter claimed a vast superiority over them this campaign.

Upon the return of *Mostafa* to *Constantinople*, he found his subjects, of all ranks, greatly dejected by the events of the preceding summer; nor, indeed, could he, with all his efforts, keep up his own spirits. Sometimes, like his predecessors, he went in disguise through the streets of his capital, that he might learn the sentiments of his people; but he heard nothing but the language of despondency. "God," said they, "has declared himself on the side of the infidels; "it is therefore impossible for the *Othmans* to defeat the *Germans*: and to shed more *Moslem* blood, in fighting against "God as well as man, is impious and fruitless" This was not only the language of the vulgar, but of the *Othman* ministry. The vizier himself had a pacific turn, and, being no enemy to wine, he sometimes opened himself, in that respect, to the *English* and *Dutch* ambassadors, who still attended the court, but thought it below the dignity of their masters to press the renewal of a mediation that had been so often rejected.

A negotiation for peace,

The *German* emperor, on the other hand, had still more powerful motives for peace than *Mostafa* had. The low state of the king of *Spain*'s health, and the daily expectation of his death, required all his attention to prevent the *French* from becoming masters of that monarchy; and the situation of his affairs in *Europe* became every day more critical. It is difficult to say, whether the *Othmans* or the *Austrians* were the most ridiculous and unremitting in their punctilios. Both equally desired peace, but neither would ask it of the other.

Alexander Maurokodatus, a *Greek*, who had been employed in the late ambassy to *Vienna*, then served as interpreter for

the

porte ; and, being a perſon of great ſagacity and penetration, he freely opened himſelf to the vizier upon that ſubject. This miniſter acknowledged, he did not expect that the imperialiſts would make any advances towards peace; and he knew that his maſter would ſuffer all extremities before he did. *Maurokordatus* aſked his leave to undertake the arduous employment, which he promiſed to effect without drawing any imputation upon the glory of the *Othman* throne ; adding, that he had ſufficient reaſon to believe, that the *Germans* were as much tired of the war as the *Othmans*. *Maurokordatus*, having brought the vizier to conſent to this, paid a viſit to the *Dutch* and *Engliſh* ambaſſadors, ſeemingly to deſire them to tranſmit to the *German* emperor his thanks for the civilities he had received at *Vienna* ; and, in the courſe of his converſation, pretending a great affection for the *Chriſtian* intereſt, he ſaid, that he would not diſcover to the *Othmans* the very great reaſons which he knew the *German* emperor had to wiſh for peace, leſt it ſhould make them advance in their demands ; but that, if they would leave the matter to him, he did not doubt but to finiſh it to the glory and ſatisfaction of his imperial majeſty. The ambaſſadors ſeeming not to diſlike the propoſal, *Maurokordatus* bound them to ſecrecy by an oath ; a very neceſſary precaution in his ſituation ; and the ambaſſadors recommended to him the taking the affair upon himſelf, as they knew that his imperial majeſty would diſavow all kinds of advances for peace that could be made in his name ; but that they believed he would not be averſe to liſten to an equal plan of accommodation. *Maurokordatus* made the vizier, who had heard him with raptures, believe that the ambaſſadors had expreſſed a greater readineſs for peace than they really had done, and he committed the whole to his conduct, with the moſt extravagant promiſes of reward, if he ſhould ſucceed in reſtoring tranquillity to the empire.

The artful agent managed with ſo much addreſs, that the material points of the treaty were ſettled, without either of the miniſters having met together ; and, at laſt, there being now no longer a neceſſity for ſtanding upon forms, the negotiation became public. *Feriole* had now ſucceeded *Chateauneuf* as ambaſſador from *France*. Under a notion of ſupporting his character to the full, he acted more like a madman than a miniſter (and indeed he fell ſoon after into a phrenzy) and ſpared neither promiſes, money, nor threats, to break off the negotiation ; pretending, that his maſter had made only a ſhort truce with the *German* emperor, and that, next ſpring, he would invade *Germany* with one hundred thouſand men. But the *Othmans* had been ſo long impoſed upon by *French* promiſes, that they were as much diſregarded as the the ambaſſador's perſon was hated, and the negotiation went on.

It

It did not, however, prevent both parties from making all the advantages they could in the field. The fultan marched to *Adrianople*, whence he fent the vizier with his army to *Hungary*; whilft he himfelf retired to a hunting-feat in the neighbourhood of *Adrianople*, there to wait the events both of the war and the negotiation. The vizier advanced to *Belgrade*, and the imperialifts to *Peterwaradin*. The *Ruffians* and *Poles* continued inactive on their refpective frontiers. The *Venetians* alone kept up the fpirit of the *Chriftian* confederacy, and beat the *Turkifh* fleet near *Mitylene*; but were repulfed in an attack they made upon *Stolaz*, in *Dalmatia*; where the *Turkifh* ferafkier was forced to abandon the fiege of *Cing*, upon the approach of the *Venetians*.

By this time, the negociations for peace were fo far advanced, that the plenipotentiaries were named by all parties. *which is concluded* Thofe for the *Othmans* were *Rami Mehemed Reis Effendi* and *Alexander Maurokordatus*; who, upon this occafion, were honoured with diftinguifhed titles and ranks. The imperial plenipotentiaries were count *Pettingen* and count *Schlik*. *Propius Bogdanowitz* acted for the czar; the waywod of *Pofnama* for the *Poles*, and *Ruzini* for the *Venetians*. Lord *Paget*, the *Englifh*, and *Collier*, the *Dutch*, ambaffadors, were the mediators. The place where they met lay near *Carlowitz*, between *Peterwaradin* and *Belgrade*; but their obftinate difputes about precedency had almoft prevented the conferences from taking place, till *Maurokordatus* contrived a round building, with different doors for the different treating powers, by which thofe ambaffadors were to enter all at the fame time, and each to take his feat, which was fo placed as to leave no room for any difpute about precedency; while the guards confifted of an equal number of *Turks* and *Germans*. This arrangement feems to have been the moft difficult part of the negociation, the material points having been fettled before-hand. The treaty was figned on the fifteenth of *January*, 1698—9.

The heads of it were, That a truce fhould take place between the porte and the *Germans* for twenty-five years; that *The terms* *Tranfylvania*, as held by *Mikhael Apaffi* and his predeceffors, fhould be ceded to the emperor; that the *Othmans* fhould remain in poffeffion of *Temefwar*; and, that the forts of *Lippa*, *Khonad*, *Karanfebes*, *Lugos*, *Herkomifia*, *Bech*, *Bechkerek*, and *Sabbia*, were to be difmantled, for the greater fecurity of *Temefwar*. The navigation of the *Teiffe* and *Maros* were to be free to both parties, and the emperor was to have poffeffion of the territory between the *Teiffe* and the *Danube*. A line drawn from the mouth of the *Maros* to that of the *Boffut*, where it falls into the *Saave*, was to be the boundary of the eaftern part of *Hungary* belonging to the *Germans*; and the *Saave* was to part the *Turkifh* from the imperial limits, on the fouth, till its junction with the *Unna*; and, that no new fortifications fhould be erected within thofe boundaries.

The

The terms made for the *Ruffians*, at firft, were no other than, that a truce fhould be concluded, for two years, upon the footing of *uti poffidetis*. This term was enlarged to thirty years, after fome further negotiation ; and it was agreed, that the *Ruffians* fhould remain mafters of *Afof*, and all that they had taken from the *Turks* on the *Nieper* ; but, that *Kafikermen*, being difmantled, fhould remain with the *Othmans*. The *Poles*, who, at firft, ftood upon very high terms, were to give back to the fultan feveral places in *Moldavia* ; but *Kaminiek*, *Podalia*, and *Ukrania*, were to be reftored to them. The *Venetians* were to remain in poffeffion of the *Morea* as far as the *Hexamilos* ; but *Lepanto*, *Prevefa*, and the caftle of *Romania*, were to return to the *Othmans* : *Leucade* was to remain with the *Venetians*, whofe tribute to the *Turks* in the *Archipelago* was to be difcontinued ; and the boundaries of their dominions were fixed in *Dalmatia*. Such, with a great number of leffer provifions, which are as immaterial as they proved afterwards ineffectual, was the famous treaty of *Carlowitz* ; in which the lord *Paget*, the *Britifh* ambaffador, obtained the greateft honour. We have omitted the incidents that retarded fo long the conclufion of the treaty ; and likewife the pompous formalities that preceded it : all which are minutely recorded by *Rycaut*, together with a copy of the treaty itfelf ; which lafted from the middle of *November*, 1698, to the time fpecified, during a bitter cold feafon.— We are now to return to the affairs of the *Turks* in other quarters.

In the beginning of the year 1698, the *Tartar* khan, as he is called, had a conference at *Conftantinople* with the fultan, mufti, and vizier, concerning the operations of the future campaign, in cafe the negociations for peace fhould not take place. They informed him, that their cavalry had fuffered but little in the battle of *Zenta* ; and, that they could have no difficulty in replacing the infantry in the enfuing campaign. The khan feemed, on this information, inclinable to continue the war. He knew that the *Ruffians* were embroiled with the *Swedes*, and that the koffaks and *Poles* were too much employed in the election of their king, to be formidable either to the *Turks* or *Tartars*. This conference being ended, the fultan applied himfelf, with great vigour, to repair, at once, his armies and his finances. He fent the proper officers to raife men and money in *Afia*, and gave orders for cafting a great quantity of heavy artillery at *Conftantinople* ; and *Mezzo Morto* was continued in his poft of high-admiral, with orders to take the firft opportunity of fighting the *Venetians* Notwithftanding thofe warlike appearances, the miniftry got over the khan of *Tartary* to their party, and gave themfelves very little trouble, in reality, concerning the *German* war ; but were greatly alarmed at the rebellion of the *Arabs* lying on the borders of *Perfia*, under one *Bebck Soleyman*. The *Othman* miniftry did not, it feems,

think

think themfelves able to quell this rebellion; and applied to the *Perfian* ambaffador, to defire that he would prevail with his mafter to furnifh a body of troops for fuppreffing the rebels. The ambaffador, at firft, declined to meddle in the affair, becaufe of *Soleyman's* great intereft among the *Arab* princes. The truth is, the fophi of *Perfia* himfelf wanted to make good fome claims he had upon the *Othmans*; and had received an ambaffador from the pope with diftinguifhed honours. Upon this, the fultan named an ambaffador to the court or *Ifpahan*; and orders were fent to the ferafkier of *Egypt*, who had likewife the government of *Baghdad* beftowed upon him, to endeavour to fubdue the rebels, who had taken poffeffion of *Baffora*.

It is obferved, in the hiftories of thofe times, that the *Othman* court never was fo fplendid as it then was. Almoft all the courts in *Europe* had their ambaffadors at *Conftantinople*, where the *Othmans* feemed to have laid afide their harfh, rigid manners, though they would not fuffer the *French* ambaffador to approach the fultan with his fword by his fide; upon which he returned to *France* without an audience. They were as magnificent in their prefents, entertainments, and equipages, as the *Chriftians* were; and as fond of pomp and fhew: though certain mifunderftandings happened occafionally on fettling the limits according to the treaty of *Carlowitz*.

The court of *France* juftified its ambaffador in refufing to fubmit to the *Turkifh* ceremonial of laying afide his fword; and he was fo foolifh as to build a gondola, for diverting himfelf on the water, every way like that made ufe of by the fultan for the fame purpofe. The *Othman* government, at firft, remonftrated upon this want of refpect; but *Feriole* refufing to make any alteration in his gondola, it was cut in pieces, and the *Turk* who had the care of it feverely baftinadoed.

But, notwithftanding all this fhew of magnificence and tranquility, the *Turkifh* government never was in a more difagreeable fituation than at that time. The common people could not bear with the pomp and fplendor of the court, after a peace which they confidered as being inglorious and detrimental to their empire. *Soleyman*, the *Arab* rebel, had obtained many advantages over the ferafkier of *Egypt*, and had cut in pieces a great caravan of pilgrims going to *Mecca*; and it now happened that he was fupported in his rebellion by the fophi of *Perfia*. Many other circumftances, and even fuperftition itfelf, contributed towards bringing the difcontents of the people to a head. Thofe difcontents firft broke out at *Belgrade*, where the garrifon, mutinied for want of pay, and forced the ferafkier to take refuge in the city; but the mutineers bringing cannon before the wall of the citadel, took it by ftorm, and put the ferafkier, and all who were with him, to death;

The

Splendor of the Othman court.

The vizier, who was well acquainted with the fultan's humour, endeavoured to ftop all difagreeable events from coming to his ears, by feverely punifhing thofe who prefumed to report them; and informed his mafter that the peace of his dominion was now fo well eftablifhed, he might fafely take fome repofe: upon which, *Moftafa*, having committed the reins of government to the vizier, retired to *Karifhtiran*, to amufe himfelf with hunting. This brought to the minds of the foldiery and populace, the fate of *Mohammed* IV. the fultan's father; and comparifons, very difadvantageous to the reigning fultan, were formed between him and his father. It was obferved, that the former, in the early part of his reign, had fupported the *Othman* glory with great luftre; and, that his paffion for hunting had alone undone him; that the prefent fultan, though young and vigorous, had difmembered the empire of its ftrongeft places and faireft territories: and their conclufion was, that, as he had the failings, fo he muft meet with the fate, of his father. Thofe murmurings coming to a great height, the vizier advifed the fultan to leave his retirement, and remove to *Adrianople*, where he remained all the winter of the year 1699.

Intelligence from *Tartary*.

Moftafa II. throughout his whole reign, was ill ferved either by his troops or his minifters. The difcontents of the former loft him the decifive battle of *Zenta*; and the attention of the latter was generally employed in concealing from him the true ftate of his affairs, and in lulling him into a fatal fecurity; in which they were but too much affifted by his mother, the fultana-valide, whom he moft tenderly loved, and who had an irrefiftible turn for pleafure and magnificence. Notwithftanding this, he appears to have been a prince of found judgment. While he remained at *Adrianople*, he received letters from the khan of *Tartary*, of whom he had a great opinion, informing him, that the whole fyftem of power in the north, and upon the *Black-fea*, was threatened with a total revolution by the ambition of the czar of *Mufcovy*, who had obliged his fubjects to conform themfelves to the *German* habit, and his foldiers to the *German* difcipline, who was building forts upon the *Don* and the *Nieper*, raifing numerous armies, and preparing fleets that would foon give him the maftery of the *Black-fea*. In fhort, that he had more to apprehend from this northern, than he had from the *German*, gyawr; and, that he would be in a condition to over-run all *Krim-Tartary*, if it was not fpeedily fupported, before the *Othmans* could march to its relief. This intelligence was quite the reverfe of what the fultan had received from his vizier, who was ftill negociating with the *Ruffian* minifters, and entertaining them with great magnificence. *Moftafa*, fufpecting the khan's intelligence to be true, refolved to employ a fecret agent, whom he could truft, to examine things with his own eyes; but made an unfortunate choice of *Kibeli Ogli*, who was the vizier's nephew.

phew. This person, afraid of undertaking a commission of such importance, without acquainting his uncle, discovered to him all that had passed between himself and the sultan. The vizier charged him to repair to *Krim-Tartary*, according to the sultan's orders ; but to make his report to him, the vizier, and receive his instructions as to the answer he was to make to the sultan. *Kibleli* performed his journey, and found the *Russians* in even greater forwardness, in building ships, fortifying places, raising armies, and in compleating every plan of greatness, than even the khan had represented them. All this, upon his return, he imparted to his uncle; who advised him to conceal from the sultan the disagreeable circumstances, and only acquaint him, that the *Russians* had indeed begun some works and fortifications, but that they had discontinued them, and were about to send an ambassador to renew their peace with the sublime porte; and that, upon the whole, the khan had aggravated matters only that he and his subjects might have an opportunity to gratify their favourite passion for plunder. *Kibleli* punctually obeyed his uncle, and appeared before the sultan in his travelling habit, as if just alighted from his journey. The sultan, exasperated at the khan, wrote him a letter full of reproaches; to which the khan sent an answer, by a trusty hand, in which he insisted upon the truth of his information, and recriminated upon *Kibleli*. The sultan, startled at the khan's firmness, sent for *Kibleli*, and, by threatening him with the rack, he got from him the truth. *Kibleli* was soon after put to death; and the vizier was disposted, his office being held vacant for forty days, till he was succeeded by *Dultaban Mostafa Pasha*, governor of *Baghdad*.

This *Dultaban* was an excellent officer, and had been employed against the *Arabs*, who were now very formidable. Being accused by one of the courtiers of favouring the enemy, a capigi was sent to take off his head; but, upon his arrival at *Dultaban*'s camp, he found that he had obtained a complete victory over the rebels; which rendered it dangerous for him to execute his commission. He therefore returned to the sultan, who approved of what he had done. *Dultaban*, in the mean time, receiving intelligence of his narrow escape, sent a large present to the avaricious mufti, who had been the sultan's tutor, and was then his favourite, and who offered to procure for *Dultaban* the viziership, as *Husseyu Pasha* had now drank away his senses; which he accordingly performed.

Dultaban made grand-vizier.

The new vizier pursued a system very different from those of his predecessors. He called for a state of the empire, on pretence of his being ignorant of its situation towards *Europe*; and perceiving that many towns beyond the *Saave*, which he himself had taken from the *Christians* while he was pasha of *Bosnia*, had been ceded by the *Othmans*, he exclaimed most bitterly against the authors of the late peace, as being bad gyawrs as the *Germans* themfelves. Above all, he inveighed againft the giving up *Kaminiek*, the glory and ftrength of the *German* empire on that fide, where a magnificent jami, or mofque, had been erected, as a trophy of the *Moflem* religion; but was now difgracefully yielded up to infidels, in exchange for three fmall places on the *Moldau*, full of *Chriftians*. In fhort, underftanding that a general war, on account of the *Spanifh* fucceffion, was like to break out all over *Europe*, he refolved to have no regard to the late peace; but to attack *Poland*, with the weaknefs of which he was beft acquainted.

who refolves to break the peace.

The *Poles*, ever fince the conclufion of the peace, had behaved with fo much circumfpection towards the *Othmans*, that the vizier could find no pretext for breaking with them, but that the *Othman* ambaffadors had exceeded their inftructions, and had acted againft the principles of their faith; and that they fhould atone, with their heads, for their treachery. Perceiving that the mufti's credit with the fultan ftood in his way, that high-prieft having confirmed the peace with his fetvah, and having always patronized the negotations of it, he refolved to difpatch him privately, and that it fhould be done by fome of his domeftics ftrangling him with a cord, at an entertainment in the vifier's own houfe; to which the mufti, out of a fhew of friendfhip, was to be invited. The vizier intrufted this fecret to his kyehaya-aga, who betrayed it to the mufti. The latter having fortified his party, efpecially by the karab-pafha, or chief butcher, one of the richeft fubjects in the empire, pretended ficknefs; and, when the ceremonial, which is very rigorous among the *Turkifh* minifters, brought the vizier to wait upon the mufti, to conduct him to his own houfe, he found him in bed; and, appearing to be very fick, he evaded going to the entertainment. The vizier retired; and the mufti fent for *Rami* and *Maurokordatus*, the negotiators of the late peace, whom he made acquainted with their danger; and it was agreed among tnem, that the vizier fhould be ruined. The mufti undertook to be the agent for his deftruction; and he informed the fultan, that *Dultaban* was raifing an army officered by his own dependants, with a view of breaking the peace and depofing his imperial majefty. The credulous fultan believed him; loaded *Dultaban* with reproaches; and, without fuffering him to fpeak in his own defence, commanded

but is put to death.

him to be put to death. The vizier begged hard for a private audience of the fultan, to whom he faid he had fomewhat very particular to impart; but was hurried to the place of execution, where the fecret died with him, and where he reproached the fultan with his injuftice and ingratitude.

Dultaban was fucceeded in the vizierfhip by *Rami*. He was of low original, but had raifed himfelf by the quicknefs of his parts, his fkill in poetry and mufic; but, above all, by his fine hand of writing; a quality which is in great efteem

among

among the *Turks* and *Arabs*. He had been only nominally joined with *Maurokordatus* in the late treaty. His preferment was very difagreeable to the clergy, and all ranks of people at *Conftantinople*; whilft *Dultaban's* memory was revered. The mufti was both hated and envied, for his avarice and for filling the chief pofts of the empire with his own relations and children, amongft whom every thing was venal. He was likewife accufed of having perfuaded the fultan to retire to *Adrianople*, and to abandon the capital of his empire; with various other charges.

Kioprili Abdollah Pafha, the fon of the great *Kioprili*, who was killed in the battle of *Salankemen*, was then kaymakan of *Conftantinople*, though but a youth of eighteen, and had married the mufti's daughter. On a certain day, after the janifaries had received their pay, the jebeji, who are the next corps, applied for their pay likewife; and, upon *Kioprili* putting them off with fome excufes, about forty of them behaved fo mutinoufly, that he ordered them to be apprehended and put to death. Matters being ripe for a revolt all over *Conftantinople*, the jebeji made refiftance, and were refcued by their fellow-foldiers. Upon their return to their quarters, they were encouraged by *Karakafh Mehemed*, a bold demagogue, to depofe young *Kioprili*, and to attempt a change of government. Next day, being joined by the janifaries and great numbers of the citizens, they met at the atmeydan, or the hippodrome, near the church of St. *Sophia*, and bound themfelves, by oath, to deftroy the mufti, vizier, and the other enemies of the republic, or to perifh in the attempt. *Kioprili*, hearing of his danger, efcaped out of his palace by a back-door; and one *Firari*, after ftrangling *Kapigi Pafha*, who had been fent to take off *Firari's* head, was chofen kaymakan by the infurgents. The mufti was depofed at the fame time; and *Kiazibi*, who had been mufti in the reign of *Mohammed* IV. was chofen mufti in his room; and one *Dorojan Pafha* was made grand-vizier. In fhort, the infurgents filled up all the chief pofts of the empire with officers of their own chufing.

To infure the fuccefs of their defigns, they fhut the gates of *Conftantinople*, and armed themfelves from the public magazines. By thofe precautions, the fultan was kept ignorant, for fome time, of their tranfactions; but, on the eighth day of the infurrection, *Moftafa Effendi*, principal fecretary of ftate, appeared before the gates of *Conftantinople*, as a meffenger from the fultan, to enquire into the caufe of the infurrection, and to promife redrefs of all grievances. The people treated the fecretary as a fpy, and had almoft beaten him to death. It was now dangerous for them to ftop; and, being fifty thoufand ftrong, they fet out for *Adrianople*, which they threatened to deftroy if they met with any refiftance from the inhabitants.

An infurrection at Conftantinople.

Y 2

When

When they had marched as far as *Hapsa*, a town in the neighbourhood of that city, they affected more moderation, and sent private notice to the inhabitants of *Adrianople*, not to oppose them in arms, because they were come to redress public grievances, and not to shed the blood of *Othmans*. They dispatched, at the same time, a messenger to inform the sultan, that he must give up his wicked minister to the justice of his country; and, that they were resolved to repel force by force. The sultan, not intimidated by this insolent message, gave his vizier the command of his army against the rebels, who were declared gyawrs by a fetvah of the mufti. When the two armies were near each other, *Nakib Effendi*, the rebel mufti, pulling out a *Koran*, held it up to the imperial troops; whom he conjured, by all the ties of blood and religion, not to oppose the insurgents, who were come only to vindicate the faith, laws, and constitution of the empire, and to bring public offenders to justice. When his speech was finished, the imperial troops saluted the insurgents as their friends and brethren, and promised to join with them in all their attempts.

The rebels march to *Adrianople*, It was with difficulty that, on this occasion, the vizier escaped in disguise, with two servants, to *Varna*; from whence he reached *Constantinople*, where he concealed himself in the suburbs. The fate of the mufti, and his family, was more terrible. The sultan would have saved him if possible, and had sent him away, under a guard, which had orders to bring him back if necessary. The rebels were then encamped within a mile of *Adrianople*, at a place called *Solak*; from whence they dispatched a messenger, to demand the heads of the mufti and vizier, those of the mufti's two sons, and that of *Maurokordatus*. The sultan, finding them intractable, ordered the mufti to be brought back, and delivered him up, with his two sons, into the hands of the rebels, who put him to death with the most excrutiating torments, which they inflicted upon him to force a discovery of his treasures; but, being a man of great resolution, he suffered all their tortures, and died without revealing them.

where they depose the sultan. The sultan, being now abandoned by all his subjects, sent the seal of the viziership to *Dorojan*, the rebel vizier, and confirmed all the other officers they had nominated in their posts; promising, at the same time, to grant all their demands, and to deliver up the late vizier, with *Maurokordatus*, as soon as they could be taken. This condescension served only to encrease the insolence of the rebels; and they privately dispatched an express to *Ahmed*, the sultan's brother, offering, if he would repair to their camp, to proclaim him emperor. The sultan intercepted this dispatch; and the few friends he still had about his person, advised him to put his brother to death; but, unwilling to commit such barbarity, he came to a resolution of resigning the empire.

With

With this view he went to *Ahmed*'s apartment, and, embracing him with great affection, gave him the appellation of fultan, and, requefting the fame liberty to be allowed him that he, *Ahmed*, had enjoyed under his reign, informed him that he was come to raife him to the throne. " But," continued he, " remember, that, however juft your title may be to " the *Othman* throne, you afcended it by means of traitors, " whom, if they are not cut off, will furprize you in the " fame manner as they have done me." Having finifhed his fpeech, he retired to his brother's apartment, where, it is faid, he died of melancholy, fix months after his abdication, having reigned eight years and fome months.

The chief failing of *Moftafa* II. appears to have been his love of favourites, efpecially the mufti. But, if we examine his hiftory by facts, which alone ought to take place in fuch cafes, he, perhaps, may appear not to be fo blameable as he has been reprefented by *Othman* writers. The want of difcipline among his troops, was evidently, as we have already feen, the occafion of his being defeated at *Zanta*. They were, in no refpect, comparable to thofe of the *Germans*, who, with all the advantages on their fide, of arms, artillery and difcipline, were commanded by, perhaps, the greateft general of his age. *Moftafa* feems to have been fenfible of his inferiority in thofe refpects, and thought it eligible to facrifice part of his dominions rather than rifque the whole; which it is more than probable he muft have been ftripped of, had he refufed to make peace at the time he did it. This peace was, by his fubjects, confidered as being difhonourable; but *Moftafa*, from an honeft principle, was refolved to maintain it: and, if we look even into the *Turkifh* accounts of *Dultalor*'s conduct, we muft conclude, if they are true, it was highly blameable, if not treafonable. In fhort, it is plain, through the whole of *Moftafa*'s cataftrophe, that he fell a victim to his good faith and the mutinous difpofition of the *Othmans*, who judge of every thing by events. His greateft enemies have acknowledged, that he was a prince naturally juft and humane; that his judgment was folid; his inclinations generous, without profufion; and the manner in which he conducted the peace of *Carlowitz* fhews him to have had great application and knowledge of bufinefs. His perfon, which was of a middle fize, was well fhaped, his complexion was fair, and his face handfome. He excelled in archery and horfemanfhip, and was ftrict to all the duties of his religion. So little do the *Europeans* know of *Turkifh* affairs, that they know not whether *Moftafa* II left any fons. Some fay that he left three; but others pretend that he was fo fond of *Ibrahim*, the fon of his uncle *Ahmed*, that he intended to have made him his fucceffor. Notwithftanding this, it feems to be certain, that the fultan *Mohammed*, who fucceeded his brother *Ahmed* III. was one of *Moftafa*'s fons.

Y 3

The

love of Moftafa II.

his hiftory by facts

The Reign of Ahmed III.

Accession of Ahmed III. THE chief transactions of the *Turkish* history, during this reign, will fall under the history of the *European* states, or are to be found in the preceding parts of this work. We shall, however, for the sake of order, continue the great lines of it, as near as we can, to the present times. *Ahmed* III. succeeded his brother in the *Othman* throne in 1703. As he was a prince of great understanding, he complied so far with the general voice, that he dismissed from his court his own mother, who was looked upon to be the protectress of the mufti in the late reign, and the main spring of all its unpopular measures. We shall have an opportunity, in the histories of *Russia* and *Sweden*, to give an account of the generous reception that *Ahmed* gave to *Charles* XII. king of *Sweden*, after the battle of *Pultowa*; and of the success of his **War with** arms against the czar *Peter* of *Russia*. It is sufficient here to **Russia,** say, that, in the year 1711, war having been, at the instigation of *Charles* XII. of *Sweden*, declared against the *Russians*, the grand-vizier passed the *Danube* with the *Othman* troops, and hemmed in the czar, who commanded his own army, in such a manner, upon the banks of the river *Pruth*, that all the *Russians* must have either been cut in pieces, or starved into a surrender, had not the great address of the famous *Catharine*, afterwards empress of *Russia*, prevailed with the vizier to agree to a peace. It has been the general opinion, that this cost the vizier his head; but later, and better, authorities inform us, that he only was dismissed from the viziership, and sent to govern a province. It is certain that the peace concluded by the vizier was ratified by the sultan; and by it the *Russians* gave up *Asoph*, and demolished all the forts that gave offence to the *Othmans*.

and Germany. After this, great preparations for war were made by the porte, without any of the powers of *Europe* knowing their destination. The *Christian* states, however, were so much alarmed, that they formed alliances to stand by one another in behalf of whatever power the storm should fall upon. It happened to be directed against the *Morea*; and, in 1715, war was declared against the *Turks* by the *Venetians*. The grand-vizier assembled the *Othman* army near the isthmus of *Corinth*, the only pass by which the *Morea* can be attacked by land. The chief officer under him was *Topal Osman*, a man of such eminent virtues, that the bare mention of him is not sufficient in this place. When young, he had been charged, by the sultan, with a commission to the pasha of *Cairo*; but, in his voyage thither, he had the misfortune to be taken by a *Spanish* privateer, who carried him to *Malta*, where he was ransomed by one *Arnaud*, a *Frenchman*, who was an entire stranger to *Topal*, but was struck with the noble

ble addrefs and manly affurance he difcovered, in his manner of entreating *Arnaud* to ranfom him; which this *Frenchman* did, at the rate of three hundred pounds fterling. *Topal* having thus recovered his liberty, repaid *Arnaud* with vaft generofity, and made him fome valuable prefents befides. He then proceeded to *Cairo*, where he executed the commiffion he had been charged with by the fultan; and, returning to *Conflantinople*, where he was well received by his mafter, he was the firft who brought to that capital the news of his having been a captive.

The vizier charged *Topal* with a command to force the pafs of *Corinth*; which he not only did, but took that city itfelf by ftorm: and he was rewarded by being made a pafha of two tails. It is well known that this important blow was followed by the *Othmans* reducing all the *Morea*, of which *Topal* was made the governor. To counterballance this conqueft, war having been proclaimed between the *Turks* and the *Germans*, *Ahmed*, in the year 1716, fent an army into *Hungary*, confifting of near two hundred thoufand men, who entrenched themfelves near *Carlowitz*. Prince *Eugene* commanded the confederates, and, though his army did not amount to above fixty thoufand men, he attacked them on the fifth of *Auguft*, and defeated them with a moft prodigious flaughter. The *Turks*, at firft, defended themfelves very bravely; but there was no refifting the *German* veterans, who, upon this occafion, made an immenfe booty. They took all the *Turkifh* artillery, confifting of one hundred and feventy pieces of cannon, tents, baggage, and ammunition, and their military cheft, which contained five millions of florins in fpecie. The plunder of the grand-vizier's tent amounted to above three hundred thoufand florins; and two hundred of his women, from fourteen to twenty-fix years of age, fell into the hands of the victors. In this battle, the grand-vizier himfelf, and ten pafhas, were killed. Prince *Eugene*, after this, invefted *Temefwar*. On the firft of *September*, he opened the trenches againft it; and it was furrendered on the fourteenth of *October*, after being in poffeffion of the *Othmans* for one hundred and fixty-four years.

Great defeat of the *Turks* at *Carlowitz*,

It was thought that this blow would have rendered the *Turks* quiet for the following year, the campaign of which prince *Eugene* intended to open with the fiege of *Belgrade*. To the amazement of all *Europe*, the *Turks* affembled a more numerous, and better appointed army than they had loft the year before. The prince marched one part of his army over the *Teiffe* by a bridge of boats, and took poft on the oppofite fide of the *Danube*, in fight of *Belgrade*. The *Othmans* were fo much ftruck with the boldnefs of this paffage, that they fled in confufion; which gave an opportunity to the other part of the imperial army, to pafs the *Danube* likewife upon a bridge of boats.

Prince

Prince *Eugene*, fenfible that the *Turks* would attempt to relieve the city, loft no time in drawing lines of circumvallation and contravallation from the *Saave* to the *Danube*; and rendered his camp fo ftrong, that, when the town was invefted, it feemed as if one fortrefs was befieging another. The *Turks* recovered their confternation; and it has been faid, that they never had in the field a better army than the grand-vizier, who was commanded to relieve *Belgrade* at all events, brought againft the imperialifts on this occafion. Prince *Eugene's* difpofitions were fo admirable, that, though the *Othman* army exceeded in ftrength what he had conceived, he continued his attacks, and, at the fame time, defended his camp; which the *Turks* found to be fo ftrong, that they were obliged to open trenches to approach the *German* lines: and thereby two fieges may be faid to have been carried on at once. The imperialifts were fhut up, on one fide, between two great rivers; on the other, by *Belgrade*, one of the ftrongeft fortrefles in *Europe*; and by the *Othman* camp, which, as ufual, was well fortified. The prince knew, in this fituation, the prodigious advantage which attends an attack; and, inftead of being attacked, he led his army out of their lines againft the enemy. This intrepidity did not, at firft, daunt the *Turks*, who made a moft gallant refiftance; but all was in vain; for, though they kept up the hotteft fire that ever was known to come from the *Othmans*, they were compleatly defeated. The *Germans* took, in this battle, one hundred and thirty-one brafs, befides other cannon, thirty-feven mortars, fifty-two pair of colours, and nine horfe-tails, or ftandards. Such was the difcipline of the *Germans*, that not one of them entered the *Othman* camp to plunder, till the general gave them permiffion, after rallying his army, and putting it in order. The lofs of the *Germans*, efpecially of the cavalry, in this battle, was very confidera-

ble; but, two days after, the important city of *Belgrade* furrendered to the *Germans* by capitulation. By an exact lift of the artillery taken in the town and the battle, it appears that, in both, the *Othmans* loft four hundred and fifty-fix brafs cannon, two hundred and nine of iron, and one hundred and three brafs mortars. The garrifon was computed to confift of twenty thoufand foldiers, and above fixty thoufand *Turks* marched out of the place by capitulation.

Thofe prodigious blows made fuch an impreffion upon *Ahmed*, that he fet on foot a negotiation for peace; which was accordingly concluded at *Paffarowitz*, in 1718; and, by that treaty, the imperialifts were left in poffeffion of all they had taken. The difputes between *Ahmed* and *Thomas Kouli Khan*, and the complete victory gained by the latter over the *Othman* army near *Tauris*, have been already mentioned; as alfo that the *Perfians* not only retook all that the *Turks* held in their dominions, but carried their arms into thofe of

Ahmed

Ahmed. The latter being then at peace with the *Christians,* recalled his forces from *Europe,* and, paffing the *Bofphorus* with his whole court, he took up a camp at *Scutari,* with an intention to march to *Aleppo,* to oppofe the progrefs of the *Perfians.* But, by this time, the *Turks,* through the immenfe lefes they had fuftained, were difgufted with the fultan; and he, to fave himfelf, threw all the mifcarriages of the empire upon the great officers of ftate. This did not quiet the populace; for, on the twenty-eighth of *September,* 1730, a fellow, one of the meaneft of the people, erected, in one of the public ftreets of *Conftantinople,* a rent-ftandard; to which, with a loud voice, he invited all good *Moflems* to repair. In the morning, this fellow's following became fo formidable, that the fultan retired to *Conftantinople*; and the janifaries, joining in the tumult, demanded the heads of the grand-vizier, the reis-effendi, and the captain-pafha, who were accordingly put to death. Even this compliance could not avert the fate of the fultan, who was depofed from his throne; and *Mohammed,* the fon of *Moftafa* II. was taken out of prifon that he might fill it.

Ahmed furvived his depofition five years. He was a magnanimous, virtuous prince, and would have made a moft glorious figure, had he reigned over any other people than the *Turks.* He was fo great a lover of learning, that he introduced, contrary to the *Othman* maxims, the art of printing into *Conftantinople*; which was fo difagreeable to thofe barbarians, that it is faid to have been one of the principal caufes of his depofition.

The Reign of Mohammed V.

THIS prince being advanced from a prifon to the throne, at firft diftinguifhed *Patrona Alli,* the perfon who had been the principal engine of his exaltation, with exemplary honours; which ferved only to encreafe the fellow's infolence fo much, that, making every day frefh demands, the fultan found himfelf, at laft, under a neceffity to put him to death. Three grand-viziers had been difpofted in a fhort time; but, in *September,* 1731, *Topal Ofman* was called from the beglerbegfhip of *Romania,* one of the greateft governments of the *Turkifh* empire, to fill that high ftation. After he arrived at *Conftantinople,* he defired the *French* ambaffador to write to *Malta,* to acquaint his benefactor *Arnaud* with his promotion, and to invite him to come to *Conftantinople,* that he might give him farther proofs of his gratitude. *Arnaud,* who was then feventy-two years of age, when he came to *Conftantinople,* brought with him his fon, and, amongft other prefents, twelve *Turks* whom he had ranfomed from

slavery.

[marginal notes:] Acceffion of Mohammed V. Account of Topal Ofman.

flavery. The vizier received him with great form, in preſence of all the high officers of ſtate, to whom, in a moſt pathetic ſpeech, he related *Arnaud*'s generous treatment, and they ſtood aſtoniſhed that ſuch noble ſentiments ſhould reſide in the breaſt of an infidel. *Topal* diſtributed the preſents which *Arnaud* brought amongſt the ſultan, the ſultana mother, and the kiſler-aga; but told *Arnaud* in private, that ſo many eyes were upon him, he could not act as he deſired; and, "that a paſha is lord and maſter in his own province, but that a grand-vizier at *Conſtantinople* has a maſter." Notwithſtanding this reaſon, he made *Arnaud* ſeveral very generous preſents; and indulged him in ſome privileges of trade which brought him in a conſiderable profit.

The morals of the *Othmans*, at this time, were degenerated beyond all conception, to the diſregard, not only of civil and military diſcipline, but of induſtry and manufactures of all kinds; ſo that the common people could not be ſupplied even with the neceſſaries of life. *Topal* applied himſelf, with vaſt aſſiduity and fortitude, to reform the people; and had amazing ſucceſs: but the ſeverities he was obliged to inflict, formed a party at court againſt him, and his diſmiſſion was reſolved on. This being ſignified to him by order of the ſultan, he repaired in perſon to court, and delivered up the ſeals of his office. Upon his returning home, perceiving his friends to be diſconſolate, he thanked God for his diſmiſſion, as being one of the moſt favourable circumſtances of his life. But, though *Topal* was diſmiſſed, he was not diſgraced. As he had always taken the opinion of the mufti, before he put any one to death, his enemies could fix nothing upon his conduct; and the ſultan expreſſed ſo high an eſteem for his perſon, that he appointed him to be paſha of *Trebeſond*; but he detained his ſon at *Conſtantinople*, and declared that he would take care of his fortune. In a few days, the ſon preſented to the ſultan the preſent which his father had intended to make him at the bayram; which was a horſe with furniture to the value of fifty thouſand crowns. Soon after, the father was ordered to take upon himſelf the command of the army that was to act upon the frontiers of *Perſia*. He diſcharged his duty as a general with great abilities; but he ſunk under the genius of *Thamas Kouli Khan*. Upon his death, which ſhall be mentioned hereafter, though the ſultan raiſed his ſon to the high poſt of beglerbeg of *Romania*, yet he had the meanneſs to ſtrip him of all his father's perſonal eſtate.

Though every thing was now quiet on the ſide of *Europe*, yet that was far from being the caſe in *Aſia*; where the *Perſians*, taking advantage of the tumults that had been raiſed at *Conſtantinople*, and the defeat of the *Turks* near *Tauris*, attacked the *Othman* empire in 1730; but, by the good conduct of the *Turkiſh* ſeraſkier, who commanded againſt them, they were brought to terms of accommodation. In the year 1734,

Thamas

Thamas Kouli Khan being then absolute in *Persia*, resolved to break with the *Turks*, in the manner we have already dedescribed. It is sufficient here to say, that, among the other pretexts for declaring war, one was, that the treaty had been extorted by the *Turks* ; and he demanded, in the name of the infant sophi of *Persia*, that all the places ceded by that peace, should be given up. The answer of the porte being as haughty as the demand of the *Persian*, hostilities commenced ; and *Kouli Khan* not only recovered all the provinces and places ceded by the late treaty, but great part of the antient dominions of *Persia*. *Topal Osman* was sent to command against him with eighty thousand men. By this time, *Kouli Khan* had formed the siege of *Baghdad* itself. *Topal Osman* had orders to risk all to raise the siege ; which he did, after fighting a bloody battle with *Kouli Khan*, who was at the head of seventy thousand men, each army losing thirty thousand. The *Turkish* general having collected together an army of one hundred thousand men, again opposed *Kouli Khan*, who had made an irruption into another part of the *Othman* dominions ; in which the latter was again defeated, on the twenty-fifth of *October* ; and the *Turks*, in general, imagined, that, in this battle, *Kouli Khan* was killed ; but, before the end of the campaign, some accounts say the very next day, he attacked *Topal Osman*'s army with so much intrepidity, that the *Othmans* were totally routed, with the loss of forty thousand men and their excellent com- who is mander, besides their military chest and all their baggage. It killed in was happy for the *Turks*, that the state of affairs in *Persia* the war was too unsettled for him to pursue this blow that year ; but with *Per-* he afterwards defeated an army of one hundred and sixty *sia.* thousand *Othmans*, commanded by *Kioprili*,. who is said to have left half that number dead on the field ; and then the conqueror retook the important city of *Erivan*, which completed the conquest of all the *Persian* dominions that had been dismembered by the *Turks*.

That great general and politician having become sophi of *Persia*, by the death of the infant above-mentioned, thought that he could not do better than to make peace with the *Turks*, upon condition of their guarantying his title, and that of his family, to the throne of *Persia*, and their solemnly recognizing him as sophi. Though he was then in the height of a prosperous war, he found means to insinuate to the porte, that they might have peace, provided those points were settled as preliminaries. He likewise hinted, that he would abolish, amongst his own subjects, many of those religious distinctions which had so long kept them and the *Turks* at irreconcileable variance. Those condescensions were more than sufficient to induce the *Turks* to enter into the negotiation ; which was concluded at *Constantinople*, in *September*, 1736, on the following conditions: That the sultan should formally acknowledge *Thamas Kouli Khan*'s right to

the

the throne of *Perſia*, and guaranty his and his family's ſucceſſion to the ſame ; that the *Perſians* ſhall have liberty to viſit the tomb of *Mohammed*; that priſoners ſhould be delivered up on both ſides ; and, to prevent the uſe of the diſagreeable word " ceſſion," it was agreed, in general, that the limits of the two empires ſhould be fixed as in the time of *Morad* I.

War with the porte, Ruſſia, and Germany
Both the emperor and the czarina had, at that time, ſome apprehenſion from the preparations of the *Turks* ; and had entered into engagements to aſſiſt each other, which afterwards ended in an offenſive and defenſive alliance ; and each power was to furniſh the other with forty thouſand men. Both of them had depended greatly upon the diverſion which they expected would be given to the *Othmans* by *Thamas Kouli Khan* , but the late treaty, concluded at *Conſtantinople*, put an end to all expectations of that kind. A congreſs had been opened at *Nemerow*, in *Poland*, for accommodating the differences between the czarina and the porte, on account of the injuries her ſubjects had ſuffered from the *Tartars* ; but thoſe conferences proving ineffectual, the emperor ordered his miniſter at the porte to declare, that, if ſatisfaction was not given to his ſiſter, the czarina, he would join her in war againſt the ſultan. The porte was ſurprized at this declaration, becauſe, upon the expiration of the treaty of *Paſſarowitz*, the imperial miniſter at the porte had declared his maſter's readineſs to renew the ſame. It muſt be acknowledged, that, on this occaſion, the good faith of the emperor towards the *Othmans* was very queſtionable. The ſultan's miniſters had received, from the *French*, information of the engagements entered into between the emperor and the czarina ; and ſeveral divans had been held upon the expediency of declaring war againſt the *Germans* ; and the *French* influence at the porte was ſo ſtrong, that it was generally believed the deciſion would have been in the affirmative. This being communicated by the *Dutch* and *Britiſh* ambaſſadors to their reſpective principals, they received orders to counteract the *French* ; which they did ſo ſucceſsfully, that the porte reſolved to continue the pacific ſyſtem ; and his *Britannic* majeſty actually received the emperor's thanks on that account. It is therefore no wonder if the *Othman* miniſtry received the imperial declaration with great indignation.

They treated it with indifference at the ſame time, but proceeded in the moſt vigorous preparations for war. A grand divan being held, it was there reſolved to act offenſively on the ſide of *Germany*, and defenſively only on that of *Ruſſia*. On the other hand, the allies agreed upon the operations of the war ; that the imperialiſts, under count *Seckendorf*, ſhould attack *Widin*, in *Servia* ; and that the *Ruſſians*, under count *Munich*, ſhould penetrate into the *Ukraine*, and beſiege *Oczakow*, on the *Boriſthenes*, the bulwark of the *Turkiſh* frontiers on that ſide, and garriſoned by twenty thouſand of the braveſt of the *Othman* troops ; while count *Laſcy*, another

Ruſſian

Ruffian general, fhould penetrate, with another army, into the *Krim*; by which the *Ruffians* would become mafters of all the *Black-Sea*.

Thofe latter operations were carried o with vigour and proportionable fuccefs. Though *Oczakow*, befides its ftrong garrifon, was defended by eighteen gallies, yet the attacks of *Munich* were conducted with fo much judgment and intrepidity, that the place muft have been taken by ftorm, had it not capitulated. In this fiege, the famous field-marfhal *Keith*, the fame who was afterwards killed in the fervice of the king of *Pruffia*, bore a diftinguifhed part. But the acquifition coft the *Ruffians* fo many men, that *Munich* was difabled from farther purfuing his conquefts that campaign. In the mean while, *Lacy* had marched towards *Precop*, and took up his winter-quarters in the *Krim*. But matters were far from being fo fuccefsful on the part of the *Germans*. *The Ruffians take Oczakow.*

The duke of *Lorrain*, who that year fucceeded to the dutchy of *Tufcany*, had the nominal command of the imperial troops; but the acting general was count *Seckendorf*, an old man, and a proteftant; and, being a favourite of the diet of the empire, to which the emperor had applied for affiftance, this command was, out of compliment to that body, conferred upon him. We have already mentioned, that *Seckendorf* was firft to attack *Widin*. This he attempted, but found it impracticable to fucceed without the affiftance of a body of fhips upon the *Danube*; and therefore he fuddenly fell upon *Niffa*, which he took, though it was then thought to be one of the ftrongeft forts upon the *Turkifh* frontiers: but this was the only fuccefsful operation of the campaign. *Seckendorf*, who never had been an enterprizing general, befides the caution incident to old age, had the misfortune of being hated by the *Roman-catholics* and jefuits, who had the chief direction of the imperial court; and therefore he was never properly fupplied with either men, artillery, or money. *Unfortunate campaign of the imperialifts.*

Having reduced *Niffa*, he formed the blockade of *Widin*; but the heats, and the unwholefome dampnefs of the foil, deftroyed vaft numbers of his troops; and he was forced to abandon the blockade with fome lofs from the enemy. The baron *de Raunach*, another imperial general, by this time, had penetrated, with fix thoufand men, into *Croatia*, where he was entirely defeated; as was the prince of *Saxhilburghaufen*, who had formed the fiege of *Bagnalac* with fourteen thoufand men, moft of whom were cut off by a fuperior body of *Turks*, who attacked the pofts of the imperialifts upon the *Danube*, took the fort of *Padudil*, and burnt the town of *Ilas*, in *Walachia*; befides plundering the country. But the greateft blow the imperialifts met with, was the retaking *Niffa*; which was furrendered to the *Turks* by general *Doxat*, who was tried by a council of war, and loft his head on that account;

account; though it was thought, by those who were best informed, that the misfortune was owing to the imperial court itself not having sufficiently provided him with the means of defence. As to count *Seckendorf*, he was accused of having wasted a fine army in marches and countermarches, without doing any thing of importance but the taking of *Nissa*, which had been as suddenly retaken. He was therefore sent for home, to give an account of his conduct. A court-martial was appointed to try him; and it was with difficulty that he escaped with life, after long and severe imprisonment.

Notwithstanding the *Turks* were thus successful in *Hungary, Bosnia*, and *Servia*, yet they seemed, all the while, willing to renew the conferences for peace; and those of *Nemerow* were again opened: but they proved ineffectual by the *Russians* absolutely refusing to part with the possession of *Asoph* and *Oczakow*. Next year, the diet of the empire granted a subsidy of fifty *Roman* months to the emperor, that he might take the field the more early; but this liberality produced little effect. *Ragotski*, waywod of *Transylvania*, declared himself against the house of *Austria*, and put himself under the protection of the sultan with a considerable army; for which he was proclaimed a rebel by the court of *Vienna*. The *Turks* took the field more early than the imperialists, and, after reducing the forts of *Usitza* and *Meadia*, they formed the siege of *Orsova*; but abandoned it upon the approach of the grand-duke of *Tuscany* and count *Konigseg*. Being afterwards reinforced, they attacked the imperialists, and were repulsed; but the latter not being able to stand their ground, repassed the *Danube*.

Ragotski's terms with the Turks, Those disgraces were not owing so much to the incapacity or misconduct of the imperial generals, as to the indigence and mismanagement of their court; who either would not, or could not, supply their wants. This brought them into infinite contempt, and the porte concluded a treaty with prince *Ragotski*; by which he was to be acknowledged free sovereign of *Hungary* and *Transylvania*; that his *Christian* subjects should have free exercise of their religion all over the *Othman* empire; that the election of his successors should be free, and only directed by the laws of the country; but that both he and they were to be ready, with a large body of men, to assist the *Turks*, in case of war with the *Germans*. Sir *Everard Fawkner* and *Villeneuf* were then residing at the porte, on the part of their *Britannic* and most *Christian* majesties, in the quality of mediators; and therefore refused to receive a copy of this treaty: but *Calkoen*, the *Dutch* ambassador, accepted of it when tendered by *Ragotski's* minister; for which he was severely reprimanded by his masters.

The *Turks* then attacked *Meadia*; which, though untenable, made a gallant resistance, and repulsed the besiegers, till the

the governor received an order from *Vienna* to deliver up the place, to avoid being put to the fword with all the garrifon. The imperial army, at this time, had not taken the field; and the *Turks* had laid fiege to *Orfova*.

On the twenty-third of *June*, the imperial army, being who are now affembled, attacked the *Turks* near *Meadia*, and routed defeated. them after a fharp difpute. Upon this, *Meadia* furrendered to the imperialifts on the firft fummons, and the *Turks* raifed the fiege of *Orfova*, leaving behind them thirty pieces of cannon, with other warlike ftores and large quantities of provifons, which they are faid to have poifoned. The grand-duke of *Tufcany* narrowly efcaped being taken or killed in the above battle. The *Othmans* broke the left wing and center of his army, and penetrated to his tent, where they cut off his furgeon's head.

This, and fome other, advantages, rendered the imperial court fo inhuman, that one colonel *Heifrich* was fent to *Almas*, with a detachment of the duke of *Tufcany's* regiment of foot, with orders to butcher all the inhabitants, without regard to age, fex, or other diftinction, for having favoured the *Othmans*. Notwithftanding their boafted victories, the *Auftrians* were obliged to march back towards the *Danube*; upon which the *Turks* retook *Meadia*, and a grand army laid fiege to *Orfova*.

By this time, the court of *Peterfburgh*, fenfible of the *Auftrian* inability to fulfil their engagements, hinted to *Jahya*, the ferafkier of *Oczakow*, who was a prifoner in their camp, that they would not be averfe to treat of peace. The ferafkier, upon this, fent a meffenger to the grand-vizier for full powers to treat. "Tell *Jahya*," anfwered that minifter, "that his fublime highnefs is not accuftomed to treat of "peace by means of flaves or prifoners."

On the twenty-fixth of *July*, general *Lacy* forced the *Lacy's* fucamazing lines of *Precop*, which were defended by forty cefs in the thoufand *Turks* and *Tartars*, commanded by *Soltan Galga*. *Krim*. He then took the fortrefs itfelf, in which he found eighty brafs cannon; the garrifon, confifting of two thoufand men, furrendering themfelves, with their commander, prifoners of war. Soon after, his van-guard, which was formed of *Ukraine* coffaks, was in danger of being cut off by thirty thoufand *Turks*, moft of them fpahis; but, being fupported by fome battalions of regulars, the *Othmans* were, at laft, defeated, with the lofs of above three thoufand men.

Count *Munich* had now paffed the *Bog*, in his march to *Munich's* *Bender*, but was furrounded, near that river, by a numerous campaign, body of *Turks*; whom he defeated after an engagement of five hours. In like manner, he was oppofed by another body on the banks of the *Savrana*; which he likewife defeated with great flaughter: but, upon the whole, thofe victories were of little more importance than that he thereby faved his army from being cut in pieces, as the event of the campaign

campaign difcovered; for the *Neifter* proved an infurmount-able barrier to his fortune. The *Tartars* in thofe parts have an irreconcileable averfion to the *Ruffians* and their coffaks; and live free and happy under the protection, rather than the government, of the *Turks*. Their numbers are inexhauftible, and feemed to encreafe as *Munich* advanced. He gained a third victory when he was within a few leagues from the *Neifter*; in which the prince of *Wolfenbuttle*, and the earl of *Crawford*, greatly diftinguifhed themfelves.

On the twenty-fixth of *July*, he arrived within two leagues of that river, between the *Molokifch* and the *Bielocz*. Here the fultan of *Bialogrod*, the chief of the *Budziac Tartars*, refolved to make his principal ftand; and, being re-inforced by a confiderable body of *Turks*, he fell upon the *Ruffians* with prodigious fury, and continued the engagement for fix or feven hours before he was repulfed. *Munich* then took up his camp upon the borders of the *Neifter*. After fome cannonading, he found the *Othmans* entirely mafters of the river, the banks of which they had ftrongly fortified. In fhort, he faw it impracticable to pafs; and, on the twenty-ninth, he drew off towards the *Bielocz*. In his retreat he was harraffed by a body of twenty-five thoufand janifaries, befides the *Tartar* army; but, according to his account, he obtained over them a fifth victory. Thus *Munich* was covered with laurels as a hero, but baffled as a general. At firft, he gave out that he would undertake the fiege of *Choczim*, but declined it on pretence that the country round about it was infected; and returned, by another way than he had advanced, to his old winter-quarters in the *Ukraine*.

and that of *Lacy*, unfuccefs-ful in the main. *Lacy's* fortune was pretty fimilar to that of count *Munich*. After he had taken *Precop*, and laid all the *Krim* open to an invafion, he found his army in danger of being famifhed by the fuperiority which the *Turkifh* fleet had over that of the *Ruffians* under *Bredal*, which was to have furnifhed him with provifions. *Bredal* perceiving his inferiority, ran his tranf-ports into creeks; but the kapudan-pafha landed his men; and, according to the *Turkifh* accounts, which appear moft probable, he took and deftroyed eighty veffels, with their ftores and crews, notwithftanding the batteries that had been erected to defend them. This obliged *Lacy* to blow up the fortifications of *Or*, and other places he had taken, and to demolifh the lines of *Precop*; which feems to have put an end to the campaign in that quarter; for *Lacy* was obliged, after that, to evacuate the country. It cannot, therefore, be denied, that the *Turks* had manifeftly the advantage of the *Ruffians*, as well as of the *Germans*, in this war. Had their accounts of the two laft campaigns been publifhed, inftead of thofe of their enemies, we might have, perhaps, en-tertained very different ideas of the *Ruffian* operations and victories. What makes this the more probable, is, that before count *Munich* arrived in the *Ukraine*, he fent the baron

Stoffele

Stoffelen to demolish the fortifications of *Oczakow* and *Kim-burn*; and we are even told that the baron left the artillery of those forts behind him.

The town of *New Orsova*, in *Hungary*, still continued to hold bravely out; and the *Turks* are said to have lost a great number of men before it. On the tenth of *July*, a battle was fought, between the imperialists and them, near *Mea-dia*; in which the latter pretended to have the advantage: but the imperialists, finding it impossible to subsist in that country, retired to *Karansebes*; and the siege of *New Orsova* went on. The grand-vizier, for some time, remained inactive, on pretence that he waited for the event of the *Russian* operations; but, all of a sudden, it was known, by authority, that that important fortress was taken; and that count *Cornberg*, the governor, had been arrested, and was to be tried for giving up the place, in which the imperialists lost two hundred and fifty cannon and mortars. *Orsova taken.*

The consequence was, that the imperial army was obliged to withdraw within the lines of *Belgrade*; that the *Turks* took *Semendria*, *Vipalanka*, and many other places; but the pasha of *Bosnia* was obliged to raise the siege of *Ratcha* upon the approach of some *Saxon* and *Bavarian* troops. The grand-vizier led his army back to *Nissa*; and the bannat of *Temeswar*, being now open to the infidels, was most unmercifully ravaged. Those losses entirely dispirited the court of *Vienna*, who employed every art to bring about a separate peace with the *Othmans*, notwithstanding the severe remonstrances of the czarina, who offered to lend the emperor thirty thousand men. But we are now to attend operations of another kind.

Sare Bey Oglu was son of an officer supposed to be the richest in the *Othman* dominions; and, upon his death, the sultan seized all his effects, and shut up his daughter in his seraglio. *Oglu's* mother exhorted him to revenge these wrongs; and he, having still a considerable real estate in *Natolia*, retired, with some malecontents, to the mountains of *Bosdag* and *Diogli Bogasse*, where they chose him their head; his chief residence being an old castle in a very strong situation. At first, he affected great courtesy to travellers, especially caravans, and sent a formal account to the grand-vizier of his situation, with a peremptory demand of an equivalent for his father's effects. This demand was rejected with great indignation; and one of the kyehaya's was strangled for corresponding with him. *Oglu* then plundered the estates of the sultan and his courtiers, wherever he could reach them. At last, he found himself obliged to lay the towns and villages under contribution, and to rifle the caravans which he had before protected. The porte was informed of his proceedings; but, being engaged in other wars, no measures were taken for suppressing him. *History of Oglu, the head of the Turkish banditti.*

One of his parties appeared before the gates of *Smyrna*, one of the moſt conſiderable cities in the *Othman* dominions, rich, large, populous, and defended by a citadel. The *Europeans*, who had immenſe magazines of effects there, hurried all they could on board their ſhips, excepting the *Dutch* conſul, who fortified his houſe, armed his country-men, kept a patrole all night on the watch, and had a veſ-ſel ready to carry him and his effects off in caſe of neceſſity. As to the other inhabitants, their conſternation was inex-preſſible.

In the morning, *Oglu*'s lieutenant, who commanded the party, demanded an interview with the magiſtrates, to ſettle their contribution; that their city, which contained forty thouſand men fit to bear arms, might not be plundered. This demand, ſo aſtoniſhingly impudent, was complied with. The banditti-chief, who had with him no more than eight hundred armed men, entered the city, received fifteen thouſand crowns contribution-money, beſides preſents, and returned in ſafety. On his departure, the citizens being ſomewhat recovered from their conſternation, were aſhamed to look one another in the face; and it was owing to the in-ſtances of the *Britiſh*, and other *European* miniſters at the porte, that two thouſand troops were ſent to protect the city.

He is de-feated and put to death.

While they lay within two leagues of it, a new alarm was ſpread, that the banditti were within ſight. This threw the inhabitants into a freſh conſternation, which was ſpread to their guards, and they retired with precipitation within the cannon of the citadel. Next day, it was known that this was a falſe alarm, raiſed by the neighbouring boors, that they might plunder the *Turkiſh* camp; which they had begun to do, when the regulars returned, and impaled ſome of them for their preſumption. The main-body of the banditti were, at this time, in the neighbourhood of *Epheſus*; and the *Oth-mans*, being reinforced with ſome freſh battalions and ar-tillery, overtook, and, having defeated them, ſent the heads of the ſlain to *Conſtantinople*; where they were publicly ex-poſed as trophies of a victory. It does not appear whether *Oglu* was preſent at this battle or not; but it is certain he was obliged, with no more than four hundred men, to aban-don his caſtle; and, being cloſely purſued, he was overtaken, and his head being cut off, it was ſent to *Conſtantinople*.

Great pre-parations of the *Turks*, and their terms.

The winter of the year 1738 was ſpent in various negotia-tions; but the *Othman* miniſters continued firm to their own terms; and, while they were treating, orders were given for raiſing an army of two hundred thouſand fighting men. The *French* ambaſſador interpoſed with great earneſtneſs; but the *Turks* were ſo much the more determined, as they knew that the *Poles* had refuſed to grant a paſſage through their country to thirty thouſand auxiliaries which the czarina propoſed to ſend to the emperor. The terms which the *Othmans* inſiſted upon

upon, as an indifpenfible bafis for a negotiation, were, That the court of *Vienna* fhould abfolutely give up the imperial *Wallachia*, *Orfova*, and its dependencies, and that part of *Servia* which lies between the *Morava* and the *Timock*. With regard to *Ruffia*, they demanded the reftitution of *Afoph* and *Oczrkow*, and that the treaty of *Pruth* fhould be carried into full execution. To fhew that they were in earneft, *Wali Pafha*, ferafkier of *Bender*, three pafhas who commanded in *Hungary*, and two on the *Niefter*, loft their heads, for mifbehaving in the laft campaign; and the troops had orders to provide themfelves with bayonets; in the ufe of which they were to be inftructed according to the *European* exercife. Before the campaign opened, the grand-vizier repaired, with the ufual ceremonies, to the temple of St. *Sophia*; from whence he took the ftandard of *Mohammed*, as a fign that he was refolved to make the campaign decifive.

The imperialifts knew not how either to accept or refufe the terms prefcribed by the *Turks*; but, at laft, pride and obftinacy determined them upon another campaign. As to the emprefs of *Ruffia*, fhe, without any hefitation, refolved that *Munich* fhould recommence his operations on the *Niefter*, and *Lacy* his in the *Krim*. The campaign began early. A body of *Tartars* made an irruption firft into the *Ukraine*, where they were repulfed; and then into *Poland*, where they committed moft dreadful ravages, and carried off three thoufand nine hundred *Poles* into flavery; but a good underftanding then fubfifting between the porte and that republic, the foltan of *Bialogrod* fet them at liberty, and undertook to make good the damages that it had fuftained. In the mean while, the *Turks* were bufied in repairing the fortifications of *Oczakow* and *Kimburn*, and rendering them much ftronger than ever.

Before the campaign opened, the fultan, perceiving that the grand-vizier *Jahya* had made himfelf difagreeable to the janifaries, by his unpopular behaviour, thought proper to depofe and banifh him to an ifland in the *Archipelago*; and to fend the feal of his office to *Ayvas Mehemed*, ferafkier of *Widin*, who was a favourite with the army. On the other hand, the court of *Vienna* made its utmoft efforts to affemble an army of eighty thoufand men. under count *Wallis* at *Belgrade*. The foltan of the *Calmuk Tartars*, who are tributary to the *Ruffians*, beat the *Cuban Tartars*, who are fubject to the *Turks*; count *Munich* took up his camp in the neighbourhood of *Kiow*; and the czarina purpofed to carry on the campaign with great warmth, though fhe had reafon to apprehend that the court of *Vienna* was meditating a feparate peace, and that the *Swedes* were arming againft her in *Finland*.

On the fifth of *June*, count *Munich* left *Kiow*, at the head of feventy-five thoufand men, including *Tartars* and *Calmuks*; and, in two days, arrived at *Berduczow*, on the frontiers of *Poland*, with intention to befige *Choczim*: after which he

Grand-vizier depofed.

Glorious campaign,

Z 2 was

was to attempt the conqueſt of all *Moldavia*, by the aſſiſtance of the imperial troops, who were to join him from *Tranſylvania*. *Munich* ſoon found reaſon to alter this plan, and he puſhed on to *Tranſylvania*, in hopes of being joined by prince *Lobkowitz*. *Lacy*, according to order, again entered the *Krim*, repaired the lines of *Precop*, and the other fortifications of that country; and, as the khan had laid it waſte, upon the approach of his army, it was agreed that he ſhould be ſupplied with proviſions from *Aſoph*. *Munich* continued his march with incredible conſtancy; and, having paſſed the river *Bokitna*, he found himſelf oppoſed by a *Turkiſh* ſeraſkier, at the head of twenty thouſand ſpahis and ſixty thouſand *Tartars*, who retired towards *Choczim* at his approach, where they took up a ſtrong camp, in hopes that the *Ruſſians*, having no magazines, or means of ſubſiſtence, would be obliged to ſurrender themſelves priſoners of war.

and conqueſts of *Munich*. The diſpoſitions of the ſeraſkier were ſuch as to force *Munich* to come to the deſperate reſolution of attacking his enemies in their camp; which he did with ſo much reſolution, that, though the janiſaries made a brave reſiſtance, the *Othmans* were defeated, and the *Ruſſians* took poſſeſſion of their camp; in which they found nineteen cannon, four braſs mortars, with all kind of military ſtores, and, what was ſtill m ꝛe agreeable, plenty of proviſion and forage. The conſequence was, that *Choczim* immediately ſurrendered on condition that the garriſon ſhould obtain quarter for life. Here the *Ruſſians* found very rich magazines, and one hundred and thirty-eight pieces of cannon. *Yaſſi*, the capital of *Moldavia*, opened its gates to the conqueror, as did *Bender*; and then the ſoltan of *Bialogrod*, and the *Budzian Tartars*, ſubmitted likewiſe.

The *Ruſſians* were equally fortunate on the ſide of the *Krim*, where the *Turks* had formed, by means of their ſuperiority at ſea, a deſign upon *Aſoph*; but their fleet being almoſt deſtroyed in a ſtorm, *Lacy* remained maſter of the country, and his army was plentifully ſupplied by *Bredal*, the *Ruſſian* admiral. But we are now to attend the operations in *Hungary*.

In *Auguſt*, the *Turkiſh* army rendezvouſed at *Razuna*, with an intention to paſs the *Morava*; but they left ſtrong encampments at *Semendria* and *Crotſca*, which laſt place they were fortifying. Upon this intelligence, marſhal *Wallis* ſent for general *Nieperg*, to join him with the troops under his command; but, in the mean while, it was judged neceſſary to attack the *Turks*, before they completed their fortifications at *Grotſca*. We ſhall, in the hiſtory of *Germany*, have an opportunity of deſcribing this unfortunate battle. It is ſufficient here to ſay, that, though the attack was made with prodigious courage and reſolution, the *Germans* were entirely defeated, and *Wallis* was obliged, next day, to ſhelter himſelf within the lines of *Belgrade*. The *Othmans*, ſoon after

th.

this, received a fevere check at *Kabouka*; but that did not hinder the grand-vizier from carrying on the fiege of *Belgrade*, which he was preparing to ftorm, when it was known that a negotiation of peace was far advanced, under the mediation of the *French* ambaffador at *Conftantinople*.

The *Turks*, and perhaps the czarina likewife, were not a little influenced to this ftep by the prodigious progrefs which the *Kouli Kan*, the *Perfian* fophi, was making in *India*; where he had amaffed a treafure fuperior to all that the *Turkifh* and *Ruffian* empires contained. The *French* ambaffador came from *Conftantinople* to the vizier's camp before *Belgrade*, to which count *Nieperg* repaired likewife as plenipotentiary; and, on the firft of *September*, 1739, the treaty was figned. The terms were, That the emperor fhould abandon *Belgrade* and *Servia* to the grand-fignior, as well as *Orfova*; that the *Danube* and the *Saave* fhould, for the future, form the limits of the two empires; that the bannat of *Temefwar*, and the town of that name, fhould remain in the poffeffion of his imperial majefty, with the territory thereupon dependent, comprehending therein *Meadia*; that *Orfova* fhould continue in the condition it was then in; but, that the fortifications of *Belgrade* fhould be demolifhed. Thofe terms were fo humiliating to the court of *Vienna*, that the emperor thought fit to difown what had been done, and to put both *Nieperg* and *Wallis* under arreft; and, at the fame time, he emitted a manifefto, difapproving of their conduct, and pretending that count *Nieperg* had exceeded his powers: notwithftanding all which, he ratified the articles. The public knew the character of the houfe of *Auftria* too well, not to be fenfible of the emperor's motives for this fcandalous proceeding; which was meant to gratify his own pride by faving fome kind of appearances. We are not, therefore, with fome authors, to imagine, that he publifhed this manifefto, with a view of appeafing the refentment of the czarina, who fent an officer, on purpofe, to the *Turkifh* camp, to prevent, if poffible, a feparate peace.

It was owing to the vaft fuccefles of *Munich*, that the czarina obtained fo good a peace as fhe did; for the porte had always been obftinate in excluding her from the negotiation. The certainty of *Munich*'s progrefs having been notified to the *Turks*, a new negotiation was begun between them and the *Ruffians*, before the camp at *Belgrade* broke up; and the following preliminaries were agreed to: viz. That *Afoph* fhould remain to *Ruffia*, but be demolifhed, and its territory laid defart, to form a barrier between the two empires; that *Ruffia* might build a fortrefs on this fide of the *Don*, and the porte another on their fide of the river; but the city of *Taganrock*, built by *Peter the Great*, on the fea of *Afoph*, fhould not be reftored, that the *Ruffians* fhould have no veffels on that or the *Black-fea*, but fhould ufe the *Turkifh* fhips in their

Peace between the Turks, Germans, and Mufcovites.

commerce in thofe feas; that the limits of the two empires, weft of the *Nieper*, fhould be the fame as regulated in 1706, *Kudack* remaining to the porte; and the limits to the eaft of the *Nieper* to be fettled by a new convention. Upon the conclufion of thofe preliminaries, count *Munich* evacuated *Moldavia*, with his army; and returned, through the *Polifh* territories, to the *Ukraine*. He carried with him numbers of *Greeks* and natives who, upon his firft irruption, had joined him; and who, no provifion having been made in their fa-vour by the convention, could expect no mercy under an *Othman* government. It was computed that, in this expedi-tion, he took from the *Turks* eight hundred pieces of brafs cannon; and, that the booty carried off with him amounted to above feven hundred thoufand pounds fterling.

Good faith of the *Turks*. It is to the honour of the *Othman* government that we mention the good faith with which both the above treaties was kept on their part, notwithftanding all the inftances made, on the part of *France*, to prevail with them to break them. But the fultan was, at this time, apprehenfive of a revolt in *Egypt*; where *Kouli Kan*, who was not yet returned from his *Indian* expedition, had a great party; and it was known that his late fucceffes had elated him fo, that he was refolved to break with the porte. It is hard to fay what pro-vocations he might have received from the *Turkifh* pafhas and fera/kiers, or what the confequence muft have been, had he not loft the greateft part of his army and treafures in his re-turn homewards.

Soon after the conclufion of the convention with *Ruffia*, the porte very wifely entered into a defenfive one with *Swe-den*, for mutually fupporting each other if attacked by the *Ruffians*; and the porte engaged, that the governments of *Al-giers*, *Tunis*, and *Tripoli*, fhould conform themfelves to the fame. Scarcely was this negotiation ended, when, through the ravages committed, during the late war, all provifions grew fo dear at *Conftantinople*, that many infurrections hap-pened, which were foon quelled. But the grand-vizier be-ing no friend to the clergy, the fultan was informed by them, that, if he expected to keep his throne in peace, he muft part with his minifter. The fultan was obliged fo far to comply, as to deprive him of his poft; but he made him go-vernor of *Gedda*, and fuffered him to keep all his treafure and effects. This, perhaps, would not have fatisfied the populace, had not the ceffion of *Belgrade* been proclaimed, and the imperial ambaffador made a moft magnificent entry into *Conftantinople*. This reconciled the people fo well to the late meafures, that the fultan ventured to exact a new oath of fidelity from the janifaries; and all foreigners who had re-fided four years in that capital, without marrying, were obliged to leave it. The revolutions which happened at the court of *Ruffia*, about this time, occafioned fome motions of the

the *Othman Tartars* on the frontiers of that empire; and a divan was held concerning a new war: but the *English* ambassador, who had great credit at the porte, informed the *Turkish* ministers so minutely concerning the state of affairs in *Europe*, that a resolution was taken to observe the treaties of *Belgrade*; and the *Russian* ambassadors received assurances accordingly.

A peace was the more necessary at this time, as *Kouli Kan* had now returned from his *Indian* expedition, and was still threatening to invade the *Othman* dominions. For this purpose, he had sent a most magnificent ambassy to prevail with the *Russians* to declare against the porte; and, a war then raging between *Russia* and *Sweden*, the ambassador of the latter, at *Constantinople*, demanded from the porte the assistance stipulated by the late treaty; but the grand-vizier drily answered, That his master must previously examine, whether *Russia* or *Sweden* was the aggressor.

About this time, an ambassador from *Kouli Khan* had an audience at the porte; in which, besides many other claims, he insisted upon his master having the same authority at *Mecca* with the *Othman* emperor. This demand being denied him, he invaded the *Turkish* dominions, and proceeded as far as *Erzerum*; but was obliged to desist by the rebellious commotions which broke out in *Persia* under his own son; who was thought to have been instigated thereto by the *Othmans*. After this, the sultan enjoyed some repose; which he employed in cultivating the arts of peace, and in putting his fleets and armies on a respectable footing. His turbulent subjects could not bear with his pacific dispositions; and, in *May*, 1742, they forced him to depose his grand-vizier *Mehmed Pasha*; and to raise to the viziership *Ali Pasha Kekim Oglou*, a professed enemy to the *Christians*. This change seems to have quieted the minds of the people for some time.

Kouli Khan, now called *Nadir Shah*, had never laid aside his ambitious designs; and, having achieved the conquest of the *Mogul*, he meditated that of the *Turkish* empire. For this purpose, he had entered into a close friendship and correspondence with the empress of *Russia*; but so faithfully had the porte kept its engagements, that they could find no subject for a quarrel with it but religion. The reader, from the foregoing part of this history, may perceive that religion was always the true prerogative of the *Mohammedan* sovereigns; and to have yielded a point of precedency in that, was more dangerous than the loss of a province. *Nadir Shah* had done all he could to extinguish those ridiculous notions among his subjects, but without effect; for he perceived an invincible disposition in many of the inhabitants of the provinces he had acquired, or conquered, in favour of the *Othman* emperors, on the foolish supposition of their being the descendants of the antient califs.

Kouli Kan invades their empire.

His progress.

After some arrogant demands of having his pretensions to an equality in this respect settled, he desired that some *Turkish* doctors should be sent to his court. This was refused; and, in the beginning of the year 1743, he sent to acquaint the sultan, that, as his ministers refused to gratify his request, in sending the doctors to instruct him, he was resolved to come in person to the frontiers of *Turkey*, that he might be more near at hand to have his doubts cleared up. To this message the grand-vizier facetiously answered, That the doctors were just setting out to wait on his highness, and that they only stayed for an escorte of thirty thousand janisaries and some other troops. *Nadir Shah* soon invaded the *Othman* dominions, destroyed one of their frontier towns, and directed his march to *Baghdad*. The news of this arriving at *Constantinople*, the horse-tail was erected at the gates of the seraglio, as a signal for assembling a great army; but the people were so much alarmed, that it was with difficulty the grand-vizier escaped with his life in an insurrection, and the levies went slowly on.

Under this disability to oppose a great conqueror, the *Othman* court, which had of late changed several viziers, set up a young man as a descendant from the antient sophis of *Persia*, who pretended that he had escaped from the common calamity of his family, and taken refuge in an island of the *Archipelago*. Him they declared shah of *Persia*, and gave him an army to oppose *Shah Nadir*, who continued still to make a formidable progress in the *Othman* empire. His demands were, To have all the provinces, that ever had been dismembered from *Persia* by the *Othmans*, restored to his crown; which must have included a most valuable part of the *Turkish* empire. He took *Kirkut*, put all its garrison to the sword, and defeated an army of the *Turks* who came to raise the siege; but was repulsed at *Mosul*, after having blocked up *Baghdad*. The news of an insurrection in his own dominions prevented his farther progress, and he offered to treat. The *Othmans* knew the difficulty he was under, and sent supplies to *Shah Rhade*, the sophi they had set up, who lay encamped between *Erzerum* and *Kars*. The serafkier *Ahmed Pasha*, who had the actual command of the *Turkish* army, was defeated, and obliged to take refuge under the cannon of *Kars*; where *Nadir Shah* attacked him, but was defeated in his turn. The *Turkish* ministers, who had carefully concealed from the people all the defeats and disgraces their arms had received from the *Persians*, made the most extravagant rejoicings on this occasion; and, though we have no authentic account of that war, but what they are pleased to transmit, it seems to be very certain, that *Nadir Shah*, at this time, failed in his invasion.

The progress he had made, and the contradictory accounts published by the ministry, but, above all, the vast number of *Othman* subjects whom *Shah Nadir* had driven to *Constantino-*
ple,

le, created such uneasiness in the minds of the inhabitants of that capital, that daily tumults happened, and great debates were held in the divan, whether the strength of the empire should be directed against *Shah Nadir*, or against the *Christian* powers. The famous renegade count *Bonneval*, who assisted at those divans, under the title of the pasha *Osman*, was of the latter opinion; but the former prevailed. In the mean while, an account arrived, that *Ahmed Pasha* had revolted, and made himself master of *Baghdad*, and had been acknowledged sovereign of that city, and all *Mesopotamia*, by *Nadir Shah*. *Ahmed* was then eighty years of age, and without children, but had a nephew who was a very gallant officer, and the shah engaged to support him with thirty thousand *Persians*. At this time, the war, which was raging in christendom, was the subject of many serious considerations at the porte; where it was firmly believed that the *Russians*, and the queen of *Hungary*, had spirited up *Nadir Shah* to invade the *Othman* dominions. This induced the grand-signior to act a part very different from the policy of his ancestors, by offering his mediation to the powers at war, on pretence that their dissentions ruined the trade of his subjects in the *Levant*. His vizier had a conference on the same head with the *Austrian* ambassador, but neither of them found any encouragement to proceed in their offer of mediation. About this time, a most dreadful fire broke out at *Constantinople*; which raged for five days, and destroyed the arsenal: and, to complete the mortification of the *Turks*, they received several very severe checks from the *Persians* in the year 1745.

Grand-signior offers his mediation to the Christians.

Ridiculous as the late offer of the sultan's mediation was, the *French* took advantage of it; for, on the fifteenth of *December*, that year, their ambassador had a most magnificent audience of the sultan; and informed him, that his master had, with great pleasure, accepted of his mediation. This procured him a very gracious dismission; and the sultan, to shew his pacific disposition, recognized the consort of the queen of *Hungary*, as emperor of *Germany*. Soon after this, a peace was proposed between the porte and *Nadir Shah*, whose situation at home rendered that measure necessary. He demanded that the grand-signior should deliver up the pretender to his throne, and give one of the princesses of the *Othman* blood in marriage to his grandson, with one of the principal frontier towns towards *Persia* for her dowry, and liberty for the *Persians* to visit the tomb of *Mecca* on the same footing with their own subjects. The sultan had too much honour to agree to the first demand; but, after some negotiations, peace was concluded: by which the limits of the two empires were to stand as they were settled in the reign of *Morad* IV. and the *Persians* were to enjoy equal privileges at *Mecca* with the *Othmans*. Upon the conclusion of this important treaty, the sultan renewed his treaties with the

Accepted by the French.

courts

courts of *Vienna* and *Ruffia*; by all which fteps, peace was not only reftored, but fecured, to his dominions. Soon after, the *Othman* empire was delivered from its greateft fcourge by the affaffination of *Kouli Khan.*

Affairs of Perfia,   The *Turkifh* hiftory, after this, is barren of any great events till the fecond of *May*, 1748; when an ambaffador from the new fophi of *Perfia* had an audience at the porte: in which he confirmed the late treaty between the two empires. A time of profound peace with foreign powers is always dangerous to the internal repofe of the *Othman* empire, and we now find feveral feditions prevailing at *Conftantinople*; by which fome of the great officers of the empire loft their lives, and the fultan himfelf was obliged to fly to *Adrianople.* There he affembled his army, and, at the head of the janifaries, he attacked the infurgents with great vigour, and, at firft, with fome fuccefs. Next day, the infurrection grew to fuch a heighth, that the fultan was obliged to depofe his grand-vizier, and foon after to declare his brother's fon, *Ibrahim*, who was looked upon to be an enemy to the *Chriftians*, his fucceffor in the empire. Thofe conceffions reftored the public tranquillity; to which the unfettled ftate of affairs in *Perfia* greatly contributed. This, however, was interrupted in 1749, by the revolt of the pafha of *Baffora*; who attacked *Baghdad*, and five ferafkiers were employed to reduce him; which they did with fome difficulty.

At this juncture, we find Mr. *Porter*, who was ambaffador from *England*, complaining of fome engagements the porte had entered into with certain northern powers, to the prejudice of the emprefs of *Ruffia*; but the grand-vizier, whofe name was *Abdallah Pafha*, affured him that the report was groundlefs; and that the fultan had only renewed his defenfive alliance with *Sweden.* On the twenty-third of *December*, 1749, this vizier was depofed, and his feal given to *Mehemed Pafha*, his kyehayah, whofe fentiments were as pacific as thofe of his predeceffor. About this time, a project was fet on foot for erecting a woollen manufactory near *Conftantinople.*

and Barbary.   In the beginning of the year 1759, the ftates of *Barbary* implored the protection of the grand-fignior; who cautioned them not to provoke the maritime powers; but, at the fame time, recommended to the latter, that they would ufe their utmoft endeavours to prevent their fubjects from coming wilfully to any difagreement with the regencies of *Barbary. Conftantinople* was, at this period, infefted with a number of wretches who fet fire to different quarters of the city, partly for the fake of plunder, and partly to bring about a revolution; in which they muft have fucceeded, had it not been for the prefence and prudence of the fultan, who quelled the janifaries. It appears as if the government of the porte, notwithftanding their pacific difpofitions, was this year obliged to keep the people in temper, by ordering their armies

mies to make feveral marches and counter-marches, as if they had been on the eve of a war with the two empires of *Ruſ-ſia* and *Germany*. Notwithſtanding this, the government had the art to keep the janiſaries on their ſide ; and, the plague breaking out, the public tranquility continued during the year 1751, in an almoſt unexampled manner, if we conſider the general diſpoſitions of the people towards a war. In *July*, 1752, the people became uneaſy with the ſtate of affairs at court, and obliged the ſultan to baniſh both the grand-vizier and the aga of the janiſaries, and to ſtrike off the head of the chief eunuch ; whoſe wealth amounted to the immenſe ſum of ten millions ſterling, including his jewels and diamonds. The only crime charged upon thoſe unhappy delinquents, was their love of peace ; and even the mufti was put to death on the ſame account. It is hard to ſay what prevented the grand-ſignior from gratifying his people in this reſpect, eſpecially as the *European* powers were but juſt recovering from a long and bloody war.

His preſervation, at this time, probably was owing partly to the earthquakes, plagues, and other calamities which then afflicted the empire, and made impreſſions on the minds of the ſuperſtitious *Othmans* ; and partly to the addreſs of the aga of the janiſaries, who, by the prevailing aſſiſtance of proper donatives, kept that formidable body quiet. In the beginning of the next year, the authority of the ſultan was ſo well re-eſtabliſhed, that he ventured to baniſh twenty-two members of the divan to different places, becauſe they had declared for war. This ſeverity renewed the mumurs of the janiſaries ; upon which a reſolution was taken to aſſemble a body of fifty thouſand men to oppoſe the progreſs of prince *Heraclius*, who had become very powerful in *Perſia* ; and, that a body of janiſaries ſhould march to quell the *Tartars* of *Oczakow*, who had mutinied. About the ſame time, a vaſt number of diſtant paſhas were ſummoned to the divan at *Conſtantinople*, to deliberate on the operations of the enſuing campaign. The miniſters of *Great-Britain*, *Vienna*, and *Ruſſia*, demanded the reaſons of the vaſt armaments making throughout the empire ; but they received no ſatisfaction : and three ſerafkiers being ſent to command in the *Krim*, the *Ruſſians* made no doubt of the ſtorm falling upon them ; and prepared themſelves accordingly. Nothing, however, was more foreign than a war to the intentions of the ſultan. All he did, was to ſubdue ſome rebellious mountaineers on the frontiers of *Perſia*, and to give orders for marching and counter-marching his troops. As a proof of his pacific diſpoſition, when a *Malteſe* renegade, who had been an engineer on that iſland, preſented him with a plan of its fortifications, he threw it into the fire ; and, in a ſhort time, the warlike humour of the people blowing over, the public tranquillity returned, and the emperor refuſed to receive any propoſals for

breaking

Earth-quakes, fires, and inſurrections.

breaking it. He thought proper, however, to give orders that his troops fhould be held to a ftrict difcipline, and frequently exercifed.

Pacific difpofitions of the fultan. Towards the end of the year 1753, the *Britifh* and *Ruffian* minifters had an audience of the grand-vizier on the affairs of *Europe*; and that minifter affured them, that his mafter did not intend to interfere in any differences among *Chriftian* princes which did not affect the glory or profperity of the *Othman* empire. On the fixteenth of *March*, next year, on a report of the grand fignior's health declining, fome commotions happened among the janifaries; but they were appeafed by the punifhment of the ring-leaders, and, upon the recovery of the fultan, all was quiet. On the fixteenth of *September*, the fame year, a moft dreadful earthquake was felt all over the *Othman* empire; which did incredible damage, the fhocks being repeated for feveral days. Three minarets, or towers, were thrown down at *Conftantinople*, for which the *Othmans* had a particular reverence, on account of a tradition, that, when they fell, their empire was near an end. The confternation of the people, on this occafion, was fo great, that the fultan was obliged to come to *Conftantinople*, from a country-feat, to encourage and reaffure them.

His death, On the thirteenth of *December* following, the grand-fignior, fultan *Mohammed*, died fuddenly of a fit of an aftma, about one o'clock; and, at three the fame morning, his brother, *Ofman* III. notwithftanding the former appointment, was proclaimed his fucceffor from the minarets of the mofques, and the *Britifh* ambaffador was the firft foreign minifter who was admitted to congratulate him after his inauguration.

and character. The deceafed fultan appears to have been a prince of uncommon qualifications and addrefs in managing the turbulent fpirit of his people, which had been fatal to fo many of his anceftors; and his reign, upon the whole, muft be confidered as happy and glorious; and himfelf was one of the moft fortunate princes, efpecially during his laft years, that had ever filled the *Othman* throne; and *Ofman*, fenfible of the difadvantages he was under in fucceeding fo great a prince, began his reign by diftributing immenfe treafures among the janifaries and the army, and by giving the minifters of the *Chriftian* powers the ftrongeft affurances that he would maintain his brother's pacific fyftem.

Ofman

Ofman III.

SULTAN *Ofman*, according to public report, was the fon of fultan *Moftafa*, by a young *Hungarian* lady, who had been prefented to him by pafha *Heken*, one of his generals in that country; and who being alive at the time of his acceffion, was, for that reafon, preferred to the vizierfhip; from which, however, he was foon depofed; though, among the fultan's firft meafures, he had degraded and banifhed his grand-vizier *Moftafa Pafha*, who before appeared to be his favourite; but, notwithftanding four bankers were tortured to make them difcover where he had placed his riches, no more than fifty thoufand chequins could be difcovered.

About the beginning of this fultan's reign, no fewer than fifteen thoufand houfes were deftroyed at *Conftantinople*, and upwards of one thoufand perfons perifhed in the flames. Very little interefting matter appears during the remainder of fultan *Ofman*'s reign, which feems to have been employed in preferving the tranquility of his empire by martial appearances, to keep his people in temper; which was the more eafy, as the *European* powers were fo far from fhewing any difpofitions to provoke him, that they treated him with all the deference which the *Othman* pride expects or requires. *Ofman* III. died on the twenty-eighth of *October*, 1757, in the fifty-ninth year of his age; and he was fucceeded by his brother *Moftafa* III. who was born in 1723. Having no fons, the people began to be very uneafy about the fucceffion; and fo dangerous a ferment arofe in *Conftantinople*, that a revolution was apprehended; efpecially when his brother *Bajazet* produced a fon whom he faid he had by a woman during his confinement. As this was pointing out to the emperor a fucceffor, he gave orders for his brother's head to be taken off; but the latter was befriended, not only by the populace, but the great officers of ftate, and the execution was prevented.

In this reign, a *Turkifh* fhip of the line, called *The Otto-* *man Crown*, being maftered by the *Chriftian* flaves on board, was carried into *Malta*, where the prize was divided among the captors. This was complained of by the fultan, as being a moft lawlefs infult upon his flag; and he made fuch preparations for war as indicated that he was refolved to extirpate the order. This alarmed the emprefs-queen fo much, that, for fear of embroiling herfelf with the porte, fhe gave orders, that none of her fubjects, who were knights of *Malta*, fhould repair to the defence of that ifland. Other *Chriftian* powers thought themfelves equally interefted not to provoke his fublime highnefs; and it is probable that the knights muft have been left to defend themfelves, had not the *French* king, with great prudence and delicacy, bought the fhip, and fent it to *Conftantinople* guarded by *Britifh* cruizers,

cruizers, as a prefent to the fultan, who declared himfelf fatisfied with that attonement.

Since then, the *Othman* empire has afforded no matter of
hiftory; the prefent emperor invariably purfues the pacific
fyftem of his two immediate predeceffors, and the *Turkifh* government feems to be fenfible, that their troops, by a long
difufe of arms, muft be a very unequal match either for the
Ruffians or the *Germans*; and, of late, they have been at
great pains to cultivate a friendfhip with the king of *Pruffia*, as a proper ballance againft the houfe of *Auftria*. For
that purpofe, towards the end of the year 1763, they fent an
ambaffador, under the title of internuncio, to his *Pruffian*
majefty, who received and entertained him with the higheft
marks of diftinction; nor, indeed, can he have a more natural ally than the *Othman* porte, fhould his differences be
renewed with the houfe of *Auftria*. Upon the whole, the
Othmans feem now to be emerging from barbarity, particularly in the cruel executions of the fucceffors to their empire,
and many other ridiculous cuftoms.

T H E

THE

HISTORY

OF

GERMANY.

GREAT part of that tract which is now called *Germany*, was included in the antient *Gaul*; and, in the former part of this history, the reader will find the various viciffitudes it underwent during its government under the *Romans*. *Germany* pretends to the glory of giving to *Europe* its prefent fyftem of liberty; but whether it is properly of *German* extraction, is juftly to be queftioned. The *Gothic* conftitution may be traced to countries far north of *Germany*, and to ages long before the *Germanic* empire had an exiftence. *Germany* was the intermediate fpot between the feats of the barbarous nations, as they are called, and *Italy*, when they over-ran it ; and the *Goths* and *Vandals*, moft of them the anceftors of the modern *Tartars*, with a mixture of the *Danes*, *Swedes*, and *Pomeranians*, and the inhabitants of the country now called *Mecklenburgh*, or *Wandalia*, imported their laws and conftitutions into *Italy*, and other fouthern countries ; where they flourifhed till they were choaked up by the papal power. The emperors of *Germany*, as will be illuftrated in the fucceeding hiftory, long refifted that execrable tyranny over the temporal, as well as fpiritual, interefts of mankind ; and therefore their *Gothic* conftitutions remain more pure than any on the continent. As to the time when they took place, it cannot be traced ; for it reached as high as the exiftence of the *Celts*, when hiftory ends in fable. It is certain that the *Romans* themfelves had many forms of proceedings, particularly in the cafe of juries, exactly correfponding to the *Gothic* (or what is fometimes called the *Saxon*) conftitutions; which, at this very time, form the bafis of the laws of *England*; and that the *Romans* could have them only from the *Celts*. If they remain more pure in *England* than even in *Germany* itfelf, it is owing to its fituation as an ifland.

It would be idle and unentertaining for us to give a particular hiftory of *Germany* from the moft early ages, becaufe we have nothing to truft to for its veracity, but what is to be found in *Greek* and *Roman* writers. It is neceffary for us, however, to connect it flightly with that of the *Roman* empire. After *Conftantine* had transferred the feat of his government from *Rome* to *Byzantium*, or *Conftantinople*, he divided

vided his empire under the denominations of Eastern and Western; which were often governed by different princes, as may be seen in the former parts of this history. Before his death, which happened in the year 337, he left the former to his son *Constantine*, and the latter to his other son *Constantius*.

Constantine invaded his brother's dominions, and lost his life at the the battle of *Aquileia*. *Constantius* then finding himself sole emperor of the western empire, assumed that title, but lost his life by *Magnentius*. He was defeated by *Constans*, the only surviving son of the great *Constantine*, who thereby became the heir of his father's undivided empire. From this time, to the year 397, the western and eastern empires were often seperated, but were reunited under *Theodosius*, who divided them before his death between his two sons, *Arcadius* and *Honorius*: to the former was allotted the eastern empire, and to the latter the western. The irruption of the northern nations extinguished the race of the *Cæsars* in the western empire; and *Pepin*, king of *France*, having reduced to his power the various leaders (or, as they are called, kings) seperated himself entirely from any dependence on the eastern empire; so that the heads of it were rather dependents upon him; and he left his dominions to his son *Charles the Great*, who succeeded, in time, to the power of the western emperors; and we shall therefore consider him as the first emperor of *Germany*.

The Reign of Charles the Great, *emperor of the West.*

PEPIN, king of *France*, divided his kingdom between his sons *Charles* and *Carloman*. *Charles*, at the time of his father's death, was twenty-five years of age, and, in every respect, an extraordinary man. Though his father, from the lowness of his stature, was called *the Little, Charles* was seven feet high, well proportioned, strong, and his person fitted to bear all the fatigues of the field. It is doubtful whether his ruling passion was ambition or religion; but he had the art to make each in its turn subservient to the other. He was brave, magnanimous, and politic beyond any prince of his age; but he seems to have been endowed with those qualities for the ruin of mankind; because he was superstitious and ignorant, though he is supposed to have been one the most learned, not only of the princes, but men, of that age. By the death of *Carloman*, *Charles* became the sole master of the *French* monarchy, which included a great part of *Germany*, though his brother left a son, whose mother carried him, for protection, to the court of *Desiderius*, king of *Lombardy*. All the northern part of *Germany* was then called

. Saxon,

Saxony, and the *Saxons* were idolaters in the moſt groſs ſenſe of the word. Their country comprehended a vaſt extent of territory; being bounded, on the weſt, by the *German Ocean;* on the eaſt, by *Bohemia ;* by the ſea on the north; and, on the ſouth, by *French Germany.* The part that lay towards the ſeas was called *Weſtphalia ;* the *Eaſtphalians* had their habitations on the borders of *Bohemia,* in the countries now called *Miſnia, Luſatia,* and *Sileſia ;* and the *Angrians* inhabited the countries that bordered upon *France.* The government of thoſe *Saxons* ſubjected them and their neighbours to infinite inconveniencies. Their territory was divided into ſeparate dukedoms, marquiſates, and counties; but without any principle of union againſt a common enemy : for every chief was independent. *Charles* pretended that the *Saxons* owed him tribute, as ſovereign of *French Germany.* The *Saxons* reſolved to live free, and, though they had none of the improvements of life, unleſs the feeding their flocks may be deemed one, they preferred their barbarous idolatry to *Charles*'s more ſavage *Chriſtianity ;* upon which he entered their country with a powerful army; and his hiſtory, as emperor of *Germany,* commences at this period.

Witikind was the chief prince of the *Saxons,* and the anceſtor of moſt of the princes who now govern the northern parts of *Germany ;* but, though he is ſtiled, in general, duke of *Saxony,* yet he only poſſeſſed a large portion of that country; and all his pre-eminence aroſe from his martial endowments; which induced the *Saxons,* in time of war, to make him their commander in chief. The *Abodrites,* a nation of *Saxons,* then held the dutchy of *Meclenburgh,* and its adjacent territories, and were governed by a king of their own, who, having ſubmitted themſelves to pay tribute to *Pepin* and *Charles,* proved uſeful allies to the latter ; and he ſometimes preſided in their meetings, and even brought them to promiſe not to moleſt the miſſionaries he ſhould ſend amongſt them.

In 770, *Charles* paſſed his *Chriſtmas* at *Mentz,* and his *Eaſter* at *Heritſtal ;* circumſtances that, unimportant as they ſeem, form diſtinguiſhed æras in the hiſtories of thoſe times; becauſe, on ſuch occaſions, the ſovereign prince appeared in all the grandeur of his royalty ; was ſurrounded by his nobles, who then paid him their homage ; and, if any one was abſent, he was immediately ſuſpected of diſaffection : for which reaſon ſuch meetings were called Plenary-courts. *Charles,* at that time, was powerfully ſollicited by the pope, and ſome of the *Italian* ſtates, to paſs into *Italy,* and to deliver them from the tyranny of *Deſiderius,* or *Didier,* king of *Lombardy ;* the ſame who had given refuge to his brother's wife and ſon. Though *Charles,* for that, and other, reaſons, which ſhall be mentioned, was extremely intent upon this expedition, yet he thought it impolitic to undertake it before he had chaſtized the *Saxons,* and conſummated a marriage which had been propofed to him, with *Hildegrade*, daughter to *Hildebrand*, duke of *Suabia*.

In the year 772, *Charles* entered the country of the *Saxons* with a powerful army, in confequence of what had been refolved on in the diet of *Worms*; and, at firft, defeated his enemies in feveral encounters: but a moft dreadful drought happening, he durft not venture to leave the river *Lippa* behind him; and there he halted for three days: but, according to the fuperftitious authors of that time, a miraculous fupply of water fell from the mountains; and then upon his advancing towards the *Wefer*, the *Saxons* were fo aftonifhed at the warlike appearance of his army, that they offered to fubmit to him: but nothing lefs would content *Charles* than the abolition of their idolatry; and he marched to *Erefburg*, near *Paderborn*, where they were ftrongly entrenched, though without walls to defend them, or fuch as were very flight.

Here was the temple of *Irminful*, or, as others fay, of the goddefs *Tanfana*, mentioned by *Tacitus*. The *Saxons* defended this poft with great obftinacy, and *Charles* loft a confiderable number of men in forcing it; but having gained it, he moft barbaroufly put all the inhabitants to the fword, and flew the priefts of their idols upon their own altars. It is faid that *Charles*'s army was, for three days, employed in deftroying this temple; which was as facred among the *Saxons* as that of *Jerufalem* was among the *Jews*; and, that there was found within it an immenfe treafure in gold and filver. He then advanced towards the *Wefer*; and the *Saxons*, feeing it in vain to refift, fubmitted to give him twelve hoftages for their future obedience. It is more than probable, that *Charles* would not have accepted of this fubmiffion, had not the ftate of his affairs in *Italy* abfolutely required his prefence there; but, before he left their country, he gave ftrict orders for erecting certain forts to bridle the inhabitants.

Didier, next to *Charles*, was the moft powerful prince then in *Europe*, and *Charles* had married his daughter *Hermengard*. As religion, perfidy, and treachery, in that age, went hand in hand, *Charles* no fooner heard that *Didier* had humanity enough to protect his brother's widow and orphan, than he repudiated his queen, on pretence of her having an hereditary leprofy; a ridiculous charge that had been fuggefted to him by the pope. *Charles* found fome difficulty in perfuading his nobility, then the moft free of any in the world, to enter into an *Italian* war; but having made an offer of accommodating matters amicably with *Didier*, who rejected all his advances, he perfuaded them that he was forced into the war. This he did in a general affembly which he held at *Geneva*, where he complained fo pathetically of the pope's oppreffions by *Didier*, and the haughtinefs of the latter, that his nobles unanimoufly concurred in his paffing the

Alp

Alps at the head of a powerful army. *Didier* continued to persecute the popes, and *Adrian* I. had been shut up by him within the walls of *Rome*, after *Didier* had stripped him of all his other dominions. The latter was not insensible of *Charles*'s power and military character, but he trusted to the unwillingness of the *French* to pass the *Alps* and the places which he had fortified in the mountains, by which he hoped to retard the march of *Charles* till he could completely extinguish the papal power.

Charles divided his army into two columns; the one was commanded by himself, and the other by duke *Bernard*, the natural son of *Charles Martel*, who forced the passage of *Mount St. Bernard*, whilst *Charles* penetrated into *Lombardy* by *Mount Cenis*. This was not done without prodigious difficulty; and, had not a panic seized *Didier*'s army, *Charles* must have been obliged to return. While *Charles* was descending into the plains of *Lombardy*, *Didier* shut himself up in *Pavia*, as his son *Adalgise* did in *Verona*. *Charles*, understanding that duke *Hunalde*, of *Aquitain*, his old enemy, was with *Didier* in *Pavia*, and that the widow of *Carloman* and her sons were with *Adalgise* in *Verona*, laid siege to both places. Each of them made a noble defence; but *Adalgise*, despairing at last of being succoured, made his escape in the night-time to *Constantinople*. The unhappy widow of *Carloman*, with her two sons, fell into the hands of the conqueror, and were never more heard of.

Pavia continued to hold out; and *Charles*, after giving orders for continuing the blockade, or siege, of that city, marched to *Rome* with a strong detachment of his troops. The pope would willingly have dispensed with his visit, but the artful behaviour of *Charles*, and the vast appearance of devotion which he assumed, captivated all ranks of the *Romans* to such a degree, that the pope's senate and the people are said to have joined in offering to him the same sovereign power as the former emperors had over them and their city, and to have confirmed it by a solemn decree published by *Adrian*. *Charles*, however, was contented with the title of king of *Italy* and patrician of *Rome*, which had been assumed by the kings of *Lombardy*; and he not only confirmed, but enlarged, his father's donation to the pope.

This visit, the particulars of which are variously represented, being over, *Charles* returned to the siege of *Pavia*; which, during his absence from it, had made but a very small progress: but the plague raging within the place, *Didier*, after a siege of six months, was obliged to give it up. The only favour he could obtain was the preservation of his own life; and he died a monk at *Corbie*, or, as others say, at *Liege*; but some affirm that he was beheaded. Be this as it will, it is certain that in him ended the kingdom of the *Lombards*; and *Charles* caused himself to be crowned at *Pavia* king of *Italy*, with the iron crown which was used by

them,

them, and is still preserved at *Monsa*, a little town near that city. In all other respects, *Charles* behaved like the deliverer of *Italy* from the power of the *Lombards*; but subjected the people to what was, perhaps, a worse tyranny; the papal dominion; which may be said to date its greatness from that æra. He emancipated the old *Italian* nobility from their subjection to all the *Lombard* government; and, excepting the provinces which he restored to the pope, he invested them with as much independency as his own superiority could admit of.

The *Saxons* revolt, His moderation was, perhaps, greatly owing to the accounts he had received from *Germany* of the dispositions the *Saxon* princes were making for re-asserting their independency, which obliged him to return to *Germany*. They had already made incursions into his *French* dominions, and were preparing to retake *Eresburg*; which they actually effected before he returned from his *Italian* expedition. They likewise took and demolished the fort which he had erected there, and carried a very great booty from his subjects in the neighbourhood; but abandoned *Eresburg*, on hearing of the approach of *Charles* and his army. The news of this revolt exasperated *Charles* so much, that he entered *Saxony* at three different places, and, as usual, butchered the defenceless inhabitants.

Historians, in general, say, that, when he returned, his army was laden with plunder; but, at the same time, they have represented the country as being void of every thing that could incite either avarice or ambition for any purpose but that of conquest.

In *May*, 774, he held an assembly of his nobles at *Duren*; where it was agreed to prosecute, to the utmost, the *Saxon* war. He then passed the *Rhine*, and again took possession of *Eresburg*, and other strong posts in the country; and passing the *Weser*, he completely defeated the *Saxons*, who were drawn up on the opposite banks. One division of his army, however, was cut off by those barbarians; and a revolution which was threatened in *Italy* determined him once more to accept of their submission, after he had built a new, but stronger, fortress at *Eresburg*. Not satisfied with this, he transported into *France* and *Italy* about twenty thousand of the chief *Saxon* families; and obliged the remainder to swear that they would renounce idolatry and receive Christian missionaries.

By this time, the *Italian* princes began to cabal for independency; in which they were encouraged by *Adalgise*, who still resided at *Constantinople*, where he afterwards died. The archbishop of *Ravenna* quarrelled with the pope about the temporalities; the great feudatories whom *Charles* had left in *Italy*, set up claims of sovereignty; and the duke of *Friuli* was in the field at the head of an army. The vast expedition of *Charles* in his marches, broke in pieces all their schemes.

The

The duke of *Friuli* was defeated and put to death; the authority of *Charles* reconciled all differences between the pope and the archbishop of *Ravenna*; and, having put the *French* garrisons into the chief fortresses of *Italy*, he returned to *Germany*, in the year 776, after an absence of no more than four months.

A zeal for idolatry, and a love of liberty, continued to animate the *Saxons*, who recovered *Eresburg* and laid siege to *Sigebourg*. That place was strong, and its garrison numerous; so that the *Saxons* were obliged to raise the siege with great loss, just at the time when *Charles* arrived in *Germany*. The certainty of his arrival being known, the *Saxons* again submitted; and *Charles*, after ordering new forts to be raised, and fresh precautions to be taken, passed the winter at *Herstal*. On the return of the spring, he again entered into the heart of *Saxony*, where *Witikind* had made fresh efforts to recover the liberties of his country, and he ordered the *Saxon* leaders to meet him at *Paderborn*, in *Westphalia*; which many of them did, and there renewed their submission to *Charles* in the most solemn manner; but *Witikind* fled to *Denmark*. *Charles* then ordered the fortress of *Eresburg* to be rebuilt, and bridled all the country of the *Saxons* with forts and garrisons.

Charles very properly affected great splendor in his pacific appearances among the *Saxons*; and, when he held his diet at *Paderborn*, which he did through necessity, perhaps, rather than conveniency, a *Moslem* emir, who is dignified in the *European* histories with the title of count *Ibinalarabi*, and was governor of *Saragossa*, repaired thither with a large retinue, imploring his protection, in his own name and those of his friends, against *Abderame*, the *Moorish*, or rather the *Moslem*, king of *Spain*. *Charles's* ambition was flattered by this application. He granted the *Moslem's* request, and marched into *Spain* at the head of an army. One division of it entered into *Roussillon*, while he himself, marching by the way of *Navarre*, took *Pampelona* and *Saragossa*, and received the homages of many *Moslem* emirs and governors, whom he reinstated in their posts.

In repassing the *Pyrenees*, the rear of his army was attacked and defeated; and the vast plunder he and his army had acquired, fell into the hands of the *Gascons*, his enemies. This defeat, which is so famous both in romance and history, happened near *Roncevaux*, and was fatal to *Roland*, or *Orlando*; who is said to have been related to *Charles*, and was incomparably the greatest of modern legendary heroes. Notwithstanding this great loss, in which many of his bravest officers were cut off, he continued his march to *France*; where he quelled some commotions that had happened during his absence; and then, once more, set out for *Saxony*, where all was again in confusion. *Witikind* returning from *Denmark* had

and are subdued by Charles

who is defeated in his return from Spain.

headed

headed a general infurrection; expelled the bifhop and the *Chriftians* from *Bremen*; and, if we are to believe the hiftorians of *Charles*, had been guilty of many barbarities. It was no wonder if thofe naked pagans, without arms or difcipline, retreated before *Charles's* well-armed veterans. He purfued them, came up with them, defeated and butchered them; for he ordered his troops to give them no quarter. He then held a diet at *Heriftal*; where his nobility (for he now affected the dominion of all *Gaul* and *Germany*, in their utmoft extent) made a moft fplendid appearance. Here he

Legifla-
tion and
policy of
Charles.

enacted feveral laws, ftill to be found in his capitularies; and, indeed, if we confider the education of *Charles*, his ambition, his cruelties, and the genius of the people he had to deal with, his legiflation, in general, is admirable. After this, he took a tour through great part of *Saxony*, and once more received the homage of the natives; whom he obliged to give hoftages for the fafety of the *Chriftian* miffionaries he was to fend among them.

It is unjuft to believe that mere motives of religion ftimulated *Charles* to thofe horrid barbarities which he inflicted upon the unhappy pagans. He was refolved to be their fovereign, and knew no other way of humanizing them, or bringing them into the habits of civil life, but by making them *Chriftians*; fo that, in fact, introducing *Chriftianity* among the *Saxons* by *Charles*, was no more than his enforcing a police that was to render them peaceable and ufeful fubjects; and the maffacres he committed, he looked upon as only cutting off fo many brutes, who were incapable of fubmitting to civil-government. Having fettled his affairs in *Saxony*, he returned to *Franconia*; where he made preparations for another expedition into *Italy*, which was again in confufion through the intrigues of *Adalgife*, who ftill remained at *Conftantinople*.

The *Greek* emperor, in 780, ftill held the kingdom of *Naples*, where he had a governor who joined fome of the great *Lombards* in oppofing pope *Adrian*. *Charles* marched to the relief of the pope, and took with him his wife *Hildegrade*, with his two younger fons, *Pepin* and *Lewis*; who being baptized by the pope, *Pepin* was crowned king of *Lombardy*, and *Lewis* of *Aquitain*. The reputation of *Charles* was then fo high, that all divifions and factions funk before him; and the *Lombard* lords outvied one another in their profeffions of loyalty. *Charles* diffembled with all; paffed his winter at *Pavia*; and, upon his return to *France*, he left his fon *Pepin*, with a council to affift him, at *Pavia*, in his kingdom. Before his departure, he concluded a treaty with the *Greek* emprefs *Irene*; promifed his eldeft daughter in marriage to the emperor *Conftantine* VI. reconciled *Adrian* and the governor of *Naples*; and left the *Italians*, to all appearance an united people.

Upon

Upon his return to *France*, he fettled his other fon, *Lewis*, Duke of at *Orleans*; and fummoned *Taffilon*, duke of *Bavaria*, to pay homage to himfelf and the young king; which *Taffilon*, tho' much againft his nature, was obliged to comply with. *Charles*, in imagination, now enjoyed fecurity for himfelf and family; and refolved once more to vifit the *Saxons* in perfon, but at the head of an army. Having paffed the *Lippe*, he was waited upon by the kings of the *Normans*, or *Danes*, as they are now called; the *Huns*, and the *Abodrites*; and *Charles* readily promifed them his friendfhip, provided they refrained from all hoftilities on his fubjects. Returning to *France*, *Witikind* again appeared among the *Saxons*; whom he perfuaded, with very little difficulty, that *Chriftianity* and flavery were the fame; and, in an inftant, thofe barbarians were in the field with fuch arms as they could procure. *Witikind* gave out, that this was to repel an inroad of the *Sclavonians*. This pretext being foon detected, *Charles* fent four generals againft the *Saxons*; but three of them being jealous of count *Thieri*, the fourth, rafhly attacked the enemy and was defeated. To repair this misfortune, *Charles* advanced with a fifth army, and joining that under *Thieri*, which was intrenched on the banks of the *Wefer*, he marched into the heart of *Saxony*, and the *Saxons* again fubmitted to him, laying all the blame of the rebellion upon *Witikind*, who, they faid, was fled to *Denmark*. *Charles*, on this occafion, was guilty of unparalleled barbarity. "If *Witikind* is fled," faid he, "his accomplices are here;" and, immediately furrounding the *Saxons*, he ordered four thoufand five hundred of them to be feized, and their heads to be cut off, in cold blood, before his face.

Right margin: Lewis, Duke of Bavaria fubmits to him. His butchery of the Saxons.

This butchery is the more remarkable as it happened after *Charles* began to cultivate a connection with *Alcuin*, archbifhop of *York*, *Willebrod*, probably a *Scotch* or *Englifhman*, and feveral other learned divines and fcholars of that age, and valued himfelf upon the progrefs he made in letters. The barbarity he had committed did not anfwer his purpofe, for, in the year 783, the rebellion of the *Saxons*, if it can be fo called, became more general and more obftinate than ever. This year, his fecond wife, *Hildegrade*, died in *April*. *Charles*, after celebrating her funeral, put himfelf at the head of a frefh army, and made his head-quarters at the fort of *Erefburg*; while the *Saxons*, under *Witikind*, and another chief, who is called *Albion* in hiftory, were divided into two bodies; one pofted at *Ticmel*, in *Weftphalia*, and the other near the river *Hafis*.

The campaigns during this and the two following years, prefent but one continued fcene of butchery. *Charles* advanced with his two eldeft fons, at the head of his army, into the heart of the *Saxon* country, mowing down the inhabitants wherever he went, but without converting them; and he

foon

soon saw himself in danger of being a sovereign without subjects.

He spends three years in subduing them

In the winter of the first campaign, he married *Fastrade*, daughter to the duke of *Franconia*; and next year he recommenced his barbarities in *Thuringia*, but not with the same success as before, as the barbarians were now become more cautious, and did not venture to attack him, as before, in great bodies. *Charles* having some intimations of a conspiracy being formed against him in *Thuringia*, returned to *Eresburg*, and gave the command of his army in *Westphalia* to his son *Charles*. His name being less formidable than that of his father, he was attacked by a great army of the *Saxons*, of whom he killed seventeen thousand, and completely defeated them.

The history of *Charles*, at this period, is somewhat dark; nor do we clearly perceive the nature of the dangers with which he is said to have been surrounded, by conspiracies and other machinations. It seems, however, to be pretty certain, that he was either tired of the war, or apprehended himself to be in danger; and that he resolved to alter his atrocious conduct. He sent for some of the chief of the *Saxon* prisoners, and, after soothing them in terms of great affection for themselves and their countrymen, they agreed to find out *Witikind* and *Albion*, and to persuade them to appear in person before *Charles*, who, they said, was ready to take them into his protection and friendship. The chiefs demanded hostages for their safety; and *Charles*, who was then holding a diet at *Paderborn*, sent *Almasin*, one of his chief ministers, with the hostages that were demanded; and furnished them with the proper arguments to persuade the *Saxons* to embrace *Christianity*.

Witikind and *Albion* submit to him.

This negotiation seems to have taken up some time; for *Charles*, during its dependence, had returned to *France*; where, at *Attigri sur l'Aine*, the two *Saxon* chiefs (*Albion* is called duke of *Friesland*) presented themselves before him. *Charles* received them with great politeness, and, even, appearance of affection; commended their patriotism and love of liberty, and assured them of his friendship and protection. In short, the chiefs were converted and baptized; and *Witikind* never again gave *Charles* any disquiet. It is said that he returned to *Saxony*, where he was highly instrumental in converting his countrymen to *Christianity*

Charles rebuilds *Florence.*

Saxony being thus quieted, *Charles* had leisure to reduce his open and secret enemies both in *France* and *Germany*; and, passing into *Italy*, he ordered the walls of *Florence* to be rebuilt; and was everywhere received, by the common-people, as the father and deliverer of the *Italian* states. Very different were the sentiments of the pope and the great feudatories, who perceived now that they had a superior, who was in a condition to make them answer for their horrid oppressions

and

and abufe of power. They endeavoured to diffemble their difquiet; but *Charles* faw through all their intrigues. *Areguife*, duke of *Apulia* and *Benevento*; and *Taffilon*, duke of *Bavaria*; had married the two fifters of *Adalgife*, who was ftill protected by *Irene*; and, by his means, they had been able to form a fecret confederacy of the *Italian* princes againft *Charles*; to which even pope *Adrian* and the *Romans* were privately not averfe. *Charles* was perfectly well apprifed of this; and, being poffeffed of proper proofs, he laid the whole before the fenate of *Rome*, and defired the members to advife him how he was to proceed. The moft guilty were for the fevereft meafures, and the duke of *Apulia*, at laft, was forced to implore the pardon of *Charles*; which he granted, on condition of his fending his two fons as hoftages for his fidelity: and this the duke was obliged to comply with. But *Charles* generoufly fent back the eldeft fon to his father, and give the younger an education fuitable to his birth; but, at the fame time, he obliged the inhabitants of *Benevento* to take an oath of homage to his ambaffadors. During the whole of this tranfaction, the pope, and the other great feudatories, were continually folliciting *Charles* for favour to the duke of *Bavaria*.

Charles, upon his return to *Germany*, affembled a diet at Confpi- Worms, after refufing to give his daughter in marriage to the racy *Greek* emperor. He perceived that the confederacy againft againft him reached farther than he, at firft, apprehended; and that him, it extended over great part of *Germany*, as far as the banks of the *Danube* and the *Drave*; where the *Huns*, and the other northern nations who had been fo terrible to *Rome*, were then fettled. His danger feemed to encreafe his activity. He advanced with his army to the bank of the *Lech*, and ordered the *Auftrians*, the *Saxons*, and the *Lombards*, to enter the territories of the confederates by different quarters; fo that *Taffilon*, finding himfelf hemmed in on all fides, privately repaired to *Charles*'s camp, threw himfelf at his feet, and, upon profeffing his repentance, was again pardoned. Soon after, he relapfed, by entering into new intrigues with the *Huns* and *Adalgife*; but they were difcovered to *Charles*, who gave orders for him and his fon to be arrefted; and they were, by the diet, condemned to lofe their heads: but that fentence was remitted, and they were fhut up, during their lives, in a convent.

The detection and punifhment of *Taffilon* did not extin- in *Ger-* guifh the confpiracy. The *Huns*, the *Sclavonians*, and the *many de-* other barbarians in the confederacy, armed againft *Charles*; feated. and were by him twice defeated with prodigious flaughter. *Grimoald*, the fecond fon of *Aregife*, was then a hoftage with *Charles*; while his father had joined *Adalgife*, who was at the head of an army in *Italy*. Here *Charles* exhibited a noble proof of his magnanimity. He gave the command of the firft divifion of his army to *Grimoald*, on the fuppofition that he would

be

grateful for the vaſt benefits he had received from him, tho'
it was well known that the young prince's mother had a
great ſway over his affections; and, at the ſame time, he
gave him his father's forfeited eſtate and title. It was in
vain that the friends of *Charles* endeavoured to diſſuade him
from giving *Grimoald* ſo important a command, which the ſe-
quel, however, proved him to deſerve. *Adelgiſe*, chiefly thro'
his valour, was entirely defeated in *Calabria*; and all hopes of
reviving the *Lombard* kingdom were dropped. *Charles* receiving the news of this defeat, returned immediately into *Bavaria*; and now, for the firſt time, he breathed, after the
toils of war were over, the ſweets of peace; and employed
his leiſure in laying the foundations of civil empire; in mo-
delling the conſtitutions, the manners and government of the
various nations over whom he ruled, and, above all, in im-
preſſing his ſubjects with a ſenſe of religion, and giving his
courtiers, generals, and ſtateſmen, a taſte for literature.
For this purpoſe, he allotted the greateſt part of his time to
the company and converſation of the moſt learned men that
the age produced, whom he ſpared no pains or expence to
bring to his court; and whom he employed in making the
neceſſary extracts and compilations for the ſchemes of his
civil and legiſlative policy. But the truth is, *Charles* appears
to have had a genius far ſuperior to the moſt learned and in-
telligent men about his court; whom he employed chiefly in
inſtructing him in matters of antiquity, till he ſhould acquire
(which he in time did) ſufficient knowledge in the dead languages to judge for himſelf.

**Tranqui-
lity of
Charles,**

diſturbed.

Some commotions broke in upon the tranquility of *Charles*'s
government at this glorious and happy period of his reign.
The *Arabs*, or, as they are called, the *Saracens*, the greateſt
and the moſt poliſhed people then in the world, made irruptions into *France*; and the *Saxon* pagans renewed their commotions: but all of them were eaſily quieted by *Charles*;
who gave the government of *Bavaria* to count *Gerald*, a
prince of great virtue, and brother to his ſecond wife *Hildegrade*. Part of the numerous nations that are diſtinguiſhed,
in general, by the name of *Northern*, and more particularly
under thoſe of *Huns, Sclavonians, Goths, Vandals, Abodrites,
Abares*, and many other diſtinctions, acknowledged *Charles*
for their maſter; poſſibly becauſe he was beſt able to protect
them from the reſentments of the others, who mortally hated
them for becoming *Chriſtians*. This reſentment carried the
barbarians to incredible extremes; nor could all the maſſa-
cres which *Charles*, whoſe dominions now reached to the
Baltic, committed amongſt them, keep them in ſubjection.
He endeavoured to form a kind of a militia of the natives
who acknowledged themſelves to be his ſubjects, by which
he might counteract the other barbarians; but, as moſt of
them were ſtill pagans in their hearts, this expedient ſeems
to have proved ineffectual. He, at the ſame time, conſtructed

ftructed bridges upon the *Elbe*, and other great rivers, for penetrating into their country; but no fooner did he return home, than they were again in arms.

Of all thofe nations, the *Huns* were the moft determined enemies of *Charles*; and they acted with a degree of enthufiafm in defence of their country; for they more than once obliged *Charles* to repafs the *Rhine*, and to return to *Ratifbonne*; where he held the chief feat of his government in *Germany*. Eight whole years, from 790, were employed in thofe wars. *Charles*, or his generals, every fummer entered the countries of the barbarians, and put numbers of them to the fword. Sometimes they made a fhew of fubmiffion, but winter no fooner came on, than they were again in the field, and recovered all they had loft. In the campaign of 792, *Charles* purfued them as far as *Raab*, upon the *Danube*; but difeafes breaking out among his troops through their fatigues, he was obliged to return to *Ratifbonne*, and to leave the barbarians in poffeffion of all the country he had overrun.

His eight years war with the *Saxons*.

In 793, he ordered his favourite general, *Thiery*, who the laft campaign had commanded one of the divifions of the army, and was affigned as tutor in the art of war to young *Pepin*, *Charles*'s eldeft fon, to take the field at the head of an army of *Frifons* and loyal *Saxons*, againft the *Abares* and the *Huns*, the inhabitants of the modern *Auftria* and *Hungary*. *Thiery* found that the progrefs of *Charles*, during the preceding year, inftead of daunting, had exafperated the barbarians.

As we are now writing the hiftory of *Germany*, we fhall, as far as poffible, confine our narrative to that country. The enemies of *Charles* (perhaps becaufe they were fo) are everywhere reprefented as lawlefs barbarians; but whatever advantages the troops of *Charles* might have over them in armour and difcipline, it feems to be certain that they made a glorious ftand in defence of their liberties. As they were the defcendants of the antient *Celts*, they retained the manner of fortifying their country which was practifed by their anceftors; in cutting ditches, and forming lines, to a moft amazing extent; which they fortified with prodigious beams of timber, as defcribed by *Cæfar*, and other hiftorians, to have been in ufe amongft the antient *Britons*. With regard to the civil arts of life, all we know particularly in that refpect is, that they had amongft them a jurifprudence, courts of juftice, and different forms of fucceffion, according to the different conftitutions of their feveral tribes; but we know of no confufion or wars that this diverfity occafioned; for every tribe appears to have been unmolefted in the enjoyment of their modes of property and freedom. We are not, at the fame time, to forget that their country is one of the fineft and moft fruitful in *Europe*; that they were in poffeffion

fion of the fpoils of the *Roman* empire; and, that they confequently were poffeffed of vaft riches, not only in coin and
bullion, but in plates and the moft precious moveables. In
fhort, before the invafion of *Charles*, they were thought to
be the moft contented and happy people in the world. But
they were pagans, and therefore they were to be plundered,
enflaved, and maffacred.

who de-
feat his
armies,
but are
fubdued.

Thiery, as we have hinted before, found them in arms;
and they were fo well prepared to receive him, that they defeated and deftroyed his army. The news of this difafter arrived at the time when *Charles* had juft received accounts that
his affairs in *Spain* and *Italy* were in the utmoft confufion;
but having fent proper orders to his fons and generals there,
he applied all his cares to quell the *Germans* and *Huns*. He
entered their country with frefh troops, and the virtue of the
barbarians proved their fcourge; for *Charles* declared that
they were fo brave a people, it was an act of devotion to
force them to be *Chriftians*. The refiftance they made was
brave, but ineffectual; they were unequal to regular troops
and generals who were animated by enthufiafm, as they were
by liberty; and, at laft, a decifive battle was fought at *Raab*, in *Hungary*; where *Charles* loft two of his beft generals;
Henry, duke of *Friuli*; and *Gerard*, governor of *Bavaria*;
but obtained a complete victory. Above fixty thoufand barbarians, as they are called, were killed, befides chiefs and
generals; and *Charles* remained abfolute mafter of their country. The fpoils he got are faid to have been immenfe, and
he fettled the fineft part of their lands upon churches and religious foundations, without forgetting the officers and foldiers who had ferved in the expedition.

While *Charles* was thus victorious in one part of *Germany*,
Godofred, the king of *Denmark*, and feveral other leaders,
inftigated by the *Saxons*, who never had been reconciled to
his government, broke into *Friezeland* and the *Lower Saxe*.
Their progrefs was fuch, that it is hard to fay what would
have been the event, had not the fon of *Godofred* confpired
with fome of his father's domeftics, who ftrangled him, to
revenge his having repudiated the prince's mother. Upon
his death, *Charles* eafily recovered the countries he had over-
run.

A plot
againft
Charles
difcover-
ed.

About this time, or, perhaps, a little before, a natural fon
of *Charles*, called *Pepin the Humpback*, confpired in *Italy* with
fome *French* and *Germans*; but the plot being difcovered,
fome of the confpirators were put to death; and *Pepin* was,
by his father's order, fhaved, and fhut up in a monaftery.
This is faid to have been difcovered by a prieft at *Ratifbonne*,
and fome fay it was difcovered by *Arnold*, a *Lombard* prince.
The reft of the year 794, and part of 795, was fpent by
Charles in introducing into *Germany* great numbers of *Frank*
families, to be incorporated with his new pagan fubjects,
whom he pardoned on condition of their admitting *Chriftian*
                                                    miffionaries

miffionaries to convert them, and giving hoftages for their future good behaviour, and that he fhould be at liberty to difpofe as he pleafed of one third of their army.

This convention was in force no longer than the terror of his arms hung over their heads. The hatred they had for the *Abodrites*, who profeffed themfelves to be *Chriftians*, and who were employed by *Charles* to fubdue them; his introduction of *Frank* colonies to take poffeffion of their country; the maffacres and plundering his armies had committed; all confpired to revive the ftruggles of thofe pagans for their liberties, and to revenge the barbarities of *Charles*. He therefore gave them up to the fwords of his foldiers, commanded by his fon *Pepin*, king of *Italy*, who cut in pieces above thirty thoufand of the *Abares*. Upon the whole, there is not in hiftory an inftance of a more inhuman tyrant than this military propagator of *Chriftianity*, who had all the great qualities of a *Jenghiz Khan*, a *Tamerlan*, and the other illuftrious monfters mentioned in the foregoing parts of this hiftory; and was equally inhuman towards thofe who were of a different faith, or who valued their freedom above their lives. Even the *Chriftian* hiftorians, who have been at the greateft pains to blazon his virtues, have never been able to. tranfmit any juftifiable grounds for the maffacres he committed: and, from relations, favourable as they are, which they have left us, there is reafon to believe, that *Germany* has not, to this day, recovered the depopulations his army made in that country.

He depopulates *Germany*.

All the time that *Charles* was thus butchering his cotemporaries, he was bufy in providing for the happinefs of pofterity. He now chofe for his refidence *Aquis-Granum*, fince called *Aix-la-chapelle*; which he moft magnificently rebuilt or repaired. He formed the noble project of uniting the *Danube* and the *Rhine*, and of interfecting the inland parts of *Germany* by canals, for the benefit of commerce and the conveniency of travelling. But the bufinefs of ambition did not fuffer him to put thofe glorious projects into execution; and none of his fucceffors in the *German* empire have had either the genius or the power of purfuing them. In his religious character, he was as defpicable as he was dreadful in his military, and great in his civil, capacity. He kept four hundred bifhops fitting in a council, bare-footed, to difpute upon ridiculous points of faith; he oppofed, with warmth, the emprefs *Irene* in the points of image-worfhip, and rejected all alliance with her, though fhe offered him her perfon and empire. But the conduct of *Charles* towards the fee of *Rome* was entirely unaccountable, and fhews his weakeft fide.

Though, upon the diffolution of the *Lombard* government, he had affected, under the title of patrician, to be abfolute lord of *Rome*, to which he was encouraged by the *Romans* themfelves, who had been difgufted by the *Greek* emperor;

and,

and, though he even was proud of that dignity; yet *Charles* laid the real foundations of the papal power, which afterwards proved so fatal to his posterity. Having established pope *Adrian* in his dignity, he admitted his legates to the first seats in the council of *Nicea*, which *Charles* himself had called; he omitted no opportunity of contributing to his greatness; **Death of the pope.** and, when that pope died, in 795, *Charles* is said to have honoured his memory by composing some *Latin* verses in his praise.

Leo III. succeeded *Adrian*, and gave notice of his election to *Charles*; who, in the letter he wrote in answer, commended him for his obedience and fidelity. *Leo*, at the same time, presented him with the city standard; and desired him to send a proper minister, in his name, to receive homage of the *Romans*. This was disagreeable to them; and they had, in a tumult raised on that account, almost murdered his holiness, whom they scarcely looked upon as a private citizen. He escaped their fury by what was looked upon as a miracle, and he fled to *Charles* at *Paderborn*. Though the latter was then employed in the most important concerns, he seems to have postponed every consideration to give satisfaction to his holiness.

Charles marches into *Italy*, Upon some new commotions of the *Saxons*, he had sent for his son king *Pepin* out of *Lombardy*, and put him at the head of his armies. At the same time, he held a dyet of his vassals and great nobility on the *Elbe*; and the king of the *Abodrites*, who was a vassal to *Charles*, was murdered by the pagans as he was repairing to it. *Charles*, upon this, charged his son to give the rebels no quarter; and they were next to exterminated. All who remained were, by *Charles*, planted upon the maritime coasts of *Holland* and *Flanders*; where they did him excellent service against the *Norman* pirates, who then infested the *European* seas. Immediately after this, he made an hasty settlement of his affairs in *Spain* and *France*, and, having sent back *Leo* under a guard to *Rome*, in 799, he called a dyet, or assembly, at *Mentz*; where he concerted measures for a grand expedition into *Italy*; and then, as the summit of his ambition, he intended to assume the authority and title of emperor of *Rome*.

where he is crowned emperor. It was easy for such a prince as *Charles*, backed by a numerous party amongst the *Romans* themselves, and by a still more numerous army, to succeed in this. Upon his arrival at *Rome*, he held an assembly of all the principal nobility and inhabitants, who cleared the pope of all the charges that had been brought against him; and then he was, with vast pomp and formality, crowned, by the appellations of *Charles Augustus*, emperor of the *Romans*. *Charles*, who well knew the impression which exteriors make upon a people, omitted no piece either of civil or sacred pageantry upon this occasion. He was saluted, and acknowledged as, emperor by the pope and all his nobility; his picture was exposed in public;

to *Augustus* he joined the title of *Cæsar*; he wore not only the dress, but the badges, of the antient *Roman* emperors, even to the taking an eagle for his devise, or armorial bearing; but to this eagle he gave two heads; intimating that he, in fact, considered himself as the head of the eastern, as well as of the western empire; but the two heads were difused by some of his succeffors. Amidst all this profusion of grandeur, *Charles* affected a singular modesty, and even to decline the honour that was done him; pretending, that, had he known what was defigned, he would not have appeared in public. Notwithstanding this self-denial, it is certain that *Charles* was fo fond of this dignity, that he never would fuffer it to be omitted in his titles; and, ever after, he infifted upon its being bestowed upon him; and, that he fhould be confidered as being upon an equality with the *Greek* emperor. If we examine his right to that great honour, we fhall find it to be founded upon conquest and the consent of the *Roman* people, who, being no longer under the protection of the *Greek* emperors, were at liberty to chufe *Charles* to defend and govern them. As to the power of the pope to confer fuch a dignity, it is justly to be despised; it not being his to confer: and he acted, in the whole transaction, only as the head agent of the people.

Charles, however, was as kind to the pope as if he had been folely indebted to him for his new dignity. He confirmed to him his father *Pepin*'s gift of the exarchate and fee of *Ancona*, to which he added various other territories; but still with a refervation of the imperial fovereignty to himself and his fucceffors.

His generofity to the pope.

Upon the return of *Charles* to *France*, he found there an affembly of ambaffadors fent from various ftates and princes to congratulate him upon his new dignity: particularly from *Scotland*, *Morocco*, *Perfia*, and *Conftantinople* itfelf; from whence the eaftern emperor, *Nicephorus*, fent him a ceffion of the titles of emperor of the weft, *Cæfar*, and *Auguftus*. As we are now writing the hiftory of *Charles* only as the head of the *Germanic* empire, we fhall omit what relates to him as king of *France*. His power feems to have been confirmed by his new dignity; for he was, in a manner, all powerful on the continent of *Europe*, from *Benevento* in *Italy*, to *Bavaria* in *Germany*. But, while he was thus at the fummit of his glory, and forming his empire, by his laws and inftitutions, to peace, order, and regularity, the *Danes*, *Normans*, and *Saxons*, took arms againft him, about the year 803. This war carried *Charles*, for the eighth time, at the head of an army, into the country of the *Saxons*; where, inftead of putting them to the fword, as ufual, he tranfplanted vaft numbers of them to *Flanders*, *Provence*, *Switzerland*, *Italy*, and even *Rome* itfelf; and fettled the *Abodrites*, who had been faithful to him, in the *Saxon* country. This expedient proved fuccefsful, and the *Saxons* ever after continued quiet.

Charles

Charles then advanced with his army towards the *Elbe*, to oppofe *Godfrey*, king of *Denmark*, who had got together a large fleet to invade *Charles's* dominions. This war ended in a treaty of mutual forbearance and friendfhip.

Deaths of the children of Charles. About this time, two of *Charles's* fons, *Pepin* and *Charles*, died; the one at *Milan*, the other in *Bavaria*. Their deaths, with that of a beloved daughter, funk deep into the fpirit of *Charles*; and, in a few years after, *Godfrey*, king of *Denmark*, who proved to be the moft dangerous enemy *Charles* ever had to deal with, broke into the country of the *Abodrites*, which he conquered, and hung up one of their princes, but retired in the winter to make preparations for renewing his invafions in the fpring. *Charles* was then at *Aix-la-Chapelle*, and, being well acquainted with *Godfrey's* martial abilities and vaft power, he gave way to another treaty being fet on foot. That proving abortive, *Godfrey* threatened to lead his arms to the gates of *Aix-la-Chapelle*; but he was prevented by the diverfion which the generals of *Charles* gave him acrofs the *Elbe*; where they gained many advantages, and carried the war to his frontiers. *Godfrey*, in the mean time, was not idle. Leaving a large army to fupport the *Sclavonians* in their revolt againft *Charles*, he embarked a great body of land-troops on board a fleet of two hundred fail; by which, all of a fudden, he reduced the iflands on the coaft of *Friefland*: from thence he invaded the continent, where he carried all before him.

Charles, who was then at *Aix-la-Chapelle*, raifed a numerous army, with which he marched to oppofe *Godfrey*; who being affaffinated by one of his guards, was fucceeded by his fon, a perfon of lefs turbulent temper; and a ceffation of arms being agreed upon, the *Danes* reimbarked on board their fhips.

who makes Bernard king of Italy. In the year 810, *Charles*, with confent of his fon *Lewis*, king of *Aquitain*, declared *Bernard*, the infant fon of *Pepin*, king of *Italy*, though illegitimate, his father's fucceffor in that kingdom. He had, at this time, three great armies on foot; one of which lay on the other fide of the *Elbe* to watch the motions of the northern nations; while another acted againft the barbarians on the fide of *Pannonia*, or *Hungary*; and a third in *Britany*.

He provides a marine. Being fenfible of the defencelefs ftate of his fea-coafts, he gave orders for fortifying them. The multiplicity of his affairs, and fatigues (notwithftanding the incredible vigour of his conftitution) and the age of 70, had brought infirmities upon him; for which reafon he affociated with himfelf into government his fon *Lewis* at *Aix-la-Chapelle*. This was done in a moft magnificent affembly of thofe nobles whom he confulted on all great occafions, and whofe confent gave a fanction to his laws. To them he declared his fon *Lewis*, and his heirs, his fucceffors in the imperial dignity; and he was recognized accordingly, and proclaimed emperor. After

entering

entering upon the exercise of that high office, he returned to *France*, where his presence was necessary; while his father applied himself to settle the civil and ecclesiastical affairs of his vast dominions, which were enlarged two thirds since his father's death. He gave the city of *Ulm* to the monks, and settled all his temporal concerns in *Germany* with great equity.

He had, by this time, provided a sufficient marine to op- **His death,** pose that of the northern nations, and he had stationed a fleet at *Boulogne*; but, about the middle of *January*, 814, he felt himself feverish; and his disorder turned to a pleurisy, which carried him off on the twenty-seventh of the same month, aged seventy-eight years; having reigned, in *France*, forty-eight years, four months, and four days; in *Italy*, about forty years; and fourteen in the empire. He had made his will some time before his death; in which he stiled himself *Charles*, emperor, *Cæsar*, the most invincible king of the *Franks* He left his son *Lewis* all the countries from *Spain* to the *Rhine*; *Italy* and *Bavaria* to *Pepin*: and *France*, from the *Loire* to *Ingolstadt*; and *Austria*, from the *Schelde* to the confines of *Brandenburgh*; to his son *Charles*: but the two last princes died before himself. This will was made some years before his death, and it is said he made another much more in favour of *Lewis*. He was buried at *Aix* (where he had built a chapel, from which it is now called *Aix-la-Chapelle*) with great funeral-pomp. When he died, he left many noble plans unfinished; particularly with regard to his marine; which, however, he had very considerably improved.

Authors have been greatly divided with regard to the cha- **and character.** racter of *Charles the Great*, for such he certainly was. All agree that he had an uncommon genius both for arms and government; and nature pointed him out, by his endowments both of body and mind, as the master of that great empire which he inherited or acquired; but, in other respects, his character is doubtful. Though he was the author, not only of the civil, but the ecclesiastical, government of his dominions; it is not easy to defend him with regard to his brother's widow and family. When he married his wife *Desiderata*, daughter to *Dedier*, king of the *Lombards*, he is said to have had another wife alive; a practice not uncommon in those days: and his repudiating that lady, on account of the humanity her father shewed to the widow and children of his brother *Carloman*, is an indelible stain upon his memory; especially as, without any regard to their rights, he caused himself, on *Carloman*'s death, to be crowned king of *Austrasia*. No encomiums can be made on the chastity of *Charles*; for, besides wives, he entertained an abundance of concubines; or, according to the rude *Christianity* that prevailed in those days, and some remains of which still subsist in *Germany*, wives of an inferior order. It is therefore a difficult matter to afcertain the number, or rank, either of his wives or con-cubines; and, confequently, of his legitimate or illegitimate iffue; for it is certain he gave the fame education to both. He was, as we have already hinted, paffionately fond of learned men and learning; in which, if we believe his hi-ftorians, and confider the rudenefs of that age, with his own avocations to war and bufinefs, he made a very furprifing progrefs. There is too much reafon to believe that *Charles*, according to the barbarous bigotry of the times, thought that all crimes might be atoned for by an unbounded liberality to the church and churchmen; which he accordingly exer-cifed.

In his private deportment towards his minifters, courtiers, and his own family, he was amiable beyond defcription. In his nature he was open, generous, and unfufpecting. Though a great œconomift, he appeared, on folemn occa-fions, with prodigious magnificence and fplendor; fo that the princes of the continent, fome of whom had great terri-tories, took a kind of pride at appearing in his parliaments or diets, and in being ranked among his vaffals. Though affa-ble, he knew how to maintain ftate to the full. His appli-cation to bufinefs of every kind was exceffive, and he was grateful for all fervices done him; but it was remarked that he feldom beftowed different offices on the fame perfon. He is juftly accufed of inhumanity towards the *Saxons* and pa-gans, whom he fought to convert to *Chriftianity* by the power of the fword. If an apology can be made for him, on this head, it muft arife from the woful prepoffeffions of the times of ignorance and bigotry in which he lived; and which often rendered the extinction of the human fpecies, who refufed to be *Chriftians*, meritorious in his eyes. But we fhall have farther opportunities of mentioning this great man.

2. Lewis the Debonnair.

Acceffion and firft acts of *Lewis*.

THIS prince was in *Aquitain* when he heard of his fa-ther's death, but he immediately haftened to *Aix-la-Chapelle*. During his father's life-time, he had behaved fo well towards his fubjects, and eftablifhed fo wonderful a re-formation among them, that *Charles* was often heard to thank God for having given him fuch a fon. He was born in the year 778; and he had married *Ermengarde*, the daughter of *Enguerand*, count of *Hefbai*, in the diocefe of *Leige*. In other refpects, he was thought to refemble his father in all the accomplifhments of body and mind, and to be but little his inferior in either. Upon his acceffion, his empire was bounded, on the north, by the *Baltic* and *Denmark*; on the weft, by the *Ocean*; on the fouth, by the *Mediterranean*, the *Adriatic*,

Adriatic, and the *Pyrenean* mountains ; and, on the eaft, by the *Viftula* and the *Teiffe* : fo that he fucceeded to a much greater extent of territory than any prince fince his time has ever poffeffed in *Europe*.

Upon his acceffion, being apprehenfive that his nephew, *Bernard*, king of *Italy*, would create him fome trouble, he difpatched an army, under the command of his generals *Baldener*, *Waldener*, *Landbrecht*, and *Junghrecht* ; who were to take poffeffion of *Aix-la-Chapelle* till his arrival. They were oppofed by *Hatwin*, mayor of the palace in the late reign ; who killed one of the generals, but was himfelf defeated and killed in his turn. *Lewis* arrived at *Aix* thirty days after, and foon began to difcover fymptoms of a difpofition very different from what the world thought him poffeffed of.

After he had been again proclaimed emperor, and given audience to the ambaffadors of foreign princes, he received the homage of the duke of *Benevento* ; who was to pay him annually feven thoufand crowns of gold, as a tribute for his dutchy : and then he ordered his nephew *Bernard* to appear before him, to do him homage for the kingdom of *Italy*. In the mean time, he fent his fon, *Pepin*, to govern *Aquitain* ; and *Lothair*, *Bavaria* ; and kept his third fon, *Lewis*, about his own perfon. After which, he feverely punifhed the accomplices of *Hatwin* in the late infurrection. *Bernard*, upon his arrival at *Aix-la-Chapelle*, found that many of his friends had, under that pretence, been put to death, or profcribed ; but the emperor having confirmed him in his kingdom, he ftifled his indignation at that time. *Lewis*, under pretence of reforming his court, and providing better for his fifters, fhut them up in convents, and fent their male-favourites to prifon.

He then affembled a diet at *Paderborn*, where he received intelligence of a confpiracy, againft the life of pope *Leo*, at *Rome* ; which being difcovered, the pope had, by his own authority, put fome of the ring-leaders to death ; and this action of his holinefs was refented by *Lewis* as being an invafion upon his fovereignty. He ordered *Bernard* to repair from *Paderborn* to *Rome*, and to fettle affairs there. In the mean while, pope *Leo* died, after making his fubmiffion for what had happened ; and *Stephen* V. who fucceeded him, immediately upon his election, fet out for *France*, where *Lewis* was, and crowned him emperor at *Rheims* ; the emperor, for this mark of refpect, forgiving all that had happened, though the pontif had taken upon himfelf to act as pope, without waiting for the imperial confirmation.

Lewis had penetration enough to fee the power of the church every day encreafing in his dominions, and that churchmen not only affected to be independent of his government, but, in right of their fiefs and abbeys confirmed by the late emperor, they headed armies of their own tenants

He difobliges the clergy.

B b 2

in the field, sometimes to the amount of ten thousand; and they lived with all the temporal pomp of the greatest princes. *Lewis* assembled a diet at *Aix* for regulating all kinds of abuses, both ecclesiastical and civil; and especially to inhibit ecclesiastics from meddling in temporal affairs, and wearing gold, silver, and jewels upon their ordinary cloaths. This proposal, though reasonable in itself, produced a kind of combination against *Lewis* among the ecclesiastics; which went so far as even to form a design for deposing him, and to substitute another emperor in his stead. The *Italian* clergy were the chiefs of this conspiracy, and they chose *Bernard*, king of *Italy*, for their head.

Rebellion and death of *Bernard*, king of *Italy*. About this time, he convened the states of his empire; and, in imitation of his father, who was very fond of seeing his sons sovereigns in his life-time, he associated his eldest son, *Lothair*, in the empire; made his second son, *Pepin*, king of *Aquitain*; and his third, *Lewis*, king of *Bavaria*. *Bernard*, king of *Italy*, had now made such a progress in the schemes he had undertaken, that he had persuaded most of the cities and states in the kingdom to throw off their dependency upon the empire; and being, as we have already seen, backed by a powerful body of the clergy, he obliged them to take an oath of fidelity to himself. *Bernard*, in this, did not follow the dictates of his own ambition singly; the *Italians*, in general, affected independency upon all *German* connection, and wanted a prince only of power and spirit to head them. *Bernard* offered them his best services for that purpose, and raised an army, but they were afraid to support him. The emperor, *Lewis*, prepared to pass the *Alps* with an army far superior to that of his nephew; who was so terrified, that he disbanded his forces, and, passing the *Alps*, threw himself at the emperor's feet. *Lewis* refused to determine his fate, and referred him, and the chief of his accomplices who surrendered themselves at the same time, to the next meeting of parliament at *Aix*. There they were tried. *Bernard* and the bishop of *Orleans*, with others of the ring-leaders of the rebellion, as it was called, were condemned to suffer death. Others, less culpable, lost their eyes, or were imprisoned for life. *Bernard*'s sentence was commuted to the loss of his eyes, but the operation being performed by an unskilful hand, he died three days after it.

Other rebellions in *Germany*, Other rebellions broke out at the same time. The *Abodrites*, who had hitherto been so faithful to the house of *Charlemagne*, revolted; and *Morman*, the count *de Bretagne*, a vassal of the empire, declared himself an independent king. *Lewis* raised an army, and, marching into their country, *Morman*'s subjects murdered him. *Lewis*, upon this, declared *Nomenon* count of *Britany*.

Soon after, as he was returning back to *Germany*, his empress, *Hermengrade*, died; and. proceeding to *Herislul*, he found his *German* and *Italian* affairs in great disorder. One

Sigon

Sigon had murdered *Grimoald*, and made himfelf duke of *Benevento*; but was pardoned and confirmed by *Lewis*, on account of the rich prefents he made him. *Linderif*, the leader of the *Huns*, complained of the duke of *Friuli*; but received no fatisfaction from *Lewis*. The count of *Gafcony* revolted, but was defeated by the king of *Aquitain*; and *Sclaomir*, formerly the prince, or leader, of the *Abodrites*, having called in the *Normans* to his affiftance againft the imperial deputy, was likewife defeated; and, both thefe rebels being taken, were, by the diet of *Aix-la-Chapelle*, fentenced to die; but *Lewis* converted their fentence into exile.

About this time, *Lewis* was fo much affected by the death of his wife, that he fell into a ftate of melancholy, and appeared defirous of retiring to a convent. With fome difficulty, he was perfuaded to marry *Judith*, the daughter of *Guelph*, count of *Ravenfburg* and *Aldorf*; and a lady of fuch perfections both in mind and body, that fhe obtained a complete afcendancy over her hufband. About the time of this marriage, *Pepin*, the emperor's fon, king of *Aquitain*, died.

Lindevit, already mentioned, whom fome call duke of *Sclavonia*, and who had large territories in *Hungary*, defpairing of making his peace with *Lewis*, for having cut off a part of the imperial troops in their march to *Italy*, was, at this time, in rebellion; but was defeated by the duke of *Friuli*; and, being hunted from place to place, he was, at laft, put to death by a *Dalmatian* lord, with whom he had taken refuge.

and Hun-gary.

In the year 820, the emperor held a parliament of the *French* and *German* nobility at *Thionville*; where his fon *Lothair* was married to *Ermengarde*, the daughter of a *German* count. About this time, *Lewis* exhibited many proofs of weaknefs, if not infanity. Though devout, even to fuperftition, he quarrelled with the bifhops about their non-refidence; and he took into his confidence *Adelard*, abbot of *Corbie*, who had been the chief prompter of *Bernard's* rebellion; and was elder brother to *Walla*, one of the wifeft men in the empire, and a favourite with *Charles the Great*; but who, being difgraced, had turned monk. *Adelard* not only got from *Lewis* the pardon of all his affociates in the rebellion of *Bernard*, but prevailed with him to fubmit to public penance for the death of *Bernard*, and the feverity with which he had treated his natural brothers, whom he had banifhed to *Bavaria*. The emperor fuffered *Pafchal* I. to impofe fo far upon his good-nature, that he exercifed the papal function without being confirmed by him; but pretending to be independent of the imperial authority, he thereby rouzed *Lewis* from his lethargy; who fent his fon *Lothair* into *Italy* with an army which over-run *Pafchal*, who invited him to *Rome*, where he crowned him emperor, and humbly retracted all his arrogant pretenfions. Upon the departure of *Lothair*, how-

ever,

ever, from *Rome*, two noble *Roman* ecclesiastics, *Theodore* and *Leo*, great sticklers for the imperial interest, had their eyes put out, and were beheaded in the pope's palace. When the emperor was preparing to punish this flagrant insult upon his authority, the pope purged himself by oath from all knowledge of the murder, and the emperor was satisfied.

Affairs of Italy.

Eugene II. succeeded *Paschal*; and the *Roman* clergy, as well as the people, were, at that time, so abandoned and irregular, that the emperor *Lothair* was obliged, once more, to take a journey to *Rome*; where he again confirmed the imperial authority, and re-established the tranquility of the public. About this time, *Germany* was visited by many natural calamities; such as earthquakes, inundations, and the like; which swept off half the inhabitants of the empire A diet, in the year 825, was assembled at *Nimeguen*, upon the affairs of *Brittany*, which was still in arms; but, by the vigour of the diet, those commotions were quelled; and *Lothair*, having settled affairs at *Rome*, met his father at *Aix*; where, by the states, he was declared his successor to the empire; and then sent, by his father, back to *Italy*. The emperor now added to the kingdom of *Bavaria*, which he had given to his son *Lewis*, *Bohemia*, *Moravia*, *Hungary*, and *Vindmarch*; but he lost *Catalonia* to the *Moors*, and *Navarre* by an insurrection of the natives; and *Heriolt*, a *Christian* king, whom he had imposed upon *Denmark*, was driven out of his kingdom by a rebellion of his subjects. The successes of the *Moors* were chiefly attributed to the misconduct of *Lothair* and *Pepin* on the side of *Spain*.

Charles the Bald born.

By this time, *Judith*, the emperor's beloved wife, had brought him a son, who was baptized *Charles*. *Lewis* having disposed of all his dominions, the empress found great difficulty in providing for her son; which, at last, was effected out of *Lothair*'s territories; and the latter was obliged to swear that he would be the child's guardian and protector. Afterwards he bestowed upon the young *Charles* all that part of *Germany* which is situated between the *Maine*, the *Rhine*, the *Neckar*, and the *Danube*; together with the countries that now form the republics of *Geneva* and *Swisserland*; so that *Charles*, in effect, was now king of *Germany*, and the emperor was entirely governed by his wife.

Distractions of the empire.

The affairs of the empire, through the mismanagement of the emperor's sons, especially *Lothair* and *Pepin*, were, at this time, in the utmost disorder; and the emperor was himself obliged, for the reformation of his empire, to establish a court of enquiry; the members of which were called *missi dominici*, and *Walla* was at its head. It appears that the empire was then divided into two parties. The one consisted of the emperor's sons by his former marriage, who resented the dismembering their dominions to provide for young *Charles*. The other party was headed by the empress *Judith*. *Walla* having made a very unfavourable report from

the

the court of enquiry, concerning the emperor and his government, *Judith* prevailed with her husband to send him back to his cell; and to employ *Bernard*, count of *Barcelona*, as his first minister, whom she was said to be in love with, as he was with her, to the great scandal of the public. Be this as it will, it is certain that *Bernard*, who was a man of great courage and abilities, under colour of subduing the *Bretons*, raised an army, and summoned *Lewis*, king of *Bavaria*, and *Pepin*, king of *Aquitain*, to join it; but both of them united with the malecontents against their father. *Lewis* was no match for this rebellion. His wife fled to a monastery, and *Bernard* obtained leave to retire to his government of *Catalonia*. The empress was drawn from her convent by *Pepin*; and she promised, not only to become a recluse, but to persuade her husband to turn monk. *Judith* then went to her husband, and, by her advice (his army having abandoned him) he demanded a conference with the nobles of his empire. An assembly was accordingly held at *Compeigne*, where he behaved with great appearance of contrition, and promised that his wife should turn nun. *Adelard* was at the head of this rebellion, but both he and *Pepin* were disappointed, for they imagined that the emperor would resign his throne to *Pepin*; for, instead of that, the assembly was so much affected by the appearance of distressed majesty, that he was desired to resume it.

Soon after, *Lothair*, upon whom the malecontents chiefly depended for support, arrived with his army; and, though he did not insist upon his father resigning his empire, he placed about his person certain monks, who were instructed to persuade him to quit the world. *Pepin* and *Lewis*, seeing that *Lothair* aimed at being sole emperor, retired with disgust to their own dominions; and *Gombaud*, one of the monks who had been placed about the old emperor's person, being gained over by him, succeeded so well, in exciting the public indignation at the imprisonment of *Lewis*, that the *Germans* took his part against his sons, and delivered him from his confinement. A general diet was held at *Nimeguen*, where the sense of the public was so much in favour of *Lewis*, that the heads of the malecontents were obliged to abscond; and *Lothair* himself, not only made his submission, but gave up the chiefs of his party; who, in a subsequent diet, held at *Aix*, were punished as their crimes deserved; some by being beheaded, some by excæcation, and some by being drowned. *Lewis* then sent for his empress, but she had taken the veil; and some dispute was held, whether she could quit it without leave of the pope; who declared that she might, as she had taken it against her will.

The empire was then in a woful condition; the emperor's sons, who were as weak, but far more wicked, than their father, were at the head of all public treason. The church was every day gaining ground in power and territo-

The emperor prevails against his sons,

ries,

ries ; so that *Germany* seemed to be no better than an eccle
fiaftical ariftocracy ; and, in *Italy*, the papal power had al
moft extinguifhed the imperial. The emperor, by his wife'
advice, did the beft he could to oblige his fons to return to
their duty, and to unite among themfelves ; but with little
effect. She had recalled count *Bernard* to court, and had
been obliged to take an oath that nothing criminal had paffed
between them.

who again
rebel.

    The recall of *Bernard* added to the court intrigues. *Pepin*
and *Lewis* were difgufted afrefh, as was alfo *Gombaud* the
monk at not being made firft minifter. The emprefs and
her favourite held the reins of the empire with a firm hand.
They obliged all who were concerned in the late commotions, to fubfcribe to the partition of the empire in favour of
young *Charles*. *Lothair* was depofed from being emperor,
but allowed to keep the empty title of king of *Italy* ; and
was obliged to promife to do nothing without his father's allowance.

    About this time, a breach happened between count *Ber-*
nard and the emprefs *Judith* ; and he privately reconciled
himfelf to *Pepin*, who had been detained at court as a kind
of prifoner ; but he now efcaped to his kingdom of *Aquitain*,
where he raifed an army, and the three fons again united to
dethrone their father. *Lewis* raifed an army, and fummoned
his nobility to affemble at *Orleans* ; but he no fooner fet out
on his march, than he heard that his fon *Lewis*, king of
Bavaria, had revolted likewife ; which obliged the emperor
to change the place of the diet to *Mentz*. *Lewis* was not
fupported in his rebellion, and he threw himfelf at his father's feet, who exacted from him an oath of future obedience. *Lothair* feeing their treafons thus difconcerted, reconciled himfelf to his father at *Frankfort* ; and then the emperor marched againft *Pepin*, who, being in no condition to
ftand his ground, furrendered himfelf, and was fent prifoner
to *Treves*, the emperor taking his kingdom of *Aquitain* into
his own hands, and fettling it upon his youngeft fon *Charles*,
who was then about nine years of age.

    Lothair had now returned to *Italy*, and, perceiving that the
attachment of the *Germans*, by means of the ecclefiaftics,
was every day growing ftronger towards the papal fee, he
found means, by the moft abject fubmiffion, to gain over
the pope, *Gregory* IV. to his intereft ; and even to prevail
with him to accompany him to *Germany* ; where he was in
hopes the very name of a pope would create a general infurrection in his favour, which it actually did ; for the *German*
ecclefiaftics, with *Walla*, who was now abbot of *Corbie*, at
their head, declared for the rebels. Some of the *German* bifhops however (among whom was *Dreux*, bifhop of *Mentz*,
the emperor's natural brother) kept firm to their allegiance,
and reproached the pope, in the moft bitter terms, for abet-
ing fo unnatural a rebellion.

Lothair,

Lothair, at firft, pretended he was come at the head of his army to oppofe *Pepin*, who had efcaped from his guards and was again in arms; and the pope, the better to deceive the emperor, had prefented himfelf as a mediator between him and his fons. This intercourfe proved fatal to the emperor *Lewis*; for the pope found means, during the negotiation, to debauch the imperial army to the fide of the filial rebels, on pretence of his being excommunicated. The emperor was weak enough, from the ridiculous reverence he had for the pontif, to contribute towards his own depofition; for, inftead of fighting the rebels, he threw himfelf into their hands. He was confined in their camp; his emprefs was fent a prifoner to *Tortona*, and his youngeft fon, *Charles*, to a caftle in the foreft of *Ardenne*.

Matters being brought to this pafs, the three brothers be- Difgrace-ful pe-nance of the em-peror, gan to difagree in dividing the fpoils of the empire; and *Lewis* and *Pepin* retired to their refpective dominions. *Lothair*, who pretended to fucceed his father as fole emperor, fummoned together a parliament, of which the greateft part was compofed of ecclefiaftics, at *Soiffons*, in *France*; where one *Ebbon*, an archbifhop of *Rheims*, whom *Lewis* had elevated from the loweft ftation to that dignity, was appointed to degrade his fovereign from the exercife of royalty. This ceremony was performed with circumftances that difgrace human nature. *Lewis* was obliged to kneel upon a hair-cloth fpread before the altar, after he had, by the archbifhop's orders, furrendered up his fword, its belt, and his royal habit, and cloathed himfelf in penitential robes. A lift of his mifdemeanours was then produced, and he was obliged to read and acknowledge them. Among many other articles charged againft him, was his having fet out on a march on *Afh-Wednefday*, and fummoning a parliament on *Holy-Thurfday* The emperor performed his penance with the greateft meeknefs; nor did thofe haughty ecclefiaftics, or his unnatural fon, in the procefs they made out againft him, deign to give him even the appellation of emperor.

This infamous ceremony being over, *Lothair* afcended the imperial throne, and fhut his father up, without either the comforts or neceffaries of life, a prifoner in the abbey of St. *Medard*. A thoufand ftratagems were employed to induce him to turn monk; but he bore all his mortifications with fo refigned a firmnefs, that the public were touched with his misfortunes. This, perhaps, was not a little owing to the weaknefs of *Lothair*, and the ill ufe which he made of his power. Even the monks exclaimed againft him; and the bifhop of *Mentz*, together with count *Bernard*, at laft, prevailed with the king of *Bavaria* to take his father's part. An army was foon raifed by the *Bavarian*, and it was joined by the *Saxons*. *Lothair* was fo much detefted, that few of the *Germans* joined him; and *Pepin* added his forces to thofe of *Lewis* of *Bavaria*. *Lothair* committed his father and brother

Charles

Charles to the abbey of St. *Dennis*, and retired to *Burgundy*.

The father was re-eftablifhed on the imperial throne, but not before he was reconfecrated by the bifhops; and all the punifhment the traitor *Ebbon* met with, was the deprivation of his fee, and his making a public recantation.

During thofe tumultuous tranfactions, the northern nations, or *Normans*, as they were called, piratically infefted the coafts of the empire; burnt *Hamburgh*, and plundered *Friefland*; and obliged the *Germans* to buy their abfence by a fum of money. In all other refpects, the empire m.   .ave been faid to be without any form of government. 'I .. .edy this, the emperor iffued out a commiffion of reforma.. ..n and refumption of his ufurped rights.

Lothair, who ftill continued in *Burgundy*, feemed, at firft, well difpofed towards his father's re-eftablifhment on the throne; and threw all the blame of his fufferings upon the ecclefiaftics. But thofe appearances vanifhed when he was himfelf fupported by the *French* and *Italian* nobility, who hated the *Germans*. He retired to *Burgundy*, kept his army on foot, and more than once defeated his father's generals. The emprefs *Judith* was, by this time, returned to court; and, notwithftanding all that fhe and her family had fuffered, fhe renewed her intrigues. Finding the kings of *Bavaria* and *Aqu-tain* not very inclinable to enter into her views, for the aggrandizement of her fon *Charles*, fhe applied herfelf to *Lothair*, who had been defeated in *Burgundy* by the imperial troops, and had thrown himfelf at his father's feet, by whom he was received and pardoned with tears of joy.

At this time, the emperor *Lewis* feemed, more than ever, to be confirmed in the imperial throne. He had returned, with his fons *Lewis* and *Pepin*, to *Aix-la-Chapelle*; and held a parliament, with great fplendor, at *Thionville*; where the accomplices of *Lothair*, in his rebellion, had been feverely cenfured and punifhed. *Lothair* made no refiftance to thofe proceedings, but fecretly ftrengthened his intereft, while he was treating with the emprefs *Judith*. In this his power clafhed with that of the pope, who had on his fide many of the *Italian* nobility, and they carried their complaints to the emperor againft *Lothair*'s encroachments. The emperor promifed them redrefs, and propofed marching to *Italy* with an army; but he was diverted from this defign by a frefh invafion of his dominions by the *Normans*, which he foon fuppreffed.

The treaty between the emprefs and *Lothair* being now at an end, fhe had recourfe to her power over her hufband; and, no good underftanding fubfifting among his fons, he ventured to declare his fon *Charles*, who was then about fourteen, king of *Neuftria*; which comprehended Upper *Burgundy*, *Alface*, *Swifferland*, and *Suabia*; *Lewis*, king of *Bavaria*, fubfcribing the declaration. The death of *Pepin* king

king of *Aquitain*, who left two fons, *Pepin* and *Charles*, gave a new turn to the affairs of the empire. *Judith* ufed her influence with the emperor, her hufband, to call a diet at *Worms*, to deprive his grandfon, *Pepin*, of his father's kingdom of *Aquitain*. *Lothair* was invited to this diet, where he came with a very bad grace; but the emprefs pretended that fhe was his friend, and offered her intereft towards procuring him fome of *Pepin*'s dominions. In fhort, a frefh partition of *Lewis*'s empire was made. The king of *Bavaria* oppofed this project, and raifed an army, as his father did another, with which he advanced within four leagues of *Frankfort*. The king of *Bavaria*, or, as he is fometimes called, of *Germany*, finding his authority weakened by the prefence of his father, fubmitted; to the great difguft of his nobility, who refufed to agree to the ambitious fchemes of the emprefs, or to any partition of power that was to render them more dependent than they were. The emperor and the king of *Bavaria* ftruck up an agreement that matters fhould continue on the fame footing with regard to the kingdom of *Germany*.

Frefh troubles now ftarted up in *Aquitain*, where many of the nobility were difgufted at the injuftice done to the young *Pepin*; but the emperor over-ruled them, though *Pepin*'s party refufed to deliver up that prince to his grandfather. The emperor paffed his winter at *Frankfort*, his Lent at *Coblentz*, his Eafter at *Conftance*; and, in *May*, he went to *Worms*, where he was waited upon by his fon *Lothair*; and here the laft partition of his dominions was made. It was agreed, that *Lothair* fhould be mafter of all *Italy*, and of the country from the *Maefe* to the *Alps*; *Lewis* was to retain the kingdom of *Bavaria*; and *Charles* was to poffefs all that lies between the *Loire*, the *Rhone*, the *Maefe*, and the *Ocean*.

In the mean while, the nobility of *Aquitain* chofe young *Pepin* for their fovereign; but the emperor fent him prifoner to *Metz*, and forced them to accept of his fon *Charles*. *Lewis* of *Bavaria* refented the late partition, and again put himfelf and his fubjects in arms. *Lewis*, though now aged and infirm, took the field, to crufh this unnatural-fon, who had created him fo many difquietudes. In his march, he was **Death** attacked by a defluxion upon his lungs; and an eclipfe happening, it had fuch an effect upon his fpirits, that he was carried, for his recovery, to an ifland in the *Rhine*; a fpot which was thought to be peculiarly healthful. From thence he fent for his brother, the archbifhop of *Mentz*, and other ecclefiaftics; while the king of *Bavaria*, not daring to keep the field againft his father, had retired to his own dominions. *Lewis*, by his will, divided his treafures and rich moveables among his family, ecclefiaftics, and the poor. He confirmed the donations of *Pepin* and *Charles the Great* to the church of *Rome*; and expired, partly by old age and difeafe, and partly through

through heart-break at the behaviour of his son *Lewis of Ba-varia*, on the twenty-first of *June*, 840.

and cha-racter of Lewis.

From a review of his life, we may pronounce, that no so-vereign prince ever went through a greater variety of fortunes than *Lewis* did ; or had a greater variety of ingredients in his personal disposition. Though he is called *the Weak* by some authors, yet, when left to himself, he acted with great pru-dence and steadiness, even during his most bitter reverses of fortune. He was a brave man, and an accomplished gene-ral ; and his misfortunes were owing to his superstition and the religious weaknesses of the times, which rendered him the reverse of what he was by nature. His following the exam-ple of his father, in parcelling out his dominions among his younger children, was the source of all his calamities; from which his patience, firmness, and natural courage, more than once delivered him : nor do we find that any of his re-bellious sons or subjects were ever equal to him in the field. From the gracefulness of his person, and manner, he was stiled *the Debonnair.*

3. Lothair.

Accession of Lothair.

LOTHAIR was surrounded with the enemies of his father's government at the time of his accession to the imperial dignity. He arrived at *Aix*, and, by his proceed-ings, he soon shewed to the world, that, as eldest son, he was resolved to be sole heir to his father's dominions. Hav-ing forced the states of *Germany* to swear obedience to him, his two brothers (*Lewis* of *Bavaria*, and *Charles the Bald*, king of *France*) began to make remonstrances upon his pre-cipitate conduct. He told them, that he had, in his father's life-time, been raised to the empire; that he was determined to maintain the right of his birth ; but he would so far con-descend, as to suffer his brother *Lewis* to possess *Bavaria*, or *Germany*; and his other brother, *Charles*, to hold *France*; but both of them as vassals to his empire. The two brothers rejected that condition ; upon which *Lothair* seized *Worms*, and advanced with his army towards *Frankfort*. *Lewis*, the *Bavarian*, having now no longer the authority of a father to contend with, offered him battle ; but a three month's truce was concluded on.

His wars with his brothers.

Lothair made use of this small interval in practising upon the subjects of his brother *Charles* ; and in making young *Pepin*, his nephew, son to the deceased *Pepin*, of *Aquitain*, subservient to his purposes. *Charles* saw through his schemes, and endeavoured to divert him from pursuing them. He was assisted by some of his nobility ; but *Pepin*, the son of *Ber-nard*, king of *Italy*, declared against him, and besieged

Bourges,

Bourges, where the empress *Judith* resided. *Charles* raised the siege and defeated *Pepin*. A negotiation succeeded; and it was agreed, that all differences between *Charles* and *Lothair* should be settled in a diet that was to be held at *Attigni*; but that, in the mean time, the truce with the king of *Bavaria* should be prolonged. *Lothair* made a most insidious use of this interval, by attempting to surprize the king of *Bavaria*, whom he found provided to resist him; and, in the mean time, *Charles*, having passed the *Seine*, obliged *Lothair* to march back into *France*, where he endeavoured to debauch the officers belonging to *Charles*. The latter was soon joined by his brother *Lewis* of *Bavaria*, who had defeated the troops *Lothair* had left near the *Rhine*; and then advanced to join *Charles*.

The junction being effected, *Lothair* having made up matters with *Pepin*, the nominal king of *Aquitain*, left every thing to the decision of a battle; which was fought in the neighbourhood of *Fontenoy*, on the twenty-third of *June*, 842. This battle lasted from seven in the morning till night, and is thought to have been one of the most bloody that had been fought for a long time in *Europe*. About one hundred thousand men on both sides were killed on the spot, but *Lothair* and *Pepin* were defeated. *Lothair* escaped with great difficulty; and, being a prince fruitful in expedients, he raised a new army, and once more invaded *Neustria*. *Lewis*, at this time, had precipitately returned to *Bavaria*; and *Charles* was pursuing *Pepin* into *Aquitain*: so that *Lothair* invaded *Neustria* with great advantage. His irresolution, and the swelling of the *Seine*, hindered him from following his good fortune. *Charles* once more joined his brother of *Bavaria* with his army, and *Lothair* was obliged to abandon *Austrasia* and part of *Burgundy*.

In this situation both parties applied to the clergy, who readily undertook the arbitration, and a kind of process was instituted, by which *Lothair*, from his repeated breaches of faith, was declared to have forfeited all title to his dominions. This seems to have been an expedient intended only to render him the more pliable; for, at length, they entered into a compromise; by which an equal partition was to be made of the empire. The kingdoms of *Italy*, *Aquitain*, and *Bavaria*, were to be divided, as nearly as could be judged, into three equal portions; of which *Lothair* was to have his choice, and the two brothers were to possess the other two. Forty commissioners were named by each of the princes, and twelve months were spent before the divisions could be settled.

It was, at last, agreed, that *Lothair* should possess *Italy* and *Rome*, with the titles of emperor and *Augustus*, and all the territory lying within the *Rhone*, *Rhine*, *Saone*, *Meuse*, and *Scheld*. In short, this kingdom was called *Royaume Lothai-* *rence,*

Origin of the kingdom of Lorrain.

enne; whence, corruptly, we have *Lorrain*; a dutchy which is but a very small part of that vast kingdom.

Pope *Gregory* and the empress *Judith* were now dead, and *Sergius* II. being elected pope, took possession of his see without any application for the emperor's leave. *Lothair*, upon this, sent his son *Lewis* into *Italy*; where he brought the pope to a sense of his duty, and was crowned king of the *Lombards.* In the mean while, the empire was attacked by the *Huns*, the *Normans*, and the *Bohemians*; and universal confusion prevailed in the dominions of *Lewis*, *Charles*, and *Lothair*. The clergy was at the head of many insurrections, the *Normans* ravaged the coasts of *France*, and *Charles the Bald* purchased his peace with them, by paying them fourteen thousand silver marks; while *Lothair* was obliged to yield *Friesland* to them.

Such was the state of this unhappy empire when *Lothair* made his last will, by which he ordained his eldest son *Lewis*, his successor in the empire. He gave his second son, *Charles*, who died without issue, in 862, the kingdoms of *Provence* and *Austrasia*, with one part of *Burgundy*; and bequeathed the other part, together with *Lorrain*, to his third son, *Lothair*; who likewise died without issue, in the year 869.

Death of Lothair. This emperor being a widower, by the death of his wife *Ermengrade* in 851, retired to the abbey of *Prum*; where he lived as a monk, and died, in the year 855, with a most contemptible character.

---

4. Lewis II.

Accession of *Lewis* II. THIS prince was unfortunate through the juncture in which he acceded to the crown; for his two uncles (*Lewis*, king of *Bavaria*; and *Charles the Bald*, king of *France*) aggrandized themselves at his expence; nor did he enjoy above one ninth part of the dominions left him by *Charles the Great*. He was a prince of great natural endowments as well as virtues. He drove the *Saracens*, or *Moors* of *Africa* from the coasts of *Italy*, and retook *Benevento*, which had revolted.

Some passages of this emperor's life are unworthy to be transmitted by history, as they turn upon the amours of his kinsmen, particularly the king of *Lorrain*, and the incredible authority assumed by the popes in granting them dispensations for divorces and marriages.

The pope declared the marriage of *Lothair* with his concubine *Waldrade* to be unlawful; and excommunicated the archbishop of *Treves* and *Cologne*, together with the senate who had pronounced it to be lawful. The emperor called

Lothair

Lothair into *Italy* to affift him againft the *Saracens*; and there the pope made him fwear, even at the altar, to a palpable untruth, that he had had no communication with his wife.

Young *Pepin*, the great-grandfon of *Charles the Great*, and His death. fon of *Pepin*, king of *Aquitain*, during all this time, led a moft miferable life; and was driven to fuch defpair that he renounced *Chriftianity*; but, being taken prifoner, he died fhut up in a convent. The king of *Lorrain*, foon after, abjuring his miftrefs, died; but left *Lorrain* to a baftard, who never enjoyed it; his kingdom being divided between *Lewis*, called *the Germanic*, and *Charles the Bald*. The reader is to obferve, that the emperor, *Lewis* II. of whom we treat, refided chiefly in *Italy*, and had very little intereft in *Germany*. Pope *John* VIII. during the life-time of the emperor, fold the reverfion of the empire to *Charles the Bald*; but the emperor *Lewis* had always the fpirit to oppofe the papal pretenfions; and died, in 875, at *Milan*. He is mentioned in hiftory as being the only defcendant, then alive, of *Charles the Great*, who inherited any of that prince's fpirit.

---

5. Charles the Bald.

UPON the death of *Lewis* II. his two uncles (*Lewis*, Reign of king of *Germany*; and *Charles the Bald*) difputed his *Charles* fucceffion. *Charles* being more politic and active than his *the Bald*, competitor, paffed the *Alps*; gained over pope *John* VIII. and was crowned emperor on *Chriftmas-day*, 875, in defiance of the falic-law; which, undoubtedly, muft have decreed the empire to the eldeft branch of *Lewis the Germanic*. Whoever confults the hiftory of that time, muft perceive that the popes were now arrived to fuch a pitch of infolence, that they arrogated to themfelves the right of beftowing the imperial dignity, which *Charles* was mean enough to purchafe from them, and thereby fet a precedent which proved fatal to pofterity.

Lewis, king of *Germany*, intended to have gone to affert his right at *Rome*; but he died at *Frankfort*, on the twenty-eighth of *Auguft*, 876. He left three fons by his wife *Emma*; *Carloman*, *Lewis*, and *Charles*; among whom, according to the pernicious practice of thofe times, the father's dominions were divided. *Carloman* inherited *Bavaria*, *Auftria*, *Bohemia*, and *Moravia*. *Lewis* poffeffed *Saxony*, *Thuringia*, *Friefland*, *Franconia*, and that part of *Lorrain* which had been difmembered at the death of *Lothair*. The younger fon, *Charles*, furnamed *the Grofs*, had *Suabia* for his inheritance.

Charles the Bald died, after a fhort reign of two years and who is two months, on the fixth of *October*, 877, of poifon, as is poifoned faid, adminiftred to him by his phyfician, one *Zedechias*, a by his *Jew*. phyfician.

Jew. His firft wife was *Richilda*, daughter of a count of *Altorf*, in *Swabia.* By his fecond wife, who was *Hermantrade*, fifter to *Bofon*, king of *Provence*, he had iffue *Lewis*, furnamed *the Stammerer*, who fucceeded him; *Lothair*, *Charles*, *Carloman*, and a daughter named *Judith.*

---

6. Lewis III. *or* the Stammerer.

Acceffion of *Lewis* the Stammerer.

THE reader may perceive that, properly fpeaking, we are not writing the hiftory of *Germany*, but of the *German* emperors, who retained that title with fcarce any *German* dominions; and refided, for the moft part, in *Italy.* It muft be acknowledged, that, during the time of *Charles the Bald*, the governmental fyftem of *Europe* underwent many material alterations.

Alterations in the fyftem of *Europe.*

The great land-holders rendered themfelves, in fome degree, independent of the emperor in point of property, by his accepting of their fervices in the field as an acknowledgment for their poffeffions; and hence arofe the code of feudal government. Some of the moft powerful of thofe landholders rendered even their military offices hereditary, and the diftinctions of nobility then took place. The leader of an army was called a duke, and his fons inherited the fame title. A warden of the marches was called a margrave, and that title became hereditary in his family; and a courtier who attended the perfon of an emperor, or king, and had lands in a particular diftrict, was created the count of that diftrict. The title of baron was entirely territorial; and, on the continent, it was fwallowed up in the titles we have already mentioned; but in *England* it ftill fubfifts. The invafions of the *Saracens* contributed greatly towards thofe alterations; as the emperors and kings on the continent of *Europe* could not, without fuch conceffions, have made head againft thofe infidels.

Lewis the Stammerer was fo called from a hefitation in his fpeech, and it is with very little propriety that his name ftands in the lift of the emperors of *Germany*; for that title was always difputed with him by *Carloman*, the eldeft fon of *Lewis the Germanic*, whofe right to it, undoubtedly, was preferable to that of *Lewis.* The latter, however, was crowned king of *France*, in the year 877; and emperor, on the feventh of *September*, 878. Numbers of the *German* and *Italian* princes adhered to *Carloman.* They feized upon the city of *Rome*, and even upon the perfon of the pope, whom they accufed of injuftice for fuffering *Lewis* to be proclaimed emperor. In fhort, *Carloman* would probably have dethroned his competitor, had he not been ftruck with the palfy, and then he refigned all his right to the empire to his youngeft brother

brother to *Charles the Grofs*. He himself retired to *Oetingen*, where he died, in the year 880, without any lawful issue. As to *Lewis the Stammerer*, he undertook a journey into *Germany*, to settle some differences he had with the king of *Bavaria*; but, upon his return to *France*, he died, in 872, at *Compeigne*, leaving his eldest son to the care of the count of *Bourges* and *Auvergne*, the marquis of *Nevers*, and *Thierri*, count of *Maçon*. His other son was about fourteen years of age at the time of his death.

---

7. Charles the Grofs.

CARLOMAN had no more right to appoint *Charles the Grofs* his successor in the empire, than *Lewis the Stammerer* had to supplant *Carloman*. But the principles of hereditary right were, in those days, arbitrarily set aside by the popes, who most unaccountably found means to render all titles venal; nor was there a prince in *Europe* who had the spirit to oppose them. *Charles the Grofs*, upon the death of *Lewis the Stammerer*, went to *Italy*; where he was, by pope *John* VIII. crowned emperor, after having secured to himself *Lombardy*. His coronation, as emperor, was on the twenty-fifth of *December*, 880. The pope, at this time, actually put up the imperial dignity to auction; and had so little regard to the right of succession, that he declared he would bestow it upon that prince who should first come to his assistance against the *Mahometans*.

Lewis of *Germany* was set up as emperor in competition with *Charles the Grofs*; and *Boson*, king of *Arles*, likewise claimed the empire. *Charles* and *Lewis* confederated against *Boson*, but *Lewis* dying in the year 882, without issue, *Charles the Grofs* became the heir of his dominions; and, had it not been for the interruption he met with from the *Normans*, he must have been almost as powerful a prince as *Charles the Great*. Those barbarians penetrated as far as *Metz*; destroyed *Aix-la-Chapelle*; and obliged *Charles the Grofs* to purchase his quiet by an immense sum of money; which, in fact, was no other than leaving them at liberty to renew their incursions.

The papal authority had, by this time, set at naught that of the emperor; and pope *Martin* II. who was successor to *John* VIII. published an order, by which the *Romifh* clergy were no longer to wait for the imperial permission to elect a pope. In the mean while, a chieftain, called *Zwentibold*, at the head of the *Moravian* pagans, laid *Germany* waste; and the emperor was obliged to purchase peace from them, as he had done from the *Normans*. The sons of *Lewis the Stammerer* dying without issue, *Charles the Grofs* succeeded to their dominions; and thereby became, by far, the most powerful

Charles Unfortunate reign of Charles the Grofs.

prince in *Europe:* but he was unhappy in his conftitution both of body and mind. This, however, was not obferved till towards the latter part of his reign; and was attributed to an accidental cut which he had received in his head, and which impaired his intellects.

The firft blow his dignity met with, came from *Hugues,* the abbot of St. *Dennis,* who was a baftard of *Lothau,* and claimed *Lorrain* for his patrimony. *Charles the Grofs* defeated this pretender, though he was fupported by the *Normans,* and put out his eyes. We are not here to follow the hiftory of *Charles the Grofs,* as king of *France;* and, therefore, we muft omit the many mortifications he received from the *Normans;* whom he was again obliged to buy off at a fhameful price, and thereby raifed the fiege of *Paris.*

who is de-
pofed, *Charles the Grofs* returned to *Germany,* where his infanity became fo manifeft, that, in a diet held there by the *Turingians, Saxons,* and *Bavarians,* he was deprived of the empire; and reduced to fo much mifery, that, it is faid, he muft have died of hunger, had it not been for the compaffion of an archbifhop of *Mentz,* who gave him a fcanty fubfiftence. He died on the twelfth of *January,* 888, after divorcing his wife *Richarda,* whom he fhut up in a convent.

---

8. Arnold.

and fuc-
ceeded by
Arnold, a
baftard. THIS prince was natural fon to *Carloman,* king of *Bavaria;* and therefore utterly deftitute of any legal pretence to the imperial crown, but what arofe from the affection of the *German* princes, who were defirous to fee their countryman their emperor. He had ferved with reputation under *Charles the Grofs,* in his wars againft the *Normans;* and, by his father's will, he inherited the provinces of *Carinthia* and *Suria.* When the late emperor's incapacity for government became too evident to be longer concealed, *Arnold* was chofen, by an affembly of the *German* princes at *Frankfort,* to fucceed him, though in prejudice to *Charles the Simple,* the younger fon of *Lewis the Stammerer,* but a minor. Their excufe for this injuftice was, that the empire wanted a man of courage and capacity to defend it againft the ravages of the *Normans,* the *Danes,* and other northern nations.

Though the name of emperor was, at this time, little better than a phantom, yet *Arnold* proved himfelf worthy of the imperial dignity. He repelled the barbarians, and gave them a great defeat near *Louvain;* where, it is faid, he killed one hundred thoufand of them: but this did not happen till they had committed moft dreadful ravages upon the empire. *Zwentibold,* who affumed the title of duke of *Moravia,* was now fo powerful, that he obliged *Arnold* to yield

to

to him *Bohemia*; which *Zwentibold* pretended to hold as an allodial fief, without any dependence upon the empire. *Arnold*, upon this, applied to the dukes of *Hungary* and *Poland*; who assisted him in reducing *Zwentibold* to his duty, and to deliver up his son as a pledge for his fidelity.

Arnold then went to *Italy*, where he crushed the factions of *Guy*, duke of *Spoleto*, and his son *Lambert*, who, because they were *Italians*, pretended to the imperial dignity, and disputed the right of the *Germans* to chuse an emperor. Upon the return of *Arnold* to *Germany*, he made his son *Zwentibold* king of *Lorrain*; and held a diet at *Worms*; where he raised troops and money. He then marched back to *Italy*, the greatest part of which he held; and, with great difficulty, he got himself crowned emperor by pope *Formosus* I. in the year 896.

Though *Arnold* appears to have been a brave and worthy prince, yet he reigned no otherwise than as a substitute to the fee of *Rome* and other ecclesiastics. It is said that a lady, one *Agiltrude*, mother to *Guy* of *Spoleto*, sent him a poisoned draught, when he was besieging her in the city of *Fermo*, which he drank; and, though it did not kill him, yet it made a very disadvantageous impression upon his health and intellects. It is certain that he raised the siege, and returned, with a disorder upon him, to *Germany*; where, during his absence in *Italy*, his rights had been invaded, without his having any remedy. The churchmen, who were then all-powerful, erected themselves into temporal princes, and had other princes subordinate to them. *Arnold* lost all spirit His death. at finding this to be the situation of his affairs after his return to *Germany*; and is said to have died of the lousy disease, at *Oetingen*, in the year 899.

---

9. Lewis IV.

THE *Germans* had so great a sense of *Arnold*'s merits, that Accession, they chose for their emperor his son *Lewis* IV. though he was, at the time of his election, no more than seven years of age, *Hatto*, archbishop of *Mentz*, and *Otho*, duke of *Saxony*, being appointed his governors. When he grew up, he waged war with his brother *Zwentibold*, king of *Lorrain*, whom he defeated and killed About the year 900, the *Hungarians*, who were in the possession of *Transylvania*, by the cession of the late emperor, invaded *Bavaria* with great cruelty. The duke of *Bavaria* raised an army to oppose them, and, indeed, defeated them; but not following his blow, in five years after, they renewed their invasions with the same barbarity as before. The emperor then took arms, but he was defeated at *Augsburg* by the barbarians, and lost the duke

of

of *Bavaria*, who was one of his generals. A scene of intestine misery to *Germany* followed this. The counts of *Bamberg*, *Franconia*, *Hesse*, and the bishop of *Wurtsburg*, were at perpetual war with one another; and did more mischief to their native country than ever had been done by the barbarians, whom their dissentions invited to return. The emperor was young, and had not sufficient authority to suppress the insurgents. He therefore, by a stratagem, decoyed *Albert*, of *Bamberg*, by means of *Hatto*, archbishop of *Mentz*, into his power, and beheaded him. This treachery rendered *Lewis* hateful to the *Germans*, and his dominions were invaded by the *Normans*, who defeated him in two great battles; which had such an effect upon him, that he died of a fever, on the twenty-first of *January*, 912, without any lawful male-issue.

and death, of Lewis IV.

The empire, at the death of *Lewis* IV. who was the last of the male-line descended from *Charles the Great*, comprehended *Franconia*, the province of *Bamberg*, *Swabia*, *Constance*, *Basil*, *Berne*, *Lausanne*, *Besançon*, *Lorrain*, *Metz*, *Liege*, *Cambray*, *Arras*, *Flanders*, *Holland*, *Zealand*, *Utrecht*, *Bologn*, *Treves*, *Mentz*, *Worms*, *Spires*, *Strasbourg*, *Friesland*, *Saxony*, *Hesse*, *Westphalia*, *Thuringia*, *Wetteravia*, *Misnia*, the marquisate of *Brandenbourg*, *Pomerania*, *Rugen*, *Stetin*, *Holstein*, *Denmark*, *Sweden*, *Poland*, *Bohemia*, *Austria*, *Carinthia*, *Stiria*, *Tirol*, and the *Grisons*, with all the countries dependent upon those provinces. The kingdom of *Burgundy*, as it was called, likewise belonged to the empire; as did *Rome*, *Italy*, *Lombardy*, and their fiefs.

Reflections on his succession.

This mighty empire departed from the descendants of *Charles the Great* through his own mistaken policy. His fondness to divide his dominions among his sons, descended to the other princes of his race, who imitated his example, till the title of emperor was torn from the kings of *France*, who were, in general, but weak men. The truth is, the imperial power, at the decease of *Lewis* IV. who was but twenty years of age when he died, was little better than a shadow; and the great fiefs of the empire were held, in reality, independent of his authority. A principle of union, however, was necessary, on account of the invasions of the barbarians, and the continual quarrels that happened among the *Germans*; and this principle naturally fell upon the emperor.

It is in vain for the *French* writers to pretend that the empire could not be lawfully transferred from the kings of *France*; those kings were unable to protect their dominions, and their great subjects therefore had a right to protect themselves. Add to this, that *Charlemagne*, and his descendants, had consulted them, and obtained their consent, in all the family dispositions they made; and thereby they obtained a right to look upon themselves as parties, whose approbation and election were absolutely necessary to constitute a right to

the

the empire; the electors having a reciprocal right of being elected: and, upon this principle, rests the foundation of the *Germanic* constitution. Who those electors were, or what right or title they acted under, is uncertain. Most probably, popularity and power gave them authority. Their ancestors, the antient *Germans*, by what we learn from *Tacitus*, and the best authors, had no other system of government.

Had hereditary right taken place, the empire must, indisputably, have fallen to the share of *Charles the Simple*, king of *France*: but that prince was unable to assert his title; and the great *German* lords paid no regard to it, but assembled at *Worms* to chuse themselves a head. *Otho*, duke of *Saxony*, by whom we are to understand, a prince who, by his valour, without any other consideration, had raised himself to that title, (though the extent of his dominions is, at this time, undetermined) would have been chosen, but he declined the honour on account of his great age; and recommended to their choice *Conrade*, duke of *Franconia* and *Hesse*, though he was his enemy. There is some reason to believe, from this circumstance, which was not in the character of those times, that the imperial dignity was then a post of danger, rather than of power and emolument.

---

10. Conrade I.

CONRADE is, properly, the first *German* emperor of Germany; his predecessors being denominated of the *Carlowingian* line. It is generally thought that some kind of family-compact had been entered into between him and *Lewis IV.* but, be this as it will, it is certain that the empire, with all the dangers and disadvantages attending it, was still a desirable object to a young and vigorous prince, such as *Conrade* was. Some of the nobility of *Lorrain* disclaimed his authority, and adhered to *Charles the Simple*; but *Conrade* marched into their country, and acted with so much prudence and generosity, that he fixed them to his party.

Henry, the son of *Otho*, was then duke of *Saxony*; and so powerful a prince, that *Conrade* refused to him the investiture of *Thuringia* and *Westphalia*. *Henry* leagued himself with *Burchard*, duke of *Swabia*, and *Arnold*, duke of *Bavaria*. *Conrade* found means to detach *Burchard* from the confederacy; and *Arnold* was obliged to return to his dominions, which were invaded by the *Hungarians*, whom he defeated. *Henry* being thus unsupported by his allies, consented to a truce with *Conrade*, who returned into *Franconia*. Here he was opposed by a rebellion of *Erchanger* and *Berthold*, two noblemen who had assisted the duke of *Bavaria* in *Franconia*,

Conrade, the first German emperor,

in

in defeating the *Hungarians*, under pretence of their being descended from *Charles the Great*; but they were difarmed by *Conrade*, convicted of treason, and executed. *Arnold*, duke of *Bavaria*, next took the field against *Conrade*; but was defeated and mortally wounded. *Conrade*, at last, had so many enemies on his hands, that he was obliged to purchase a peace with the *Hungarians*, that he might turn his arms against the duke of *Saxony*, by whom he was defeated.

The last will of *Conrade* shews that the imperial crown was lined with thorns while it was upon his head; for, after a restless reign of seven years, he recommended, on his death-bed, his capital enemy, *Henry*, duke of *Saxony*, to be his successor, in preference to his own brother *Everard*, count of *Franconia*; and he is said to have sent to *Henry* the imperial regalia. *Conrade* died in the year 919.

---

11. Henry I. *surnamed* the Fowler.

succeeded by Henry the Fowler.

THIS prince was employed in his favourite diversion of fowling, from which he took his appellation, when he had notice that *Conrade* had nominated him to the empire; and he repaired to *Fritzlar*; where the dukes of *Bavaria*, *Franconia*, *Suabia*, and other powerful *Germans*, with the deputies of the imperial cities, which were now become very independent, confirmed the nomination of *Conrade*, by electing *Henry the Fowler* emperor. Some of the *Italian* nobility had assumed that title; and the pope, to shew his power, offered to confer it on *Henry*, by formally creating him emperor of the *Romans*; but he declared himself satisfied with the right which his election gave him, and applied all his cares to promote the internal unanimity of his empire. In this he succeeded so well, that, when the *Hungarians* invaded it, he assembled an army of his subjects, who joined him as one man, and he killed eighty thousand of them in a battle fought near *Merfbourg* The empire was next attacked by the *Vandals*, they were likewise defeated by *Henry*, who pursued them into their own country, and is said to have killed one hundred and twenty thousand of them. He had the like success against the *Danes*, *Sclavonians*, and *Dalmatians*. He killed *Gonnen*, a northern king. He took prisoner *Weneflaus*, the king, or duke, of *Bohemia*; but reinstated him in his dominions. He quelled a rebellion of the *Abodrites*, and cleared *Lorrain* and his empire of the adherents to *Charles the Simple*

That prince was a formidable rival to *Henry*, on account of his descent from *Charles the Great*, which supplied all the defects of his capacity. *Henry* was so sensible of this, that he

gave

gave him a meeting at *Bonn*; and there the famous compact, called *Pactum Bonnense*, was drawn up · which was a kind of feeble effort made by *Charles* to assert his eventual hereditary right to the empire. An assembly of *French* and *German* bishops, which afterwards met at *Coblentz*, confirmed this treaty.

Henry, being now in full possession of *Lorrain*, that is, of part of the kingdom of *Lotharingia*, applied himself indefatigably to strengthen his empire against the invasions of the barbarians, and the encroachments of his own nobility, He curbed the former, by collecting his people into cities; which repelled their incursions: and he brought the latter to their duty, by obliging them to contribute, according to their respective fees, to the defence of the empire. He built towns and cities in *Bradenburgh*, *Misnia*, and *Sleswick*; and erected marquisates, which he parcelled out among his nobility for their defence against the barbarians. Those towns were garnisoned by every ninth person of the marquisate, or district, to which they belonged; the other eight inhabitants being employed in providing subsistence for their countrymen who were doing military duty. *Henry* was as zealous in his religious, as he was in his civil, capacity. He persuaded one of the kings of the *Abodrites* to be baptized, and founded a bishopric in *Holstein*. He assisted *Charles the Simple* in his wars against his rebellious subjects, and especially against *Raoul*, duke of *Burgundy*; and *Gislbert*, duke of *Lorrain*, whom he forced to do him homage, but afterwards gave him his daughter in marriage. He introduced among his subjects a taste for military politeness, by instituting the practice of jousts and tournaments. Those meetings were, in fact, regular assemblies of his courtiers and great men, where they exercised themselves in feats of arms; and were rewarded, according to their merit, by the smiles of the fair and the favour of the emperor. Till his reign, no regular fortifications had been raised in *Germany*; and he abolished the disgraceful tribute which his predecessors had been forced to pay to the *Hungarians*; by sending them, when they demanded it, a mangy dog, by way of contempt. He suffered none to be admitted, or inrolled, among his nobility, who were defective either in morals or religion; and he kept a catalogue of above a thousand who enlisted themselves into the service of his government. *Henry*, however, was not always fortunate; he sometimes met with checks in *Lorrain*, and was obliged, not only to bestow that dutchy upon the undutiful *Gislbert*, but to publish an amnesty in favour of his other rebellious subjects.

Germany was, at this time, far from being cleared of paganism. *Dragomire*, mother to *Wenceslaus*, duke of *Bohemia*, was a bigotted pagan; and had incited *Ladislaus*, a *Polish* nobleman, to invade her son's dominions. The emperor went to his assistance; and not only forced *Ladislaus* to retire, but

His great actions.

established

established the *Christian* religion in *Bohemia*, and *Wenceslaus* in his dominions. The *Lorrainers* took advantage of his absence to rebel; but they were soon reduced: and the emperor *Henry*, in the year 929, ordered *Bernard*, duke of *Lunenburg*, and other *German* noblemen, to suppress a confederacy of the barbarians; but they were defeated. *Henry*, upon this, called together an assembly of the states of his empire; in which he reformed many abuses, and then put himself at the head of his army to oppose the *Hungarians*, who had invaded his empire to the number of three hundred thousand men; but they were defeated by the emperor, with the loss of above forty thousand.

Death and character of *Henry* the Fowler.

This defeat of the barbarians restored tranquility to the empire, and *Henry* prepared to march to *Italy*, in order to recover the imperial rights in that country, and to be crowned by the pope. For this purpose, he put himself at the head of a great army; but was seized with an apoplexy upon his march, and obliged to return to *Mansleben*; where he named his son *Otho* for his successor; and died, in the sixtieth year of his age, and the seventeenth of his reign.

His wife was *Matilda*, daughter of *Theodoric*, count of *Aldenburg*; and by her he had three sons; *Otho*, who succeeded him; *Henry*, and *Bruno*. *Henry the Fowler* was, by far, the greatest prince who had filled the imperial throne since the days of *Charles the Great*, whom he resembled in his political capacity. He brought the government and constitution of the empire, civil, ecclesiastical, and military, to a consistency which it had never known before. He had the art of making pagans and barbarians good subjects; and, though he is accused of superstition, it is a charge upon which we cannot hastily pronounce. The age had superstition for its distemper. The people were governed by churchmen, whose arms were the abuse and degeneracy of *Christianity*; and their temporal, was as formidable as their spiritual, authority. Where such an inundation of depravity prevailed, *Henry* must have been endowed with more than human talents to have opposed it; and therefore he was obliged, at least, to seem to join it. This is the best reason we can give for the acts of enthusiasm and credulity ascribed to him by historians, as the weakness of which they accuse him is utterly incompatible with the great capacity he discovered in the government of his empire.

Otho

12. Otho I. *called* the Great.

THIS prince, at the time of his accession to the empire, *Otho* inherited, from his father, the dutchy of *Saxon* , *West-* chosen *phalia, Angria, Thuringia, Hesse, Wetteravia,* and the coun- emperor. tries situated on the *Weser* adjacent to *Minde,* and those on the *Elbe* towards the confines of *Lunenburg*; the cities of *Wertemburg, Misnia,* and *Lusatia*; the eastern country towards the *Plesse* and the *Ester*; the country of *Northeim*; the dutchy of *Brunswick,* and all the country about the city of *Magdebourg.* His natural endowments corresponded with his great possessions. *Aix-la-Chapelle* had been laid in ashes by the barbarians; but the partiality which *Charles the Great* had shewn towards it, gained the spot a degree of reverence, and a wooden hall was run up to serve as the place of election. Most of the electors were ecclesiastics; among whom were the archbishops of *Mentz, Magdebourg, Triers* and *Besançon*; the bishops of *Ratisbon, Tresingen, Augsbourg, Constance, Eichstet, Worms, Spire, Brixen,* and *Hildesheim.* Besides those, were the abbots of *Fulde, Herchfelt,* and *Erbach.* The temporal electors were the king of *Bohemia,* and the dukes of *Saxony, Bavaria, Austria, Moravia,* and *Lorrain.* The ceremony of this election, which is the first regular one we have on record, was very complicated. *Otho* was, indeed, unanimously chosen by the clergy and nobility we have mentioned; but it does not appear that that election was conclusive, even though they swore allegiance to him and did him homage.

They attended him from the throne, on which he had re- Forms of ceived homage, to the great church, where he was received his elec- by *Hildebert,* archbishop of *Mentz,* and his clergy. They tion. presented the emperor to the people, whose assent to his election the archbishop demanded; which being granted, he was anointed, and inaugurated with ceremonies not very different from those made use of at the coronation of a king of *England*; and the admonitions he received from the archbishop were much in the same strain. All the ceremony of election was gone through with a punctuality, that fully indicated, the electors, as well as the elected, were resolved to make it a precedent on all future occasions. The elect was anointed with consecrated oil, and the archbishop of *Mentz* placed the crown upon his head. On his return to his palace, we find the commencements of personal services for great fees. His chief officers of state served him during his dinner, but the prelates sat at his table.

The first storm that fell upon his government was from Subdues the *Hungarians,* who invaded the province of *Franconia,* and the *Hun-* desolated both the *Saxonies.* They were defeated by *Otho,* garians. who fortified *Magdebourg,* and, passing the *Elbe,* checked the incursions incurfions of other barbarians. He then detached *Efic*, count of *Afcania*, againft *Bodeflaus*, who had murdered his brother *Winceflaus*, duke of *Bohemia*, and taken poffeffion of his dominions. This proved a long and a bloody war. *Efic*, tho' victorious at firft, was total'y defeated ; and the war lafted for feventeen years before *Otho* could oblige *Bodeflaus* to fubmit to his authority.

While this *Bohemian* war was depending, another broke out in *Bavaria*. The fucceffion of *Arnold*, the laft duke, was difputed amongft three of his fons, who agreed in nothing but difowning the fovereignty of the emperor. He afferted it with a very high hand, for he beftowed the inveftiture of the dutchy upon *Bertolf*, the brother of the laft duke, whofe eldeft fon, *Everhard*, was recognized by the pope, *Leo VII* and he found means to make this inveftiture good ; but *Otho* provided for the young princes in other principalities. The truth is, we know but little of the real hiftory of the empire at this time. All the accounts tranfmitted to us are, generally, from monks or ecclefiaftics, who had received favours from the emperors, and were by them raifed to an impolitic pitch of greatnefs, that they might counterballance the temporal nobility, whom they thought to be lefs manageable.

His ambitious conduct Amongft the other palatine princes whom *Otho* created, by virtue of his imperial prerogative, was *Everhard*, duke of *Franconia*. He imagined, that, in this quality, he had a right to be independent. A quarrel broke out between him and *Henry*, duke of *Brunfwick*, who was the emperor's brother ; which being attended with difagreeable circumftances to the latter, *Otho* interpofed. At firft, he fentenced *Henry*, and his oppofers, each of them to carry a live dog from the place of their habitation to *Magdeburg*. Such was the punifhment then inflicted in *Germany* upon the difturbers of public tranquility. *Everhard* was pardoned ; but differences ftill continuing between him and *Henry*, the latter was taken prifoner ; and *Everhard* found means to perfuade him that he had a better title to the imperial crown than *Otho*, as having been born after his father was emperor, which *Otho* was not ; and they, with *Sigebert*, duke of *Auftrafia*, confederated together to dethrone *Otho*. At the fame time, they invited *Lewis the Ultramarine*, king of *France*, to defend their feudal rights ; which, they faid, were invaded by *Otho*.

Before the confederates could be joined by *Lewis*, *Otho* attacked, and totally defeated, them, on the banks of the *Rhine* ; *Everhard*, the general, being killed ; *Sigebert* drowned in endeavouring to efcape ; and *Henry* flying to *Merfburg* ; where he came to an engagement with his brother, and then with the king of *France*. After this, *Otho* made himfelf mafter of *Briffac*, *Mentz*, and *Cheuremont*, and drove the *French* entirely out of *Lorrain*.

Otho

Otho made an arbitrary use of his victories. He stripped towards *Conrade*, the son of *Everhard*, of the title of count-palatine, the Ger-and gave it to *Herman*, third son to *Arnold*, duke of *Bavaria*, man together with as many towns and lands as laid a foundation princes. for the house of count-palatine of the *Rhine*. The *Sclavoni-ous* having made an irruption into *Bohemia* and *Brandenburgh* about this time, they were entirely defeated by the imperial general, who put to death such of the chiefs as fell into his hands. A great party of the *French* nobility had joined *Otho*, as those of *Germany* had *Lewis*, and for the same reason, to protect them against their sovereign. *Lewis* was driven from *Champagne* to *Burgundy* with great loss ; but *Otho* was recalled to *Germany* by fresh conspiracies that had broken out against him His brother *Henry*, to whom he had given part of *Lor-rain*, had leagued with many of the *Saxon* chiefs, and, ac-cording to the uncertain histories of those times, they in-tended to have assassinated *Otho* ; but he defeated and punished them, and confined *Henry* to the castle of *Ingelheim*. But, soon after, we find them not only reconciled together at *Franckfort*, but *Otho* bestowing upon this brother *Henry*, who had so often rebelled against him, the dutchy of *Bavaria*, in prejudice of its lawful heirs.

The empire seems to have been in great confusion at this time, and the emperor erected a tribunal at *Bonn* for trying all breaches of the public peace. *Ruthbert*, bishop of *Triers*, and *Richard*, bishop of *Tongres*, were tried for felony, upon a charge brought against them by *Conrade*, the new duke of *Lorrain* : but they were admitted to justify themselves upon oath ; and the see of *Triers* was erected, in favour of *Ruth-bert*, into a sovereign principality, and an archbishopric, with the rights of regality through all his diocese.

Otho, about the year 945, marched, with a numerous ar-my, to the assistance of *Lewis the Ultramarine*, against his vassal *Hugh the Great*, duke of the isle of *France*, of whose power the emperor was jealous. *Lewis* was joined by the count of *Flanders* near *Cambray*, and he undertook the siege of *Rouen* ; but, by a series of mismanagements, he and his confederates were obliged to raise the siege with great loss ; and *Lewis*, being abandoned by the count of *Flanders*, re-turned home with the shattered remains of his army.

In the year 947, the emperor called together an assembly of his nobles at *Ingelheim*, the king of *France* having resigned all his pretensions to *Lorrain*; and there some measures were fixed upon for assisting him against *Hugh the Great*, whom *Otho* procured to be excommunicated by the pope's legate. *Otho* having nominated proper ministers and officers for ma-naging his government in his absence, undertook an expedi-tion against the *Danes*, who had murdered the *Saxon* mar-grave in the town of *Slefwick*, and put the *German* garrison there to the sword. It is probable, though we have but dark accounts of the particulars, that *Otho* was successful in this expe-

He marches into France.

Subdues the Danes.

expedition; for he re-eftablifhed the *German* garrifon at *Slef-wick*, and obliged the *Danes* to tolerate *Chriftian* miffionaries in their country.

Upon *Otho's* return to *Germany*, he procured a reconciliation between *Lewis the Ultramarine* and *Hugh the Great*, who was now tired of war. He then, in perfon, reduced *Boleflaus*, duke of *Bohemia*, who had renewed his treafons; obliging him to do penance for his brother's murder, and to hold his dukedom as a fief of the empire. In 951, the emperor's fon, *Ludolph*, whom he had named his fucceffor in the empire, married *Idda*, daughter and fole heirefs of *Herman*, a prince of great power and riches; all which fell to *Ludolph*.

Otho had long entertained a defign to re-eftablifh the empire of *Charles the Great* in *Italy*; but the *Italian* princes, in general, were now fo independent, and fo averfe to the *Germans*, that he could find no means to effect it, till, this year, *Alix*, or *Alicia* (fome call her *Adelaide*) the widow of *Lothair*, king of *Italy*, had been perfecuted, and fhut up in *Caniffe*, by an ufurper, *Berengar the Younger*; and had recourfe to *Otho* for affiftance; being feconded by pope *Agapetus*, who was afraid of the fame ufurper. *Otho's* emprefs, *Ethea*, an *Englifh* princefs, had left him a widower; and he concluded, that nothing could happen fo favourable for his views in *Italy* as a marriage with *Alix*. He accordingly raifed a very powerful army, marched to her deliverance, defeated *Berengar*, and married her. *Berengar* threw himfelf at the emperor's feet, and obtained not only his pardon, but a confiderable part of his dominions, and provifions of territory for his brothers.

Otho having made a triumphal entry into *Pavia* with his bride, left *Italy* to prefide in a council of ecclefiaftics at *Augfburg*; and gave the command of his army to his fon-in-law the duke of *Lorrain*; by which he, in a manner, forfeited all the fruits of his *Italian* conquefts and marriage. His fon *Ludolph* was difobliged, not only at his father having retracted his nomination of him to the empire, but at his marriage with *Alix*; which feems, indeed, to have been difagreeable to the *Germans* in general. *Otho* having deprived *Conrade* of the command of his army, the latter came over to *Ludolph's* party, and was joined by feveral other powerful princes. The progrefs of this confederacy was, at firft, very alarming; and *Ludolph*, among other cities of importance, feized upon, and fortified *Mentz*; where he took up his head-quarters. The emperor befieging him there, he fled to *Ratifbon*; which finding likewife untenable, he privately departed from the place, in a mournful habit, and threw himfelf at his father's feet, while the latter was hunting, in fo moving a manner, that the old man raifed and pardoned him, and even gave him the command of an army; but *Ludolph*, during his rebellion, had invited in the *Huns* and the *Sclavonians* to invade the empire. This gave great trouble

to

to *Otho*; who, at laft, defeated them with a moft amazing flaughter.

Otho's character was, at this time, very high in *Europe*. He had effectually eftablifhed the imperial authority through all his dominions, and had gone fo far as even to ftrike off the hereditary fucceffion to great fiefs, and to give them to thofe perfons who could beft perform the feudal fervices, and were moft attached to his own perfon and government. This arbitrary conduct kept him in perpetual wars with thofe whom he had difinherited or difobliged; but he generally was conqueror, though he fometimes wɛs hard preffed by the prodigious fwarms of barbarians that invaded his dominions, which had no fufficient barrier to defend them. The arts of peace, in thofe days, in their moft flourifhing ftate, under the imperial patronage and encouragement, confifted in the regulation of feudal tenures, and adjufting the various conftitutions of the nations of which *Germany* was compofed, to fome general confiftency with the imperial conftitutions; to the practice of agriculture and manufacturing of arms. As to the clergy, they were more ignorant and barbarous than the flocks they pretended to inftruct. *Otho* was far from being deficient as a legiflator, but he was obliged to fupport his dignity by well-difciplined armies; and this procured him refpect and reverence. The *Arabs*, the moft polifhed and powerful people then in the world (if, perhaps, we except the *Chinefe*) courted his alliance; and we are told that a queen of *Ruffia* requefted him, by her ambaffadors, to fend her fome *Chriftian* miffionaries for the converfion of her dominions. But the glory of *Otho* was not complete, as he was not, at this time, mafter of *Italy*, and poffeffed of all the power of *Charles the Great* there.

Berengar, whom we have already mentioned, had conquered the kingdom of *Lombardy*, and was attempting that of *Rome*; the fee of which was held by pope *John* XII. the baftard of a famous ftrumpet called *Marofia*, and a *Roman* patrician *Alberic*, and no more than eighteen years of age. *Otho* thought the juncture favourable for re-eftablifhing his authority in *Italy*. His fon *Ludolph* marched thither at the head of an army, and defeated *Berengar*, but foon after died; fome fay of the plague, and others of poifon, adminiftred to him through the invincible hatred which all *Italians* have of *German* dominion. *Berengar* recovered himfelf fo far, that he affembled another army, and fhut up the pope in *Spoleto*, from whence *Otho* received an invitation to come to his affiftance. The latter ftipulated his terms. He was to be crowned king of *Lombardy* by the archbifhop of *Milan*, and emperor of *Rome* by the pope; which being granted, he put himfelf at the head of an army. Before he began his march, he ordered his young fon, *Otho*, by his wife *Alix*, to be elected king of *Germany*, and crowned at *Aix-la-Chapelle*;

though

Profperity
and glory
of *Otho*.

though he was then no more than eight years of age. The emperor's brother *Otho*, archbifhop of *Cologne*, performed the ceremony of the coronation.

He is crowned king of Lombardy,

The affairs of *Germany* being properly fettled, *Otho* paffed the *Alps*, entered *Pavia*, and was crowned king of *Lombardy*, with the famous iron crown, at *Monfa*. *Berengar*, unable to ftand before him, fled; and the emperor, without refiftance, entered *Rome*, where he accordingly was crowned. Here he acted as fovereign mafter, and, as fomewhat more than, the fucceffor of *Charles the Great*. *Adelbert*, the fon of *Berengar*, and his affociate, would have oppofed him; but the *Lombard* nobility, in hatred to the father, would not follow him.

and emperor of the Romans.

In the month of *February*, 962, *Otho*, with great formality and pomp, received the imperial crown from the ftripling pope; but he obliged the *Romans* to take an oath of allegiance to him as being their fovereign lord. He forced the pope to take the fame oath, on the body of St. *Peter*; and an inftrument written in letters of gold, which is faid to be ftill preferved in the caftle of St. *Angelo* at *Rome*, was extended; by which, imperial commiffaries were re-eftablifhed at *Rome*, that, without their confirmation, no election of a pope fhould be deemed valid; and that even the temporal adminiftration of juftice fhould be fubject to their controul. The emperor, in return, promifed to reftore to the church all that had been granted to it by *Pepin* and *Charles the Great*, and made it moft magnificent prefents.

He fubdues Lombardy.

Otho having fhewn the fame fpirit for fovereignty in *Italy* as he had done in *Germany*, exhibited a new fcene to the papal court; but fcarcely had he left *Rome*, in purfuit of *Berengar*, when the pope, reflecting on what he had done, entered into a fecret alliance with his greateft enemy, *Adelbert*; and they agreed, not only to drive the *Germans* out of *Italy*, but to invite the *Huns* to invade *Germany*. In the mean while, the pope had feized upon the perfons of *Berengar* and his wife, and, after being tried, they were condemned to perpetual imprifonment, where they actually died. The pope's treaty with *Adelbert* foon came to *Otho*'s ears; and he underftood that the pretext of it was, his having invaded the rights of the church. Mutual embaffies and defiances paffed between both parties; and *Otho*, who had, by this time, completed the conqueft of *Lombardy*, marched, with part of his army, to *Rome*; from whence the pope, with *Adelbert*, fled.

He was received by the *Roman* nobles, who renewed their oath of allegiance to him; and he gave orders for a council to meet, to try the pope for crimes of the deepeft die. He was accufed of having fet fire to houfes, of rendering his palace a brothel, of having ravifhed a widow of quality, of having lain with his own father's concubine, of being a

common

common fimoniac, and of felling a bifhopric to a boy of no more than ten years of age; alfo of being an affaffin, and of various other crimes; fome of which feem to have been youthful, but impious, frolics. Though feveral of thofe charges were undoubtedly true, yet *John*'s chief crime was the league he had made againft the emperor. *Otho* himfelf prefided in the affembly, which was very auguft; and the facts alledged againft the pope being proved, the members unanimoufly pronounced, that he had forfeited the holy fee; and his fecretary, though a layman, was chofen in his place, and took the name of *Leo* VIII. The new pope was fo grateful, that he granted a bull, enlarging the powers over the church that had been granted to *Otho* before; and even bound up himfelf and his fucceffors from the liberty of confecrating a bifhop without the emperor's leave,

It does not precifely appear where pope *John* hid himfelf Revolutions in at this time; but, however debauched and abandoned he the popemight be in his perfon, he appears to have been a man of dom. great fpirit and abilities. The *German* noblemen always ferved with reluctance in *Italy*; and *John*, before the end of the year 963, found means to raife fuch a revolt among the *Romans*, that they almoft furprized the emperor, who quelled them with fome difficulty, and obliged them to give him one hundred hoftages for their good behaviour; but thefe, at the requeft of pope *Leo*, who fought to be popular in *Rome*, were foon releafed. New commotions arifing in *Italy*, *John*, by means of his intrigues, both amorous and political, got admittance to *Rome*; where he reverfed all that had been done, and inflicted fome fignal punifhments upon the heads of the oppofite faction; particularly by ordering the right hand of a cardinal to be cut off for writing the fentence of his depofition. He then paffed a decree, that an inferior fhould never have the power of degrading his fuperior: meaning, that no future emperor fhould ever fit as judge upon a pope. In fhort, *John* had the art to unite all parties againft the *Germans*; but, while he was in the middle of his arduous enterprizes, he was affaffinated by a rival in the arms of one of his miftreffes,

Pope *Leo* had taken refuge in the camp of the emperor, who was then befieging *Camerini*; but the *Romans*, inftead of recalling him, chofe a cardinal deacon in his ftead, who affumed the name of *Benedict*. The emperor immediately raifed the fiege, and marched againft the *Romans*, who refolutely fhut their gates againft him; but famine obliged them to give him admittance. *Benedict* prefented himfelf, with great humility, before a council fummoned by pope *Leo*; where he confeffed his ufurpation, and, at the interceffion of the emperor, the pope fuffered him to retain his deacon's orders, on condition that he fhould refide at *Hamburgh*.

The

The *Germans* saw the imperial authority thus raised at their expence, and shewed so much reluctance to remain longer in *Italy*, that *Otho* was obliged to return to *Germany*, leaving the affairs of *Italy* in the utmost confusion; but not without compelling the *Roman* nobility to swear, that they never would chuse any other than a *German* for their emperor. He held a diet at *Cologne*, where he confirmed the division of the kingdom of *Lorrain* into two provinces; one of which, bounded by *Luxembourg*, (the foundation of which illustrious family was likewise at this time laid) and *Franche Compte*, was given to *Frederick*, earl of *Bar*; and the other, comprehending the dutchies of *Balant*, *Juliers*, and *Guelderland*, with many other noble provinces, was assigned to *Brunc*, archbishop of *Cologne*, the emperor's brother. The first of those divisions is now what is properly called *Lorrain*.

By this time, the *Italians* had recalled *Adelbert* from *Corsica*, to which he had fled; and he raised a revolt in *Lombardy*, which cost *Otho* great trouble in suppressing. In 965, pope *Leo* died; and *Otho*, by virtue of his prerogative, sent two deputies to authorize the election of a new pope; which fell upon a bishop who took the name of *John* XIII. He declared for the emperor; for which the *Romans* threw him into prison. Those commotions obliged *Otho* to return to *Italy*, at the head of an army before which all opposition fell. Having punished the authors of the revolt of *Lombardy*, he proceeded to *Rome*, where he ordered a number of the senators to be hanged, and banished the rest; but *Rodred the Perfect*, who was meditating to restore the form of the antient *Roman* government, was ignominiously scourged through the streets of *Rome* on the back of an afs, and then thrown into prison, where he died. Proceedings which sufficiently demonstrated the arbitrary disposition of *Otho*.

Treachery of the Greek emperor. After establishing a new police at *Rome*, he caused his son *Otho* to be crowned there, as his associate in the empire. *Nicephorus*, the *Greek* emperor, held still some places in *Calabria* and *Apulia*; and had pretensions to others that were possessed by *Otho*; to whom he sent an ambassador to demand them. *Otho*, in pursuance of his plan to be sole master of *Italy*, refused to deliver them up; but offered to accept of those held by *Nicephorus* in dowry with his daughter *Theophania*, if *Nicephorus* would agree to her marrying his son *Otho*. *Nicephorus* seemed to approve the proposal; and a most magnificent embassy of *Germans* was sent to *Constantinople*, to receive the princess, consisting of his chief nobility; who were all of them treacherously slaughtered in their journey by order of *Nicephorus*, who could not bear that *Otho* should put himself on an equality with a *Greek* emperor. *Otho*, upon this, sent an army to expel the *Greeks* from *Calabria*, under the command of the counts *Gonther* and *Sigifrid*.

The

The fuccefs of this expedition is fomewhat dark in hiftory; all we know is, that the *Germans* got a great booty in fighting againft the *Saracens*; and, at laft, defeated the *Greeks*; and fent fuch of them as efcaped the fword, to *Conftantinople*, with their nofes cut off. By this time, *Nicephorus* was dethroned and murdered by the *Greeks*; and his fucceffor, *John Zemifces*, not only releafed all the *German* prifoners at *Conftantinople*, but fent the princefs *Theophania*, with a noble retinue, to *Italy*; where fhe was married to young *Otho*.

In the year 971, *Otho the Great*, having put his *Italian* affairs in better order than they had ever known before, returned victorious to *Germany*; where he fpent the remainder of his days in eftablifhing bifhoprics; particularly the archbifhopric of *Magdeburg*, and the bifhoprics of *Merfhourg*, *Zell, Havelberg*, and *Mifnia*; all which he endowed with a profufion of revenues. We are not, however, to forget, that, during his abfence in *Italy*, a duke of *Bohemia* found means to deprive him of *Moravia* and to annex it to his own dukedom.

In the year 973, he ordered a general thankfgiving to be put up through all his dominions, for the profperous ftate of his affairs; and he died, of an apoplectic fit, at *Mirleben*, in *Saxony*, on the feventh of *May*, that fame year, after a glorious, but turbulent, reign of thirty years. *Death, &c.*

Otho refembled *Charles the Great*, the neareft of any of his fucceffors, both in his civil and military abilities; and poffeffed, likewife, many of his defects. The donations he made, and the inftitutions he formed, conftitute great part of the municipal laws both in *Germany* and *Italy*; under which laft head we fhall often have occafion to mention them. *Otho*'s firft wife was *Editha*, daughter to *Edmund*, king of *England*; and his fecond wife was *Alix*, or *Adelaide*; who, upon his death, retired to a convent. *and character, of Otho.*

---

13. Otho II. *called* the Bloody.

THIS prince having been recognized in his father's lifetime as his fucceffor, difpenfed with the forms of an election, and was proclaimed emperor at *Magdeburg*. His coufin *Henry*, duke of *Bavaria*, oppofed his promotion, and was proclaimed emperor at *Ratifbon*. His caufe was efpoufed by *Denmark, Poland*, and *Bohemia*, which laft now afpired to the dignity of a kingdom. Thofe princes were not in arms time enough to fupport the *Bavarian*, who was not only defeated, but driven out of his dutchy, which *Otho* gave to the duke of *Suabia*. As to the *Bavarian* himfelf, he was afterwards firft imprifoned at *Quidlembourg*, and then banifhed to *Elrick*, with his friend the bifhop of *Augfburg*. *Commotions in Germany upon the acceffion of Otho II.*

Otho, after that, marched againſt *Harold*, king of *Denmark*; whom he obliged to promiſe him an annual tribute, and to give up his ſon as an hoſtage for his fidelity. *Otho* then marched againſt the dukes of *Bohemia* and *Carinthia*, whom he likewiſe reduced, re-annexed the city of *Paſſau* to his dominions, and forced the *Bohemians* to accept of a peace. Thoſe wars ſerve to prove the dread the *Germans* were under from the imperial authority being veſted in the houſe of *Otho*.

His wars with *France*. — *Lothair* was then king of *France*, which began to recover from its late weakneſs; and he revived his claims upon *Lorrain* and ſome of the adjacent provinces. By his conduct, he ſeems to have intended to enlarge thoſe claims. The lords of *Lorrain* had ſhewn diſpoſitions to prefer their being feudatories to *France* rather than *Germany*; and ſome of them, thro' the help of *Hugh Capet*, had recovered, by force of arms, their paternal eſtates, which had been given away by *Otho* I. The emperor was ſenſible of this, and offered to give the dutchy of *Lorrain* to *Lothair's* brother, if he would hold it as a fief of the empire. *Lothair* rejected this condition, which, we are told, *Charles* accepted of, to the great ſcandal of the *French* nation, who looked on the ſuperiority of the emperor as no better than a proſperous uſurpation. *Lothair* raiſed an army, with which he had almoſt ſurprized the emperor at *Aix-la-Chapelle*. *Otho* eſcaped with great difficulty, and, invading *France*, in his turn, he ravaged all *Champagne* and the iſle of *France*. Being afraid of having his retreat cut off, he returned towards *Germany*; but loſt a great number of men in recroſſing the river *Aine*. This gave an opportunity to *Geffrey*, count of *Anjou*, the *French* general, to come up with *Otho*, and to challenge him to ſingle combat, which the emperor declined. Many reaſons, notwithſtanding the obſcurity of hiſtory, prove that the emperor had the better in this expedition; for *Lothair* conſented, at laſt, to make peace with him upon the terms he had rejected at firſt; and his brother *Charles* did homage to *Otho* on his knees, upon his receiving the inveſtiture of *Lorrain*.

He marches into *Italy*. — *Otho* II. retained the imperial, *German*, weakneſs of thinking they could be maſters of *Italy*, without making it the ſeat of their empire. The *Romans* had already revolted, and had choſen *Boniface* VII. for their pope; and he had offered to be ſubject to the *Greek*, rather than the *German*, emperor. The *Greeks* of *Apulia* and *Calabria*, with their ſpirit of hatred to the *Germans*, called the *Moſlems* of *Africa* to their aſſiſtance, and thoſe two people, in conjunction, became maſters of *Naples*. Had it been left to the pope's option, he would have held his ſee of the *Mohammedans* rather than the *Germans*, as he found the *Greek* emperor too weak to ſupport him ſingly.

Such was the ſtate of *Italy*, when *Otho*, in 980, having made peace with *Lothair*, entered it with an army. He marched to *Rome*, where his party was ſtrong enough to procure

procure him admittance. Having reinforced his army there *Defeated* by the *Italians* of his party, who obeyed him only out of ha- *by the* tred to the pope, he marched against the *Greeks* and *Saracens*, *Greeks and* to whom he gave battle; but being deserted by his *Italian* *Saracens.* troops, he was completely defeated, and, with great difficulty, escaped to the sea-side. There he found a vessel, into which he threw himself. This vessel was taken by the *Saracens*, and the emperor offered the captor a sum of money if he would set him on shore at *Capua*. The pirate was then lying off that place, and, being ignorant of his prisoner's quality, or country, because he spoke good *Greek*, he was musing whether or not he should accept of the offer, when the emperor jumped into the sea and swam ashore. Some writers pretend that he was carried to *Sicily*, and that he purchased his return to *Italy* by money. It is certain that he rejoined the remains of his army, and raised new forces.

By this time, the *Greeks* and *Saracens* had quarrelled; so *His cru-* that they could make no head against *Otho*, who is said to *elty*, have exterminated them out of *Italy*. The first use he made of his victories, was to chastize the *Beneventines*, who, during the course of the war, had favoured his enemies, by suffering his army to plunder the town for three days, and then to set it on fire. In 983, he declared his son *Otho*, who was no more than ten, or at most twelve, years of age, emperor at *Verona*; and then proceeding to *Rome*, he is said there to have invited the prætor *Cincius*, and the chief nobility of *Rome*, to a banquet; and, in the midst of the festivity, soldiers, by the emperor's order, entered the hall; where they cut the throats of all the guests whom he had devoted to destruction by name; but he entertained the rest with great splendour and politeness. There is some reason for doubting the manner in which this massacre was committed, authors disagreeing as to the time; but that *Otho* put great numbers of the *Romans* to death, is past question; and that he thereby got the epithet of *the Bloody*.

Hearing that the troubles of *Germany* were renewed by the *death,* irruptions of the *Sclavonians*, he ordered his subjects of *Saxony* and *Thuringia* to make head against them; which they did so successfully, that they defeated and killed thirty-seven thousand of the barbarians. *Otho*, instead of marching against the *Greeks* and *Saracens*, his capital enemies, held a council at *Rome*; where he confirmed the erection of *Hamburgh* and *Bremen* into an archiepiscopal see; and died, on the seventh of *September*, of a wound which, they say, he received from a poisoned arrow in his battle with the *Greeks*; and which festered through the grief he conceived at the exultation of his empress *Theophania* upon the victory her countrymen had got over her husband.

The historians of that age give but an indifferent character *and cha-* of this emperor; probably through the aversion he enter- *racter.*

tained

tained for the *Italians*. It is certain he ordained, by one of his laws, that no *Italian* should be believed upon his oath; and, that, when they were parties in any doubtful point, the affair should be decided by duel.

---

14. Otho III.

Remarks on the accession of Otho. THE accession of a boy to the imperial throne was what had not been known before to the *German* empire. *Henry*, duke of *Bavaria*, nephew to *Otho* I. was still in being, and claimed the tutelage of the young prince, whose person he seized at *Cologne*; not with an intention to reserve him to empire, but to remove a rival to his own pretensions till he could make them good. The parties in the disposal of the empire were, at this time, divided into three. The *Italians* chose one of their own countrymen, *Cressentius*, consul and governor of *Rome*; one part of the *Germans* espoused the title of *Henry* of *Bavaria*; and another, that of young *Otho*; for no other reason but because they thought that his inability to govern would leave to themselves the greater power. The last proved to be the strongest; and *Henry* of *Bavaria*, upon an assurance given him that he should be re-instated in his dutchy, delivered *Otho* into the hands of his friends, who proclaimed him emperor, with the usual titles, at *Weisemstadt*; and committed the care of his future education to the archbishop of *Mentz* and the bishop of *Heildeshem*. The ceremony was attended by all the usual services. *Henry* of *Bavaria* acted as his steward; the count-palatine as his cupbearer; the duke of *Saxony* as his master of the horse; and the dukes, or kings as they are called, of *Bohemia* and *Poland*, had other services allotted them.

The *Danes* vanquished. The king of *France* and the barbarians thought the juncture favourable for their distressing the empire. *Lewis* V. of *France*, son of *Lothair*, was then dead; and *Charles* of *Lorrain*, his uncle, claimed his succession. He was opposed by *Hugh Capet*, who, amongst other things, objected to him the disgraceful homage he had performed to the emperor for the dutchy of *Lorrain*. *Capet* prevailed, and made *Charles* his prisoner. The beginnings of an usurping reign are always favourable to neighbouring powers; and *Verdun*, about this time, reverted to the empire of *Germany*. *Otho*, who is said to have had a pregnant genius, no sooner arrived at the age of fourteen, than he marched in person to the frontiers of his empire, which he cleared of the *Sclavonians* and other barbarians; and, when more advanced in years, he visited the internal parts of his dominions; where he settled many regulations, and won the hearts of the ecclesiastics by his compliances

ances and liberality. He was diverted from this laudable attention by an invasion of the *Danish* fleet in the *Lower Saxony*, with a considerable body of land-forces on board. These, at first, defeated the imperial generals; but, being weakened by sickness, and laden with booty, they were defeated, in their turn, by *Sigefroi*, governor of *Standen*; and *Sweno*, their king, in 989, was obliged to return, with great loss, to his ships. Soon after, *Sweno* was defeated by *Eric*, king of *Sweden*, who made himself master of *Denmark*; and *Otho*, with a right policy, entered into an alliance with *Eric*, to prevent any future depredations of the *Danes* upon his empire.

In the mean while, *Cressentius* had left nothing unessayed to establish his authority as emperor at *Rome*; and, indeed, he seems to have deserved that dignity. He imprisoned pope *John* XIV. for his adherence to the *German* emperor; and his successor, *John* XV. upon his death under his confinement, would have met with the same fate, for the same reason, had he not fled to *Tuscany* and implored *Otho's* protection. The memory of the *German* emperor was so terrible to the *Romans*, that *Cressentius* could not prevent their sending a reconciliatory message to *John*, imploring him to return *John* accordingly returned, and *Otho* sent his empress, *Theophania*, with an army, under the marquis of *Brandenburg*, into *Italy*, to over-awe the *Romans* and the other states there. This she did for two years, and, leaving the management of the emperor's interest to the marquis, she died at *Nimeguen* on her return to *Germany*. The emperor was then carrrying on a war with the *Sclavonians*, who had taken *Brandenburg*; but they were, at last, subdued, and obliged to deliver up all their conquests. *[margin: Affairs of Italy. to which he marches,]*

In the year 995, the state of affairs in *Italy* demanded the emperor's presence; but, as *Germany* was to furnish him with the means of carrying on the war, he was obliged to summon a diet at *Magdeburg*. He appeared there attended by the pope's nuncios, and by *Landolph*, archbishop of *Milan*, who had been expelled from his see by the rebels. The diet granted him supplies for his *Italian* expedition, and he marched into *Italy* at the head of an army. He found all *Lombardy* in arms against him. He took *Milan*, and restored the archbishop, who crowned him king of *Lombardy*. The reduction of *Milan* awed the rest of that country into obedience to his will. Hearing that the pope was dead, by his own prerogative, he raised *Bruno*, one of his relations, to the popedom; and, at the new pope s request, pardoned *Cressentius*. *[margin: and makes a pope.]*

On his return to *Germany*, he is said to have ordered a count of *Modena* to be beheaded for an attempt upon his wife's chastity. Finding afterwards, by means of the count's wife, who was at the expence of a miracle to prove her veracity, that the count had been sacrificed to the resentment *[margin: A fable concerning his wife.]*

of the empress, who was in love with him, because he refused to comply with her lewdness, he ordered the empress to be burnt, and settled an annuity upon the widow. The credibility of this story is justly questionable. The count, perhaps, was beheaded, and the empress burnt; but the causes assigned for those events are too improbable for belief. Upon *Otho*'s return to *Germany*, he found that the barbarians had renewed their ravages in his absence; and he soon received news that his pope had been expelled by *Cressentius*; and that another, under the name of *John* XVI. had been

His hatred to the Italians. raised to the papal see. The emperor flew again into *Italy* with an army, besieged and took *Rome*, and then the castle of St. *Angelo*, which was bravely defended by *Cressentius*; and ordered the anti-pope, after having his eyes put out, and his nose and ears cut off, to be thrown from its summit. As to *Cressentius*, he is said to have died in arms; others, with greater probability, think that he was put to death by *Otho*, after surrendering himself upon promise of mercy: but the general report is, that he and his accomplices, to the number of twelve, after being most ignominiously scourged and tortured, were gibbetted, as a warning to other rebels. The reason for those differences in opinion, may be accounted for by *Otho* being in love with the beautiful widow of *Cressentius*, whom he took for his mistress; and, it is said, he promised to marry her. It is certain, that, about this time, he performed severe penances for the crimes he had committed.

Before he left *Italy*, he published a decree, importing that the *Germans* alone should have the exclusive right and power of chusing the *Roman* emperors from among their own princes; and, that the pope should have no farther concern in the election than to announce it in public, and to crown the elected whenever he came to *Rome*. Pope *Gregory* confirmed that decree; and, at this time, it is said the basis of the *Germanic* constitution in chusing emperors was fixed; the number of the electors being limited by the pope and the emperor to seven. *Otho*, before he left *Italy*, made many other regulations, which are immaterial here, with regard to its government.

Affairs of Germany. Pope *Gregory* V. dying, the emperor bestowed the papacy on *Gerberg*, archbishop of *Rheims*, one of the most learned men of that age, who took the name of *Silvester* II. He then returned to *Germany*, where he quieted some commotions, and gave the title of king to *Boleslaus* of *Bohemia*, who agreed to hold his dominions as a fief of the empire. He afterwards went to *Aix-la-Chapelle*, where he ordered the tomb of *Charles the Great* to be opened, and found his body placed on a golden throne, with a sceptre and crown richly adorned with jewels. This discovery is thought, by some, to be far from probable; because the *Normans* were, for some time, in possession of, and pillaged that, city. The fact, however, is too well attested to be destroyed by that suggestion.

geſtion. We know not that the *Normans* ever looked for plunder into the repoſitories of the dead ; or, that they were acquainted with the ſpot where *Charles the Great* was buried.

Neither their own vows, nor the chaſtizements of the emperors, could fix the *Italians* in their duty. About the year 1001 (the *Greek* being too weak to keep poſſeſſion of the kingdom of *Naples*) the *Saracens* were called in by the *Romans*, and the other *Italians*, to ſupport their liberties againſt their *German* oppreſſors. *Otho* again paſſed the *Alps*, drove the infidels out of *Capua* ; ſuppreſſed his enemies in *Rome*, where he kept his *Chriſtmas* ; and puniſhed the ſeditious with moſt ignominious deaths. As ſome atonement for his ſeverity, he eſtabliſhed a chamber for reſumptions all over *Italy*. But nothing could reconcile the natives to his government. The *Tiburtines* revolted ; and, upon his return to *Rome*, it was with difficulty that he was readmitted, with a few troops, into that capital. After reſiding there for a few days, the *Romans*, by the inſtigation of a *Tuſcan* prince, beſieged him in his palace. He was in no condition to reſiſt ; but the duke of *Bavaria*, the governor of *Florence*, amuſed the inſurgents till he and the pope eſcaped.

He was collecting his army, which had been lately re-inforced from *Germany*, and preparing to take a ſevere revenge for this inſult, when he died. The cauſe of his death is variouſly related. Some ſay that his miſtreſs, the widow of *Creſſentius*, poiſoned him with a pair of gloves, becauſe he would not fulfil his promiſe of marrying her. Perhaps, the love of her country (a paſſion not unuſual with the ladies of thoſe days) might operate with her reſentment of his infidelity. Other authors ſay that he died of the ſmall-pox at *Paterno*, when he was about thirty years of age, and without iſſue.

Otho, like his predeceſſors, was the ſpiritual ſlave, and the temporal tyrant, of the church ; to which, it is thought, he and his two predeceſſors gave two thirds of its eccleſiaſtical eſtates in *Germany*. But this opinion is to be received with caution ; for, though they were immeaſureably liberal to the church, that liberality is not to be ſuppoſed to ariſe out of their patrimony. Their numerous confiſcations of great eſtates was the main ſource of their bounty. When they re-granted thoſe eſtates, it was either to church-men, in whoſe hands they thought them ſafer than in thoſe of lay-men ; or to laymen (frequently to their former poſſeſſors) with ſome diſmemberment of their territory in favour of the church : and in this ſenſe the three emperors may very juſtly be ſaid to have given away to eccleſiaſtics, eſtates amounting to two thirds above what they formerly poſſeſſed.

Otho III through all the courſe of his reign, diſcovered great abilities for government ; being brave, juſt, and generous.

The emperor returns to Italy.

His death,

and character.

rous. He entered on the exercise of empire and war as early as any prince we read of in history, and acquitted himself equally well in both.

15. Henry II.

Henry II. chosen emperor.

THE *Germans* in the emperor's army endeavoured to conceal his death from the *Italians*; who, having some intimation of it, attacked them in their return with the body to *Germany*; but they were always repulsed. Three capital candidates for the empire immediately started up. *Henry*, duke of *Bavaria*; *Herman*, duke of *Suabia* and *Alsatia*; and *Eckard*, marquis of *Saxony*. *Henry* had the advantage of being grandson to *Otho* II. as well as that of being the most powerful of the competitors; and therefore was chosen by the electors, who, according to the constitution established in the late reign between the pope and the emperor, were now, for the first time, seven in number. It is, however, said that *Eckard* stood the fairest chance for being elected, had he not been assassinated by the *Bavarian* party. *Henry* was crowned at *Mentz*, on the sixth of *June*, 1002. His competitor, the duke of *Suabia*, though powerfully supported, was declared an enemy to the empire, and his estates were ravaged; so that he was obliged to submit to the emperor, who had accepted of a challenge to fight him in single combat. *Henry* having reduced this powerful rival, exacted an oath of allegiance from *Boleslaus*, king of *Bohemia*, the duke of *Saxony*, the counts-palatine, and the archbishops of *Magdeburg* and *Bremen*. He, at the same time, obliged the *Sclavonians* in *Pomerania* to submit to his authority.

His marriage.

Being unmarried, he took to wife *Cunegund*, a daughter to the first count of *Luxemburg*; and, to satisfy some of his scrupulous subjects, he was, for a second time, crowned at *Aix-la-Chapelle*. After this, the *Lorrainers* interrupting the peace of the empire, *Henry* ordered the castle of *Mulsberg*, on the *Rhine*, to be demolished, to cut off their communication with *Germany*. *Boleslaus*, king of *Bohemia*, left a son of the same name, a worthless prince; and his dominions were seized by the king of *Poland*. This producing vast commotions in that country, *Henry* interposed, and demanded that the king of *Poland* should do him homage for *Bohemia*, and the other fiefs which he held of the empire. The king, instead of obeying, entered into an association with the marquis of *Franconia*; *Ernest*, duke of *Suabia*; and *Bruno*, archbishop of *Augsburg*, *Henry*'s brother. *Henry*, who did nothing of moment without the advice of his states, summoned them on this occasion; and they supported him so well, that the

Franconian

Franconian fled to *Poland*; *Erneft* was beheaded, but *Bruno* was pardoned.

This rebellion was fcarcely fuppreffed, when the *Holftein-* ers invaded the empire; which obliged *Henry* to ravage *Hol-* *ftein* in return, after defeating the invaders. It was this peri- od that gave rife to the title of " Apoftolic," lately revived in the perfon of the emprefs-queen of *Hungary*. *Stephen*, duke, or rather the chief, of the *Hungarians*, being probably lefs barbarous than his fubjects, or neighbours, demanded from *Henry* his fifter *Gifella* in marriage. The lady would not con- fent till *Etephen*, who was a pagan, fhould embrace *Chrifti-* *anity*; which he did, as is faid, by the perfuafion of *Henry*. The marriage then taking place, *Stephen* converted his fub- jects; and *Henry* was weak enough to fuffer the pope to erect *Hungary* into a kingdom, and to prefent *Stephen* with the title of King and Apoftle.

Hungary made a kingdom.

It would be tedious and uninftructive, and indeed unne- ceffary, to particularize the jarring interefts of this time. There fcarcely was a petty prince in the empire who did not quarrel with his neighbours, but the imperial authority held the ballance between the ftronger and the weaker; which was all the emolument it received, as the contending parties were generally fupported by powerful confederates. *Henry*, at laft, found means either to fupprefs, or over-awe, all di- fturbances; and he was the more active, as his prefence was now abfolutely neceffary in *Italy*.

The *Italian* ftates were as divided as turbulent and as re- fractory to the imperial authority as thofe of *Germany*; and, had it not been for their divifions, the power of the *German* intereft there muft long before have been extinguished The period we now treat of, was, as they thought, the moft fa- vourable that had occurred, fince the days of *Charles the Great*, for their afferting their independency upon the em- pire. The inhabitants of *Lombardy* chofe one *Ardouin*, marquis of *Ivrea*, to head them; and, the better to unite other ftates under his command, he affumed the fuperb title of king of *Italy*. *Arnold*, the archbifhop of *Milan*, oppofed this nomination; and fent repeated advices to *Henry* to fup- port him in his oppofition to the new king. *Henry* was too much immerfed in the affairs of *Germany* to attend an expe- dition into *Italy* in perfon. He therefore gave the command of a body of troops to *Otho*, duke of *Carinthia*, who was to penetrate into *Italy*. *Ardouin* found means to take pof- feffion of the long neglected paffes of the *Alps*, which he guarded with fifteen thoufand men, and defeated *Otho*, who was obliged to return to *Germany*.

Henry marches to *Italy*.

When the affairs of the empire were fettled, *Henry*, who had ftill a very ftrong party in *Italy*, raifed an army, and marched into *Bavaria*; where his brother-in-law, *Henry*, duke of *Luxemburg*, was elected duke by the ftates of that province. He then paffed the *Alps*, and was crowned king

of

of *Lombardy*, by the archbifhop of *Milan*, at *Pavia*. It is difficult to account for the reafon why *Ardouin* did not fortify the paffes of the *Alps* againft *Henry* as he had done againft *Otho*. Moft probably he was engaged in *Italy* againft *Henry's* party, and trufted to the loyalty of his fubjects. There feems to have been a fettled defign laid in *Pavia* to cut the empe- ror off. The inhabitants of that city, while the *German* troops were encamped without their walls, attempted to mur- der him; but he was faved by his troops, who fcaled the walls, and quelled the infurrection by blood: after which, *Henry*, with the greateft profeffions of clemency, pardoned the furviving inhabitants; and, having paid a vifit to *Milan*, he fet out on his return to *Germany*.

His wars with the Poles.   *Henry*, all this while, was convoking affemblies and ftates for the reformation of his empire, both in fpiritual and tem- poral concerns; but, as the members of thofe parliaments were moft of them, in fome fhape or other, parties in the abufes complained of, their refolutions, when attempted to be carried into execution, feldom, or never, had any good effect: but, to do *Henry* juftice, the fault did not lie in him. Upon his return from *Italy*, he drove the king of *Poland* out of *Bohemia*, and gave the dukedom to *Jaromir*, the brother of *Boleflaus*, its former duke. He then paffed the *Elbe*, and, after defeating the *Poles* in their own country, he prefcribed peace, on his own terms, to their king. After this, *Henry* obtained the pope's confent for erecting the powerful diftrict of *Bamberg* into a bifhopric.

Rife of the Pruffians.   It was about this time that the *Boruffians*, a migrating co- lony from the fource of the *Tannis*, but then fettled in the uncultivated defarts between *Poland* and the *Baltic*, were firft heard of as a people. They are reprefented, at this time, to have been the moft barbarous of all barbarous pagans; and yet this defpicable people, fince fo well known by the name of *Pruffians*, became objects of prey to the *Poles*, who plun- dered them. In 1007, *Henry* gave the province of *Low Lorrain* to *Godfrey*, count of the *Ardennes*; *Otho*, its late poffeffor, and the laft of the pofterity of *Charles the Great*, being now dead. This donation produced great troubles; and, the late duke having left fifters, their hufbands entered their claims to his fucceffion; and were patronized by the king of *France*, who wanted to lay hold of that opportunity to revive his claims upon *Lorrain*. The emperor, however, acted with fo much vigour, that he quelled all oppofition, and effectually fup- ported his own nomination. With equal prudence and firm- nefs, he fuppreffed the troubles arifing at the fame time in *High Lorrain*; and put *Henry*, duke of *Bavaria*, who fo- mented them, to the ban of the empire.

Commo- tions in Germany.   All *Germany* feems, at this time, to have been agitated by the ambition of its great lords. The marquis of *Mifnia*, having caballed with *Boleflaus*, king of *Poland*, was by him divefted of his-eftates; which were given to *Herman*, the fon of of *Eckard*, count of *Thuringia*. To punish *Boleslaus*, the imperial troops ravaged his dominions; and *Henry* seized the passes on the *Oder* to prevent his future irruptions into the empire. He then assembled a diet at *Coblentz*, where the duke of *Bavaria*, with the bishops of *Mentz* and *Triers*, who had been concerned in the late rebellious practices, threw themselves at his feet and were pardoned.

It is no wonder if a life so tumultuous as that which *Henry* was obliged to lead, disgusted him with the world; and, as a convent, in those times, was the only place were tranquility could be enjoyed, he thought of becoming a canon of *Strasbourg*; and, though he was then dissuaded from this intention, he founded a rich prebendary there, with a view of one day filling it himself. The restlessness of *Boleslaus*, king of *Poland*, contributed not a little to divert *Henry* from his thoughts of retirement; for that *Pole* once more made himself master of *Bohemia*, but was again dispossessed by *Henry*, to whom he sued for peace.

In the year 1013, notwithstanding an irruption of the *Slaves*, or *Sclavonians*, who were then plundering the territory about *Bamburgh*, *Henry* was again prevailed on by the archbishop of *Milan*, to march into *Italy*, that he might reduce *Ardouin*, who was then become the absolute master of *Lombardy*. *Ardouin* made an ineffectual opposition to the great army which *Henry* headed; and he, and his wife *Cunegunda*, received the imperial crown at *Rome* from the hands of pope *Benedict* VIII. That pontif knew the weak side of *Henry*, and the force which a solemn act acquires. While the imperial pair were upon their knees before him, he asked *Henry*, Whether he would always observe his fidelity to him and his successors; to which the simple prince answered in the affirmative: and this concession was, by the after popes, construed into a homage paid by the head of the empire to the holy see. *(marginal note: Henry again marches to Italy.)*

The affairs of *Germany* would not suffer *Henry* to remain long in *Italy*; but he relapsed into his fits for a monastic life, and was guilty of a thousand extravagant acts of devotion. When he passed through *Burgundy*, he visited the abbey of *Clugni*, where he was entered as an associate. He endeavoured to be admitted a monk in the abbey of St. *Val*. The abbot gravely asked him, Whether he would obey him in every thing. *Henry* answered, That he would. " Then," said the abbot, " I enjoin you to return to the government of " your empire." This salutary advice came very seasonably to *Henry*, who followed it; for his absence had again set the empire in arms.

In 1015, *Boleslaus*, the warlike and intriguing king of *Poland*, was summoned to appear before a diet at *Mersbourg*, to answer to a charge brought against him of having conspired with the duke of *Bohemia* and *Ardouin* to disturb the peace of *(marginal note: Wars with Poland.)*

the

the empire. *Boleſlaus* laughed at this ſummons ; he raiſed an army ; and a prædatory war enſued, which ended by another deceitful peace ; and *Boleſlaus* promiſed to pay tribute to the empire for *Poland* and *Moravia.* After this, *Henry* received, from *Rodolph* III. king of *Transjurane Burgundy*, a ceſſion of his dominions ; but the inhabitants not receiving him as their ſovereign, he gave them up to be plundered and maſſacred by his troops ; and *Werner*, biſhop of *Straſbourg*, his lieutenant-general, gave them a complete defeat near *Geneva*, while the emperor was reducing the duke of *Saxony*, who tyrannized over his ſubjects, to a good behaviour.

Trial of the empreſs.

Here we are to place the famous trial of the empreſs *Cunegunda*, for being unfaithful to her huſband's bed It happens unfortunately for the character of the ladies of thoſe days, that their honour never is vindicated but at the expence of credibility. *Cunegunda* approved herſelf innocent by going through the ordeal trial unhurt. Either the ſtory itſelf muſt be falſe, or the empreſs muſt have impoſed upon her huſband and the judges. *Henry's* ſuſpicions, however, were very natural, as we ſhall ſee hereafter.

About the year 1019, the *Greeks*, having regained their footing in *Apulia* and *Calabria*, defeated the *Normans*, whom the *Italians* had called to their aſſiſtance ; and pope *Benedict* VIII. was obliged to fly to *Bamberg* for the imperial protection. Upon this occaſion a diet was held at *Aix-la-Chapelle*, where the laws he had formerly enacted at *Pavia*, and which rendered the pope a vaſſal of the empire in temporal matters, were confirmed ; and meaſures were taken for inſuring the peace of the empire, and for ſending an army into *Italy*, where the *Saracens* had ravaged *Tuſcany.* In 1021, *Henry*, at the head of an army, the general officers of which were chiefly biſhops, who commanded their own regiments, re-conquered all *Apulia* and *Calabria*, and expelled, or otherwiſe reduced, the *Italian* noblemen and prelates, who had favoured the *Greeks* or *Saracens* In ſhort, he diſabled his enemies ſo, that *Italy* was reſtored to an uncommon ſtate of tranquility.

Henry then repaſſed the *Alps*, and expreſſed a deſire of having an interview with *Robert*, king of *France.* This was in order to ſtrengthen the tranquility of his empire. *Robert* conſented ; but ſome diſputes happening concerning the ceremonial, *Henry*, with great magnanimity, cut them ſhort, by going in perſon to the *French* camp ; where *Robert* received him like a brother, and all former differences between them and their ſubjects were ſettled. This was the laſt illuſtrious action of *Henry's* life ; for, after reſtoring *Germany* and *Italy* to a ſtate of greater tranquility than they had known for many years before, he died, in 1024, at *Grone*, when he was but fifty-two years of age, of which he reigned twenty-two. It is ſaid, upon good authority, that, on his death-

Death,

bed,

bed, he declared, to the parents of *Cunegunda*, his wife, that he reſtored her a virgin to their care. This, if true, eaſily accounts for his jealouſy.

Henry had as many epithets as he had defects or virtues, and character of *Henry*. cha- or what were eſteemed ſo in thoſe times. He had a halt in walking, and therefore he was called *the Lame* ; he had a cold conſtitution, which gained him the appellation of *the Chaſte*; he was devout, and therefore he was called *the Saint*; and his *Chriſtian* zeal got him the name of *the Apoſtle*. That *Henry* was a prince of great abilities, muſt appear to any one who reflects upon the length and proſperity of his reign, the powerful enemies he had to contend with, the turbulence of the times, and the tranquility in which he left his empire. His great art ſeems to have conſiſted in his ballancing parties among his chief vaſſals, and keeping the *German* ecclefiaſtics on his ſide. This laſt meaſure coſt him ſometimes too dear; for he is ſaid to have muttered a curſe while a biſhop of *Paderborn* was beſtowing a benediction upon him for his liberality to his ſee.

---

16. Conrade II. *ſurnamed* the Salic.

HENRY of *Bavaria* dying without iſſue, a moſt prodigious number of *German* dukes and nobility aſſembled in the open fields between *Worms* and *Mentz*, to proceed to the choice of a new emperor. We cannot pronounce any thing deciſive concerning this meeting, whether all thoſe princes had actually a voice in electing the emperor ; or, whether their preſence was not neceſſary for adjuſting certain differences among the ſeven electors. The dukes of *Saxony, Bohemia, Bavaria, Carinthia, Suabia, Franconia, Lorrain,* and *Holland* and *Frieſland*, were preſent. The multitude of prelates, and other noblemen, was prodigious ; as was the number of retinues they brought with them. After a canvaſs of ſix weeks, their choice fell upon *Conrade* II. called *the Salic,* from his being born near the river *Sala*, or deſcended from the *Salian* princes. The choice of the electors ſeems to have been determined by the opinion they had of his virtue and his inability to oppreſs them, as his patrimonial dominions were inconſiderable ; whereas, the imperial authority devolving upon a prince of great ambition and power, might have rendered him abſolute over the other electors.

Conrade is ſaid to have begun his reign by purſuing the plan of his predeceſſor in continuing the public tranquility, and eſtabliſhing the practice of juſtice and true policy among his ſubjects. While he was intent on this, an account came that ſome of the great fiefs of *Italy* were inclined to put themſelves

Election of Conrade, (margin note)

felves

felves under the protection of the king of *France*, who had refufed their offer; and that *Lombardy* was on the point of revolting. The pope, *John* XX. continued firm in the *Germanic* intereft; and he invited *Conrade* into *Italy* in 1026, whither he repaired with incredible expedition.

who is crowned at *Rome*. Like his predeceffors, his prefence, at the head of a great army, bore down all oppofition; and, after chaftizing the infurgents of *Lombardy*, he went, accompanied by *Canute*, king of *England*, and *Rodolph* III. king of *Transjurane Burgundy*, to *Rome*; where, on *Eafter-day*, he received the imperial crown from the pope. Having intelligence that *Erneft*, duke of *Suabia*; *Albert*, duke of *Carinthia*; and *Conradin*, duke of *Worms*, were in arms againft him in *Germany*; he left *Italy*, and caufed his fon *Henry*, who was then but twelve years of age, to be elected and crowned king of *Germany* at *Aix-la-Chapelle*; and then taking the field, he thoroughly defeated the rebels. *Erneft* was killed; the reft were made prifoners, and adjudged, by an affembly of the *Germanic* body, to have forfeited their dominions. *Mifico*, fon of *Boleflaus*, king of *Poland*, had taken upon him that title; and pretended to be independent of the empire. *Conrade* marched againft him with an army; defeated him; and forced him to throw himfelf upon the protection of *Othalric*, duke of *Bohemia*; who ungeneroufly fent a letter to the emperor, offering to give up his gueft. The emperor privately fent the letter to *Mifico*, who thereupon threw himfelf at *Conrade*'s feet. The emperor reftored him to his dominions, and *Othalric* fued for pardon and peace, which were granted him.

Affairs of *Germany* and *Poland*. Soon after, *Otho*, *Mifico*'s brother, being affaffinated, as was thought, by *Mifico*, *Conrade*, by his imperial authority, divided *Mifico*'s kingdom into three parts: one he left to *Mifico* himfelf, but the other two were given to two *Polifh* noblemen, who were fuppofed to be well affected to the empire. They foon fhewed themfelves unworthy of their truft, for each fet up for himfelf; *Silefia* was entirely detached from *Poland*; and *Moravia* was annexed to *Bohemia*, where duke *Othalric* became thereby very powerful. His fon, *Bretiflaus*, about the year 1032, after thofe partitions had taken place, had forcibly carried off a lady, one *Judith*, the daughter of a nobleman who, in hiftory, is called count *Albert Otho*. The father threw himfelf at the emperor's feet, who immediately marched to punifh the ravifher; but matters were made up while the two armies were on the point of coming to a bloody battle. *Bretiflaus* fubmitted, and *Conrade* pardoned him. The emperor then chaftized fome of the pagan inhabitants of the county of *Mecklenburgh*; but frefh commotions drew his arms towards *Hungary*. *Stephen*, the king of that country, demanded the dutchy of *Bavaria*, in right of his wife, fifter and heirefs to the late emperor. *Conrade* not only rejected his claim, but entered *Hungary* with

with a powerful army; and *Stephen* was obliged to sue to him for a peace. It was obſerved that one *Babo*, count of *Auremberg*, ſerved in this expedition with thirty-two of his ſons, all bearing arms and born of one mother.

Rodolph, king of *Transjurane Burgundy*, being dead, *Con-* King Rorade claimed his ſucceſſion under *Rodolph*'s laſt will, rather dolph's than as being the huſband of *Giſella*, his younger ſiſter. ſucceſſion *Eudes*, count of *Champagne*, the ſon of the elder ſiſter, diſputed. *Bertha*, diſputed *Conrade*'s title to the whole; but, after a bloody war, he was killed in a battle which he loſt near *Barleduc*; by which a very conſiderable acquiſition fell to *Conrade*. A number of the biſhops and noblemen, in *Transjurane Burgundy* aſſembled at *Soleuvre*, confirmed his ſucceſs by taking an oath of allegiance to him, and acknowledged his ſon ſucceſſor to their kingdom. *Miſico*, king of *Poland*, being dead, the *Poles* revolted from his widow *Ricliza*, who acted as regent for her young ſon *Caſimir*, and ſhe put herſelf under the emperor's protection; but *Conrade* could not prevent the *Bohemians* from ravaging *Poland*, where they carried off a vaſt booty. As to young *Caſimir*, he was ſhut up in a monaſtery; from whence he was releaſed by the *Poles* themſelves, and he mounted the throne of his anceſtors.

Conrade then celebrated the marriage of his ſon *Henry* with Affairs in *Gunhilda*, daughter of *Canute*, king of *England*. This is the *Italy*. lady whoſe chaſtity was vindicated, when accuſed, by a young *Engliſhman*, of ſmall ſtature, who became her voluntary champion, and killed the giant who was champion for the proſecution. This fact, though but ſparingly mentioned by *German* authors, is well atteſted by the *Engliſh*, who wrote the neareſt to thoſe times. The feſtivities of this marriage were broken off by the account that *Conrade* received of the archbiſhop of *Milan* having declared againſt him in *Italy*; which he entered, with a great army, in 1037. His march was ſo ſudden, that he entered *Milan* without oppoſition; and ordered *Heribert*, the archbiſhop, with the prelates of his party, to be put under arreſt. The biſhops were ſent priſoners to *Germany*; but *Heribert* made his eſcape, by making his guards drunk; and, entering *Milan*, he fortified it, and ſhut his gates againſt the emperor. *Conrade* was, at this time, buſied in reducing other parts of *Italy* to their duty; but he marched to *Milan*, which he beſieged, though in vain; and this ruined his credit in *Italy*. *Conrade*, exaſperated to the laſt degree, revenged himſelf by deſolating the country; and by prevailing with the pope, who is ſaid to have been a boy of ſeventeen years of age, to excommunicate *Heribert*.

The troubles and commotions of *Italy*, where *Conrade* loſt great part of his army, every day encreaſed; and *Henry* pardoned ſome and puniſhed others; but a contagious diſtemper breaking out in his army, he was obliged to return to *Germany*,

many, and to leave *Italy* in a more diſtracted ſtate than when he entered it ; the *Normans* having now made a great progreſs in *Apulia* and *Calabria*. *Conrade*, before he left *Italy*, ſeems to have entered into ſome compromiſe with *Heribert*; for we are told that he came to *Milan*, where he was crowned; and that he received the bleſſing of *Benedict* IX. who had ſucceeded *John* XX.

Conrade's death and character. *Conrade*, ſoon after his return from *Italy*, being ſeized with the gout in his legs, died ſuddenly at *Utrecht*, in the fifteenth year of his reign. According to the beſt accounts, he was a prince of great virtue and magnanimity, and remarkable for his generoſity towards thoſe who ſerved him well. A gentleman who had loſt his leg in his ſervice, received his boot full of gold, as the emperor told him, to pay for his cure. Upon the whole, however, notwithſtanding all the virtues of the late emperors, *Germany* was, at this time, more barbarous and uncivilized than it was at the death of *Charles the Great*. This was owing to the impolitic diviſions of the empire made by that prince and his ſucceſſors among their children, which was productive of perpetual war, the great enemy of civilization.

17. Henry III. *ſurnamed* the Black.

Henry's wars with the Hungarians. THIS prince aſcended the imperial throne in conſequence of his former election, without any difficulty; and was crowned at *Aix-la-Chapelle* by *Philigrin*, archbiſhop of *Cologne*. In 1040, he had reduced the duke of *Bohemia*, who had refuſed to pay him tribute. He then marched againſt *Ovon*, who, it is ſaid, had uſurped the crown of *Hungary* from *Peter*, a relation of king *Stephen*, who was called *Peter the German*, becauſe he owed his dignity to the emperor *Conrade*. This war was undertaken in the year 1042. *Henry's* view was to revive the ſuperiority of his empire over the *Hungarians* irreconcileable to *Peter*, and to every other prince he preſented to their choice ; but ſtrongly diſpoſed in favour of *Ovon*, with whom he was obliged to enter into an alliance for a ſhort time. Next year, he defeated *Ovon* in a pitched battle near *Raab*, and, entering *Alba Regalis*, he was acknowledged ſovereign of the kingdom by the ſtates ; and he reeſtabliſhed *Peter* on the throne. Soon after, *Ovon* was taken priſoner, and *Peter* ordered his head to be ſtruck off.

State of affairs at Rome. In conſequence of the imperial rights, *Henry* beſtowed the archbiſhopric of *Lions* upon a prelate whom he inveſted with a ring and a crown. The counts of *Tuſcany* had, of late, directed the affairs of the papacy at *Rome*, but they were now oppoſed by *Ptolemy*, the conſul ; and they expelled *Benedict* IX. on account of the ſcandalous life he led; and one

of

of their own faction, who took the name of *Silvester* III. was raised to the papacy. The latter was deposed in three months time, and *Benedict* re-established; but finding himself universally detested, he sold part of the papacy to one *John*, and all the three competitors entered into a kind of compromise to divide the revenues of the holy see among them, and to indulge themselves in pleasure, without taking any concern about the public. This triumvirate was too infamous to last; and a priest, called *Gratian*, prevailed with the three popes to accept, each of them, a sum of money, and to resign the dignity of pope; which they did, and were succeeded in it by *Gratian*, who assumed the name of *Gregory* VI. The emperor, *Henry*, looked upon all those revolutions as so many invasions of his prerogative; and, in 1046, he passed the *Alps* at the head of an army; was crowned at *Milan* by the archbishop; waited upon by pope *Gregory* VI. at *Placentia*; and ordered a council to be assembled at *Sutri*. There the deposition of the papal triumvirs was confirmed; *Gregory* was deposed for simony; the papal see was declared vacant; and *Hedegar*, bishop of *Bamberg*, immediately took possession of it, by the express order of the emperor, under the title of *Clement* II.

Henry having thus re-asserted, in its fullest extent, the exercise of the imperial rights at *Rome*, was crowned there, on *Christmas-day*, with his empress, by the new pope; and obliged the senate, and people of *Rome*, to swear, that they never would afterwards chuse a pope without the consent and permission of the emperors of *Germany*. *Henry* found the *Norman* princes in *Italy* too powerful to think of recovering the territories they had taken from the *Greeks* and the *Saracens*; and was contented with their receiving from him, as a mark of his superiority, the investiture of *Apulia*, *Calabria*, and the *Beneventine*. *Henry* then returned to *Germany*, where he received news of the death of pope *Clement* II. and, notwithstanding the intrigues of the *Italians*, nominated *Poppo*, bishop of *Brescia*, to succeed him; which he did, under the name of *Damasus* II. but he enjoyed his papacy only twenty-three days. The emperor, to keep up his dignity to the full, refused to admit of any applications from the *Romans*; and immediately nominated *Bruno*, bishop of *Toul*, to the papal see; and obliged him directly to assume the pontifical vestments, and to set out on his journey for *Rome*. He was attended thither by the famous *Hildibrand*, a monk of *Clugni*, who won the pope's confidence, and persuaded him, as a matter of conscience, to divest himself of the pontifical robes till he should be formally elected at *Rome*; where *Hildebrand* artfully embarrassed his election, that the pope, who took the name of *Leo* IX. might think he owed it entirely to him.

In 1050, a new war broke out between the emperor and the *Hungarians*. The latter had deposed *Peter*, the emperor's king; and chose, in his room, *Andrew*, his cousin;

where the papal Henry nominates the the popes.

He is defeated in Hungary.

who had defeated *Peter*, and, after putting out his eyes, had murdered him in prison. The circumstances of the war carried on, upon this occasion, by *Henry* against *Andrew*, are so variously related, that we have nothing but conjecture to guide us. It is most propable that the emperor, upon the whole, was unsuccessful; though the *German* historians pretend that he defeated *Andrew* in several bloody battles, stripped him of a great part of his dominions, and obliged him to pay a tribute both in men and money: but the fact is, that *Andrew*, who was a *Christian*, which more than half of his subjects were not, kept possession of the crown of *Hungary*; and, according to some authors, married one of the emperor's daughters.

All *Bavaria* was, at this time, in agitation, on account of the tyranny of young *Conrade*, its duke. *Henry* summoned him to appear before him at *Mersbourg*, where he deprived him of his dominions, which he gave to his son *Henry*, a child of no more than three years of age, though he was, about the same time, elected and crowned king of the *Romans*, that the accession to the empire might be assured to him. As a proof that the emperor had not subdued *Hungary*, the deprived duke of *Bavaria* retired thither, and received both shelter and assistance from the *Hungarians*.

In 1055, the emperor, with the assistance of the diet of *Aix-la-Chapelle*, marched with an army into *Flanders*, the count of which had invaded *Lorrain*, and plundered *Triers*, with the other towns upon the *Moselle*. This obliged count *Baldwin* to leave *Lorrain*, to defend his own territories, from which *Henry* withdrew. But we are now to attend the affairs of *Italy*.

Affairs of *Italy*.   Upon the death of *Leo* IX. *Hildebrand* intrigued so artfully, that he prevailed with the *Romans* to chuse a pope, and with the emperor to pardon them for not having obtained his consent. The *Normans*, at this time, were very powerful in *Italy*; where they defeated an army which had been lent by the emperor to the late pope, whom they took prisoner and carried captive to *Benevento*. He was succeeded, as we have already hinted, by *Victor* II. who came to *Germany* to implore the emperor's protection against the *Normans*. *Henry* accordingly marched into *Italy*, and summoned a council at *Florence*; where he complained that *Ferdinand* of *Castile* had refused to do him homage for the fiefs he held of the empire, and had even usurped the title of emperor. The pope sent his admonitions to *Ferdinand*; but he, instead of obeying them, sent *Roderigo*, the cid, with an army across the *Pyrenees*. A negotiation soon put an end to their differences *Ferdinand* dropped the title of emperor, and *Henry* his claim of homage.

During *Henry*'s abode in *Italy*, he had a quarrel with his own sister, *Beatrice*, the widow of a marquis of *Tuscany*, and the wife of *Godfrey*, a *German* nobleman, to whose son he had

had promised her daughter, *Matilda*, who was heir to her father's estates. The husband was obliged to fly to *Flanders* and the lady was sent prisoner to *Germany*. Before *Henry* left *Italy*, he made an alliance with *Contarini*, duke of *Venice*, which was, even at that time, a powerful state ; and, upon his return to *Germany*, he obliged his own uncle, *Jebhard*, bishop of *Ratisbon*, to appear before the diet, for having fomented an insurrection in *Bavaria* ; for which he was condemned to perpetual imprisonment, but released by the emperor's clemency.

In 1056, all *Germany*, and the greatest part of *Europe*, was visited with a most dreadful famine, pestilence, and earthquakes. *Henry* did all he could to relieve his subjects, who were over-run by the *Sclavonians*, those barbarians being pressed by the same calamities. The sufferings of his subjects, it is thought, made an impression upon the emperor's health ; and, after causing his son, for a second time, to be elected king of the *Romans*, he died, at *Burfelt*, in *Saxony*, in the twenty-ninth year of his age, and the sixteenth of his reign. His character was much the same with those of his two immediate predecessors ; all of them were endowed with ambition and magnanimity, had the same interests to support, and the same enemies to combat. *The emperor's death and character.*

---

18. Henry IV. *surnamed* the Great.

THE history of the infancy of this reign is as unentertaining as it is barbarous. The name of the empress-mother was *Agnes*, daughter to the duke of *Guienne*, a woman of sense and spirit. The young emperor was no more than five years of age when he was recognized by a diet of the princes, convoked at *Cologne*, with so much unanimity, that the count of *Flanders*, and the marquis of *Tuscany*, were then reconciled to the empress-regent, who was acknowledged as such by all present. The inexpressible ignorance, vice, pride, and ambition, which then over-run *Germany*, created infinite trouble to the regent. She conferred the great dutchy of *Suabia* upon *Rudolph* of *Rhirfield*, in preference to count *Berthold*; and thereby made the latter her enemy. *Poland* renounced its dependence upon the *German* empire, and attacked *Hungary*. The regent gave that king some support, but he and his queen were obliged to take refuge in *Ratisbonne*. Wars likewise broke out amongst the counts of *Holland* and the bishops of *Cologn* and *Liege*, for matters so trivial that they are not worthy of being mentioned in history. *Accession of Henry IV. a minor.*

The wisdom of the empress-regent prevented all foreign quarrels, but could not compose the turbulent spirits of the *Government of his mother* empire. Every woman of high rank, in those days, who had a minister to whom she was obliged to trust, was supposed to be in love with him. The empress-regent's minister was the bishop of *Augsburg*, and the dukes of *Saxony* and *Bavaria* laid hold of that circumstance to calumniate her; and found means to get the person of the emperor, who was nephew to them both, into their possession. They committed his education to the care of the archbishops of *Cologne* and *Bremen*, men of very different characters. The former endeavoured to render his august pupil worthy of empire, but the latter to make himself necessary to his vicious inclinations, which he sought by all means to gratify. We do not find that the empress renounced her regency after she was deprived of the tuition of her son.

Pope *Nicholas* took the opportunity of the emperor's nonage to enact a decree, that the popes should be elected by the curates of *Rome*, who are now called cardinals. The empress-regent, in a diet which she convoked, deposed pope *Alexander* II. who had been chosen under that decree, and substituted, in his room, *Honorius* II. A schism naturally ensued, and it had great consequences. *Alexander* was supported by *Geoffrey* of *Lorrain*, the husband of *Matilda*, heiress of *Tuscany*, and one of the most powerful of the Italian princes; so that, when *Henry*, at the age of twenty-two, in 1072, entered upon the exercise of government, he found every thing in confusion. His mother, disgusted with the opposition she met with, had retired to a convent; and *Germany*, in general, was a scene of public robbery and depredation.

Henry strove to remove those abuses. He made *Goslar* the seat of his government, and erected forts for bridling the public abuses. The expence with which his government was attended, produced murmurings among his great subjects; who, glad of any pretext for emancipating themselves from the imperial authority, sided with pope *Alexander*. That pontif had the insolence to summon the emperor to appear before him at *Rome*, to give an account both of his moral and civil conduct. Though the emperor despised this summons, yet the states of *Saxony* made a handle of it to distress him in the administration of government. They demanded that he should demolish all his new-erected forts in *Saxony* and *Thuringia*; that he should re-instate *Otho*, the duke of *Saxony*, in the dutchy of *Bavaria*, of which he had been deprived for treason against the emperor's person; and that, in all his private life, he should conform himself to their desires. Those treasonable requests were backed by an association consisting chiefly of churchmen. The heads of it were *Werner*, archbishop of *Magdeburg*; *Burchar*, bishop of *Halberstadt*; *Henry*, bishop of *Hildesheim*; *Werner*, bishop of *Mersbourg*; *Heilberg*, bishop of *Minden*; *James*, bishop of *Paderborn*; *Frederic*, bishop of *Mimmegardefurt*; *Benno*, bishop

bishop of *Misnia*; *Otho*, duke of *Saxony*; the marquises of *Thuringia*, *Uko*, and *Dedo*; and *Frederic*, count-palatine of *Saxony*.

The emperor offered them all the constitutional redress that was in his power to afford; but, as some of their demands were not only unreasonable, but ridiculous, he underhand strengthened himself by forming a counter-party in the empire. His own vices proved to be his greatest enemies. His complection was amorous, and he had about him a haughtiness extremely disgusting to his subjects. In short, he was deserted by all his friends; and obliged, at last, to have recourse to the poor expedient of sending personal challenges to his subjects, who declined them; and, in the end, he was forced to take refuge in *Worms*. Distressed majesty has always been known to be a powerful advocate. The inhabitants of *Worms* compassionated their emperor, who came to implore their protection; and he prevailed with some of his chief subjects to give him a meeting at *Oppenheim*, where his address and eloquence conquered the most obstinate among them. One *Reginger*, who had formerly been his domestic, had likewise been particularly active in stirring up the rebellion against him. Him the emperor defied to single combat, in those days the sacred tribunal of justice; but *Reginger*, either declining the combat, or being secretly made away with, *Henry* thereby established his own character.

The *Saxons*, however, having settled a plan of rebellion, again appeared in arms; but *Henry* defeated them in the year 1075, and their heads publicly asked him pardon. Cardinal *Hildebrand*, whom we have already mentioned, upon the death of *Alexander* II. had been chosen pope, and assumed the name of *Gregory* VII The emperor was not consulted in this election, and complained of it. The pope temporized, as being in no condition to resist; but, when *Henry* confirmed his election, he threw off the mask, and excommunicated all the *German* princes who opposed his will. The papal artillery, upon this occasion, was chiefly levelled at the ecclesiastics for their submitting to take investitures from laics. The pope omitted nothing in his power to stir up a rebellion in *Germany* against *Henry* He sent four legates thither to hold a council, and to charge the emperor with simony He even employed emissaries to stir up the *Saxons* to rebellion; and treated the emperor, in all respects, as an excommunicated person. *Henry*, though he acted with great vigour in the field, and subdued the *Saxons*, was obliged to give way to the torrent of religious zeal. He wrote a letter to the pope, acknowledging his faults, and begging forgiveness. This was granted him by *Gregory*, who, at the same time, proposed to head an army of *Christians*, to rescue the holy sepulchre from the infidels; and that the emperor should serve under him as a volunteer. The pontif's presumption

He is excommunicated by the pope.

did

did not ſtop here; for he rebuked a king of *Hungary* for paying homage for his crown to the emperor, inſtead of the holy ſee.

Donation of Matilda to the ſee of Rome. The emperor hated *Gregory* in his heart, and, notwithſtanding his ſubmiſſion, he continued, as before, to grant eccleſiaſtical inveſtitures by the croſs and the ring. This exaſperated *Gregory*, who accuſed the emperor, perhaps with ſome reaſon, of ſelling thoſe inveſtitures; and had the inſolence to cite *Henry*, under pain of excommunication, to appear before him, as a criminal, at *Rome*. This drove *Henry* from all his moderation, and he ſummoned an aſſembly of biſhops at *Worms*, who pronounced ſentence of deprivation againſt the pope. *Gregory*, on the other hand, called together a council, which declared the emperor to be excommunicated. The *German* princes, even ſuch of them as owed their dominions to *Henry*'s bounty, laid hold of that pretext to render themſelves independent; and the very men who, but a little before, had voted *Gregory* to be deprived of the pontificate, now joined him againſt *Henry*, who was ſummoned to appear before the pope at *Augſburg*. The emperor, on this occaſion, ſeemed to be deſerted by all the world. His couſin, the famous counteſs *Matilda*, had an implacable hatred to him and his houſe; but was proportionably attached to *Gregory* and the church. In her own right, ſhe poſſeſſed great part of *Tuſcany, Mantua, Parma, Reggio, Placentia, Ferrara, Modena, Verona*, and almoſt all that is now called the patrimony of St. *Peter*, from *Viterbo* to *Orvieto*; together with part of *Umbria, Spoleto*, and *the March of Ancona*. Thoſe vaſt poſſeſſions were by her, in the madneſs of her zeal, beſtowed upon *Gregory*, who lived with her, in no very decent manner, at her caſtle of *Canoſſa*, in *Italy*.

Henry's humility and penance. Nothing but diſtreſs and difficulty preſented itſelf to *Henry*, who, in ſhort, was obliged to appear at *Canoſſa* like a ſuppliant, and to wait, bare-footed, in the midſt of ſnow, from morning to evening, during three days, to implore pardon of his holineſs, who, with difficulty, was prevailed upon to grant it. This happened in the month of *January*, 1077. The reader is miſtaken, if he imagines that all the laity in thoſe days were enthuſiaſts for the pope. Religion was then, as ſince, worn as a maſk for temporal motives. The noble *Italians* could have borne with the inſolence of the pope, becauſe it ſerved them as a defence againſt the imperial authority; but, when they ſaw *Gregory* exalt himſelf above the higheſt pretenſions of the emperor, they took part with the latter, and, in very ſtrong terms, expreſſed their hatred of the pontifical inſolence. Matters were very different in *Germany*, where a jealouſy of the imperial power prevailed, and the princes ſided ſo entirely with the pope, that they laid hold of the excommunication which had been pronounced againſt the emperor, to declare him divested of the empire; and, in his

his ſtead, they elected *Rodolph*, duke of *Suabia*, who was actually crowned at *Mentz*. *Henry* was then in *Italy*, collecting forces againſt the pope; but, hearing he had been depoſed in *Germany*, he ſet out for that country; and, having haſtily aſſembled an army, he gave battle, near *Wurtzburg*, to his rival *Rodolph*, who was completely defeated.

In 1080, *Gregory* VII. who had, for ſome time, been blocked up by the *Lombards* in *Canoſſa*, eſcaped and confirmed the depoſition of *Henry*. *Rodolph*, about the ſame time, was again defeated by the emperor, who made himſelf maſter of *Suabia*; and, marching into *Saxony*, he gave *Rodolph* a third defeat. This ſerved only to animate the haughty pontif againſt *Henry*. He ſent to *Rodolph* a golden crown, with a ſtupid verſe, intimating, That, as our Saviour gave dominion to *Peter*, ſo he, *Gregory*, gave the empire to *Rodolph*, in the following words: *Petra dedit Petro, Petrus diadema Rodolpho*. *Henry* was no ways diſconcerted, and turned the pope's artillery upon himſelf. He aſſembled the *German* biſhops at *Brixon*, and they depoſed *Gregory*; ſubſtituting in his room *Gilbert*, archbiſhop of *Ravenna*, who took the title of *Clement* III. *Rodolph* was again in arms. The count of *Provence*, and the *Norman* princes, declared themſelves for *Gregory*; but *Godfrey of Bouillon*, one of the greateſt warriors of that age, ſided with *Henry*, and a deciſive battle was fought at *Merſburg*, in which *Godfrey* cut off *Rodolph*'s hand; and mortally wounded him. *Henry* being victorious, ſaw, without emotion, the magnificent interment which *Rodolph*'s friends beſtowed upon him; ſaying, That he wiſhed all his enemies were as pompouſly buried.

The death of *Rodolph* completed the triumphs of *Henry* in *Germany*, where he revenged himſelf ſeverely upon his opponents; and then marched to *Italy*, that he might place his own pope, *Clement*, upon the papal throne. *Gregory* made a vigorous reſiſtance. The *Romans* ſhut their gates againſt the emperor, and defended themſelves for two years and a half. Their city, at laſt, was taken by ſtorm, in 1084; but *Gregory* retired to the caſtle of St *Angelo*, which was too well fortified for *Henry* to take. *Robert Guiſcard*, the *Norman* duke of *Apulia*, marched to *Gregory*'s relief; and while *Henry* was in *Lombardy*, he delivered him and carried him to *Salem*. In the mean while, *Henry* publiſhed his reaſons for depoſing *Gregory*, and ſubſtituting *Clement* in his room; with which the *Romans* appeared to be ſo well ſatisfied, that the latter was crowned at St. *Peter*'s with the uſual ceremonies; after which he put the imperial diadem upon the head of *Henry*.

It is remarkable, that, while the *Romans* and the *Lombards* were almoſt unanimous in ſupporting the imperial dignity againſt the pope, the *Germans* were uniting againſt it. The emperor had given his daughter in marriage to *Frederic*, baron of *Stenffen*, and the dutchy of *Suabia* for her dowry; but

Death of his rival Rodolph.

The emperor takes Rome.

but the *Saxons* once more confederated, under the shadow of *Gregory*'s authority; and, in 1085, they elected count *Herman*, of *Luxembourg*, king of the *Romans*; and destroyed the estates of *Henry* and his adherents in *Franconia*. Those disturbances carried *Henry* back to *Germany*; and, calling a general assembly of ecclesiastics at *Mentz*, all the anathemas of *Gregory* against *Henry* were annulled; and the emperor's ordinances against the pope were confirmed; and all the prelates who befriended count *Herman* were deprived of their benefices, as the count himself was of his new title.

Death of pope Gregory. Upon the breaking up of this assembly, an account came of the death of *Gregory* at *Salerno*; and, that the *Romans*, without regarding *Clement*, the *German* pope, had fixed upon cardinal *Didier*, the abbot of *Monte Casino*, to succeed him. *Henry* was then too much employed in *Germany* to support his pope's title. *Herman*, though deprived, was still a dangerous rival; but the emperor, at last, after driving him from place to place, he obliged him to fly to *Thuringia*; from whence he came and surrendered himself at the emperor's feet, and afterwards died by the hands of a woman who threw a stone from a battlement upon his head. The rebels chose *Egbert*, marquis of *Thuringia*, king of the *Romans* in his room; but *Henry* defeated him in a decisive battle, and he was killed in his flight.

State of Henry's affairs in Germany. The emperor's affairs no sooner began to wear a favourable aspect in *Germany*, than they went to wreck in *Italy*. The countess *Matilda* vigorously espoused the cause of *Victor* III who had succeeded pope *Gregory* VII. and afterwards of *Urban* II. both of them raised to the popedom in prejudice of pope *Clement*. *Matilda* had married, for her second husband, young *Guelph*, of *Bavaria*, whose father had received that dutchy from *Henry*, and from whom the faction of the *Guelphs* had their name. She headed her troops in person, and spirited up the emperor's son and wife to declare against him, which they did, and invited the *Normans* to their assistance. The emperor being resolved to march to *Italy*, gave the marquisate of *Misnia* to the count of *Lansberg*, the ancestor of the electors of *Saxony*; and then crossing the *Alps*, he made a most rapid progress against his enemies in *Italy*. He took all the towns on this side the *Po*; reduced *Mantua*, after a twelve month's siege; and, at last, all *Lombardy*.

Origin of the Guelphs. Those conquests were more splendid than they were substantial. His pope was shut up in the *Lateran* at *Rome*. *Conrad*, the emperor's son, and the empress *Adelaide*, whom *Henry* had maltreated, had joined with *Matilda*, and the *Normans* were actually in the field. Pope *Urban* continued to thunder out his excommunications against him; and the bishops of *Constance* and *Passau*, being in *Urban*'s interest, were perpetually exciting his subjects to rebel. That pope was then holding the famous council of *Clermont*, in *Auvergne*,

Beginning
of the
crufades.

for promoting a crufade againft the infidels for the recovery
of the *Holy Land*; and the inconftant *Romans*, dreading of the
Henry's refentment, had efpoufed the caufe of his pope *Clement*. But this prelate was deftitute of authority; and *Milan*, with many cities of *Lombardy*, had declared for *Conrade*,
who had married the daughter of *Roger*, king of *Sicily*; and
was actually crowned king of *Italy* by the archbifhop of *Milan*. This revolution gave a new, and a ruinous, turn to
the affairs of *Henry*, who was obliged to return to *Germany*.
Here he put his fon to the ban of the empire; and, in 1099,
he caufed his fecond fon, *Henry*, to be elected king of the
Romans.

All *Europe* was, at this time, frantic with the fpirit of
crufading; which did not much infect *Henry*: and we muft
refer the reader to the former part of this hiftory for the fuccefs of thofe adventurers. The emperor had not power to
fupprefs them; they filled all the places through which they
went with murders and defolation, but the firft fwarms of
them were almoft all extinguifhed in their route through
Hungary. The inequality of *Henry's* temper, rather than
any habitual practice of vice, appears to have been the great
fource of his misfortunes. His fon *Conrade* is mentioned in
hiftory as having been an inoffenfive prince; and his power
was fo well fixed in *Lombardy*, that he died in poffeffion of
the throne which he had mounted. After he was put to the
ban of the empire, *Ratifbon* was affigned for the refidence of
his other fon, *Henry*, king of the *Romans*. An accommodation was effected between the emperor, the *Saxons*, and
Bavarians.

Young
Henry re-
bels
againft his
father the
emperor,

Henry was now in hopes of fubduing all oppofition; efpecially as young *Guelph* had quarrelled with his wife *Matilda*,
from whom he had feparated. The archbifhop of *Mentz*
had fled, for his treafonable practices, into *Thuringia*; but, against his
all of a fudden, *Henry's* troubles were renewed. Pope *Urban* had raifed the power of the holy fee to an immeafurable
height, by the fupport of the *Normans*, *Matilda*, and young
Conrade; and his footfteps were followed by *Pafchal* II. who
encouraged the archbifhop of *Mentz* and the bifhop of *Conftance*, to oppofe the emperor; who had, by his own authority, fet up three popes, but with no effect, after the
death of *Urban*. It is true, the election of a pope, without
his leave, was an invafion of his authority, but, on the
other hand, the fanction of a pope, acknowledged as fuch
by the cardinals, the *Romans*, and the great powers of *Italy*,
was too ftrong to be oppofed by *Henry's* prerogative; and rebellion and ambition laid hold of it to juftify every kind of
crime.

The reigning doctrine now all over *Europe* was, that a
prince excommunicated by the pope, was unworthy, not
only to reign, but to live; that his fubjects and children
owed him neither obedience nor affection, and, that all
mankind

mankind ought to be confederated againſt him. Thoſe were maxims extremely well ſuited to young *Henry*, who privately linked himſelf with his father's enemies; and *Paſcbal* undertook to give him the empire. For this purpoſe he called a council at *Rome*, where he excommunicated *Henry*; and the ſon, out of pure duty to God and the church, declared that his father had forfeited the empire, and that he himſelf was now its lawful head. This impious doctrine prevailed ſo ſtrongly, that, notwithſtanding all the elder *Henry's* admonitions, he ſaw his ſon at the head of a greater army than his own. All that young *Henry* could be brought to, was, to offer to lay down his arms if his father was abſolved from his excommunication. The father and ſon met, at the head of their armies, near *Ratiſbon*; but the former, finding himſelf too weak to hazard a general battle, fled to *Bohemia*; and the ſon ſeized *Spire*, with all the imperial treaſure.

Such unparalleled ingratitude, together with a declaration the elder *Henry* made that he would enter into the cruſade, procured him many powerful friends; and he ſet out, at the head of an army, to break up the aſſembly which his ſon and the pope's legates had convoked at *Mentz* for his depoſition. The ſon dreaded this; and, when the father was advanced as far as *Coblentz*, he threw himſelf at his feet, and affected ſo much penitence for his undutiful behaviour, that his father not only pardoned him, but, as a ſign of his entire reconciliation, diſmiſſed his army, the ſon undertaking to make up all differences between him and the aſſembly at *Mentz*; but, when the unhappy father came to *Bingenheim*, he found himſelf under an arreſt by his ſon's order. This happened in the year 1106.

who is depoſed with great barbarity, After this treachery, the patricide repaired to *Mentz*, where the legates again excommunicated his father, who was declared to be diveſted of the imperial dignity, and his ſon was proclaimed in his ſtead. The archbiſhops of *Mentz* and *Cologne* were ſent to notify to *Henry* his depoſition; to demand of him the imperial regalia; and to acquaint him with the crimes he had been guilty of, among which was the charge of ſimony. The emperor expoſtulated with them moſt pathetically upon this accuſation, and appealed to themſelves whether he had not gratuitouſly given them the two beſt biſhoprics he had in his diſpoſal. They were deaf to all his remonſtrances; forcibly threw him to the ground; tore the imperial crown from his head, the mantle from his back, and wreſted the ſceptre out of his hand.

Young *Henry* being thus poſſeſſed of the imperial dignity, could not be eaſy till his father had made a voluntary reſignation of the empire in his favour. The elder *Henry's* ſpirit was by this time broken, though he was no more than fifty-five years of age. He complained, at firſt, that he had been condemned unheard; but, being obliged to appear before an aſſembly of his great ſubjects at *Ingelheim*, he there made a voluntary

voluntary refignation of the empire to his fon; afked pardon of all whom he had offended; threw himfelf at the feet of the pope's legate, and begged him to take off the fentence of his excommunication: but this requeft was refufed, on pretence that none could abfolve him but the pope himfelf.

Few princes were ever driven to the diftrefs that now overwhelmed *Henry*, who, literally fpeaking, had not bread to eat. He, in vain, begged to be admitted a canon in his own church at *Spire*; and wrote letters, which are ftill extant, imploring his fon to fuffer him to live in obfcurity at *Liege*, that he might be no longer forced to go begging about for a place where to lay his head.

The fon was as deaf, as the ecclefiaftics had been, to his entreaties; but the emperor, at laft, found fome relief in defpair. Efcaping from his jailors, he fled to *Cologne*; where the citizens admitted him as their fovereign. From thence he propofed a reconciliation with the pope; and wrote circular letters to all the powers of *Europe*, exhorting them to take the part of diftreffed majefty. The bifhop of *Liege*, the dukes of *Limbourg* and *Lower Lorrain*, and many other princes of the empire, took his part; and a powerful army was raifed for him in the *Low Countries*. This difquieted his fon, who, under pretence of exacting homage from the ftates of *Alface*, wanted to furprize his father at *Liege*; but his army was beaten, and he himfelf put to flight. It is difficult to fay what the event might have been, had *Henry* furvived this crifis; but he died, on the feventh of *Auguft*, 1106, in the fifty-fixth year of his age, and the forty-ninth of his reign. His laft words are faid to have been full of bitternefs againft the parricide his fon and his accomplices.

Nothing can fill the mind with more horrible ideas of ecclefiaftical tyranny, than the melancholy fate of the emperor *Henry* IV. who, according to the beft accounts, was, both in perfon and mind, notwithftanding the inequalities of his conduct, one of the moft amiable princes that ever exifted. He was bleffed, by nature, with irrefiftible eloquence and undaunted courage. He was beneficent and charitable almoft to a degree of weaknefs; for he is faid to have fed the needy, lame, wounded, and diftreffed of all kinds; and to have provided apartments and medicines for them under his own eye and in his own palaces. When but twelve years of age, he headed his armies in perfon, and was prefent in fixty-two pitched battles, in which he was generally victorious. He is faid to have been guilty of fome irregularities in his youth, efpecially towards his emprefs, whom, it feems, he difliked; but, as he grew up, he difcovered greater talents for government than any prince of his time, by the wife provifions he made, and the regulations he eftablifhed for the peace of his empire. He never was known to punifh any of the numerous confpirators who plotted againft his life, even when they

[marginal notes:] but efcapes to *Liege*, where he dies.

His character.

they were taken in the fact of affaffination ; and his juftice and liberality in remitting his revenues, when his fubjects were diftreffed, were equal to his other virtues.

To conclude, *Henry* might have lived and died a great and a happy prince, had he been poffeffed of but a middling genius. The popes he had to do with admitted of no equal, far lefs a fuperior, as fovereigns ; and the more that *Henry* fuffered from their power and infolence, he was the more impatient under their dominion. His virtues, in other refpects, undid him. The liberalities he beftowed were placed upon perfons who connected themfelves with his enemies, that they might eftablifh an independency upon his power ; gratitude being, in thofe days, no common virtue ; and no prince ever met with fewer returns of it than *Henry* did.

---

19. Henry V. *furnamed* the Young.

Affairs of Germany at Henry's fucceffion. THIS emperor, to diftinguifh him from his father, was called *the Young* ; and, at his acceffion, *Germany* was upon the eve of a total alteration in her internal fyftem. He had raifed himfelf to his unnatural greatnefs by the crimes of rebellion and ingratitude to his friend, father, and fovereign. To carry on the fame, he advanced to *Liege* ; where he forced the inhabitants, who had given a noble burial to his father's body, to raife it out of the grave, as being the carcafe of an excommunicated wretch ; and he flung it into a vault at *Spire*, where it continued unburied for five years. This complaifance to the church was, in the main, far from eftablifhing his authority. The great vaffals of the empire purfued their fcheme of being independent of the emperor; and acknowledged no other fubjection than a feudatory relation, or political confederacy, with their co-ordinate ftates: and they actually began, about this time, to affect the name of *co-imperantes*, or fellow-emperors. Soon after the late emperor's death, *Pafchal* II. fummoned a council at *Guaftalla*, on the *Po*; where all the decrees that had paffed againft the imperial right of inveftitures were confirmed : by which the imperial diadem loft its faireft diamond, and *Henry* himfelf was ftripped of his moft fubftantial prerogative.

His wars with Hungary and Poland. The emperor thought to mitigate the feverity of this alienation, but it was too late ; for the princes and cities of *Italy* had entirely broken off all connection with the imperial authority. The wrath of the pope hung over the emperor's head; and *Philip*, king of *France*, found it his intereft to fupport his holinefs. In fhort, the emperor was obliged to diffemble, and even to apply to *Philip*'s mediation. *Henry* at laft, had the courage to difpute the right of inveftitures, and

and was supported by some of the German bishops, who preferred his dominion to that of the pope; but Henry was required to leave the matter to a general council, where he was sure of losing the cause.

Those disputes never failed to foment intestine divisions. A rebellion broke out in Bohemia, where all was in confusion; and the emperor, for a sum of money, deserted the cause of the lawful duke, and suffered an usurper to possess his dignity. Henry then invaded Hungary, which, at that time, was governed by Coloman. His expedition was unfortunate. He was obliged to raise the siege of Presburg, and to retire, with great loss, into Bavaria; Coloman having entered into an alliance with Boleslaus, king of Poland. The emperor soon recruited his army; invaded Silesia, then belonging to Poland; and defeated the Poles in a general battle. Boleslaus, finding Henry determined to revive the German claims of superiority over Poland, raised a new army, defeated Henry, and drove him out of Silesia.

The emperor had now leisure to consult the sentiments of his German subjects concerning the pope's usurpations; and he found them disposed to support the rights of the empire. While he was raising an immense army to do himself justice, he married Matilda, the daughter and heiress of Henry I. of England; and the immense sum he received as her dowry, was of infinite service to his affairs. He then crossed the Alps, at the head of eighty thousand men, to assert his double right, that of investitures, and the sovereignty over the Italian states. He reduced many places in Tuscany, and entered Florence as its master. He brought along with him, out of Germany, a number of persons who had made the constitutions of the empire their study. Them he employed to negotiate with pope Paschal, who would have paid them very little regard, had not their master been at the head of an army to enforce their arguments. Paschal was therefore obliged to dissemble, and granted the emperor all he desired, but not without great difficulty. Henry marched his army into Rome. There he massacred numbers of the citizens, and shut the pope, his cardinals, and the Roman nobility, up in prison; where he kept them, for above six weeks, till the pope should comply with his demands concerning the investitures. As Paschal appeared to be obstinate on that point, Henry ordered the heads of the Roman nobility to be struck off before his eyes, upon which Paschal complied. and signed the accommodation in Henry's own terms. The pope next crowned the emperor, and omitted no appearance of respect or cordiality to prevail with him to return to Germany, which, at last, he effected.

Henry was no sooner returned than he found all Germany in a flame, and matter more embroiled than ever. The Lateran council disavowed all that his holiness had done in the affair of the investitures, which, as was indeed the fact, they said

He forces the pope to grant him the right of investitures.

Rebellion against him in Germany.

said had been extorted from him by force. The *French* bishops excommunicated the emperor, and those of *Germany* refused to receive the bull of investiture in his favour. A rebellion soon after broke out in *Saxony*, fomented by the clergy and headed by duke *Lothair*. *Henry* marched thither, laid waste the country, and took an archbishop into custody; but, in his return, he was defeated by *Lothair* and the *Saxon* nobility. *Lothair* called an assembly at *Goslar*, consisting of ecclesiastics and laymen; and there the emperor was excommunicated.

This had so pernicious an effect on his affairs, that, like his father, he must have sunk under the intrigues and power of the church, had not the duke of *Stauffen-Suabia*, whom we have already mentioned, marched to his assistance with an army, and delivered him out of his distresses. The famous countess *Matilda* was, by this time, dead; but had confirmed all the donations she had made of her great estates to the church. The emperor, as being her next heir, claimed her succession, both as kinsman and emperor. With this view, he once more marched into *Italy* to demand justice of the pope, who refused to see his ambassadors, or to revoke his sentence of excommunication; and he once more annulled all the bulls he had granted in the affair of investitures. *Henry*, seeing that his holiness was bent upon his ruin, marched with his army to *Rome*, and the pope fled to *Apulia*. The emperor took that opportunity to be again crowned; which was performed by the hands of the archbishop of *Braga* in *Portugal*; as thinking his former coronation to be invalid, because of the pope's perjury.

Pope
Gelasius
chosen, Being obliged, on account of the heats, to retire to *Tuscany*, *Paschal* seized that opportunity to re-enter *Rome*; where he began to make new cabals, but died in two days; and the *Norman* soldiers, who had come to support his cause, returned home after plundering *Rome*. Cardinal *Cajetan*, without the emperor's knowledge, was raised to the popedom, and assumed the name of *Gelasius* II. but *Henry* returning with his army to depose him, and to substitute the archbishop of *Braga* in in his stead, *Gelasius* excommunicated him. This provoked *Frangipani* (who was consul at *Rome*, and a friend of the emperor) so much, that he broke into the assembly of the cardinals, seized *Gelasius* by the throat, knocked him down, and kicked him before him into prison. This occasioned an attempt of the *Romans*, and the *Normans* who were at *Rome*, against *Frangipani*'s house; and he was beginning to repent of what he had done, when the emperor as is *Gregory*VIII. arrived with his army. *Gelasius* escaped with difficulty, and the emperor caused, or rather nominated, the archbishop of *Braga* to be elected pope. This prelate, whose name was *Bourdin*, took the name of *Gregory* VIII. and solemnly reversed all that had been done by his predecessors to the emperor's prejudice. Notwithstanding this, *Gelasius*, who, after

various

various adventures, escaped to *France*, was, by far the greatest part of *Christendom*, recognized as the true pope; and *Gregory* supported himself only by the force of the imperial arms.

The affairs of *Germany*, as usual, recalling the emperor thither before he had fully completed any one purpose of his expedition, he left a guard with *Gregory* at *Rome*; but an account of the death of *Gelasius* arriving, the cardinals elected the archbishop of *Vienne*, who was of the house of *Burgundy*, and related to the blood-royal of *France*, to be pope; and he took upon him the name of *Calixtus* II. After his consecration, he held a numerous council at *Rheims*; and the *German* princes of *Saxony* and *Westphalia* entered into a confederacy, in his favour, against *Henry*, on account of the investitures which they demanded; and which the emperor, by virtue of his prerogative, refused to grant them. This confederacy produced a great deal of blood-shed. The neutral princes of the empire interposed; and, both sides being tired of the quarrel, the emperor expressed an inclination to compromise matters under the mediation of the king of *France* and the pope promising, in that case, to take off the ecclesiastical censures against him, they agreed to finish the accommodation at *Mouzon*, while the council was still sitting at *Rheims*, to give it the greater sanction. Every thing but the formality of signing being concluded, *Henry* set out for the conference at the head of thirty thousand men. This startled the pope, and he sent to know whether the emperor intended to stand by the terms agreed on. *Henry* returned a conditional answer, because he waited for the advice of the diet, which was sitting at *Tribur*, between *Mentz* and *Worms*. The pope thought that this was an evasion contrived to surprize him. He returned in haste to *Rheims*, where he renewed the decree against the investitures, and again excommunicated *Henry* and the anti-pope *Gregory* VIII.

It is uncertain to what those sudden revolutions were owing, whether to the ambition of the emperor or the pope; but it is reasonable to believe that the former, in the confused situation of his affairs, durst not make any ultimate agreement with his holiness without the concurrence of the diet. Upon the return of *Calixtus* to *Rome*, he raised an army, and besieged his rival *Gregory* in *Sutri*; and, becoming master of his person, he treated him with as much ignominy as he could devise, and then he shut him up in a monastery.

The removal of *Gregory* was of infinite advantage to *Calixtus*; and, consequently, of detriment to the emperor. The confederacy against him in *Germany*, with the archbishop of *Mentz* at its head, daily gathered strength; and the bishops, in general, being less afraid of the papal than the imperial authority, refused to receive their investitures from the emperor, who found himself on the point of being overwhelmed

(margin note: Pope Ca-lixtus II.)

(margin note: excommunicates the emperor.)

whelmed by the confederacy. He took the wifeft courfe he could in fuch a fituation. While the two parties were in arms, the ftates of the empire addreffed him to give peace to the church and their country. *Henry* fhewed the moft placable difpofition for that purpofe. A diet was called at *Wurtzburg*; and there it was determined, that a folemn ambaffy fhould be fent to *Rome*, to befeech the pope to call a council, wherein all differences might be accommodated. *Calixtus* fhewed himfelf equally difpofed for peace, and called a council, confifting of three hundred bifhops and feven hundred abbots, who gave audience to the imperial ambaffadors.

Henry's agreement with the pope. The matter, after this, was compromifed in the following manner: That the emperor fhould leave the elections free to the chapters and communities, and no longer confer inveftitures by the crofier and ring; that he fhould reftore the poffeffions belonging to the holy fee and the churches; that the elections fhould be made in the emperor's prefence, or his deputy's, by canonical methods; that, in cafe there fhould be any difpute about the election, the emperor, affifted by the metropolitan and his fuffragans, fhould be judge thereof; that the perfon elected fhould receive the inveftiture of the fiefs and lordfhips of the empire, not with the crofier, but the fceptre, or fome wand, and fhould be faithful to him on account of the faid lordfhips; and, that, for the countries diftant from *Germany*, the emperor fhould allow fix months to receive the like inveftitures.

Troubles of Germany continued. This important affair being finifhed, the pope named a legate, who attended the ambaffadors to *Germany*, and there gave abfolution to the emperor. But, though this compromife was ratified by the diet of *Worms*, it was far from reftoring peace to *Germany*. *Holland* revolted; as did *Worms*, and feveral other places; and the emperor was put to great trouble and expence in reducing them.

About the year 1122, *Henry*, by the force of his father-in-law's *Englifh* money, was prevailed upon to take part with him in his differences with *Lewis the Grofs*, king of *France*, and actually invaded that kingdom. But we do not find that he was fupported in this attempt by the princes of the empire, who generally fought refuge with the kings of *France* againft the encroachments of their own emperors. *Henry* therefore returned without effecting any thing

He had, in his late treaty with *Rome*, tacitly given up all concern in the election of a pope; and, upon the death of *Calixtus*, the cardinals, without the emperor's participation, proceeded to a new election; which was carried on fo tumultuoufly, that a double return was made, though *Honorius* II. was foon acknowledged to be the true pope. The emperor, by giving up this right, and likewife that of the inveftitures, gave a mortal blow to the imperial authority. All *Hungary*, *Bohemia*, and *Alface*, were over-run with cabals againft his prerogative; which had now loft all its force, and

and the emperor himself was more than once put in hazard of his life by sudden tumults, especially by one at *Ruffac*.

Those disgraces are said to have affected his spirits so Death. much, that he died at *Utrecht*, in 1125, on the twenty-third of *May*, aged forty-four.

The character of this prince, after he came to the empire, and cha- was pretty much the same with that of his father; but he racter of cast an indelible stain upon the former part of his life, by his *Henry V.* rebellion, treachery, and parricide. Notwithstanding all the pains which papal writers have taken to blacken him, he certainly was brave and active in his person, and an undaunted asserter of the independency of his empire. Upon the whole, if he was guilty of faults in his government, they were owing to the treachery, ambition, and bigotry of his over-grown subjects, spirited up by the see of *Rome* to every act of rebellion; for he appears to have had a proper regard for the legal constitution of his empire.

---

20. Lothair II.

HENRY V. died without issue of his own body, but Election he left two nephews by his sister, *Conrade*, duke of of *Lothair* *Franconia*; and *Frederic*, duke of *Suabia*, both of them popular in the empire on account of their excellent qualities. It was not the interest of the popish faction, that any of the blood, or principles, of *Henry* should succeed to the empire. The archbishop of *Mentz*, who was at the head of that faction, pretended that he was in the party of the two princes; and, getting possession of the imperial regalia, he leagued himself with the *French* court; who sent the famous *Suger*, abbot of St. *Dennis*, the historian of those times, to the diet at *Mentz*; where the number of the electing princes were reduced to ten; and they chose for emperor *Lothair*, duke of *Saxe-Supplenbourg*; who was crowned in *September*, 1126. The two princes did all they could to traverse this election; and their party actually chose *Frederic*, duke of *Suabia*, king of the *Romans*.

The great motive which determined the archbishop of to what *Mentz*, and his party, in favour of *Lothair*, was his having owing. generally been the lay-head and champion of their faction. From this principle, the beginning of his reign was marked by an expedition against the *Bohemians*, who had always espoused the party of the late emperor. His declared pretext was to settle the guardianship of the young duke of *Bohemia*; and, after a bloody contest, he forced *Boleslaus*, the regent of that country, to do him homage. *Conrade* took advantage of this war to repair to *Italy*, where he was crowned king of *Lombardy* at *Milan*. The emperor, notwithstanding his devotion to the fee of *Rome*, was a juft and generous prince; and, though he had obtained vaft advantages over the brothers in *Germany*, yet he offered them his friendfhip, which they afterwards accepted; and he diftinguifhed *Conrade* with particular marks of his favour and affection.

The fyftem of power in the empire was thus again altered, and we cannot fay to the detriment of public liberty; the imperial prerogative being rather bounded than abolifhed; and the fucceffion to the great feudal eftates was now hereditary, inftead of dependifig, as formerly, upon the will of the emperor. It is true the popes had acquired vaft power, but it was fubmitted to by the enemies of the imperial prerogative only through conveniency; and they knew that the pontifs did not dare to exercife the fuperiority which they had acquired, to opprefs them.

All thofe great alterations, however, did not take place without violent ftruggles and oppofition made by the princes and people who depended on the empire, and they reached as far as *Denmark*. They wanted themfelves to be independent both of the pope and the emperor; but having no principle of unity to conduct their oppofition, it was crufhed by the now united interefts of the papal and imperial fovereignty. In the year 1130, pope *Honorius* II. who had fo effectually fupported the claims of his fee, died; and the cardinals elected, in his place, *Innocent* II. but the *Roman* people chofe one *Leo*, who was of *Jewifh* parentage. He took the name of *Anacletus*, and drove *Innocent* out of *Rome* into *France*; where his caufe was efpoufed by the apoftle of that age, St. *Bernard*, and who had the greateft perfonal intereft of any man in *Europe*. By his perfuafion, *Lothair* befriended *Innocent*, and they had an interview at *Liege*. Their meeting was difgraceful to the emperor, who alighted from his horfe to affift the pope in defcending from his. At firft, the emperor, perhaps to pleafe the dukes of *Franconia* and *Suabia*, pretended to make fome terms with his holinefs concerning the inveftitures; but St. *Bernard* taking the part of *Innocent*, who appeared to be inflexible on that head, *Lothair* receded from his claim, and even engaged to re-eftablifh his holinefs in the papal chair. At parting, the pope went to *France*; where he received a large contribution. When the emperor came to *Rome*, he found that *Anacletus*, the anti-pope, had been joined by *Conrade*'s party, which was very ftrong in *Italy*; but *Lothair* being refolute in *Innocent*'s intereft, the antipope was forced to fhut himfelf up in the caftle of St. *Angelo*; while *Lothair*, upon his knees, received the imperial crown from the hands of *Innocent*.

Upon the return of *Lothair* to *Germany*, he endeavoured to give a greater confiftency to the legiflation of the empire, by abolifhing the provincial and particular modes of juftice that prevailed in its different diftricts, and often occafioned inteftine commotions, through the frequent intercourfes and

inter-

He takes part with the pope,

introduces the civillaw into Germany,

intermarriages among the people, who lived under separate jurisdictions. For this purpose, by the advice of one *Werner Ursperg*, a great civilian, he ordered that distributive justice should be exercised according to the laws collected or enacted by *Justinian*; and that a new code of feudal-laws should be drawn up.

While he was employed in this laudable undertaking, the intention of which was afterwards perverted into chicanery, *Anacletus*, the antipope, befriended by *Roger*, duke of *Apulia*, drove *Innocent* from *Rome* to *Pisa*; where he again implored the assistance of *Lothair* for his re-establishment, which the emperor promised him: but, by this time, *Anacletus*, having promised to erect the dukedom of *Apulia* into a kingdom, had made himself master of almost all St. *Peter's* patrimony.

It appears as if *Lothair's* zeal for the pope was not quite disinterested. He had a passionate desire for the estates bequeathed by *Matilda* to the holy see. *Innocent* gratified him in giving him the profits of those possessions; but he required that the emperor should hold them in vassalage: in token of which, *Lothair* kissed *Innocent's* feet, and led his mule for some paces. Before *Lothair* set out upon his second expedition to *Italy*, he obliged the king of *Poland* to take an oath of fidelity to his empire; and he re-settled its tranquility according to the new system of laws which he had adopted. *and does homage to the pope.*

The progress of *Roger*, who is now designed king of *Sicily*, rendered it necessary for *Lothair*, on his account, as well as that of the pope, to march once more, at the head of a powerful army, into *Italy*. Having formed it into two divisions, he took the command of the one to himself, and, giving the command of the other to his son-in-law, the duke of *Bavaria*, he soon drove *Roger* from all his conquests, and forced him to retire to *Sicily*; while *Innocent* entered *Rome* in triumph, to the violent mortification of *Anacletus*, who died of spite. *Lothair* then pushed his conquests into *Apulia* and *Calabria*; both which he took from *Roger*, and formed them into a principality. This he bestowed upon *Renaud*, one of his *German* relations, who received the investiture thereof jointly from the hands of the emperor and the pope, each pretending to be lord-paramount, and the point remaining undetermined. The emperor, during this glorious expedition, was assisted by a fleet of forty stout gallies, equipped by the city of *Pisa* alone from the profits of its commerce, and they did him infinite service. *His successful expedition into Italy.*

Lothair, in his return to *Germany*, was overtaken by sickness at *Verona*; but, being in hopes that his native air might recover him, he proceeded on his journey; and died in the *Alps*, near *Trent*, on the third of *December*, 1138, after a reign of twelve years. *His death,*

This prince's character was the reverse of that of most of his predecessors; and therefore he does not, in the history of *and character.*

F f 2

his

his own times, make the great figure he merited. Superior to the barbarous prepoffeffions of the *Germans*, he fuffered himfelf to be governed by prudential confiderations, and by well-timed conceffions, as to exteriors, to fecure himfelf important advantages. His perfonal humiliations before the pope were indeed fhameful ; but the hiftory of two ages had taught him, that, without thofe compliances, if he reigned, he muft live in blood, and die in mifery. This melancholy alternative took its rife from the invincible attachment which the common people, in thofe days, influenced by the inferior clergy, had for the facred character of the vicar of *Chrift*. *Lothair* could neither cure nor conquer their prejudices; therefore he fought to avail himfelf of the difputes about the popedom, and to fecure the beft bargain that could be made (which he certainly did) for the imperial authority. He was an inflexible lover of juftice, and he may be termed the laft legiflator of the *German* empire.

---

21. Conrade III.

Conrade's election oppofed by the duke of Bavaria.

LOTHAIR had the unufual good fortune to die in the arms of glory and conqueft : and he owed it, in a great meafure, to the good underftanding in which he lived with his former competitors of *Franconia* and *Bavaria* ; whom he had fupplanted in the empire, and whofe intereft there was ftill very powerful. It was natural for *Lothair* to recommend his fon-in-law, *Henry*, of *Bavaria*, to be his fucceffor ; and it is faid, that, with this view, he gave him, in his own lifetime, poffeffion of the imperial ornaments, of which *Henry* availed himfelf to claim the empire ; but he was difappointed. The princes of *Germany* met at *Coblentz*, and nominated feven electors, being three archbifhops and four princes, who unanimoufly chofe for emperor *Conrade*, duke of *Franconia*. *Henry's* power and arrogance contributed greatly to this event. They hated a man who, from his manners, was furnamed *the Haughty* ; and they were jealous of a prince who was poffeffed of *Bavaria*, *Saxony*, *Mifnia*, and *Thuringia*, befides vaft eftates in *Italy*, particularly that of *Matilda*, which had been bequeathed to him by the late emperor. Depending on this vaft power, *Henry* thought to have forced himfelf upon the imperial throne, and refufed to deliver up the regalia ; but the princes of *Germany* uniting againft him at *Goflar*, put him to the ban of the empire, and gave his dutchy of *Bavaria* to *Leopold*, marquis of *Auftria* ; and that of *Saxony*, to *Albert*, marquis of *Brandenburgh*. *Henry the Haughty* oppofed thofe deftinations, but died in the year 1139.

His brother, *Guelph*, duke of *Bavaria*, fucceeded to his dominions and contefts ; and was fupported by *Roger*, king of
Sicily,

Sicily; who made ufe of the diffentions in *Germany* to regain poffeffion of *Apulia* and *Calabria*. It is faid by fome, that, at this period, the famous diftinction of *Guelph* and *Gibelin* commenced. After feveral bloody battles had been fought between *Guelph* and the duke of *Suabia*, the emperor's brother and general, the former was forced to fhut himfelf up in the caftle of *Weinfburg*. *Guelph* refolving to make a defperate fally, gave his own name as the word to his foldiers; while the duke of *Suabia* gave to his the word *Gibelin*, the place where he had been educated; and the two words paffed afterwards to denote two parties; the former, the papal; the latter, the imperial. We are to obferve that *Gueplh* had been long the furname of the *Bavarian* family. *Guelph* was unfortunate in his fally, and, being reduced to extremity, he demanded an honourable capitulation, which was granted him by the emperor.

We fhould be cautious of tranfmitting the adventure that followed, were it not unqueftionably well attefted. The dutchefs of *Bavaria* fufpected, from the readinefs with which the emperor granted the capitulation, that he intended to violate it, efpecially in the perfon of her hufband, whom he remarkably hated. The capitulation bore, That *Guelph* and his garrifon might retire in fafety; but the dutchefs infifted upon a particular capitulation being granted to herfelf and the ladies of her train, and that they might be permitted to leave the caftle each with as great a load as fhe could carry. The emperor, imagining that this was meant of their paraphernalia and effects, agreed to the terms; but was amazed to fee the ladies, with the dutchefs at their head, each tottering under the weight of her hufband, when they evacuated the caftle. The emperor is faid to have melted into terms of tendernefs at this fpectacle, and, notwithftanding the oppofition he met with from his generals, he generoufly gave very advantageous terms to *Guelph*; faying, at the fame time, That a fovereign who broke his word was unworthy of empire. *Remarkble exploit of German ladies.*

The flourifhing ftate of the popedom, at this period, had almoft overturned it. The people of *Italy* retained ftill fome glimmerings of a diftinction between the temporal and ecclefiaftical power; and it was ftrongly enforced by one *Arnold*, of *Brefcia*, a difciple of the famous *Abelard*. This perfon went through the towns of *Italy*, where he diffeminated the doctrine of his mafter, who, upon that account was excommunicated; and gained great numbers of profelytes, efpecially among the *Roman* people and nobility, who had not forgot that their anceftors made and unmade popes; and that *Charlemagne* himfelf, at firft, was, at *Rome*, no more than a patrician. The civil-wars in *Germany* had given an opportunity for almoft every ftate and city in *Italy* to erect itfelf into an independent government. This fpirit was communicated *An attempt to reftore the Roman commonwealth.*

F f 3   municated

municated to the *Romans*, who once more attempted to re-establish their antient republic, and proceeded with a regularity seldom known in popular commotions. *Lucius* II. was then pope; and the *Arnoldists*, as the reformers were called, sent him a formal message, requiring him to divest himself of his temporal, and to confine himself to the exercise of his spiritual, authority, with the lawful perquisites annexed to it as their bishop. To support their demand, they conferred the post of patrician, with the same authority that *Charles the Great* held it, upon one *Giordani*, whom they likewise invested with the tribunitial power. At the same time, they emitted manifestos that they intended nothing against the imperial authority, and that they only wanted to abolish the usurpations of the popes.

The pope applies to *Conrade*, *Lucius* being thus applied to, had recourse to *Conrade*, and implored his assistance; but the other party seized all the temporal revenues of the popedom, and took possession of the capitol. *Lucius* had still a strong party at *Rome*, and, putting himself at the head of some troops to reduce the insurgents, he besieged the capitol, but was killed by a stone from its battlements. The cardinals chose in his place *Eugene* III. whose history we are not obliged to follow farther than it is connected with that of the empire. *Conrade* had declared himself for the late pope, and the rest of *Italy* condemned the proceedings of the *Romans*; so that *Eugene* found means to repossess himself of the popedom and all its temporalities.

The spirit of crusading was now higher in *Europe* than ever; and, being most zealously encouraged by St. *Bernard*, it infected *Conrade* himself, and he took the cross at *Spire* from the hands of that enthusiast. Before he set out, he put the affairs of the empire upon the best footing he could, by procuring his son to be crowned king of the *Romans*, and establishing the imperial council at *Rotwel* (some remains whereof still subsist) which was, in his absence, to be the supreme judicature of the empire. *Henry the Lion*, duke of *Saxony*, one of the most powerful of the *German* princes, laid hold of that opportunity to reclaim the dutchy of *Bavaria*, which had been dismembered from his family. *Conrade* promised to adjust the affair upon his return from the *Holy Land*, and employed *Wiebold*, abbot of *Corbie*, to persuade the duke to undertake a crusade for the conquest and conversion of the numerous tribes of northern pagans.

who goes to the *Holy Land*. *Conrade* set out for *Palestine* at the head of a well-appointed army of sixty thousand men; and the reader will meet with a full account of his adventures there, in the preceding part of this work. It is sufficient, for the sake of historical connection, to say here, that he was attended by his nephew, afterwards the famous emperor *Frederic Barbarossa*, and duke *Guelph*; that he approved himself to be as intrepid a warrior as he was a credulous prince; and, notwithstanding the prodigies of valour he and his troops performed, he was, almost on every occasion, defeated by the *Saracens* and *Turks*; and returned, with scarce the shadow of an army, in vessels furnished him by his brother-in-law *Manuel Comnenus*, the *Greek* emperor. About this time, another crusade of *Germans* and *English* took *Lisbon* from the usurping *Moors*, and restored it to king *Alphonso Henriquez*.

Though *Henry the Lion* had taken the abbot's advice in undertaking the crusade against the pagans, yet he did it only that he might have a pretext for raising and disciplining an army. He was assisted by the bishops of *Magdebourg*, *Halberstadt*, *Munster*, *Mersbourg*, and *Bradenburg*, with many abbots; but no sooner did *Conrade* return to *Germany*, than *Henry* renewed his claim to *Bavaria*, having performed his crusade by laying the country, he wanted to convert, waste with fire and sword. The merit of *Conrade*'s expedition into the *Holy Land*, and a pilgrimage he made to *Jerusalem*, was so popular among the *Germans*, that *Henry* was defeated in his attempt, and *Bavaria* remained with *Guelph*, who, soon after, revolted likewise, but was unable to make good his pretensions, though they were supported by *Roger*, king of *Sicily*; and, by the mediation of the duke of *Suabia*, an accommodation was effected between him and the emperor.

His expedition unfortunate.

The death of *Conrade*'s eldest son, who had been elected king of the *Romans*, which happened about this time, and his inability to have the imperial throne filled by his younger son, who was in his non-age, affected *Conrade* so much that he fell into an incurable distemper. Being sensible of his approaching end, he convoked a diet of the empire at *Bamberg*; where he recommended to their choice, for his successor, *Frederic*, duke of *Suabia*; to whom the imperial ornaments were, by way of investiture in the empire, accordingly delivered; and, soon after this destination, *Conrade* expired.

Death,

He was a prince endowed with the popular virtues of that age, which consisted in an unbounded courage and zeal for the church; and his misfortunes in the *Holy Land*, instead of depressing, exalted him, in the eyes of his subjects. He died in the sixtieth year of his age; and he left, by his wife *Gertrude*, who was daughter of a count of *Sultzbach*, *Frederic*, count of *Rothenbourg*, a minor; and a daughter named *Judith*, who was married to *Lewis*, landgrave of *Thuringia*.

and character.

22. Frederic I. *surnamed* Barbaroſſa, *and* Father of his Country.

Acceſſion and difficulties of Frederic,

THE inveſtiture that had been conferred on this prince, at the recommendation of *Conrade*, operated ſo ſtrongly in his favour, that he was unanimouſly elected emperor at *Francfort*, in the preſence of many *Roman* noblemen of high diſtinction; which was a tacit acknowledgment of their owning him to be the *Roman* emperor. He was crowned, by the archbiſhop of *Cologne*, at *Aix-la-Chapelle*, when he was about twenty-nine years of age. His character was then ſo high, that his authority was recognized by all the powers of *Europe*.

which he finiſhes,

Frederic, at his acceſſion, took cognizance of the long ſtanding conteſt concerning the dutchy of *Bavaria*, which then ſubſiſted between *Henry*, duke of *Saxony*, and the duke of *Bavaria*. All the *German* princes took part in this quarrel, which *Frederic* finiſhed by decreeing, in a diet, which was held at *Spire*, that the dutchy of *Bavaria* ſhould revert to *Henry*, duke of *Saxony*; and, that *Auſtria* ſhould be detached from *Bavaria* and erected into a dutchy, in favour of the other competitor; who was, at the ſame time, forced to reſign to the emperor all his claims upon the dutchies of *Tuſcany* and *Spoleto*, and the iſland of *Sardinia*. This important affair being ſettled, *Frederic* proceeded, by virtue of his imperial authority, to take cognizance of the quarrel between *Sueno* and *Canute*, who were competitors for the crown of *Denmark*. *Sueno* had defeated *Canute*, who, while the diet of the empire was ſitting at *Merſbourg*, put himſelf under the emperor's protection; and *Frederic* ſummoned *Sueno* to appear before his tribunal. *Sueno* obeyed, but was informed, that, if he expected to keep the crown of *Denmark*, he muſt hold it as a fief of the empire, and gratify his competitor with certain eſtates in *Jutland* and *Scania*; to all which *Sueno* agreed.

and prepares for an expedition into Italy.

Frederic reſumed the old policy of the *German* emperors; and, though his predeceſſor never had been crowned in *Italy*, he held a diet at *Wurtzburg*, where the noblemen of *Apulia* laid before him their complaints againſt *Roger*, king of *Sicily*, who had driven them from their country. *Frederic* laid hold of this application to revive the claim of his empire upon the ſovereignty of *Italy*; and the diet promiſed to ſupport him againſt *Roger*, who was conſidered in the light of an uſurper and a tyrant. Pope *Eugene* III. who then filled the ſee of *Rome*, was ſenſible of *Frederic*'s intentions, and quarrelled with him upon his having raiſed the biſhop of *Zeitz* to the archbiſhopric of *Magdeburg*. *Frederic* ſupported what he had done, and drove the pope's legates out of *Germany*. The next pope, who took the name of *Anaſtaſius*, ſent cardinal

Gerhard

Gerhard into *Germany* to support the papal rights in the same
affair; but the emperor, who was thoroughly acquainted
with the disputes between the popes and his predecessors,
laid hold of some insolent expressions made use of by the legate to force him likewise to fly into *Italy*, where he died of
grief in his journey to *Rome*.

The pope, from those proceedings, became as sensible of
the emperor's intentions, as the latter was of his influence;
and, for some time, neither of them durst venture upon a
breach; for *Anastasius* confirmed the nomination of the archbishop of *Magdeburg* to that see; he having, by the emperor's
order, repaired to *Rome*, to plead his own cause. Notwithstanding this, *Frederic* resolved to prosecute the imperial
claims to their height; and, without consulting the pope,
he repudiated his wife *Adelaide*, daughter to the marquis of
Vohenburg. **He repudiates his wife.**

The affairs of *Germany*, for some time, detained *Frederic*
from marching into *Italy*; and the cities and states there took
advantage of that interval to renew their claims of independency. Pope *Adrian* IV. an *Englishman*, had raised himself
to that see from the most abject degree of beggary; and, under him, the *Romans* returned to their old republican principles; being instigated thereto by *Arnold*. *Adrian* was supported by the bishops, and other ecclesiastics residing at
Rome, who were rich and powerful, and considered his case
as their own. A cardinal was murdered in the streets of
Rome, and the pope laid that city under an interdiction.
The laity found themselves unable to make good their point.
Arnold and his adherents were banished, and the interdiction
was taken off. The popedom, by this time, was deprived
of the powerful protection of *Roger*, king of *Sicily*; and the
republicans, renewing their schemes, *Adrian* was forced to
fly to *Viterbo*; from whence he implored the assistance of the
emperor, who was then ready to set out for *Italy* at the head
of a numerous army, attended by *Henry the Lion* and a great
number of the chief *German* nobility. One of his pretexts
for this invasion was, to seize, in the name of his ward, son
of the emperor *Conrade* III. the inheritance of the countess
Matilda. The situation of *Italy*, at this time, is necessary
to be known before the reader can form an idea of the history
of *Germany*. **Affairs of Italy.**

Though we have often mentioned the *Italian* states and
cities having thrown off their dependency upon the emperor,
yet the independency they recovered served only to make
them miserable. In every community two factions started
up, and, after cutting one another's throats, the strongest
always expelled the weakest; the partizans of which declared
themselves to be either *Guelphs* or *Gibelins*, and flew for protection either to the pope or the emperor. *Frederic* held an
assembly in the plains of *Roncalia*, where all the exiles of his
party repaired to his standards, and the *Gibelin* states and ci- **which Frederic enters.**

ties

ties sent their deputies. Thus, in fact, all the power the emperor possessed in *Italy*, was owing to the divisions of the people among themselves; and, with regard to the pope, the *Italians* and *Romans* were not near so bigotted to him as the *Germans* and other *Europeans*.

Frederic having thus strengthened his party, reduced all the rebellious towns in *Lombardy*, and, proceeding into *Pavia*, he was there crowned king of *Italy*. From thence he sent a message to desire an interview with the pope at *Sutri*, in order to prepare for his coronation at *Rome*. The pope, though an exile from his capital, did not abate the least in his pontifical pride; and, before he granted him the interview, he settled the ceremonial at meeting. *Frederic* was somewhat awkward at holding the stirrup of his holiness, which the cardinals, his attendants, interpreted so suspiciously, that he fled to the strong fortress of *Citta di Castello*. The pope refused *Frederic* the kiss of peace till he complied with every punctilio of the ceremony; and the emperor, being instructed that it was only a matter of form, and had been practised by some of his predecessors, submitted to the disagreeable office of holding the pope's stirrup, and leading his mule by the bridle.

and is crowned at Rome. *Frederic* then being superior to all resistance, conducted the pope to *Rome*, and there received the imperial crown from his hands, but with mutual distrust on both sides, though each had taken an oath that neither should attempt to kill or mutilate the other. The *Romans*, previous to the ceremony, had sent the emperor a deputation, expressing their readiness to receive him, though he was a stranger, as their master; but he cut the deputies short in the beginning of their speech, "You were conquered," said he, "by *Charles the Great* and *Otho*, therefore you are my subjects;" and then he drove them from his presence.

The Romans exasperated. The *Romans* were exasperated at this treatment of their deputies, and laid a scheme for revenging it. Being in no condition to interrupt the ceremony of the coronation, they suffered the pope to return to his camp; which, by way of precaution, he had pitched without the gates of *Rome*; and then taking arms, they killed several bishops of the imperial party, on pretence that the pope had no right to crown the emperor without their permission and consent; while the pope, on the other hand, proclaimed to the public, in his bulls, that he had given *Frederic* the *Roman* empire as a fief of the holy see. The emperor no sooner heard of this new commotion, than he flew to the assistance of the pope, and, with the loss of no more than one *German* killed, and another taken, he cut in pieces one thousand of the insurgents, and took two hundred prisoners; who, at the pope's intercession, were restored to their liberty.

This seasonable service done to the pope made no impression of gratitude upon his mind, which continued as haughty

as

as ever; and he prohibited *Frederic* from accepting of the keys of *Tiburtum*, because, he said, it belonged to the holy see. Upon his leaving *Rome*, he was accompanied by the pontif, who did not think himself safe in that city. He marched to *Spoleto*; which he took, plundered, and burnt, for the contumacy of its inhabitants. When he came to *Ancona*, he was waited upon by a deputation from the patriarch of *Jerusalem*, with a complaint against the *Knights Hospitallers*; but he was obliged to refer the matter to the cognizance of his holiness. He then gave his protection to the exiles of *Apulia*; and sent an abbot, his ambassador, to the *Greek* emperor, who had invited him to march against *William*, king of *Sicily*, a common enemy to them both.

Though *Frederic* had done very little towards the tranquility of *Italy*, and the re-establishment of the imperial power there, yet he was obliged to return to *Germany*, where every thing was now in confusion. The count-palatine, assisted by other counts of the empire, had destroyed the city of *Mentz*, and ravaged the country round it; and, when the emperor returned to *Germany*, he summoned a diet at *Worms*, where all parties were convened, and some condemned as disturbers of the public peace. The penalty of the counts, and those who were above that degree, was to carry a dog on their backs from one county to another; that of gentlemen was to carry a joint-stool, and the peasants a cart-wheel. Neither the archbishop of *Mentz*, aged as he was, nor the elector-palatine, were exempted from this sentence; but the execution of it was remitted by the emperor. *Frederic obliged to return to Germany.*

The more that *Frederic* prospered in *Germany*, the greater was the pope's passion to humble him. He laid hold of a complaint of a bishop of *Lunden*, who pretended that he had been robbed in the imperial territories, without obtaining any redress; and sent legates to demand satisfaction, with letters addressed to the emperor and the diet, in which the papal insolence was carried to an unusual height. *Frederic* was treated as the slave and subject of his holiness, who reproached him for cowardice, and threatened that he would transfer the imperial dignity, which he held by his gift and favour, from the *Germans* to the *Greeks*; with many other expressions, if possible, still more provoking. "We are," said this letter, "appointed by God to rule over kings and "nations; and we may destroy, pluck up, build, plant, and treat them as we please."

The count-palatine of *Bavaria* would have cut the legates, whose behaviour was as insolent as their message, into pieces, but they were saved by the moderation of the emperor, and they fled back to *Italy*. This legation did service to *Frederic*, by uniting all his lay-subjects in his support. He published manifestos, asserting, in the strongest terms, the rights of his imperial sovereignty, and his independency upon the papal see, *Differences with the pope.*

fee. The pope, on the other hand, by the advice of the *German* bifhops, fent him a mollifying letter; which did not, however, prevent *Frederic* refolving to take the firft opportunity to humble him. The better to effect this, he reduced *Boleflaus*, of *Poland,* who had revolted, and erected *Bohemia* into a kingdom; its former erection to that dignity being only temporary. After this, he made a progrefs through his empire, to reform abufes, and fecured the fidelity of the king of *Hungary*. Before he repaffed the *Alps*, he fent commiffaries to infpect into the ftate of his affairs in *Lombardy*, and to take a new oath of fidelity from the ftates and cities there; and obliged *Waldemar*, king of *Denmark*, to receive in perfon, from his hands, the inveftiture of his kingdom at *Augfburg*.

Great profperity of the empire.

The empire, and its head, fince the time of *Charlemagne*, had never known fuch days of profperity as it enjoyed about the years 1157 and 1158. *Frederic* having affembled his army at *Augfburg*, paffed the *Alps*, took *Brefcia*, received the contingents and homages of all his vaffals in *Italy*, iffued new orders for civil and military regulations, obliged *Milan* to furrender, and was crowned king of *Lombardy* at *Monza*. To prevent any confufion, or uncertainty, concerning the imperial claims in *Italy*, he held an affembly on the plains of *Roncalia*, where they were produced, proved, and adjufted; and then he obliged all his feudatories, not excepting the bifhops themfelves, to do him homage. Many other general regulations, with regard to diftributive juftice, feudal fervices, and reformation of abufes of all kinds, were enacted. In fhort, a new fyftem of police took place. For this purpofe, we are told, by that accurate hiftorian *Sigonius*, who writes from the records of the univerfity of *Bologna*, that *Frederic* called to his affiftance four of the profeffors of the civil-law of that univerfity, the moft eminent then in *Europe* for that ftudy. They thinking themfelves unequal to fo great a tafk, he employed eighteen more, whom he called from the other cities of *Lombardy*. It was by their advice, and with their affiftance, that all thofe regulations were made; and the *Bolognefe* civilians had credit enough with him to obtain feveral very important privileges in favour of their univerfity; by which he became, though not the founder, the father, of that illuftrious mother of learning. We have been the more follicitous to be particular on this head, as it does great honour to the memory of *Frederic*; and proves, not only his love for letters, but, what is of far greater importance, that his revival of the imperial rights in *Italy* was not an arbitrary act of power, but the moft deliberate refult of juftice.

Feudal regulations.

Among other regulations, fub-vaffals, in the oaths they made to their lords-paramount, when they fwore them to fidelity againft all their enemies, were obliged to do it with
an

an exprefs exception to the emperor. This excellent regulation did not take place in other parts of *Europe* till some centuries after.

The pope, finding himfelf in danger of lofing his temporal authority in *Italy*, fent legates to remonftrate with *Frederic* upon the part he was acting; but he juftified his conduct, not without fome farcaftic hints at the pope's ambition and injuftice, in pretending to withdraw from *Cæfar* that tribute-money which had been paid him by the author of his religion. The *Milanefe*, partly fpirited up by the pope, but more ftrongly influenced by the lofs of that independency which they had fo long enjoyed, rebelled; *Milan* being then incomparably the moft powerful town in *Lombardy*. *Frederic* ravaged their territory; burnt down *Crema*. which was in confederacy with them; and rejected a fum of money which the *Milanefe* offered for the prefervation of their independency; but was not able to make himfelf mafter of the city, though his emprefs, *Beatrix*, had brought with her, out of *Germany*, a ftrong reinforcement to his army. During thofe tranfactions, negotiations of an accommodation were ftill going on between *Frederic* and the pope; but they were broken off by the death of the latter. *Roland*, chancellor of the church, was chofen by one part of the conclave; and *Octavian*, canon of St. *Cæcilia*, by the other; the firft taking the name of *Alexander* III. and the latter that of *Victor* IV. and a moft ridiculous fquabble happened between them, each forcibly plucking from the other the pontifical robe.

Alexander, with his party, retired to the caftle of St. *Angelo*; where he was invefted, but not with the fame robe that had been taken from him by his competitor. *Frederic* confidered himfelf as being the umpire between the two parties. He did not, however, chufe to annul the election becaufe it had not been made by his confent, but he fummoned a council at *Pavia*, and feemingly left the decifion to their uninfluenced voices, though it was known that he favoured *Victor*, with whom he had always been connected. *Alexander*, fenfible of this, refufed to acknowledge the validity of that council; and the members recognized *Victor* as the true pope. *Frederic* confirmed their choice by holding the ftirrup of his horfe while he alighted, kiffing his feet, and leading him to the altar. Thofe ceremonies were well placed, as they were paid by the emperor to a creature of his own, not upon any temporal confiderations, but becaufe he acknowledged him to be the head of the church.

Alexander, who had the right of election on his fide, filled all *Europe* with his manifeftos, with fo much fuccefs, that his caufe was efpoufed by the kings of *France* and *England*, by the *Milanefe*, and all the *Italian* ftates who were not immediately fubject to *Frederic*; and *Lewis the Young*, king of *France*, gave him refuge in his dominions, he not

thinking

Affairs of *Italy*.

thinking himfelf fafe at *Rome*, where the imperiálifts were all powerful. When *Alexander* came to *Torcy*, on the river *Loire*, he was met by the two kings of *France* and *England*, who alighted from their horfes, and, each taking a rein of his mule in his hand, conducted him to his lodging. *Alexander* had already thundered out his excommunications againft *Frederic* and his competitor *Victor*; and *Frederic* was, at this time, in no condition to oppofe him with any other arms than counter-manifeftos.

Milan re-
duced.
The fiege of *Milan* ftill continued, and the inhabitants made fo brave a defence, that, though they were obliged to feed upon the moft loathfome animals, they gave *Frederic* several fevere defeats, particularly one 'near *Carentia*, a few miles from *Lodi*; but not being feconded by the other ftates of *Italy*, they were obliged to capitulate in the beginning of the year 1162; and to give hoftages to deliver up their city to the emperor at difcretion. *Frederic* granted the inhabitants their lives, and diftributed them through different diftricts of *Lombardy*. He then ordered the town to be demolifhed. Moft writers imagine that this demolition was total, and that not a houfe in the city was left ftanding; but we apprehend, from the beft authorities, that it extended only to the public fortifications, works, and buildings; for *Frederic* appointed the bifhop of *Liege* to be its governor, and ordered it to be re-inhabited by *Germans*. The reduction of *Milan* difpirited the other *Italian* ftates, and, one after another, they fubmitted to him. He was, at this time, meditating an expedition againft *Naples*, *Sicily*, and *Capua*; and the *Genoefe*, who had depended upon the empire, but had likewife revolted, bought their pardon from *Frederic*, by promifing to fit out a fleet in his fervice for his *Sicilian* expedition.

The emperor-having thus conquered all *Lombardy*, gave the inhabitants a new fyftem of government, compofed partly from the civil, and partly from the feudal, conftitutions; and appointed new governors, moft of them *Germans*, to all the cities, as well as thofe of *Ancona*, *Tufcany*, and *Romania*; where the pope, at this time, feems to have poffeffed no temporal property. The feverities which *Frederic* inflicted upon *Milan*, and fome other cities, can only be excufed by their repeated breaches of fidelity to his government. He had no idea of their enjoying any liberty but what depended on him as emperor; and he difmantled *Placentia*, and even his favourite city of *Bologna*, with moft of the other cities in *Italy*, that they might not become, as he called them, The nefts of rebellion. To keep his prerogative entire, he inftituted feveral petty magiftracies and commonwealths, which were independent of the greater fiefs, and fome of them are at this time fubfifting.

Profperity
of Frede-
ric.
The emperor being, at this time, in the height of power and reputation, fent colonies from *Germany*, *Flanders*, and
Brabant,

Brabant, to *Mecklenburg*, the inhabitants of which country had hitherto been pagans, but were conquered by the duke af *Saxony*. *Waldemar*, the king of *Denmark*, with the kings of *Bohemia* and *Hungary*, recognized his fuperiority; and, when pope *Alexander* fled to *France*, he iffued out his orders for thofe powers to fend their bifhops, and to repair themfelves to a council, which was to be held at St. *Jean de Laon* for terminating the fchifm. He then returned victorious to *Germany*, which he found involved in feuds and troubles; but they were food fettled by his prefence. He then repaired to St. *Jean de Laon* with a body of troops; which intimidated the *French* king *Lewis* fo much, that he fled from thence, and pope *Alexander* fhut himfelf up in a convent. The council at St. *Jean de Laon* proving ineffectual, *Frederic* returned to *Mentz*, expecting to receive homage from *Waldemar*, king of *Denmark*, in perfon. That prince made a diftinction between his crown of *Denmark*, which he refufed to hold from any earthly power, and the country of *Wandalia*, for which he paid the emperor his homage; but on the condition of him and his fucceffors not being obliged to furnifh any contingencies towards the fervice of the empire or emperor. After this, he difmantled the city of *Mentz*, where the archbifhop had been murdered; and fortified the town of *Haguenau*, where he erected a college of juftice, and made it the feat of the imperial treafury.

In the year 1164, the privileges of the hans-towns in *Germany* took their rife. *Frederic*, from a liberal turn of mind, declared *Lubec* to be an imperial town, though it belonged to *Henry the Lion*, duke of *Saxony*, who, he thought, was beginning to grow too powerful in the empire; and he gave it even the privilege of coining money. *Hamburgh*, and other towns in *Germany* and the north, were affociated in the like freedom, which they have preferved ever fince. The emperor took the hint of this noble inftitution from *Pifa*, and the other trading cities of *Italy*; the inhabitants of which, becaufe they were free and independent of any territorial lord, not only grew wealthy themfelves, but enriched their indigent neighbours, and introduced plenty all round them. Thofe *Italian* and *German* towns were, at this time, the feats not only of plenty but liberty; and that too a liberty jealous of domination.

The rigour with which *Frederic* had treated *Milan*, gave them pain for themfelves, and they confederated together againft him. They were infpirited to this by pope *Alexander*; and, if their condition is difpaffionately confidered, the popes of thofe days were the afferters of the liberty of *Italy*, which the imperial power always endeavoured to crufh. But we do not prefume to affirm that the popes had any other motive for this than their oppofition to the emperors; or, that the papal yoke, when writhed about the necks of the people, was not more intolerable than the imperial. This

Powerful confederacy againft him.

confederacy

confederacy obliged *Victor*, the emperor's pope, to fly to *Germany*, and *Frederic* resolved upon another *Italian* expedition. The *Venetians* had headed the confederacy; and *Venice*, at this time, had acquired, by commerce, more wealth than belonged to any crowned head in *Europe*, except *Henry* II. of *England*. The very appellation of pope, in those days, being venerable, *Frederic* sent *Victor* before him into *Italy* to confirm his party there, and bring over others; but *Victor* died at *Lucca*. The emperor, by his own prerogative, convened a council at *Wurtzburg*, where the members chose a pope, who assumed the name of *Paschal* III. and bound themselves to obey no pope who was not acknowledged by the emperor, or who presumed to dictate in temporal affairs.

When *Frederic* and his empress *Beatrix* had passed the *Alps*, they found the confederacy against the imperial power very strong. Not only the *Romans* and the *Venetians*, but the inhabitants of *Vicenza*, *Verona*, *Padua*, and other cities, were parties in it, and complained loudly of being oppressed by the imperial governors. *Frederic* did all he could again to dismantle the towns which had presumed to rebuild their walls; and, finding the confederacy against him too strong to be shaken, he endeavoured to divide it. He did not attempt this by acts of power, but by clemency and liberality. He enlarged the privileges of all the states and communities who had stood firm in his interests, and he rendered them more free than even those who opposed him. He released *Mantua* and *Pavia* from their taxes, but he imposed rigorous penalties upon all defaulters. The archbishops of *Cologne* and *Mentz* were, upon this occasion, his generals and collectors. He established himself as umpire of the differences which subsisted between *Genoa* and *Pisa*. He laid *Bologna* under cotribution, as he did *Imola*, *Faenza*, and *Forli*; and he reduced *Ancona* to obedience. He made one of the bailiffs of *Sardinia* a king; and, in short, he over-stretched his power to such a degree, that he broke it; the oppression of his *German* governors being too great for human nature to bear.

Rebellion of the Italians. The *Milanese* rebuilt their walls, bade him defiance, and took the castle of *Trea*, where all his treasure was deposited; but the *Romans* were defeated by the archbishop of *Cologne*; while *Frederic* himself beat *William* II. king of *Sicily*, and again reduced *Ancona*, which had rebelled. The emperor then forced his entrance into *Rome*, where he was crowned by his anti-pope *Paschal*, *Alexander* having stolen away in disguise to *Benevento*. *Frederic*, at this time, seems to have been at the summit of his glory, which declined ever after. A plague broke out in his army, so that he scarcely commanded soldiers sufficient to keep in awe the open country of *Italy*. This rendered him contemptible in the eyes of the *Italian* states. His formidable enemy, pope *Alexander*, was

supported

supported by the *Greek* emperor; and it was with the utmost difficulty that *Frederic* escaped the *Milanese*, who pursued him, after he had lost his army, to the dominions of the count *de Morienne*, who favoured his retreat into *Germany*. All *Italy* then combined to oppose his return; and a new town, called *Alexandria*, in honour of the pope, was built between *Asti* and *Tortona*, as a future barrier of *Italy* against the *Germans*. *Frederic* being returned to *Germany*, quelled the commotions of *Saxony*, and assembled a diet at *Wurtzburg*; where he prevailed with the great lords of *Germany* to chuse his eldest son, *Henry* (who, by marriage, afterwards acquired the crown of *Naples*) king of the *Romans*.

However powerful the emperor was in *Germany*, he grasped but the phantom of power in *Italy*, where the confederacy against him still gathered strength; and the pope, sollicited by presents from *Constantinople*, was on the point of declaring *Manuel*, the *Greek* emperor, emperor of the *Romans*, on the promise of a union between the *Greek* and *Romish* churches. All that *Frederic*, though he proceeded upon right principles, did, could not prevent the *Italians* from strengthening their confederacy against him; and pope *Alexander*, in a full consistory, rejected the applications he was obliged to make for a reconciliation. *The emperor's interest declines in Italy,*

The second son of *Frederic* was, about this time, crowned king of *Germany*; and the duke of *Saxony* departed for the *Holy Land*, with a great number of crusaders under his command. The emperor, who seems to have had a contempt for the weakness of the times, assembled a diet at *Worms*; where he laid before the members his own and their importance, with a detail of the insolence of the holy-see, which they unanimously agreed upon ought to be checked. For this purpose, the members voted him a supply to enable him to undertake another expedition into *Italy*; and the archbishop of *Mentz* marched thither with an army to support his interests. A dispute at this time happened between *Genoa* and *Pisa*, concerning the property of the island of *Sardinia*; and the *Pisans*, being dissatisfied with the award pronounced by the archbishop of *Mentz*, were put to the ban of the empire, as were the *Florentines*, who took their part.

The emperor, by this time, gave orders to besiege *Ancona*, but without effect, because it held a correspondence with his enemy, the *Greek* emperor. On the other hand, the cities and states of the confederates assembled at *Modena*, where they entered into very spirited resolutions against the imperial yoke, and bound themselves to resist it. *Frederic* was, all this time, in *Germany*, employed in settling the affairs of *Bohemia*, which he committed to the care of one *Sobieslaus*. The peace of the empire being thereby, in some measure, restored, a rendezvous of the imperial army was appointed to be held at *Ratisbon*; and *Frederic*, receiving the *where he is defeated.*

neceſſary ſupplies, ſet out with his army for *Italy*, by way of mount *Cenis.* He quickly reduced *Aſti, Tortona, Cremona*, and *Como*; but, in beſieging the new city of *Alexandria*, he received ſo ſevere a repulſe, that he was obliged to retire to *Pavia*, which ſtood firm in his intereſt, though the army of the confederate ſtates was then beſieging it.

The confederacy was ſtrengthened by the fulminations of pope *Alexander* againſt the emperor, which incredibly operated to his diſadvantage. His vaſſals, who aſpired to independency, and particularly *Henry the Lion*, duke of *Saxony*, withdrew from their allegiance, on pretence that they could not ſerve againſt the holy-ſee; and, though the confederates were obliged to raiſe the ſiege of *Pavia*, yet the emperor could not take *Alexandria*, and was obliged to content himſelf with ravaging the adjacent country. The imperial general, *Chriſtian*, archbiſhop of *Mentz*, was ſomewhat more fortunate; for, after taking many cities in the marche of *Ancona*, and reducing the dutchy of *Spoleto*, he offered *William*, king of *Sicily*, peace, if he would conſent to a marriage between that king's ſon and the emperor's daughter; which *William* declined, leaſt he ſhould thereby give umbrage to his allies.

Affairs of The excommunications launched out by the pope affected
Germany. the courage of *Frederic*'s ſoldiers; and, though he was one of the beſt generals of his age, and had received a ſtrong reinforcement from *Germany*, yet he was defeated by the confederates, in a pitched battle, near *Cignano*, where he narrowly eſcaped with his life; and the few remains of a fine army were obliged to take refuge under the walls of *Pavia*. This was not the only mortification which *Frederic* moſt undeſervedly underwent at this time. His fleet was defeated by the *Venetians*; and his eldeſt ſon, prince *Henry*, was taken priſoner in the engagement. This was the triumphal period of liberty in *Italy*. The *Milaneſe* had received their freedom; the pope was everywhere victorious, and had the art to throw out the lure of the *Holy Land* to the *German* princes, who were otherwiſe well inclined to the emperor's ſervice. *Lunenburg* was now a free town, and the biſhop of *Wurtzburg* had eſtabliſhed a temporal juriſdiction in *Franconia*. *Guelph*, who was deſcended from a duke of *Bavaria*, whom we have already mentioned, left the emperor the dutchy of *Spoleto*, and the marquiſate of *Tuſcany*, with the iſland of *Sardinia*, and ſeveral other eſtates, to which he had a claim, but never was poſſeſſed of. This legacy ſerved only to embroil the emperor the more. All *Frederic*'s hopes of ſucceeding in *Italy*, now lay in his diſuniting the confederates; in which he partly ſucceeded, by his general, the archbiſhop of *Mentz*, having prevailed upon the *Venetians* to detach themſelves from the common alliance. In other reſpects, the allies, though united againſt him, were jealous of each other. The

Lucqueſe

Lucquese hated the *Pisans*, as the *Genoese* did the *Florentines*; but all conspired towards the diminution of the imperial power in *Italy*.

The emperor, haughty and over-bearing as he was, could not, without the greatest concern, see the storm gather round him; and he offered his friendship, in the way of accommodation, to pope *Alexander*; who gave him the meeting at *Venice*, after various intermediate negotiations had proved ineffectual. The reception of the emperor at *Venice* was very pompous, and, when he approached the pope, he humbled himself at his feet; which brought tears into the eyes of his holiness, so that he raised, and embraced, him. Soon after they retired together, and an accommodation between them was concluded. The pope, during the whole of this negotiation, maintained his superiority; and *Frederic* even held his stirrup when he mounted his mule. Other circumstances, of great discredit to *Frederic*, attended this accommodation. The pope preached in *Latin*, a language which the emperor pretended he did not understand; and said whatever he pleased concerning his own importance; and he proclaimed aloud, That, though he was an old man, and a priest, he had triumphed over a great and a powerful emperor. Some writers have said that the pope, on this occasion, put his foot upon the emperor's neck; but this is by no means probable, as we do not find that *Frederic* was reduced to a state of being obliged to suffer such an indignity; and we perceive, that, though he understood *Latin*, he had spirit enough to maintain his dignity, by refusing to answer *Alexander* in any other tongue than the *German*. But, to say the truth, this was the only species of equality which he preserved. towards his holiness.

The treaty of accommodation, which was concluded in the year 1177, comprehended the king of *Sicily*; and the emperor, on the thirteenth of *September*, set out for *Ravenna*. This accommodation was attended with great effects in favour of both parties. The confederated states and cities of *Italy*, having now no farther pretexts for disobedience, submitted to the emperor; and the pope remained on the papal throne without a competitor, as *Calixtus* acknowledged his right. At this time, *Alexander* called a general council; where it was decreed, that no pope should be looked upon as duly elected, without his having two thirds of the electors in his favour: a regulation which prevails to this day.

Frederic could not have remained so long in *Italy*, had not his great subjects in *Germany* been so much embroiled among themselves that they could attempt nothing to his prejudice. *Henry the Lion*, duke of *Saxony*, had behaved as the tyrant of the empire; and *Frederic*, upon his return to *Germany*, was not displeased to find that duke to be extremely unpopular, and that he might safely humble him. For that purpose, he

Margin notes: *Frederic's* accommodation with the pope. — Duke of *Saxony* forfeits his estates.

called a diet at *Worms*; where many articles of accusation were preferred against *Henry* by the great vassals of the empire. He did not deign to attend; and *Frederic*, from a principle of moderation, adjourned the diet to *Magdeburg*, and offered to acquit *Henry*, if he would pay five thousand marks into the imperial treasury; which he refused to do. A third diet was convoked at *Goslar*, where *Henry the Lion* was put to the ban of the empire; and *Philip*, archbishop of *Cologne*, was constituted the imperial commissary for executing the sentence. *Philip*, being joined by the troops of *Brabant*, *Flanders*, and *Guelderland*, laid waste the duke of *Saxony's* estates; and the bishop of *Halberstadt* excommunicated him. *Henry the Lion*, by this time, had got together an army; with which he defeated all his enemies in *Thuringia*, retook all the places he had lost in *Westphalia*, and made the bishop of *Halberstadt* his prisoner, after destroying his dominions.

Partition of them. *Frederic* began now to apprehend that his dignity was incompatible with the vast power of the duke of *Saxony*, who was son-in-law to the king of *England*. Fortunately for the emperor, the princes of the empire were as jealous as he was of the duke; and it was no difficult matter for *Frederic* to form an effectual confederacy to undo him. He convened a diet at *Wurtzburg*, which, at the request of the *English* ambassadors, he ajourned to *Gelnhausen*, in *Wetteravia*; where *Henry the Lion* was dispossessed of his estates, which were conferred upon different noblemen; and the emperor himself carried the sentence into execution. *Henry the Lion*, when the sentence was pronounced, was more powerful than the emperor himself was in *Germany*. The house of *Anhalt* partook largely of his spoils, by receiving a gift of *Saxony* and part of *Westphalia*; and *Otho*, count of *Vitelsbach*, the ancestor of the present house of *Bavaria*, received that dukedom as his portion of the spoil. The archbishop of *Cologne* took *Brunswic*; and *Waldemar*, king of *Denmark*, being gained over by *Frederic*, equipped a fleet, with which he blocked up the mouth of the *Trave*; while *Frederic* took *Lubec* by land, and *Henry the Lion* fled to *Holstein*. The emperor having compassed his ends, in humbling so powerful a subject, who, at this time, prostrated himself at his feet, begging him to restore him part of his dominions, was inclined to have shewn him favour; but, as his great fees had been granted away under a ban of the empire, *Frederic* was obliged to refer him to a diet that was convoked at *Quedlemburg*, and from thence adjourned to *Erfurt*.

When the princes assembled there, *Frederic* perceived he had done what he could not undo; for they who had shared in the *Saxon* spoils refused to resign them; and *Frederic* advised the duke of *Saxony* to reside for some time in *England*, till he could soften matters in his favour; but promised, in the mean time, to take care of his children, and to protect for him the territories of *Brunswic* and *Lunenburg*, the only

lands

lands that remained to him unforfeited in *Germany*. *Henry* Duke of *Saxony* retires to *England*. *Henry* accordingly retired to *England*, where his wife bore him a son called *William*, who was the anceftor of the prefent houfe of *Brunfwic* and all its branches.

The inhabitants of *Rome* were, at this time, free from all the imperial ufurpations; though the emperor's general, the archbifhop of *Mentz*, was ftill in *Italy* with an army. Pope *Alexander* III. dying in 1181, the cardinals, without confulting the *Roman* clergy or people, advanced to the popedom *Ubaldo*, a *Lucquefe* bifhop of *Oftia*, who affumed the name of *Lucius* III. but he was driven out of *Rome* by its inhabitants, and he applied to the *German* general for protection. It appears as if *Lucius* had been in the interefts of the emperor, whofe general marched his army towards *Rome*, but he died at *Tufculum*. The fpiritual and the temporal orders, at this time, were confounded. Every prelate exercifed temporal and military jurifdiction; and his ecclefiaftical preferments were only matters of conveniency, not of duty.

Frederic, and the other powers of *Europe*, furnifhed the pope with money, which enabled him to re-enter *Rome*; from whence he was again expelled by the fenators, who were fo barbarous as to put out the eyes of feveral of his ecclefiaftical adherents, and, in derifion, fend them to him with mitres on their heads. *Lucius* was obliged to retire to *Verona*, where all he could do was to fulminate excommunications againft his enemies. In the mean while, a very black ftorm hung over *Germany*. *Revolutions in Italy,* *Henry* II. of *England*, who was, by far, the moft powerful prince in *Europe*, and whofe poffeffions in *France* exceeded thofe he held in *England*, interpofed in favour of his fon-in-law *Henry the Lion*. *Frederic* began to repent of his aggrandizing other princes out of the *Saxon* fpoils; for *Otho de Vitelfbach* difcovered fuch talents for government as bade fair for rendering himfelf independent of the empire. The emperor, to curb him as much as he poffibly could, erected many parts of his dominions into imperial fiefs, and declared *Ratifbon* a free city.

In the year 1183, *Frederic* laid a plan of a general accommodation for all his eftates in *Italy*; and a congrefs was held for that purpofe at *Placentia*. *and Germany.* There, by the intervention of *Henry*, king of the *Romans*, the emperor's eldeft fon, all matters were accommodated. The *Italian* vaffals of the emperor were obliged to take an oath of allegiance to their head; and, in his *Roman* expedition (for fo his journey to *Rome* was called) they were obliged to furnifh him with provifions and forage in lieu of all other impofts. They were entitled to raife troops and erect fortifications, and to decide pecuniary and other caufes according to their own municipal laws; but, when the bifhop of a place was not a count, the nomination of confuls, or podeftas, was to revert to the emperor. This pacification, fo authentically concluded, was, by the *Italians*, juftly confidered as the æra of their public liberty.

liberty. The inhabitants of *Alexandria*, at that time, called *de Paglia*, becaufe their houfes were covered with thatch, confidered themfelves as holding the ballance of power in *Italy*, and refufed to accede to this accommodation; but they were afterwards obliged to atone for their obftinacy by applying, in the moft fubmiffive manner, to the emperor at *Nuremburg*, and confenting to hold their privileges from him.

Henry, king of the Romans, knighted, After this, in the year 1184, *Frederic* again declared his fon *Henry*, king of the *Romans*; and formally knighted him, and his brother *Frederic*, at *Mentz*, where he held a diet. He then went to *Italy*, with a fincere defire of accommodating fome differences with the pope, *Lucius* III. concerning the fucceffion of *Matilda*. Nothing decifive was fettled on that head, the pope being inflexible, and refufing to crown the young man king of *Lombardy*; but *Henry*, by his own power, had that ceremony performed at *Milan*. He then returned to *Germany*, where he quelled fome difturbances that had been raifed by the ambitious archbifhop of *Cologne*. Returning to *Verona*, where the council was ftill fitting, he met with *Heraclius*, the patriarch of *Jerufalem*, who was folliciting a crufade in favour of king *Baldwin*; but, inftead of entering upon fo wild a propofal, *Frederic* afferted his right to the fucceffion of the countefs *Matilda*.

He had a meeting with the pope at *Verona*, where they agreed upon having a council convoked for reforming the errors and abufes of the church; and, upon the return of *Henry the Lion* to take poffeffion of *Brunfwic* and *Lunenburg*, *Lucius* appeared to be inflexible with regard to the fucceffion to *Matilda*'s dominions; neither would he give *Frederic*'s fon, prince *Henry*, the imperial crown; but the father had him crowned king of *Lombardy*, and then fet out for *Germany*; where he chaftized the archbifhop of *Cologne*, whofe ambition and avarice raifed fome difturbances. A council was then fitting at *Verona*, where the patriarch of *Jerufalem* endeavoured to excite a new crufade, but without effect; and the emperor infifted upon his right to the long difputed fucceffion of *Matilda*. He feized the towns of *Aquapendente*, *Chieffa*, *Balfena*, *Bagnarea*, and, after a fiege of two years, took *Orvieto*.

Frederic prevails againft the pope, *Frederic* then undertook a progrefs through *Lombardy* and *Tufcany*, and reconciled moft of the towns there to his dominion, till the death of pope *Lucius*, who was fucceeded by *Urban* III. The popes were always jealous of the *German* intereft in *Italy*, and *Urban* could not, without uneafinefs, behold a match which was concluded between *Henry*, *Frederic*'s eldeft fon, and *Conftance*, the fifter and heirefs of *Wilham*, king of *Sicily*. He fufpended the bifhops who had affifted at the ceremony; and the emperor, in return, difmantled *Cremona*; but enlarged the privileges of *Milan*, which he had fo lately punifhed for its difobedience.

The

The cuſtoms of *Germany* were, at this time, inexpreſſibly barbarous. Where living witneſſes were wanting to decide a law-ſuit, the parties had recourſe to ſingle combat; which was performed in the biſhop's court-yard before him or his officers. This ridiculous and cruel practice, about the year 1186, began to abate; and *Bernard*, biſhop of *Mentz*, firſt ſhewed the *Germans* the method of keeping regiſters in writing for the ſecurity of private and public property.

Frederic gave the government of his *Italian* dominions to his ſon *Henry*, and returned to *Germany*, where he found every thing in diſorder. The archbiſhop of *Mentz* ſtood in oppoſition to him in raiſing an archbiſhop to the ſee of *Triers*; and *Canute*, king of *Denmark*, refuſed to pay him homage for *Wandalia*. *Frederic* employed *Bugeſlaus*, whom he had made duke of *Pomerania*, to make war upon the *Danes*; but he was defeated by *Abſalom*, biſhop of *Lunden*, who blocked up the mouth of the river *Pena*; and, next year, *Canute* obliged *Bugeſlaus* to hold *Pomerania* as a fief of *Denmark*. This was extremely mortifying to the emperor, who invited *Canute* to be preſent at the nuptials of his ſon *Frederic* with *Canute*'s ſiſter *Chriſtina*. *Canute*, ſuſpecting that the emperor deſigned to entrap him, as he probably did, declined the invitation; which exaſperated *Frederic* ſo much, that he ſent home the princeſs with contempt; while *Canute*, in revenge, ravaged the northern parts of *Germany*.

In the year 1187, a quarrel happened between *Bela*, king of *Hungary*, and his brother *Emeric*. The latter fled to *Sobieſlaus*, the duke of *Bohemia*, who put him under an arreſt, and ſent him to his brother; for which *Frederic* ſummoned *Sobieſlaus* to the diet of the empire, and deprived him of his dominions; which were given to *Frederic*, the ſon of *Uladiſlaus*, his predeceſſor. This new duke receiving ſome aſſiſtance from the biſhop of *Saltſburg*, ſettled himſelf at *Prague*; where the people, who hated *Uladiſlaus*, willingly received him. After this, being ſummoned to attend the diet at *Ratiſbon*, *Sobieſlaus* aſſembled an army, which defeated him in his attempt to return to *Prague*; but was, in his turn, defeated by *Frederic*, who thereby gained poſſeſſion of *Bohemia*. His tyranny, and his raiſing foreigners to the principal poſts of the magiſtracy, loſt him the hearts of the *Bohemians*, who elected, for their duke, *Conrade*, marquis of *Znain*, in *Moravia*; for which they were put to the ban of the empire. This daring violation of the imperial dignity was reſented by the emperor, who reinſtated *Frederic* in his dukedom.

The popes ſeldom failed to improve every difficulty of an emperor to their own purpoſes. *Urban* was diſobliged at the marriage of *Henry*, king of the *Romans*, with *Conſtance of Sicily*; and he laid hold of certain intermedlings of *Frederic* with the eccleſiaſtical revenues to ſtir up the *German* prelates

Returns to Germany,

and puts his enemies to the ban of the empire.

againſt

against him; though the true cause of his disquiet lay in his having seized the estates of *Matilda*. The emperor, aware of his design, had the address to convoke an ecclesiastical assembly at *Gelnhausen*; where he laid open the encroachments of the pope in so strong a light before them, that he prevailed with them to join in a remonstrance against his conduct. A paper was accordingly drawn up, accusing him of having invaded the imperial rights in *Italy*, and of having stirred up the vassals of the empire to rebellion; with various other charges of the same nature. *Urban's* death, just as he was about to have launched the bolt of excommunication against the emperor, prevented farther consequences at that time; but the papal cause was supported by *Philip*, the warlike archbishop of *Cologne*, who was apostolical legate in *Germany*.

Urban was succeeded by *Gregory* VIII. who died in the second month of his reign; and *Frederic*, in a diet at *Worms*, brought over the princes of the empire to declare against the archbishop of *Cologne*, and to cut off all communication between him and the rest of *Germany*. *Frederic*, about the same time, was embroiled with *Hubert*, count of *Savoy*, who was a declared partizan of the see of *Rome*, because he aimed at being independent of the empire. *Frederic* had erected the sees of *Turin* and *Geneva* into imperial fiefs, which *Hubert* opposed, and the emperor therefore destroyed his estates. Upon the death of *Hubert*, his son *Thomas* fell under the tutelage of the marquis of *Montferrat*, who prevailed with *Henry*, king of the *Romans*, to revoke the decree which erected the bishopric of *Turin* into a fief of the empire: but the count of *Savoy*, on the other hand, was obliged to do homage to the emperor for the jurisdiction and lordship of that city, which he acquired from the bishop.

He undertakes a crusade. In the year 1188, all *Europe* was thrown into consternation by the accounts of *Saladin* having retaken *Jerusalem*. *Clement* III. who succeeded *Gregory* VIII. in the popedom, was an enthusiast in the cause, and preached up a new crusade, which the emperor *Frederic* most unaccountably embraced; and was thereupon reconciled to the pope: and he sent a *German* count, who formally demanded from *Saladin* restitution of the holy city and sepulchre. All *Christendom* seemed to be smitten with the same religious rage. The reader, in the former parts of this work, has been made acquainted with the madness of *Frederic's* conduct on this occasion. Not only he himself, but his son *Frederic*, duke of *Suabia*, with sixty-eight of the chief princes in *Germany*, took the cross; and, though *Frederic* decreed that none should enlist himself as a crusader who could not afford to spend three marks of silver, yet the numbers who enlisted amounted to one hundred and fifty thousand men; all of them well appointed, armed, and accoutred. That no revolution might

happen

happen in the empire during his abſence, he reconciled himſelf to *Henry the Lion*, duke of *Saxony*; and that prince ſwore
he would attempt nothing to injure *Frederic* during his abſence.

The emperor then applied himſelf, by the aſſiſtance of the
pope, who indulged him to the utmoſt, to raiſe money for
his expedition; and the ſums he amaſſed were incredible,
both from eccleſiaſtics and laics. He then ſettled the ſucceſſion to his empire, and marched through *Auſtria* and *Hungary* at the head of one hundred thouſand enthuſiaſts; the
odd fifty thouſand having, it ſeems, thought proper to buy
off their ſervices by the conſent of the pope. He then fell His death.
upon *Iſaac Angelus*, the emperor of *Conſtantinople*, whom he
defeated, becauſe he denied him a paſſage through his dominions, as he alſo did the ſultan of *Iconium*; and he filled
all *Aſia* with the terror of his name, where he died; but the
manner of his death is uncertain, as we have already ſeen.
He moſt probably caught it by bathing in the river *Cydnus*,
though ſome ſay he was drowned.

He was a prince of great accompliſhments; and the ſtrik- and cha-
ing inequalities of his temper and conduct may be well ac- racter.
counted for by the turbulence of the times in which he lived.
He has been accuſed, by ſome, of atheiſm; but this charge
probably aroſe from the ſettled contempt and hatred he had
for the papal power. His embarking ſo late in life as he
did in the cruſade, plainly evinces that he had a ſenſe of
religion, however miſtaken it might be. His death happened
in 1190, and he is ſaid to have been buried in the city of
Tyre.

By his firſt wife, *Alice*, who was a daughter to the marquis of *Urſbourg*, and whom he repudiated, he had not any
children. His ſecond wife was *Beatrix*, a daughter of *Bernard*, duke of *Burgundy*; and by that princeſs he had five
ſons and two daughters; viz. *Henry*, who ſucceeded him;
Frederic, duke of *Suabia*, who attended him in his expedition; *Conrade*, duke of *Rottenburg*; *Otho*, duke of *Burgundy*, which came by the mother; and his youngeſt ſon
was *Philip*, for whom he made up an eſtate out of the eccle-
ſiaſtic lands and revenues which he ſeized. *Sophia*, one of
his daughters, was wife to *Conrade*, duke of *Miſnia*, and
ſome ſay the marquis of *Montferrat*. His ſecond daughter,
Beatrix, was married to the duke of *Lorrain*, and was afterwards abbeſs of *Quedlemburg*.

23. Henry

23. Henry VI. *surnamed* the Severe.

Acceffion of *Henry* VI.

UPON the death of *Frederic Barbaroffa*, his fon, the duke of *Suabia*, headed the remains of his army, which was reduced to about eight thoufand men; but he died at the fiege of *Ptolemais*. Moft part of the furviving *Germans* returned to their own country, under the landgrave of *Thuringia*, the duke of *Guelderland*, and the count of *Holftein*; and they who remained ranged themfelves under the banners of *Leopold*, duke of *Auftria*.

New diffentions in the empire.

About the time of *Frederic Barbaroffa*'s death, died *William*, king of *Sicily* and *Naples*; by which *Henry*, in right of his wife, came to the poffeffion of that crown. Upon the departure of his father from the *Holy Land*, *Henry the Lion*, without regard to his oath, ftirred up new diffentions in the empire, and leagued himfelf with *Hartwick*, archbifhop of *Bremen*, who plundered great part of the *Northern Germany*, and reduced *Lubec*, *Hamburgh*, and other places of importance, before the king of the *Romans*, in the then exhaufted ftate of *Germany*, could affemble an army to oppofe them. At laft, he gave battle to *Henry the Lion*, and defeated him, near *Ferden*; forced him to fly to *England*; but afterwards admitted him to peace, on condition of one of his fons being delivered up as a hoftage, while the eldeft was to attend him to *Italy*; and the chief feats of his rebellion to be difmantled.

The peace of *Germany* being thus reftored, *Henry* prepared to march into *Italy*, where *Tancred*, his wife's natural brother, had been proclaimed king of *Sicily*. *Henry*, to ftrengthen his party in *Italy*, confirmed and encreafed the privileges of the *Lombard* ftates and cities, and likewife thofe of *Genoa* and *Pifa*; which laft he erected into a free republic, on condition of their affifting him with a fleet againft *Tancred*.

Pope *Celeftine* chofen.

Celeftine III. about the year 1191, fucceeded to the papal throne; being, at the time of his election, eighty-fix years of age. The emperor thought it was of great confequence for him and his wife to be crowned at *Rome*. This could not be done till the pope (who was a layman) was made a prieft and bifhop, and exalted into the papal chair; which was performed with a thoufand ridiculous ceremonies. Next day, the imperial pair were crowned; and it is faid, that, after the crown was put upon the emperor's head, the haughty old man kicked it down, to teach that prince what he owed to the papal fee.

Though this fact is queftioned by fome, yet it is too ftrongly attefted to be denied. What makes it the more probable, is, that the friendfhip of his holinefs was fo important at this time, that he gave him up the town of *Tufculum*;

tulum; which was demolished by the *Romans*, and *Frescati* was built upon its ruins. Though *Tancred* was a usurper, yet he was a less formidable neighbour than *Henry*; and *Celestine* commanded that emperor, on the severest penalties, not to proceed in his expedition against *Naples* and *Sicily*. *Henry* was well supported by the *German* princes, who probably proposed to conquer those fine countries, as the *Normans* had done before, and to hold them under himself. The latter, therefore, notwithstanding the pope's prohibitions, proceeded in his expedition; and, after reducing almost all *Campania*, *Apulia*, and *Calabria*, he laid siege to *Naples* itself; and must have become master of it, by the help of the *Genoese* fleet, had not an uncommon mortality attacked his army and reduced its numbers, so that he was obliged to discontinue his operations. Among other great men, died *Philip the Warlike*, archbishop of *Cologne*, with *Otho*, duke of *Bohemia*; and it was with the greatest difficulty that *Henry* himself recovered from that contagion. The people of *Naples* and *Sicily* were far better satisfied in being subjects to *Tancred* than to *Henry*, from whom they revolted as soon as they saw him disabled from continuing the war; and the *Salernians*, with whom the empress had taken refuge, treacherously delivered her up to *Tancred*; who, with great honour, restored her to her husband.

[margin: Ruin of the emperor's army in Italy.]

This loss of *Henry's* army did not discourage him from pursuing his undertaking, unsuccessful as it had hitherto been. He went to *Genoa*, where he entered into a new convention for the use of the *Genoese* ships; and he performed a progress over all the towns of *Lombardy*, which he again confirmed in their allegiance, and then he repaired to *Worms*. There he knighted *Lewis* IV. of *Bavaria*; gave *Suabia* to his brother *Conrade*; and the dutchy of *Spoleto*, with large estates in *Tuscany*, of which he had stripped the *Guelph* family, to his other brother, *Philip*.

About this time, the *Teutonic* order was established in *Germany*, and forms an important period in that history. They took their rise from the remains of those *German* noblemen and gentlemen who had so bravely served in the *Holy Land* under the duke of *Suabia*, after the death of his father *Barbarossa*. Being incorporated under the order of a knighthood, they got possession of a *Greek*, or *Teutonic*, chapel on the mount *Zion*, and put themselves under the protection of the Blessed Virgin. Thus their order was partly military and partly charitable, their employment resembling that of the *Knights-Templars*, in guarding and entertaining pilgrims in their journeys to and from *Jerusalem*; and, by their oath, they were obliged to protect the church, the clergy, the widow, the orphan, the poor, and the distressed. They quickly became favourites with the emperor, *Henry* VI. who recommended them to the pope; and *Celestine* confirmed them in all their privileges and possessions; assigned them a proper

[margin: Original of the Teutonic knights.]

habit

habit to wear, and gave them an armorial bearing ; which was a black crofs upon a white banner ; with feveral rules in the romantic fpirit of thofe times. The original number was not to exceed forty, but none of them was to be under the degree of a gentleman by birth ; and one *Henry Walpot*, a *German*, was chofen their firft grand-mafter. After the *Chriftians* had entirely loft the *Holy Land*, this order became quite military, and was of great confequence in the affairs of *Europe*. The firft houfe they had in *Germany* was built by the emperor at *Coblentz*.

Affairs of Germany

The vaft application which *Henry* gave to the affairs of his empire, his affiduous adminiftration of juftice in perfon, the popular manner in which he behaved towards all ranks of fubjects, and his liberalities towards the cities, both of the empire and *Italy*, had two great objects in view: the one was, the renewal of his expedition againft the two *Sicilies* ; and the other was, the rendering the empire hereditary in his family : but he found both thefe projects to be attended with great difficulty. He had given the inveftiture of the bifhopric of *Liege* to one *Lothair* ; but *Albert*, another ecclefiaftic, had been elected by the canons, and confirmed by the pope. *Albert* was found murdered by two *German* knights. The archbifhop of *Mentz* flew to arms ; and the emperor, being fufpected of having fome concern in the murder, was in danger of being depofed, had he not convened an affembly of the ftates at *Coblentz*, where he folemnly afferted his innocence, gave orders that the murderers fhould be profecuted to the utmoft, and that *Lothair* fhould be deprived of the fee, which was given to *Albert de Cuck*.

About this time, *Henry the Lion*, notwithftanding his great age and the variety of his misfortunes, refufed to evacuate *Holftein*, according to agreement, to duke *Adolphus*. The latter could expect no affiftance from the emperor, who then was entirely bufied in raifing troops for his *Italian* expedition. But duke *Bernard* of *Saxony*, the marquis of *Brandenburg*, and the other princes who enjoyed *Henry the Lion's* fpoils, gave *Adolphus* fuch affiftance as drove *Henry* out of *Holftein*, and procured the inveftiture of it from the emperor, with all its dependencies.

and Denmark.

The fucceffes of *Adolphus* rendered duke *Bernard* jealous. He pretended that fome part of his conquefts ought to belong to his family. Hoftilities commenced. *Bernard* prepared to befiege *Lubec*, and *Adolphus* reduced *Lawenberg*. This quarrel reached, at laft, to *Denmark*. The party of *Adolphus* efpoufed the caufe of *Waldemar*, the pretender to that crown ; while *Canute*, the reigning king, acted with fo much addrefs, that *Waldemar* was taken prifoner ; and *Adolphus*, being driven out of *Slefwic*, was obliged to receive the law from *Canute*. But another, and more important, fcene was now opened in *Germany*.

Richard

Richard I. king of *England*, who had exhibited prodigies *Henry* de-
of valour, to no purpofe, in the *Holy-Land*, having taken tains *Ri-*
leave of that grave of the *Europeans*, was, upon his return *chard*,
to his own dominions, fhip-wrecked on the *Adriatic* coaft; king of
and, though he endeavoured to conceal himfelf, by travel- *England*,
ing, in the habit of a pilgrim, through the territories of in chains.
Leopold, duke of *Auftria*, yet he was difcovered, made prifoner, and moft fhamefully loaded with irons. The emperor, as the head of the empire, claimed the cuftody of the
royal prifoner, which *Leopold* yielded to him upon pecuniary
confiderations. *Henry* was too mercenary to attend to the
requefts of *Richard*'s friends and *Englifh* fubjects, to have
him fet at liberty; but, to give fome colour for his detention, he accufed him, before the diet of *Haguenau*, of feveral
malverfations in his conduct as a crufader; and of his having
entered into an alliance with *Tancred*, the ufurper of the two
Sicilies. Though thofe charges were in themfelves unjuft and
ridiculous, and though *Richard* was not amenable to any tribunal, yet he pleaded his own caufe with great ftrength of
reafon and evidence, and turned all the charges againft him
upon his accufers; infomuch that, barbarous as that age was,
the princes of the empire interceded with *Henry* for *Richard*'s
liberty.

Two great obftacles lay to this; the firft was *Henry*'s own He is ran-
avarice, and his defire of amaffing money for his expedition fomed.
to *Italy*. The next was the intrigues of *Philip*, king of
France, who found his account in *Richard*'s detention. He
therefore fixed the royal ranfom to about three hundred
thoufand pounds fterling; a moft amazing fum in thofe
days; which was raifed by the affiduity of *Richard*'s mother
and the zeal of his *Englifh* fubjects. The emperor infifted
likewife upon *Richard* giving orders for fetting at liberty the
tyrant king of *Cyprus*, whom he had dethroned; and his
giving to the duke of *Auftria*'s eldeft fon his niece *Eleanore* of
Britany in marriage. *Richard* knew the value of liberty, at
that juncture when his crown was threatened by the practices of his brother *John*, better than to difpute any of the
terms; but, fo very fordid was the emperor, that, though
the queen-mother paid two thirds of the ranfom, it is thought
that he would ftill have detained the royal prifoner, that he
might get a farther fum from the king of *France*, had he not
been deterred by the interpofition of the princes of the empire, who demanded the liberty of *Richard* in very high
terms. The emperor gave orders accordingly, but foon after retracted them; and *Richard* muft have been again arrefted, had he not got out of the imperial dominions with
amazing difpatch. *Richard* had left hoftages behind him for
the payment of the refidue of his ranfom which was to go
into the pocket of the duke of *Auftria*. *Richard* finding
fome difficulty in the impoverifhed ftate of *England*, the duke
moft unmanfully was about to have put the hoftages to death
when

when the money arrived, with the princess *Eleanore* of *Brittany*. Before she came to *Vienna*, *Leopold* died of a fall from his horse; but, in his last moments, he ordered the *English* hostages to be set at liberty. It is difficult to say what pretext *Leopold*'s son and succeffor could have for oppoſing this order; but it is certain that he not only broke off his match with *Eleanore*, whom he fent back, but would have detained the hoſtages, had he not been compelled by the biſhops and ſtates of his dominions to ſet them at liberty.

The proceedings of *Henry* againſt the king of *England* had been fo ſhameful, that, when *Henry* was preparing to ſet out on his *Italian* expedition, he fent ambaſſadors to aſk *Richard*'s pardon for what had happened, and even to promiſe reſtitution of the ſum he had ſo ſcandalouſly extorted from him. A competition, about this time, happening concerning the dukedom, or kingdom, of *Bohemia* (for it was both by turns) *Henry* fold the inveſtiture of it to the biſhop of *Prague*, upon the death of *Wenceſlaus*. *Henry the Lion* continued as reſtleſs as ever; but all his ſchemes failing, he endeavoured to recover the good graces of the emperor, who took into his favour *Henry*'s ſon, the duke of *Brunſwic*; and, at laſt, by the interceſſion of *Conrade*, the count-palatine, he was reconciled to himſelf. Soon after, *Henry the Lion* died, at the age of ſeventy, leaving behind him three fons, the eldeſt of whom was in poſſeſſion of *Brunſwic*. The affairs of *Germany* being thus pacified, *Henry* ſent an army towards *Naples*, under the command of his general *Berthold*, who reduced feveral places. *Tancred*, in the mean while, loſt his ſon *Roger*; and was fo affected with grief, that he died himſelf in a few days after; but his ſubjects declared his infant ſon *William*, who was in his cradle, his ſucceſſor.

Henry courts his friendſhip.   This news determined *Henry* to paſs, in perſon, into *Italy*. He had always continued his ſubſidies to the *Piſans* and *Genoeſe*; and they lent him their joint fleets to reduce *Naples* by ſea, which he himſelf attacked by land. That city ſoon fell into his hands, as did all *Apulia* and *Calabria*. He took *Palermo* by ſtorm, and exerciſed moſt horrid cruelties upon the inhabitants. In ſhort, nothing could withſtand his fortune. He purſued the widow and infant ſon of *Tancred*, and, after beſieging them in *Salerno*, they ſurrendered upon a capitulation offered by himſelf; by which the young prince was to return to the principality of *Tarentum*. The emperor, however, no ſooner got him into his power, than he moſt inhumanly ordered him to be caſtrated, and his eyes put out; and ſhut up his mother, and her two daughters, in a monaſtery in *Alſace*. This imperial monſter's next ſtep was to feize all their effects, and the treaſures which had been amaſſed by *Tancred* and his predeceſſors. He then new modelled his government of the two *Sicilies*, which he had entruſted in the hands of *Germans* as rapacious and cruel as himſelf;

himfelf; and carried with him, by way of hoftages, into *Germany*, the chief prelates and noblemen of the country. The fufferings of the *Sicilians* were beyond what human nature could bear. They rebelled, and the emperor ordered all his hoftages to lofe their eyes.

While he remained in *Sicily*, a moft extraordinary event of nature happened. His emprefs, *Conftance*, the heirefs of that noble crown, though confiderably paft fifty years of age, grew pregnant; and *Henry*, to put the reality of her delivery beyond all difpute, ordered a fpacious fcaffold to be erected on the plains of *Palermo*; where fhe was delivered, in fight of his people and army, of a fon, whofe name was *Frederic*, and who afterwards was emperor.

Wonderful birth of Frederic II.

Till this time, *Henry* had been indefatigable in aggrandifing his brothers. On the death of *Conrade*, duke of *Suabia*, he had beftowed all his dominions on his brother *Philip*, who had married the daughter of the *Greek* emperor; and, upon the death of *Conrade*, count-palatine, he beftowed the inveftiture of his dominions upon his fon-in-law *Henry*, duke of *Brunfwic*. The emperor was, at this time, the terror of all *Europe*; but, powerful as he was, he durft not refufe to liften to the pope's admonitions that he would take upon him the crofs; and, in imitation of his father, ordered an army to march to the *Holy Land*. *Henry* knew that the pope follicited this only becaufe he was afraid of his prefence in *Italy*; but he was obliged actually to fend thither fome troops under the command of the archbifhop of *Mentz* and other princes, and even to promife folemnly to take the crofs upon himfelf as foon as he fhould return from finifhing his affairs in *Sicily*, where the inhabitants now threatened a general revolt.

A new crufade.

The fpirit of crufading was, at this time, fo ftrong in *Germany*, that *Margaret*, queen-dowager of *Hungary*, fifter to the king of *France*, took upon herfelf the crofs; and actually joined, with an army, the archbifhop of *Mentz*, who marched through her dominions. A fecond army went by fea, in fhips provided by the inhabitants of *Holftein* and the *Hans* towns; and *Henry* took hold of the occafion to lead a third army into *Italy*, in the year 1196, with an exprefs promife to fend it into the *Holy Land* as foon as the affairs of *Sicily* were fettled.

The emperor found every thing in confufion in *Sicily* and *Naples*, through the horrid cruelty and perfidy he had been guilty of. The *Genoefe* had demanded of him to fulfil the ftipulations he had contracted for the ufe of their fleet; but he laughed at their ambaffador's requeft; and told him, That, as he was their fuperior, they were obliged to furnifh him with fhips. The bifhop of *Worms*, and the other *German* deputies, continued to opprefs the people, particularly thofe of *Palermo*, *Naples*, and *Capua*; fo that they ran to arms, and applied to *Roger*, count *de Acerra*, to head them. The count of *Moloffa* was likewife very active in ftirring up

Henry's cruelties in Sicily.

the

the other towns of *Sicily* to throw off the imperial yoke. The count *de Acerra* was unfuccefsful and crufhed by the emperor's governors; and *Henry*, upon his arrival, diveſted the rebellious cities of all their properties and privileges, which he beſtowed upon his *German* adherents. Even this feverity was far from quelling the revolt; and *Henry* propoſed a congreſs to be held at *Capua*, to give fatisfaction to the malcontents. He there promiſed to redreſs all their grievances, and to reſtore them to their eſtates and privileges; but no fooner had the affembly broken up, and the *Sicilians* laid down their arms, than he moſt perfidiouſly broke the terms, filled *Sicily* with his troops, feized the perſons of the chief infurgents, put fome of them to death, and carried others to *Germany*.

As the empreſs *Conſtance* confidered *Sicily* not only as her native country, but her inheritance, fhe could not, without horror, reflect upon the miferies it had fuffered; and regarded her own huſband as the faithleſs butcher of her kindred, who had been exterminated by his cruelty. Perhaps the infidelity, and the brutal indifference, of her huſband towards her, contributed not a little to her refentment, which fhe purfued like a woman of fenfe and fpirit. She is faid to have privately engaged one count *Jordani*, a *Sicilian* nobleman, and fome of his friends, in a confpiracy, to fortify themfelves in the ifland of *Lipara* till fhe could openly declare for them. In this fhe was warranted, by her duty as fovereign of the two *Sicilies*, the emperor being no other than her fubſtitute. Another reafon might concur, not taken notice of by hiſtory. He had caufed his fon *Frederic*, though in his cradle, to be chofen king of the *Romans* by fifty-two noblemen and bifhops, who durſt not oppofe his will. He had obliged them to concur with him in declaring the empire hereditary; and he had annexed to it, for ever, the kingdoms of *Naples* and *Sicily*. This laſt meafure muſt have been very difagreeable to the empreſs, as it took from her and her poſterity the independency of her crown. *Jordani* was betrayed, and, being taken prifoner, he was put to death with the moſt exquifite torments, and his followers were executed likewife.

Henry now imagining that it would be impoffible for the *Sicilians* ever after to diſturb his government, no longer refifted the importunities of his army to go to the *Holy Land*; and they marched off with the bifhop of *Wurtzburg* at their head. The empreſs had watched for this juncture, and fhe employed *Renaldo* and *Landolph* to fpirit up a general infurrection. They were fo fuccefsful, that *Landolph* was chofen head of the infurgents; and he immediately publifhed an edict, abolifhing all the taxes and penalties that the emperor had laid upon the *Sicilians*. This had the defired effect. The empreſs now openly acted, and advanced, at the head of an army which joined her, againſt her wicked huſband, who was

obliged

A rebellion againſt him, headed by the empreſs.

obliged to fhut himfelf up in a caftle, where he was befieged, but found means to enter into a negotiation; by
which he partly recovered his liberty: but happening to His death,
fleep in an unwholefome air, after hunting, he contracted a
difeafe, of which he died. Some have faid that he was poifoned by the emprefs; but this charge agrees ill with the
general tenour of her conduct. He died in the year 1197,
in the feventh year of his reign, and the thirty-fecond of his
age.

Never did any prince make a worfe ufe than *Henry* did of and cha-
the advantages which nature and education gave him. His racter.
perfon was tall, beautiful, and well-fhaped; his manner of
addrefs noble: his elocution irrefiftible; his judgment true
and penetrating; his views extenfive, but well compacted;
and his courage and conduct in war equal to that of any general of the age. With all thofe accomplifhments, his ambition, avarice, meannefs, and perfidy, could only be exceeded by the cruelties he exercifed, efpecially upon the *Sicilians*. His ambition was fo great, that he fummoned the
Greek emperor to pay him homage for his empire; and, as
he died in the flower of his age, it is more than probable,
that, had he lived, he would have attempted either to have
poffeffed himfelf of it, or to have rendered it tributary by
force. Two obftacles lay in the way of this fcheme. The
firft was the violent impulfe which prevailed among the
Germans to enter upon the crufade, which was fo ftrong that
it fwallowed up all other confiderations of policy and ambition. The next was the dreadful misfortunes which attended the *Germans* who were employed in thofe expeditions;
for there is little reafon to doubt, that, had any confiderable
number of them furvived, *Henry* intended to have put himfelf
at their head, and to have attacked the *Greeks*, whom they
hated worfe than they did the infidels themfelves. *Henry's*
great principle of government was, that all the difmember-
ments which had been made from the empire fince the days
of *Charles the Great*, were only fo many profperous ufurpations; and therefore it was lawful for him to employ all the
means that were in his power to refume them. He found it
not eafy to break the power of the great princes of his empire,
but, at laft, he fucceeded by weakening the abfurd dependence of the vaffal upon his fuperior. His father had begun
to attack that principle of the feudal-law, but did not go fo
far as the fon did towards abolifhing it. *Henry*, at the time
of his death, was the terror of *Europe* and *Afia*; and he had
the peculiar happinefs of being well ferved by his brothers,
who merited all the great favours he heaped upon them.

24. Philip I. *of* Suabia.

Philip
chofen
king of
the *Ro-
mans.*

IT is evident, from what follows, that neither the princes of the empire, nor the pope, thought themfelves bound by what they were forced to agree to in the reign of *Henry* VI. The duke of *Suabia* was upon his march towards *Italy* when he received an account of his brother's death near *Meffina*, together with the regalia, and his laft will, conftituting him guardian to his nephew, *Frederic* II. during his minority. He, at the fame time, received intelligence that all the *Sicilians* were in arms under the emprefs *Conftance*, and that a general maffacre had been committed upon the *Germans* in the two *Sicilies*. Thofe events determined him to return to *Germany*, to affert his own, and his nephew's, rights.

Innocent III. had fucceeded *Celeftine* III. in the popedom, and was difpofed to carry the pontifical pretenfions to their utmoft height; but he was obliged to conceal his ambition during the reign of the late emperor. *Henry* was no fooner dead than *Innocent* abfolved from their oaths the *Germans* who had recognized young *Frederic* king of the *Romans*, and exhorted the archbifhops of *Triers* and *Cologne*, and all the *German* princes with whom he had any influence, to proceed to a new election, and tranffer the empire from the houfe of *Suabia*. In confequence of thofe letters, the two archbifhops, with the count-palatine of the *Rhine*, the landgrave of *Thuringia*, and feveral other princes, both fpiritual and temporal, met at *Cologne*, to elect an emperor, who fhould not be formidable by his paternal dominions; and their choice fell upon *Berthold*, duke of *Zeringia*, a fmall diftrict in *Swifferland*; but he declined the honour: and their fecond choice fell upon *Otho*, of *Saxony*, fon of *Henry the Lion*.

*Oppofed
by Otho.*

Germany was then in a moft dreadful fituation. The houfe of *Suabia* was fupported by the archbifhops of *Mentz*, *Magdebourg*, and *Befançon*; the king of *Bohemia*; the dukes of *Saxony*, *Bavaria*, *Auftria*, and *Moravia*; with many other bifhops and princes of great power and influence. *Otho*, affembling his party, was crowned, at *Aix-la-Chapelle*, by the archbifhop of *Cologne*; and his election was confirmed by the pope, who excommunicated *Philip* and all the adherents of the houfe of *Suabia*. Young *Frederic's* party, on the other hand, affembled at *Arnfberg*, where they confirmed his election as emperor; but chofe his uncle *Philip* king of the *Romans*, and gave him the executive power of the government. *Otho* was fupported by *Richard* I. of *England*, and *Philip* by *Philip Auguftus* of *France*, who himfelf had an eye upon the empire. Nothing was feen all over *Germany* but devaftations and fire; and the party of *Philip*, in general, was prevalent.

It

It feems, by the complexion of hiftory, as if *Philip* had been, by his party, elected, not only king of the *Romans*, but emperor of *Germany*; and he is accordingly mentioned in hiftory as fuch. It is probable that even many of the friends of the houfe of *Suabia* did not think the election of *Frederic* II. to be king of the *Romans*, regular; and *Philip* was again crowned at *Mentz* by the archbifhop of *Tarentum*, who acted for the archbifhop of that city and the archbifhop of *Triers*, who had quitted *Otho*'s party.

Philip, after this fecond coronation, burnt the towns of *Philip* Bonn, *Coblentz*, and others belonging to the oppofite party, prevails. and laid fiege to *Brunfwic*; but he was obliged to raife it, and retire to *Alface*, where he forced the inhabitants to fwear allegiance to him in the city of *Strafbourg*. About this time, *Premiflaus*, king of *Bohemia*, one of *Otho*'s moft fanguine partizans, joined *Philip*, in confideration of a family marriage between the daughter of the one and the fon of the other, both of them in their cradles. This marriage proving a difappointment to the count-palatine, *Otho*'s brother, he befieged *Wurtzburg*; but an accommodation took place between the count and *Philip*, who promifed him the inveftiture of *Brunfwic*, which, however, he never could obtain from *Otho*. *Richard*, king of *England*, who, by means of the vaft treafures he had furnifhed him, had been *Otho*'s chief fupport, was now dead, and was fucceeded by his brother *John*, who refufed to pay *Otho* the legacy which *Richard* had bequeathed to him, and leagued himfelf with the king of *France*.

In the mean while, the emprefs *Conftance* died in *Sicily*, Death of where fhe was regent, and gave her fon an excellent educa- the emtion. He had been crowned king of *Sicily* by the confent of prefs *Con-* pope *Celeftine*; but, upon his death, a new inveftiture being *ftance*. demanded from *Innocent* III. in his favour, the pope infifted upon the kings of *Sicily* renouncing the right which they had obtained from former popes of being legates, and filling up vacant fees in their own dominions, and of judging ecclefiaftical matters in the laft refort, without any appeal to the holy fee; but thofe matters were not decided at the time of the death of *Conftance*, who, however, left the regency of her kingdom to the pope during the minority of her fon.

His holinefs having gained this great point, he renewed and redoubled his efforts in favour of *Otho*, and for excluding his pupil *Frederic*, as well as *Philip*, from the imperial throne, of which he pretended, by the authority of almighty God, to be the fole difpofer, as fucceffor to St. *Peter*; for in thofe terms his manifeftos ran. In other letters he declared that *Philip* muft either lofe the empire or he the papacy. This haughtinefs hurt him with the *German* princes as well as with *Philip*, king of *France*; for, though his legates had again excommunicated *Philip*, and confirmed *Otho*'s election, yet the intereft of the latter daily dwindled away.

A new

A new crufade was fet on foot about this time. The *Venetians* were at the head of it; and their doge, *Dandalo*, af- ter reducing *Zara*, a town in *Dalmatia*, which had formerly belonged to the *Venetians*, took *Conftantinople*, and reftored the emperor *Ifaac Angelus*, who had been dethroned, and de- prived of his eye-fight, by his brother *Alexius Comnenus*.

Confuſed ſtate of the em- pire,

Though many *Germans* were engaged in this crufade, yet it was not an object of their public attention. All the empire was then in confufion; *Adolphus*, count of *Holſtein*, was de- feated by *Waldemar*, in an invafion he made upon the pro- vince of *Ditharmiſe:* the *Danes* were, in their turn, defeated by *Otho*, marquis of *Brandenburgh*, who fided with *Adolphus;* but the *Danes* fucceeded at laft; for they took *Adolphus* pri- foner, added his dominions to their own crown, and reduced the cities of *Hamburgh* and *Lubec*. Thofe conquefts of the *Danes* were favoured by the anarchy in which the affairs of *Germany* lay, through the conteft for power which ftill continued between *Philip* and *Otho*. The great *German* princes paid no regard to either farther than their own inte- reft, or conveniency, led them; and thus there was a per- petual fluctuation of parties in the empire. The princes who efpoufed one fide in one week, joined with the other in the next; till the fword, at laft, gave law; and a moft cruel civil-war took place; fathers, fons, and brothers, butchered each other; and no rank or order was regarded. *Philip* depopulated *Thuringia*, and degraded *Premiſlaus* from the throne of *Bohemia* and the title of royalty. In fhort, *Philip* had both virtues and abilities fuperior to his competi- tor. The landgrave of *Thuringia* fubmitted to him; the count-palatine declared againft his own brother *Otho*, who was, at the fame time, deferted by his capital friend, the archbifhop of *Cologne*.

which is poffeffed by *Philip* without a rival.

Philip, though he was ftill ftrongly oppofed by the pope, had now no rival in the empire. He was acknowledged by the duke of *Brabant*, and *Otho's* moft powerful friends; and, in token of his triumph, he was, a fecond time, crowned at *Aix-la-Chapelle*, by the hands of that very archbifhop of *Co- logne* who had crowned his rival. The pope, though unable to fupport *Otho* againft *Philip*, found fo much employment for the latter, that he became more powerful than ever in *Italy*, and confirmed himfelf in great part of the litigated eftates of the famous *Matilda*.

He and *Otho* concurred, about the year 1203, in inftituting a new order of *German* knights, who had the title of *Enſ- feri* from their wearing long fwords, and were bound by the ufual laws of chivalry, but entitled to all the conquefts they could make upon the pagans.

Otho, notwithftanding his expedients, was, at laft, for- faken by all but the army, which he and the pope paid. A vacancy of the archbifhopric of *Cologne* happening, the new archbifhop efpoufed his caufe, and received him and his ar- my

my into his capital, where they were fhut up by *Philip*, tho'
he ftood, at the time, excommunicated by the pope. *Otho*,
in defpair, made a fally, which terminated in a general engagement, wherein his troops were entirely routed. The
new archbifhop of *Cologne* was taken prifoner, and *Otho* fled
to *England*, his never failing afylum. The important city
of *Cologne* then fell into the hands of *Philip*, who kept the
pope's archbifhop in ftrait durance, and began now to think
of reftoring tranquility to the empire. For this purpofe, as
wifely as generoufly, he pardoned all paft offences againft
his perfon and dignity; he beftowed one of his daughters in
marriage upon *Wenceflaus*, whom he had made king of *Bohemia* by his imperial authority; he gave another to the eldeft
fon of the duke of *Brabant*, who had been a ftrenuous afferter
of his intereft; and fuch was his zeal for peace, that he even
attempted to purchafe it by acts of liberality and munificence;
nay, he went fo far as to propofe terms to his two capital
enemies, his competitor *Otho* and the *Roman* pontif. The
latter demanded, as the price of his friendfhip, and in confideration of his taking off *Philip's* excommunication, that
he would give his fifter in marriage to the nephew of his
holinefs, together with the dutchies of *Spoleto* and *Tufcany*,
and the marche of *Ancona*. *Philip* rejected the propofal; and He is ab-
the pope, feeing that he had power on his fide, abfolved him folved,
from his excommunication upon his releafing the captive
archbifhop of *Cologne*, and granting his holinefs fome other
trifling advantages.

This reconciliation could not have been fo eafily effected,
had not *Otho*, who had great family alliances, again appeared
in *Germany*, and brought the *Danes*, who were then the moft
powerful neighbours of the empire, to favour his pretenfions,
and to march a body of troops towards *Saxony*. *Philip* was
waiting for his army at *Bamberg*, and under confinement in
his chamber through a flight indifpofition. While he was and affaf-
there, count *Otho*, of *Wittelfbach*, a *Bavarian* palantine, came finated.
into the room, and, without any provocation, thruft his
fword through *Philip's* throat; and, favoured by the confternation of his attendants, made his efcape; while *Philip* died
with the lofs of blood.

Various are the conjectures concerning the murderer's motives, but they moft probably were of a family kind. Some
fay, that, having been declared infamous for a former murder, *Philip* had refufed to perform a promife he had given
him of one of his daughters in marriage. Others pretend
that *Philip* had promifed to marry the palatine's daughter;
but refufed, for the fame reafon, to fulfil the contract.

Philip, according to all accounts, inherited, by nature,
every quality of an accomplifhed prince; as appears from the
vaft difficulties which he had furmounted at the time of his
death.

25. Otho IV.

WE are under fome difficulty in pronouncing either *Philip* or *Otho* to have been real emperors of *Germany*, as young *Frederic*, who had been acknowledged king of the *Romans*, was ftill alive in *Sicily*; but, as they poffeffed the entire power of the empire, we have followed the general arrangement of the *German* hiftorians. An accommodation, at the time of *Philip*'s death, had been fo far advanced between him and *Otho*, that hiftorians are in doubt whether the latter was not married to *Philip*'s daughter *Beatrix*. The contrary opinion is moft probable.

Succeeded by Otho, who marries his daughter. Upon *Philip*'s death being divulged, *Otho* took upon himfelf the adminiftration of the empire; and, in a diet which he called at *Holberftadt*, he was recognized by the princes of *Saxony*, *Thuringia*, and *Mifnia*. At this diet *Beatrix* appeared in perfon, and demanded juftice from the princes upon the murderer of her father, who was accordingly put to the ban of the empire, and foon after killed by a count of *Pappenheim*. A kind of coalition of parties then took place, by *Otho* marrying *Beatrix*, who foon after died. Nothing could be more agreeable to the pope than *Otho*'s thus becoming mafter of the empire, and he offered to give him the imperial crown if he would receive it in *Italy*. *Otho*, on the other hand, promifed to gratify the pope in all his demands, and to relinquifh the exercife of feizing the eftates and effects of deceafed ecclefiaftics. In the year 1209, *Otho* promifed, by letter, to yield to pope *Innocent* III. all the obedience which the emperors, his predeceffors, had paid to former popes; and he not only confirmed him in the poffeffion of *Viterbo*, *Orvieto*, and *Perufa*, but promifed to reinftate him in the whole inheritance of *Matilda*, and to admit his claim of a territorial fuperiority over *Naples* and *Sicily*.

Otho then called a diet at *Haguenau*, where he appointed *Rodolphus*, count of *Hafpurg*, to be vicar of the empire during his abfence in *Italy*, and to reprefent his perfon in *Germany*. He then marched, at the head of an army, to *Rome*; where he received the imperial crown from the hand of the pope, to whom he confirmed the ceffion he had made him of *Matilda*'s inheritance.

Otho's differences with the pope. It foon appeared that *Otho* was far from being fincere in thofe compliances; and, indeed, at that time, the interefts of a pope and an emperor of *Germany* were incompatible. During *Otho*'s refidence at *Rome*, a quarrel happened between his foldiers and the *Romans*; and, one thoufand *Germans* being killed in the fcuffle, the emperor complained to the pope and demanded juftice. The pontif looked upon this demand as being little better than infolence, and the emperor left

Rome

Rome without receiving fatisfaction, but fecretly refolved to do himfelf right by his fword. He wintered in *Lombardy,* and, early in the fpring of 1210, he publifhed his intention of reannexing to the empire all the dominions that had been difmembered from it. Thefe comprehended all the inheritance of *Matilda* and the dominions of young *Frederic.* As the *Germans* were incomparably better foldiers than the *Italians, Otho* met with no great difficulty in feizing *Apulia.* It was in vain for the pope to expoftulate with him, for he retracted all that he had promifed in favour of the holy fee: upon which *Innocent* III. thundered out an excommunication againft him, and fent it to be promulgated, by the archbifhop of *Mentz,* throughout all the *German* empire. This proved the ruin of *Otho.* His fubjects were abfolved from their allegiance; and, at a diet held at *Bamberg,* the king of *Bohemia,* the dukes of *Bavaria* and *Auftria,* the landgrave of *Thuringia,* and the other great princes of the empire, renounced their allegiance to him; and chofe, in his room, young *Frederic,* who was then about feventeen years of age, fon to the emperor *Henry* VI.

Otho, upon this, returned to *Germany,* and called a diet of the princes of his party at *Nuremberg;* where he laid before them his reafons for feizing *Apulia,* and the other imperial fiefs of *Italy;* which they approved of. Encouraged by this recognition, *Otho* beftowed the crown of *Bohemia* upon the fon of that king, who had repudiated his wife and married an *Hungarian* princefs. *Otho* then proceeded vigoroufly againft the landgrave of *Thuringia,* the archbifhop of *Mentz,* and the other princes who had fided with the pope. Thofe proceedings embroiled him with *Philip Auguftus,* king of *France,* who had fhewn a great contempt for his perfon and underftanding, and who was, at that time, at war with *England.* He feizes the imperial fiefs in *Italy,*

In the mean while, young *Frederic* paffed the *Alps;* feized upon *Alface;* was joined by the duke of *Lorrain* and a number of other princes; and *Germany,* from its one end to the other, became a fcene of civil-war. Notwithftanding thefe unpromifing appearances againft *Otho,* his great intereft in *England* fupported him. He was joined by the dukes of *Limburg* and *Lorrain* (who, it feems, had changed his party, unlefs there were more dukes of *Lorrain* than one) and the counts of *Holland* and *Flanders;* and, being at the head of one hundred and ten thoufand fighting men, he drove young *Frederic* out of *Germany* into *Swifferland,* and advanced to fight the *French,* who were encamped at *Bovines,* near *Tournay.* Here one of the moft remarkable battles of that age was fought; but the reader who has no knowledge of the antient armour can form but a very indifferent idea of it. The generals and great men of thofe days were immured in fteel, in proportion to the property they held and the men they brought to the field. A count was better armed than a but lofes the empire in the battle of *Bovines.*

knight,

knight, a knight than an esquire, and an esquire than a peasant, who was almost defenceless. Thus few men of any
rank were killed in the most bloody battle. In this of *Bovines* the king of *France* was thrown from his horse and rode
over; but, so impenetrable was his armour, that, though
he lay at the mercy of his enemies, they could not fall upon
a way to kill him. Notwithstanding this accident, his troops
got a complete victory; and the battle of *Bovines* is dwelt
upon, with great pleasure, by the *French* historians. Thirty
thousand *Germans*, by whom are meant ill-armed peasants, are
said to have died on the spot; but no man, of any rank or
consideration, on the part of the *French*, except one *William
Longchamps*; nor are we made acquainted with the precise
number of the *French* slain. The victory of *Philip* was owing to his superiority in cavalry over the *Germans*, which,
undoubtedly, gave him a decisive advantage. The loss of
the *French*, however, must have been very considerable, as
Philip Augustus, the most designing and ambitious prince
of his age, did not improve his victory on the side of *Germany*. *Otho*'s imperial standard, which resembled the mast of
a ship, surmounted with a dragon, and fixed in the midst of
a huge machine, drawn by oxen, was taken by *Philip*, who
sent it to young *Frederic* as the badge of empire. As to *Otho*,
he escaped with difficulty, but never could recover the blow
he then received.

Successes
of *Frede
ric* II.

Frederic was in *Swisserland*, where he secretly cultivated
the friendship of that people and many of the *German* princes,
when he received the joyful news of *Otho*'s defeat; and, that
his friends, the counts of *Flanders* and *Boulogne*, who had
been taken prisoners, were carried to *Paris*, loaded, after
the barbarous manner of that time, with heavy irons. As
the *Swisses* shewed a particular attachment to *Frederic*, he distinguished them, upon this happy turn of his fortune, with
great immunities; and, by his bounty and noble behaviour,
he captivated the hearts of the *Germans* in general; so that
every thing seemed now to yield to his fortune. He gave the
kingdom of *Arles* to *William* V. prince of *Orange*, in vassalage to the empire. He bestowed the temporalities of *Strasbourg* upon its bishop, and conferred particular favours upon
the other principal towns of *Alsace*.

Having passed the *Moselle*, the towns which had been the
most attached to *Otho*, submitted to his authority, as did the
duke of *Brabant*, with all the counties of *Juliers* and *Westphalia*. *Waldemar*, king of *Denmark*, was the only power
whom he had now to dread; and the price of his friendship
was a formal cession of *Holstein*, with the towns of *Lubec* and
Hamburgh, which were to be dismembered from the empire
and annexed to the *Danish* crown; to which *Frederic* agreed.
This stipulation was resented by the count-palatine, the
margrave of *Brandenburg*, the bishop of *Bremen*, and some
other princes, who exclaimed against it as being injurious
and

and difgraceful to the empire; but, though they feized *Ham-burgh*, they were foon obliged to fubmit, by the prevailing arms of *Frederic* and *Waldemar*.

Here, properly fpeaking, ends the reign of the emperor *Otho*; who, finding himfelf abandoned by all the princes of the empire, retired to *Brunfwic*, where he betook himfelf to a private life for four years, and ended his days in indolence and ignominy.

---

26. Frederic II.

THIS prince came to the empire with great advantages arifing from his illuftrious anceftors, and *Otho* having left behind him no male iffue. He had a noble education from his mother, and, befides the *Italian*, is faid to have been mafter of the *Greek*, *Latin*, *German*, *French*, and *Turkifh* languages; and, to thofe liberal accomplifhments, he joined an elevated genius and moft engaging manners. He was not, however, free from the religious follies of the times. Perceiving himfelf to be at the head of the empire without a rival, and, by the death of his uncle, having added to his great patrimonial eftate the dutchy of *Suabia* and the county of *Rottenburg*, he took upon himfelf a vow to go in perfon to the *Holy Land*. Being crowned at *Aix-la-Chapelle*, and eftablifhed in the empire, the count-palatine of the *Rhine*, brother to the late emperor *Otho*, was put to the ban of the empire; and his dominions were given to the duke of *Bavaria*, whofe eldeft fon was married to the count-palatine's daughter. *Frederic* then applied himfelf to refettle the police of his dominions, which a long continuance of civil-wars had almoft abolifhed.

In the year 1216, pope *Innocent* III. who had made fo diftinguifhed a figure during his pontificate, died; and he was fucceeded by *Honorius* III. Nothing contributed more to the papal intereft, than the finding employment for the emperors of *Germany*; and *Honorius* eagerly preffed *Frederic* to fulfil his vow of going to the *Holy Land*. *Frederic*, who had, by this time, probably repented of his rafhnefs, begged to be excufed till he fhould eftablifh his authority in *Germany*, and receive the imperial crown from his holinefs in *Italy*. This backwardnefs on the part of the emperor did not daunt the fpirit of the crufade, which, as ufual, infected all ranks of men: *Germany*, *Sweden*, *Denmark*, *Bohemia*, and *Hungary*, embraced it; and the pope declared *Andrew* II. king of *Hungary*, commander in chief. Three hundred fail of fhips were provided at *Venice*, *Genoa*, *Meffina*, and other ports of the *Mediterranean*, for the *German* adventurers only. In their voyage, being driven by ftrefs of weather to *Lifbon*, they

(marginal note: who is arifing chofen emperor.)

(marginal note: Death of pope Innocent III. who is fucceeded by Honorius III.)

they defeated the *Moors*, and replaced *Alphonso*, king of *Portugal*, upon his throne. The king of *Hungary*, and his army, was joyfully received at *Acra* by the king of *Jerusalem* and the various orders of knights; but, being unfortunate in every expedition he undertook, he returned to his own dominions; as did the duke of *Austria*, whom he left behind, and several other crusaders.

Frederic prepares to go to Italy,

The absence of those great men was a favourable circumstance for the emperor *Frederic*; but the cities of *Milan* and *Placentia*, and other imperial fiefs in *Italy*, having tasted the sweets of liberty, refused, while *Otho* lived, to acknowledge him for their master; and, upon *Otho*'s death, most unwillingly submitted to his authority. *Frederic*, finding the pope's friendship absolutely necessary to his affairs, promised to bestow the kingdom of *Sicily* on his own son *Henry*, as soon as he received the imperial crown in *Italy*; and, having held a diet at *Goslar*, where he was reconciled to the count-palatine, he quelled some public commotions in the empire; and, in another diet, held at *Francfort*, he declared his resolution of going to receive the imperial crown at *Rome*; upon which a vote passed by the princes for providing him with whatever could contribute towards his appearing with the utmost splendour in *Italy*. It had been always the custom of the emrors, when they undertook that journey, to send before them a bishop, or some other ecclesiastic, as their harbinger, with credentials to prepare the way for their reception. *Frederic* made use of his chancellor, *Conrade*, bishop of *Spire*, who was to administer the oath of allegiance to the emperor's subjects in *Italy*. He then gave his young son, *Henry*, in charge to the count of *Boland*, and appointed a council for the management of public affairs; well knowing that the miscarriages of his predecessors in *Italy* were owing to the intrigues and the wars of secular and temporal princes in *Germany* during their absence. He issued out charters of immunity in favour of both; and, in particular, he enacted that the effects of deceased bishops should devolve to their successors; and, that no emperor, by his own prerogative, should encrease the taxes or alter the coin. He next reconciled all the differences among his great men; and then passed the *Alps* at the head of his army.

and is crowned at Rome.

The *Milanese* refused him admittance into their city, and he was obliged to content himself with receiving the submissions of other places, who were willing to own him as their sovereign. Above all, he took care to keep in friendship with the pope, by renewing his promise not to re-annex the kingdoms of *Naples* and *Sicily* to the empire, but to give them to his son. Not chusing to venture his person among the *Romans* without a sufficient force, he was joined by the army he had in *Italy*; and then he received the imperial crown from *Honorius* III. but swore to defend all the rights and privileges of the holy see, including *Matilda*'s inheritance; and to march,

whenever

whenever the pope should require him, with his army, against the infidels.

Notwithstanding those fair appearances, *Honorius* suspected the emperor's sincerity. He declared, by virtue of his own prerogative, and the consent of the *German* princes, his son *Henry* king of the *Romans*; and he betrothed him to *Margaret*, daughter to *Leopold*, duke of *Austria*. He then visited the kingdom of *Naples*, out of which he drove two brothers of pope *Innocent*, who had been practising against his authority. The death of *Otho*, which happened, near *Brunswic*, in 1218, was of great service to *Frederic*, as it took from the *Lombard* cities all pretext of their disowning him for emperor. To keep the pope easy, however, he issued many bloody decrees against the heretics, or the *Albigenses*, of those times; particularly, that the son of a heretic should not inherit his father's estate. He likewise was obliged to wink at the protection which the pope gave to some of his *Neapolitan* rebels; and to send a good fleet, and army, under the duke of *Bavaria*, to join the crusaders in the east. The pope strenuously pressed him to go in person; but *Frederic* excused himself by marching against the *Saracens* of *Sicily*, whom he had entirely reduced; and by multiplying favours on the holy see at the expence of other princes and states.

In the year 1223, while *Frederic* was laudably employed in aggrandizing and embellishing his favourite city of *Naples*, and rendering it a seminary of learning, the archbishop of *Cologne* crowned his son *Henry* at *Aix-la-Chapelle*, that *Germany* might not be without a head; and the young prince immediately entered upon the exercise of sovereignty. The great grievance of *Germany*, at that time, consisted in the abuse of the feudal powers; and the policy of the emperors was to encourage the erection of free cities and towns, who attempted to render themselves independent of the great fiefs. *Henry* held a diet at *Aix-la-Chapelle*, where many regulations were made for the better administration of justice; and made a progress through the principal towns of *Germany*, where he abolished many oppressive powers, particularly in *Alsace*. That same year, *Henry*, by order of his father, renewed his treaties with the crown of *France*, in the person of *Lewis* VIII. who had succeeded *Philip Augustus*; and, among other stipulations, he promised never to assist *England* against *France*.

At this time, an opportunity presented itself to the empire for its resuming its superiority over *Denmark*. *Waldemar* II. king of *Denmark*, who had extended his dominions over almost all the countries bordering on the *Baltic*, was, together with his son, surprized, seized, and made prisoner, upon a family quarrel, by the count of *Meclenburgh Schwerin*. *Waldemar*, and his friends, applied to the emperor and the pope for their deliverance; but the diet of the empire informed them,

Honorius suspected Differ-ence between him and the pope, on account of the holy war.

Confederacy in Italy against the emperor.

them, that, if *Waldemar* expected any affiftance from the princes, he muft, as his predeceffors had done, hold his crown of the empire. The pope, on the other hand, laid claim to the fame dependence, on pretence that the kingdom of *Denmark* was a fief of the holy fee. *Waldemar* and his fon rejecting thofe terms, their enemies divided their fpoils. The count of *Schwerin*, the archbifhop of *Bremen*, the princes of the houfe of *Saxony*, and others, reduced *Holftein* and *Hamburgh*, and the country to the north of the *Elbe*; and the knights of the *Teutonic* order feized *Revel*, and the adjacent territory on the coaft of the *Baltic*. The *Vandals*, *Sclavonians*, *Pomeranians*, and other ftates and people, threw off the *Danish* yoke; and each had a fhare of *Waldemar*'s plunder: but, at laft, after a long and fevere captivity, they were fet at liberty, upon promifing to pay a ranfom of forty-five thoufand marks of filver.

About the fame time, violent difputes happened in *Alface* about the inheritance of the countefs of *Dafburg*; to which the bifhops of *Mentz*, *Liege*, and *Strafbourg*, the duke of *Brabant*, the marquis of *Baden*, and other princes, laid claim. After a great deal of blood had been fpilt by the competitors, the affair was, at laft, compromifed by the interpofition of the emperor and *Engelbert*, archbifhop of *Cologne*, who was foon after affaffinated. This prelate was looked upon as the wifeft of all the *German* princes. He was tutor to the young king of the *Romans*, in which office he was fucceeded by *Lewis*, duke of *Bavaria*.

Affairs of the *Holy* Land. We have, in the former part of this work, given a full account of the bad fuccefs of the crufaders of that time, who loft the important city of *Damietta* to the infidels. *John de Brienne*, who was little more than a nominal king of *Jerufalem*, and the grand mafter of the *Teutonic* order, were folliciting frefh recruits of crufaders, to fave the little that was ftill left to the *Chriftians* in the eaft; and the pope reproached the emperor, as having, through the breach of his vows, occafioned the lofs of *Damietta*; and threatened even to excommunicate him if he did not immediately fet out upon the expedition. *Frederic* had eftablifhed his authority too firmly in *Italy* to dread the thunder of the vatican. He even feemed glad of an opportunity to refume the full extent of imperial power, as exercifed by his predeceffors, both as emperors and kings of *Sicily*. He revived the rights of legation in *Naples*, by which he actually became a pope in his *Italian* dominions. He filled up vacant fees, and banifhed the bifhops who had been put in by the pope. *Honorius* renewed his threatenings, and *Frederic* defpifed them; and it was now plain that the latter intended to found a new empire in *Italy*, and to make that country his refidence; which might, in time, have annihilated the papal power. *Honorius* began to think he had gone too far, efpecially as *Frederic* had publifhed a manifefto

to juſtify his own conduct. He applied to the emperor in a *Frederic*
ſoothing, ſubmiſſive manner ; and they were not only recon- *marries*
ciled, but *Frederic*, being now a widower by the death of his *the king*
wife, *Conſtance*, of *Arragon*, *Honorius* had the addreſs to en- *of Jeruſa-*
gage him to marry the princeſs *Yolanda*, daughter to the king *lem's*
of *Jeruſalem*; to which crown ſhe was heireſs in right of her *daughter.*
mother *Iſabella*. It is uncertain what *Frederic's* motives
might be for this impolitic, unprofitable, marriage. Though
he was a great and a wiſe prince, he was not, perhaps, proof
againſt the vanity (to ſay nothing of religious principles) of
adding the honour of being king of *Jeruſalem* to the other
titles of his family. He likewiſe might have been influenced
by the hopes of recovering part of the territory which the
Chriſtians had conquered and loſt in the eaſt. Whatever may
be in thoſe conſiderations, it is certain that the pope exerted
himſelf, in an unuſual manner, to ſupport *Frederic* in his expedition ; but it was two years before the princeſs *Yolanda*
arrived in *Italy* from *Ptolemais.*

The *German* princes, in general, ſhewed themſelves well *Confede-*
diſpoſed to ſupport the enterprize ; and preparations were *racy in*
made accordingly, when *Frederic* received undoubted intel- *Italy*
ligence that the chief towns in *Lombardy* were confederated *againſt*
againſt him. It was eaſy for the emperor to ſee that the pope *Frederic.*
himſelf was at the bottom of this confederacy, and that it
would break out the moment he left *Italy*. The confederate
towns, beſides others of leſs note, were *Milan, Bologna, Verona,*
Placentia, Breſcia, Mantua, Vercelli, Lodi, Bergamo, Turin,
Alexandria, and *Vicenza*; and their troops were to be commanded by *Boniface*, marquis of *Montferrat*. No confederacy
was, perhaps, ever formed upon truer principles of liberty
than this was. The cities did not pretend to ſeparate themſelves from the empire, but to aſſert thoſe immunities and
privileges which ſome of them had bought, and others obtained, from former emperors, particularly *Frederic Barba-*
roſſa ; which the reigning emperor refuſed to confirm. *Fre-*
deric ſeems to have held a dangerous maxim, that no anceſtor can renounce the rights of his poſterity. This is a principle that tends to unhinge every acquiſition of liberty, and
is in itſelf deteſtable. The truth is, the popes, in this queſtion, were on the ſide of freedom ; for that of *Italy* was in
danger of ſinking under the imperial power. *Frederic* again
refuſed to ſet out on his cruſade ; but promiſed, under pain
of excommunication, to do it in two years ; to which *Hono-*
rius was obliged to conſent.

Frederic ſummoned a general aſſembly at *Cremona*, to
which all the towns and ſtates of *Italy* were invited to ſend
deputies. He, at the ſame time, ordered his ſon, the king
of the *Romans*, to attend him, at the ſame place with a body
of troops. The confederates then avowed, and renewed,
their aſſociation, and placed troops in the defiles of the *Alps,*
which prevented that prince from penetrating into *Italy*.

The

The breach now widened, every day, between *Frederic* and the pope. The latter did all he could to prohibit the meeting of the affembly at *Cremona*; and, at laft, a paper war was kindled up, in which each loaded the other with the moft opprobrious and illiberal language. The pope had a great party in *Germany*, and the emperor had the fame in *Italy*; but *Frederic* perceived plainly that the *Italians* in general were diffatisfied with his government. He had been again refufed admittance into *Milan*, which he had put to the ban of the empire; and he had tranflated the univerfity of *Bologna* to *Naples*: but thofe meafures ferved only to make him more and more unpopular in *Italy*; and, at laft, he deigned to admit the pope as umpire between him and the confederate ftates, who agreed to the arbitration. The award of his holinefs was, That the emperor fhould lay afide all refentment towards the confederates for what had paffed, and revoke all his penal edicts; but, that the confederates fhould furnifh him with four hundred knights, for two years, to ferve under him in the *Holy Land*. Soon after this accommodation was effected, pope *Honorius* died, and was fucceeded by *Gregory* IX. who was nearly related to the difcontented part of *Frederic*'s fubjects in *Naples*, and adopted all the principles of his predeceffor, but was ftill of a more haughty difpofition. We are now to attend the affairs of *Germany*.

Agnes, wife to the king of the *Romans*, in the year 1227, was crowned at *Aix-la-Chapelle*, where *Henry* accommodated feveral differences among the *German* ftates. That fame year, a quarrel broke out between *Henry* and the houfe of *Saxony*, on account of the fucceffion to the eftates of the count-palatine of the *Rhine*; which were claimed (he dying, without iffue) by the marquis of *Baden*, who had married his eldeft daughter, but had refigned his right to *Brunfwic* in favour of the emperor. The duke of *Saxony* had recourfe to the king of *Denmark*, who had, by the pope, been abfolved from the oath he was obliged to make while a prifoner, and defended *Brunfwic* againft the king of the *Romans*. *Waldemar*, by *Otho*'s affiftance, foon got poffeffion of *Lubec*, but as quickly loft its garrifon, by being expelled by the inhabitants; and, a commiffion arriving from the emperor to the counts of *Meclenburg* and the other northern princes of the empire, they compleatly defeated *Waldemar*, and recovered *Lawenburg*, *Holftein*, and all the *Lower Saxony*, to the empire. This was fome difappointment to pope *Gregory*, who preffed the emperor's departure for the *Holy Land* with fo much earneftnefs, that *Frederic* was, at laft, obliged to comply; and, having equipped a fleet, at a vaft expence, he actually failed from *Bundifi* with a powerful army and magnificent attendance. He had not been at fea above three hours, when, pretending ficknefs, he returned, but ordered his army to proceed. The pope, and all *Italy*, was convinced

that

that *Frederic's* return was owning to his diftruft of him and the *Italian* ftates ; and *Gregory* excommunicated him. The emperor, on his part, kept no farther meafures with his holinefs. He juftified himfelf to the *Germans*, and publifhed manifeftos in his own vindication, which he fent to all the princes of *Europe*. He then expelled from his dominions all who had treated him as an excommunicated prince, and laid his hands upon the effects of the *Knights Templars* wherever he could find them.

In the year 1228, he carried his army to *Rome*, *Frederic* whence the pope fled to *Perugia* ; but, after all, neither *Frederic's* power, nor fpirit, could conquer the temper of the *to Rome.* times. He was confidered as a prince who had incurred the heavy cenfure of excommunication by perjury ; and his wife *Yolanda*, who had brought him a young fon, *Conrade*, being dead, he prepared himfelf for the expedition in good earneft ; not fo much with a view of fighting the infidels, as of fecuring the remains of his fon's inheritance. He affembled his chief officers and noblemen at *Barletta*, in *Sicily* ; where he communicated to them his intention ; the execution of which was oppofed by the pope till his excommunication fhould be taken off. *Frederic* left full powers with *Renald*, duke of *Spoleto*, to treat with *Gregory* in his abfence ; and, without minding the papal inhibition, he fet fail for *Cyprus*, from whence he proceeded to *Ptolemais*. *Frederic* marches to *Rome.*

The pope had now carried his great point, that of confolidating the confederacy of the *Italian* ftates. He refufed to treat with *Renald*, who entered St. *Peter's* patrimony, and laid it wafte, with an army of *Germans* and *Sicilian Saracens*. The pope oppofed them with an army, the command of which he gave to *John de Brienne*. The reader, in the place referred to, will learn, from the beft *Moflem* and *Chriftian* authors, the fuccefs of *Frederic* in the *Holy Land*, where he entered *Jerufalem* in triumph ; and concluded, with *Camel* and *Moadhem*, a wife, and indeed a glorious, peace for the *Chriftians*. This was far from anfwering the views of the pope, who would have been glad to have heard of *Frederic's* ruin, and who difapproved of the treaty. See Vol. vii. Page 233.

Frederic returned to *Naples*, and found his affairs in *Italy* in great diforder; and he had now no chance for their being fettled, but his obliging the pope to take off the fentence of excommunication. For this purpofe, he marched againft his holinefs at the head of that very army which he had carried with him into *Syria*, and retook all the places which he had loft during his abfence. *Gregory* renewed his fulminations againft him and all his friends and followers, and abfolved his fubjects from their allegiance. He, at the fame time, complained of *Frederic* to all the princes of *Europe*, who paid him but very little attention. The *Italian Guelphs*, however, who were confederated againft *Frederic*, and whofe Diforders in *Italy*.

caufe

cause was really that of liberty, stuck by his holiness, because they were in no danger from his temporal power, and
might be served by his spiritual. But their troops had no
experience in war, and were not comparable to *Frederic's*
veterans; so that the emperor was everywhere victorious.
His successes seemed to inspire him with moderation; and,
at the desire of St. *Lewis*, king of *France*, he sent a deputation of prelates, with *Leopold*, duke of *Austria*, to treat with
his holiness at *Rome*. The pope, notwithstanding his distresses, refused to come to any equitable agreement, depending upon certain intrigues he was carrying on against *Frederic* in *Germany*, by his legate *Otho*, who offered the imperial
crown to the duke of *Brunswic*; but the latter refused it.
Otho then, in a diet held at *Wurtzburg*, exhorted the princes
to elect a new emperor; but they received his speech with so
much indignation, that he was in danger of being put to
death.

Reconcili-   His ill success inspired the pope, his master, with more
ation be-   moderate sentiments, which he found means to convey to
tween the   the emperor, and a peace was accordingly concluded; by
pope and   which *Frederic* engaged to give his holiness a pecuniary in-
emperor.   demnification for his damages, and the pope took off from
Frederic the sentence of excommunication under which he
lay. This treaty was executed at *Anagni*, with great appearances of cordiality on both sides. It was soon seen that the
Italian Guephs had less regard for the pope than their liberties;
for they refused to accede to the treaty, by which they were
to return in subjection to the emperor. Finding that they
were unable to stand against *Frederic* in the field, they joined
against him in a variety of intrigues in *Naples*, *Sicily*, and *Germany*. *Frederic*, in an assembly which he held at *Aquileia*,
had declared his resolution to reduce the confederates; but,
through the avocations he met with from the conspiracies
that broke out against him, he found he could do nothing effectual, unless he marched a new army of *Germans* into
Italy.

While he was preparing for this, a conspiracy, of the most
dangerous nature against him, was discovered; for it was
headed by his son *Henry*, king of the *Romans*. The cities of
Milan and *Bologna* had promised to join with *Henry*, as did
the duke of *Austria*, the bishop of *Strasbourg*, and almost all
the towns upon the *Rhine* from *Basil* to *Cologne*. *Henry*, having thus strengthened his party, ventured to hold a diet at
Boppart; where he complained of the injuries which the empire received by the continual dissentions between his father
and the pope, and the little power which he had in the empire; though, as king of the *Romans*, he was entitled to be
sole regent in his father's absence. The duke of *Bavaria*,
and the marquis of *Baden*, dissented from the rest of the assembly, who approved of what he said; and those two dukes

pressed

preſſed *Frederic* to come in perſon to *Germany*, which he accordingly did, and held a diet at *Mentz*. *Frederic*, on this occaſion, behaved with wonderful moderation. He applied himſelf to correct the real abuſes that had crept into *Germany* during his abſence, which had continued for fifteen years; and all the reſentment he ſhewed againſt his ſon, was to remove him to *Sicily*, that he might be at a diſtance from his dangerous *German* connections.

From thoſe proceedings, it appears very plain, that the views of *Henry* and his friends were founded on the emperor's abſence from *Germany*; for, on his arrival there, his ſon's party could make no head againſt him. *Frederic* then compoſed the differences that had ariſen between him and the houſe of *Savoy*, particularly the duke of *Lunenburg*, who had ſeized *Brunſwic*, as being heir-male to *Henry the Lion*, father to the late count-palatine. *Otho* obtained from the emperor the inveſtitures both of *Brunſwic* and *Lunenburg*; and the inhabitants of thoſe two dutchies were enjoined to receive him as their lawful lord, according to the laws and conſtitutions of the empire. This moderation was the more neceſſary, as it reconciled the princes of the empire to his ſcheme of carrying a new *German* army into *Italy* for the reduction of *Lombardy*. The pope offered to bring the confederates to a ſenſe of their duty, provided *Frederic* would remain in *Germany*; but, finding the emperor reſolute, he, and the confederate cities, renewed their intrigues with the king of the *Romans*, who promiſed to find the emperor ſufficient employment in the empire. *Frederic* coming to the knowledge of thoſe parties, made his ſon the principal object of his reſentment, and eaſily detached the pope from his intereſt.

Frederic returns to Germany,

In the year 1236, he once more marched into *Italy* with an army. Such of the cities and ſtates of *Lombardy* as could not reſiſt, ſubmitted to him; but the moſt powerful among them, encouraged by the aſſiſtances they expected from the king of the *Romans* and the *Venetians*, and depending upon a rebellion in *Germany*, refuſed him admittance. The pope took part with the emperor on this occaſion, and iſſued fulminations againſt all the adherents of *Henry* who ſhould abett him in his rebellion. None were ſo hardy as to do it; and the young prince, being ſeized, by his father's order, was ſhut up in *Apulia*, where he died. *Frederic*, duke of *Auſtria*, who had been the main inſtrument of *Henry*'s rebellion, ſtill was in arms againſt the emperor; who gave a commiſſion to the dukes of *Bohemia* and *Bavaria* to make head againſt him, till his affairs in *Italy* ſhould permit him to return to *Germany* and reduce him in perſon.

quells his ſon's rebellion,

Frederic, being now friends with the pope, had little to apprehend in *Italy*; and, returning to *Germany*, he entered the duke of *Auſtria*'s dominions, and took his capital, *Vienna*; where he founded the univerſity which ſtill ſubſiſts in

and ſubdues Auſtria.

that city: and his fon *Conrade* was elected, and crowned, king of the *Romans* at *Spire*. He then returned to *Italy* with a very numerous army, and there found the confederacy against him more powerful than ever. *Frederic*'s great failing was his arbitrary difposition towards thofe ftates whom he confidered as lawlefs ufurpers of his authority. The pope advifed him to moderate meafures, and to confirm the privileges that had been granted them by *Frederic Barbaroſſa* and other emperors. *Frederic* rejected this counfel. He forced his way into *Pavia*, and, to ſtrike the greater terror into his opponents, he abandoned feveral other places, which had been in the confederacy, to ſtorm and pillage.

Defeats the *Milaneſe*. The confederate army, commanded by *Tiepolo*, fon to the doge of *Venice*, was then lying at *Milan*, and as numerous as that of the emperor, who attacked and defeated them after a moft bloody battle, which lafted for feveral hours. Ten thoufand of the confederates were killed; and *Frederic* ordered the chief prifoners who fell into his hands to be put to death, as traitors, by common executioners. This victory, great as it was, was far from being decifive. The city of *Milan* was populous, ftrong, and rich; and *Frederic* forbore to attack it till he could reduce other places. After being inactive for a time at *Cremona*, he reduced fome towns in *Piedmont*; and confirmed fome of the *Lombard* cities, which were in his intereft, in their antient privileges, in an affembly at *Pavia*. *Mantua* being among the ftrong cities which *Frederic* had reduced in *Italy*, none of any confequence now held out againſt him but *Milan*, *Bologna*, *Alexandria*, and *Breſcia*.

Frederic was now arrived at that precife crifis of power in *Italy* which had always rendered the holy fee the enemy of the *German* emperors. He had made his natural fon, *Enzo*, a young man of great accomplifhments, count, fome call him king, of *Sardinia*; which the pope pretended to be a fief of the holy fee. He had publifhed fome decrees for the reformation of ecclefiaftical tribunals, and had feized the revenues of certain vacant bifhoprics in *Sicily*. In fhort, all his conduct pointed at an abfolute independence upon his holinefs.

The *Milaneſe*, all this while, were preparing for a vigorous defence; but offered, through the mediation of the pope, to fubmit to *Frederic* if he would confirm their privileges. Nothing could appeafe him but an unconditional furrender, and they refolved to defend themfelves to the laft extremity. *Gregory* gave up all other confiderations, that he might make head againft the emperor. He reconciled himfelf to the *Romans*, who were as jealous as he was, of *Frederic*, and entered their capital in triumph; and then he publicly declared himfelf the patron and protector of the *Lombard* confederacy. *Frederic* defpifed all he could do, and difmiffed the cardinals and meffengers fent to him by the pope,

withouc

without deigning to give them a hearing. His holinefs then had recourfe to his ufual arms. He folemnly excommuni-cated the emperor, and fent an excommunicatory bull againft him to be publifhed by the archbifhop of *Mentz*, and others, all over *Europe*. Thofe bulls are conceived in terms of ran-cour and malice not to be credited were they not exifting. The pope there accufes *Frederic* of rebellion againft *Jefus Chrift*; of atheifm; and of having declared, that the world had been deceived by three impoftors, *Jefus Chrift*, *Mofes*, and *Mahomet*; but that the two laft had fupported their glory to the ends of their lives. *Frederic*, in his manifeftos, was little behind hand with his holinefs, whom he termed, The great dragon, who was the forerunner of *Antichrift*; *Balaam*, the prince of darknefs, and fuch other epithets. *(He is ex-communicated,)*

The pope, to give force to his excommunications, en-deavoured to intereft St. *Lewis*, of *France*, in his favour; and offered to transfer the imperial crown to his brother *Robert* of *Artois*; but *Lewis* not only rejected his propofal, but intimated, That his holinefs had no power to difpofe of crowns. *Frederic* ordered his chancellor, the famous *Peter de Vineis*, to read, at the head of his army, his anfwer to *Gregory's* invectives; and they were heard with loud applaufes: and he then ordered it to be circulated all over *Germany*, where it raifed an univerfal fpirit of deteftation againft his holinefs, and united the inhabitants in their allegiance to *Frederic*. The great objects of the latter's refentment were now the *Romans*, inftead of the *Milanefe*. He had expelled, out of *Naples* and *Sicily*, all the ecclefiaftics, of every deno-mination, who favoured the pope; and had forbid his letters to be received in any part of his *Italian* dominions. He kept a fecret correfpondence with the *Gibelin* party at *Rome*, where the other party formed a crufade againft him, and wore the crofs accordingly.

Before *Frederic* could march to *Rome*, he was defeated, by the *Milanefe*, at land; and by the *Venetians*, who had feized *Ravenna*, at fea. This weakened his army, and gave fuch fpirits to his enemies in *Rome*, that he was repulfed in at-tempting to enter that city, and obliged to retire towards *Naples*. During his march, he ordered all the prifoners who had taken the crofs againft him, to be put to death with tor-tures. Having recruited his army in *Naples*, and ravaged the *Beneventine*, he again entered the *Milanefe*, intending to befiege that city. Practice and difcipline had, by this time, rendered the confederates good troops; and the *Milanefe* fought a pitched battle with this great emperor, in which his army was entirely routed; and he himfelf muft have been taken in the purfuit, had he not ordered the bridges over which he fled towards the *Placentine* to be broken down. In *Tufcany* he recruited his army; and the wars between the *Guelphs* and *Gibelins* in *Italy* raged now with redoubled fury. *(He is repulfed from Rome, and de-feated.)*

I i 2 Such

Such of the *Christian* states as thought that *Frederic* had pushed his resentment against the pope too far, sent him liberal supplies, especially *England* and *France*; and, a general council having been indicted at *Rome* by the pope, against the emperor's express command, the *French*, and other prelates, embarked on board the combined fleets of the pope and the *Genoese*; which were beaten and destroyed by the emperor's fleet: and three cardinals, with many archbishops, bishops, and other ecclesiastics, were made prisoners. This was a terrible blow to the papal interest, because, without those prelates, the assembly could not have had the face of a council. In this critical period died the pope, and he was succeeded by *Celestine* IV. who lived but eighteen days after his election. *Frederic* pressed the cardinals to chuse another pope, which they refused to do till their brethren were released. *Frederic* complied with their request, but, in the mean time, they took such measures, that their choice fell upon *Innocent* IV. the friend and favourite of *Frederic*. It is said, on good authority, that he rejected, on this occasion, the congratulations of his nobility, upon *Innocent*'s promotion; " because," said he, " in the pope I must lose the " friend." The event did justice to his penetration. *Innocent* began his pontificate by taking steps to oblige the emperor to leave *Italy*; and he not only demanded restitution of all the towns that he had taken from the holy see, but that *Frederic* should do him homage for the kingdom of *Naples*. The latter offered to leave their differences to the arbitration of the kings of *England* and *France*; but *Innocent* rejected that proposal, though he offered to have a personal conference with *Frederic*; which the latter agreed to; but his holiness invented pretexts for declining it, and fled to *France*, where he convoked a general council to be held at *Lyons*.

Innocent summoned the emperor to appear at this council, to purge himself from the crimes alledged against him: and he complied so far, that he sent his ambassadors to the council; where they cleared his conduct to the satisfaction of all its impartial members. This did not prevent his being excommunicated, and a bull issuing, commanding the princes of the empire to proceed to a new election, but reserving the disposal of the crown of *Naples* to his holiness. *Frederic* received the news of this audacious proceeding with a mixture of rage and contempt, openly declaring that he withdrew all obedience from the see of *Rome*. Though *Innocent* repented of his having carried matters to such an extremity, yet perseverance was now his only safety. He intrigued so artfully in *Germany*, that some of the electors chose *Henry*, the landgrave of *Thuringia*, king of the *Romans*; and, the majority of the meeting being ecclesiastics, the people of *Germany* called him " The king of priests."

The

The pope follicited fupplies from all the powers of *Chrift-endom* to fupport this election; and fucceeded fo well, that he prefented *Henry* with five and twenty thoufand marks in filver to enable him to make head againft *Conrade*; whom he defeated. He then made an irruption, but with no fuccefs, into *Frederic*'s paternal dominions; and was killed by an arrow while he befieged *Ulm*. The advantages obtained in the field againft a pope, feldom, in thofe days, filenced the fpiritual thunder; with which *Frederic* found himfelf fo affected, that he went to *France* to juftify his conduct in perfon; leaving the adminiftration of his affairs in *Italy* to his favourite fon *Enzo*, king of *Sardinia*. The *Guelphs* made fo good a ufe of *Frederic*'s abfence, that they furprized *Parma*; the news of which reaching him while was on the road, the emperor hurried back, and laid fiege to that important city, which baffled his moft vigorous attempts. He therefore endeavoured to take it by famine, and formed a new kind of a blockade, by building another city oppofite to it called *Victoria*; which, in a fhort time, became as populous as *Parma* itfelf.

In the mean while, *Frederic* unaccountably applying himfelf more to his diverfions than the affairs of war, the papal party chofe *William*, count of *Holland*, king of the *Romans*; and, as fuch, he was recognized by the cities of *Cologne,* *Mentz*, and *Strafbourg*. The hiftory of *Frederic*, at this time, becomes very myfterious. We are told, that, while he was intent upon this ridiculous fiege of *Parma*, his enemies prevailed upon his firft minifter, *Peter de Vineis*, and his chief phyfician, to poifon him. *Frederic*, though we know not by what means, difcovered the confpiracy; and, the effects of the poifon being clearly proved, by its being adminiftered to a malefactor, who died of it, the phyfician was executed, and the minifter's eyes were put out. *Frederic*'s ruling weaknefs was for women, and thofe punifhments might have been the confequence of fome female intrigues, though the apparent cauf.es were as we have here related them. The fequel proves that *Frederic* had given himfelf entirely up to a life of fenfuality. He lived at *Victoria* in as much feeming fecurity as if he had been in the capital of the empire, but ftill continued the fiege of *Parma*.

Confpiracy againft him.

The pope's legate, *Gregory Monte Longo*, who conducted the defence of that city, was apprized of *Frederic*'s way of life; and made fo furious a fally, at the head of the *Parme-fans*, that the imperial army was cut in pieces. *Frederic* himfelf, half naked, efcaped, with difficulty, to *Cremona*; and his admired city of *Victoria* was levelled with the ground. This defeat ferved to roufe *Frederic*'s fpirit; and, his party being ftill very ftrong in *Italy*, he was preparing to retrieve it, when he received an account, that his darling fon, *Enzo*, was taken prifoner by the *Bolognefe* in an unadvifed attempt he made upon their city.

He is defeated at Parma.

The

The fate of *Enzo* is another of those events which characterize the spirit of that age and country. However unequal the *Bolognese* were to *Frederic*'s power, yet *Enzo* was a king and a *Gibelin*; and those republicans, for so they then declared themselves, had the glory of defeating and making him their prisoner. A glory which they prized so much, that, by a public decree of their commonwealth, it was enacted, That *Enzo* (who, according to *Sigonius*, was but twenty-five years of age, and, by far, the most graceful man of his time) should be kept in perpetual imprisonment, and maintained at the public charge, be the ransom proposed for him ever so great. *Frederic*, who was passionately fond of him, offered immense sums for his deliverance; but they were rejected: nor could all his power and paternal affection, ever free *Enzo* from his prison. This blow dispirited *Frederic* so much, that he retired with his army to his kingdom of *Naples*; where he began to think seriously of his latter end, finding that the pope was too firmly protected by the king of *France* for his army to reach him at *Lyons*, which *Frederic* attempted.

His death, This was the last expedition of his long and tumultuous reign. While he was busy in recruiting his army, he was seized by a fever, which carried him off, on the seventeenth **testament;** of *December*, 1251, in the fifty-fifth year of his age. By his last will, which is said to be still extant, he left the kingdoms of *Naples*, *Jerusalem*, and *Italy*, and all the rights he had in the empire, to his son *Conrade*. He bequeathed the principality of *Tarentum* to *Mainfroi*, another of his natural sons. He left to his grandson *Frederic*, by his eldest son *Henry*, the dutchy of *Austria*, which he had erected into a kingdom; but the creation was deemed to be void on account of his excommunication. His eldest daughter was unfortunately married to the landgrave of *Thuringia*, and his second to the landgrave of *Hesse*.

and cha- As to *Frederic*'s character, it may be collected from the good **racter.** and bad qualities of his predecessors; but he inherited qualities of both kinds that were peculiar to himself. He seems to have been a free-thinker, in the utmost extent of the word, with regard to religion; insomuch, that he took *Mahometans* and infidels into his pay; as thinking no set of men were so detestable as the *Guelphs*. With an irresistible propensity to pleasure, he was active, brave, and indefatigable. Had he been succeeded by princes of equal learning and abilities with himself, the house of *Medicis*, and the *Italian* patrons of learning of the fifteenth century, would not have been deemed the revivers of literature; but *Frederic*'s death brought with it a barbarism which those *Italians* had the glory to reform. He encouraged true learning as much as his cotemporaries and successors did the miserable jargon which they termed learning; and he was so far above the vulgar prepossessions of the age, that he had recourse to the

Arab

Arab authors; which he ordered to be tranflated for the pro-
pagation of the fine arts and true literature, as he did feveral of the antient *Greek* writers, particularly *Ariftotle*, that
fountain of fcience. His cruelty towards the *Guelphs* of *Italy*
is unpardonable, but he could not view the papal ufurpations
in any other light but as fo many attempts to erect a ridiculous, illiberal, and illiterate hierarchy above all civil power.
His notions of government feem to have been vaft and com-
prehenfive, but founded upon injuftice and defpotifm. By
the fame principles upon which he deprived the *Lombard*
ftates and cities of their rights and privileges, and attempted
to revive the feat of the *Roman* empire in *Italy*, he might have
called upon the kings of *France* and *England*, and the other
powers of *Europe*, to become his vaffals, becaufe their countries had formerly belonged to the *Roman* empire; nor is it
unreafonable, had he fucceeded in his ambitious fchemes, to
fuppofe that he actually would have done fo. Some writers
of good note have faid that *Frederic*, in his laft illnefs, was
ftifled by his wicked fon *Mainfroi*.

---

27. Conrade IV.

MANY writers have here introduced an inter-regnum; Uncer-
but, though the times were troubled, as the right of tainty of
empire ftill fubfifted in *Conrade*, who had been twice crowned hiftory.
king of the *Romans*, and had maintained that dignity with
undaunted refolution, we fhall treat of him as the immediate
fucceffor of his father.

We have already mentioned his having been defeated by
the landgrave of *Thuringia*, commonly called, The king of
the priefts; and an accident happened to him, at that time,
which plainly difcovers the flavifh fubordination of the civil
to the ecclefiaftical power; or, rather, the triumph of fuperftition over humanity itfelf. After the above defeat, he fled
to *Ratifbon*, where he put himfelf under the protection of
the bifhop; and, that confecrated monfter, confpiring with
the abbot of St. *Emeran*, fent fome affaffins to murder him
in his apartment in the night-time. *Conrade* had changed
his bed, and, in the dark, the affaffins killed two of his domeftics; but, during the fact, *Conrade* was alarmed with the
noife, and efcaped to his army, which was encamped without the walls. Next day, the bifhop and abbot were apprehended, tried, and convicted; but *Conrade* durft not venture
to punifh either of them capitally; for the bifhop was only
imprifoned for life; a punifhment which, according to the
papal doctrine of thofe times, the civil power had no authority to inflict; and the abbot was deprived of his benefice.

William,

Difputes
between
Conrade
and the
count of
Holland.

William, count of *Holland*, who, as we have already mentioned, had been chofen king of the *Romans*, in oppofition
to *Conrade*, continued ftill to be fupported by the pope and
the princes of *Germany* who were difaffected to the houfe of
Suabia. William was then no more than twenty years of age,
and, being engaged in a war with the countefs of *Hainault*,
on account of her hufband's fucceffion, he was, by *Conrade*,
forced to fly to the pope at *Lyons*, where his holinefs confirmed him king of the *Romans*; promifed to give him the imperial crown at *Rome*; and preached up a crufade of the *European* powers and *German* princes againft *Conrade* and his
brother *Mainfroi*, who acted as his deputy in *Italy*.

Diforders
in Ger-
many and
Italy.

Conrade was fo well fupported by his party in *Germany*, that
he thought himfelf fafe in undertaking an expedition into
Italy, though he and all his adherents ftood excommunicated
by *Innocent*. The pope's agents exerted themfelves fo ftre-
nuoufly, that *Naples, Capua*, and *Aquina*, refufed to fubmit
to his allegiance. *Conrade* reduced *Naples* after a fiege of
eight months, but found himfelf embroiled with the court of
Rome, who had offered the imperial crown to *Charles*, count
of *Anjou*, brother to the king of *France*. Powerful as the
pope was then in *Europe*, he was a fugitive from *Rome*, from
whence the citizens had expelled him; but, through their
natural inconftancy, they now recalled him; and he appeared there at the fummit of pontifical glory. *Conrade* was
fenfible of his power, and endeavoured fecretly to form a
party in *Rome* againft him; but, failing in that, he fued for
an accommodation; which was rejected by *Innocent*, who excommunicated both him and *Ezzelino*. The latter was a
free-booter, and had been a fuccefsful commander under
Frederic II. Under a pretext of acting fometimes for the
pope, and fometimes for the emperor, he made himfelf
mafter of *Verona* and *Padua*; and might have laid the foundation of an independent power in *Italy*, could he have acted
with the fmalleft degree of moderation; but, fuch was his
cruelty, that he was, by the *Italians* in general, termed, The
fon of the Devil. After an uninterrupted courfe of robberies, for forty years, he was taken prifoner, in confequence
of the crufade the pope had preached up againft him; and
died raving mad, to the great joy of the *Romans*.

Conrade did not long enjoy his conqueft of *Naples*, for he
died on the twenty-firft of *May*, 1254. Some time before
his death, he had fent for his younger brother, prince *Henry*,
to whom his father had bequeathed the kingdom of *Sicily*,

Death of
Henry,
king of
Sicily.

who died likewife; and his death happening at fo critical a
time, has given room for fome authors, who make no allow-
ances for the change of climates, and the accidents to which
youth are expofed, to fuppofe him to have been poifoned by
Conrade. It is more probable that *Conrade* himfelf was poifoned by *Mainfroi. Conrade*, at his death, left, by his wife
Elizabeth

Elizabeth of *Bavaria*, a son, *Conradin*, who was no more than three years of age, and *Mainfroi* became his guardian.

William, count of *Holland*, continued, all this time, to act as king of the *Romans*; and omitted nothing that could en- gage the subjects and vassals of the empire in his interest. He gave the investiture of *Turin*, and the chief fiefs of *Savoy* and *Piedmont*, to the count of *Maurienne*; from whence the family of his present *Sardinian* majesty may be said to date its greatness. As *Frederic* II. had applied his cares towards literature, *William* extended his towards commerce. The union of the hans-towns had rendered them rich, powerful, and independent; and the feudal-law, which is ever an enemy to trade, introduced a most pernicious distinction between the landed and the commercial interest in *Germany*. Every petty prince, or land-holder, under the pretext of being the superior of his tenant, robbed him of the honest gains he had acquired by trade; and exacted tolls upon all commodities and manufactures that went from place to place, either by land or water. The cities of *Mentz*, *Francfort*, *Cologne*, *Worms*, and *Spire*, associated together to defend themselves against those depredations; and in this they were encouraged and protected by *William*. The benefits arising from this confederacy were so visible, that, in a short time, many towns, not only of *Germany*, but *Flanders*, sued for admission into it. Some noblemen, of enlarged ideas, who saw themselves enriched by the wealth of their subjects through commerce, forwarded the institution; and, in about twelve months after its commencement, it included no fewer than threescore towns. *Lubec*, *Hamburgh*, and *Bremen*, the original associated hans-towns, at this time, were engaged in a quarrel with the king of *Denmark*, who was murdered by his brother *Abel*; and therefore they could not exert themselves in this confederacy, which had great consequences for the good of *Germany*. The projectors of it, to whose memory history has been ungrateful, established a paper credit, which supplied the place of money, and answered all the purposes of commerce. The bills of one city of the confederacy passed current in another, and the cause of one city or town became that of the whole. Thus, in *Germany*, a commercial repulic was settled about the year 1254. It would be no difficult attempt to prove that this noble institution was confirmed by the troubles of *Germany*, which was now without a head; and, had they not happened, it never could have been established. Succeeding emperors and princes of the empire looked with a jealous eye upon this association, but they never could entirely ruin it, for its remains subsist to this day.

Germany, at this time, was under the influence of the civil and religious differences that had so long distracted *Italy*. The *Gibelin* faction refused to acknowledge the count of *Holland* for emperor, because his election was effected merely by

the

and the Teutonic knights. the papal intereſt; but they choſe no other emperor: The knights of the *Teutonic* order laid hold of this opportunity to convert the pagans of *Pruſſia* and *Brandenburg*; for one third of *Germany* and *Hungary* at this very time were pagans. They ſucceeded, by the aſſiſtance of fire and ſword. A king of *Bohemia* headed them, and two of the *Pruſſian* chieftains were beaten into baptiſm; and *Koningſberg* was, at his requeſt and direction, repaired, or rather refounded, by the *Teutonic* knights. But a very extraordinary ſcene was, at this time, forming in *Italy*.

Succeſs of Mainfroi againſt the pope. *Mainfroi*, as guardian to young *Conradin*, adminiſtred the affairs of *Sicily*, which belonged to his ward. The pope claimed *Sicily*, and excommunicated *Mainfroi* for not giving up his adminiſtration. Young *Conradin's* claim, and that of the pope, were equally deſtructive of *Mainfroi's* ſcheme, which was that of ſeizing *Sicily* for himſelf; and he reſolved to eſtabliſh it by making himſelf ſerviceable to both. He found the papal intereſt in *Naples* and *Sicily* too ſtrong to be cruſhed; and, by making proper ſubmiſſions to the pope, he not only abſolved from his excommunication, but confirmed him in his principality of *Tarentum*, and appointed him lieutenant to his holineſs in that kingdom. The latter, however, was a diſagreeable commiſſion; and the pope, ſuſpecting his true intentions, reſolved to put him to the trial. A friend to his holineſs being killed, *Mainfroi* was accuſed of the murder; and the pope cited him to appear before him as a criminal. *Mainfroi*, inſtead of obeying him, threw himſelf into the hands of the *Saracens* and defeated the papal troops.

Pope *Innocent* dying, at this time, was ſucceeded by *Alexander* IV. who purſued the maxims of his predeceſſor, and appointed the marquis of *Honebruc* his adminiſtrator for the kingdom of *Naples*; but *Mainfroi's* intereſt there being ſuperior to his, he ſubmitted to a treaty; which the pope refuſed to ratify, and declared the throne of *Sicily* to be vacant. In conſequence of this declaration, he offered it to *Edmund* II. ſon of *Henry* III. of *England*; which flattered *Henry's* ambition ſo much, that he gave his holineſs money, with which he recruited his army; but it was defeated by *Mainfroi*, who ſoon after made himſelf maſter of *Naples* and *Sicily*, while his holineſs was obliged to ſhut himſelf up in *Viterbo*.

Diſtreſſes of the houſe of Suabia. All thoſe incidents contributed to the ruin of the houſe of *Suabia*. *Mainfroi* acted only for himſelf, and not for his pupil. The pope was the declared enemy of both; and *William*, his king of the *Romans*, was at war with the *Frieſlanders*, who refuſed to be ſubject to him as count of *Holland*, and, as ſuch, he was himſelf a feudatory of the empire. This rebellion proceeded ſo far, that he diſfranchiſed them from the privileges which their anceſtors had obtained from *Charles the Great*, and marched an army into their country. In one of thoſe unguarded moments in which great princes, often to
their

their coft, want to examine things with their own eyes, he went to reconnoitre a little fortrefs without any attendants. The ice on which he rode broke under him, and, not being known by the natives, he was killed, and buried as a common man. At the time of his death, which happened in 1256, he was not above twenty-five years of age, and had difcovered great talents for government. Had it not been for the affociation of the free towns, which we have already mentioned, *Germany* muft, at that time, have been entirely ruined; but they became fo powerful by commerce, that the count-palatine, and feveral of the *German* princes defired, for their protection againft the lawlefs violence that raged in every corner of the empire, to become members of their confederacy; which they obtained. Some of thofe confederates afterwards abufed this excellent inftitution to their own ends; but, upon the whole, after the deceafe of *William*, count of *Holland*, whom fome rank as emperor, the empire was not thought worthy of acceptance by any prince who knew its diftracted ftate.

The archbifhop of *Cologne*, who had been the principal agent in raifing the landgrave of *Thuringia*, and the count of duke of *Holland*, to royalty, offered the imperial dignity to *Richard*, duke of *Cornwal*, brother to *Henry* III. of *England*. He feems to have been a weak prince. He paid a vaft fum of money, fome fay no lefs than feven hundred thoufand pounds, which is equal to as many millions at prefent, for his title, invalid as it was; and releafed the archbifhop of *Mentz*, who was prifoner to the duke of *Brunfwic*, that he might concur in his election. *Richard's* electors were the two archbifhops, the count-palatine, and his brother, with other princes of lefs note who had been bribed to give him their fuffrages. The archbifhop of *Triers*, and fome other princes of the empire, chofe *Alphonfo*, king of *Caftile*, who is fo well known by the name of *the Aftronomer*, to be their emperor, but *Richard* was crowned at *Aix-la-Chapelle*; after which he was abandoned by his mock-greatnefs: for his money failing him, his venal electors formally withdrew from him their allegiance, and he was obliged to return to *England*. His election, however, ought to make a more diftinguifhed period in hiftory, efpecially that of *England*, than it does. When he left *Germany*, he committed the care of the empire to three vicars. He invefted *Ottocar* (a name in common to all the kings of *Bohemia* fince their attachment to the emperor *Otho*) with the kingdom of *Bohemia*; he received homage from *Guy de Dampier* for the county of *Hainault*; and, in fhort, he acted, in every refpect, as the fovereign of *Germany*. It is true, having no patrimonial revenues in the empire, he could not fupport his authority; but fome contemporary hiftorians inform us, that he not only bore the title of king of the *Romans*, but acted as fuch, to the day of his death.

Richard, duke of Cornwal, brother to Henry III. of England. He chofen king of the Romans.

Alphonfo,

Alphonfo, *Richard*'s competitor, was under the fame difad-vantage of having no property in *Germany*. He was involved in a war with the *Saracens*, and could not repair to the empire in perfon. In other refpects he exercifed all acts of fovereignty; but the confufion, the mifery, and anarchy that then prevailed in *Germany*, is inexpreffible; as no law but the fword was known. The pope was applied to, to interpofe his authority; but he preferved his importance, by fiding with neither party. When fome public fpirited princes convoked affemblies for fettling the government, they commonly ended in blood-fhed; and his holinefs put a negative upon the elevation of young *Conradin* to the imperial dignity, merely becaufe he was the grandfon of the emperor *Frederic* II. Self-prefervation at laft operated among the princes of the empire to give themfelves a head. But all was in vain; rapine and anarchy had got too great a fway to be extinguifhed by any confideration. All they could do was to appoint a fpecies of officers, called *auftreques*, who had in charge to preferve the public peace, and to form confederacies together for the adminiftration of diftributive juftice. Thofe auftreques were found to be fo ufeful, that their authority lafted for a long time, even after the reftoration of the imperial dignity.

Charles of
Anjou be-
comes
king of
the two
Sicilies.

Young *Conradin* was the innocent victim of the public confufion. His uncle, *Mainfroi*, feized the title and kingdom of *Naples*, which the pope offered to *Charles* of *Anjou*, who accepted of the prefent, and was crowned, at *Rome*, by *Clement* IV. on condition of holding his kingdom as a fief of the holy fee, and paying for it to the pope an annual tribute of fixty thoufand ducats. *Charles* was joined by the *Italian Guelphs*, and *Mainfroi* was defeated and killed in a pitched battle near *Benevento*. *Charles*, though a brother to *Lewis*, king of *France*, to whom that ignorant age gave the appellation of *Saint*, was a monfter of cruelty, and that too with the approbation of his holy brother, who never appears to have checked, but rather to have encouraged, him in his acts of inhumanity. He fuffered the wife and children of *Mainfroi* to languifh in prifon, and then, by way of mercy, he put them to death; and permitted his army to commit all manner of enormities wherever he marched; but, at laft, he became the peaceable poffeffor of the two *Sicilies*.

Conradin was educated under *Lewis*, duke of *Bavaria*, his maternal uncle, and, at the time of the *Anjouvine* ufurpation, he was no more than fixteen years of age. The *Guelphs* were then all powerful in *Italy*; and the *Gibelins*, who dreaded an univerfal maffacre, invited *Conradin* to come to their refcue. He fet out accordingly with an army for *Italy*, attended by the duke of *Bavaria*, his father-in-law; the count of *Tirol*; and his beloved coufin the duke of *Auftria*, whofe inheritance was likewife in the hands of an ufurper

Though

Though *Clement* IV. who was then pope, dreaded *Charles* of *Anjou*, he was still in more fear of *Conradin*, and invested the former with the office of imperial vicar in *Tuscany*, as the holy see was *Matilda's* heir and executor. *Conradin* had the hearts of the *Italians*, and even the *Guelphs* favoured his claims upon the crown of *Sicily*, to which he had a most indisputable title. He defeated an *Italian* army that had been raised by *Charles*. He took the title of king of the two *Sicilies*, and, in right of his father, assumed that of emperor of *Germany*, to which he had no just claim, though he was received as such at *Rome* by *Honorius*, a senator, who was his relation; and by *Don Henry* of *Castile*, the governor of that city, a true 'knight-errant, who had been banished by his brother *Alphonso*, the nominal emperor. *Conradin* was likewise supported by the citizens of *Rome*, over whom that very pope who could thus dispose of kingdoms and empires, had very little influence; and by the *Moslems* of *Africa*, who, at the sollicitation of their countrymen, the *Neapolitan Saracens*, lent him a fleet and money. *Charles* of *Anjou* had no dependence but upon his countrymen, who, by their wars with the *English*, were become much better soldiers than either the *Italians* or the *Germans* in *Conradin's* army. He went to *France*, from whence he brought a powerful reinforcement, and returning defeated *Conradin*, who was by this time master of *Naples*, in a pitched battle, so completely, that *Conradin*, his cousin of *Austria*, and *Don Henry* of *Castile*, fell into the hands of the conqueror.

The politics of those times were more barbarous than their manners. *Charles*, monster as he was, hesitated how he should dispose of his illustrious captives. Pope *Clement*, tho' himself upon his death-bed, advised him to put them to death; and the heads of *Conradin*, and his beloved cousin of *Austria*, were accordingly struck off in the market-place of *Naples*, after a formal sentence had been pronounced upon them by a prothonotary of *Charles*. *Conradin*, when he appeared on the scaffold, cut off, as he was, from all resources of human justice, threw his glove among the numerous spectators, desiring that it might be carried, as a signal of revenge for his death, to his cousin *Peter* of *Arragon*. The glove was taken up by the chevalier *Truchses de Walbourg*, who fulfilled the dying bequest of the unfortunate young prince, whose head was struck off while he was kissing that of his cousin of *Austria*, who had been first beheaded, and watering it with his tears. Those, and some other executions, put a period to the illustrious house of *Suabia*, with which we shall conclude this volume.

who loses his head on a scaffold,

END OF THE EIGHTH VOLUME.

Lightning Source UK Ltd.
Milton Keynes UK
UKOW07f0041131216

289858UK00009B/533/P